BLACK
CULTURE
AND
BLACK
CONSCIOUSNESS

*This book has been published with the aid of a
Bicentennial Grant from the Phi Beta Kappa Society*

BLACK CULTURE AND BLACK CONSCIOUSNESS

Afro-American Folk Thought
from Slavery to Freedom

Lawrence W. Levine

New York · Oxford University Press · 1977

Lyrics from the following songs are used with the kind permission of their publishers:

Harold Arlen and Johnny Mercer: "Out of This World," copyright 1945 by Edwin H. Morris & Company.

Harold Arlen and Johnny Mercer: "That Old Black Magic," copyright © 1942 by Famous Music Corporation; copyright renewed 1969 by Famous Music Corporation.

Lovie Austin and Alberta Hunter: "Down Hearted Blues," © copyright 1922 by Alberta Hunter and Lovie Austin. © copyright renewed 1949 and assigned to MCA Music, a division of MCA, Inc. © copyright 1963 by MCA Music, a division of MCA, Inc., New York, N.Y. Used by permission. All rights reserved.

Alex Bradford: "He Makes All My Decisions for Me," copyright 1959, Martin and Morris. "My Reward Is in Heaven," copyright 1953, Martin and Morris.

Walter Donaldson: "My Blue Heaven," copyright 1927, renewal 1955, Leo Feist, Inc. Used by permission.

Thomas A. Dorsey: "I Don't Know Why I Have To Cry," copyright © 1937 by Hill and Range Songs, Inc., copyright renewed, assigned to Unichappell Music, Inc. International copyright secured. All rights reserved. Used by permission.

"Jesus Lives in Me," copyright © 1937 by Hill and Range Songs, Inc., copyright renewed, assigned to Unichappell Music, Inc. International copyright secured. All rights reserved. Used by permission.

"Life Can Be Beautiful," copyright © 1940 by Hill and Range Songs, Inc., copyright renewed, assigned to Unichappel Music, Inc. International copyright secured. All rights reserved. Used by permission.

"Take My Hand, Precious Lord," copyright © 1928 by Hill and Range Songs, Inc., copyright renewed, assigned to Unichappell Music, Inc. International copyright secured. All rights reserved. Used by permission.

Thomas A. Dorsey and Hudson Whittaker: "It's Tight Like That," copyright © 1928 by Edwin H. Morris & Company, Inc., copyright renewed. International Copyright secured. All rights reserved. Used by permission.

George and Ira Gershwin: "Our Love Is Here To Stay," © 1938 by Gershwin Publishing Co.

Porter Grainger and Everett Robbins: "'Tain't Nobody's Biz-ness If I Do," © copyright 1922 by MCA Music, a division of MCA Inc., © copyright renewed 1949 and assigned to MCA Music, a division of MCA Inc. © copyright 1960, 1963 MCA Music, a division of MCA Inc., New York, N.Y. Used by permission. All rights reserved.

Lorenz Hart and Richard Rodgers: "Blue Moon," copyright © 1934, renewed 1961 Metro-Goldwyn-Mayer Inc. Rights throughout the world controlled by Robbins Music Corporation.

Richard M. Jones: "Trouble in Mind," © copyright 1926, 1937 by MCA Music, a division of MCA Inc. © copyright renewed 1953 and assigned to MCA Music, a division of MCA Inc., © copyright 1962 by MCA Music, a

To Cornelia

PREFACE

This study rests upon two related convictions which I hold even more firmly at the conclusion of my work than I did at its inception: It is time for historians to expand their own consciousness by examining the consciousness of those they have hitherto ignored or neglected. It is time that the study of human intellect be broadened to embrace Joseph Levenson's admirable definition of intellectual history as "the history not of thought, but of men thinking." This is such an attempt. It can be repeated for many other groups in American history. It focuses upon the orally transmitted expressive culture of Afro-Americans in the United States during the century that stretched from the antebellum era to the end of the 1940s, and is primarily concerned with two major questions: What were the contours of slave folk thought on the eve of emancipation and what were the effects of freedom upon that thought?

The significance of this study lies not only in its subject matter but also in its quest. I have attempted to present and understand the thought of people who, though quite articulate in their own lifetimes, have been *rendered* historically inarticulate by scholars who have devoted their attention to other groups and other problems. Historians are the prisoners not only of what Jack Hexter has called their "tracking devices"—the scholarly tools of perception that prevail among them at any given time—but also of their sources or what they perceive to be their sources. The effect of the embarrassment of documentary riches confronting modern

American historians is to relieve them of the desperate and innovation-producing need to examine every last bit and piece of evidence; to squeeze out of every remnant of the past whatever meaning, whatever understanding, whatever perception might lie hidden within. The abundance of those sources United States historians have considered accessible and important has produced a poverty of understanding of those groups which have not left behind them traditional written remains or have not been in the mainstream of American society and politics. The result has been that we know infinitely more about the clergy than about their parishioners; more about political spokesmen than about their constituents; more about union leaders than workers; more about troop movements during America's various wars than about the migrations that transformed the face of the United States from generation to generation; more about the aspirations and life styles of large entrepreneurs than about those of small shopkeepers, merchants, or artisans; more about social workers than about the poor to whom they ministered; more about men than women; more about Protestants and whites than about members of other religious and racial groups.

This catalogue—which of course could be extended—is not meant to be an indictment of the history that has been written most frequently. Obviously, there can be no meaningful historiography which does not take as one of its central tasks the re-creation of the background, thought, and action of those who direct the important institutions and movements of any society. No one who understands the historian's craft would plead seriously that all groups should receive equal time. We know more about some groups than others not only because of the predilections of historians or the nature of their sources but frequently because we should know more about some groups of individuals in terms of their importance and their effects upon others. The problem is that historians have tended to spend too much of their time in the company of the "movers and shakers" and too little in the universe of the mass of mankind. I began this study with a sense of isolation from the mainstream of current historiography. I conclude it with the recognition that it is part of what hopefully is a growing effort on the part of historians to restore a greater balance in historical writing.

Greater balance is necessary not only in the amount of attention we devote to neglected groups of people, but also in the nature of that attention. This book may dismay some because it abandons the popular formula which has rendered black history an unending round of degradation and pathology. The familiar urge to see in heroes only virtue and in villains only malice has an analogue in the desire to see in the oppressed only unrelieved suffering and impotence. This ideal construct—the pure victim—is no more convincing or supported by what we know of human psychology and history than the ideals of pure hero or villain. Yet such are the realities of our current racial and political situation that it remains necessary to stress that which should be obvious: to argue, as this book does, that even in the midst of the brutalities and injustices of the ante-bellum and postbellum racial systems black men and women were able to find the means to sustain a far greater degree of self-pride and group cohesion than the system they lived under ever intended for them to be able to do, is not to argue that the system was more benign than it has been pictured, but rather that human beings are more resilient, less malleable, and less able to live without some sense of cultural cohesion, individual autonomy, and self-worth than a number of recent scholars have maintained.

Upon the hard rock of racial, social, and economic exploitation and injustice black Americans forged and nurtured a culture: they formed and maintained kinship networks, made love, raised and socialized children, built a religion, and created a rich expressive culture in which they articulated their feelings and hopes and dreams. My aim has not been to reiterate the difficult conditions that Negroes have faced in this country—though certainly these conditions do emerge in the following pages—but rather to examine the folk sources without which it is impossible to understand the history and culture of the bulk of black Americans. My efforts have led me to depart from the traditional historical practice of viewing the folk as inarticulate intellectual ciphers, as objects who were continually acted upon by forces over which they had no control, and to recognize them as actors in their own right who not only responded to their situation but often affected it in crucial ways. Those who would restrict intellectual history to the educated, the intelligentsia, the elite, would do well to look carefully at the richness of expression, the sharpness of perception, the uninhibited imagination, the complex imagery that form the materials upon which this study has been based. I have utilized these materials as fully as possible in order to explore and reconstruct the mind of the black folk.

Inevitably, this task is simpler to state than to accomplish. Having worked my way carefully through thousands of Negro songs, folktales, proverbs, aphorisms, jokes, verbal games, and the long narrative oral poems known in Afro-American culture as "toasts," I am painfully aware of the problems inherent in their use. They are difficult, often impossible, to date with any precision. The identity of their creators and their point of origin are lost in the obscurity of the past. Their geographical distribution is usually unclear. They were collected belatedly, frequently by men and women who had only a rudimentary knowledge of the culture from which they sprang, and little scruple about altering or suppressing them. The historian's frustration can only mount as he reads in one collection after another variants of the admission of Howard Odum and Guy Johnson that they failed to publish "a great mass" of their material "because of its vulgar and indecent content" and that many of the songs they did print "have been shortened by the omission of stanzas unfit for publication," or John Burma's lament that many of the "most illustrative" jokes he collected "are too crude and obscene for the printed word." The offending material not only went unpublished, it seems to have gone unpreserved as well. Of the major collectors of black folklore, only Newman White in the papers he left to Harvard University and John and Alan Lomax in many of the recordings and tapes they deposited in the Library of Congress' Archive of Folk Song appear to have followed the admonition of Cecil Sharp that unexpurgated texts be placed in libraries "where they may be examined by students and those who will not misunderstand them."

Censorship was not the exclusive province of folklorists. The black folk from whom they collected their material were often extremely selective and circumspect in choosing the songs and stories they related to the dignified whites who came among them. When Elsie Clews Parsons accused James Murray, a resident of the South Carolina Sea Islands, of deleting salacious material from one of his tales, he replied, "Yes, I leave out a little bit. I know twenty-five or t'irty man stories, funny too, but I *wouldn' tell dem.*" During the 1930s an interviewer for the Federal Writers' Project heard a story from a South Carolina black, Lewis Small, and promptly related it to one of Small's Negro neighbors who exclaimed, "I heard that story all my life but that ain't the way I hear it! The way I hear it had such a disgraceful ending that I didn't tell you that one. But Lewis fix it up all right!" "No, honey," a black stevedore told Mary Wheeler, "I don't know no rouster songs fittin' fo' a nice lady to write down." Nor was it merely material of a sexual nature that occasioned this reticence. As this study will demonstrate, black singers and storytellers were often extremely self-conscious and self-protective in the presence of folklorists, white and black alike. Their attitudes and actions were succinctly expressed in a song sung by generations of Negroes:

> Got one mind for white folks to see,
> 'Nother for what I know is me;
> He don't know, he don't know my mind.

That these folkoristic documents are not perfect sources should hardly surprise historians whose quest by its very nature engages them in an incessant struggle to overcome imperfect records. They have learned how to deal with altered documents, with consciously or unconsciously biased firsthand accounts, with manuscript collections that were deposited in archives only after being filtered through the overprotective hands of friends and relatives, and with the comparative lack of contemporary sources. The scholarly challenge presented by the materials of folk culture is very real, but it is neither unique nor insurmountable.

I could not have written this book without the past and present work of scholars in the fields of folklore, ethnomusicology, and anthropology, and my debt to them is incalculable. Nevertheless, my aims and procedures remain those of the historian. While I have utilized with great profit such aids to research as the various folkloristic indices of tale types and motifs, I have not felt it necessary to make extensive comparative considerations part of my own scholarly apparatus. I am aware that many of the materials I analyze have their origins or parallels in the folk thought of other peoples, and whenever it was relevant to my purposes I have explored these avenues, but for the most part I have assumed that once these materials made their way firmly into the network of Afro-American thought and culture they could be used to shed light upon black consciousness without constant reference to their existence in other cultures. Such comparative studies are important, of course, and much remains to be done in this area. My own aims have been different. I have attempted to write a history of the thought of a group of people who have been too largely neglected and too consistently misunderstood. If I have succeeded at all then this study should serve the dual purpose of helping to establish the contours of Afro-American folk thought in the United States and of calling to the attention of other historians the importance of an entire body of sources which, until very recently, they have chosen to ignore.

Where I have utilized folk materials collected after 1950 it has been to illustrate the continuance of patterns present before then rather than to detail the emergence of new lines of thought. I have ended my inquiry with the 1940s, since it seems to me that the major patterns of change wrought by freedom were observable by then. Of course I am aware that changes have continued to take place since then in black music, black religion, and black consciousness in general, but these are the subject of a different study than the one I have undertaken.

I have attempted not only to understand the materials of Afro-American expressive culture but also to present them to readers to whom they are unfamiliar. I have quoted more frequently and at greater length than historians commonly do because the materials upon which this study is based are extremely difficult to present in summary or paraphrase. They must be experienced directly to be comprehended. Thus while this book contains an argument or, more accurately, a series of arguments, it is not intended exclusively as a vehicle for purveying my own analysis. I have been at least equally interested in communicating a sense of black folk thought. I have tried to include sufficient material so that whether or not readers are convinced by my arguments they will come away with a feeling for and a comprehension of the folk materials upon which my work is based. These materials, like all folk materials, are extremely redundant and relatively long-lived. In order to limit repetition I generally have not told the same story, song, saying, or joke again and again no matter how frequently it was told throughout the period of this study. Since I have chosen representative materials the reader should assume redundancy; that is, most of the material quoted in these pages was known over a relatively wide area and was repeated over and over in seemingly endless variation.

Finally, it is important to bear in mind that folk expression is only one part of a people's culture. As Bruce Jackson has written: "It is not all of culture, it is not all of action. It is one way of handling some things, but only one way, appropriate only to certain circumstances at certain times." This, then, does not pretend to be a study of all of Afro-American culture but only of one crucial and much neglected aspect of it. Even within these confines I have no illusions of definitiveness. I have attempted to inaugurate not end discussion, to open up not seal off new avenues of research and understanding.

L.W.L.

Berkeley, California
December 1975

A NOTE ON BLACK DIALECT

The numerous quotations which document this study make it evident that Afro-American oral culture was distinctive not only in content but in structure and sound as well. The language employed in these quotations, of course, is not invariably the language actually spoken by black Americans but representations of that language recorded by observers and folklorists, the great majority of whom were white and a substantial proportion of whom were southern. The language I have been forced to rely upon is a mélange of accuracy and fantasy, of sensitivity and stereotype, of empathy and racism. The distortions, where they exist, were not always conscious; people often hear what they expect to hear, what stereotype and predisposition have prepared them to hear. Thus the variety and subtlety of Negro speech was frequently reduced to what the auditor thought Negroes spoke like. Even when the pronunciation of a given word was precisely the same as that of the collectors, their desire to indicate the exotic qualities of black speech led them to utilize such misleading and superfluous spellings as *wen* for "when," *fo'ks* or *fokes* for "folks," *w'ite* or *wite* for "white," *wuz* for "was," *bizness* for "business," *neer* for "near," *wurst* for "worst," *frum* for "from," *reel* for "real," *cullered* for "colored," *cundemn* for "condemn," *fast'n* for "fasten," and so on and on.

The temptation to delete the most obvious distortions from the documented dialect has been great but in the end I have resisted it and have utilized the language as it was recorded. Any attempt to standardize it into some ideal form of Afro-American dialect would have the effect of distorting it even more, since there was no standard black dialect covering all sections of the country and all periods from the antebellum South through the 1940s. Indeed, it was the very attempt at standardization that has led to the distortions that appear throughout the collections upon which my research is based, and I have been reluctant to compound the problem by any further and necessarily futile attempts in this direction. The record we have, in spite of its errors, is closer to what prevailed than any mid-twentieth-century reconstruction could be. I have utilized the language as I found it in the reports of nineteenth- and twentieth-century observers and folklorists because for all of its manifold mistakes and inaccuracies, it does have the ultimate effect of conveying the enduring distinctiveness and creativity of black speech.

ACKNOWLEDGMENTS

I have received generous help and courtesy from the staffs of the Houghton Library, Harvard University; the New York Public Library and its branches, the Schomburg Collection in Harlem and the Library of the Performing Arts in Lincoln Center; the University of California Library at Berkeley and particularly the staff of its interlibrary loan division. I am especially indebted to the Archive of Folk Song and the Music Division of the Library of Congress. Alan Jabbour, who was then the head of the Archive, Joseph Hickerson, its present head, and their staff not only gave me expert help but treated me with great warmth. They simultaneously facilitated my work in the Library's rich collections and made it one of my more rewarding and enjoyable research experiences.

Funds from the Social Science Research Council enabled me to devote the academic year 1965-1966 to begin my education in the field of Afro-American history. National Institute of Mental Health grant no. MH18732-02 provided indispensable funds for research, travel expenses, and time off from my teaching duties. The Committee on Research and other agencies of the University of California at Berkeley generously granted me funds for research and typing expenses. And, finally, Phi Beta Kappa awarded me a Bicentennial Fellowship which enabled me to complete the writing of this study.

I have been even more richly endowed with human resources. At the very beginning of my work on this book, I met the poet and scholar

Sterling A. Brown who gave me warm words of encouragement and sent me a copy of his unpublished manuscript collection of Negro jokes. An early version of Chapter 1, which I delivered as a paper at the 1969 meetings of the American Historical Association, was perceptively criticized by J. Saunders Redding, Mike Thelwell, and my friend Nathan Huggins. Professor Huggins also read an early version of part of Chapter 4. In the process of writing Chapter 5, I was fortunate enough to meet Linda Morris who shares my interest in exploring what makes people laugh. She spent time helping me to formulate a number of my ideas as well as reading and improving a draft of the chapter. I benefited also from my conversations on Afro-American culture with VèVè Clark. Lisa Rubens helped me for a time with my research, but she has been even more important as a friend who was always willing to talk out matters relating to this work and who invariably buoyed my spirits by her unwavering faith that somewhere, somehow, amid the mass of notes and documents piled high on my desk, a book was taking shape.

Kenneth Stampp read and helped me to improve early drafts of my chapters on slavery and shared with me his vast knowledge of the antebellum United States. Paula Fass read the entire final draft of the manuscript with perception and sensitivity. I found myself incorporating her suggestions again and again. Alan Dundes, of Berkeley's Anthropology Department, never begrudged the time and energy necessary to guide a historian through some of the intracacies of folklore scholarship. He has read the entire manuscript and encouraged and stimulated me to explore these unfamiliar sources with more confidence than I might otherwise have mustered.

From the inception of this work five friends have shared some of its burdens and, I hope, some of its joys as well. Leon Litwack, Robert Middlekauff, and Irwin Scheiner of Berkeley's History Department, Sheldon Meyer of Oxford University Press, and my wife, Cornelia Levine, read various drafts, listened with patient understanding to my compulsive conversation about folk history, and responded in ways that have made this a richer book in every respect.

CONTENTS

BLACK
CULTURE
AND
BLACK
CONSCIOUSNESS

1

THE
SACRED
WORLD
OF
BLACK
SLAVES

Y ou t'inks I'm mistaken, honey! But I know t'ings dat de wite
folks wid all dar larnin' nebber fin's out, an' nebber sarches
fo' nudder. . . .
No, honey! De good Lawd doan gib ebery'ting to his
wite chilluns. He's gib 'em de wite skin, an' larnin', an' he's made 'em
rich an' free. But de brack folks is his chilluns, too, an' he gibs us de
brack skin an' no larnin', an' hab make us t' work fo' de wite folks.
But de good Lawd gibs us eyes t' see t'ings dey doan see, an' he comes
t' me, a poor brack slave woman, an' tells me be patient, 'cause dar's no
wite nor brack in hebben. An' de time's comin' when he'll make his
brack chilluns free in dis yere worl', an gib 'em larnin', an' good homes,
an' good times. Ah! honey, I knows, I knows!

"Aunt Aggy"—a Virginia slave in the 1840s[1]

The Africans brought to the English colonies as slaves in the seventeenth,
eighteenth, and nineteenth centuries did not carry with them a network
of beliefs, customs, institutions, and practices constituting what might be
called with accuracy a unified "African" culture. No such monolithic
cultural entity existed. The peoples of Africa created a myriad of languages, religions, customs, social, political, and economic institutions
which differentiated them and gave them separate identities. These marked

differences have been cited frequently to illustrate the insuperable obstacles slaves in the British colonies of North America faced in keeping a semblance of their traditional cultures alive. With few exceptions—the most notable being W. E. B. Du Bois and Melville Herskovits—most scholars until very recently have assumed that because United States slavery eroded so much of the linguistic and institutional side of African life it necessarily wiped out almost all of the fundamental aspects of traditional African cultures. "The Negro," Robert Park wrote in 1919, in a statement that typifies much of twentieth-century scholarship on this question, "when he landed in the United States, left behind him almost everything but his dark complexion and his tropical temperament. . . . Coming from all parts of Africa and having no common language and common tradition, the memories of Africa which they brought with them were soon lost." This inability to transmit and perpetuate African culture on American soil, Park maintained, made the Negro unique among the peoples of the United States. "Other peoples have lost, under the disintegrating influence of the American environment, much of their cultural heritage. None have been so utterly cut off and estranged from their ancestral land, traditions and people."[1]

What has been lost sight of too easily in these pronouncements is that culture is more than the sum total of institutions and language. It is expressed as well by something less tangible, which the anthropologist Robert Redfield has called "style of life." Peoples as different as the Lapp and the Bedouin, Redfield has argued, with diverse languages, religions, customs, and institutions, may still share an emphasis on certain virtues and ideals, certain manners of independence and hospitality, general ways of looking upon the world, which give them a similar life style.[2] This argument applies with special force to the West African cultures from which so many of the slaves came. Though they varied widely in language, institutions, gods, and familial patterns, they shared a fundamental outlook toward the past, present, and future and common means of cultural expression which could well have constituted the basis of a sense of common identity and world view capable of withstanding the impact of slavery.

The terms which scholars utilize in their search for the manifestations of this traditional world view are important. To think of them as "survivals" is to prejudge the issue, to make the prior decision that even if they did continue to exist within the contours of a slave world they did so vestigially, as quaint reminders of an exotic culture sufficiently alive to render the slaves picturesquely different but little more. Scholars must be receptive to the possibility that for Africans, as for other people, the journey to the New World did not inexorably sever all associations with the Old World; that with Africans, as with European and Asian immigrants, aspects of the traditional cultures and world view they came with may have continued to exist not as mere vestiges but as dynamic, living, creative parts of group life in the United States.

To insist that only those elements of slave culture were African which remained largely unchanged from the African past is to misinterpret the nature of culture itself. Culture is not a fixed condition but a process: the product of interaction between the past and present. Its toughness and resiliency are determined not by a culture's ability to withstand change, which indeed may be a sign of stagnation not life, but by its ability to react creatively and responsively to the realities of a new situation. The question, as VèVè Clark recently put it, is not one of survivals but of transformations.[3] We must be sensitive to the ways in which the African world view interacted with that of the Euro-American world into which it was carried and the extent to which an Afro-American perspective was created. There is no better place to search for these transformations than in the numerous folk expressions of nineteenth-century slave cosmology.

THE CONTOURS OF SLAVE SONG

White southerners, no matter how much they might denigrate the culture and capacities of their black bondsmen, paid tribute to their musical abilities, from Thomas Jefferson's observation that musically the slaves "are more generally gifted than the whites with accurate ears for tune and time," to the northern Mississippi planter who told Frederick Law Olmsted more than half a century later that "Niggers is allers good singers nat'rally. I reckon they got better lungs than white folks, they hev such powerful voices." "Compared with our taciturn race, the African nature is full of poetry and song," an anonymous correspondent in *Dwight's Journal of Music* wrote in 1856. "The Negro is a natural musician. He will learn to play on an instrument more quickly than a white man. They have magnificent voices and sing without instruction. . . . They go singing to their daily labors. The maid sings about the house, and the laborer sings in the field." The slaves seem to have agreed. "That's one thing the colored folks is blessed," an ex-slave exclaimed. "They certainly got the harp in their mouths."[1] An examination of the shape and content of slave song reveals much about slave culture and consciousness.

Alan Lomax's argument that musical style appears to be one of the most conservative of culture traits and that even when an entirely new set of tunes, rhythms, or harmonic patterns is introduced a musical style will remain intact and yield to change only very gradually, certainly seems borne out by slave music.[2] As this chapter will demonstrate, black slaves engaged in widespread musical exchanges and cross-culturation with the whites among whom they lived, yet throughout the centuries of slavery and long after emancipation their song style, with its over-riding antiphony, its group nature, its pervasive functionality, its improvisational character, its strong relationship in performance to dance and bodily movement and expression, remained closer to the musical styles and performances of West Africa and the Afro-American music of the West Indies and South America than to the musical style of Western Europe. In their songs, as in their tales, aphorisms, proverbs, anecdotes, and jokes, Afro-American slaves, following the practices of the African cultures they had been forced to leave behind them, assigned a central role to the spoken arts, encouraged and rewarded verbal improvisation, maintained the participatory nature of their expressive culture, and utilized the spoken arts to voice criticism as well as to uphold traditional values and group cohesion.

While observers have collected and ex-slaves have remembered songs containing some African words and phrases, specific African songs do not seem to have remained an important element in antebellum slave song, though their history in the colonial period still requires investigation.[3] The disappearance of a specific song literature, of course, is not synonymous with the disappearance of the structure of that literature or the purposes to which it had been put. Slaves, in fact, continued to utilize song in much the way their African ancestors had. Music remained a central, living element in their daily expression and activities. "I used to pick 150 pounds of cotton every day," an ex-slave recalled and then, perhaps to explain what helped to make that tedious, grueling task bearable, she added, "We would pick cotton and sing, pick and sing all day."[4] Slaves not only picked cotton but planted rice, husked corn, rowed boats, rocked babies, cooked food, indeed performed almost every conceivable task to the accompaniment of song with an intensity and style that continually elicited the comments of the whites around them. During the Second Seminole

War in Florida in the 1830s, a white passenger on a boat propelled by "a dozen stout negro rowers" described a scene which could have as easily taken place in Africa as on the St. Johns River. As the boat shot through the quiet waters, the black rowers timed the strokes of their oars by singing. A song leader sang a line, the other rowers joined in on a short chorus, then came another solo line and another brief chorus, followed by a longer chorus. Some of the lines seemed to be standard ones known by all, but as soon as these were used up lines relating to the surrounding scenes and people were extemporized. "Some of these were full of rude wit, and a lucky hit always drew a thundering chorus from the rowers, and an encouraging laugh from the occupants of the stern-seats." The singers paid little attention to rhyme or even to the number of syllables in a line: "they condensed four or five [syllables] into one foot, or stretched out one to occupy the space that should have been filled with four or five; yet they never spoiled the tune. This elasticity of form is peculiar to the negro song."[5]

Fannie Berry, an ex-slave, described a similar use of song when she told of how the hired slaves from her plantation cut down trees and sawed them into ties for the railroad that was being built through her section of Virginia during the late 1850s. As the slaves felled pine trees in the morning mist and fog, they sang:

> A col' frosty mo'nin'
> De niggers feelin' good
> Take yo' ax upon yo' shoulder
> Nigger, talk to de wood.

The voices of hundreds of slaves ringing through the woods created a memorable scene, but the purpose of their song was not exclusively aesthetic any more than that of the slave rowers had been.

> Dey be paired up to a tree, an' dey mark de blows by de song. Fus' one chop, den his partner, an' when dey sing TALK dey all chop togedder; an' purty soon dey git de tree ready for to fall an' dey yell "Hi" an' de slaves all scramble out de way quick.[6]

Throughout slavery black workers continued to time their work routines to the tempo of their music in much the same manner as their African ancestors.

Black song, of course, had many additional functions both in Africa and America. In Africa, songs, tales, proverbs, and verbal games served the dual purpose of not only preserving communal values and solidarity but also providing occasions for the individual to transcend, at least symbolically, the inevitable restrictions of his environment and his society by permitting him to express deeply held feelings which ordinarily could not be verbalized. Among a number of African peoples, for example, periods were set aside when the inhabitants were encouraged to gather together and through the medium of song, dance, and tales to openly express their feelings about each other and their leaders. William Bosman, the Dutch traveler and official who lived in Africa from 1688 to 1702, described a ceremony which he had twice witnessed on the Gold Coast: "This Procession is preceded by a Feast of eight Days, accompanied with all manner of Singing, Skipping, Dancing, Mirth, and Jollity: In which time a perfect lampooning Liberty is allowed, and Scandal so highly exalted, that they may freely sing of all the Faults, Villanies and Frauds of their Superiors as well as Inferiors without Punishment, or so much as the least interruption."[7] More than two hundred years later the English anthropologist R. S. Rattray witnessed this same annual eight-day *Apo* ceremony. All around him the Ashanti freely chanted their normally repressed feelings:

> All is well to-day.
> We know that a Brong man eats rats,
> But we never knew that one of royal blood eats rats.
> But to-day we have seen our master, Ansah, eating rats.
> To-day all is well and we may say so, say so, say so.
> At other times we may not say so, say so, say so.

"Wait until Friday when the people really begin to abuse me," the chief told him, "and if you will come and do so too it will please me." In their custom of *bo akutia* the Ashanti practiced an ingenious vituperation by proxy in which a person brought a friend to the home of a chief or some other official who had offended him but of whom he was afraid. In the presence of this personage, the aggrieved individual pretended to have an altercation with his friend whom he verbally assailed and abused freely. Once he had thus relieved himself of his pent-up feelings in the hearing of the person against whom they were really intended, the brief ritual ended with no overt acknowledgment by any of the parties involved of what had actually taken place.[8]

In the days of their kings, the Dahomeans too had annual rites in which the subjects were encouraged to invent songs and parables mocking their rulers and reciting the injustices they had suffered. They possessed numerous additional outlets as well. Melville and Frances Herskovits witnessed the monthly social dance known as *avogan* in which the residents of a given quarter of the city of Abomey satirized those of another section. "Crowds come to see the display and to watch the dancing, but, most of all, to listen to the songs and to laugh at the ridicule to which are held those who have offended members of the quarter giving the dance. Names are ordinarily not mentioned, . . . However, everyone who is present already knows to whom reference is being made." In everyday work situations also, Dahomean men and women wove songs in which they commented on the generosity or scant hospitality of their last host, recounted gossip, and articulated attitudes of reproach and protest. In these songs indirection was typical. Thus a Dahomean woman masked her ridicule of her co-wife, a princess, by referring to her as a "man of rank."

O son of King Hwegbadja
To you I bring news
With you I leave word
That a man of rank who kills and then steals is here.
Something has been lost in this house
And the owner has not found it.
The man of rank who kills and then steals
Has been here.[9]

The psychological release these practices afforded seems to have been well understood. "You know that everyone has a *sunsum* (soul) that may get hurt or knocked about or become sick, and so make the body ill," an Ashanti high priest explained to Rattray. "Very often . . . ill health is caused by the evil and the hate that another has in his head against you. Again, you too may have hatred in your head against another, because of something that person has done to you, and that, too, causes your *sunsum* to fret and become sick. Our forbears knew this to be the case, and so they ordained a time, once every year, when every man and woman, free man and slave, should have freedom to speak out just what was in their head, to tell their neighbours just what they thought of them, and of their actions, and not only their neighbours, but also the king or chief. When a man has spoken freely thus, he will feel his *sunsum* cool and quieted, and the *sunsum* of the other person against whom he has now openly spoken will be quieted also."[10] Utilization of verbal art for this purpose was widespread throughout Africa and was not confined to those ceremonial occasions when one could directly state one's feelings. Through innuendo, metaphor, and circumlocution the Ashanti, Dahomeans, Chopi,

Ibo, Ewe, Yoruba, Jukun, Bashi, Tiv, Hausa, and other African peoples could utilize their songs as outlets for individual release without disturbing communal solidarity.[11]

There is abundant evidence that the verbal art of the slaves in the United States served many of these traditional functions. Priscilla McCullough recalled that when young women on the plantation where she was a slave misbehaved, their fellow slaves "put um on duh banjo," a practice which she explained as follows: "When dey play dat night, dey sing bout dat girl and dey tell all bout uh. Das puttin uh on duh banjo. Den ebrybody know an dat girl sho bettuh change uh ways."[12] On a boat trip to Edisto Island in South Carolina in the early 1840s, the leading oarsman, Big-Mouth Joe, used song to criticize one of his fellow slaves who was not pulling his weight:

> One time upon dis ribber,
>   Long time ago—
> Mass Ralph 'e had a nigger,
>   Long time ago—
> Da nigger had no merit,
>   Long time ago—
> De nigger couldn't row wid sperrit,
>   Long time ago—
> And now dere is in dis boat, ah,
>   A nigger dat I see—
> Wha' is a good for nuthing shoat, ah,
>   Ha, ha, ha, he—
> Da nigger's weak like water,
>   Ha, ha, ha, he—
> 'E can't row half quarter,
>   Ha, ha, ha, he—
> Cuss de nigger—cuss 'e libber,
>   Ha, ha, ha, he—
> 'E nebber shall come on dis ribber,
>   Ha, ha, ha, he—[13]

In the 1840s slaves on a Louisiana plantation sang songs in which the actions of their fellow slaves were commented upon and lampooned:

> Ebo Dick and Jurdan's Jo,
> Them two niggers stole my yo'.
>   *Chorus.* Hop Jim along,
>   Walk Jim along,
>   Talk Jim along, &c.

Old black Dan, as black as tar,
He dam glad he was not dar.
      Hop Jim Along, &c.[14]

The precise meaning of the song is difficult to decipher and may be only
a compilation of nonsense verses, but we should not come to this conclusion too easily as contemporary whites were wont to do. Slaves frequently
sang songs about each other which were incomprehensible to white listeners. In the late 1830s on the Altamaha River in Georgia, Frances Kemble
heard this rowing song which provided "an unmistakable source of satisfaction" for the black oarsmen but only a source of puzzlement for Miss
Kemble who quickly concluded that, with few exceptions, "I have never
heard the Negroes on Mr. [Butler]'s plantation sing any words that could
be said to have any sense."

Jenny shake her toe at me,
    Jenny gone away;
Jenny shake her toe at me,
    Jenny gone away.
Hurrah! Miss Susy, oh!
    Jenny gone away;
Hurrah! Miss Susy, oh!
    Jenny gone away.[15]

Chadwick Hansen has shown that in all probability what Miss Kemble
heard was not the English word "toe" but an African-derived word referring to the buttocks. The Jenny of whom the slaves were singing with
such obvious pleasure was shaking something more interesting and pro-
vocative than her foot.[16] Negro tales frequently featured music as a device
to get around and deceive the whites. In one such story a master dropped
in on his slave on a rainy day to hear him play the fiddle. The slave had
just stolen a shoat and hidden it under his bed. Afraid that his master
would notice the pig's leg sticking out, he sang as he played the fiddle:
"Ding-Ding a Dingy—Old Lady put the pig's foot further on the bed."
His wife walked to the bed while harmonizing, "Ummmmmmmmmm,"
and jerked the cover down over the pig's foot. "Yessir, that's a new one,"
the master said, delighting in the improvised song. "Yessir, that's a new
one."[17]

Inevitably, the slaves used the subtleties of their song to comment on the
whites around them with a freedom denied them in other forms of expression. In her fictionalized biography, *Recollections of a Southern Matron*

(1838), Caroline Gilman included a superb example of this type of song. During a boat trip down the Ashley River in South Carolina, Juba, the head oarsman, led his fellow slaves in a song about the boat *Neely*, which was named for the young mistress Cornelia who was aboard:

> Hi de good boat Neely?
> She row bery fast, Miss Neely!
> An't no boat like a' Miss Neely,
>   Ho yoi'!
>
> Who gawing to row wid Miss Neely?
> Can't catch a' dis boat Neely—
> Nobody show he face wid Neely,
>   Ho yoi'!

Almost imperceptibly, Juba shifted the song's focus from the boat to its namesake and her suitor Lewis who was also present:

> Maybe Maus Lewis take de oar for Neely,
> Bery handsome boat Miss Neely!
> Maus Lewis nice captain for Neely,
>   Ho yoi'![18]

Slave songs about whites were not invariably this good-natured. In 1774 an English visitor to the United States, after his first encounter with slave music, wrote in his journal: "In their songs they generally relate the usage they have received from their Masters or Mistresses in a very satirical stile and manner."[19] Songs fitting this description can be found in the nineteenth-century narratives of fugitive slaves. Harriet Brent Jacobs recorded that during the Christmas season the slaves would ridicule stingy whites by singing:

> Poor Massa, so dey say;
> Down in de heel, so dey say;
> Got no money, so dey say;
> Not one shillin, so dey say;
> God A'mighty bress you, so dey say.[20]

"Once in a while among a mass of nonsense and wild frolic," Frederick Douglass noted, "a sharp hit was given to the meanness of slaveholders."

> We raise de wheat,
> Dey gib us de corn;
> We bake de bread,
> Dey gib us de crust;
> We sif de meal,
> Dey gib us de huss;

We peel de meat,
Dey gib us de skin;
And dat's de way
Dey take us in;
We skim de pot,
Dey gib us de liquor,
And say dat's good enough for nigger.[21]

During their Christmas-time John Kuners or John Canoe festival, slaves in Wilmington, North Carolina, dressed in gayly colored tattered costumes with grinning masks, horns, and beards on their heads and faces, wound their way from house to house accompanying their songs and dances with bones, triangles, cow's horns, and an assortment of homemade instruments. They improvised verse after verse and quickly identified those whites who did not respond to their offerings with generosity:

Run, Jinnie, run! I'm gwine away,
    Gwine away, to come no mo'.
        Dis am de po' house,
            Glory habbilulum![22]

Abram Harris remembered a satirical song sung by himself and his fellow slaves which was to become one of the most long-lived songs in the black repertory:

My old Mistis promised me
Dat when she died, she gwine set me free.
But she lived so long en got so po
Dat she lef me diggin wid er garden ho.[23]

The slaves were able to use even their most seemingly inconsequential songs to communicate with each other and those around them. In 1808 John Lambert took a twenty-five-mile trip down the Savannah River and recorded one of the songs he heard from the slave rowers:

	Chorus
We are going down to Georgia, boys,	Aye, aye.
To see the pretty girls, boys;	Yoe, yoe.
We'll give 'em a pint of brandy, boys,	Aye, aye.
And a hearty kiss, besides, boys.	Yoe, yoe.
&c. &c. &c.	

"The words were mere nonsense; any thing in fact, which came into their heads," Lambert noted, but then added an insight which indicated that he understood the limits of his own generalization: "I however remarked that brandy was very frequently mentioned, and it was understood as a hint to the passengers to give them a dram."[24] In the 1850s the Swedish visitor Fredrika Bremer took a steamship trip on the Ohio River and was escorted to the lowest deck, where she observed the black stokers stripped to the waist passing wood to each other and feeding the immense fires. She admired the "fantastic song" with which the slaves timed their actions and noted that they quickly incorporated into their song "a hint that the singing would become doubly merry, and the singers would sing twice as well, if they could have a little brandy when they reached Louisville, and that they could buy brandy if they could have a little money, and so on."[25]

If slaves used their work songs to laugh at each other and the whites around them and to communicate their momentary desires, they used them as well to speak of the forces that affected their lives profoundly. They sang of the white patrols and the whippings that continually harassed them:

Run, nigger, run, patteroler'll ketch yer,
Hit yer thirty-nine and sware 'e didn' tech yer.[26]

They used their omnipresent humor to articulate dreams that would not come true in their lifetimes:

Harper's creek and roarin' ribber,
Thar, my dear, we'll live forebber;
Den we'll go to de Ingin nation,
All I want in dis creation,
Is pretty little wife and big plantation.[27]

They sang especially of the enforced separations that continually threatened them and haunted their songs. In Maryland, John Dixon Long heard the slaves sing:

William Rino sold Henry Silvers;
    Hilo! Hilo!
Sold him to de Gorgy trader;
    Hilo! Hilo!
His wife she cried, and children bawled,
    Hilo! Hilo!
Sold him to de Gorgy trader;
    Hilo! Hilo![28]

In the midst of their comic corn shucking songs, slaves on a South Carolina plantation sang this "wild and plaintive air" in 1843:

Johnny come down de hollow.
    Oh hollow!
Johnny come down de hollow.
    Oh hollow!
De nigger-trader got me.
    Oh hollow!
De speculator bought me.
    Oh hollow!
I'm sold for silver dollars.
    Oh hollow!
Boys, go catch de pony.
    Oh hollow!
Bring him round the corner.
    Oh hollow!
I'm goin' away to Georgia.
    Oh hollow!
Boys, good-by forever!
    Oh hollow![29]

Emma Howard remembered the following song as "one of de saddest songs we sung en durin' slavery days. . . . It always did make me cry."

Mammy, is Ol' Massa gwin'er sell us tomorrow?
Yes, my chile.
Whar he gwin'er sell us?
Way down South in Georgia.[30]

Slaves, then, had frequent recourse to their music, and they used it in almost every conceivable setting for almost every possible purpose. The accounts of contemporaries, white and black, and the numerous interviews with former slaves are filled with evidence that the variety of nonreligious songs in the slaves' repertory was wide. There were songs of in-group and out-group satire, songs of nostalgia, nonsense songs, children's songs, lullabies, songs of play and work and love.[31] Nor was slave music confined to song. Louise Jones, who had been a slave in Virginia, remembered the Christmas festivities her master allowed his slaves: "de music, de fiddles an' de banjos, de Jews harp, an' all dem other things. Sech dancin' you never did see befo. Slaves would set de flo' in turns, an' do de cakewalk mos' all night."[32] Slaves brought the banjo, the musical bow, several other stringed instruments, and a number of percussive instruments with them from Africa. In the New World they learned the use of the guitar, violin, and a variety of instruments common to the Europeans.[33] In 1753 one planter advertised in the *Virginia Gazette* for "an orderly Negro or mulatto who can play well the violin," another offered to sell "a young healthy Negro fellow . . . who [plays] extremely well on the French horn," while a third begged for the return of his escaped slave who "took his fiddle with him."[34] Slaves played their instruments primarily for their own pleasure and that of their fellow slaves but facility on an instrument could have other rewards as well. Solomon Northup wondered how he could have endured his long years of bondage without his beloved violin: "It introduced me to great houses—relieved me of many days' labor in the field—supplied me with conveniences for my cabin—with pipes and tobacco, and extra pairs of shoes, and oftentimes led me away from the presence of a hard master, to witness scenes of jollity and mirth. It was my companion. . . . It heralded my name round the country—made me friends, who, otherwise would not have noticed me—gave me an honored seat at the yearly feasts, and secured the loudest and heartiest welcome of them all at the Christmas dance."[35]

In America as in Africa Negro music, both vocal and instrumental, was intimately tied to bodily movement. John Bernard, an Englishman who lived in the United States from 1797 to 1811, wrote of slaves who would walk five or six miles after a hard day's work "to enjoy the pleasure of flinging about their hands, heads, and legs to the music of a banjo, in a manner that threatened each limb with dislocation."[36] Ella Lassiter, who had been a slave in Florida, told of the slaves' love of dancing: "Did us uster dance? . . . When some plantation niggahs give a frolic dey sont de word aroun bout three weeks ahaid time so us all be ready and git Massa to say we kin go. Sometimes us walk fifteen miles to de frolic but us don min dat."[37] While slaves often learned the dances of the whites—the quadrille, the reel, the cotillion, and even the waltz—their own dance style remained distinctive. There is a wealth of evidence in contemporary accounts and slave recollections to buttress Melville Herskovits' assertion that the dance "carried over into the New World to a greater degree than almost any other trait of African culture."[38] The basic characteristics of African dance, with its gliding, dragging, shuffling steps, its flexed, fluid bodily position as opposed to the stiffly erect position of European dancers, its imitations of such animals as the buzzard and the eagle, its emphasis upon flexibility and improvisation, its concentration upon movement outward from the pelvic region which whites found so lewd, its tendency to eschew bodily contact, and its propulsive, swinging rhythm, were perpetuated for centuries in the dances of American slaves and ultimately affected all American dance profoundly.[39]

Dance no less than song could become an instrument of satire at the

expense of the whites. In 1772 the *South Carolina Gazette* printed an account of a clandestine country dance attended by sixty slaves on the out-
skirts of Charleston. "The entertainment was opened," the anonymous
correspondent reported, "by the men copying (or *taking off*) the manners
of their masters, and the women those of their mistresses, and relating
some highly curious anecdotes, to the inexpressible diversion of that company."[40] At the close of a corn shucking he attended in 1843 on a South
Carolina plantation, the poet William Cullen Bryant described a series of
slave dances which gradually turned into a mock military parade, "a sort
of burlesque of our militia trainings, in which the words of command and
the evolutions were extremely ludicrous."[41] In 1901 an ex-slave recalled
that when she was young in the 1840s she was particularly fond of dancing: "Us slaves watched white folks' parties where the guests danced a
minuet and then paraded in a grand march, with the ladies and gentlemen
going different ways and then meeting again, arm in arm, and marching
down the center together. Then we'd do it, too, *but we used to mock 'em,*
every step. Sometimes the white folks noticed it, but they seemed to like
it; I guess they thought we couldn't dance any better."[42] Shephard Edmonds described how the slaves in Tennessee would do the cakewalk: "It
was generally on Sundays, when there was little work, that the slaves both
young and old would dress up in hand-me-down finery to do a high-kick-
ing, prancing walk-around. They did a take-off on the high manners of
the white folks in the 'big house,' but their masters, who gathered around
to watch the fun, missed the point."[43]

It was not merely the satirical element in slave secular song and dance
but the entire rich vein of secular music itself that many contemporary
whites missed. Touring a Richmond, Virginia, tobacco factory in 1843,
William Cullen Bryant listened to the slave workers sing religious songs
and was told by one of the proprietors: "What is remarkable, their tunes
are all psalm-tunes, and the words are from hymn-books; their taste is
exclusively for sacred music; they will sing nothing else."[44] Writing in
1862 James McKim noted that the songs of the Sea Island freedmen "are
all religious, barcaroles and all. I speak without exception. So far as I
heard or was told of their singing, it was all religious."[45] Others who
worked with recently emancipated slaves recorded the same experience,
and Colonel Thomas Wentworth Higginson reported that he rarely heard
his black Union troops sing a profane or vulgar song. With a few exceptions "all had a religious motive."[46] Whether they were aware of secular
song or not—and some whites quite consciously eschewed the "simple

airs" of the oarsmen and corn huskings in favor of the spirituals—it was black religious song that fascinated and attracted the early collectors of slave music. Consequently, we have long known far more about slave spirituals than about any other form of slave music. Spirituals were collected by the hundreds directly from slaves and freedmen during the Civil War and the decades immediately following, and although they came from widely different geographical areas they share a common structure and content which seem to have been characteristic of Negro music wherever slavery existed in the United States.

It is possible that a greater number of religious than nonreligious songs have survived because slaves were more willing to sing these ostensibly innocent songs to white collectors who in turn were more eager to record them since they fit easily with their positive and negative images of the Negro. But I would argue that the vast preponderance of spirituals over any other sort of slave music rather than being merely the result of accident or error is instead an accurate reflection of slave culture during the antebellum period. Though slaves never abandoned secular song, by the time of the Civil War the widespread conversion of slaves to Christianity and the impact of the revivals had made important inroads. "When I joined the church," Willis Winn of Texas recalled, "I burned my fiddle up."[47] Sir Charles Lyell visited the Hopeton plantation in Georgia during his second trip to the United States in the 1840s and reported that "above twenty violins have been silenced by the Methodist missionaries."[48] During the next decade Fredrika Bremer toured the South and heard that the Methodist missionaries were condemning as sinful the slaves' love of dancing and music. "And whenever the negroes become Christian, they give up dancing, have preaching meetings instead, and employ their musical talents merely on psalms and hymns."[49] In 1842 Charles C. Jones observed with satisfaction that one of the advantages of teaching the slaves psalms and hymns "is that they are thereby induced to lay aside the extravagant and nonsensical chants, and catches and hallelujah songs of their own composing; and when they sing, which is very often while about their business or of an evening in their houses, they will have something profitable to sing."[50] The planter Henry William Ravenel remembered that after the 1830s and 1840s slave Christmas festivities continued to be marked by "dancing and merrymaking . . . but it was in a more subdued form, and under protest from some of the elders."[51]

These pressures were certainly important but they were not primarily responsible for the primacy of the spirituals in antebellum slave culture.

Spirituals were not merely quantitatively but qualitatively the antebellum slaves' most significant musical creation. Contemporaries found the slaves' secular music less impressive than their religious songs, I suspect, because in reality it was less impressive. Secular song was more strictly occasional music: as varied, as narrow, as fleeting as life itself. Afro-American religious music seemed far superior because slaves used it to articulate many of their deepest and most enduring feelings and certainties. As valuable as secular songs are as a record of slave consciousness, it is to the spirituals that historians must look to comprehend the antebellum slaves' world view, for it was in the spirituals that slaves found a medium which resembled in many crucial ways the cosmology they had brought with them from Africa and afforded them the possibility of both adapting to and transcending their situation.

A QUESTION OF ORIGINS

The subject of slave religious music has produced a large and varied literature, the bulk of which has focused upon matters of structure and origin. This latter question especially has given rise to a long and heated debate.[1] The earliest collectors and students of slave music were impressed by how different that music was from anything familiar to them. Following a visit to the Sea Islands in 1862, Lucy McKim sounded a note which generations of folklorists were to echo when she despaired of being able "to express the entire character of these negro ballads by mere musical notes and signs. The odd turns made in the throat; and that curious rhythmic effect produced by single voices chiming in at different irregular intervals, seem almost as impossible to place on score, as the singing of birds, or the tones of an Aeolian Harp."[2] Although some of these early collectors maintained, as did William Francis Allen in 1865, that much of the slaves' music "might no doubt be traced to tunes which they have heard from the whites, and transformed to their own use, . . . their music . . . is rather European than African in its character,"[3] they more often stressed the distinctiveness of the Negro's music and attributed it to racial characteristics, African origins, and indigenous developments from the slaves' unique experience in the New World.

This tradition, which has had many influential twentieth-century adherents,[4] was increasingly challenged in the early decades of this century. Such scholars as Newman White, Guy Johnson, and George Pullen Jackson argued that the earlier school lacked a comparative grounding in Anglo-American folk song. Comparing Negro spirituals with Methodist and Baptist evangelical religious music of the eighteenth and nineteenth centuries, White, Johnson, and Jackson found similarities in words, subject matter, tunes, and musical structure.[5] Although they tended to exaggerate the degree of similarity, their comparisons were often a persuasive and important corrective to the work of their predecessors. They proved without question the existence of significant relationships between white and black religious song. But their work was weakened inevitably by their ethnocentric assumption that similarities alone settled the argument over origins. In 1918, for instance, Louise Pound totally dismissed H. E. Krehbiel's claim that the spiritual *Weeping Mary* was an Afro-American song, solely on the ground that her grandmother had learned a similar spiritual from a white woman who had heard it at a Methodist camp meeting in Hamilton, New York, sometime between 1826 and 1830.[6] This was evidence enough for Miss Pound. If whites knew the song it must have been they who originated and disseminated it. Neither she nor many of her fellow scholars could contemplate the possibility that the direction of cultural diffusion might have been from black to white as well as the other way. At the heart of their inability to give credence to such a possibility was the attitude articulated by Frederick W. Root in his introductory address to the International Folk-Lore Congress of the World's Columbian Exposition in Chicago in 1893. Armed with the fashionable and comfortable evolutionary predispositions of his day, Root envisioned the panorama of music as a development "from the formless and untutored sounds of savage people to the refined utterances of our highest civilization." Therefore, he told those gathered to hear the Congress' Concert of Folk Songs and National Music: "Excepting some selections representative of the music of our North American Indians, the utterances of the savage peoples were omitted, these being hardly developed to the point at which they might be called music."[7]

In fact, insofar as white evangelical music departed from traditional Protestant hymnology and embodied or approached the complex rhythmic structure, the percussive qualities, the polymeter, the syncopation, the emphasis on overlapping call and response patterns that characterized Negro music both in West Africa and the New World, the probability that it was influenced by the slaves who attended and joined in the singing at religious meetings is quite high. The contemporary accounts of one observer after another make it indisputably clear that during the period when the spirituals were being forged and were beginning to supplement or even supplant the established psalms and hymns, black men and women, slave and free, were commonly present at religious revivals and regular church services alongside whites throughout the South, and that the contributions of the black singers were often distinctive enough to be noted.

The Reverend Samuel Davies, who preached to whites and blacks in Virginia between 1747 and 1774, wrote a friend in London that "The Negroes, above all the human species that ever I knew, have an ear for music and a kind of extatic delight in psalmody," and described to another correspondent the pleasure he took during Sabbath services listening to the slaves in their segregated gallery "breaking out in a torrent of sacred harmony, enough to bear away the whole congregation to heaven."[8] The Reverend Lucius Bellinger described a quarterly Methodist meeting during the 1820s in South Carolina: "The crowd continues to increase, and song after song climbs the hills of heaven, . . . The negroes are out in great crowds, and sing with voices that make the woods ring."[9] At a camp meeting attended by seven thousand near Hagerstown, Maryland, in 1838, an observer reported that after the preaching the black participants formed a circle: "Their shouts and singing was so very boisterous that the singing of the white congregation was often completely drowned in the echoes and reverberations of the colored people's tumultous strains."[10] Fredrika Bremer mingled with the thousands attending a Georgia camp meeting in 1850 and marveled at the music: "They sang hymns—a superb choir! Strongest of all was the singing of the black portion of the assembly, as they were three times as many as the whites, and their voices are naturally pure and beautiful."[11] On the eve of the Civil War D. R. Hundley observed that "the loudest and most fervent camp-meeting singers amongst the whites are constrained to surrender to the darkeys in *The Old Ship of Zion*, or *I Want to Go to Glory*."[12] "Our white folks," an ex-slave recalled, "when they have camp meeting would have all the colored come up and sing over the mourners. You know they still say that colored can beat the white folks singing."[13] For blacks and whites who were commonly, though not invariably, separated at southern camp meetings, song easily breached the bounds of racial barriers and became the chief means of communication. Even at those camp meetings where the races were separated, the plank partition was removed on the final day of the meeting and blacks and whites joined together in a song festival or "singing ecstasy."[14]

Religious interaction, of course, was not confined to music. Whether segregated or not, many blacks and whites shared similar religious experiences and reactions. The Virginia minister Thomas Rankin was forced to interrupt his sermon again and again on July 7, 1776, to beg his parishioners to compose themselves, but to no avail. "Crying mightily to God," they fell to the floor, some on their knees, some on their faces. "Hundreds of Negroes were among them," Rankin wrote, "with the tears streaming down their black cheeks."[15] In these numerous encounters there was ample opportunity for white and black to influence and learn from each other, and the music they left behind attests to the fact that this is precisely what they did.

The scholars of the white derivation school used the similarities between black and white religious music to deny the significance of slave songs in still another way. Newman White, for example, argued that since white evangelical hymns also used such expressions as "freedom," the "Promised Land," and the "Egyptian Bondage," "without thought of other than spiritual meaning," these images when they occurred in Negro spirituals could not have been symbolic "of the Negro's longing for physical freedom."[16] The familiar process by which different cultural groups can derive varied meanings from identical images is enough to cast doubt on the logic of White's argument. In the case of white and black religious music, the problem may be much less complex since it is quite possible that the similar images in the songs of both groups in fact served similar purposes. Many of those whites who flocked to the camp meetings of the Methodists and Baptists were themselves on the social and economic margins of their society and had psychic and emotional needs which, qualitatively, may not have been vastly different from those of black slaves.[17] Interestingly, George Pullen Jackson, in his attempt to prove the white origin of Negro spirituals, makes exactly this point: "I may mention in closing the chief remaining argument of the die-hards for the Negro source of the Negro spirituals. . . . How could any, the argument runs, but a natively musical and sorely oppressed race create such beautiful things as 'Swing Low,' 'Steal Away,' and 'Deep River?' . . . But were not the whites of the mountains and the hard-scrabble hill country also 'musical and oppressed'? . . . Yes, these whites were musical, and oppressed too. If their condition was any more tolerable than that of the Negroes, one certainly does not get that impression from any of their songs of release and escape."[18] If this is true, the presence of similar images in white music would merely heighten rather than detract from the significance of these images in Negro songs.

The existence of similarities in the content of white and black spirituals should not blind us to the presence of some evident differences as well. In his detailed comparison of the two bodies of song, Jackson concentrated on tunes not words. A careful scrutiny of Jackson's evidence shows that even when the melodies of a white and black spiritual are similar, the texts are by no means inevitably close. Indeed, they are often quite disparate. Thus it was not uncommon for whites to have sung of Jesus: "O when shall I see Jesus / And reign with him above," while to a markedly similar tune blacks sang of the Hebrew people: "O my Lord deliver'd Daniel, / O why not deliver me too?" Where whites sang "Lord, I believe a rest remains / To all thy people known," blacks used the same tune to sing of Moses leading his people out of Egypt.[19] These differences were not random. From those few analyses of white spirituals that exist it is possible to hypothesize tentatively that while white spiritual songs shared a number of textual characteristics with their black counterparts—a sense of community, a frequent use of martial imagery, the depiction of Heaven as a place containing many of those joys denied in this world, an emphasis on the need to prepare oneself for the coming glory, and a tendency to dwell upon the imminent and permanent reunion of loved ones in death—there were significant differences in content and emphasis. White spirituals seem to have been informed by a more pervasive otherworldliness, a more marked rejection of the temporal present, and a tendency to concentrate upon Jesus, which were never as typical of black spirituals, while they lacked much of the vivid Biblical imagery, the compelling sense of identification with the Children of Israel, and the tendency to dwell incessantly upon and to relive the stories of the Old Testament that characterized the religious songs of the slaves. It would be unwise to make too much of these comparisons until we have more comprehensive and detailed studies of the content, function, and meaning of white religious music in the late eighteenth and early nineteenth centuries. In the interim we must be wary of allowing the mere existence of similarities to deter us from attempting to comprehend the cultural dynamics and meaning of slave music.

Many contemporary scholars, tending to transcend the stark lines of the old debate, have focused upon the process of syncretism to explain the development of Negro music in the United States. Their analyses emphasize a number of factors: the rich West African musical tradition common to almost all of the specific cultures from which the slaves came; the comparative cultural isolation in which large numbers of slaves lived; the tolerance and even encouragement which their white masters accorded to many of their musical activities; the fact that, for all the divergences in rhythm, harmony, and performance style, nothing in the European musical tradition with which the slaves came into contact in America was totally alien to their own traditions while a number of important features such as the diatonic scale were held in common and a number of practices such as the lining-out of hymns in Protestant denominations and the Africans' antiphonal call and response pattern were analogous. All of these conditions were conducive to a situation which allowed the slaves to retain a good deal of the integrity of their own musical heritage while fusing to it compatible elements of Euro-American music. The result was a hybrid with a strong African base.[20]

We have only gradually come to recognize not merely the sheer complexity of the question of origins but also its irrelevancy for an understanding of consciousness. It is not necessary for a people to originate or invent all or even most of the elements of their culture. It is necessary only that these components become their own, embedded in their traditions, expressive of their world view and life style. Interestingly, no one engaged in the debate over origins, not even advocates of the white derivation theory, denied that the slaves possessed their own distinctive music. Newman White took particular pains to point out again and again that the notion that Negro song is purely an imitation of the white man's music "is fully as unjust and inaccurate, in the final analysis, as the Negro's assumption that his folk-song is entirely original." He observed that in the slaves' separate religious meetings they were free to do as they would with the music they first learned from the whites, with the result that their spirituals became "the greatest single outlet for the expression of the Negro folk-mind."[21] Similarly, George Pullen Jackson, after admitting that he could find no white parallels for over two-thirds of the existing Negro spirituals, reasoned that these were produced by Negro singers in the true folk fashion "by endless singing of heard tunes and by endless, inevitable and concomitant singing differentiation." Going even further, Jackson asserted that the lack of deep roots in Anglo-American culture left the black man "even freer than the white man to make songs over unconsciously as he sang. . . . The free play has resulted in the very large number of songs which, though formed primarily in the white man's moulds, have lost all recognizable relationship to known white-sung melodic entities."[22] This debate over origins indicates clearly that a belief in the direct continuity of African musical traditions or even in the process of syncretism is not a necessary prerequisite to the conclusion that the slaves' music was their own, regardless of where they received the components out of which it was fashioned; a conclusion which is crucial to any attempt to utilize these songs as an aid in reconstructing the slaves' consciousness.

Equally important is the process by which slave songs were created and transmitted. When James McKim asked a freedman on the Sea Islands during the Civil War where the slaves got their songs, the answer was eloquently simple: "Dey make em, sah."[23] Precisely *how* they made them worried and fascinated Thomas Wentworth Higginson, who became familiar with slave music through the singing of the black Union soldiers in his Civil War regiment. Were their songs, he wondered, a "conscious and definite" product of "some leading mind," or did they grow "by gradual accretion, in an almost unconscious way"? A freedman rowing Higginson and some of his troops between the Sea Islands helped to resolve the problem when he described a spiritual which he had a hand in creating:

> Once we boys went for some rice and de nigger-driver he keep a-callin' on us; and I say, "O de ole nigger-driver!" Den anudder said, "Fust ting my mammy tole me was, notin' so bad as nigger-driver." Den I made a sing, just puttin' a word, and den anudder word.

He then began to sing his song:

> O, de ole nigger-driver!
>   O, gwine away!
> Fust ting my mammy tell me,
>   O, gwine away!
>
> Tell me 'bout de nigger-driver,
>   O, gwine away!
> Nigger-driver second devil,
>   O, gwine away!

Higginson's black soldiers, after a moment's hesitation, joined in the singing of a song they had never heard before as if they had long been familiar with it. "I saw," Higginson concluded, "how easily a new 'sing' took root among them."[24]

This spontaneity, this sense of almost instantaneous community which so impressed Higginson, constitutes a central element in every account of slave singing. The English musician Henry Russell, who lived in the United States in the 1830s, was forcibly struck by the ease with which a slave congregation in Vicksburg, Mississippi, took a "fine old Psalm tune" and, by suddenly and spontaneously accelerating the tempo, transformed it "into a kind of negro melody."[25] "Us old heads," an ex-slave told Jeannette Robinson Murphy, "use ter make 'em up on de spurn of de moment, . . . Notes is good enough for you people, but us likes a mixtery." Her account of the creation of a spiritual is typical and important:

> We'd all be at the "prayer house" de Lord's day, and de white preacher he'd splain de word and read whar Ezekial done say—
>
> > Dry bones gwine ter lib ergin.
>
> And, honey, de Lord would come a'shinin' thoo dem pages and revive dis ole nigger's heart, and I'd jump up dar and den and holler and shout and sing and pat, and dey would all cotch de words and I'd sing it to some ole shout song I'd heard 'em sing from Africa, and dey'd all take it up and keep at it, and keep a'addin' to it, and den it would be a spiritual.[26]

This "internal" account has been verified again and again by the descriptions of observers, many of whom were witnessing not slave services but religious meetings of rural southern Negroes long after emancipation. The essential continuity of the Negro folk process in the more isolated sections of the rural South through the early decades of the twentieth century makes these accounts relevant for the slave period as well. Natalie Curtis Burlin, who had a long and close acquaintance with Negro music, never lost her sense of awe at the process by which these songs were molded. On a hot July Sunday in rural Virginia, she sat in a Negro meeting house listening to the preacher deliver his prayer, interrupted now and then by an "O Lord!" or "Amen, Amen" from the congregation.

> Minutes passed, long minutes of strange intensity. The mutterings, the ejaculations, grew louder, more dramatic, till suddenly I felt the creative thrill dart through the people like an electric vibration, that same half-audible hum arose,—emotion was gathering atmospherically as clouds gather—and then, up from the depths of some "sinner's" remorse and imploring came a pitiful little plea, a real "moan," sobbed in musical cadence. From somewhere in that bowed gathering another voice improvised a response: the plea sounded again, louder this time and more impassioned; then other voices joined in the answer, shaping it into a musical phrase; and so, before our ears, as one might say, from this molten metal of music a new song was smithied out, composed then and there by no one in particular and by everyone in general.[27]

Clifton Furness has given us an even more graphic description. During a visit to an isolated South Carolina plantation in 1926, he attended a prayer meeting held in the old slave cabins. The preacher began his reading of the Scriptures slowly, then increased his tempo and emotional fervor, assuring his flock that "Gawd's lightnin' gwine strike! Gawd's thunder swaller de ert!"

> Gradually moaning became audible in the shadowy corners where the women sat. Some patted their bundled babies in time to the flow of the words, and began swaying backward and forward. Several men moved their feet alternately, in strange syncopation. A rhythm was born, almost without reference to the words that were being spoken by the preacher. It seemed to take shape almost visibly, and grow. I was gripped with the feeling of a mass-intelligence, a self-conscious entity, gradually informing the crowd and taking possession of every mind there, including my own.

In the midst of this increasing intensity, a black man sitting directly in front of Furness, his head bowed, his body swaying, his feet patting up and down, suddenly cried out: "Git right—sodger! Git right—sodger! Git right—wit Gawd!"

> Instantly the crowd took it up, moulding a melody out of half-formed familiar phrases based upon a spiritual tune, hummed here and there among the crowd. A distinct melodic outline became more and more prominent, shaping itself around the central theme of the words, "Git right, sodger!"
> Scraps of other words and tunes were flung into the medley of sound by individual singers from time to time, but the general trend was carried on by a deep undercurrent, which appeared to be stronger than the mind of any individual present, for it bore the mass of improvised harmony and rhythms into the most effective climax of incremental repetition that I have ever heard. I felt as if some conscious plan or purpose were carrying us along, call it mob-mind, communal composition, or what you will.[28]

These postbellum accounts are verified by the contemporary evidence attesting to the presence of a compelling communal ethos at slave religious meetings which threatened continually to transform observers into participants. In the 1850s Frederick Law Olmsted attended a slave service in New Orleans. Amidst the singing, the shouting, the cries of ecstasy, the stamping, jumping, and clapping of hands, Olmsted noted: "I was at once surprised to find my own muscles all stretched, as if ready for a struggle—my face glowing, and my feet stamping. . . ."[29] Nehemiah Adams, a Boston minister traveling through the South in 1854, witnessed a Methodist prayer meeting of slaves in which the "seraphic expressions in the prayer of a slave brother" raised "involuntary shouting from the whole meeting, in which I almost wished to join. . . ."[30] During the first year of the Civil War, Mary Boykin Chesnut visited the praise house on her South Carolina plantation and listened to Jim Nelson, one of her slaves, lead the prayer. On his knees, his eyes shut, Nelson faced his fellow slaves and became "wildly excited." His voice rose shrilly yet musically, his words rang out passionately, his hands clapped to punctuate each sentence. "I wept bitterly," Mrs. Chesnut recorded. "The Negroes sobbed and shouted and swayed backward and forward, some with aprons to their eyes, most of them clapping their hands and responding in shrill tones: 'Yes, God!' 'Jesus!' 'Savior!' 'Bless de Lord, amen,' etc. It was a little too exciting for me. I would very much have liked to shout, too."[31]

Shortly after the Civil War, Elizabeth Kilham witnessed a similar scene among the freedmen and described it in terms by now familiar to us. As they stamped, groaned, shouted, clapped, shrieked, and sobbed, the black congregation embroidered chorus after chorus of an "utterly indescribable, almost unearthly" spiritual:

Jesus said He wouldn't die no mo',
  Said He wouldn't die no mo',
So my dear chillens don' yer fear,
  Said He wouldn't die no mo'.

De Lord tole Moses what ter do,
  Said He wouldn't die no mo',
Lead de chillen ob Isr'el froo',
  Said He wouldn't die no mo'.

"A fog seemed to fill the church," Miss Kilham wrote, ". . . an invisible power seemed to hold us in its iron grasp; the excitement was working upon us also, . . . a few moments more, and I think we should have shrieked in unison with the crowd." Pushing their way through the worshippers, she and the other whites rushed outdoors and inhaled the evening air, but the mood was not broken easily: "More than one of the party leaned against the wall, and burst into hysterical tears; even strong men were shaken, and stood trembling and exhausted."[32]

Kilham's experience was shared by many other observers. In 1868 John Mason Brown listened to the freedmen sing a slave revival song filled with the imagery of the Apocalypse and commented: "The effect can hardly be overstated. . . . Such a chorus, sung with the energy of a people of simple and literal faith and strong and inflammable emotions, has often quickened the pulse and set aglow the heart of those whose social position or philosophy made them ashamed to acknowledge the effect."[33] In the

1880s W. E. B. Du Bois was to experience the truth of Brown's observation. Born and raised in Great Barrington, Massachusetts, Du Bois was accustomed only to the "quiet and subdued" Congregationalism of his boyhood, when as a young country school teacher in Wilson County, Tennessee, he encountered his first southern black revival meeting. He thrilled to the "rhythmic cadence of song," he was struck by "the air of intense excitement that possessed that mass of black folk," and suddenly, inexplicably, uncomfortably, he found himself affected: "A sort of suppressed terror hung in the air and seemed to seize us,—a pythian madness, a demoniac possession that lent terrible reality to song and word."[34]

The similarity of these accounts, not only in their details but in their very language, is impressive. They make it clear that even outsiders had difficulty resisting the centripetal pull of black religious services and song. Created within this atmosphere, spirituals both during and after slavery were the product of an improvisational communal consciousness. They were not, as some observers thought, totally new creations, but were forged out of many pre-existing bits of old songs mixed together with snatches of new tunes and lyrics and fit into a fairly traditional but never wholly static metrical pattern. They were, to answer Higginson's question, *simultaneously* the result of individual and mass creativity. They were products of that folk process which has been called "communal re-creation," through which older songs are constantly re-created into essentially new entities.[35] Anyone who has read large numbers of Negro songs is familiar with this process. Identical or slightly varied stanzas appear in song after song; identical tunes are made to accommodate completely different sets of lyrics; the same song appears in different collections in widely varied forms. In 1845 a traveler observed that the only permanent elements in Negro song were the music and the chorus. "The blacks themselves leave out old stanzas, and introduce new ones at pleasure. Travelling through the South, you may, in passing from Virginia to Louisiana, hear the same tune a hundred times, but seldom the same words accompanying it. This necessarily results from the fact that the songs are unwritten, and also from the habit of extemporizing, in which the performers indulge on festive occasions."[36] Another observer noted in 1870 that during a single religious meeting the freedmen would often sing the words of one spiritual to several different tunes, and then take a tune that particularly pleased them and fit the words of several different songs to it. On one occasion she heard the hymn *When I Can Read My Title Clear* sung six different times during the course of one service to a different tune each time.[37] Slave songs, then, were never static; at no time did slaves create a "final" version of a spiritual. Always the community felt free to alter and re-create them.

The two facts that I have attempted to establish thus far—that slave music, regardless of its origins, was a distinctive cultural form, and that it was created or constantly re-created through a communal process—are essential if one is to justify the use of these songs as keys to slave consciousness. But these facts in themselves say a good deal about the nature and quality of slave life and personality. That black slaves could create and continually re-create songs marked by the poetic beauty, the emotional intensity, the rich imagery which characterized the spirituals— songs which even one of the most devout proponents of the white man's origins school admits are "the most impressive religious songs in our language"[38]—should be enough to make us seriously question those theories which conceive of slavery as a closed system which destroyed the vitality of the slaves and left them dependent children. For all of its horrors, slavery was never so complete a system of psychic assault that it prevented the slaves from carving out independent cultural forms. It never pervaded all of the interstices of their minds and their culture, and in those gaps they were able to create an independent art form and a distinctive voice. If North American slavery eroded the Africans' linguistic and institutional life, it nevertheless allowed them to continue and to develop the patterns of verbal art which were so central to their past culture. Historians have not yet fully come to terms with what the continuance of the oral tradition meant to blacks in slavery.

THE QUEST FOR CERTAINTY: SLAVE SPIRITUALS

It is significant that the most common form of slave music we know of is sacred song. I use the term "sacred" not in its present usage as something antithetical to the secular world; neither the slaves nor their African forebears ever drew modernity's clear line between the sacred and the secular. The uses to which spirituals were put are an unmistakable indication of this. They were not sung solely or even primarily in churches or praise houses but were used as rowing songs, field songs, work songs, and social songs. Seated in a long cypress bark canoe on the Altamaha River in Georgia in 1845, Sir Charles Lyell listened to the six slave rowers improvise songs complimenting their master's family and celebrating a black woman of the neighborhood by comparing her beauty to that of the red bird. "Occasionally they struck up a hymn, taught them by the Methodists, in which the most sacred subjects were handled with strange familiarity, and which, though nothing irreverent was meant, sounded oddly to our ears, and, when following a love ditty, almost profane."[1] Mary Dickson Arrowood recalled slave boatmen in the late 1850s singing the following spirituals which, characteristically, were as congenial to the work situation as to the praise house:

Breddren, don' git weary,
Breddren, don' git weary,
Breddren, don' git weary,
Fo' de work is most done.

De ship is in de harbor, harbor, harbor,
De ship is in de harbor,
To wait upon de Lord. . . .

'E got 'e ca'go raidy, raidy, raidy,
'E got 'e ca'go raidy,
Fo' to wait upon de Lord.[2]

On the Sea Islands during the Civil War, Lucy McKim heard the spiritual *Poor Rosy* sung in a wide variety of contexts and tempos:

On the water, the oars dip "Poor Rosy" to an even andante; a stout boy and girl at the hominy-mill will make the same "Poor Rosy" fly, to keep up with the whirling stone; and in the evening, after the day's work is done, "Heab'n shall-a be my home" [the final line of each stanza] peals up slowly and mournfully from the distant quarters.[3]

For the slaves, then, songs of God and the mythic heroes of their religion were not confined to a specific time or place, but were appropriate to almost every situation. It is in this sense that I use the concept sacred— not to signify a rejection of the present world but to describe the process of incorporating within this world all the elements of the divine. The religious historian Mircea Eliade, whose definition of sacred has shaped my own, maintains that for people in traditional societies religion is a means of extending the world spatially upward so that communication with the other world becomes ritually possible, and extending it temporally backward so that the paradigmatic acts of the gods and mythical ancestors can be continually re-enacted and indefinitely recoverable. By creating sacred time and space, Man can perpetually live in the presence of his gods, can hold on to the certainty that within one's own lifetime "rebirth" is continually possible, and can impose order on the chaos of the universe. "Life," as Eliade puts it, "is lived on a twofold plane; it takes its course as human existence and, at the same time, shares in a trans-human life, that of the cosmos or the gods."[4]

Claude Lévi-Strauss, who found these same cosmological outlooks in South America and Asia, has eloquently expressed the difficulties modern Westerners have in relating to them. As a boy he lived with his grandfather, the rabbi of Versailles, in a house which was linked to the synagogue by a long inner corridor. To the young Lévi-Strauss that long passage was appropriately symbolic: "Even to set foot in that corridor was an awesome experience; it formed an impassable frontier between the profane world and that other world from which was lacking precisely that human warmth which was the indispensable condition to my recognizing it as sacred."[5] For men and women of traditional societies, such as those the slaves had originally come from, such corridors were absent. This is not to deny that the slaves were capable of making distinctions between this world and the next. Of course they were, and some of their songs do reflect a desire to release their hold upon the temporal present. "Why don't you give up de world?" they sang at times. "We must leave de world behind." Or, again:

> This world is not my home.
> This world is not my home.
> This world's a howling wilderness,
> This world is not my home.[6]

But for the most part when they looked upon the cosmos they saw Man, Nature, and God as a unity; distinct but inseparable aspects of a sacred whole.

This notion of sacredness gets at the essence of the spirituals, and through them at the essence of the slave's world view. Denied the possibility of achieving an adjustment to the external world of the antebellum South which involved meaningful forms of personal integration, attainment of status, and feelings of individual worth that all human beings crave and need, the slaves created a new world by transcending the narrow confines of the one in which they were forced to live. They extended the boundaries of their restrictive universe backward until it fused with the world of the Old Testament, and upward until it became one with the world beyond. The spirituals are the record of a people who found the status, the harmony, the values, the order they needed to survive by internally creating an expanded universe, by literally willing themselves reborn. In this respect I agree with the anthropologist Paul Radin that

> The ante-bellum Negro was not converted to God. He converted God to himself. In the Christian God he found a fixed point and he needed a fixed point, for both within and outside of himself, he could see only vacillation and endless shifting. . . . There was no other safety for people faced on all sides by doubt and the threat of personal disintegration, by the thwarting of instincts and the annihilation of values.[7]

The spirituals are a testament not only to the perpetuation of significant elements of an older world view among the slaves but also to the continuation of a strong sense of community. Just as the process by which the spirituals were created allowed for simultaneous individual and communal creativity, so their very structure provided simultaneous outlets for individual and communal expression. The overriding antiphonal structure of the spirituals—the call and response pattern which Negroes brought with them from Africa and which was reinforced in America by the practice of lining out hymns—placed the individual in continual dialogue with his community, allowing him at one and the same time to preserve his voice as a distinct entity and to blend it with those of his fellows. Here again slave music confronts us with evidence which indicates that, however seriously the slave system may have diminished the central communality that had bound African societies together, it was never able to destroy it totally or to leave the individual atomized and psychically defenseless before his white masters. In fact, the form and structure of slave music presented the slave with a potential outlet for his individual feelings even while it continually drew him back into the communal presence and permitted him the comfort of basking in the warmth of the shared assumptions of those around him. Those shared assumptions can be further examined by an analysis of the content of slave songs.

The most persistent single image the slave songs contain is that of the chosen people. The vast majority of the spirituals identify the singers as "de people dat is born of God," "We are the people of God," "we are de people of de Lord," "I really do believe I'm a child of God," "I'm a child ob God, wid my soul sot free," "I'm born of God, I know I am." Nor is there ever any doubt that "To the promised land I'm bound to go," "I walk de heavenly road," "Heav'n shall-a be my home," "I gwine to meet my Saviour," "I seek my Lord and I find Him," "I'll hear the trumpet sound / In that morning."[8]

The force of this image cannot be diminished by the observation that similar images were present in the religious singing of white evangelical churches during the first half of the nineteenth century. White Americans could be expected to sing of triumph and salvation, given their long-standing heritage of the idea of a chosen people which was reinforced in this era by the belief in inevitable progress and manifest destiny, the spread-eagle oratory, the bombastic folklore, and, paradoxically, the deep insecurities concomitant with the tasks of taming a continent and developing an identity. But for this same message to be expressed by Negro slaves who were told endlessly that they were members of the lowliest of races *is* significant. It offers an insight into the kinds of barriers the slaves had available to them against the internalization of the stereotyped images their masters held and attempted consciously and unconsciously to foist upon them.

Not only did slaves believe that they would be chosen by the Lord, there is evidence that many of them felt their owners would be denied salvation. On a trip through the South, Harriet Martineau recorded the instance of a mistress being told by one of her slaves, "You no holy. We be holy. You in no state of salvation."[9] "Slaves knew enough of the ortho-dox theology of the time to consign all bad slaveholders to hell," Fred-erick Douglass wrote in his autobiography.[10] Some went even further than this. "No white people went to Heaven," a correspondent in the *Southern Workman* noted in 1897, summing up the attitude of his fellow slaves before the Civil War and added, "Many believe the same until this day."[11] The fugitive slave Charles Ball insisted that his fellow slaves re-fused to picture Heaven as a place where whites and blacks lived in per-fect equality and boundless affection. "The idea of a revolution in the conditions of the whites and the blacks, is the corner-stone of the religion of the latter," he maintained. "Heaven will be no heaven to him [the slave], if he is not to be avenged of his enemies."[12] One hundred years later a former slave bore witness to Ball's assertion: "This is one reason why I believe in a hell. I don't believe a just God is going to take no such man as that [her master] into His Kingdom."[13] Martha Harrison re-counted how her master, "Old Bufford," who beat her mother savagely for refusing to sleep with him, offered on his death bed to spend seven thousand dollars to pay his way out of hell, "but he couldn'ta got out of hell, the way he beat my mammy."[14] Another former slave recalled that when her mistress died the slaves filed into the house "just a hollering and crying and holding their hands over their eyes, just hollering for all they could. Soon as they got outside of the house they would say, 'Old God damn son-of-a-bitch, she gone on down to hell.' "[15] Mary Reynolds described the brutality of Solomon the white overseer on the Louisiana plantation where she had been a slave and concluded simply, "I know that Solomon is burning in hell today, and it pleasures me to know it."[16]

Whether or not these reactions were typical, it is clear that a great many slaves agreed with H. B. Holloway that "It's going to be an awful thing up yonder when they hold a judgment over the way that things was done down here."[17] The prospect pleased slaves enough to become part of their repertory of jokes. The fugitive slave Lewis Clarke recounted two anecdotes with which the slaves on his Kentucky plantation used to delight each other. The first described the final conversation between a dying master and his slave: "Good-by, Jack; I have a long journey to go; farewell." "Farewell, massa! pleasant journey: you soon be dere, massa—*all de way down hill.*" The second told of a slave's reaction to the news that he would be rewarded by being buried in the same vault with his master: "Well, massa, one way I am satisfied, and one way I am not. I like to have good coffin when I die [but] I fraid, massa, when the debbil come take you body, he make mistake, and get mine."[18]

The confinement of much of the slave's new world to dreams and fantasies does not free us from the historical obligation of examining its contours, weighing its implications for the development of the slave's psychic and emotional structure, and eschewing the kind of reasoning that has led one historian to imply that, since the slaves had no alternatives open to them, their fantasy life was "limited to catfish and watermelons."[19] Their spirituals indicate clearly that there *were* alternatives open to them—alternatives which they themselves fashioned out of the fusion of their African heritage and their new religion—and that their fantasy life was so rich and so important to them that it demands understanding if we are even to begin to comprehend their inner world.

The God the slaves sang of was neither remote nor abstract, but as intimate, personal, and immediate as the gods of Africa had been. "O when I talk I talk wid God," "Mass Jesus is my bosom friend," "I'm goin' to walk with [talk with, live with, see] King Jesus by myself, by myself," were refrains that echoed through the spirituals.

In de mornin' when I rise,
  Tell my Jesus huddy [howdy] oh,
I wash my hands in de mornin' glory,
  Tell my Jesus huddy oh.

Gwine to argue wid de Father and chatter wid de son,
The last trumpet shall sound, I'll be there.
Gwine talk 'bout de bright world dey des' come from.
The last trumpet shall sound, I'll be there.

Gwine to write to Massa Jesus,
To send some Valiant soldier
To turn back Pharaoh's army, Hallelu!

"Good news, member, good news member," the slaves sang jubilantly, "And I heard-e from Heav'n today."[20]

The images of these songs were carried over into slave religious experiences. In a small South Carolina town in the 1850s, a white visitor questioned a young slave about his recent conversion experience:

"An den I went to hebben."
"What!" said I.
"An' den I went to hebben."
"Stop, Julius. You mean you had a dream, and thought you went to heaven."
"No, Sah: an' den I went to hebben, and dere I see de Lord Jesus, *a sittin' behind de door an' a reading his Bible.*"

There was no question, the white interrogator concluded, of the slave's "unmistakable sincerity" or of the fact that his fellow slave parishioners believed him implicitly.[21] "We must see, feel and hear something," an ex-slave exclaimed, "for our God talks to his children."[22] During a slave service in New Orleans in January of 1851, Fredrika Bremer witnessed the conversion of a black woman who, transported by religious enthusiasm, lept up and down with outstretched arms crying out "Hallelujah! Hallelujah!" and then, falling prostrate on the floor, lapsed into rigid quiescence. Gradually she recovered consciousness: "she talked to herself in a low voice, and such a beautiful, blissful expression was portrayed in her countenance that I would willingly experience that which she then experienced, saw, or perceived. It was no ordinary, no earthly scene. Her countenance was, as it were, transfigured."[23]

In these states of transfiguration slave converts commonly saw and conversed with God or Christ: "I looked to the east and there was . . . God. He looked neither to the right nor to the left. I was afraid and fell on my face. . . . I heard a voice from God saying, 'My little one, be not afraid

for lo! I am with you always.' " "I looked away to the east and saw Jesus.
. . . I saw God sitting in a big arm-chair." "I first came to know of God
when I was a little child. He started talking to me when I was no more
than nine years old." "I seen Christ with His hair parted in the center."
"I saw Him when he freed my soul from hell." "I saw in a vision a snow-
white train once and it moved like lightning. Jesus was on board and He
told me that He was the Conductor." "I saw the Lord in the east part of
the world. . . . His hair was parted in the middle and he looked like he
had been dipped in snow and he was talking to me."[24] For the slave,
Heaven and Hell were not concepts but places which could well be experienced during one's lifetime; God and Christ and Satan were not symbols but personages with whom meetings or confrontations were quite
possible.

The heroes of the Scriptures—"Sister Mary," "Brudder Jonah," "Brudder Moses," "Brudder Daniel"—were greeted with similar intimacy and
immediacy. In the world of the spirituals, it was not the masters and mistresses but God and Jesus and the entire pantheon of Old Testament figures who set the standards, established the precedents, and defined the
values; who, in short, constituted the "significant others." The world described by the slave songs was a black world in which no reference was
ever made to any white contemporaries. The slave's positive reference
group was composed entirely of his own peers: his mother, father, sister,
brother, uncles, aunts, preacher, fellow "sinners" and "mourners" of
whom he sang endlessly, to whom he sent messages via the dying, and
with whom he was reunited joyfully in the next world.

The same sense of sacred time and space which shaped the slave's portraits of his gods and heroes also made his visions of the past and future
immediate and compelling. Descriptions of the Crucifixion communicate
a sense of the actual presence of the singers: "Dey pierced Him in the
side . . . Dey nail Him to de cross . . . Dey rivet His feet . . . Dey
hanged him high . . . Dey stretch Him wide. . . ."

> Oh sometimes it causes me to tremble,—tremble,—tremble.
> Were you there when they crucified my Lord?[25]

In 1818 a group of white Quaker students observed a Negro camp meeting. They watched in fascination and bewilderment as the black worshippers moved slowly around and around in a circle chanting:

> We're traveling to Immanuel's land,
>   Glory! Halle-lu-jah.

Occasionally the dancers paused to blow a tin horn. The meaning of the ceremony gradually dawned upon one of the white youths: he was watching "Joshua's chosen men marching around the walls of Jericho, blowing the rams' horns and shouting, until the walls fell."[26] The students were witnessing the slaves' "ring shout"—that counterclockwise, shuffling dance which frequently lasted long into the night. The shout often became a medium through which the ecstatic dancers were transformed into actual participants in historic actions: Joshua's army marching around the walls of Jericho, the children of Israel following Moses out of Egypt. The shout, as Sir Charles Lyell perceived in 1845, frequently served as a substitute for the secular dance. It was allowed even where dancing was proscribed—"Hit ain't railly dancin' 'less de feets is crossed," "dancin' ain't sinful iffen de foots ain't crossed," two participants explained—and constituted still one more compelling feature of black religion. "Those who have witnessed these shouts can never forget them," Abigail Christensen has written. "The fascination of the music and the swaying motion of the dance is so great that one can hardly refrain from joining the magic circle in response to the invitation of the enthusiastic clappers, 'Now, brudder!' 'Shout, sister!' 'Come, belieber!' 'Mauma Rosa kin shout!' 'Uncle Danyel!' 'Join, shouters!' "[27]

The thin line between time dimensions is nowhere better illustrated than in the slave's visions of the future, which were, of course, a direct negation of his present. Among the most striking spirituals are those which pile detail upon detail in describing the Day of Judgment: "You'll see de world on fire . . . see de element a meltin', . . . see the stars a fallin' . . . see the moon a bleedin' . . . see the forked lightning, . . . Hear the rumblin' thunder . . . see the righteous marching, . . . see my Jesus coming . . . ," and the world to come where "Dere's no sun to burn you . . . no hard trials . . . no whips a crackin' . . . no stormy weather . . . no tribulation . . . no evil-doers . . . All is gladness in de Kingdom."[28] This vividness was matched by the slave's certainty that he would partake of the triumph of judgment and the joys of the new world:

> Dere's room enough, room enough, room enough in de heaven, my Lord
> Room enough, room enough, I can't stay behind.[29]

Continually, the slaves sang of reaching out beyond the world that confined them, of seeing Jesus "in de wilderness," of praying "in de lonesome valley," of breathing in the freedom of the mountain peaks:

Did yo' ever
Stan' on mountun
Wash yo' han's
In a cloud?[30]

Continually, they held out the possibility of imminent rebirth: "I look at de worl' an' de worl' look new, . . . I look at my hands an' they look so too . . . I looked at my feet, my feet was too."[31]

These possibilities, these certainties were not surprising. The religious revivals which swept large numbers of slaves into the Christian fold in the late eighteenth and early nineteenth centuries were increasingly based upon notions of individual, volitional conversion and, in the words of one southern minister, "a free salvation to all men thro' the blood of the Lamb." They were based on a practical and implied, if not invariably theological or overt, Arminianism: God would save all who believed in Him; Salvation was there for all to take hold of if they would. This doctrine more and more came to characterize the revivals of the Presbyterians and Baptists as well as those of the more openly Arminian Methodists.[32] The effects of this message upon the slaves who were exposed to and converted by it are illustrated graphically in the spirituals which were the products of these revivals and which continued to spread the evangelical word long after the revivals had passed into history. "What kind o' shoes is dem-a you wear? . . . Dat you can walk upon de air?" slaves asked in one of their spirituals, and answered by emphasizing the element of choice: "Dem shoes I wear am de gospel shoes; . . . An' you can wear dem ef-a you choose." "You got a right, I got a right," they sang, "We all got a right to de tree ob life."[33]

The religious music of the slaves is almost devoid of feelings of depravity or unworthiness, but is rather, as I have tried to show, pervaded by a sense of change, transcendence, ultimate justice, and personal worth. The spirituals have been referred to as "sorrow songs," and in some respects they were. The slaves sang of "rollin' thro' an unfriendly world," of being "a-trouble in de mind," of living in a world which was a "howling wilderness," "a hell to me," of feeling like a "motherless child," "a po' little orphan chile in de worl'," a "home-e-less child," of fearing that "Trouble will bury me down."[34]

But these feelings were rarely pervasive or permanent; almost always they were overshadowed by a triumphant note of affirmation. Even so despairing a wail as *Nobody Knows The Trouble I've Had* could suddenly have its mood transformed by lines like: "One morning I was a-walking down, . . . Saw some berries a-hanging down, . . . I pick de berry and I suck de juice, . . . Just as sweet as de honey in de comb." Similarly, amid the deep sorrow of *Sometimes I Feel Like a Motherless Chile*, sudden release could come with the lines: "Sometimes I feel like / A eagle in de air. . . . Spread my wings an' / Fly, fly, fly."[35] Slaves spent little time singing of the horrors of hell or damnation. Their songs of the Devil pictured a harsh but almost semicomic figure (often, one suspects, a surrogate for the white man), over whom they triumphed with reassuring regularity:

> The Devil's mad and I'm glad,
> He lost the soul he thought he had.[36]

> Ole Satan toss a ball at me.
> O me no weary yet . . .

> Him tink de ball would hit my soul.
> O me no weary yet . . .

> De ball for hell and I for heaven.
> O me no weary yet . . .[37]

> Ole Satan thought he had a mighty aim;
> He missed my soul and caught my sins.
> Cry Amen, cry Amen, cry Amen to God!

> He took my sins upon his back;
> Went muttering and grumbling down to hell.
> Cry Amen, cry Amen, cry Amen to God!

> Ole Satan's church is here below.
> Up to God's free church I hope to go.
> Cry Amen, cry Amen, cry Amen to God![38]

For all their inevitable sadness, slave songs were characterized more by a feeling of confidence than of despair. There was confidence that contemporary power relationships were not immutable: "Did not old Pharaoh get lost, get lost, get lost, . . . get lost in the Red Sea?"; confidence in the possibilities of instantaneous change: "Jesus make de dumb to speak. . . . Jesus make de cripple walk. . . . Jesus give de blind his sight. . . . Jesus do most anything"; confidence in the rewards of persistence: "Keep a' inching along like a poor inchworm, / Jesus will come by'nd bye"; confidence that nothing could stand in the way of the justice they would receive: "You kin hender me here, but you can't do it dah," "O no man, no man, no man can hinder me"; confidence in the prospects of the future: "We'll walk de golden streets / Of de New Jerusalem." Religion, the slaves sang, "is good for anything, . . . Religion make you happy, . . . Religion gib me patience . . . O member, get Religion . . . Religion is so sweet."[39]

The slaves often pursued the "sweetness" of their religion in the face of many obstacles. Becky Ilsey, who was sixteen when she was emancipated, recalled many years later:

> 'Fo' de war when we'd have a meetin' at night, wuz mos' always 'way in de woods or de bushes some whar so de white folks couldn't hear, an' when dey'd sing a spiritual an' de spirit 'gin to shout some de elders would go 'mongst de folks an' put dey han' over dey mouf an' some times put a clof in dey mouf an' say: "Spirit don talk so loud or de patterol break us up." You know dey had white patterols what went 'roun' at night to see de niggers didn't cut up no devilment, an' den de meetin' would break up an' some would go to one house an' some to er nudder an' dey would groan er w'ile, den go home.[40]

Elizabeth Ross Hite testified that although she and her fellow slaves on a Louisiana plantation were Catholics, "lots didn't like that 'ligion."

> We used to hide behind some bricks and hold church ourselves. You see, the Catholic preachers from France wouldn't let us shout, and the Lawd done said you gotta shout if you want to be saved. That's in the Bible.
> Sometimes we held church all night long, 'til way in the mornin'. We burned some grease in a can for the preacher to see the Bible by. . . .
> See, our master didn't like us to have much 'ligion, said it made us lag in our work. He jest wanted us to be Catholicses on Sundays and go to mass and not study 'bout nothin' like that on week days. He didn't want us shoutin' and moanin' all day 'long, but you gotta shout and you gotta moan if you wants to be saved.[41]

Slaves broke the proscription against unsupervised or unauthorized meetings by holding their services in secret, well-hidden areas, usually referred to as "hush-harbors." Amanda McCray testified that on her Florida plantation there was a praying ground where "the grass never had a chance ter grow fer the troubled knees that kept it crushed down," and Andrew Moss remembered that on the Georgia plantation where he grew up all the slaves had their private prayer grounds: "My Mammy's was a ole twisted thick-rooted muscadine bush. She'd go in dar and pray for deliverance of de slaves."[42] Even here the slaves were often discovered by the white patrols. "Den dey would rush in an' start whippin' an' beatin' de slaves unmerciful," West Turner of Virginia reported. ". . . an' do you know some o' dem devils was mean an' sinful 'nough to say, 'If I ketch you here servin' God, I'll beat you. You ain't got no time to serve God. We bought you to serve us.' "[43] Slaves found many ways to continue to speak with their gods. Patsy Larkin recalled that on her plantation the slaves would steal away into the cane thickets and pray in a prostrate position with their faces close to the ground so that no sound would escape. Kalvin Woods, a slave preacher, described how slave women would take old quilts and rags and soak them before hanging them up in the shape of a small room, "and the slaves who were interested about it would huddle up behind these quilts to do their praying, preaching and singing. These wet rags were used to keep the sound of their voices from penetrating the air." On a Louisiana plantation the slaves would gather in the woods at night, form a circle on their knees, and pray over a vessel of water to drown the sound.[44] The most commonly used method, in which the slaves had great confidence, was simply to turn a large pot upside down. "All the noise would go into that kettle," an ex-slave explained. "They could shout and sing all they wanted to and the noise wouldn't go outside."[45]

Religious services were not confined to formal meetings, open or secret, but were often informal and spontaneous. One former slave remembered how religious enthusiasm could begin simply with a group of slaves sitting in front of their cabins after supper on a summer evening. Someone might start humming an old hymn; the humming would spread from house to house and would be transformed into song. "It wouldn't be long before some of them got happy and started to shouting. Many of them got converted at just such meetings."[46] Wherever the slaves practiced their religion—in formal church settings, in their own praise houses, in camp meetings, in their secret hush-harbors—it was characterized by physical and spiritual enthusiasm and involvement. A white visitor observing a slave religious gathering on a Georgia plantation noted that they sang "with all their souls and with all their bodies in unison; for their bodies rocked, their heads nodded, their feet stamped, their knees shook, their elbows and their hands beat time to the tune and the words which they sang with evident delight. One must see these people singing if one is rightly to understand their life."[47] Attempting to explain why the slaves shouted, an old slave preacher testified, "There is a joy on the inside and it wells up so strong that we can't keep still. It is fire in the bones. Any time that fire touches a man, he will jump."[48]

The slaves were no more passive receptors of sermons than they were of hymns and spirituals; they became participants in both forms of worship. Attending à slave service in New Orleans in the 1850s, Frederick Olmsted carefully recorded a single passage of the black preacher's sermon which was punctuated every few sentences with cries from the parishioners of "yes, glory!" "that's it, hit him again! hit him again! oh, glory! hi! hi! glory!" "glory, glory, glory,!" "Glory!—oh, yes! yes!—sweet Lord! sweet Lord!" "yes, sir! oh, Lord, yes!" "yes! yes!" "oh! Lord! help us!" "Ha! ha! HA!" "Glory to the Lord!" The responses were not confined to ejaculations of this kind, "but shouts, and groans, terrific shrieks, and indescribable expressions of ecstacy—of pleasure or agony—and even stamping, jumping, and clapping of hands, were added. The tumult often resembled that of an excited political meeting."[49] For many slaves shouting was both a compelling personal need and a religious requirement. A well-known joke told of a master who was so embarrassed by the uproar his slave made every Sunday at church that he promised him a new pair of boots if he would stop making so much noise. The slave agreed to try, and at the next meeting he did his best to keep quiet so that he might win his prize, but the "spirit" proved too great a force to contain. "Glory to God!" he finally cried out. "Boots or no boots, glory to God!"[50]

The slaves clearly craved the affirmation and promise of their religion. It would be a mistake, however, to see this urge as exclusively otherworldly. When Thomas Wentworth Higginson observed that the spirituals exhibited "nothing but patience for this life,—nothing but triumph in the next," he, and later observers who elaborated upon this judgment, were indulging in hyperbole. Although Jesus was ubiquitous in the spirituals, it was not invariably the Jesus of the New Testament of whom the slaves sang, but frequently a Jesus transformed into an Old Testament warrior whose victories were temporal as well as spiritual: "Mass Jesus" who engaged in personal combat with the Devil; "King Jesus" seated on a milk-white horse with sword and shield in hand. "Ride on, King Jesus," "Ride on, conquering King," "The God I serve is a man of war," the slaves sang.[51] This transformation of Jesus is symptomatic of the slaves' selectivity in choosing those parts of the Bible which were to serve as the basis of their religious consciousness. Howard Thurman, a Negro minister who as a boy had the duty of reading the Bible to his grandmother, was perplexed by her refusal to allow him to read from the Epistles of Paul.

When at length I asked the reason, she told me that during the days of slavery, the minister (white) on the plantation was always preaching from the Pauline letters—"Slaves, be obedient to your masters," etc. "I vowed to myself," she said, "that if freedom ever came and I learned to read, I would never read that part of the Bible!"[52]

This experience and reaction were typical. Slaves simply refused to be uncritical recipients of a religion defined and controlled by white intermediaries and interpreters. No matter how respectfully and attentively they might listen to the white preachers, no matter how well they might sing the traditional hymns, it was their own preachers and their own songs that stirred them the most. Observing his black soldiers at religious services, Colonel Higginson wrote: "they sang reluctantly, even on Sunday, the long and short metres of the hymn-books, always gladly yielding to the more potent excitement of their own 'spirituals.' "[53] In Alabama, Ella Storrs Christian noted in her diary: "When Baptist Negroes attended the church of their masters, or when their mistress sang with them, they used hymn books, but in their own meetings they often made up their own words and tunes. They said their songs had 'more religion than those in the books.' "[54] "Dat ole white preachin' wasn't nothin'," Nancy Williams observed. "Ole white preachers used to talk wid dey tongues widdout sayin' nothin' but Jesus told us slaves to talk wid our hearts." "White folks can't pray right to de black man's God," Henrietta Perry agreed. "Cain't nobody do it for you. You got to call on God yourself when de spirit tell you."[55]

Of course there were many white preachers who were able to reach the slaves they preached to and who affected them in important ways. But even the most talented and devoted among them faced certain grave obstacles resulting from the tension between their desire to spread the Gospel and their need to use Christianity as a form of social control. In his autobiographical *Sketches from Slave Life*, published in 1855, the black minister Peter Randolph wrote that when he was a slave in Prince George County, Virginia, he and his fellow slaves had the rather uninspiring choice of listening to the white Reverend G. Harrison who taught them: "Servants obey your masters. Do not *steal* or *lie*, for this is very wrong. Such conduct is sinning against the Holy Ghost, *and is base ingratitude to your kind masters, who feed, clothe and protect you*," or the white Reverend James L. Goltney who warned: "It is the devil who tells you to try and be free."[56] The Reverend A. F. Dickson, whose Charleston congregation included over four hundred blacks and whose published

sermons served as a model for other whites ministering to the slaves, reduced the Judeo-Christian ethic to a triad stressing humility, patience, and
fear of sin.[57] The Reverend Charles C. Jones, who devoted so much of his
life to propagating the Gospel among slaves, illustrated exactly what it
was that limited his influence with them in the *Catechism* he published in
1844:

> Q. What command has God given to Servants, concerning obedience
> to their Masters?
> A. "Servants obey in all things your Masters . . . fearing God."
> Q. How are they to try to please their Masters?
> A. "With good will, doing service as unto the Lord and not unto
> men." . . .
> Q. But suppose the Master is hard to please, and threatens and punishes
> more than he ought, what is the Slave to do?
> A. Do his best to please him.
> Q. When the Slave suffers *wrongfully*, at the hands of his Master, and
> to please God, takes it patiently, will God reward him for it?
> A. Yes.
> Q. Is it right for the Slave *to run away*, or is it right to harbour a
> runaway?
> A. No. . . .
> Q. Will Servants have to account to God for the manner in which they
> serve their Masters on earth?
> A. Yes.[58]

In a catechistic exchange between a Methodist minister and a slave in
Alabama, the message was even less subtle:

> Q. What did God make you for?
> A. To make a crop.[59]

This attempt to reduce Christianity to an ethic of pure submission was
rejected and resented by the slaves. After listening to the white minister
counsel obedience to whites, an old black worshipper in the African
Church in Richmond declared: "He be d——d! God am not sich a
fool!"[60] Slaves generally suffered these sermons in silence but there were
exceptions. Victoria McMullen reported that her grandmother in Arkansas
was punished for not going to church on the Sabbath but still she refused,
insisting: "No, I don't want to hear that same old sermon: 'Stay out of
your missus' and master's henhouse. Don't steal your missus' and master's
chickens. Stay out of your missus' and master's smokehouse. Don't steal
your missus' and master's hams.' I don't steal nothing. Don't need to tell
me not to."[61] In the midst of a white minister's sermon, Uncle Silas, an

elderly slave in Virginia, cried out: "Is us slaves gonna be free in Heaven?" The preacher looked up in surprise and anger, paused a moment, and then continued his sermon, but the old man persisted: "Is God gonna free us slaves when we git to Heaven?" A slave who was present described the rest of the encounter:

> Old white preacher pult out his handkerchief an' wiped de sweat fum his face. "Jesus says come unto Me ye who are free fum sin an' I will give you salvation." "Gonna give us freedom 'long wid salvation?" ask Uncle Silas. "De Lawd gives an' de Lawd takes away, and he dat is widdout sin is gonna have life everlasin'," preached de preacher. Den he went ahead preachin', fast-like, widdout payin' no 'tention to Uncle Silas.[62]

The dilemma that white ministers faced was simple to grasp but not to resolve: the doctrine they were attempting to inculcate could easily subvert the institution of slavery—and both they and the slaves realized it. Thus tensions and contradictions were inevitable. William Meade, Episcopal Bishop of Virginia, could teach slaves in one sermon that "what faults you are guilty of towards your masters and mistresses are faults done against God Himself . . . I tell you that your masters and mistresses are God's overseers, and that, if you are faulty towards them, God Himself will punish you severely for it in the next world," while in another sermon he assured the slaves that "God is no respector of persons" and specifically applied the case of the rich man who went to Hell while the beggar at his gate went to Heaven to the life of the black slave.[63] The Methodist minister John Dixon Long, who preached in Maryland from 1839 to 1856, was continually disturbed by the "elementary and abstract preaching" he was forced to engage in and the "adulterated Gospel" he was forced to embrace because of slavery. "When you want to denounce sin," he wrote, "you must go to Adam and Eve, and to the Jews in the wilderness. You must be careful, however, when slaves are present, how you talk about Pharaoh making slaves of the Hebrews, and refusing to let the people leave Egypt. At any rate, you must make no direct application of the subject." During one of his sermons on the conduct of Cain toward Abel, a slave asked him if he thought it was right for one brother to sell another. Long was at first confused and finally could do no better than to counsel: "Colored friends, it is best for you not to discuss such questions here." "What preachers in the South," he complained, "can say with Paul that they have not shunned to declare the whole counsel of God?"[64] During a debate in the South Carolina legislature over a bill (ultimately passed in 1834) prohibiting slaves from learning to read and write, Whitemarsh B.

Seabrook put it more succinctly: anyone who wanted slaves to read the *entire* Bible was fit for a "room in the Lunatic Asylum."[65]

Until such recent studies as Eugene Genovese's,[66] the important role of the Negro preacher in slavery was largely ignored by scholars, though the historical record is clear enough. In 1790 John Leland of Virginia noted that in their religious services the slaves "seem in general to put more confidence in their own colour, than they do in whites; when they attempt to preach, they seldom fail of being very zealous; their language is broken, but they understand each other, and the whites may gain their ideas."[67] Traveling in Alabama some fifty years later, Sir Charles Lyell observed, "the negroes like a preacher of their own race."[68] Touring the slave states of the eastern seaboard, Frederick Olmsted noted that black preachers were common: "On almost every large plantation, and in every neighborhood of small ones, there is one man who has come to be considered the head or pastor of the local church. The office among the negroes, as among all other people, confers a certain importance and power."[69] Henry Ravenel of South Carolina wrote that the slaves on his plantation "had local preachers of their own who conducted their services in the absence of the other [the white preacher]. This colored preacher was always one of great influence. . . ."[70] Amanda McCray, who had been a slave in Florida, recalled that the slave minister on her plantation was not obliged to engage in hard labor, went about the plantation "all dressed up" in a frock coat and store bought shoes, and was held in awe by the other slaves.[71] Northern whites who went South to work with the freedmen during and directly after the Civil War often commented upon the "great power which the chief elders of their churches possess over the rest of the negroes." Referring to an old slave preacher, a federal official in Alexandria, Virginia, exclaimed, "this old negro has more influence over the blacks, and does more good among them, than all the missionaries and chaplains who have been sent here."[72] "Mostly we had white preachers," Anthony Dawson of North Carolina remembered, "but when we had a black preacher that was heaven."[73]

Given the precariousness and delicacy of their position, it is not surprising that black preachers often repeated the message of their white counterparts. "We had some nigger preachers," an ex-slave in Tennessee recalled, "but they would say, 'Obey your mistress and marster.' They didn't know nothing else to say."[74] Frank Roberson described a typical service on the plantation where he was a slave. First the white minister rose and preached variations on the theme "Obey your master"; then his black colleague, Parson Tom, would get up and repeat everything that the white preacher had said, "because he was afraid to say anything different."[75] Nevertheless, the evidence indicates that the behavior of black preachers would vary radically with altered circumstances. William Parker, a Methodist minister in Virginia, told Helen Ludlow shortly after the Civil War that in the 1820s he had been made a preacher when the white parson on his plantation discovered he could read. His duties consisted of assisting in the singing, leading the prayer meetings, and preaching when his white superior was absent, which was often. "You know de cullered people was obleege to hab white ministers in slavery times. He use' to come down onst in a while and preach up 'Sarvants, obey your marssas,' an' den I'd preach de gospil in between times 'cep' when he was to hear me; den I'd hab to take his tex'."[76] Parker's distinction between the "Gospel" and the message generally promulgated by the whites was commonly held among the slaves who knew the Scriptures had more to teach them than obedience. Anderson Edwards, a black preacher in Texas, was forced to preach what his master told him to: "he say tell them niggers iffen they obeys the master they goes to Heaven; but I knowed there's something better for them, but daren't tell them 'cept on the sly. That I done lots. I tells 'em iffen they keep praying, the Lord will set 'em free."[77]

Occasionally it was possible for a slave minister to disagree openly with his white colleague and to insist upon his own interpretation of the Scriptures. In 1847 an observer at a slave service in New Orleans wrote that as soon as the white minister had finished his sermon the black minister rose and corrected him:

> My brudder call your 'tention to de fact dat God did temp Abra'am; and den he go on to tell you 'bout Abra'am's temptation. Now I don't like dat word "temp-tation." "God can not be tempted wid evil; neither temp-test he any man." Suppose we read that word temp *try.* Ah, my brudder (turning to the white preacher), why you no say *try?*—"After dese things God did *try* Abra'am." He try his people *now.* Who hasn't trials and triberlations from God? But I don't like dat word *temp.* I—*tell-you* (to the congregation) *God—don't—temp—any-body!*

Several years later this same white observer lived in a South Carolina courthouse town and found that week after week the slaves, tired from a hard day's work, would sleep through the white sermon at the Saturday evening services. "But let the congregation be surprised by the unexpected visit of some colored preacher, or let the exercises consist wholly of prayer, exhortation, and singing, and the fervor, vivacity, and life of the meeting would continue for the hour without diminishing." "None can move the negro," he concluded, "but a negro."[78]

There was great exaggeration in the last remark, of course. White preachers often moved the slaves, especially at the camp meetings. But it is true that slaves preferred black preachers who, all things considered, were in a better position to understand the kind of message the slaves wanted to hear, as in this sermon delivered by a Negro Baptist minister named Bentley to a congregation of Georgia slaves in 1851:

> I remember on one occasion, when the President of the United States came to Georgia and to our town of Savannah. I remember what an ado the people made, and how they went out in big carriages to meet him. The clouds of dust were terrible, and the great cannon pealed forth one salute after another. Then the president came in a grand, beautiful carriage and drove to the best house in the whole town, and that was Mrs. Scarborough's! And when he came there he seated himself in the window. But a cord was drawn around the house to keep us negroes and other poor folks from coming too near. We had to stand outside and only get a sight of the president as he sat at the window. But the great gentlemen and the rich folks went freely up the steps and in through the door and shook hands with him. Now, did Christ come in this way? Did He come only to the rich? Did He shake hands only with them? No! Blessed be the Lord! He came to the poor! He came to us, and for our sakes, my brothers and sisters!

It is not surprising that the same slaves who would sit silently through sermons admonishing them to treat their masters and mistresses as they would treat the Lord, greeted Bentley's offering with several minutes of laughter, tears, stamping feet, and cries of "yes, yes! Amen! He came to us! Blessed be His name! Amen! Hallelujah!"[79]

Like other forms of Christianity, that preached to the slaves contained elements of what Karl Mannheim has identified as *ideology* and *utopia*.[80] The former, conducive to order and stability, and the latter, conducive to transcending and shattering the existing order, were so intermeshed that it is difficult to separate them into totally antithetical forms of slave religion. The teachings of white sermons and songs contained the seeds not merely of submission and docility but of egalitarianism and fundamental change, while those of black sermons and songs certainly can be seen as fostering the promulgation of stability as well as of discontent and the urge toward a different order of things. In spite of this important overlap, distinctions can be made: the religion the masters attempted to inculcate was laced with an emphasis upon morality, obedience, and right conduct as defined by the master class, while that which filled the sermons of black preachers and the songs of black folk was characterized by the apocalyptic visions and heroic exploits of the Scriptures. This was particularly true of slave spirituals, which were informed not by the Epistles of Paul but by the history of the Hebrew Children.

Judging from the songs of his black soldiers, Colonel Higginson concluded that their Bible was constructed primarily from the books of Moses in the Old Testament and of Revelations in the New: "all that lay between, even the life of Jesus, they hardly cared to read or to hear." "Their memories," he noted at another point, "are a vast bewildered chaos of Jewish history and biography; and most of the great events of the past, down to the period of the American Revolution, they instinctively attribute to Moses."[81] Many of those northerners who came to the South to "uplift" the freedmen were deeply disturbed at the Old Testament emphasis of their religion. H. G. Spaulding complained that the ex-slaves needed to be introduced to "the light and warmth of the Gospel," and reported that a Union army officer told him: "Those people had enough of the Old Testament thrown at their heads under slavery. Now give them the glorious utterances and practical teachings of the Great Master."[82] Shortly after his arrival in Alabama in 1865, a northern army chaplain wrote of the slaves, "Moses is their *ideal* of all that is high, and noble, and perfect, in man," while Christ was regarded "not so much in the light of a *spiritual* Deliverer, as that of a second Moses."[83]

The essence of slave religion cannot be fully grasped without understanding this Old Testament bias. It is important that Daniel and David and Joshua and Jonah and Moses and Noah, all of whom fill the lines of the spirituals, were delivered in *this* world and delivered in ways which struck the imagination of the slaves. Over and over their songs dwelt upon the spectacle of the Red Sea opening to allow the Hebrew slaves past before inundating the mighty armies of the Pharaoh. They lingered delightedly upon the image of little David humbling the great Goliath with a stone—a pretechnological victory which postbellum Negroes were to expand upon in their songs of John Henry. They retold in endless variation the stories of the blind and humbled Samson bringing down the mansions of his conquerors; of the ridiculed Noah patiently building the ark which would deliver him from the doom of a mocking world; of the timid Jonah attaining freedom from his confinement through faith. The similarity of these tales to the situation of the slaves was too clear for them not to see it; too clear for us to believe that the songs had no worldly content for blacks in bondage. "O my Lord delivered Daniel," the slaves observed, and responded logically: "O why not deliver me, too?"

> He delivered Daniel from de lion's den,
>   Jonah from de belly ob de whale,
> And de Hebrew children from de fiery furnace,
>   And why not every man?[84]

In another spiritual the slaves rehearsed the triumphs of the Hebrew Children in verse after verse, concluding each with the comforting thought: "And the God dat lived in Moses' [Dan'el's, David's] time is jus' de same today." The "mighty rocky road" that "I must travel," another of the slaves' songs insisted, is "De rough, rocky road what Moses done travel."[85]

These songs state as clearly as anything can the manner in which the sacred world of the slaves was able to fuse the precedents of the past, the conditions of the present, and the promise of the future into one connected reality. In this respect there was always a latent and symbolic element of protest in the slave's religious songs which frequently became overt and explicit. Frederick Douglass asserted that for him and many of his fellow slaves the song, "O Canaan, sweet Canaan, / I am bound for the land of Canaan," symbolized "something more than a hope of reaching heaven. We meant to reach the *North*, and the North was our Canaan," and he wrote that the lines of another spiritual, "Run to Jesus, shun the danger, / I don't expect to stay much longer here," had a double meaning which first suggested to him the thought of escaping from slavery.[86] Similarly, when the black troops in Higginson's regiment sang:

> We'll soon be free,
> We'll soon be free,
> We'll soon be free,
>   When de Lord will call us home.

a young drummer boy explained to him, "Dey tink *de Lord* mean for say *de Yankees*."[87] These veiled meanings by no means invariably eluded the whites. At the outbreak of the Civil War slaves in Georgetown, South Carolina, were jailed for singing this song, and Joseph Farley, who had been a slave in Virginia and Kentucky, testified that white patrols would often visit the slaves' religious services and stop them if they said or sang anything considered offensive: "One time when they were singing, 'Ride on King Jesus, No man can hinder Thee,' the padderollers told them to stop or they would show him whether they could be hindered or not."[88]

There is no reason to doubt that slaves may have used their songs as a means of secret communication. An ex-slave told Lydia Parrish that when he and his fellow slaves "suspicioned" that one of their number was telling tales to the driver, they would sing lines like the following while working in the field:

O Judyas he wuz a 'ceitful man
　He went an' betray a mos' innocen' man.
Fo' thirty pieces a silver dat it wuz done
　He went in de woods an' 'e self he hung.[89]

As many writers have argued and as some former slaves have testified, such spirituals as the commonly heard "Steal away, steal away, steal away to Jesus!" could be used as explicit calls to secret meetings. Miles Mark Fisher was correct in seeing the slaves' songs as being filled with innuendo and hidden meaning. But it is not necessary to invest the spirituals with a secular function only at the price of divesting them of their religious content, as Fisher has done.[90] While we may make such clear-cut distinctions, I have tried to show that the slaves did not. For them religion never constituted a simple escape from this world, because their conception of the world was more expansive than modern man's.

Nowhere is this better illustrated than during the Civil War itself. While the war gave rise to such new spirituals as "Before I'd be a slave / I'd be buried in my grave, / And go home to my Lord and be saved!" or the popular *Many Thousand Go*, with its jubilant rejection of all the facets of slave life—"No more peck o'corn for me, . . . No more driver's lash for me, . . . No more pint o'salt for me, . . . No more hundred lash for me, . . . No more mistress' call for me"[91]—the important thing was not that large numbers of slaves now could create new songs which openly expressed their views of slavery; that was to be expected. More significant was the ease with which their old songs fit their new situation. With so much of their inspiration drawn from the events of the Old Testament and the Book of Revelation, the slaves had long sung of wars, of battles, of the Army of the Lord, of Soldiers of the Cross, of trumpets summoning the faithful, of vanquishing the hosts of evil. These songs especially were, as Higginson put it, "available for camp purposes with very little strain upon their symbolism." "We'll cross de mighty river," his troops sang while marching or rowing,

We'll cross de danger water, . . .
O Pharaoh's army drownded!
My army cross over.

"O blow your trumpet, Gabriel," they sang,

> Blow your trumpet louder,
> And I want dat trumpet to blow me home
> To my new Jerusalem.

But they also found their less overtly militant songs quite as appropriate to warfare. Their most popular and effective marching song was:

> Jesus call you. Go in de wilderness,
>   Go in de wilderness, go in de wilderness,
> Jesus call you. Go in de wilderness
>   To wait upon de Lord.[92]

Black Union soldiers found it no more incongruous to accompany their fight for freedom with the sacred songs of their bondage than they had found it inappropriate as slaves to sing their spirituals while picking cotton or shucking corn. Their religious songs, like their religion itself, was of this world as well as the next.

Slave songs present us with abundant evidence that in the structure of their music and dance, in the uses to which music was put, in the survival of the oral tradition, in the retention of such practices as spirit possession which often accompanied the creation of spirituals, and in the ways in which the slaves expressed their new religion, important elements of their shared African heritage remained alive not just as quaint cultural vestiges but as vitally creative elements of slave culture. This could never have happened if slavery had so completely closed in around the slave, so totally penetrated his personality structure as to reduce him to a kind of *tabula rasa* upon which the white man could write what he chose.

Slave songs provide us with the beginnings of a very different kind of hypothesis: that the preliterate, premodern Africans, with their sacred world view, were so imperfectly acculturated into the secular American society into which they were thrust, were so completely denied access to the ideology and dreams which formed the core of the consciousness of other Americans, that they were forced to fall back upon the only cultural frames of reference that made any sense to them and gave them any feeling of security. I use the word "forced" advisedly. Even if the slaves had had the opportunity to enter fully into the life of the larger society, they might still have chosen to retain and perpetuate certain elements of their African heritage. But the point is that they really had no choice. True acculturation was denied to most slaves. The alternatives were either to remain in a state of cultural limbo, divested of the old cultural patterns but not allowed to adopt those of their new homeland—which in the long run is no alternative at all—or to cling to as many as possible of the old ways of thinking and acting. The slaves' oral tradition, their music, and their religious outlook served this latter function and constituted a cultural refuge at least potentially capable of protecting their personalities from some of the worst ravages of the slave system.

The argument of Professors Tannenbaum and Elkins that the Protestant churches in the United States did not act as a buffer between the slave and his master is persuasive enough, but it betrays a modern preoccupation with purely institutional arrangements.[93] Religon is more than an institution, and because Protestant churches failed to protect the slave's inner being from the incursions of the slave system, it does not follow that the spiritual message of Protestantism failed as well. Certainly the slaves themselves perceived the distinction. Referring to the white patrols which frequently and brutally interfered with the religious services of the slaves on his plantation, West Turner exclaimed: "Dey law us out of church, but dey couldn't law 'way Christ."[94] Slave songs are a testament to the way in which Christianity provided slaves with the precedents, heroes, and future promise that allowed them to transcend the purely temporal bonds of the Peculiar Institution.

Historians have frequently failed to perceive the full importance of this because they have not taken the slave's religiosity seriously enough. A people cannot create a music as forceful and striking as slave music out of a mere uninternalized anodyne. Those who have argued that Negroes did not oppose slavery in any meaningful way are writing from a modern, political context. What they really mean is that the slaves found no *political* means to oppose slavery. But slaves, to borrow Professor Hobsbawm's term, were prepolitical beings in a prepolitical situation.[95] Within their frame of reference there were other—and from the point of view of personality development, not necessarily less effective—means of escape and opposition. If mid-twentieth-century historians have difficulty perceiving the sacred universe created by slaves as a serious alternative to the societal system created by southern slaveholders, the problem may be the historians' and not the slaves'.

Above all, the study of slave songs forces the historian to move out of his own culture, in which music plays a peripheral role, and offers him the opportunity to understand the ways in which black slaves were able to perpetuate much of the centrality and functional importance that music had for their African ancestors. In the concluding lines of his perceptive study of primitive song, C. M. Bowra has written:

> Primitive song is indispensable to those who practice it. . . . they cannot do without song, which both formulates and answers their nagging questions, enables them to pursue action with zest and confidence, brings them into touch with gods and spirits, and makes them feel less strange in the natural world. . . . it gives to them a solid centre in what otherwise would be almost chaos, and a continuity in their being, which would too easily dissolve before the calls of the implacable present. . . . through its words men, who might otherwise give in to the malice of circumstances, find their old powers revived or new powers stirring in them, and through these life itself is sustained and renewed and fulfilled.[96]

This, I think, sums up concisely the function of song for the slave. Without a general understanding of that function, without a specific understanding of the content and meaning of slave song, there can be no full comprehension of the effects of slavery upon the slave or the meaning of the society from which slaves emerged at emancipation.

THE QUEST FOR CONTROL: SLAVE FOLK BELIEFS

The sacred world of the slaves was not confined to Christianity. There existed as well a network of beliefs and practices independent of yet strongly related to the slaves' formal religion. If religion is, as Anthony F. C. Wallace has defined it, "That kind of behavior which can be classified as belief and ritual concerned with supernatural beings, powers, and forces,"[1] then the slaves' religion went beyond the creeds of the Protestant denominations that converted them. The slaves' sacred folk beliefs may not have been part of their formal religion, but they were *religious* beliefs nonetheless, and many slaves would have had some difficulty disentangling the web that bound their formal creed and their folk religion into an intelligible whole.

These interconnections have frequently been obscured by a tendency—usually imprecise and ethnocentric—to separate "superstition" from "religion," forgetting that, as Gustav Jahoda has observed, one man's religion is another man's superstition. Alexander Krappe, for instance, has defined superstition as "any belief or practice that is not recommended or en-joined by any of the great religions such as Christianity, Judaism, Islam and Buddhism."[2] It is obviously still necessary to recall Voltaire's warning that the boundaries of superstition are difficult to delineate: "A French-man travelling in Italy finds almost everything superstitious, and is hardly wrong. The archbishop of Canterbury claims that the archbishop of Paris is superstitious; the Presbyterians levy the same reproach against his Grace of Canterbury, and are in their turn called superstitious by the Quakers, who are the most superstitious of men in the eyes of other Christians."[3] It is important to understand that, in the cultures from which the slaves came, phenomena and activities that we might be tempted to dismiss as "superstitious" were legitimate and important modes of comprehending and operating within a universe perceived of in sacred terms. To distin-guish these activities and beliefs from religion is a meaningless exercise. Even my own practice of separating the slaves' Christianity from their sacred folk beliefs by discussing each in different sections can be mislead-ing. The slaves' religion was multifaceted and extremely eclectic in the African tradition. For most slaves there was no unbridgeable gulf between the beliefs described in the last section and those I will discuss in this one.

Of course for some slaves such a chasm did exist. "Hoodooers," and fortune tellers, Janie Scott announced, "can't tell you nothing. When Christ was risen He carried all prophets with Him and didn't leave any wise folks able to tell things going to happen here on earth. Everything Christ wanted folks to know had already happened."[4] More commonly such divisions were permeable: some aspects of folk beliefs were rejected rather firmly, others were easily assimilated. Martha Colquitt remembered hearing her fellow slaves talking about Voodoo, but her grandmother and mother, both devout Christians, "told us chillun voodoo wuz a no 'count doin' of de devil, and Christians wuz never to pay it no 'tention. Us wuz to be happy in de Lord, and let voodoo and de devil alone." Her very next words made it clear that all folk beliefs were not similarly proscribed: "None of us liked to hear scritch owls holler, 'cause everybody thought it meant somebody in dat house wuz goin' to die if a scritch owl lit on your chimney and hollered, so us would stir up de fire to make de smoke drive him away." "I sho' does b'lieve in ha'nts," she added, " 'cause I done heared one and I seed it too, leasewise I seed its light."[5] "We didn't have no voodoo women nor conjure folks at our 'Twenty Acres,' " Anthony Dawson of North Carolina testified. "We all knowed about the Word and the unseen Son of God and we didn't put no stock in conjure. 'Course we had luck charms and good and bad signs, but everybody got dem things, even nowadays."[6]

For many other slaves there were few tensions of this sort; the various components of their religion complemented and reinforced each other. The Bible, in fact, could be used to prove the efficacy of sacred folk beliefs. "Does I believe in spirits?" Charles Hayes asked. "Sho I does. When Christ walked on de water, de Apostles was skeered he was a spirit, but Jesus told dem dat he warn't no spirit, dat he was as 'live as dey was. . . . He tol' 'em dat spirits couln't be teched, dat dey jus' melted when you tried to. So, Mistis, Jesus musta meant dat dere was sich a thing as spirits."[7] Thomas Smith of Georgia made the same point more forcefully when he insisted that the magic power used by Moses to turn his rod into a snake before Pharaoh still exists among Negroes. "Dat happen in Africa duh Bible say. Ain dat show dat Africa wuz a lan uh magic powuh since duh beginnin uh histry? Well den, duh descendants ub Africans hab duh same gif tuh do unnatchul ting."[8] If the Scriptures could be used to validate sacred folk beliefs, the latter could be helpful in making Christian beliefs more vivid and immediate, as in the spirituals depicting the Devil as a conjure man:

> Old Satan is a liar and a conjurer, too;
> If you don't mind, he'll conjer you.[9]

An arresting example of the ease with which slaves could amalgamate their various sacred beliefs can be seen in the use slaves made of one of their magical folk beliefs to protect the privacy and integrity of their Christian religious worship. There may be little foundation for the folk notion that turning over a large pot in the middle of a circle of worshippers would absorb the sounds of prayer and song and hide them from the whites, but substantial numbers of slaves believed it would work and this gave them the confidence, the courage, the power to practice their religion in their own way.

Black preachers themselves could embody the full spectrum of religious beliefs. Mary Livermore, who left her native New England to spend several years as a tutor on a large plantation in southern Virginia in the early 1840s, has described the plantation's black preacher, "Uncle Aaron," whose power over his fellow slaves was such that he could publicly denounce their sins during his sermons: "Ef you aint ready t' go t' de Debble jess yit, Ike Martin, quit youah stealin', an' ef you doan, de ole Dragon'll cotch you in de woods some dark night! Ben Solger, stop youah lyin'!"

His authority was enhanced by the slaves' belief that in addition to being a Christian preacher he was a conjurer who could "raise the spirits" and use the charm he wore to become invisible whenever he was threatened.[10] It was undoubtedly this type of preacher W. E. B. Du Bois had in mind when he wrote that the "Priest or Medicine-man" was the chief surviving institution that African slaves had brought with them: "He early appeared on the plantation and found his function as the healer of the sick, the interpreter of the Unknown, the comforter of the sorrowing, the supernatural avenger of wrong, and the one who rudely but picturesquely expressed the longing, disappointment, and resentment of a stolen and oppressed people."[11] Du Bois was characteristically ahead of the scholarly opinion of his age in his assumption that one had to look to Africa for an understanding of a substantial part of the slaves' religious consciousness.

The ethos prevailing in the African cultures from which the slaves came would have had little use for concepts of the absurd. Life was not random or accidental or haphazard. Events were meaningful; they had causes which Man could divine, understand, and profit from. Human beings could "read" the phenomena surrounding and affecting them because Man was part of, not alien to, the Natural Order of things, attached to the Oneness that bound together all matter, animate and inanimate, all spirits, visible or not. It was crucially necessary to understand the world because one was part of it, inexorably linked to it. Survival and happiness and health depended upon being able to read the signs that existed everywhere, to understand the visions that recurrently visited one, to commune with the spirits that filled the world: the spirit of the Supreme Being who could be approached only through the spirits of the pantheon of intermediary deities; the spirits of all the matter that filled the universe—trees, animals, rivers, the very daily utensils and weapons upon which Man was dependent; the spirits of contemporary human beings; the spirits of ancestors who linked the living with the unseen world. There was, as Mary Kingsley has observed, very little gap between things. She has described Africans, before hunting or warfare, rubbing a substance into their weapon to strengthen the spirit within it, talking to it, reminding it of the care they have given it, of the good fights they have had together, imploring it not to fail them: "Go not away from me." She has described Africans bending over a river, talking to its spirit with proper incantations, asking it to upset the canoes of their enemies, to carry down with it the malignant souls of unburied human beings or the ravages of the plague. She has described an individual at a bush fire or in the village palaver house suddenly turn around and say: "You remember that, mother?" to a being that she could not see but that to him was there. To the African, she concluded, "everything is real, very real, horribly real."[12]

But comfortably real as well, for if the spirits that affected mankind had to be implored and propitiated constantly, they also allowed human beings to comprehend and exercise some control over forces which otherwise would have overwhelmed them. If nothing was without meaning, then nothing was beyond understanding. Personal or family misfortunes, sudden, inexplicable illnesses, were not accidental or due to bad luck; they had a root cause which properly understood could lead to their termination or reversal. Relief might come from a better understanding of one's obligations if the source of the problem was lack of duty toward the gods or ancestors or the breaking of some taboo, or it might come from taking the proper counter-measures if the problem was that another human being had invoked the spirits against one. There was no magic so great that a more potent counter-magic could not be found. Human beings, then, were seen in perspective. If they were not at the center of the universe, neither were they ciphers; they were an integral part of the Natural Order and as such were both affected by and had an impact upon the forces and spirits with which they coexisted.[13]

Equipped with these beliefs, African slaves were transported to an environment that was unquestionably alien, yet perhaps not as invariably alien as we have supposed. Even in what Europeans like to call their Age of Enlightenment, they retained an active core of sacred folk beliefs to which slaves could relate with familiarity. In the realm of popular religion and folk beliefs, no less than in the realm of music, the African and West European systems, long assumed to be totally diverse, had enough in common to facilitate syncretism. Keith Thomas has described in admirable detail the network of magic, divination, witchcraft, astrology, and ghost-lore that informed the English world view in the sixteenth and seventeenth centuries. By the end of the seventeenth century, urbanization, the growth of science, the development of attitudes of self-help and of more efficient secular agencies of control, such as insurance companies and fire-fighting brigades, helped to diminish the force of magical folk beliefs, especially among the urban educated and middle classes, but the old patterns of thought and the traditional faiths survived among large segments of the population, particularly in rural areas, and they survived well beyond the seventeenth century. Folklorists in nineteenth-century England documented the continued popular faith in witchcraft, magical healing, omens, ghosts, and divination, which provide documentation for Jacob Burck-hardt's assertion that the religion of the nineteenth century was "rational-ism for the few and magic for the many."[14]

Thus slaves in North America came into contact with people, from other European countries as well as England, who held beliefs that the slaves could adopt or adapt without doing essential violence to their own world view. Here was a universe populated by spirits and witches, by supernatural omens and signs, by charms and magic, by conjuring and healing, that the slaves could understand and operate within. I am not put-ting forward the untenable thesis that Euro-American and Afro-American folk beliefs were either identical or barely distinguishable; only that there were significant areas of similarity and interchangeability. The African practices and beliefs which had the best chance of survival in the New World were those that had European analogues, as so many of the folk beliefs did.[15] It is within this context that one should understand the point made by Newbell Niles Puckett and other folklorists that Afro-American folk beliefs often were more specifically European in form than African.[16] In the realm of supernatural belief, black slaves could absorb so many Euro-American beliefs not because their own African culture had been reduced to a negligible force but because these beliefs fit so easily beside and often in place of their traditional outlooks and convictions. They were easily assimilable—even more so than the formal religion of the whites was—and they were accepted readily by black slaves who must have found in them a source of comfort and familiarity in a world that was hostile and unpredictable.[17]

The retention of traditional beliefs and practices was facilitated by the delay that occurred in the conversion of the African slaves to Christianity. For almost two hundred years whites debated the wisdom of giving their religion to their bondsmen, the chief deterrents being the fear that free-dom inevitably would follow baptism, that conversion would have eco-nomically negative results by prohibiting Sunday labor and consuming valuable time in church attendance, that it would imbue the slaves with dangerous notions of religious equality and make them intractable, and that African "savages" were unworthy associates for white Christians. Even though we lack an adequate study of the slaves' religion in the colo-nial period, it seems safe to say that during these years they had to ac-commodate their religious beliefs to the demands of a harsh economic and social system and to the fears and arbitrary ethnocentrism of their masters who could and did interfere in important ways with their religious practices—the suppression of the use of drums being only one example. Nevertheless, not until the Great Awakening of the 1740s, and for most slaves not until the Great Revivals half a century later, did slaves have the additional and perhaps even greater pressure of a new religion to which they owed allegiance. Thus in the last half of the eighteenth century it is common to find Protestant ministers still lamenting the hold that non-Christian religious practices continued to have upon the slaves. In 1756 Samuel Davies wrote enthusiastically of his own missionary efforts among the slaves in Virginia but complained of the otherwise "almost universal neglect of the many thousand of poor slaves . . . who generally continue Heathens in a Christian Country," and in South Carolina during the Revolution the Reverend Alexander Hewatt observed that the slaves, "a few only excepted, are to this day as great strangers to Christianity, and as much under the influence of Pagan darkness, idolatry and superstition, as they were at their first arrival from Africa."[18]

These observations continued well into the antebellum period. In 1842 Charles C. Jones observed of the slaves among whom he was spreading the Gospel: "They believe in second-sight, in apparitions, charms, witchcraft, and in a kind of irresistible Satanic influence. The superstitions brought from Africa have not been wholly laid aside." Jones' confidence that a "plain and faithful presentation of the Gospel" would reverse this situation was misplaced. When conversion did come it was not invariably at the expense of the slaves' prevalent folk beliefs. In the 1850s a Virginia correspondent of the *New York Times* wrote that in their Christian worship "negroes are excessively superstitious. They have all sorts of 'experiences,' and enjoy the most wonderful revelations. Visions of the supernatural are of nightly occurrence." Frederick Olmsted, touring the same state, observed that, while a "goodly proportion" of the slaves were received into the churches, their religion was dominated by "a miserable system of superstition, the more painful that it employs some forms and words ordinarily connected with true Christianity."[19]

If the possibilities of syncretism with European folk beliefs and the relative absence of competing religions before 1800 fostered the slaves' sacred folk beliefs, the dependent situation they found themselves in was no less important. African slaves were at no time as totally dependent upon whites as some scholars have imagined. Indeed, in some areas—colonial South Carolina is a perfect instance—the Africans were far more familiar with the environment than were the Englishmen. It was to the blacks that the Europeans looked for advice and counsel with regard to the cultivation of rice, indigo, and cotton, the use of such indigenous plants as gourds and the palmetto, knowledge of the medicinal properties of wild plants, herbs, and roots which either duplicated or resembled those the slaves had been familiar with in Africa. It was the slaves and not their masters who knew how to deal with the alligator, so exotic and frightening to Europeans and so commonplace to Africans who had long dealt with the crocodile, and it was the slaves who had the experience necessary to develop the dugout canoe as the prime means of fishing and transportation in the colony for the first several generations.[20] These are merely dramatic examples of the truth that dependency was by no means a one-way process in the daily relationship between masters and bondsmen. And yet the Peculiar Institution undeniably forced its victims into a severe state of dependency, the result largely of the lack of control they had over their own lives and destinies. This lack of control, this absence of power helped to perpetuate the slaves' sacred universe and to intensify their search for supernatural aid and solutions.

Bronislaw Malinowski has shown that on the Trobriand Islands when knowledge was systematic and conditions predictable—in the construction of fences, the weeding of gardens, the building of houses, fire-making, fishing in a well-protected inner lagoon—magic generally was not invoked. But activities and events over which there was limited knowledge and control—climate, blight, and insects in agriculture, incalculable tides, sudden gales, and unknown reefs in boating, fishing in the dangerous and uncertain open sea—all fostered the practice of magic. "We find magic wherever the elements of chance and accident, and the emotional play between hope and fear have a wide and extensive range," Malinowski concluded. "We do not find magic wherever the pursuit is certain, reliable, and well under the control of rational methods and technological processes. Further, we find magic where the element of danger is conspicuous. We do not find it wherever absolute safety eliminates any elements of foreboding."[21] Uncertainty, insufficient knowledge, or lack of control may not be prerequisites for the use of magic, as Malinowski implied, but surely they remain conducive to its use. There is plentiful evidence of this in our own culture and period. In their study of the American soldier during World War II, Samuel Stouffer and his colleagues found that in the highly unpredictable state of warfare, in which the individual soldier becomes an object to be used rather than a free person with some degree of control over his life, there was a blossoming of protective charms and amulets, and an intensified utilization of folk beliefs and rituals.[22] A still more familiar example can be found in the world of athletic competition where the practice of magic rituals is commonplace. In his study of baseball, George Gmelch found little magic associated with the activity of fielding, where the average player succeeds better than 9.7 times in 10. The far less certain and predictable activities of pitching and hitting—the average major league batter succeeds less than 2.5 times in 10—have on the contrary engendered a host of rituals, taboos, and fetishes which any baseball fan is familiar with.[23]

For slaves, who were much closer to a traditional world view and far more exposed to forces over which they had minimal control, magical folk beliefs were a central and necessary part of existence. They were no less important to the slave than his Christian myths, which they supplemented and fortified. Both were crucial sources of strength and release. Both allowed the slaves to exert their will and preserve their sanity by permitting them to impose a sense of rationality and predictability upon a hostile and capricious environment. Christianity helped to accomplish this by providing assurance of the ephemeral quality of the present situation and the glories and retribution to come, both in this world and the next, by solidifying the slaves' sense of communality, and by reinforcing their feelings of self-worth and dignity. Folk beliefs too provided hope, assurance, and a sense of group identification, but they had another dimension as well: they actually offered the slaves sources of power and knowledge alternative to those existing within the world of the master class.

One of the more obvious and common uses to which slave folk beliefs were put was the protection and preservation of health. On many plantations white doctors were employed to cure sick slaves, and on many more masters and mistresses kept a stock of medicines and were themselves skilled users of folk remedies—an area in which Indians, whites, and blacks all shared certain practices and all learned from one another. While slaves acknowledged the medical care extended to them by their masters—"Our white folks was good as dey knowed how to be when us got sick," Callie Elder testified—there is evidence that in doctoring as in preaching slaves frequently distrusted the whites and preferred their own doctors and remedies.[24] In the late eighteenth century William Dawson wrote to ask his fellow Virginia planter Robert Carter if he would send "Brother Tom," his black coachman, to treat a sick slave child on Dawson's plantation, explaining: "The black people at this place hath more faith in him as a doctor than any white doctor; . . ."[25] The South Carolina planter Henry Ravenel told of his slave, Old March, a root doctor who was so commonly consulted by his fellow slaves that the white physician who was called in to treat the slaves "complained that his prescriptions were thrown out of the window, and March's decoctions taken in their stead."[26] Rebecca Hooks testified that on the Georgia plantation where she had been a slave the white doctor was not nearly as popular as the "granny" or midwife who brewed medicines for every ailment.[27] "Well, duh root doctuh wuz all we needed," William Newkirk recalled. "Dey wuz bettuh dan duh doctuhs now-a-days. Deah wuzn all dis yuh cuttin an wen yuh sick, duh root doctuh would make some tea an gib yuh . . . sumpm tuh rub wid an das all. Den for yuh know it, yuh wuz all right."[28]

A number of slave practitioners won considerable renown for their skill. In 1729 the governor of Virginia traded an elderly slave "who has performed many wonderful cures of diseases" his freedom in return for the secret of his medicine, "a concoction of roots and barks"; the South Carolina slave Caesar's cures for poison and rattlesnake bite were so well thought of that in 1750 the legislature awarded him his freedom and ordered his prescriptions published, and more than half a century later they were still in active use as far away as upstate New York; the nineteenth-century white patients of "Doctor Jack," a Tennessee slave, petitioned the state legislature to allow him to practice medicine.[29] Instances like these are worth noting as evidence of the frequent efficacy of slave medicine and of the fact that there was no invariable gulf between black and white medical practices. Nevertheless, in the case of common diseases and ailments it would be a distortion to focus too exclusively on those who specialized in cures, for we might say of the antebellum slaves (and of many antebellum whites as well) what Nicholas Culpepper said of his own mid-seventeenth-century England: "All the nation are already physicians."[30] Indeed, this is precisely what an ex-slave from Kentucky did say: "There were no doctors back there. If you got sick, you would go dig a hole and dig up roots and fix your own medicine. . . . They would make their own pills and syrups, and so on. They were a country full of people who practiced with herbs; white and colored people did this." "They had remedies for nearly everything at that time," another former slave remembered. "Sometimes they would kill a cat and make soup out of it. I remember my uncle killed one once, and made a soup for one of us in the family who had the whooping cough. For babies, they made different kinda teas. One they called sheep's apple, made out of sheep's balls."[31]

Slaves seem to have quietly resisted those masters who attempted to proscribe these practices. "Old Master wouldn't let us take herb medicine, and he got all our medicine in Van Buren when we was sick," George Kye of Arkansas testified. "But I wore a buckeye on my neck just the same."[32] As this last remedy indicates, disease being a spiritual as well as a physical problem, it was not always necessary to ingest medicines; it was sometimes better to wear them. Thus the ubiquitous bag of asafetida, a gum resin obtained from the roots of certain plants, hung from the necks of children to ward off almost any conceivable ailment. A teething baby could be relieved by tying a string of coppers or hog's teeth around his or her neck; chills could be cured by tying the same number of knots in a piece of cotton string as the number of chills one had and then tying the string to a persimmon tree; a tarred rope worn around the waist would cure rheumatism; a nutmeg hung from the neck was effective for neuralgia; the most agonizing toothache would disappear if three deep incisions were made in the northern side of a tree at sundown and blood from the infected tooth was transferred to the tree; snake bites could be treated by splitting a living chicken open and laying it on the wound.[33] This list could be extended almost indefinitely; there is no subject in slave reminiscences more fully documented than that of folk medicine. It would be possible to construct an extensive and probably fairly complete pharmacopoeia from these recollections.

Some slaves spoke of having learned their medical lore directly from their African forebears. Rosa Grant was taught by her African-born grandmother, Ryna O'Neal, that a "misery" in the arm or leg could be cured by splitting a black chicken open and applying it to the painful area. Jack Waldburg's teacher was also his African-born grandmother: "She duh one wut lun me tuh make medicine frum root. She a midwife an tell me duh kine tuh use."[34] Africa contributed more than specific cures; it contributed a general outlook. In matters of health as in all the affairs of life it was crucial to remember Man's place in the universe and not tempt or taunt the spirits into afflicting one. Thus the slaves, like so many rural people throughout the world, rarely boasted openly of good health. This was the root of an attitude that puzzled Elizabeth Kilham when she went among the freedmen after the Civil War: "Their ideas on the subject of health are somewhat peculiar. I never knew one own to being 'very well.' Their invariable answer to inquiries respecting their health is, 'tollable,' drawled out with a slow reluctance as if they were loath to acknowledge to any thing even so robust as that. Even the children will raise their chubby faces, shining with health, and to the 'How do you do?' respond, 'Tollable, thankee, ma'am.' The elders more frequently are not even 'tollable,' but afflicted with some 'misery.' "[35] Mingling the skills and attitudes they brought with them from Africa with those of the Europeans and Indians, and learning from their accumulated experiences in the New World, slaves built up a vast store of remedies and treatments which may not have always cured diseases or saved lives but which doubtless gave them a necessary and salutary sense of competence, control, and active participation in at least one area of their lives.

If Nature provided the materials for curing illness, it also provided signs that correctly read could help one avoid or, at the very least, be prepared for a host of calamities and disasters. The universe was not silent; it spoke to those who knew how to listen. "Old people had signs for everything then," an ex-slave reported. There were signs indicating what the weather would be; signs telling of the coming of strangers or loved ones; signs prophesying bad luck or good fortune; signs warning of an impending whipping or the approach of white patrols; signs foretelling imminent illness or death.[36] Dreams were taken seriously as an important source of such signs. "When I was small I used to dream a lot," a former slave, born on a South Carolina plantation in 1844, reported. "I remember one night I dreamt that I saw Uncle Link, Uncle Jake and Uncle Peter skinning a cow and cutting her open. A lot of women and children were sitting around and seemed to be crying. I told my mother about it the next morning. She said it was a sign of death to dream about fresh meat. Sure enough that very evening Uncle Peter Price died. I used to dream so much that the old heads got so they took special notice of me and nearly every time it would come true."[37]

Signs were not merely phenomena to be accepted passively; they were often calls to action. A screech owl's cry was a sign of death which could be countered by turning shoes upside down at your door, or turning your pockets inside out and tying a knot in your apron string, or turning your pillow inside out, or putting salt on the fire; a black cat crossing your path was bad luck unless you spit on the spot where your paths met; seeing a cross-eyed person could bring on a spell unless one crossed one's fingers and spit on them; starting on a journey and then turning back brought disaster unless one made a cross in the path and spit on it. If slaves heard a kildeer "holler"—the sign that white patrollers were approaching—the remedy was obvious, and if they received one of the signs of an impending whipping, such as an itching left eye, they could try to avoid it by chewing roots, which was supposed to soften the master's hard heart, or by walking backwards and throwing dirt over their left shoulder, though they undoubtedly supplemented such rituals by acting circumspectly until the crisis had passed.[38] Once again the lesson was clear: the environment did not have to be accepted docilely; it could be manipulated and controlled to some extent at least.

The price paid for not understanding the forces around one was recounted in a stream of stories and anecdotes. Hamp Kennedy told of two of his fellow slaves who attempted to escape: "when day was passin' through de woods det night a great big old gran' daddy owl flopped his wings an' Joe said 'we'd better turn back.' I allus heard hit was bad luck fer to hear a owl floppin' like dat, but Green said 'twant nothin', jes a old owl floppin', but he jes naturally flopped diffrunt dat night, an' Green walked on 'bout fifteen steps an somebody shot him dead. Joe said he tu'ned back an' run home."[39] Another group of fugitive slaves were forced to break a taboo when they had to double back over their tracks. One of their number, Vina Still, immediately insisted: "This yer jaunt's a gwine to turn out bad, for nobody has good luck when they turns back after they's started on a long journey." She supplemented this bad omen with dreams warning of disaster should they travel by daylight. Seth Concklin, the white man leading the slaves to freedom, disregarded these warnings as mere superstition. The episode ended with his death and the slaves' recapture, and still one more instance of the efficacy of omens and visions was brought back to the plantation to become part of the oral tradition.[40]

In planning an escape from bondage in Maryland, Frederick Douglass, then still in his late teens, had a similar warning, which he also chose to ignore. Sandy Jenkins, the root man on the plantation, had a dream in which he saw a flock of angry birds of all colors and sizes, one of which held Douglass in its claws while the rest pecked at him. "Now I saw this as plainly as I now see you," Jenkins told Douglass, "and furder, honey, watch de Friday night dream; dere is sumpon in it shose you born, dere is indeed, honey." Still, Douglass and his fellow conspirators, Jenkins excepted, decided to go ahead with their plans. On the day the escape was scheduled, while spreading manure in the fields, Douglass himself had a vision: "I had a sudden presentiment, which flashed upon me like lightning in a dark night, revealing to the lonely traveler the gulf before and the enemy behind. I instantly turned to Sandy Jenkins, who was near me, and said: '*Sandy, we are betrayed!*—something has just told me so.' I felt as sure of it as if the officers were in sight. Sandy said, 'Man, dat is strange, but I feel just as you do.' " Thirty minutes later they were taken into custody, their dream of freedom a shambles.[41]

It is not surprising that magic played a role in the slaves' attempts to flee bondage. Nothing else the slaves undertook, aside from rebellion itself, was marked by more uncertainty or peril. The fugitive slave Lewis Clarke described the torment he went through once he decided to escape: "No tongue can tell the doubt, the perplexities, the anxiety which a slave feels, when making up his mind upon this subject." If his attempt should fail it would mean beatings, closer supervision, and quite possibly the ridicule and anger of fellow slaves who felt their lot too would now be harder. And if it did succeed, what then? To what extent could the slave trust the whites he would meet in the North. "All the white part of mankind, that he has ever seen, are enemies to him and all his kindred. How can he venture where none but white faces shall greet him? . . . A horror of great darkness comes upon him, as he thinks over what may befal him. Long, very long time did I think of escaping before I made the effort."[42] Thus though Frederick Douglass professed no faith in magic or omens, the situation he was in and the mood of so many of his fellow slaves made total skepticism difficult. He admitted that Jenkins' dream seriously depressed him and that he had difficulty freeing himself from its effects. "I felt that it boded no good. Sandy was unusually emphatic and oracular and his manner had much to do with the impression made upon me."[43]

Another of Douglass' encounters with Sandy Jenkins is worth exploring. In 1834, two years before Douglass' abortive escape, his master sent him for one year to the farm of Edward Covey, who specialized in "breaking in" young and spirited slaves. After six months of unceasing labor and weekly beatings with sticks and cowskins, Douglass, in the most desperate state of his life, met Jenkins:

> I found Sandy an old adviser. He was not only a religious man, but he professed to believe in a system for which I have no name. He was a genuine African, and had inherited some of the so-called magical powers said to be possessed by the eastern nations. He told me that he could help me, that in those very woods there was an herb which in the morning might be found, possessing all the powers required for my protection . . . and that if I would take his advice he would procure me the root of the herb of which he spoke. He told me, further, that if I would take that root and wear it on my right side it would be impossible for Covey to strike me a blow, and that with this root about my person, no white man could whip

me. He said he had carried it for years, and that he had fully tested its virtues. He had never received a blow from a slaveholder since he carried it, and he never expected to receive one, for he meant always to carry that root for protection.

Douglass at first rejected the suggestion as absurd and sinful: "I had a positive aversion to all pretenders to 'divination.' It was beneath one of my intelligence to countenance such dealings with the devil as this power implied." Jenkins prevailed by arguing that all of Douglass' book learning (Douglass was one of the few slaves in the area who could read) had not helped him against Covey; if the root did no good it could do no harm.

The next morning, Sunday, Douglass, admitting that perhaps "a slight gleam or shadow of his superstition had fallen on me," put the root in his right pocket and went to face his master, from whom he had run away the day before. Covey treated him so kindly that the young slave began to believe in the root, though he suspected that his treatment had more to do with Covey's Sabbath piety. When Covey attempted to beat him the following day, Douglass was certain there was no magic in the root. For the first time, however, Douglass stood up to Covey, and after a two-hour skirmish, in which he drew Covey's blood, the white man backed down, and for the remaining six months Douglass lived with him "he never again laid the weight of his finger on me in anger." For Douglass this was the turning point that ultimately led to his freedom, and he pondered the incident in some detail in his autobiography. To the question, "Whence came the daring spirit necessary to grapple with a man who, eight-and-forty hours before, could, with his slightest word, have made me tremble like a leaf in a storm," Douglass had no answer. Nor could he explain why Covey had not gone to the authorities and had Douglass publicly whipped, or worse, for using force against a white man: "I confess that the easy manner in which I got off was always a surprise to me." The root, which Douglass had in his right pocket during the entire incident, was not mentioned by him as a possible cause of his new spirit and his good fortune, though we may be certain that its presence was not lost upon Sandy Jenkins and many of Douglass' fellow slaves.[44]

Sandy Jenkins was not a unique figure. Slaves with similar beliefs and powers existed throughout the antebellum South and probably had been even more numerous in the colonial era. The fugitive slave William Wells Brown observed that "Nearly every large plantation . . . had at least one, who laid claim to be a fortune-teller, and who was regarded with more than common respect by his fellow-slaves."[45] In 1851 a southern minister lamented that "on almost every large plantation of Negroes there is one among them who holds a kind of magical sway over the minds and opinions of the rest; to him they look as their oracle. . . ."[46] These "oracles" constituted still another source of autonomous power within the slave community. To them the slaves could bring their dilemmas and uncertainties, in their knowledge slaves could try to find remedies and solutions to their numerous problems, from their aura of mystical authority slaves could attempt to draw assurance and strength.

They were, to be sure, fallible pillars of strength at best. Anthony Burns, later to win renown as a fugitive slave who became a symbol in the struggle between North and South, was only one of many slaves who lost some or all of their faith in plantation seers when the period in which it was predicted he would win his freedom passed without any change in his status.[47] In his desire to lessen the rigors of enslavement, Henry Bibb consulted a conjurer who gave him protection against whippings in the form of a powder to sprinkle and a root to chew. When a long period elapsed without a flogging, Bibb was convinced that with his new found protection he could do as he pleased. He left the plantation without permission and spoke impudently when his master questioned his absence. "He became so enraged at me for saucing him," Bibb wrote, "that he grasped a handful of switches and punished me severely, in spite of all my roots and powders." Bibb next consulted an old slave who was reputed to be an even more powerful conjurer and was given a snuff compounded of fresh cow manure, red pepper, and white people's hair, but this too failed to protect him from his master's wrath. Although he became convinced that the only effectual protection from punishment was escape, Bibb continued to patronize conjurers in his efforts to win the attention of young women on the plantation. He was given various charms to use—the bone of a dried frog, the lock of the woman's hair to be worn in his shoe—and again his results were discouraging. The point of these incidents is not that slave magic frequently failed but that in spite of failure faith in it continued. "I had been taught by the old superstitious slaves to believe in conjuration," Bibb noted, "and it was hard for me to give up the notion, for all I had been deceived by them."[48]

This persistent faith should surprise us no more than the persistence in our own time of faith in prayer or in modern medicine, both of which obtain very mixed results. When alternatives are limited, faith dies hard. Had Bibb's totally negative experiences been typical, the art and practice of conjuring would have languished long before the antebellum period. But slave magic had triumphs enough to match its failures. When seen from the perspective of Sandy Jenkins, who was not fortunate enough to write his own memoirs, Frederick Douglass' experiences seem quite the reverse of what Douglass intended them to mean. Jenkins gave Douglass a root to protect him from Covey's whippings and, however Douglass himself interpreted what ensued, in fact Covey never again whipped him. Two years later Jenkins had a dream warning against Douglass' intended escape. Douglass ignored the omen with disastrous results, while Jenkins was the only conspirator prescient enough to withdraw from the plot before it was too late. Jenkins might be excused if he viewed his efforts in both of these instances as successful. There is reason to suspect that many of his fellow slaves would have agreed.

During her stay on the South Carolina Sea Islands in 1919, Elsie Clews Parsons found stories of slave magic deeply embedded in the oral tradition. Maria Middleton, an ex-slave, told two typical tales of successful conjuring. In one a slave is beaten so severely that he goes to a conjurer who agrees to help him. The next morning the master appears powerful and happy, but as the sun sets he gradually declines: "As soon as de sun was down, he down too, he down yet. De witch done dat." The very brevity of the next tale, in which the master's wife magically receives the punishment her husband is meting out to a slave who had previously sought the protection of a conjurer, indicates that the mechanics of the magic involved were well understood in the community: "Wen' to a witch-man. When his master 'mence to whip him, eve'y cut he give de man, his [master's] wife way off at home feel de cut. Sen' wor' please stop cut lick de man. When he [master] got home, his wife was wash down wid blood."[49] Shortly after the Civil War, freedmen were still telling stories of Old Julie, a conjure woman responsible for so much death and maiming on the plantation that her master finally sold her. He personally put her on a steamboat that was to take her to her new owner deep in the South. That night she used her power and forced the boat to go backwards so that the next morning it was once again at its point of departure and the master was compelled to keep her.[50]

Stories like these were common. One Georgia practitioner was reputed to have the power to cause runaway slaves to return to their masters but also to compel their masters to pardon them without punishment.[51] Hilliard Johnson, who was a slave in Alabama, told of a spell which forced the hounds pursuing a fugitive to stop and bark at an empty tree while the slave escaped. "Dey calls hit hoodooin de dogs. And I'se seen hit more times than one."[52] A number of former slaves spoke of methods designed to elude the white patrols and their dogs, the most common being rubbing turpentine or fresh graveyard dirt on the slaves' feet or on their tracks, which prevented the dogs from finding them. A more elaborate prescription called for catching a yearling calf by the tail and while running along with it, stepping in its droppings: "Den dat is a sho conjure ter mak dem hounds loose de track, en dat nigger kin dodge de paddyrollers."[53]

Nothing seems to have led slaves to seek the aid of magic more surely than their fear of being whipped. A favorite mode of resolving their anxieties, one way or the other, was the use of a small bottle which when filled with roots, water, and sulphur was transformed into what the slaves called a "jack." Holding this on the end of a string, between his thumb and forefinger, the diviner would chant:

> By some Peter
> By some Paul
> And by the God that made us all

and ask the jack to reveal if the slave was to be beaten. If it turned to the right there would be a whipping, if it quivered without moving the master had not yet made up his mind, and if it turned left all was well. Chewing roots and spitting around the master's front door to cool his angry passion, carrying a rabbit's foot, or wearing a conjure bag were among the varied responses to a predicted whipping. "During slavery time," Amanda Syles recalled, "the master promised ter whip a nigger and when he came out ter whip him instead he just told him 'go on nigger 'bout your business.' De nigger had fixed him by spitting as far as he could spit as the master couldn't come any nearer than that spit."[54]

Many slaves felt it was well to take such precautions even without a sign or a prophecy of an imminent beating. Louis Hughes, for example, carried a little leather bag containing roots, nuts, pins, and a number of other ingredients given to him by an elderly slave who claimed it had the power to prevent anyone wearing it from being whipped. In his autobiography, written long after his escape, Hughes derided the practice as "one of the superstitions of a barbarous ancestry," but admitted, "It was the custom in those days for slaves to carry voodoo bags. It was handed down from generation to generation; and . . . it was still very generally and tenaciously held to by all classes."[55] Conjurers sometimes intervened directly and mysteriously to protect the slave. An ex-slave testified that one night a stranger appeared on the plantation with an object on the end of a foot-long string: "he was swinging it along and when it got to my father it stopped just as still. He said father was going to get whipped the next morning but he would keep him from getting the whipping. Sure enough the next morning they come got him, but they never touched him. They couldn't for that man had fixed it so they couldn't whip him. This man was a runaway nigger. He just went around keeping people from getting killed."[56]

Some slaves doubted that the power of conjure could affect their masters and mistresses. "They had in those days a hoodoo nigger who could hoodoo niggers, but couldn't hoodoo masters," an ex-slave reported. "He couldn't make ole master stop whipping him, with the hoodooism, but they could make Negroes crawl to them."[57] This attitude is important, but there is a danger in blowing it out of proportion as further evidence of the slaves' recognition of their ultimate impotence in the face of white authority. I have tried to demonstrate that the slaves commonly believed that conjure and their other magical practices did affect whites as well as blacks. But there is something more important at issue here; a question of cultural perception as well as a question of power relationships. The slaves recognized different loci of power and dealt with them pragmatically as they had to, but there is no indication that they ranked these various sources of power in terms of the neat secular hierarchy that governs modern Western Man, with temporal power standing at the apex. The slaves acknowledged and feared the masters' power and, as we shall see in the next chapter, much of their lore revolved around the problem of how to deal with that authority in a worldly context. But even if it was true that the conjurer, like the Pope, had few divisions, the slaves would have posed the question differently than Stalin did: they would have asked not "how many" but "what kinds," for within their sacred world view they understood the different sources and types of power, some of which their masters could not begin to comprehend.

It is important to ponder the statement made by a slave in the 1840s: "I knows t'ings dat de wite folks wid all dar larnin' nebber fin's out, an' nebber sarches fo' nudder." Similarly, Silvia King, in the midst of her discussion of the powers and uses of roots and barks, observed with some condescension: "White folks just go through de woods and don't know nothin'."[58] There were many things white folks did not know, and because of this their power, great as it was, was limited. This, I think, is one of the primary messages of slave magic. The whites were neither omnipotent or omniscient; there were things they did not know, forces they could not control, areas in which slaves could act with more knowledge and authority than their masters, ways in which the powers of the whites could be muted if not thwarted entirely. The question, then, was not necessarily whether the conjurers had any power over the masters; what was more significant was that conjurers had powers the masters lacked, and they were precisely the kinds of powers that a people living within a sacred context found impressive. This is what made the conjurers such awesome and respected figures to so many slaves.

Conjurers could be pictured as exotic Old Testament type prophets or magicians: "He could turn as green as grass, most, and was just as black as a man could very well be, and his hair covered his neck and he had lizards tied on it. He carried a crooked cane. He would throw it down and pick it up and say something and throw it down again and it would wriggle like a snake, and he would pick it up and it would be as stiff as any other cane."[59] At their most powerful, conjurers commanded great respect from everyone. "My ma was a black African and she sure was wild and mean," Susan Snow told an interviewer. "Dey couldn't whip her. Dey used to say she was a 'conger' and dey was all scared of her."[60] William Wells Brown described Dinkie, the conjurer and fortune teller on the plantation where Brown had been a slave. Around his neck Dinkie wore a snake's skin, in his pockets he carried a petrified frog and a dried lizard. He did little work and was neither beaten nor sold, though masters and overseers had attempted to do both. The slaves stood in "mortal fear" of him, the patrollers permitted him to pass without challenge, and white ladies visited his cabin to have their fortunes told. Dinkie, Brown concluded, "was his own master."[61] The conjurer's power over whites was the explicit message of a slave tale in which a conjurer suggests to his son one night: "Come, git up; let's go ride de overseer an' his oldes' son: I had a spite gin 'em dis long time." Entering the white man's home through a keyhole, they turn the overseer into a bull and his son into a bull yearling, mount them, and spend the night riding and whipping them.[62] Outside of the slaves' animal tales, slave lore contains few more graphic examples of reversal of power in this world.

That slaves might attempt actually to effect such a reversal preyed on the minds of many whites. In 1842 the Reverend Charles C. Jones expressed his fears concerning the impact that conjurers and magical beliefs would have on slave order:

On certain occasions they have been made to believe that while they carried about their persons some charm with which they had been furnished, they were *invulnerable*. They have, on certain other occasions, been made to believe that they were under a protection that rendered them *invincible*. That they might go any where and do any thing they pleased, and it would be impossible for them to be discovered or known; in fine, to will was to do—safely, successfully. They have been known to be so perfectly and fearfully under the influence of some leader or conjurer or minister, that they have not dared to disobey him in the least particular; nor to disclose their own intended or perpetrated crimes, in view of inevitable death itself; notwithstanding all other influences brought to bear upon them.[63]

The large scale and widespread slave insurrections that Jones seemed to have on his mind did not come to pass, but his insights were shrewd. Magical folk beliefs did give many slaves the courage and determination to indulge in acts they otherwise would have had difficulty committing: standing up to the master, moving freely about the plantation, conspiring to escape, even in some instances rebelling itself.

In planning what became known as Gabriel's Rebellion in Virginia in 1800, those conspirators who desired to utilize the slaves' folk religion and to recruit the "Outlandish People" who dealt with witches and wizards and thus could "tell when any calamity was about to befall them" lost out to the more secular, political approach of Gabriel Prosser. This, Gerald Mullin has argued, was the source of the rebellion's failure: "at a time when revivalism was a vital force among plantation slaves, those who would lead couched their appeal in political and secular terms. Unlike Nat Turner's magnificent Old Testament visions, which transfigured him and sustained his movement, Gabriel's Rebellion, lacking a sacred dimension, was without a Moses, and thus without a following."[64] If this was true, then Gabriel's Rebellion was not typical of other major slave revolts or aborted revolts in the eighteenth and nineteenth centuries. Indeed, even in Gabriel's plot, as Mullin's own evidence indicates, the Old Testament message played a role. In other revolts sacred elements were more prominent. In the 1712 slave insurrection in New York, the conspirators bound themselves to secrecy by sucking the blood of each other's hands and were given still greater determination by a free Negro sorcerer who distributed a powder which when rubbed on their clothing would make them invulnerable.[65] In 1816 George Boxley, a white Virginia storekeeper and visionary who had been attending black religious meetings, recruited a band of slaves in his insurrection plot by convincing them that a little white bird had brought him a holy message to deliver the slaves from bondage.[66]

Six years later, in South Carolina, the Denmark Vesey conspiracy combined a number of the sacred strands of the slaves' world view. The religious element in Vesey's appeal was made evident in the testimony of his fellow slaves and rebels during his trial: "he studies the Bible a great deal and tries to prove from it that slavery and bondage is against the Bible"; "his general conversation was about religion which he would apply to slavery, as for instance, he would speak of the creation of the world, in which he would say all men had equal rights, blacks as well as whites, &c. all his religious remarks were mingled with slavery"; he "read to us from the Bible, how the Children of Israel were delivered out of Egypt from bondage." At meetings in the African Church of Charleston or at his home he would quote to his fellow slaves Scriptural passages from the Books of Exodus, Zachariah, and Joshua setting precedents for the coming struggle: "Behold the day of the Lord cometh, and thy spoil shall be divided in the midst of thee." "And they utterly destroyed all that was in the city, both man and woman, young and old, and ox, and sheep, and ass, with the edge of the sword." Vesey's chief lieutenant, Jack Pritchard, known more commonly as Gullah Jack, was an Angolan-born conjurer whose role in the conspiracy was described by one of his fellow slaves: "he gave me some dry food, consisting of parched corn and ground nuts, and said eat that and nothing else on the morning it breaks out, and when you join us as we pass put into your mouth this crab-claw and you can't then be wounded, and said he, I give the same to the rest of my troops—if you drop the large crab-claw out of your mouth, then put in the small one." "Jack said he could not be killed, nor could a white man take him," one of his fellow rebels testified. "Until Jack was taken up and condemned to death, I felt as if I was bound up, and had not the power to speak one word about it."[67]

No one has better captured the sacred core of Nat Turner's 1831 rebellion than Turner himself in the confessions he dictated to Thomas R. Gray. From his early youth Turner was made to feel he was destined to be a prophet: he knew of things that had taken place before his birth, he had special markings on his head and breast, as he grew older he heard voices and had visions "which fully confirmed me in the impression that I was ordained for some great purpose in the hands of the Almighty." This conviction grew with the years:

> And about this time I had a vision—and I saw white spirits and black spirits engaged in battle, and the sun was darkened—the thunder rolled in the Heavens, and blood flowed in streams . . . while laboring in the field, I discovered drops of blood on the corn as though it were dew from

heaven—and I communicated it to many, both white and black in the neighborhood—and then I found on the leaves in the woods hieroglyphic characters, and numbers, with the forms of men in different attitudes, portrayed in blood, and representing the figures I had seen before in the heavens. And now the Holy Ghost had revealed itself to me, and made plain the miracles it had shown me. . . . And on the 12th of May, 1828, I heard a loud noise in the heavens, and the Spirit instantly appeared to me and said the Serpent was loosened, and Christ had laid down the yoke he had borne for the sins of men, and that I should take it on and fight against the Serpent, for the time was fast approaching when the first should be last and the last should be first. . . . And by signs in the heavens that it would make known to me when I should commence the great work. . . .

The sign Turner sought proved to be the solar eclipse of February 1831, following which the prophet arose "and I communicated the great work laid out for me to do. . . ."[68] Though Turner had contempt for conjuring and never directly practiced its arts, his revelations, his portents, his signs, his sense of the supernatural, and his power flowed organically from the slaves' sacred world in which magic and Christianity were integral ingredients.

If Denmark Vesey, Gullah Jack, and Nat Turner were not typical products of the slaves' sacred universe, neither were they alien to it. Their actions and beliefs outline in exaggerated relief a truth which emerges from the bulk of evidence relating to slave culture: that the religion and folk beliefs of the slaves provided them with crucial alternative standards and possibilities. These alternatives existed not only in the slaves' relations with the environment and their masters but with each other as well. The creation and administration of laws and regulations rested in the hands of the master class and frequently created a vacuum within the slave quarters. There was a genuine difference of interest at work here. While their masters were primarily concerned with the pervasive theft that slaves committed against them, the slaves, who did not always equate taking things from whites as stealing, were most concerned with the less common but still troublesome problem of intragroup theft which was a matter of much less immediate interest to the whites. In their search for alternative means of social control within their own community, slaves turned naturally to their store of magical folk beliefs. Jacob Stroyer, who was a slave in South Carolina, has described the ways slaves had of detecting thieves among them. The first two were almost identical. A Bible or a sieve was suspended from a string and asked if the person under suspicion was the thief. If the object turned at the mention of the suspect's name, he was guilty. A third procedure consisted of diluting graveyard dirt in a bottle of water and offering it to the suspects, warning them that if they were guilty and drank the mixture "you will die and go to hell and be burned in fire and brimstone."[69]

Theft was only one of the areas in which slaves took the initiative in lieu of alternative provisions. Henry Rogers recalled that his parents hid a bag containing a mixture of devil's snuff and cotton stalk roots under the front of their cabin in order to render all who came up the steps friendly and peaceful regardless of their original intentions.[70] Again and again slaves consulted conjurers or directly practiced the magic arts themselves to right wrongs they felt they had suffered at the hands of their fellow slaves. "Old folks used to conjure folks when dey got mad at 'em," Alice Green recalled. "Dey went in de woods and got certain kinds of roots and biled 'em wid spider webs, and give 'em de tea to drink." The power of conjurers to wreak retribution upon slaves when requested to do so by other slaves was believed to be almost unlimited. They could, a former slave testified, "put snakes, lizards, terrapins, scorpions and different other things in you, fix you so you can't walk, can't sleep, or sleep all the time, and so you can't have any use of your limbs. They could put you in such a state that you would linger and pine away or so that you would go blind or crazy." Other conjurers, of course, could be consulted to reverse these effects.[71]

Separated from their young children for much of the day, slaves relied not only upon the Bible and Christian morality, but upon magical folk beliefs, fear of conjuring, and ghost stories—especially tales of "Raw Head and Bloody Bones"—to teach their progeny right from wrong and to encourage them to be well behaved. On a Texas plantation, Abram Sells' great-grandfather had the task of supervising the children who were too young to work. "Us sure have to mind him," Sells remembered, " 'cause iffen we didn't, us sure have bad luck. He always have the pocket full of things to conjure with." He carried a rabbit's foot which he took out "and he work that on you till you take the creeps and git shaking all over." He invariably had a pocket full of fish scales, "and he kind of squeak and rattle them in the hand, and right then and there you wish you was dead and promise to do anything." His most potent charm was a small dried mud turtle. "With that thing he say he could do 'most anything, but he never use it iffen he ain't have to."[72]

Inevitably, the supernatural was invoked as a means of controlling the supernatural itself. To the slaves ghosts were familiar phenomena: "as common as pig tracks," Jordan Smith asserted; "de air am full of 'em," John Daniels agreed.[73] Ghosts were conceived of in the African tradition as spirits at a certain stage of their being. That is, they were *natural* phenomena and by no means invariably a source of fear. The ghosts of loved ones frequently returned to render aid and protection, give counsel, and even occasionally point the way to hidden treasure. Some satisfaction was taken, too, in stories of dead slaves who returned to demand justice from the whites who had abused or killed them. Jane Arrington told of John May, a slave who was beaten to death by two whites, Bill Stone and Oliver May, and who gave his murderers no rest for the remainder of their days: "Dey said dey could hear him hollerin' an' groanin' most all de time. Dese white men would groan in dere sleep an' tell John to go away. Dey would say, 'Go way John, please go away.' "[74] Ghosts, of course, could be evil as well as benign. As Henry Cheatam of Mississippi observed: "Dere is good spirits and bad spirits."[75] Among the latter were the spirits of masters who returned after death to continue the torment of their black bondsmen. Lewis Clarke watched two of his fellow slaves dig their master's grave six or seven feet deep and then helped them place a large stone on his coffin "so as to fasten him down as strong as possible." Slaves, he commented, preferred to be buried at the greatest possible distance away from their master. "They are all superstitious, and fear that the slave-driver, having whipped so much when alive, will, somehow, be beating them when dead. I was actually as much afraid of my old master when dead, as I was when he was alive. I often dreamed of him, too, after he was dead, and thought he had actually come back again, to torment me more."[76]

The fugitive slave Charles Ball told of two slaves who murdered a young white woman in 1805 and were themselves put to a slow and horrible death by being devoured alive by carrion crows and buzzards. The scene of the murder and execution immediately became known as Murderers' Swamp, "believed to be visited at night by beings of unearthly make, whose groans, and death-struggles were heard in the darkest recesses of the woods, . . . Whilst I remained in this neighbourhood, no coloured person ever travelled this road, alone, after nightfall; and many white men would have ridden ten miles round the country, to avoid the passage of the ridge road, after dark."[77] Slaves resorted to numerous rituals to protect themselves from these malignant spirits whether black or white: burying a corpse face down would prevent return after death; placing a broom, a sifter, or a Bible at the door would keep spirits from entering; scattering mustard seeds on the floor of a room would confine the spirit to that space until every seed was picked up; reading the Bible backwards three times provided especially ·strong protection. These and many similar prescriptions worked as well against the hostile behavior of witches who spent the nights riding their victims.[78]

While it would be possible to extend this discussion into a number of other areas, such as the practice of Voodoo, enough evidence has been reviewed to make it clear that in numerous contexts and ways slaves were able to find their own sources of power and protection. It remains valid, of course, to query the nature and meaning of these alternatives. The slaves, after all, remained slaves, the whites remained masters, and the harsh, exploitative history of the Peculiar Institution continued. If our sole criterion of judgment is physical freedom, then the slaves' sacred folk beliefs had a very limited effect, though they unquestionably encouraged some slaves to escape. If we extend the criterion to material well-being, the effects are greater, for their folk beliefs encouraged and enabled slaves to assert themselves more than they would have otherwise. If we extend it yet further into the more speculative but crucial area of the slaves' psychic and emotional state, the results are more positive still. The slaves' expressive arts and sacred beliefs were more than merely a series of outlets or strategies; they were instruments of life, of sanity, of health, and of self-respect. Slave music, slave religion, slave folk beliefs—the entire sacred world of the black slaves—created the necessary space between the slaves and their owners and were the means of preventing legal slavery from becoming spiritual slavery. In addition to the world of the masters which slaves inhabited and accommodated to, as they had to, they created and maintained a world apart which they shared with each other and which remained their own domain, free of control of those who ruled the earth.

2
THE
MEANING
OF
SLAVE
TALES

D*e buckruh [whites] hab scheme, en de nigger hab trick, en
ebery time de buckruh scheme once de nigger trick twice.*
South Carolina slave saying.[1]

*I sometimes think that I learned more in my early childhood about how
to live than I have learned since.*
Testimony of an ex-slave.[2]

For the historian interested in slave culture, the use of folk tales parallels
that of songs and folk beliefs. Although few black tales were collected
until the decades following the Civil War, their distribution was so widespread throughout the South, their content so similar, and their style and
function so uniform that it is evident they were not a sudden post-
emancipation creation. "All over the South the stories of Br'er Rabbit are
told," Octave Thanet reported in 1892. "Everywhere not only ideas and
plots are repeated, but the very words often are the same; one gets a new
vision of the power of oral tradition."[1] The variations in patterns of mobility, educational and vocational opportunities, cultural expression, and
life styles brought about by emancipation produced inevitable changes in
black folklore, and they will be examined in later chapters. Still, throughout the remainder of the nineteenth century—and well into the twentieth—

the large body of slave tales remained a vital and central core of Afro-American expression.

As with other aspects of their verbal art, slaves established in their tales important points of continuity with their African past. This is not to say that slave tales in the United States were necessarily African. Scholars will need more complete indices of African tale types and motifs than now exist before they can determine the origin of slave tales with any definitiveness. Comparison of slave tales with those guides to African tales that do exist reveals that a significant number were brought directly from Africa; a roughly similar percentage were tales common in both Africa and Europe, so that, while slaves may have brought the tale type with them, its place in their lore could well have been reinforced by their contact with whites; and, finally, a third group of tales were learned in the New World both through Euro-American influence and through independent creation.[2]

Unfortunately, extended debate concerning the exact point of origin of these tales has taken precedence over analysis of their meaning and function. Cultural continuities with Africa were not dependent upon importation and perpetuation of specific folk tales in their pristine form. It was in the place that tales occupied in the lives of the slaves, the meaning slaves derived from them, and the ways in which slaves used them culturally and psychically that the clearest resemblances with their African past could be found. Thus, although Africans brought to the New World were inevitably influenced by the tales they found there and frequently adopted white tale plots, motifs, and characters, what is most important is not the mere fact of these borrowings but their nature. Afro-American slaves did not borrow indiscriminately from the whites among whom they lived. A careful study of their folklore reveals that they tended to be most influenced by those patterns of Euro-American tales which in terms of functional meaning and aesthetic appeal had the greatest similarity to the tales with deep roots in their ancestral homeland. Regardless of where slave tales came from, the essential point is that, with respect to language, delivery, details of characterization, and plot, slaves quickly made them their own and through them revealed much about themselves and their world.

The most effective single force in popularizing these tales after the Civil War was the work of Joel Chandler Harris. Beginning with the dialect sketches he published in the *Atlanta Constitution* in the late 1870s—which he brought together in his first volume of tales, *Uncle Remus: His*

Songs and Sayings (1880)—Harris spent much of the remainder of his life deluging his countrymen with Afro-American animal tales, seven volumes of which were published before his death in 1908 and three more posthumously.[3] Harris insisted that his tales were not "cooked" but were "given in the simple but picturesque language of the negroes, just as the negroes tell them."[4] If one discounts his "character-sketches" of Remus and the other slaves who appear in his books, along with many of his anecdotes and asides, Harris, in his early volumes especially, was faithful to the themes, motifs, and plots of black animal tales. His errors were those of omission more than commission. In the introduction to his second volume, *Nights with Uncle Remus* (1883), Harris asserted that his work embodied "everything, or nearly everything of importance in the oral literature of the negroes of the Southern States." In fact, the picture that emerges from his work is a relatively frozen one which helped to establish the stereotype that slave tales were comprised almost exclusively of the adventures of Brer Rabbit. Harris did not completely slight other forms of black tales; his ten volumes included a substantial number of explanatory tales and some fifteen supernatural tales, featuring witches, ghosts, and devils. Still, his attention remained centered upon Brer Rabbit and his adversaries.

Harris' fixed emphasis was by no means a radical distortion of the nature of slave tales. As this chapter will demonstrate, antebellum slaves manifested a central feature of their consciousness graphically and dramatically through the medium of trickster tales featuring the victories of the weak over the strong. Nevertheless, while Harris captured the essence of slave animal trickster tales, his work exaggerated their dominance over the folklore of the slaves. An understanding of antebellum black culture and consciousness demands a consideration of the entire spectrum of slave tales.

SLAVE TALES AS HISTORY

Slave tales were almost totally devoid of cosmological myths which attempt to render factual accounts of all natural and divine phenomena. Something approaching myths of this nature, which Malinowski has defined as characterized by "a retrospective, everpresent, live actuality," did of course exist among antebellum slaves, but they were confined almost exclusively to the slaves' sacred songs and sermons; they played little or no role in oral tales.[1] The closest the slaves came to these myths was in their creation legends, which paralleled many of the creation stories of nineteenth-century colonized, Christianized Africans. Some of these were clearly influenced by the ubiquitous Anglo-American myths which insisted that blackness resulted from God's curse on Cain or Ham. Gus Rogers, who had been a slave in North Carolina and Alabama, explained the genesis of his race by referring to the Biblical account of Noah:

> God gave it [religion] to Adam and took it away from Adam and gave it to Noah, and you know, Miss, Noah had three sons, and when Noah got drunk on wine, one of his sons laughed at him, and the other two took a sheet and walked backwards and threw it over Noah. Noah told the one who laughed, "Your children will be hewers of wood and drawers of water for the other two children, and they will be known by their hair and their skin being dark." So, Miss, there we are, and that is the way God meant us to be. We have always had to follow the white folks and do what we saw them do, and that's all there is to it. You just can't get away from what the Lord said.[2]

Other creation legends were more imaginative though hardly less self-denigrating. One, reported as early as 1828 in the Tarboro (North Carolina) *Free Press*, told of the Devil attempting to emulate God's creation of Adam. Lacking clay, he went to the swamp and got some mud, using thick, curly moss for hair. When he looked upon his creation he was so disgusted that he kicked it on the shins and struck it on the nose, thus establishing the physical attributes of the black race.[3] A later version has the Devil becoming so furious at an ape who refused to answer any of his questions that he turns him into a black man.[4] In 1878 an aged ex-slave in Louisiana accounted for the pre-eminence of West Europeans by explaining that after God had created all the peoples of the world—Negroes, Chinese, Indians, and so on—He exhausted the mound of earth He was using and so seized a butterfly and an ant, creating a Frenchman out of the former and an Englishman out of the latter.[5] The importance of such patently white-influenced stories is obvious, but it would be a mistake to assume that slaves invariably took them literally. There are indications that the blacks telling them frequently were aware of their original source. "En dat's how de w'ite man dun 'count fo' de niggah bein' on 'Arth," a black storyteller concluded one such story.[6]

Perhaps more typical, and certainly more original, were stories which had God begin His creation with the black race. In one version the original colored peoples discovered a body of water that had the power of washing away their dark skin color. Those who reached the water first came out pure white; as the supply was used up the skin color remained darker until the last to reach it were able to dip in only their palms and the soles of their feet.[7] The assumption of a black creation allowed slaves to stand the white creation myths on their heads. In 1859 a white Baptist preacher, Harden E. Taliaferro, recalled the teachings of Charles Gentry, a black slave preacher whom he had known in the rural North Carolina country in which he grew up in the 1820s. The first men, Gentry insisted, were black: "Adam, Cain, Abel, Seth, was all ob 'um black as jet."

> Cain he kill his brudder Abel wid a great big club . . . and God he cum to Cain, and say, "Cain! whar is dy brudder Abel?" Cain he pout out de lip, and say, "I don't know; what ye axin' me fur? I ain't my brudder Abel's keeper." De Lord he gits in airnest, and stomps on de ground, and say, "Cain! you Cain! whar is dy brudder Abel? I say, Cain! whar is dy brudder?" Cain he turn white as bleech cambric in de face, and de whole race ob Cain dey bin white ebber since. De mark de Lord put on de face ob Cain was a white mark. He druv him inter de land ob Nod, and all de white folks hab cum frum de land ob Nod, jis' as you've hearn.[8]

How popular Gentry's version of the creation was is not clear, but it was known at least as early as the opening years of the nineteenth century and remained in circulation well into the twentieth century from Maryland to Mississippi.[9]

Black slaves, then, possessed their own form of racial ethnocentrism and were capable of viewing the white race as a degenerate form of the black. Significantly, precisely the same creation legends were reported from nineteenth-century Africa. Mary Kingsley, who traveled extensively in West Africa in the 1890s, asked a twelve-year-old girl in the Cameroons why she was black and received this succinct reply: "One of my pa's pas saw dem Patriark Noah wivout his clothes." This Miss Kingsley attributed to "the result of white training direct on the African mind." She was more forcibly struck by another story often told to her by Africans which held that after Cain killed Abel he carried the body around with him for years trying to hide it from God, growing gradually white with horror and fear, until observing a crow scratching a hole in the desert he buried the body there, "but all his children were white, and from Cain came the white races, while Abel's children are black, as all men were before the first murder."[10] In mid-nineteenth-century Africa the Englishman

Richard F. Burton heard exactly the same story from "converted ne-groes."[11] Africans, both those who were forcibly taken from their home-land and those who remained to live in a colonized state, were the recipi-ents of the same European racial myths and, it would appear, erected many of the same defenses against them.

Although slave tales included nothing approaching the intricate gene-alogies and historical narratives common in the African oral tradition,[12] they did contain a historical dimension. The tales slaves related to one an-other were not confined to fictionalized stories. As Richard Dorson has observed: "American Negroes (and whites) relate local traditions, family history, and personal experiences with as much gusto as any folktale—and sometimes these localized and personalized narratives prove to be folktales in disguise."[13] This was as true of slaves as of the twentieth-century Ne-groes Dorson was referring to. In 1876 the South Carolina planter, bota-nist, and writer, Henry W. Ravenel, set down his childhood recollections of life on his father's plantation which was inhabited by some two hun-dred slaves. Among his most vivid memories was the time he spent listen-ing to "the old negroes' stories, which they were very fond of telling."

> Some (the native Africans) told of the "old country," which they could remember—of the big elephants "as big as this house"—of the lions and tigers, and alligators, and monkeys—of the great snakes, "as big as your body, sir," that could crush and swallow a man or a horse—the story of their capture and march to the coast—of the "middle passage," and other marvellous things about ivory and gold. . . . Then those of the country born could tell the wonderful stories of the old war—of the "red coats" whom they had seen (when the State was overrun by British troops), of the hair-breadth escapes of old master from the British, . . . With these and like marvellous stories they fed my childish credulity, and impressed me with a respect and veneration for their stately forms which I yet retain.[14]

Although memories of Africa may have faded as the number of native-born Africans in the United States decreased with the diminution of the slave trade in the late eighteenth and early nineteenth centuries, they did not disappear entirely. In the 1870s an aged freedman spoke warmly of his African-born grandfather from whom he had learned many of the animal stories he told:

> I often yeardy [heard] him tell how 'e was bring ober from Africa in a ship when 'e was a boy. De white man lef' de ship behin' and gone asho' in a small boat; an' when dey meet up wid my gran'daddy an' a whole parcel more, young boys like, all from de same village, dey hire dem wid piece

ob red flannel an' ting for to 'long [go along] wid dem. But when dey git dem on bo'd de ship dey bring dem ober to dis country an' sell dem for slave. Dey bring my gran'daddy to Charleston an' ol' Marse Heywood buy um. When I was a small leetle boy 'e ben bery ol', too ol' for work, an' I use for hab it for my tarsk for min' um. So 'e tell me heap o' dese story.[15]

It does not appear to have been uncommon for slaves to refer to their African roots among themselves. "Whilst us was all a-wukin' away at house and yard jobs, de old folkses would tell us 'bout times 'fore us was borned," Paul Smith related as a preface to an elaborate story of how red ships were used to capture Africans.[16] "I used to set on Grandma's lap and she told me about how they used to catch people in Africa," Luke Dixon, who was born a slave in 1855 in Virginia, remembered:

> They herded them up like cattle and put them in stalls and brought them on the ship and sold them. She said some they captured they left bound till they come back and sometimes they never went back to get them. They died. They had room in the stalls on the boat to set down or lie down. They put several together. Put the men to themselves and the women to themselves. When they sold Grandma and Grandpa at a fishing dock called New Port, Virginia, they had their feet bound down and their hands bound crossed, up on a platform.[17]

Similarly, Shack Thomas, born a slave in Florida in 1834, described how his father would spend hours at night telling him and his brothers about his capture in Africa and his subsequent experiences as a slave in America.[18] African forebears were often referred to with affection and pride:

> Pappy was a African. I knows dat. He come from Congo, over in Africa, and I heared him say a big storm drove de ship somewhere on de Ca'lina coast. I 'member he mighty 'spectful to Massa and Missy, but he proud, too, and walk straighter'n anybody I ever seen. He had scars on de right side he head and cheek what he say am tribe marks, but what dey means I don't know.[19]

African-born slaves were associated with conjure and magical powers as exemplified in the frequently told stories of Africans who put up with the treatment accorded to them by whites in America as long as they could and then simply rose up and flew back to Africa. In some versions they delayed their escape until they could teach their American-born relatives and friends the power of flight as well. After relating such a story James Moore of Georgia added: "From duh tings I see mysef I blieb dat dey could do dis."[20]

While the testimony of some former slaves indicates a detailed knowledge of the customs, religion, garb, and food of their African ancestors,[21] for the most part memories of Africa became confined to stories of capture and of the Middle Passage. The scene of history shifted from the Old World to the New. If the testimony of former slaves is any indication, slaves often told stories centering upon their condition and their reaction to it. They recounted anecdotes from their daily lives; they spoke of their religious meetings and conversions; they described and relived whatever pleasures they were allowed or managed to fit in; they remembered the horrors of whippings and other punishments; and, for all their stress on the need for caution, they seemed to take delight and pride in telling stories of relatives and friends who challenged the system by escaping or by directly confronting the master or overseer.[22]

The slaves' version of history was largely but not wholly confined to the black world. In the 1880s folklorists in Washington, D.C., discovered a story deeply embedded in the local black oral tradition and "accepted as undoubtedly true by many, if not most, of the colored people over a wide area," which insisted that during his final moments on earth George Washington turned to the friends and relatives gathered around his death bed, "rolled his eyes" and pleaded, "Forever keep the niggers down."[23] The slaves had their own uncomplimentary stories about other white historical figures as well. Andrew Jackson, for instance: "Old General Jackson said before he would see niggers free he would build a house nine miles long and put them in it, and burn everyone of them up. A dirty old rascal; now he is dead and gone."[24] Abraham Lincoln emerged more positively in the stories of slaves and freedmen. Charles Davenport, a slave in Mississippi, remembered when Abraham Lincoln "come here to talk with us. He went all through de country just a-rantin' an' a-preachin' about us being his black brothers. De marster didn't know nothin' about it, cause it was sorta secret-like. It sure riled de niggers up and lots of 'em run away." There were similar legends of Lincoln disguising himself and visiting the plantations before the war to view slavery firsthand, invariably leaving the mark of his visit by carving his name on a bedstead or between the leaves of a table.[25]

Slave versions of history, like all slave tales, were enhanced by the manner of their delivery. The oral inventiveness of good storytellers, who appear to have been relatively common in black culture, was a source of delight and stimulation to their audiences. Their narratives were interlarded with chants, mimicry, rhymes, and songs. "I don't know how they do it," Emma Backus wrote at the end of the nineteenth century, "but they will say 'lipity clipity, lipity clipity,' so you can almost hear a rabbit coming through the woods. They talk animatedly, especially in the dialogues, and change the voice to represent the different animals."[26] Nothing, it seems, was too difficult for a storyteller to represent: the chanting sermon of a black preacher and the response of his entire congregation, the sounds of a railway engine, the cries of barnyard animals, the eerie moans of spectral beings, all formed an integral part of black tales. "The characteristic emphasis of Negro tales, the drawl, and the tricks of speeding up, are difficult to indicate on paper," Elsie Clews Parsons lamented. "Italics and exclamation points are but feeble indicators; and how can one express by printers' signs the significance of what is *not* said?—A significance conveyed by manner or by quietness of intonation, of which a good storyteller is past master."[27]

In addition, black storytellers would frequently supplement the rhythm and meter of their voices by utilizing their bodily rhythms to act out parts of their stories. Richard Dorson has described this aspect of black tales:

When the rabbit scoots away from the fox, or John runs from the Lord, the narrator slaps his hands sharply together, with the left sliding off the right palm in a forward direction—a manual trademark of the Negro raconteur. To indicate continuous running, rather than a sudden sharp spurt, he drops his hands to his sides, spreads the fingers, and wriggles his wrists in a sideways motion, thus suggesting steady movement. Sometimes the reciter gets to his feet and weaves, writhes, gestures, and groans, to simulate the preacher exhorting his flock, or a witch straddling her victim.[28]

And through the entire performance the audience would comment, correct, laugh, respond, making the folktale as much of a communal experience as the spiritual or the sermon. Joel Chandler Harris noted that his recitations of tales to black audiences were continually punctuated by cries of "Dar now!" "He's a honey, mon!" "Git out de way, an' gin 'im room!" and by "peals of unrestrained and unrestrainable laughter."[29] The sense of immediacy which this audience participation afforded was heightened by the tale-ending formulas frequently employed. It was not uncommon for Sea Island narrators to personalize their stories by closing with the sudden interjection, "Of course I couldn't stay any longer to see any more done," or "I was watching them very close, and I turn aroun'." In nineteenth-century Creole tales from Louisiana, storytellers would use such endings as "and there was such a wedding that they sent me to relate the story everywhere, everywhere," or "As I was there when all that happened, I ran away to relate it to you." These formulas remained popular throughout the twentieth century. In the 1950s, Sara Hall concluded her account of why the buzzard has a bald head by commenting, " 'Bout that time I stepped on a piece of tin, and it bent, and I skated on away from there," and J. D. Suggs ended another story with the observation, "And it was raining, and I had on my paper suit, and I made a short cut home as quick as I could."[30]

The nature of their content and delivery, then, allowed slave tales to evoke the past and make it part of the living present. In general, however, slaves used their songs and sermons to achieve this end; they tended to devote the structure and message of their tales to the compulsions and needs of their present situation.

OF MORALITY AND SURVIVAL

If slave tales only infrequently dealt with the sacred world, they nevertheless were often infused with a direct moral message. In Africa, tales which taught a moral, either implicitly or explicitly, were widely used for didactic purposes. "While you Whites have schools and books for teaching your children," a Dahomean told Melville and Frances Herskovits, "we tell them stories, for our stories are our books."[1] This equation of folktales with education was widespread among Afro-Americans during and long after slavery. As late as 1953 Mary Richardson, a seventy-nine-year-old southern black then living in Michigan, told Richard Dorson, "I don't know as I got one year of school if all the days was put together. . . . When it come to 'rithmetic and subtracting I'd get lost, like the dog on the rabbit's tracks. But for a piece or a speech I'd be right up there with the good scholars."[2] Slaves told some explanatory tales—why the rabbit has a short tail, why the buzzard eats carrion, why the alligator lives in the river, why the tiger has a striped back, why the frog lives in water, why the dog cannot talk, why the clay is red—but these details never constituted a central part of black folktales; they were always peripheral and incidental.[3] The didactic element in these stories was rarely specific or technical but embodied in the moral of the tale itself. Heli Chatelain's characterization of African folktales in Angola sums up Afro-American tales as well: "The didactic tendency of these stories is . . . essentially social. They do not teach how to make a thing, but how to act, how to live."[4]

Among the Dahomeans not every day of the week was devoted to work in the fields. Those engaging in agricultural labor on *Mioxi*, a day when such work was expressly prohibited, were threatened with incurring the wrath of the thunder gods, and the story was told of an ambitious man who while cultivating his lands on *Mioxi* was struck and killed by lightning.[5] Precisely the same kinds of stories were told by the slaves and freedmen. Certainly as the black man's control over his own movements and actions increased after emancipation, such stories may have become more relevant and necessary, but they clearly had a purpose during slavery as well. Some of these tales were aimed at those masters who forced their slaves to break the Biblical injunction against working on the Sabbath. Jack Brown, an ex-slave on the Sea Islands, told a tale about an over-worked mule named Jack who complained to its owner about having to work every Sunday. When the owner ran in fright, crying "Great Gawd! I never hear' de mule talk in my life befo'," his dog replied, "Me neither." That, concluded Brown, "broke him of hitchin' up Jack on Sunday an' kyarr'in him to work."[6] But such stories could be aimed at the slaves as well, for if they did not have control over whether they worked on Sundays they did have some options about what they did with those Sundays they were given off. One of the most popular of these tales is typified by the Virginia story of a slave who insisted upon fishing every Sunday in spite of the warnings of his family and friends that he would bring bad luck to himself and to them all. (Significantly, his master was indifferent to the keeping of the Lord's day and refused to order him to stop.) One Sunday, after a terrific struggle, he landed an exotic creature with a head like a duck, wings like a bird, a tail like a fish, and a human voice. Dropping his strange catch, the slave ran in fright, only to be summoned by the creature's compelling song:

> Come back, Sambo,
> Come back, Sambo,
> Domie ninky head, Sambo.

The animal then commanded him in successive verses to "Pick me up, Sambo," "Carry me home, Sambo," "Clean and cook me, Sambo," "Eat me up, Sambo," "Eat me all, Sambo," whereupon the slave burst open and the creature emerging whole and alive went back to the river singing:

Don't fish on Sunday,
Don't fish on Sunday,
Domie ninky head, Sambo.[7]

Stories like this, which resembled African moral tales not only in content but also in form—embracing a song sung in a call-and-response pattern—remained popular well into the twentieth century. In the early 1950s
the great black storyteller J. D. Suggs told, or rather chanted, almost the
identical tale featuring a black fisherman named Simon, and recalled that
he had first heard it from his father as a boy in Mississippi in the last decade of the nineteenth century:

> After my father told me that I wouldn't even pick up a fish on Sunday.
> When the rain flooded the pond you could just pick up a fish on t'other
> side the road. We cooked fish every day it rained. But Sunday we'd go to
> church. When other boys went fishing Dad would say, "They're just
> like Simon."[8]

That these stories were taken literally is attested also by an incident that
occurred when Margaret Burke, who was born free in North Carolina
around 1840, told the same tale in 1917. After she had finished, her fifty-
five-year-old daughter commented, "It's sure wrong to go fishin' on Sunday," and related how she had once done so and almost drowned.[9]

Stories which detailed the fate of those who forgot their dependence
upon God were common among the slaves and freedmen. A tale told in
the Gullah dialect of the Georgia coast pictured a hawk and a buzzard
meeting when times were bad and food scarce. The buzzard confided that
though he was so hungry he was almost ready to perish he had made up
his mind "ter keep on guine, an ter wait on de Lord." The hawk, switching his tail proudly, replied that he was smart enough to earn his own living and that Lord or no Lord he would manage to find food. Pointing
below he called out, "You see dat black chicken down yander? Me guine
ketch um now fuh me dinner." But the "chicken" turned out to be a
sharp-pointed stump, and the hawk, crashing into it, was killed. Several
days later the buzzard returned to eat the hawk's carcass and moralized:
"Enty me [haven't I] bin tell you eh heap better ter wait on de Lord
stidder trus ter you own luck? You wouldn't yeddy [hear] me, an you
see wuh happne."[10] Cap Blanks, an ex-slave from Mississippi, recalled the
similar fate of a proud lizzard:

> One day Brer Lizzud an' Deacon Frawg wuz tryin' ter get thru a
> crack in a split-rail fence. In dem days Brer Lizzud sot up lak Deacon
> Frawg do now. Ole Deacon Frawg sez, "Ah'll git thru dishyere crack ef

de Lawd spares me." He tried hit an' squeeze thru all right. Brer Lizzud wuz mo' uppity. Sez he, "Ah'll git thru dishyere crack wedder de Lawd spare me or no." He tried hit, but, kerflip, came a lawg down an' mash him flat. Dat's why de lizzud be flat terday and crawls de dus' on his belly, while de frawg sets up an' hops.[11]

The moralizing tales of the slave were by no means primarily caught up with an explicitly religious message. The majority of them centered upon everyday human relationships. Mrs. I. E. Edwards recalled that her grandmother, who had been reared in slavery, often told of the buzzard who could soar in the skies higher than any other bird except the eagle, but who still had to come down to earth to get his food. "Our grandmother told us this when she wanted to explain to us how to be kind," Mrs. Edwards commented. "From that she would tell us, regardless of what you might have, don't ever forget to be kind, because we all have to live on the same level."[12] The importance and obligations of friendship were frequently stressed. In one tale a frog trapped in a deep well begs a rattlesnake to aid him and promises to reward him. When he is saved he refuses to fulfill his obligation. Shortly afterwards they meet in the woods and the rattlesnake grabs him. "Yas, I pay yer!!! Yas, I pay yer!! Yas, I pay yer!" the frog cries, but "as Frawg tell dat, Rattlesnake chaw him up."[13] Other tales ended with such clear moral precepts as: "Eh yent [it doesn't] do, in dis wul, fuh man fuh ceive [to deceive] eh fren." "Anybody wuh gwine back on eh prommus, an try fuh harm de pusson wuh done um a faber sho ter meet up wid big trouble." "Bad plan fur stranger fuh meddle long tarruh people bidness [with other people's business]."[14] Stories featuring the reward of those who dispensed kindness and provisions to the needy and the punishment of those who refused aid or gave only begrudgingly were common.[15]

The values and importance of family ties and of the obligations of children and parents to one another played a prominent role in these tales. Disobedient children were dealt with in the story of the chick who disregarded his mother's cry of warning: "Crick, crick, kick, kick, kick!" and was devoured by a hawk. "Dat was de . . . unruly chil' dat wouldn' min' his moder," the storyteller moralized. "De hawk get him. Like we get unruly chillun now."[16] A complementary point was made in the tale told by Georgia coastal Negroes of the eagle who cared for her children until the day when she flew away telling them, "De time come fuh you fuh mek you own libbin. Me feed you long nough. Now you haffer look out fuh youself." "Do same like Buh Eagle," the story concluded. "Mine you chillun well wen dem leetle; an soon dem big nough fuh wuk, mek um wuk."[17] Children were taught proper manners in such tales as that of the man who saved his daughter from the Devil. Satan, showing his anger and frustration at losing the girl, brought his lower teeth up against his upper lip and made a sucking noise. "Dat's why it's not good for chilrun to suck deir teeth at people," the former slave who told the story pointed out, " 'cause de Devil done dat." Portia Smiley reported that in Charleston old Negroes would invariably slap a child who "sucked" his teeth, warning him: "no good will foller you if you do dat. Devil suck his teeth. Devil would foller you 'til you get to heaven's gate. He done mad now, he lost you. . . . Always suck his teeth when he lose a soul."[18]

Courting and marriage were the subject of a number of stories. In "Trackwell, Divewell, Breathewell," which Elsie Clews Parsons has judged to be of "undoubted African provenience" because its structure was intended to provoke group discussion, three young men, each with a special power, court a girl who suddenly disappears. Trackwell traces her path to the water's edge; Divewell jumps in and searches the river bottom until he finds her; Breathewell breathes life back into her. Each then claims the woman for his own, arguing as follows: Trackwell: "I am entitled to the woman, because she was los', an' I track her out." Divewell: "Your track didn' done no good, because you couldn' fin' her. . . . I had to dive out in dat ocean, take chance of my life, an' hunt until I foun' her." Breathewell: "All for what you folk have done, the woman is mine, because she was dead, an' I brought life into her again." In this particular version the narrator had the girl's father give her to Breathewell, immediately stimulating debate among the audience: "My belief is, Trackwell should have dat woman." "My belief is, Breavewell should have dat woman. It's hard, but it's fair." More often, the teller of a dilemma tale left its conclusion up to his audience, as in the story of a man whose boat capsizes throwing himself, his wife, and his mother into the water. "Which one you try to save? I ax de question," the storyteller concluded. "Dat a close point," one of his listeners responded. "Wife is lovin', bosom heart to you. Moder still better, she de one dat bring you here. Get anoder wife, kyan' get anoder moder."[19]

The importance of parental love and care was touched upon in the Georgia fable of an old bullfrog with a young, attractive wife and "a heap of leely chillun" who on his deathbed asked his friends: "who gwine tek me wife wen de breaf leff dis yer body?" The friends hollered: "Me me.

Me me. Me me." Then he inquired, "Who er you gwine mine me leely chillun?" There was a long silence followed by cries of "Yent der me [not me]. Yent der me. Yent der me."[20] The plight of such children was demonstrated in detail in the tales of the wicked stepmother who starved her husband's children, making them smear grease on their hands and mouths so that their father would think they had eaten. When he discovered the truth, she was severely punished.[21] Of course, a natural parent—in these tales invariably the mother—could betray the child as well. Easily the most grisly black tale of this period is an Afro-American version of a commonly known European tale of the murderous mother who, after eating the possum her husband brings home for the entire family to share, becomes frightened and kills and bakes one of her children, serving it to the husband at dinner. While eating, the husband is informed of the murder, either by a bird who flies in and sings of the crime or by the child's spirit which sings:

> My mother killed me.
> My father ate me.
> My brothers buried my bone
> Under a marble stone.

Again the mother is severely punished, usually by death, and again the father emerges as the chief protector and avenger of his children.[22]

The moral inconstancy and overweening pride of women was a recurrent theme. A widow, on the very day she is having her husband's body rowed across a river to the cemetery, is serenaded by the boatman:

> Don' min' de man dat's dead an' gone, but
>   min' de man dat rowed de boat a-sho'!

and marries him the next day.[23] Another series of stories focused upon the envy of a woman whose friends' husbands all brought home raccoons and possums to eat but whose own mate constantly returned from the hunt empty-handed. Driven to desperation by his wife's nagging, the husband kills the family dog and brings home its carcass disguised as that of a raccoon. Only after his wife and children have consumed the animal and call for the dog to eat the bones does the husband reveal his secret, singing:

> Eat Tommy meat,
> Suck Tommy bones,
> Call Tommy heah.
> Oh, yeah, Rover, yeah!

"She mus' have a raccoon, because her neighbor have one," a storyteller moralized. "Woman want somet'in' above his means."[24] More often than not, female pride and egocentricity are punished sternly. In one popular tale a proud woman who could find no suitors to her taste is tricked into marrying the Devil, who takes her off to Hell.[25] In a South Carolina version, a beautiful young lady vows not to marry any man who has a scratch on his back. A tiger turns himself into a man, marries her, and carries her back to the swamp. She finally escapes with the help of a fearless black man named Sambo, whom the tiger tells, "I only married um for le' um know dat a woman isn't more dan a man." The girl's mother greets her upon her return with the same message: "Daughter, I tol' you so. I tol' you dat you always speak too venomous. God had nebber made a woman for be head of a man."[26]

The caveat against undue pride and self-assertiveness was not confined to women. Throughout these tales there runs a perpetual reminder of the fate of those who forget who they are and aspire too high. A North Carolina tale told of "Ole Brer Terrapin" who went through life "a-grumbling and a-fussing, 'cause he have to creep on the ground. When he meet Brer Rabbit, he grumble 'cause he can't run like Brer Rabbit, an' when he meet Brer Buzzard he grumble 'cause he can't fly in the clouds like Brer Buzzard, an' so grumble, grumble, constant." Finally the animals could stand his complaints no longer and agreed that he should be taken high in the air and dropped to his death. Readily agreeing to go for a ride in the clouds, he ascends on the backs of a succession of birds from the crow to the eagle until he is taken so high he becomes frightened and begs to be let down, but the eagle, flying higher and higher, refuses. As he is about to fall off, he remembers a spool of thread in his pocket. Tying one end to the eagle's leg he lets himself down, "and you never hear old Brer Terrapin grumble 'cause he can't run or fly, 'cause the old man he done fly that yer day to satisfy hisself, that he did, sure's yer born, he did fly that yer day."[27]

The same message came through clearly in two other tales found throughout the South. The first, "Fatal Imitation," concerns a monkey who consistently annoyed and embarrassed his owner by imitating everything he did. Finally the owner decides to use the monkey's penchant for imitation to destroy him. One day while shaving he notices the monkey watching him intently. When he finishes, he turns the razor blunt side outward and draws it across his throat.

Sure enough, when he gone, the monkey git the bresh and rub the lather all over he face, . . . When that monkey through shaving he draw the razor quick 'cross he throat, but he ain't know for to turn it, and he cut he own throat and kill hisself.[28]

A second series of stories focuses upon older people (generally women) who try to win much younger mates and are rewarded invariably by humiliation or death.[29] These tales remained popular well into the twentieth century. In 1920, Lendy Hutto, a black schoolchild in Aiken, South Carolina, summed up their collective message in a succinct story:

One time Buh Wolf ax Buh Rabbit, "How come you got such a short tail?"—" 'Cause Gawd put it on, an' he didn' mean fur me to have any long tail."[30]

Acceptance of one's lot and identity may indicate either impotent resignation or a growing sense of autonomous independence. Stories like these contained the seeds of both attitudes—attitudes which created an uneasy duality in black thought for a century after emancipation.

I have dealt in some detail with the moralistic tales of the slaves and freedmen because their existence has been too generally ignored or slighted. They contain material of importance for a comprehension of Afro-American consciousness in the period of emancipation. They helped to reiterate and complement the slaves' religious values. They were utilized to inculcate a vision of the good and moral life by stressing the ideals of friendship, cooperation, meaningful activity, and family love. Their denigration of the aggressive woman and their tendency to celebrate the father as the family's chief protector and provider must be taken into account in any reformulation of our understanding of familial patterns and male-female relations among Afro-Americans. But as important as they were, they cannot be seen in isolation. The situation of the slave and freedman made survival a paramount concern, and it is not surprising that this need gave a practical cast to much of their folklore. It was this perhaps as much as feelings of Christian humility that led to the stress on the pitfalls of aspiring too high. It was dangerous for black men and women to forget who or where they were, and this danger constituted a motif running through Negro tales.

There can be no question that a substantial number of slaves sincerely believed in the values of the religion they embraced and in part refashioned. But their situation frequently made those values a luxury they could not afford to indulge. This certainly is the message of John Hill's recollection of the fate of runaways on the Georgia plantation where he had been a slave.

> They had dogs to trail 'em with, so they always cotched 'em, and then the whipping boss beat 'em most to death. It was awful to hear 'em hollering and begging for mercy. If they hollered, "Lord, have mercy!" Marse Jim didn't hear 'em, but if they cried "Marse Jim, have mercy!" then he made 'em stop the beating. He say, "The Lord rule Heaven, but Jim Smith rule the earth."[31]

Had slaves internalized this lesson on a mass scale then the Peculiar Institution truly would have produced the Sambos whom nineteenth-century whites and their twentieth-century descendants so liked to romanticize. But slave religion and folktales make it clear that the mass of black men and women seldom took this message too literally. A story told by Texas blacks recalled a plantation on which slave prayer meetings were forbidden. Ignoring this injunction whenever they could, the slaves would meet secretly in the woods near the big house. During one of these illicit meetings the master returned to his plantation earlier than usual and heard the slave elder, Uncle Peter, praying: "Oh, Lawdy, cum git us! Oh, blessed Savior, lay Yo' han's on us! Oh, *Master*, cum give us Yo' blessin's." Crying, "I'll come and get you all right," the master ran out into the circle of slaves and began whipping Peter. "Oh, Massa," Peter cried, "Ah didn' want yo' blessin's! Yuh's killin' Uncle Peter! Ah didn' call 'massa'; Ah called '*Master!*' "[32]

However clearly slave religion may have taught its adherents to distinguish between the eternal power and justice of the "Master" as opposed to the short-run temporal power of the "Massa," the latter still had to be dealt with. This need structured both the form and the content of slave tales. Although the repertory of slave tales included many types diffused into it from Euro-American culture in the midst of which Afro-Americans lived, European *Märchen*—the magical fairy tales so popular among American whites—were rarely represented. Tales such as "Rumplestiltskin," "Cinderella," "Jack, the Giant Killer," and "The Devil's Daughter" were occasionally told, but rarely have they constituted a standard element in Afro-American tales. Wherever found they were always more typical of young Negroes after emancipation than of older ones who themselves experienced slavery.[33] At first sight the absence of these tales from Afro-American lore is surprising. Stith Thompson has defined the

Märchen as a tale which "moves in an unreal world without definite locality or definite characters and is filled with the marvelous. In this never-never land humble heroes kill adversaries, succeed to kingdoms, and marry princesses."[34]

Ostensibly, such tales should have had a direct appeal to down-trodden and powerless nineteenth-century Negroes. That they did not is another testament to the realism that pervaded black folktales. Writing of African folktales, Paul Radin has argued: "in the main, little romanticism is found in African myths and definitely no sentimentality. It is emphatically not a literature in which wish-fulfillment plays a great role, not one where we can assume that the hero will triumph at the end or that wrongs will always be righted."[35] Largely the same generalization can be applied to Afro-American folktales. The slaves' plight was too serious, their predicament too perilous, for them to indulge in pure fantasy and romanticism. Certainly, wish-fulfillment and transference were important elements in the slaves' trickster tales, but even here they were tailored to the slaves' peculiar needs and never were permitted to obscure the reality of their situation.

Similarly, while the slaves' didactic tales attempted to inculcate elements of proper conduct and righteous living, they were also filled with strategies for survival. An excellent example is the common story of the slave who meets an animal—usually a frog or a turtle—who could speak. Rushing to inform his master of this miracle, the slave brings him back to hear the creature for himself, although the master warns him he will be punished if he is lying. The animal remains mute before the white man and the slave is severely beaten. Only when the master departs does the animal speak again saying: "ah tol' yuh de othah day, niggah, yuh talk too much." In an equally popular version, the slave discovers the head of a skeleton, which tells him, "Mouth brought me here. Mouth's goin' to bring *you* here." Ignoring this warning, the slave prevails upon his master to come and witness the wondrous talking skull. When the master is greeted only by silence from the lifeless head, he kills the slave to whom the skull now turns and says: "Didn't I tell you Mouth was goin' to bring you here?" The concluding lines of these widely told stories repeated one message over and over: "It's bad to talk too much." "I told you something that got me here would get you here. You talk too much." "I told you tongue brought me here and tongue is what brought you here." "Live in peace; don't tell all you see."[36]

There is abundant evidence that the slaves thoroughly assimilated this lesson. Even their friends and defenders testified to the slaves' duplicity and secretiveness. The Methodist minister John Dixon Long, whose opposition to slavery led him to emigrate from Maryland to Philadelphia in 1856, noted:

> The inevitable tendency of servitude is to make a slave a hypocrite toward the white man. If you approach him from the stand-point of authority, you will never get an insight into his real character. He is exceedingly shrewd. . . . Let a slave once know or suspect that you are seeking to "pump" him, and if you don't meet with your match for once, then I am mistaken. . . . You must catch him at work. Listen to his songs while seated on his ox-cart hauling wood, or splitting rails. You must overhear his criticisms in the quarters.[37]

Laura Towne, one of that early band of New England whites who flocked to the Sea Islands during the Civil War to work with the newly liberated slaves, concluded after a short residence on St. Helena Island that "the negroes are pretty cunning." She described a praise house meeting she attended in May 1862, during which "good old Marcus," one of the black elders, exhorted his fellows to "be jus' like de birds when a gunner was about, expectin' a crack ebery minute."[38] "Jes like the tarpins or turtles," is the way W. L. Bost characterized himself and his fellow slaves on a North Carolina plantation. "Jes stick our heads out to see how the land lay."[39]

These deeply ingrained attitudes and strategies remained long after slavery to plague white folklorists attempting to collect slave lore: "tarpins or turtles," they were to discover, did not make the most cooperative subjects. "Curiously enough," Joel Chandler Harris complained in 1880, "I have found few negroes who will acknowledge to a stranger that they know anything of these legends; and yet to relate one of the stories is the surest road to their confidence and esteem. In this way, and in this way only, I have been enabled to collect and verify the folklore in this volume." In the introduction to his second volume, Harris described in detail how he obtained his stories. Infiltrating a group of black workers who were resting, he began to tell several animal tales in dialect, thus stimulating his audience to join in with stories of their own.[40] He was able to collect black tales, then, only by speaking the idiom of his subjects; only, in short, by becoming black himself, however temporarily. Some forty years later, Elsie Clews Parsons was told by James Murray, in whose house she was living while collecting black folklore, that if she had chosen to live with a neighboring white family he would have told her no stories "fo' no money, not fo' a week. We pay dem [whites] fo' what we git, an' dey pay us. We don' boder wid dem, an' dey don' boder wid us. We wouldn' tell riddle [tales] befo' dem, not even if we was a servan' in deir house."[41] As if to verify this statement, Lydia Parrish's black cook on St. Simon's Island off the Georgia coast worked for her for fifteen years, from 1912 to 1927, before she revealed that she could sing the old slave songs her employer was so avidly seeking. "When I periodically ask why, in all those years, she never told me she could sing, she smiles quizically, but says nothing," Mrs. Parrish noted. "I am convinced that the average Negro enjoys intensely knowing something the white man does not, and the exquisite delight he derives from realizing that the white man has been bested in a little game makes up for any loss or indignity he may be obliged to endure."[42]

The difficulty whites had in persuading blacks to reveal their folklore was, appropriately enough, the product of that lore itself. It took Mrs. Parrish three winters of residence on St. Simon's Island to hear her first slave spiritual, nine winters to witness her first ring shout, and more than a decade to see and hear other forms of black folklore, in part because slaves and their descendants had used their tales so effectively to teach the advantages and necessity of reticence and caution. The lesson was repeated endlessly in black aphorisms: "A smart redbird don't have much to say." "De fox wants to know how de rabbit's gittin on." "De mousetrap don't go to sleep." "Don' crow tel yuh git out o' de woods; dey mought be, uh beah behin' de las' tree." "Long talk catch run 'way nigguh." "Everything good to hear is not good to talk."[43]

"Persons live and die in the midst of Negroes and know comparatively little of their real character," Charles C. Jones complained in 1842. "They are one thing before the whites, and another before their own color. Deception towards the former is characteristic of them, whether bond or free, throughout the whole United States."[44] Almost a century later Duncan Clinch Heyward, the son of one of antebellum South Carolina's largest rice planters, observed: "I used to try to learn the ways of these Negroes, but I could never divest myself of the suspicion that they were learning my ways faster than I was learning theirs."[45] The most important single mechanism produced by antebellum blacks to create this frustration among the whites and enhance survival among themselves was their cycle of trickster tales.

"SOME GO UP AND SOME GO DOWN": THE ANIMAL TRICKSTER

Although the range of slave tales was narrow in neither content nor focus, it is not surprising or accidental that the tales most easily and abundantly collected in Africa and among Afro-Americans in the New World were animal trickster tales. Because of their overwhelmingly paradigmatic character, animal tales were, of all the narratives of social protest or psychological release, among the easiest to relate both within and especially outside the group.

The propensity of Africans to utilize their folklore quite consciously to gain psychological release from the inhibitions of their society and their situation has already been described in Chapter 1, but it needs to be reiterated here if the popularity and function of animal trickster tales is to be understood. After listening to a series of Ashanti stories that included rather elaborate imitations of afflicted people—an old woman dressed in rags and covered with sores, a leper, an old man suffering from the skin disease yaws—which called forth roars of laughter from the audience, the English anthropologist R. S. Rattray suggested that it was unkind to ridicule such subjects. "The person addressed replied that in everyday life no one might do so, however great the inclination to laugh might be. He went on to explain that it was so with many other things: the cheating and tricks of priests, the rascality of a chief—things about which every one knew, but concerning which one might not ordinarily speak in public. These occasions gave every one an opportunity of talking about and laughing at such things; it was 'good' for every one concerned, he said." Customs such as these led Rattray to conclude "beyond a doubt, that West Africans had discovered for themselves the truth of the psychoanalysts' theory of 'repressions,' and that in these ways they sought an outlet for what might otherwise become a dangerous complex."[1]

Certainly this was at the heart of the popularity of animal trickster tales. Whether it is accurate to assert, as Rattray has done, that the majority of "beast fables" were derived from the practice of substituting the names of animals for the names of real individuals whom it would have been impolitic or dangerous to mention, there can be no question that the animals in these tales were easily recognizable representations of both specific actions and generalized patterns of human behavior. "In the fable," Léopold Senghor has written, "the animal is seldom a totem; it is this or that one whom every one in the village knows well: the stupid or tyrannical or wise and good chief, the young man who makes reparation for injustice. Tales and fables are woven out of everyday occurrences. Yet it is not a question of anecdotes or of 'material from life.' The facts are images and have paradigmatic value."[2] The popularity of these tales in Africa is attested to by the fact that the Akan-speaking peoples of the West Coast gave their folk tales the generic title *Anansesem* (spider stories), after the spider trickster Anansi, whether he appeared in the story or not, and this practice was perpetuated by such New World Afro-American groups as the South American Negroes of Surinam who referred to all their stories, whatever their nature, as *Anansitori*, or the West Indian blacks of Curaçao who called theirs *Cuenta de Nansi*.[3]

For all their importance, animals did not monopolize the trickster role in African tales; tricksters could, and did, assume divine and human form as well. Such divine tricksters as the Dahomean Legba or the Yoruban Eshu and Orunmila did not survive the transplantation of Africans to the United States and the slaves' adaptation to Christian religious forms. Human tricksters, on the other hand, played an important role in the tales of American slaves. By the nineteenth century, however, these human tricksters were so rooted in and reflective of their new cultural and social setting that outside of function they bore increasingly little resemblance to their African counterparts. It was in the animal trickster that the most easily perceivable correspondence in form and usage between African and Afro-American tales can be found. In both cases the primary trickster figures of animal tales were weak, relatively powerless creatures who attain their ends through the application of native wit and guile rather than power or authority: the Hare or Rabbit in East Africa, Angola, and parts of Nigeria; the Tortoise among the Yoruba, Ibo, and Edo peoples of Nigeria; the Spider throughout much of West Africa including Ghana, Liberia, and Sierra Leone; Brer Rabbit in the United States.[4]

In their transmutation from their natural state to the world of African and Afro-American tales, the animals inhabiting these tales, though retaining enough of their natural characteristics to be recognizable, were almost thoroughly humanized. The world they lived in, the rules they lived by, the emotions that governed them, the status they craved, the taboos they feared, the prizes they struggled to attain were those of the men and women who lived in this world. The beings that came to life in these stories were so created as to be human enough to be identified with but at the same time exotic enough to allow both storytellers and listeners a latitude and freedom that came only with much more difficulty and daring in tales explicitly concerning human beings.

This latitude was crucial, for the one central feature of almost all trickster tales is their assault upon deeply ingrained and culturally sanctioned values. This of course accounts for the almost universal occurrence of trickster tales, but it has not rendered them universally identical. The values people find constraining and the mechanisms they choose to utilize in their attempts at transcending or negating them are determined by their culture and their situation. "It is very well to speak of 'the trickster,'" Melville and Frances Herskovits have noted, "yet one need but compare the Winnebago trickster [of the North American Indians] . . . with Legba and Yo in Dahomey to find that the specifications for the first by no means fit the second."[5] The same may be said of the slave trickster in relation to the trickster figures of the whites around them. Although animal trickster tales do not seem to have caught a strong hold among American whites during the eighteenth and the first half of the nineteenth century, there were indigenous American tricksters from the tall, spare New Englander Jonathan, whose desire for pecuniary gain knew few moral boundaries, to the rough roguish confidence men of southwestern tales. But the American process that seems to have been most analogous in function to the African trickster tale was not these stories so much as the omnipresent tales of exaggeration. In these tall tales Americans were able to deal with the insecurities produced by forces greater than themselves not by manipulating them, as Africans tended to do, but by overwhelming them through the magnification of the self epitomized in the unrestrained exploits of a Mike Fink or Davy Crockett. "I'm . . . half-horse, half-alligator, a little touched with the snapping turtle; can wade the Mississippi, leap the Ohio, ride upon a streak of lightning, and slip without a scratch down a honey locust; can whip my weight in wildcats, . . . hug a bear too close for comfort, and eat any man opposed to Jackson," the latter would boast.[6]

It is significant that, with the exception of the stories of flying Africans, mythic strategies such as these played almost no role in the lore of nineteenth-century slaves; not until well after emancipation do tales of exaggeration, with their magnification of the individual, begin to assume importance in the folklore of Afro-Americans. Nor did the model of white trickster figures seem to have seriously affected the slaves, whose own tricksters remained in a quite different mold—one much closer to the cultures from which they had come. In large part African trickster tales revolved around the strong patterns of authority so central to African cultures. As interested as they might be in material gains, African trickster figures were more obsessed with manipulating the strong and reversing the normal structure of power and prestige. Afro-American slaves, cast into a far more rigidly fixed and certainly a more alien authority system, could hardly have been expected to neglect a cycle of tales so ideally suited to their needs.

This is not to argue that slaves in the United States continued with little or no alteration the trickster lore of their ancestral home. The divergences were numerous: divine trickster figures disappeared; such important figures as Anansi the spider were at best relegated to the dim background; sizable numbers of European tales and themes found their way into the slave repertory. But we must take care not to make too much of these differences. For instance, the fact that the spider trickster retained its importance and its Twi name, Anansi, among the Afro-Americans of Jamaica, Surinam, and Curaçao, while in the United States Anansi lived only a peripheral existence in such tales as the Aunt Nancy stories of South Carolina and Georgia, has been magnified out of proportion by some students. "The sharp break between African and American tradition," Richard Dorson has written, "occurs at the West Indies, where Anansi the spider dominates hundreds of cantefables, the tales that inclose songs. But no Anansi stories are found in the United States."[7] The decline of the spider trickster in the United States can be explained by many factors from the ecology of the United States, where spiders were less ubiquitous and important than in either Africa or those parts of the New World in which the spider remained a central figure, to the particular admixture of African peoples in the various parts of the Western Hemisphere. Anansi, after all, was but one of many African tricksters and in Africa itself had a limited influence. Indeed, in many parts of South America where aspects of African culture endured overtly with much less alteration than occurred in the United States, Anansi was either nonexistent or marginal.[8]

What is more revealing than the life or death of any given trickster figure is the retention of the trickster tale itself. Despite all of the changes that took place, there persisted the mechanism, so well developed throughout most of Africa, by means of which psychic relief from arbitrary authority could be secured, symbolic assaults upon the powerful could be waged, and important lessons about authority relationships could be imparted. Afro-Americans in the United States were to make extended use of this mechanism throughout their years of servitude.

In its simplest form the slaves' animal trickster tale was a cleanly delineated story free of ambiguity. The strong assault the weak, who fight back with any weapons they have. The animals in these tales have an almost instinctive understanding of each other's habits and foibles. Knowing Rabbit's curiosity and vanity, Wolf constructs a tar-baby and leaves it by the side of the road. At first fascinated by this stranger and then progressively infuriated at its refusal to respond to his friendly salutations, Rabbit strikes at it with his hands, kicks it with his feet, butts it with his head, and becomes thoroughly enmeshed. In the end, however, it is Rabbit whose understanding of his adversary proves to be more profound. Realizing that Wolf will do exactly what he thinks his victim least desires, Rabbit convinces him that of all the ways to die the one he is most afraid of is being thrown into the briar patch, which of course is exactly what Wolf promptly does, allowing Rabbit to escape.[9]

This situation is repeated in tale after tale: the strong attempt to trap the weak but are tricked by them instead. Fox entreats Rooster to come down from his perch, since all the animals have signed a peace treaty and there is no longer any danger: "I don' eat you, you don' boder wid me. Come down! Le's make peace!" Almost convinced by this good news, Rooster is about to descend when he thinks better of it and tests Fox by pretending to see a man and a dog coming down the road. "Don' min' fo' comin' down den," Fox calls out as he runs away. "Dawg ain't got no sense, yer know, an' de man got er gun."[10] Spotting a goat lying on a rock, Lion is about to surprise and kill him when he notices that Goat keeps chewing and chewing although there is nothing there but bare stone. Lion reveals himself and asks Goat what he is eating. Overcoming the momentary paralysis which afflicts most of the weak animals in these tales when they realize they are trapped, Goat saves himself by saying in his most terrifying voice: "Me duh chaw dis rock, an ef you dont leff, wen me done . . . me guine eat you."[11]

At its most elemental, then, the trickster tale consists of a confrontation in which the weak use their wits to evade the strong. Mere escape, however, does not prove to be victory enough, and in a significant number of these tales the weak learn the brutal ways of the more powerful. Fox, taking advantage of Pig's sympathetic nature, gains entrance to his house during a storm by pleading that he is freezing to death. After warming himself by the fire, he acts exactly as Pig's instincts warned him he would. Spotting a pot of peas cooking on the stove, he begins to sing:

> Fox and peas are very good,
> But Pig and peas are better.

Recovering from his initial terror, Pig pretends to hear a pack of hounds, helps Fox hide in a meal barrel, and pours the peas in, scalding Fox to death.[12]

In one tale after another the trickster proves to be as merciless as his stronger opponent. Wolf traps Rabbit in a hollow tree and sets it on fire, but Rabbit escapes through a hole in the back and reappears, thanking Wolf for an excellent meal, explaining that the tree was filled with honey which melted from the heat. Wolf, in his eagerness to enjoy a similar feast, allows himself to be sealed into a tree which has no other opening, and is burned to death. "While eh duh bun, Buh Wolf bague an pray Buh Rabbit fuh leh um come out, but Buh Rabbit wouldnt yeddy [hear] um."[13] The brutality of the trickster in these tales was sometimes troubling ("Buh Rabbit . . . hab er bad heart," the narrator of the last story concluded), but more often it was mitigated by the fact that the strong were the initial aggressors and the weak really had no choice. The characteristic spirit of these tales was one not of moral judgment but of vicarious triumph. Storytellers allowed their audience to share the heartening spectacle of a lion running in terror from a goat or a fox fleeing a rooster; to experience the mocking joy of Brer Rabbit as he scampers away through the briar patch calling back to Wolf, "Dis de place me mammy fotch me up,—dis de place me mammy fotch me up"; to feel the joyful relief of Pig as he turns Fox's song upside down and chants:

> Pigs and peas are very good,
> But Fox and peas are better.

Had self-preservation been the only motive driving the animals in these stories, the trickster tale need never have varied from the forms just considered. But Brer Rabbit and his fellow creatures were too humanized to be content with mere survival. Their needs included all the prizes human beings crave and strive for: wealth, success, prestige, honor, sexual prowess. Brer Rabbit himself summed it up best in the tale for which this section is named:

> De rabbit is de slickest o' all de animals de Lawd ever made. He ain't de biggest, an' he ain't de loudest but he sho' am de slickest. If he gits in

trouble he gits out by gittin' somebody else in. Once he fell down a deep well an' did he holler and cry? No siree. He set up a mighty mighty whistling and a singin', an' when de wolf passes by he heard him an' he stuck his head over an' de rabbit say, "Git 'long 'way f'om here. Dere ain't room fur two. Hit's mighty hot up dere and nice an' cool down here. Don' you git in dat bucket an' come down here." Dat made de wolf all de mo' onrestless and he jumped into the bucket an' as he went down de rabbit come up, an' as dey passed de rabbit he laughed an' he say, "Dis am life; some go up and some go down."[14]

There could be no mistaking the direction in which Rabbit was determined to head. It was in his inexorable drive upward that Rabbit emerged not only as an incomparable defender but also as a supreme manipulator, a role that complicated the simple contours of the tales already referred to.

In the ubiquitous tales of amoral manipulation, the trickster could still be pictured as much on the defensive as he was in the stories which had him battling for his very life against stronger creatures. The significant difference is that now the panoply of his victims included the weak as well as the powerful. Trapped by Mr. Man and hung from a sweet gum tree until he can be cooked, Rabbit is buffeted to and fro by the wind and left to contemplate his bleak future until Brer Squirrel happens along. "This yer my cool air swing," Rabbit informs him. "I taking a fine swing this morning." Squirrel begs a turn and finds his friend surprisingly gracious: "Certainly, Brer Squirrel, you do me proud. Come up here, Brer Squirrel, and give me a hand with this knot." Tying the grateful squirrel securely in the tree, Rabbit leaves him to his pleasure—and his fate. When Mr. Man returns, "he take Brer Squirrel home and cook him for dinner."[15]

It was primarily advancement not preservation that led to the trickster's manipulations, however. Among a slave population whose daily rations were at best rather stark fare and quite often a barely minimal diet, it is not surprising that food proved to be the most common symbol of enhanced status and power. In his never-ending quest for food the trickster was not content with mere acquisition, which he was perfectly capable of on his own; he needed to procure the food through guile from some stronger animal. Easily the most popular tale of this type pictures Rabbit and Wolf as partners in farming a field. They have laid aside a tub of butter for winter provisions, but Rabbit proves unable to wait or to share. Pretending to hear a voice calling him, he leaves his chores and begins to eat the butter. When he returns to the field he informs his partner that his sister has just had a baby and wanted him to name it. "Well, w'at you name um?" Wolf asks innocently. "Oh, I name um Buh Start-um," Rabbit replies. Subsequent calls provide the chance for additional assaults on the butter and additional names for the nonexistent babies: "Buh Half-um," "Buh Done-um." After work, Wolf discovers the empty tub and accuses Rabbit, who indignantly denies the theft. Wolf proposes that they both lie in the sun, which will cause the butter to run out of the guilty party. Rabbit agrees readily, and when grease begins to appear on his own face he rubs it onto that of the sleeping wolf. "Look, Buh Wolf," he cries, waking his partner, "de buttah melt out on you. Dat prove you eat um." "I guess you been right," Wolf agrees docilely, "I eat um fo' trute."[16] In some versions the animals propose a more hazardous ordeal by fire to discover the guilty party. Rabbit successfully jumps over the flames but some innocent animal—Possum, Terrapin, Bear—falls in and perishes for Rabbit's crime.[17]

In most of these tales the aggrieved animal, realizing he has been tricked, desperately tries to avenge himself by setting careful plans to trap Rabbit, but to no avail. Unable to outwit Rabbit, his adversaries attempt to learn from him, but here too they fail. Seeing Rabbit carrying a string of fish, Fox asks him where they came from. Rabbit confesses that he stole them from Man by pretending to be ill and begging Man to take him home in his cart which was filled with fish. While riding along, Rabbit explains, he threw the load of fish into the woods and then jumped off to retrieve them. He encourages Fox to try the same tactic, and Fox is beaten to death, as Rabbit knew he would be, since Man is too shrewd to be taken in the same way twice.[18]

And so it goes in story after story. Rabbit cheats Brer Wolf out of his rightful portion of a cow and a hog they kill together. He tricks Brer Fox out of his part of their joint crop year after year "until he starved the fox to death. Then he had all the crop, and all the land too." He leisurely watches all the other animals build a house in which they store their winter provisions and then sneaks in, eats the food, and scares the others, including Lion, away by pretending to be a spirit and calling through a horn in a ghostly voice that he is a "better man den ebber bin yuh befo." He convinces Wolf that they ought to sell their own grandparents for a tub of butter, arranges for his grandparents to escape so that only Wolf's remain to be sold, and once they are bartered for the butter he steals that as well.[19]

The many tales of which these are typical make it clear that what Rabbit craves is not possession but power, and this he acquires not simply by obtaining food but by obtaining it through the manipulation and deprivation of others. It is not often that he meets his match, and then generally at the hands of an animal as weak as himself. Refusing to allow Rabbit to cheat him out of his share of the meat they have just purchased, Partridge samples a small piece of liver and cries out, "Br'er Rabbit, de meat bitter! Oh, 'e bitter, bitter! bitter, bitter! You better not eat de meat," and tricks Rabbit into revealing where he had hidden the rest of the meat. "You is a damn sha'p feller," Partridge tells him. "But I get even wid you."[20] Angry at Frog for inviting all the animals in the forest but him to a fish dinner, Rabbit frightens the guests away and eats all the fish himself. Frog gives another dinner, but this time he is prepared and tricks Rabbit into the water. "You is my master many a day on land, Brer Rabbit," Frog tells him just before killing and eating him, "but I is you master in the water."[21]

It is significant that when these defeats do come, most often it is not brute force but even greater trickery that triumphs. Normally, however, the trickster has more than his share of the food. And of the women as well, for sexual prowess is the other basic sign of prestige in the slaves' tales. Although the primary trickster was occasionally depicted as a female—Ol' Molly Hare in Virginia, Aunt Nancy or Ann Nancy in the few surviving spider stories[22]—in general women played a small role in slave tales. They were not actors in their own right so much as attractive possessions to be fought over. That the women for whom the animals compete are frequently the daughters of the most powerful creatures in the forest makes it evident that the contests are for status as well as pleasure. When Brer Bear promises his daughter to the best whistler in the forest, Rabbit offers to help his only serious competitor, Brer Dog, whistle more sweetly by slitting the corners of his mouth, which in reality makes him incapable of whistling at all. If Rabbit renders his adversaries figuratively impotent in their quest for women, they often retaliate in kind. In the story just related, Dog chases Rabbit, bites off his tail, and nothing more is said about who wins the woman.[23]

More often than not, though, Rabbit is successful. In a Georgia tale illustrating the futility of mere hard work, Brer Wolf offers his attractive daughter to the animal that shucks the most corn. Rabbit has his heart set on winning Miss Wolf but realizes he has no chance of beating Brer Coon at shucking corn. Instead, he spends all of his time during the contest singing, dancing, and charming Miss Wolf. At the end he sits down next to Coon and claims that he has shucked the great pile of corn. Confused, Wolf leaves the decision up to his daughter:

Now Miss Wolf she been favoring Brer Rabbit all the evening. Brer Rabbit dancing and singing plum turned Miss Wolf's head, so Miss Wolf she say, "It most surely are Brer Rabbit's pile." Miss Wolf she say she "plum 'stonished how Brer Coon can story so." Brer Rabbit he take the gal and go off home clipity, lipity. Poor old Brer Coon he take hisself off home, he so tired he can scarcely hold hisself together.[24]

In another Georgia tale the contest for the woman seems to be symbolically equated with freedom. Fox promises his daughter to any animal who can pound dust out of a rock.

Then Brer Rabbit, he feel might set down on, 'cause he know all the chaps can swing the stone hammer to beat hisself, and he go off sorrowful like and set on the sand bank. He set a while and look east, and then he turn and set a while and look west, but may be you don't know, sah, Brer Rabbit sense never come to hisself 'cepting when he look north.

Thus inspired, Rabbit conceives of a strategy allowing him to defeat his more powerful opponents and carry off the woman.[25]

In the best known and most symbolically interesting courting tale, Rabbit and Wolf vie for the favors of a woman who is pictured as either equally torn between her two suitors or leaning toward Wolf. Rabbit alters the contest by professing surprise that she could be interested in Wolf, since he is merely Rabbit's riding horse. Hearing of this, Wolf confronts Rabbit, who denies ever saying it and promises to go to the woman and personally refute the libel as soon as he is well enough. Wolf insists he go at once, and the characteristic combination of Rabbit's deceit and Wolf's seemingly endless trust and gullibility allows Rabbit to convince his adversary that he is too sick to go with him unless he can ride on Wolf's back with a saddle and bridle for support. The rest of the story is inevitable. Approaching the woman's house Rabbit tightens the reins, digs a pair of spurs into Wolf, and trots him around crying, "Look here, girl! what I told you? Didn't I say I had Brother Wolf for my riding-horse?"[26] It was in many ways the ultimate secular triumph in slave tales. The weak doesn't merely kill his enemy: he mounts him, humiliates him, reduces him to servility, steals his woman, and, in effect, takes his place.

Mastery through possessing the two paramount symbols of power—food and women—did not prove to be sufficient for Rabbit. He craved something more. Going to God himself, Rabbit begs for enhanced potency in the form of a larger tail, greater wisdom, bigger eyes. In each case God imposes a number of tasks upon Rabbit before his wishes are fulfilled. Rabbit must bring God a bag full of blackbirds, the teeth of a rattlesnake or alligator, a swarm of yellowjackets, the "eyewater" (tears) of a deer. Rabbit accomplishes each task by exploiting the animals' vanity. He tells the blackbirds that they cannot fill the bag and when they immediately prove they can, he traps them. He taunts the snake, "dis pole *swear* say you ain't long as him." When Rattlesnake insists he is, Rabbit ties him to the stick, ostensibly to measure him, kills him, and takes his teeth. Invariably Rabbit does what is asked of him but finds God less than pleased. In some tales he is chased out of Heaven. In others God counsels him, "Why Rabbit, ef I was to gi' you long tail aint you see you'd 'stroyed up de whol worl'? Nobawdy couldn' do nuttin wid you!" Most commonly God seemingly complies with Rabbit's request and gives him a bag which he is to open when he returns home. But Rabbit cannot wait, and when he opens the bag prematurely "thirty bull-dawg run out de box, an' bit off Ber Rabbit tail again. An' dis give him a short tail again."[27]

The rabbit, like the slaves who wove tales about him, was forced to make do with what he had. His small tail, his natural portion of intellect—these would have to suffice, and to make them do he resorted to any means at his disposal—means which may have made him morally tainted but which allowed him to survive and even to conquer. In this respect there was a direct relationship between Rabbit and the slaves, a relationship which the earliest collectors and interpreters of these stories understood well. Joel Chandler Harris, as blind as he could be to some of the deeper implications of the tales he heard and retold, was always aware of their utter seriousness. "Well, I tell you dis," Harris had Uncle Remus say, "ef deze yer tales wuz des fun, fun, fun, en giggle, giggle, giggle, I let you know I'd a-done drapt um long ago." From the beginning Harris insisted that the animal fables he was collecting were "thoroughly characteristic of the negro," and commented that "it needs no scientific investigation to show why he selects as his hero the weakest and most harmless of all animals, and brings him out victorious in contests with the bear, the wolf, and the fox."[28]

Harris' interpretations were typical. Abigail Christensen noted in the preface to her important 1892 collection of black tales: "It must be remembered that the Rabbit represents the colored man. He is not as large nor as strong, as swift, as wise, nor as handsome as the elephant, the alligator, the bear, the deer, the serpent, the fox, but he is 'de mos' cunnin' man dat go on fo' leg' and by this cunning he gains success. So the negro, without education or wealth, could only hope to succeed by stratagem." That she was aware of the implications of these strategies was made evident when she remarked of her own collection: "If we believe that the tales of our nurseries are as important factors in forming the characters of our children as the theological dogmas of maturer years, we of the New South cannot wish our children to pore long over these pages, which certainly could not have been approved by Froebel."[29] In that same year Octave Thanet, in an article on Arkansas folklore, concluded, "Br'er Rabbit, indeed, personifies the obscure ideals of the negro race. . . . Ever since the world began, the weak have been trying to outwit the strong; Br'er Rabbit typifies the revolt of his race. His successes are just the kind of successes that his race have craved."[30]

These analyses of the animal trickster tales have remained standard down to our own day.[31] They have been advanced not merely by interpreters of the tales but by their narrators as well. Prince Baskin, one of Mrs. Christensen's informants, was quite explicit in describing the model for many of his actions:

> You see, Missus, I is small man myself; but I aint nebber 'low no one for to git head o' me. I allers use my sense for help me 'long jes' like Brer Rabbit. 'Fo de wah ol' Marse Heywood mek me he driber on he place, an' so I aint hab for work so hard as de res'; same time I git mo' ration ebery mont' an' mo' shoe when dey share out de cloes at Chris'mus time. Well, dat come from usin' my sense. An' den, when I ben a-courtin' I nebber 'lowed no man to git de benefit ob me in dat. I allers carry off de purties' gal, 'cause, you see, Missus, I know how to play de fiddle an' allers had to go to ebery dance to play de fiddle for dem.[32]

More than half a century later, William Willis Greenleaf of Texas echoed Baskin's admiration: "De kinda tales dat allus suits mah fancy de mo'es' am de tales de ole folks used to tell 'bout de ca'iens on of Brothuh Rabbit. In de early days Ah heerd many an' many a tale 'bout ole Brothuh Rabbit what woke me to de fac' dat hit tecks dis, dat an' t'othuh to figguh life out—dat you hafto use yo' haid fo mo'n a hat rack lack ole Brothuh Rabbit do. Ole Brothuh Rabbit de smaa'tes' thing Ah done evuh run 'crost in mah whole bawn life."[33]

This testimony—and there is a great deal of it—documents the enduring identification between black storytellers and the central trickster figure of their tales. Brer Rabbit's victories became the victories of the slave. This symbolism in slave tales allowed them to outlive slavery itself. So long as the perilous situation and psychic needs of the slave continued to characterize large numbers of freedmen as well, the imagery of the old slave tales remained both aesthetically and functionally satisfying. By ascribing actions to semi-mythical actors, Negroes were able to overcome the external and internal censorship that their hostile surroundings imposed upon them. The white master could believe that the rabbit stories his slaves told were mere figments of a childish imagination, that they were primarily humorous anecdotes depicting the "roaring comedy of animal life." Blacks knew better. The trickster's exploits, which overturned the neat hierarchy of the world in which he was forced to live, became their exploits; the justice he achieved, their justice; the strategies he employed, their strategies. From his adventures they obtained relief; from his triumphs they learned hope.

To deny this interpretation of slave tales would be to ignore much of their central essence. The problem with the notion that slaves completely identified with their animal trickster hero whose exploits were really protest tales in disguise is that it ignores much of the complexity and ambiguity inherent in these tales. This in turn flows from the propensity of scholars to view slavery as basically a relatively simple phenomenon which produced human products conforming to some unitary behavioral pattern. Too frequently slaves emerge from the pages of historians' studies either as docile, accepting beings or as alienated prisoners on the edge of rebellion. But if historians have managed to escape much of the anarchic confusion so endemic in the Peculiar Institution, slaves did not. Slaveholders who considered Afro-Americans to be little more than subhuman chattels converted them to a religion which stressed their humanity and even their divinity. Masters who desired and expected their slaves to act like dependent children also enjoined them to behave like mature, responsible adults, since a work force consisting only of servile infantiles who can make no decisions on their own and can produce only under the impetus of a significant other is a dubious economic resource, and on one level or another both masters and slaves understood this. Whites who considered their black servants to be little more than barbarians, bereft of any culture worth the name, paid a fascinated and flattering attention to their song, their dance, their tales, and their forms of religious exercise. The life of every slave could be altered by the most arbitrary and amoral acts. They could be whipped, sexually assaulted, ripped out of societies in which they had deep roots, and bartered away for pecuniary profit by men and women who were also capable of treating them with kindness and consideration and who professed belief in a moral code which they held up for emulation not only by their children but often by their slaves as well.

It would be surprising if these dualities which marked the slaves' world were not reflected in both the forms and the content of their folk culture. In their religious songs and sermons slaves sought certainty in a world filled with confusion and anarchy; in their supernatural folk beliefs they sought power and control in a world filled with arbitrary forces greater than themselves; and in their tales they sought understanding of a world in which, for better or worse, they were forced to live. All the forms of slave folk culture afforded their creators psychic relief and a sense of mastery. Tales differed from the other forms in that they were more directly didactic in intent and therefore more compellingly and realistically reflective of the irrational and amoral side of the slaves' universe. It is precisely this aspect of the animal trickster tales that has been most grossly neglected.

Although the vicarious nature of slave tales was undeniably one of their salient features, too much stress has been laid on it. These were not merely clever tales of wish-fulfillment through which slaves could escape from the imperatives of their world. They could also be painfully realistic stories which taught the art of surviving and even triumphing in the face of a hostile environment. They underlined the dangers of acting rashly and striking out blindly, as Brer Rabbit did when he assaulted the tar-baby. They pointed out the futility of believing in the sincerity of the strong, as Brer Pig did when he allowed Fox to enter his house. They emphasized the necessity of comprehending the ways of the powerful, for only through such understanding could the weak endure. This lesson especially was repeated endlessly. In the popular tales featuring a race between a slow animal and a swifter opponent, the former triumphs not through persistence, as does his counterpart in the Aesopian fable of the Tortoise and the Hare, but by outwitting his opponent and capitalizing on his weaknesses and short-sightedness. Terrapin defeats Deer by placing relatives along the route with Terrapin himself stationed by the finish line. The deception is never discovered, since to the arrogant Deer all terrapins "am so much like anurrer you cant tell one from turrer." "I still t'ink Ise de fas'est runner in de worl'," the bewildered Deer complains after the race. "Maybe you air," Terrapin responds, "but I kin head you off wid sense."[34] Rabbit too understands the myopia of the powerful and benefits from Mr. Man's inability to distinguish between the animals by manipulating Fox into taking the punishment for a crime that Rabbit himself commits. "De Ole Man yent bin know de diffunce tween Buh Rabbit an Buh Fox," the storyteller pointed out. "Eh tink all two bin de same animal."[35] For black slaves, whose individuality was so frequently denied by the whites above them, this was a particularly appropriate and valuable message.

In many respects the lessons embodied in the animal trickster tales ran directly counter to those of the moralistic tales considered earlier. Friendship, held up as a positive model in the moralistic tales, was pictured as a fragile reed in the trickster tales. In the ubiquitous stories in which a trapped Rabbit tricks another animal into taking his place, it never occurs to him simply to ask for help. Nor when he is being pursued by Wolf does Hog even dream of asking Lion for aid. Rather he tricks Lion into killing Wolf by convincing him that the only way to cure his ailing son is to feed him a piece of half-roasted wolf liver.[36] The animals in these stories seldom ask each other for disinterested help. Even more rarely are they caught performing acts of altriusm—and with good reason. Carrying a string of fish he has just caught, Fox comes upon the prostrate form of Rabbit lying in the middle of the road moaning and asking for a doctor. Fox lays down his fish and hurries off to get help—with predictable results: "Ber Fox los' de fish. An' Ber Rabbit got de fish an' got better. Dat's da las' of it."[37] Brer Rooster learns the same lesson when he unselfishly tries to help a starving Hawk and is rewarded by having Hawk devour all of his children.[38]

Throughout these tales the emphasis on the state of perpetual war between the world's creatures revealed the hypocrisy and meaninglessness of their manners and rules. Animals who called each other brother and sister one moment were at each other's throats the next. On his way to church one Sunday morning, Rabbit meets Fox and the usual unctuous dialogue begins. "Good-mornin', Ber Rabbit!" Fox sings out. "Good-mornin', Ber Fox!" Rabbit sings back. After a few more pleasantries, the brotherliness ends as quickly as it had begun and Fox threatens: "Dis is my time, I'm hungry dis mornin'. I'm goin' to ketch you." Assuming the tone of the weak supplicant, Rabbit pleads: "O Ber Fox! leave me off dis mornin'. I will sen' you to a man house where he got a penful of pretty little pig, an' you will get yer brakefus' fill." Fox agrees and is sent to a pen filled not with pigs but hound dogs who pursue and kill him. Reverting to his former Sabbath piety, Rabbit calls after the dogs: "Gawd bless yer soul! dat what enemy get for meddlin' Gawd's people when dey goin' to church." "I was goin' to school all my life," Rabbit mutters to himself as he walks away from the carnage, "an learn every letter in de book but *d*, an' D was death an' death was de en' of Ber Fox."[39]

Such stories leave no doubt that slaves were aware of the need for role playing. But animal tales reveal more than this; they emphasize in brutal detail the irrationality and anarchy that rules Man's universe. In tale after tale violence and duplicity are pictured as existing for their own sake. Rabbit is capable of acts of senseless cruelty performed for no discernible motive. Whenever he comes across an alligator's nest "didn' he jes scratch the aigs out fur pure meaness, an' leave 'em layin' around to spile."[40] In an extremely popular tale Alligator confesses to Rabbit that he doesn't know what trouble is. Rabbit offers to teach him and instructs him to lie down in the broom grass. While Alligator is sleeping in the dry grass, Rabbit sets it on fire all around him and calls out: "Dat's trouble, Brer 'Gator, dat's trouble youse in."[41] Acts like this are an everyday occurrence for Rabbit. He sets Tiger, Elephant, and Panther on fire, provokes Man into burning Wolf to death, participates in the decapitation of Raccoon, causes Fox to chop off his own finger, drowns Wolf and leaves his body for Shark and Alligator to eat, boils Wolf's grandmother to death and tricks Wolf into eating her.[42] These actions often occur for no apparent reason. When a motive is present there is no limit to Rabbit's malice. Nagged by his wife to build a spring house, Rabbit tricks the other animals into digging it by telling them that if they make a dam to hold the water back they will surely find buried gold under the spring bed. They dig eagerly and to Rabbit's surprise actually do find gold. "But Ole Brer Rabbit never lose he head, that he don't, and he just push the rocks out the dam, and let the water on and drown the lastest one of them critters, and then he picks up the gold, and of course Ole Miss Rabbit done get her spring house."[43] It is doubtful, though, that she was able to enjoy it for very long, since in another tale Rabbit coolly sacrifices his wife and little children in order to save himself from Wolf's vengeance.[44]

Other trickster figures manifest the identical amorality. Rabbit himself is taken in by one of them in the popular tale of the Rooster who tucked his head under his wing and explained that he had his wife cut his head off so he could sun it. "An' de rabbit he thought he could play de same trick, so he went home an' tol' his ol' lady to chop his head off. So dat was de las' of his head."[45] All tricksters share an incapacity for forgetting or forgiving. In a North Carolina spider tale, Ann Nancy is caught stealing Buzzard's food and saves herself only by obsequiously comparing her humble lot to Buzzard's magnificence, stressing "how he sail in the clouds while she 'bliged to crawl in the dirt," until he takes pity and sets her free. "But Ann Nancy ain't got no gratitude in her mind; she feel she looked down on by all the creeters, and it sour her mind and temper. She ain't gwine forget anybody what cross her path, no, that she don't, and while she spin her house she just study constant how she gwine get the best of every creeter." In the end she invites Buzzard to dinner and pours a pot of boiling water over his head, "and the poor old man go baldheaded from that day."[46] At that he was lucky. When Rabbit's friend Elephant accidentally steps on Rabbit's nest, killing his children, Rabbit bides his time until he catches Elephant sleeping, stuffs leaves and grass in his eyes, and sets them on fire.[47] Hare, unable to forgive Miss Fox for marrying Terrapin instead of himself, sneaks into her house, kills her, skins her, hangs her body to the ceiling, and smokes her over hickory chips.[48]

The unrelieved violence and brutality of these tales can be accounted for easily enough within the slave-as-trickster, trickster-as-slave thesis. D. H. Lawrence's insight that "one sheds one's sicknesses in books" is particularly applicable here. Slave tales which functioned as the bondsmen's books were a perfect vehicle for the channelization of the slaves' "sicknesses": their otherwise inexpressible angers, their gnawing hatreds, their pent-up frustrations. On one level, then, the animal trickster tales were expressions of the slaves' unrestrained fantasies: the impotent become potent, the brutalized are transformed into brutalizers, the undermen inherit the earth. But so many of these tales picture the trickster in such profoundly ambivalent or negative terms, so many of them are cast in the African mold of not depicting phenomena in hard-and-fast, either-or, good-evil categories, that it is difficult to fully accept Bernard Wolfe's argument that it is invariably "the venomous American slave crouching behind the Rabbit."[49] Once we relax the orthodoxy that the trickster and the slave are necessarily one, other crucial levels of meaning and understanding are revealed.

"You nebber kin trus Buh Rabbit," a black storyteller concluded after explaining how Rabbit cheated Partridge. "Eh all fuh ehself; an ef you listne ter him tale, eh gwine cheat you ebry time, an tell de bigges lie dout wink eh yeye."[50] Precisely what many slaves might have said of their white masters. Viewed in this light, trickster tales were a prolonged and telling parody of white society. The animals were frequently almost perfect replicas of whites as slaves saw them. They occasionally worked but more often lived a life filled with leisure-time activities: they fished, hunted, had numerous parties and balls, courted demure women who sat on verandas dressed in white. They mouthed lofty platitudes and professed belief in noble ideals but spent much of their time manipulating, oppressing, enslaving one another. They surrounded themselves with meaningless etiquette, encased themselves in rigid hierarchies, dispensed rewards not to the most deserving but to the most crafty and least scrupulous. Their world was filled with violence, injustice, cruelty. Though they might possess great power, they did not always wield it openly and directly but often with guile and indirection. This last point especially has been neglected; the strong and not merely the weak could function as trickster. Jenny Proctor remembered her Alabama master who was exceedingly stingy and fed his slaves badly: "When he go to sell a slave, he feed that one good for a few days, then when he goes to put 'em up on the auction block he takes a meat skin and greases all around that nigger's mouth and makes 'em look like they been eating plenty meat and such like and was good and strong and able to work."[51] Former slaves recalled numerous examples of the master as trickster:

> There was one old man on the plantation that everybody feared. He was a good worker but he didn't allow anybody to whip him. Once he was up for a whipping and this is the way he got it. Our young master got a whole gang of paddy-rollers and hid them in a thicket. Then he told old man Jack that he had to be whipped. "I won't hit you but a few licks," he told him, "Papa is going away and he sent me to give you that whipping he told you about." Old man Jack said, "Now, I won't take nairy a lick." Young master took out a bottle of whiskey, took a drink and gave the bottle to old man Jack and told him to drink as much as he wanted. Old man Jack loved whiskey and he drank it all. Soon he was so drunk he couldn't hardly stand up. Young Mars called to the men in hiding, "Come on down, I got the wild boar." They whipped the old man almost to death. This was the first and last time he ever got whipped.[52]

Slave tales are filled with instances of the strong acting as tricksters: Fox asks Jaybird to pick a bone out of his teeth, and once he is in his mouth, Fox devours him; Buzzard invites eager animals to go for a ride on his back, then drops them to their deaths and eats them; Wolf constructs a tar-baby in which Rabbit almost comes to his end; Elephant, Fox, and Wolf all pretend to be dead in order to throw Rabbit off guard and catch him at their "funerals"; Fox tells Squirrel that he had a brother who could jump from the top of a tall tree right into his arms, and when Squirrel proves he can do the same, Fox eats him.[53] Tales like these, which formed an important part of the slaves' repertory, indicate that the slave could empathize with the tricked as well as the trickster. Again the didactic function of these stories becomes apparent. The slaves' interest was not always in being like the trickster but often in avoiding being like his victims from whose fate they could learn valuable lessons. Although the trickster tales could make a mockery of the values preached by the moralistic tales—friendship, hard work, sincerity—there were also important lines of continuity between the moralistic tales and the trickster stories. Animals were taken in by the trickster most easily when they violated many of the lessons of the moralistic tales: when they were too curious, as Alligator was concerning trouble; too malicious, as Wolf was when he tried to kill Rabbit by the most horrible means possible; too greedy, as Fox and Buzzard were when their hunger for honey led to their deaths; overly proud and arrogant, as Deer was in his race with Terrapin; unable to keep their own counsel, as Fox was when he prematurely blurted out his plans to catch Rabbit; obsessed with a desire to be something other than what they are, as the Buzzard's victims were when they allowed their desire to soar in the air to overcome their caution.

The didacticism of the trickster tales was not confined to tactics and personal attributes. They also had important lessons to teach concerning the nature of the world and of the beings who inhabited it. For Afro-American slaves, as for their African ancestors, the world and those who lived in it were pictured in naturalistic and unsentimental terms. The vanity of human beings, their selfishness, their propensity to do anything and betray anyone for self-preservation, their drive for status and power, their basic insecurity, were all pictured in grim detail. The world was not a rational place in which order and justice prevailed and good was dispensed. The trickster, as Louise Dauner has perceived, often functioned as the eternal "thwarter," the symbol of "the irrational twists of circumstance." His remarkably gullible dupes seldom learned from their experience at his hands any more than human beings learn from experience. There was no more escape from him than there is escape from the irrational in human life.[54] The trickster served as agent of the world's irrationality and as reminder of man's fundamental helplessness. Whenever animals became too bloated with their power or importance or sense of control, the trickster was on hand to remind them of how things really were. No animal escaped these lessons; not Wolf, not Lion, not Elephant, indeed, not the trickster himself. Throughout there is a latent yearning for structure, for justice, for reason, but they are not to be had, in this world at least. If the strong are not to prevail over the weak, neither shall the weak dominate the strong. Their eternal and inconclusive battle served as proof that man is part of a larger order which he scarcely understands and certainly does not control.

If the animal trickster functioned on several different symbolic levels—

as black slave, as white master, as irrational force—his adventures were given coherence and continuity by the crucial release they provided and the indispensable lessons they taught. In the exploits of the animal trickster, slaves mirrored in exaggerated terms the experiences of their own lives.

THE SLAVE AS TRICKSTER

"Slaves have their *code of honor*, and their *tricks of trade*," the Reverend John Dixon Long wrote in 1857. "The colored people reason as rationally on some questions as we do. Their conceptions of justice and right are not very different from those of white men. They say: 'We do the work; we raise the corn and wheat; and part of it is justly ours.' "[1] To improve their lot, to effect a rough sort of justice, and to protect themselves from some of the worst features of the slave system, slaves translated many of the tactics of their animal trickster tales into their own lives. Like Brer Rabbit, slaves learned to maneuver as well as they could from their position of weakness. The practicality and realism at the core of the slave aphorism, "White folks do as they pleases, and the darkies do as they can," was repeated in proverb after proverb: "A smart man ain't gwine to buck 'gin a mud-hole; he walks 'round it eb'ry time." "It don't make much diffunce whar de rain comes fum, jes' so it hits de groun' in de right place." " 'E yent matter 'bout de road so long as 'e kah you to de right place." "All de jestice in de wul' ain't fastened up in de cote-'ouse." "Yuh mought as well die wid de chills ez wid de fever." "Better not laugh too quick at de runt pig." "Little axe cut down big tree."[2]

The meaning of these teachings was made painfully apparent to Laura Towne almost as soon as she arrived in the Sea Islands to work with the freedmen during the Civil War. "We need patience," she complained on April 28, 1862:

One day I came downstairs to make a cup of tea for an unexpected guest. No fire and no wood. No possibility of getting wood, as it was raining hard. No butter. Old Robert was sick and had the key to the dairy, and was away off somewhere; just as it was at breakfast, when we had no milk, and Robert was away at "the pen," . . . Hominy gone. Sent Lucy to ask Susannah why and where she had taken it. It came. . . .

I told Rina to come up and do our room and have not seen her since. Just now Aleck was idle and I sent him for wood to the pines with a little mule. I told him not to whip it. He yelled and doubled himself up with laughter, and lashed it before my eyes until quite out of sight, shrieking with laughter and paying no heed to my calls.[3]

The work habits that drove Miss Towne to distraction were not new to the freedmen among whom she lived but had been endemic in slavery. "So deceitful is the Negro," a Georgia planter complained, "that as far as my own experience extends I could never in a single instance decipher his character. . . . We planters could never get at the truth." Slaves were, a North Carolina planter agreed, "a troublesome property," as James Hammond discovered graphically when his bondsmen stole and killed one hundred of his hogs in a single year alone, and as Charles C. Pinckney acknowledged when he estimated that 25 per cent of his rice crop was pilfered annually. The tactics slaves resorted to in order to resist the compulsions of their situation would have been familiar enough to the creatures of their animal tales. The records left by nineteenth-century observers of slavery and by the masters themselves indicate that a significant number of slaves lied, cheated, stole, feigned illness, loafed, pretended to misunderstand the orders they were given, put rocks in the bottom of their cotton baskets in order to meet their quota, broke their tools, burned their masters' property, mutilated themselves in order to escape work, took indifferent care of the crops they were cultivating, and mistreated the livestock placed in their care to the extent that masters often felt it necessary to use the less efficient mules rather than horses since the former could better withstand the brutal treatment of the slaves.[4]

Many former slaves were completely candid about these behavior patterns and almost unanimous in defending them. "They didn't half feed us either," Robert Falls of North Carolina remembered. "They fed the animals better. They gives the mules the roughage and such, to chaw on all night. But they didn't give us nothing to chaw on. Learned us to steal, that's what they done. Why, we would take anything we could lay our hands on, when we was hungry. Then they'd whip us for lying when we say we don't know nothing about it. But it was easier to stand when the stomach was full."[5] Referring to the slaves on his plantation, one former slave asserted: "These darkies didn't get no fresh meat unless they stole it."[6] Jake Green, a slave in Alabama, told the folk story of a master who boasted to a traveler that his slave John "ain't never told me a lie in his life." The traveler bet one hundred dollars to fifty cents that he could catch John in a lie. The next morning after breakfast, he put a live mouse in a covered dish and instructed the master to inform John that he could eat whatever food was left over but that he must not open the covered dish. The white men left and when they returned the master asked John if he had obeyed his orders. John swore he had, but when the traveler lifted the cover off the forbidden dish the mouse was gone. "See dere," he said triumphantly, "John been lyin' to you all de time, you jes' ain't knowed it." "An," Green quickly added, "I reckon he right, 'caze us had to lie."[7] These attitudes were repeated again and again: "Of course they'd [the slaves] steal. Had to steal. That the best way to git what they wanted." "Those white folks made us lie. We had to lie to live."[8] The same message was reiterated long after slavery in the postbellum anecdote about the old black preacher who discovered that some members of his congregation were claiming to have donated more to the church than they actually had. "De trouble wid you," he admonished them, "is dat de white man done been dealin' wid you so long, some uv you gittin' real tricky."[9]

In these attitudes we can begin to perceive the mechanism that slaves erected to help reduce the tensions between their universal ideals and their worldly needs. Although slaves were forced by their situation to create their own practical set of values and norms of behavior, these did not necessarily replace those of their heritage, their religion, and of the outside society but rather were used to "neutralize" them. In their work on the "techniques of neutralization," Gresham Sykes and David Matza have demonstrated that deviation from certain norms may occur not because they are rejected but because a given situation may accord precedence to other norms. "Norms may be violated without surrendering allegiance to them," Matza has written. "The directives to action implicit in norms may be avoided intermittently rather than frontally assaulted. They may be evaded rather than radically rejected. Norms, especially legal norms, may be neutralized. . . . Most if not all norms in society are conditional. Rarely, if ever, are they categorically imperative."[10]

Thus it was possible for slaves to rationalize their need to lie, cheat, and steal without holding these actions up as models to be followed in all instances, without creating, that is, a counter-morality. In their dealings with whites the conditions permitting the application of their moral values were frequently absent. Not only did their masters deny them the fruits of their labor but the whites themselves practiced theft far more serious than that of the blacks. "Dey talks a heap 'bout de niggers stealin'," Shang Harris told an interviewer. "Well, you know what was de fust stealin' done? Hit was in Afriky, when de white folks stole de niggers jes' like you'd go get a drove o' horses and sell 'em."[11] The Gullah preacher Brother Coteny articulated a common feeling when he asked in one of his sermons: "Ef buckra neber tief, how cum nigger yer [here]?"[12] Black children imbibed these attitudes at a tender age. An officer of one of the Aid Societies led the following discussion in a Louisville school in 1866:

> Now children, you don't think white people are any better than you because they have straight hair and white faces?
> No, sir.
> No, they are no better, but they are different, they possess great power, they formed this great government, they control this vast country. . . . Now what makes them different from you?
> MONEY. (Unanimous shout)
> Yes, but what enabled them to obtain it?
> Got it off us, stole it off we all![13]

The masters were guilty of more "devilment" than stealing: "Look at old N. that lived on the other side of us. He forced nearly every decent looking slave woman he had. Williamson County is full of half white children he got by his slaves."[14]

It is unlikely that these attitudes completely relieved slaves of all feelings of guilt. In this respect their animal trickster tales may have served as a convenient channel for whatever guilt slaves felt about having to adopt modes of behavior which were proscribed both by their African heritage and their new religion. Rabbit's frequent transgressions of the moral frontiers, his egregious acts of violence and pure malice, can be seen not only as an expression of the slaves' fantasies or an object lesson concerning the irrationality of life, but also as a projection of the slaves' inner anxieties. But on the whole the evidence indicates that the slaves' strong convictions regarding the injustice they suffered at the hands of whites, who themselves were guilty of hypocrisy and gross immorality, were sufficient to allow them to relax or neutralize their normal standards and mores in certain situations. Touring antebellum Virginia, Frederick Olmsted noted: "everywhere on the plantations, the agrarian notion has become a fixed point of the negro system of ethics: that the result of labor belongs of right to the laborer, and on this ground, even the religious feel justified in using 'Massa's' property for their own temporal benefit. This they term 'taking,' and it is never admitted to be a reproach to a man among them that he is charged with it, though 'stealing,' or taking from another than their master, and particularly from one another, is so."[15] "They think it wrong to take from a neighbor, but not from their master," Lewis Clarke wrote of his fellow slaves. "The only question with them is, 'Can we keep it from master?' If they can keep their backs safe, conscience is quiet enough on this point. But a slave that will steal from a slave, is called *mean as master*. This is the lowest comparison slaves know how to use: 'just as mean as white folks.' 'No right for to complain of white folks, who steal us all de days of our life; nigger dat what steal from nigger, he meaner nor all.' "[16]

Slaves recounted their tactics in a number of the songs they sang:

> O some tell me that a nigger won't steal,
> But I've seen a nigger in my corn-field;
> O run, nigger, run, for the patrol will catch you,
> O run, nigger, run, for 'tis almost day.

> I fooled Old Master seven years,
>   Fooled the overseer three.
> Hand me down my banjo,
>   And I'll tickle your bel-lee.[17]

But for the most part tales were the vehicle through which slaves rehearsed their tactics, laughed at the foibles of their masters (and themselves), and taught their young the means they would have to adopt in order to survive. To this day much less is known about the slaves' human trickster cycle than about their animal trickster stories. Precisely because these tales dealt with slaves and masters instead of rabbits and wolves and were in many respects more open and direct, slaves and freedmen guarded them more closely. A number of these tales were collected in the years following emancipation, but it has not been until the twentieth century that more and more of them have come to light. It would be a mistake, however, to conclude that the continued and perhaps enhanced popularity of human trickster stories after slavery is proof that they were primarily a postbellum product. These tales mirrored the behavior patterns of large numbers of slaves so closely and were so important a part of the repertory of ex-slaves that they clearly had their origins in the years before freedom.

Frequently tales of this type were based upon actual occurrences which through constant retelling were in the process of becoming part of black folklore. Lizzie Williams told of her father's adventures when he was away from his Alabama plantation one night without a pass and saw a patrol coming his way:

He know if dey finds him what dey do. So Pappy he gets down in de ditch and throw sand and grunts like a hog. Sure 'nough, dey thinks he a hog and dey pass on, 'cept one who was behind de others. He say, "Dat am de gruntin'est old hog I ever hear. I think I go see him." But de others dey say: "Just let dat old hog alone and mind you own business." So dey pass on. Pappy he laugh about dat for long time.[18]

Many years after emancipation, Henry Johnson still remembered his craving for one of his master's turkeys which the slaves were forbidden to eat. Succumbing to temptation, he lured a turkey to his cabin, twisted its neck until it was dead and then ran to inform his mistress that one of the birds had died: "She said, 'Stop crying, Henry, and throw him under de hill.' I was satisfied. I run back, picked dat old bird, taken all his feathers to de river and throwed dem in. Dat night we cooked him. And didn't we eat somethin' good! I had to tell her about dat missin' bird cause when dey check up it all had to tally, so dat fixed dat."[19] A fellow ex-slave remembered an old slave on his plantation who became so angry at one of the steers he was plowing with that he took a rock and knocked it on the head. "He dragged him a little way off and told me to run to the house and tell the boss that one of his steers was awful sick. They never did know why that steer died. My mistress tried in every way to make me tell her what happened to cause the steer to die but the old man had warned me not to tell."[20] Another former slave recounted the way she acted when asked to brush the flies away from her elderly, sick mistress: "I would hit her all in the face; sometimes I would make out I was sleep and beat her in the face. She was so sick she couldn't sleep much, and couldn't talk, and when old master come in the house she would try to tell him on me, but he thought she meant I would just go to sleep. Then he would tell me to go out in the yard and wake up. She couldn't tell him that I had been hitting her all in the face. I done that woman bad. She was so mean to me."[21] West Turner spoke of Gabe, a fellow slave whose job it was to mete out punishment on the plantation: "Ole Gabe didn't like dat whippin' bus'ness, but he couldn't he'p hisself. When Marsa was dere, he would lay it on 'cause he had to. But when ole Marsa warn't lookin', he never would beat dem slaves. Would tie de slave up to one post an' lash another one. 'Cose de slave would scream an' yell to satisfy Marsa, but he wasn't gettin' no lashin'."[22]

It did not take much for such relatively common events to become embroidered into more elaborate and fanciful tales. Josie Jordan, born a slave in Tennessee, recalled a story her mother told her about a stingy master who fed his slaves so poorly that "they ribs would kinda rustle against each other like corn stalks a-drying in the hot winds. But they gets even one hog-killing time, and it was funny, too, Mammy said." The day before seven fat hogs were to be killed, one of the field hands ran to the master and told him, "The hogs is all died, now they won't be any meats for the winter." When the master arrived on the scene he found a group of sorrowful-looking slaves who informed him that the hogs had died of "malitis" and acted as if they were afraid to touch the dead animals. The master ordered them to dress the meat anyway and to keep it for the slave families. "Don't you all know what is malitis?" Mrs. Jordan's mother would ask while she rocked with laughter. "One of the strongest Negroes got up early in the morning, long 'fore the rising horn called the slaves from their cabins. He skitted to the hog pen with a heavy mallet in his hand. When he tapped Mister Hog 'tween the eyes with that mallet, 'malitis' set in mighty quick. . . ."[23]

The cycle of stories featuring the relations of a slave trickster, often named John, and his master were based upon the kinds of incidents related in these factual and pseudo-factual tales, but by removing them from the realm of the immediately personal it allowed storytellers even more scope for their imaginations and their psychic needs.[24] The most widely diffused tale of this type, found in a variety of cultures, captured the essence of the entire slave trickster cycle. By eavesdropping outside his master's window, learning his plans for the next day and then anticipating them, and by hiding things and then "discovering" them when his master was looking for them, John convinced his master that he was omniscient and won a privileged position on the plantation. One day the master boasted to a group of his fellow slaveowners of John's powers. The other whites were dubious and wagered a large sum that they could prove John's fallibility. On the day of the contest they hid something in a barrel and called upon John to reveal the barrel's contents. The reluctant slave, fearing that at last his careful deceptions were to be discovered, desperately walked around and around the barrel, tapped it, put his ear to it, and then in despair confessed, "Marstah, you got dis here coon at las'!" His choice of language saved him for when the barrel was removed to reveal a raccoon inside, John's master won the bet, and John was amply rewarded, sometimes by freedom itself.[25] In John, slaves created a figure who epitomized the rewards, the limits, and the hazards of the trickster. He could improve his situation through careful deception, but at no time was he really in complete control; the rewards he could win were limited by the realities of the system within which he existed, and the dangers he faced were great. Time and again the more elaborate schemes of the slave trickster failed, and he saved himself only by last minute verbal facility and role playing—two qualities which these stories emphasized were crucial for all slaves to cultivate.

As in the animal stories, the acquisition of food was a primary goal for the slave trickster. In a popular tale, a slave steals some chickens and is cooking them when his master enters his cabin, is informed that the slave is cooking a possum, and decides to wait and share some of it. After an hour of clever delays on the slave's part, the master loses patience, uncovers the pot and discovers the chicken. "Wal," the slave says quickly, "dey wuz 'possums when Ah put 'em in dar. Ef dey's chickens now, Ah's gwine th'ow 'em away."[26] In another version, related at the turn of the century by a black woman whose father heard it from his grandfather, a slave on the Hammond plantation in Georgia, the slave, hard-pressed by the master to carve the non-existent possum up, announces in desperation: "Dis possum am done to a tu'n. Mus' be all dat good spittin' we done." When the master expresses surprise, the slave explains: "Spittin'. Us nigguhs allus spits in possum gravy. Makes de meat mo' tenduh. Aunt Janie done spit in it; Uncle Amos done spit in it; de chilluns done spit in it; an' I spit in it myse'f fo' er five times. You wants nice big piece, Massa?" The latter, rushing from the cabin, cries out, "That's the most disgusting habit I ever heard of. You're a pack of damned savages."[27]

In a South Carolina story, a slave named Jack eats the leg of a baked chicken he is to serve to his master and a guest and turns the chicken on its side to hide the missing limb. When the white men finish the top side and turn the chicken over, they discover the loss and are told by the slave, "Must be one-legged chicken, suh. I has seen plenty of one-legged chickens." The next day, riding through the plantation the master and the slave come across some chickens on the road standing on one leg and huddled up to keep warm. "See, Doctor, dat been what I was talking 'bout," Jack tells his master. "All dem chicken one-legged." His master looks carefully at the chickens and says, "Sish!" whereupon they all put down their other leg. "Well, Doctor," Jack quickly counters, "if you had say 'Sish' to de chicken on de dish, he would hab stick out 'e odder leg, too."[28] In a Virginia tale a young slave is instructed to cook a duck for Sunday dinner. While preparing it he tastes first one wing, then the other, and by the time the master and the preacher return to eat, the duck is entirely consumed. Watching his master sharpening his knife for the coming feast, the desperate slave turns to the preacher and whispers, "He is sharpening his knife to kill you." The preacher begins to run and the slave shouts to the master, "There he goes with the duck!"[29]

In other tales the slave trickster had less luck. In a story which long remained popular, John was in the practice of giving big parties for all the slaves whenever his master took his annual trip North. One year the master came back early to check on his slaves, disguised himself as a slave by rubbing soot on his face, and observed the festivities. While the slaves happily consume his food and liquor and smoke his cigars, John shouts:

> Joy yourself, joy yourself,
> Master's gone to Philly-Me-York.

During the course of the evening the master's sweat gradually dissolves his disguise until John at last recognizes him and cries out in despair, "Oh marster, is dat you. Oh marster, is dat you! Aint dat you, oh marster? Um gone!"[30] An old slave named Dinna has been stealing her master's chickens for years until he discovers her one day cooking them and singing:

> Massa, ain't you glad your old game-hen
> Been on the roos' so long?
> But Ah got 'em in the pot at las'.

When she is finished, the master sings his own song:

> Aunt Dinna, ain't you glad my old game-hen
> Been on the roos' so long?
> You got 'em in the pot at las'.
> But Aunt Dinna, ain't you sorry
> You got my old game-hen in the pot,
> For Massa gwine to cut your back at last.[31]

These tales, too, paralleled real life situations. In 1899 R. R. Moton related a story told to him by an old, toothless man who as a slave used to get out of work periodically by claiming he had a toothache. One day the master appeared with a pair of pincers and pulled out twenty of the slave's teeth and a piece of his jawbone as well. "I ain't nuver had no mo' teefache from dat day to dis, dat I ain't," the old man told Moton.[32]

For all the limitations imposed upon slave tricksters and all the hazards they faced, it is not difficult to understand the pleasures slaves derived from their exploits. In spite of the role playing and subservience forced upon them and the defeats they often suffered, slave tricksters continually made the whites look foolish and always seemed one step ahead of them. In a widely told tale a master boasts of a deer he shot through the foot and eye with only a single bullet. When his friends prove to be incredulous, he turns to his slave and commands him to tell how he did it. Thinking fast, the slave explains that the deer was brushing a fly out of his eye with his hind foot when the white man fired his shot. After the others have departed, the slave tells his master: "Mossa, me willin fuh back anyting you say bout hunt an kill deer, but lemme bague you nex time you tell bout how you shoot um, you pit de hole closer. Dis time you mek um so fur apart, me hab big trouble fur git um togerruh." "Tell yo' lies a li'l' closer togedder f'om now on," the slave instructs his master in another version.[33] In a Georgia tale a newly purchased slave asks his master why he spends so much time sitting and doing nothing while the slaves have to work. The master assures him that he is not loafing but working with his head making plans and studying about things. One day the master comes upon his slave in the field sitting in the cotton and resting. When he inquires why the slave is not working, the latter informs him that he too is working with his head. Pointing to three pigeons on a tree limb, he asks the white man how many would be left if he shot and killed one. Any fool can answer that, the master replies indignantly, "two." "No mossa, you miss," the slave tells him. "Ef you shoot an kill one er dem pigeon, de odder two boun fuh fly way, an none gwine leff." "De buckra man bleege fuh laugh," the storyteller concluded, "an eh yent do nuttne ter de New Nigger case en glec eh wuk."[34]

In many of these tales the slaves prove to be superb thieves and frequently win their freedom by betting their masters they can steal the very clothes off their backs and then through elaborate maneuvers accomplish the task.[35] Slaves received not only vicarious triumph from their human trickster stories but also quite frequently explicit instruction, as in the tale of the slave who asked his master: "How much Christmas kin I have?" and was informed that he could celebrate until the back log in the fireplace burned out. Cutting a black gum log, the slave rolled it in the ditch and let it remain for several days until it was well soaked. Then he rolled it out so that it would dry on the outside. Christmas morning he put the log in the fire, where it burned for seven days, giving the slave an entire week of leisure.[36]

In some stories slave tricksters would occasionally try out their wiles on their fellow slaves. One would boast to another that he had put his hand under his mistress' dress or cursed his master with impunity. The other would try the same thing and be beaten severely, only to be told by the trickster that he had not said anything about the mistress being in the dress when he put his hand under it or the master being present when he cursed him.[37] Only rarely do these stories picture slaves stealing from one another. In a story sharing many elements with the animal tales, a slave puts a possum on to cook and goes to sleep. Just when the possum is done, a friend visits the cabin, eats the possum, scatters its bones around the hearth, and greases the sleeping slave's mouth and hands. When the latter arises, he finds his possum gone and concludes it was stolen until he notices the bones on the floor and the grease on his hands and mouth. "I mus' 'a' done it! I mus' 'a' done it!" he exclaims. "Well, all I got to say is dis: ef I did git up an' eat dat 'possum while I was 'sleep, he sets lighter on my stomach an' he gibs me less consolation dan any 'possum I ebber eat sence I was born!"[38]

For the most part, however, the trickster's art as depicted in these tales was saved for the benefit of the whites and was seldom practiced upon members of his own group. Slave tales document the distinction many slaves made between "stealing" which meant appropriating something that belonged to another slave and was not condoned, and "taking" which meant appropriating part of the master's property for the benefit of another part. In a commonly told story, an old slave, Uncle Abraham, invites his black preacher, Brother Gabriel, to eat with him on Christmas Eve. The preacher is uneasy about the roast pig and potatoes on the table since he knows they must have been stolen and refuses to eat until his host says grace and makes a confession before him. With little hesitation, Abraham prays: "A Lord, dou . . . taught dy sarvents dat it want no harm fur ter take de corn out er de barril and put it into de kag. De barril 'longs to de marster and de kag 'longs ter de marster, dar-forth it aint no diffunce when de darkie take de marster's pig out er de pen an put it into de darkie, case de darkie 'longs ter de marster, an de pig pen 'longs ter de marster." "All right, Brer Abe, dat all right," Brother Gabriel announces. "Less be gwine ter dese yere good nugs."[39]

The slaves' animal and human trickster tales shared a number of common elements: They placed the same emphasis upon the tactics of trickery and indirection, took the same delight in seeing the weak outwit and humiliate the strong, manifested the same lack of idealization, and served the same dual function which included the expression of repressed feelings and the inculcation of the tactics of survival. Their greatest point of departure was that human trickster stories were more restricted by the realities of the slaves' situation. It was in their animal trickster tales that slaves expressed their wildest hopes and fears. The human trickster might win his victories, but they were always less spectacular than those of his animal counterpart—triumphs of the spirit more than of the flesh. He could outwit his master again and again, but his primary satisfaction would be in making his master look foolish and thus exposing the myth of white omniscience and omnipotence. True, he could and did attain some material prizes: rare foods, extra leisure, fine clothing, trips to the city or town, occasionally even freedom. But these were insignificant compared to the material victories attained by the weak in the animal tales: the death of the oppressor, the love of the oppressor's woman, the inheritance of the oppressor's material empire. John could outsmart his master; Brer Rabbit could replace him and in this way give flesh and substance to the ethereal promises of slave religion. But if Rabbit won greater victories he was also forced to become more like his oppressor than the human trickster was ever allowed to. If there was any moral advantage accruing to him it was that he started from a much lower vantage point, but in the end he was as ruthless, as unmerciful, as corrupt as those who sought to control him. In the more conscious and more realistic world of the human trickster stories, slaves never enunciated either these heights or these depths. The exploits of the human trickster functioned as a carefully constructed rationale for the actions slaves found themselves resorting to. They described patterns of behavior which more often than not could with some modification be incorporated into the slaves' own life; they were largely free of ambiguity or tensions; and more than any other form of Afro-American expressive culture they clearly depicted the possibilities and the limits of slave .existence.

It can be argued that by channelizing the bondsmen's discontent, reducing their anxieties, and siphoning off their anger, slave tales served the master as well as the slave. In a sense of course they did, and the fact that tales and songs were often encouraged by the masters may indicate a gleaning of this fact on their part as well. But in terms of the values they inculcated, the models of action they held up for emulation, the disrespect and even contempt they taught concerning the strong, the psychic barriers they created against the inculcation of many of the white world's values, it would be difficult to maintain that they should be viewed primarily as a means of control. What the tales gave to the masters with one hand they more than took back with the other. They encouraged trickery and guile; they stimulated the search for ways out of the system; they inbred a contempt for the powerful and an admiration for the perseverance and even the wisdom of the undermen; they constituted an intra-group lore which must have intensified feelings of distance from the world of the slaveholder.

SLAVE TALES AND THE SACRED UNIVERSE

The practical, naturalistic universe of the slaves' trickster tales, pervaded by a dominant duplicity and ruled by bodily appetites and immediate needs, would seem to have had little in common with the sacred universe developed in the slaves' spirituals. Yet there are important points of continuity. The slaves' ready identification with animals in their tales revealed not merely a strategy for disguising their inner emotions from the whites but also a tendency to see themselves as part of a unified world in which Man, beasts, spirits, even inanimate objects, were a natural part of the order of things. Slave tales no less than slave songs or folk beliefs were fashioned within this world view and derived much of their substance and meaning from it. Equally revealing is the similar emphasis both spirituals and tales placed upon the need for the assertion of the weak against the strong and the belief that although the latter may control the earth their power is neither irrevocable nor permanent. This dynamic faith in the possibilities of transcendence and the certainties of change made the expression of a tragic sense as rare among Afro-American slaves as it was among their African ancestors.[1]

These fundamental similarities should make it clear that for all their differences in tone and spirit slave songs and slave tales were not separate expressions of diametrically opposite attitudes but parts of a continuum in which slaves gave conscious and unconscious voice to a relatively well-integrated and consistent world view. Lévi-Strauss, using the analogy of contrapuntal music, has maintained that, just as the various voices in a piece of music may go their own ways but still be held together by their relationship to each other, so the various levels and conceptual systems existing in a group's folklore may be seen as transformations "of an underlying logical structure common to all of them." The different levels of consciousness within a myth, he argues, "cannot be separated out by the native mind. It is rather that everything happens as if the levels were provided with different codes, each being used according to the needs of the moment, and according to its particular capacity, to transmit the same message."[2]

Similarly, the folk beliefs of slaves were expressed on different but complementary levels. The unremitting system of slavery made its subjects not merely idealists who created a sacred universe which promised change and triumph, allowed them to reach back to relive the victories of the past, and drew them into the rich future where the justice and goodness that had been experienced before would exist again; it also made them realists who understood the world as it operated in the present. To have acculturated their children exclusively to the world view proclaimed by their religion would have signified an impracticality that slaves rarely showed. The universe held promise and hope, but it was also dominated by malevolence, injustice, arbitrary judgment, and paradox which had to be dealt with here and now. Their tales prepared the slaves to do this by identifying the forces which shaped their lives and by giving prescriptions for overcoming or at least surviving them. At no point did slaves allow romanticism to dilute their vision of the world. The trickster was often celebrated, to be sure, since in his victories slaves could experience vicarious joy. But he was portrayed in hard and realistic terms. Slave tales anticipated Lord Acton's dictum about power corrupting but would have added to it the now familiar corollary that impotence too corrupts. Slave tales taught tactics for short-run survival and maintenance but held few illusions concerning the costs of survival or the ways in which the world as it was constituted distorted the victim as well as the oppressor. Ultimate hope and faith in miraculous and permanent transformation were compartmentalized in the slaves' sacred world view, which complemented rather than competed with their practical assessment of their temporal condition.

Aesthetically, slaves undoubtedly derived great pleasure from all forms of their folk culture. Functionally, however, these divergent levels of expression operated in very different ways and served distinct needs. Viewed in isolation they each reveal only one aspect of the slaves' consciousness. But slaves did not experience or create the various parts of their folk culture in isolation. On any given evening slaves might transcend their temporal situation by singing their sacred songs of hope, attempt to control it by putting into practice one or more of their varied store of folk beliefs, and understand it and its immediate imperatives by reciting some of their tales. All three were essential parts of the slaves' life. Their sum did not add up merely to an instrument which allowed slaves to survive their situation, but more importantly it added up to a cultural *style*. Perhaps at no other point in United States history is the term *Afro-American* a more accurate cultural designation than when it is applied to black Americans in the mid-nineteenth century. The essence of their thought, their world view, their culture, owed much to Africa, but it was not purely African; it was indelibly influenced by the more than two hundred years of contact with whites on American soil, but it was not the product of an abject surrender of all previous cultural standards in favor of embracing those of the white master. This syncretic blend of the old and the new, of the African and the Euro-American, resulted in a style which in its totality was uniquely the slaves' own and defined their expressive culture and their world view at the time of emancipation.

3

FREEDOM, CULTURE, AND RELIGION

O ne ever feels his two-ness,—an American, a Negro; two souls, two thoughts, two unreconciled strivings; two warring ideals in one dark body, whose dogged strength alone keeps it from being torn asunder.

The history of the American Negro is the history of this strife,—this longing to attain self-conscious manhood, to merge his double self into a better and truer self. In this merging he wishes neither of the older selves to be lost. He would not Africanize America, for America has too much to teach the world and Africa. He would not bleach his Negro soul in a flood of white Americanism, for he knows that Negro blood has a message for the world. He simply wishes to make it possible for a man to be both a Negro and an American, without being cursed and spit upon by his fellows, without having the doors of Opportunity closed roughly in his face.

W. E. B. Du Bois[1]

Shortly before Lee's surrender, slaves on an Alabama plantation gathered in their church to sing of "good old Daniel" who had been cast in the lion's den but was "Safe now in the promised land," and assured themselves that "By and by we'll go home to meet him. / Way over in the promised land." The passion and certainty of their refrain filled a white

auditor with a sense of foreboding: "I . . . seemed to see the mantle of
our lost cause descending."[1] The South's lost cause was the fulfillment of
a prophecy the slaves had been singing of for more than half a century.
After the northern conquest of Richmond, Virginia, slaves crowded the
streets running, leaping, singing: "Slavery chain done broke at last; slavery
chain done broke at last—I's goin' to praise God till I die."[2] In Petersburg,
Virginia, Annie Harris and her fellow slaves danced around a barn fire
singing:

> I's free, I's free, I's free at las'!
> Thank God A'mighty, I's free at las'!
>
> I fasted an' I prayed tell I came thew
> Thank God A'mighty, I's free at las'![3]

A Wisconsin soldier marching with Sherman's army through Georgia observed the jubilant slaves and commented: "To them it was like the bondsmen going out of Egypt." In Savannah he and his fellows were greeted
with shouts of "Glory be to God, we are free!" and a hymn of thanksgiving:

> Shout the glad tidings o'er Egypt's dark sea,
> Jehovah has triumphed, his people are free![4]

Biblical allusions filled the exclamations, sermons, songs, and reminiscences of the freedmen. Throughout the South the newly freed slaves sang
variants of the ubiquitous lines:

> Old master's gone away and the darkies stayed at home;
> Must be now that the kingdom's come and the year for jubilee.[5]

A Scottish visitor to the South was struck by the freedmen's "devoutness
and recognition of God's hand in everything."[6] "Lincoln died for we,
Christ died for we," a Sea Islander told Laura Towne, "and me believe
him de same mans."[7] "God said de plantations would grow up and de hoot
owls would have 'em and dey is doin' it. Growin' up into wilderness,"
Alice Sewell exclaimed. "God planned dem slave prayers to free us like
he did de Israelites, and dey did."[8] Mingo White echoed these beliefs:
"The children of Israel was in bondage one time, and God sent Moses to
'liver them. Well, I s'pose that God sent Abe Lincoln to 'liver us."[9] The
precedent of the Hebrew Children had not been false; the Lord had not
reneged on His promise. More than seventy years after the coming of
freedom, Clara Jones of North Carolina still communicated her sense of
triumph and vindication: "The white folks went off to the war. They said

they could whup, but the Lord said, 'No,' and they didn't whup. They went off laughing, and many were soon crying, and many did not come back."[10] Fannie Berry greeted the news of freedom by informing all living things on her Virginia plantation that a new day had come:

> Mammy don't yo' cook no mo'
> Yo' ar' free, yo' ar' free.
> Rooster don't yo' crow no mo'
> Yo' ar' free, yo' ar' free.
> Ol' hen, don't yo' lay no mo' eggs
> Yo' free, yo' free.[11]

The initial impact of emancipation was a glorious confirmation of the sacred world view and the expressive culture the slaves had forged and maintained through their years of bondage. Its ultimate impact was another matter: the freedom that at first seemed to reify Afro-American slave consciousness would inevitably alter it profoundly. The contours and meaning of those changes will be explored in this and the remaining chapters.

THE LANGUAGE OF FREEDOM

Freedom ultimately weakened the cultural self-containment characteristic of the slaves and placed an increasing number of Negroes in a culturally marginal situation. The terms "cultural self-containment" and "marginality" as I employ them here should not be taken as absolutes. The first refers to a group whose cultural standards and world view are determined largely by the values of the group itself and are held with a relative lack of self-consciousness. The second refers to a more obviously bi-cultural or multi-cultural situation in which a group, poised to some extent between two worlds, finds its desire to absorb and emulate the culture of a dominant group, in an attempt to attain and enjoy the latter's privileges and status, in tension with its urge to continue to identify with many of its own central cultural traditions.[1] Obviously these are ideal constructs which are not meant to describe completely the situation of any group of people in American history. Nevertheless, if they are conceived of as cultural *tendencies* or *directions*, rather than as fixed points on a cultural spectrum, they can be of use in understanding some of the major effects of emancipation upon the slaves.

Cultural marginality was a situation unknown and unavailable to most blacks before emancipation. The culture of the antebellum slave was neither static nor impermeable. As Chapters 1 and 2 have shown, there was constant interaction with the culture areas that surrounded it. But the limits were fairly well fixed. Marginality presupposes alternatives. For the vast majority of slaves there were few if any alternatives emanating from the surrounding white world. Their life style, their occupational possibilities, their prospects of change and mobility were predetermined. These limitations in turn threw slaves back upon their own cultural world whose dictates and values were accepted with a minimum of ambivalence, questioning, or inhibiting self-consciousness. While some house servants, artisans, and urban slaves may have aspired to emulate the manners, style, and culture of the master class, for the mass of slaves the peer group and role models—the significant others—remained black. Of course there was desire for things the whites possessed—the freedom, power, mobility, luxuries—but the road to these ends seemed to lie not in attempting to emulate the whites but rather by entering fully into the sacred world of one's own peers with its comforting precedents and promises, its strategies and alternative sources of power. The rewards of imitating whites were never very certain. "I was once whipped," a freedman in New Orleans told David Macrae, "because I said to missis, 'My mother sent me.' We were not allowed to call our mammies 'mother.' It made it come too near the way of the white folks."[2] The world of the whites, attractive as it might appear at times, offered little but the certainty of arbitrary and perpetual enslavement and inequality. In slavery the surest way of attaining those things that would alter life positively, short of escape or rebellion, was not outside of but through black culture itself. Thus even profound dissatisfaction could be an inducement to enter more fully into one's own culture, which seemed to offer the only promise of amelioration and change.

Emancipation and potential cultural marginality were parallel developments for the bulk of black people in the United States. In freedom the barriers became much more permeable, much more incomplete, much less predictable. For a small number of antebellum Negroes the condition so prevalent in modern mass societies—simultaneous participation in a variety of social worlds—was possible to a limited extent. After emancipation this condition broadened for blacks as well as for whites. New channels of mobility and communication were created, the number of reference groups multiplied, life styles became more segmentalized and shifting. It is within the perspective of these changes and new potentialities that black culture after emancipation must be viewed.

If it is difficult to generalize for the culture of the slaves, it is infinitely more perilous to do so for postbellum Negroes. The very cultural diversity that makes generalization increasingly difficult was one of the chief fruits of freedom. If emancipation opened up unprecedented opportunities for acculturation and accommodation, the freedmen did not necessarily exploit them either uniformly or immediately. Indeed, one of the first results of emancipation in a number of areas of black life and culture was the intensification of black separatism. In religion there was a wave of black secession from white churches and the establishment of Negro churches throughout the South. Demographically, Negroes moved not only to cities and to the North but, for both economic and social reasons, large numbers moved further South into areas already heavily black. In Alabama, for instance, the pattern of Negro migration following the Civil War tended to intensify racial polarization in the state. In education, too, the large numbers of new, eager black students created by freedom attended institutions filled almost exclusively with members of their own race.[3]

But the question of acculturation is not simply one of physical proximity or institutional intermixing. Black institutions could, and often did, become the bearers of the values and perceptions of the larger society. If the freedmen remained in a black world demographically and institutionally, their channels of communication with the outside cultures were greatly enhanced. One of the early agencies of this communication was the dedicated army of some five thousand northern teachers, the majority of them from New England, who traveled South during and after the Civil War to educate the former slaves.

Motivated by deeply rooted religious and humanitarian impulses, many of these teachers viewed the events they were part of in ways that only could have reinforced the slaves' interpretation of the meaning of the Civil War and emancipation. "Oh what a privilege to be among them, when their morning dawns; to see them personally, coming forth from the land of Egypt and the house of bondage," proclaimed Martha Kellogg, a teacher at Hilton Head, South Carolina.[4] Dedicated opponents of slavery and subscribers to the notion that Negroes as free individuals could and should become an integral part of the American democracy, these teachers could be no less patronizing toward and even less tolerant of Afro-American culture than were southern whites. If they were disturbed by the Old Testament bias of slave religion and the conversion of Jesus into an Old Testament hero, they were appalled at many of the actual practices of slave worship.

Shortly after arriving on St. Helena Island in 1862, Laura Towne, who was to devote the rest of her life to the education of the freedmen and their progeny, wrote a friend: "To-night I have been to a 'shout,' which seems to me certainly the remains of some old idol worship. . . . I never saw anything so savage. They call it a religious ceremony, but it seems more like a regular frolic to me."[5] On January 15, 1863, Lucy Chase sent her New England family her first impressions of the newly liberated slaves on Craney Island, Virginia: "At one of their prayer-meetings, which we attended, last night, we saw a painful exhibition of their barbarism. Their religious feeling is purely emotional; void of principle, and of no practical utility. . . . They must know what is *right!* in order to worship aright the God of right." Several months later she wrote of her superior, Dr. Orlando Brown, a surgeon in the 18th Massachusetts Infantry and Superintendent of Negro Affairs under General Benjamin Butler: "He loses no opportunity to impress upon the noisy worshippers that boisterous Amens, wild, dancing-dervish flourishes—'Oh that's the Devil,' exclamations— . . . and pandemoniamics generally, do not constitute religion." After a year and a half of teaching the freedmen she was still complaining of the excessive emotionalism, the wild dancing, the "horrible and startling" screeches and howls that filled black religious worship, and wondering, "how fast and how far it would be advisable for the whites to check such customs. . . . The lash and the auction block could dictate to them, but not the preacher. They *must find out* that their way is not the best way, without being told so, or they will never change it."[6]

In these letters Towne and Chase typified the conviction of many northern teachers that black emotional effervescence had to be balanced by greater understanding of the "first elementary principles of the Gospel," and their intention of working untiringly to teach the freedmen "the difference between sense and sound," and to eliminate from their worship what W. G. Kephart, a teacher in Decatur, Alabama, called the "mass of religious rubbish." In these statements the difference between northern and southern attitudes toward Negro culture begins to emerge. Both could be equally critical, but while southerners saw in black culture a confirmation of their conviction concerning Negro inferiority and childishness, the northern teachers perceived a challenge to be overcome in the attempt to educate "all men equally as members of the same great commonwealth." Where southern whites generally were perfectly content to allow the blacks to stew in their own cultural juices, the northerners pined to wipe them clean and participate as midwives at a rebirth. "Our work," a teacher in Beaufort, South Carolina, declared, "is just as much a missionary work as if we were in India or China." The Civil War had been but the first stage in the struggle. Now it was necessary for "Civilization" to triumph over "Barbarism" so that the "power that had its germ in the Mayflower" could create "one common civilization" throughout the nation. Susan Clark, a teacher in Mill Creek, Virginia, put it more simply when she wrote of her black students: "They need so much instruction."[7]

"They need so much instruction" might well stand as emblematic of the chief thrust of the northern white teachers. There were many things they admired about the former slaves, but they rarely wavered in their conviction that their pupils had to be reconstructed in almost every particular from the rudiments of their learning to their style of worship, from their habits of cleanliness to the structure of their families, from their moral fiber to their manner of speaking and pronunciation. It is difficult to gauge the freedmen's reaction to all of this solicitation. Slavery had taught them the wisdom of seeming to agree with everything the white man said, and they soon learned that the strategy retained considerable utility in freedom as well. "In school," Harriet Ware complained, "it is rather annoying to have them say, 'Yes Marm, 'zackly Marm,' before it is possible for an idea to have reached their brains."[8] David Macrae recorded a revealing instance of this. He and the Reverend E. P. Smith visited the youngest class in a Negro school shortly after emancipation. Before leaving, Smith informed the children that he and his companion were going away perhaps never to return, and then, in an attempt to close his remarks on a spiritual note, he asked them: "Are we to meet again?"

> The children, thinking he wished them to back him out in what he had said about our not returning, shouted with one voice, "No!"
> "Are you sure," asked Mr. Smith, hoping to make them reflect; "are you quite sure we shall never meet again?"
> The whole class answered with another shout, "Yes!"
> He paused a moment to think how he could put the question differently, and then said, "Now I want you to think about what I am going to ask. Do you know that I am going to die by-and-by?"
> "Yes."
> Mr. Smith, brightening at the thought that he was at last being appre-

hended: "Well, now, when I am dead and buried, is that the end of me?"
   Chorus of voices—"Yes!"
   "The last of me?"
   "Yes."
   "Does no one say 'No?'"
   All the voices—"No!"
   Mr. Smith was baffled, but not discouraged. He thought a moment, and
then tried another tack.
   "Does a horse go to heaven?"
   "Yes."
   "What!—a horse?"
   Children see from his face that they are wrong, and cry "No!"
   "Does a good man go to heaven?"
   "Yes."
   "Then sha'n't we go if we are good?"
   "Yes."
   "So even though I die, we may meet again up there?—May we not?"
   Of course the answer was "Yes."[9]

However they might mask their attitudes, there can be no doubt that
the freedmen were affected by the new models, the new standards, the
new possibilities to which they were exposed both in and out of their
schools. Emancipation took place in the midst of a society rapidly becoming industrialized, urbanized, and centralized but which in its popular culture was still mesmerized by the image of the individual as architect of his
own fortune and creator of his own universe. Young black children who
were inducted into the mysteries of *McGuffey's Eclectic Readers* and
similar textbooks were ushered into a world in which no one had to be
poor, in which there was no need to fail, in which all could be successful
if only all would follow a simple formula summed up in simple stories and
poems:

> Once or twice though you should fail
>   Try, try Again;
> If you would, at last, prevail
>   Try, try Again; . . .
> All that other folks can do,
> Why, with patience, should not you:
> Only keep this rule in view
>   Try, try Again.[10]

They were taught by teachers who agreed with Ralph Waldo Emerson
that "The reason why this or that man is fortunate . . . lies in the man,"
and who constantly reaffirmed the central political symbols of individual-

ism and the triumph of Will. Though the slaves' ethos had been primarily communal, there were important individual strains in their religion. Sinners could *choose* conversion and the Christian life; conversion and salvation were primarily *individual* experiences. The religious songs of the freedmen reiterated the message:

> I got to stan' my trial in the Judgment
>   I got to stan' there fo' myself.
> There's nobody here can stan' there fo' me
>   I got to stan' there fo' myself.[11]

To the extent that the new ethos they were urged to embrace was a secular version of the ideas of religious salvation they had long held, the former slaves were not on wholly unfamiliar ground. But never before in their experience had they been subjected to more exhortation and inducement to change individually, to embrace new models, to think along new lines, to turn their backs on the past and the traditional ways of thought and action. The end of Reconstruction and the blockage of political channels for Negroes by northern indifference and southern disfranchisement only served to intensify the urgency for change: Negroes must show themselves the equal of whites by developing their own capabilities.[12] Culturally, all of this exhortation, inducement, and exposure to outside influences produced a pervasive self-consciousness about traditional black culture even in those areas of the South where the old ways were to persist well into the twentieth century.

Her experience collecting folk tales on the South Carolina Sea Islands in 1919 led Elsie Clews Parsons to comment: "The heaviest handicap that the white recorder is under, in taking down Negro tales, is the pressure which he exerts, willy nilly, upon the use of language. In the effort to use school English, dialect tends to pass into bad grammar."[13] Six years later Elisha Kane, collecting Negro folklore along the Savannah River in Georgia, noted the same problem: "Negroes, when talking to white people, will consciously modify their speech so that it is quite hard to get a close approximation of the language as they speak it among themselves."[14] The first whites to collect folklore on the Sea Islands found a very different situation: if they were to understand the freedmen they had to learn their dialect. In 1862 Laura Towne noted in her diary that one of her fellow teachers asked his pupils what ears were made for and when they said "To yer with," he could not understand them at all.[15] Even after six months of continuous residence on Port Royal Island during the Civil War, William Francis Allen admitted he often could not understand the speech of his students unless they spoke very slowly. Nor could they always understand him. One day he asked a group of boys the color of the sky. "Nobody could tell me. Presently the father of one of them came by, and I told him their ignorance, repeating my question with the same result as before. He grinned: 'Tom, how sky stan'?' 'Blue,' promptly shouted Tom."[16] Elizabeth Hyde Botume shared Allen's experience:

> Now I wished to take down the names of these children; so I turned to the girl nearest me and said,
> "What is your name?"
> "It is Phyllis, ma'am."
> "But what is your other name?"
> "Only Phyllis, ma'am."
> I then explained that we all have two names; but she still replied,
> "Nothing but Phyllis, ma'am."
> Upon this an older girl started up and exclaimed, "Pshaw, gal! What's you'm title?" whereupon she gave the name of her old master.[17]

There was much these whites had to learn if they were to communicate with the freedmen—not only new words, expressions, and pronunciations, but new rules of grammar as well. Slaves and freedmen frequently used a zero copula and eliminated an explicit predicating verb in certain constructions. Thus "He old" was used instead of "He is old," or "He mighty keerful" instead of "He is very careful." They also tended to use a zero possessive: "Mosey house" rather than "Mosey's house," "Sandy hat" rather than "Sandy's hat," "My brudder child" rather than "My brother's child." The use of undifferentiated pronouns was common: "He pick up he feet and run," "Him lick we," "What make you leff we?" And—to give one final example, though there were a number of other grammatical differences between slave speech and what linguists have called Standard English—the slaves and freedmen tended to disregard gender and use *him* and *he* for either sex. Thus a freedmen observed of his wife, "The old hen, he mighty keerful," students commonly referred to their female teacher as "he," and a school girl asked to give the gender of *sister*, puzzled over it for a time and then exclaimed triumphantly: "Him's feminine, Miss Ellen! Him's a gal!"[18]

The freedmen were frequently delighted at the mistakes in comprehension their linguistic practices caused whites to make, just as many seemed amused at the white teachers' attempts to change black language patterns. A student of Elizabeth Botume's rushed to spread the news of a cyclone that had just leveled their schoolhouse in Beaufort:

> "Dem folks coming from the fields say we schoolhouse is done blowed down!" he exclaimed.
> "O Tom! Tom! You forget your grammar," said one of the young ladies.
> "That's so, Miss Fannie. Yur must really excuse me this time; I done forget," he replied, bowing and chuckling.[19]

The teachers who filled their letters, diaries, and memoirs with expressions of bemused amazement at what their charges were doing to the English language doubtless would have been surprised to learn that their own language created reciprocal feelings in the freedmen. Decades after emancipation a Sea Islander expressed it well when he exclaimed of some white visitors: "Dey use dem mout' so funny!"[20]

The Gullah and Geechee dialects of the South Carolina and Georgia Sea Islands were to retain vitality during the century following emancipation, as Lorenzo Dow Turner's pioneer study of Sea Island speech, *Africanisms in the Gullah Dialect* (1949), demonstrated. But in the interim Sea Islanders had learned much about outsiders and their language. "The Gullahs," Turner noted, "say that they have fared so badly at the hands of strangers that they are suspicious of anyone they do not know very well." Although black himself, Professor Turner found that it took a considerable time before the Sea Islanders would speak naturally to him. His first recordings contained far fewer African words than those he made after he became a familiar figure on the islands. He discovered that the vocabulary and syntax the Sea Islanders used when speaking to strangers differed markedly from that they employed in addressing friends and relatives.[21] This defensiveness was hardly surprising considering the attitudes of many of the folklorists who came among them. Two well-known collectors of lore along the South Carolina coast will serve as examples. In 1908 John Bennett, in one of the first studies of the Gullah dialect, called it "a grotesque patois; . . . the quite logical wreck of once tolerable English, obsolete in pronunciation, dialectical in its usage, yet the natural result of a savage and primitive people's endeavor to acquire for themselves the highly organized language of a very highly civilized race." In 1922 Ambrose Gonzales, one of the most accurate and meticulous recorders of Sea Island language, gave his version of its genesis: "Slovenly and careless of speech, these Gullahs seized upon the peasant English used by some of the early settlers and by the white servants of the wealthier Colonists, wrapped their clumsy tongues about it as well as they could, and, enriched with certain expressive African words, it issued through their flat noses and thick lips. . . ." Both Bennett and Gonzales were convinced that the Gullah dialect's economy of words and elision of syllables stemmed from the Negro's "characteristic laziness."[22]

This denigration was ridden through with ambivalence. No matter how much they might deride black speech, whites, from the teachers of the Civil War period to the folk collectors of the twentieth century, took great pains to preserve it and noted continually the striking phrases and creative terminology they so commonly encountered, such as this response by a young freedman to his teacher's request for definitions of love: "Arter [after] you lub, you lub, you know, boss. You can't broke lub. Man can't broke lub. Lub stan', he ain't goin' broke. Man hab to be berry smart for broke lub. Lub is a ting stan' jus' like tar; arter he stick, he stick. He ain't goin' move. He can't move less dan you burn um. Hab to kill all two arter he lub, 'fo you broke lub."[23] Elizabeth Botume recorded that in 1865 a young black woman exclaimed after seeing a display of Christmas gifts: "I should like to keep this in my eyes forever."[24] And in the 1920s Newbell Niles Puckett, even as he laughed at what he considered the malapropisms of black English, admitted that they were the result of the same linguistic freedom that produced such vitally expressive phrases as these from a twentieth-century spiritual:

We kin almos' see de baby (Moses)
Hide-an-seekin' 'roun' de throne.[25]

The language of the songs, tales, narrative poems, verbal games, and jokes analyzed in the remainder of this study makes it clear that Afro-American capacity for verbal creativity did not end with the coming of freedom. Nevertheless, all of the condescension, exhortation, and outside opportunities took their toll. Half a century after emancipation the Sea Islanders who had spoken with so little inhibition before their white teachers in the 1860s told the tale of a young man who came from an area where "de people talk very bad" and went to New York to study medicine. When he returns as a doctor to visit, he meets three sisters, one of whom attracts him. "So one of de sister he [she] talk so bad, so de eldes' sister say, 'Mind, now, when dat doctor come, don' you talk!' " Inevitably she does speak, but the doctor is not discouraged. "De doctor married de younges' sister, kyarried her to his country, where she learn to talk proper. Take her out travellin' an' change her woice. Dat's de reason, you go in differen' climate now, yer woice change."[26]

The story is an important reflection of events on the Sea Islands during the second decade of the twentieth century. More and more young people were going off to a different "climate"—the cities of the South and North —and were returning with "voice changes" in the form of altered speech habits. The tale, of course, is more than a commentary on events, it is also a commentary on changing values. During these years Portia Smiley heard a similar South Carolina tale with a less happy ending and therefore an even more obvious didactic purpose:

> There were three sisters, and there was a young man coming to court dem. The mother could talk nicely, but the girls couldn't talk. The mother was going out; said, "Now, if he comes to-night, don't say anything." Man came. One girl was sewing. The thread pop. Said, "Dishyer t'read rotten seaka [seem like] punk." The second girl said, "Didn' mammy tell yer musn' talk?" Third said, "T'ank Gawd, I ain't talk! Titty [Sister] talk." The young man was through.[27]

Didactic tales stressing the need for clear, well-enunciated speech were told throughout the South. Children who mumbled were informed that the Devil carried souls in his mouth, and to prevent them from escaping he would not speak when asked a question but would say either "unh hunh" or "Mhm." "So you must never say 'Mhm,' no, always say, yes, and no, because you say 'Mhm' they say youse just like the Devil."[28] "Dere is not'in' de matter wid us," Frank Murray of Defuskie Island, South Carolina, asserted in 1919, "but bad grammar."[29]

The attitudes manifest in these tales were not confined to matters of language. On the Georgia Sea Islands, Lydia Parrish complained that such "musically commonplace English game songs as 'The Farmer Takes a Wife'" were being substituted for such "joyous Afro-American melodies as 'Go roun' the Border, Susie'—for all the world like carrying synthetic coals to Newcastle."[30] Some years earlier Elsie Clews Parsons had a graphic demonstration of such substitutions. Approaching a group of school girls on the South Carolina Sea Islands in 1919, she noticed that they were performing a ring dance commonly known as dancing Juba: "Their knees were bent, their buttocks protruding; they shuffled from one foot to the other as they clapped their hands." When they realized Parsons was watching them, "they broke up their game, drew nearer, and re-formed to play 'The Farmer in the Dell.'"[31] The incident is revealing. The children were not unwilling to allow Parsons to observe their play but they were more comfortable having her see them play a game well known among white children rather than one that went back to slave tradition. Part of this reaction is certainly similar to the slaves' cautious reticence discussed in the last chapter, but by the twentieth century it seems more intensely defensive and self-conscious than the attitude exhibited by the slaves or freedmen. And what was true of the isolated Sea Islands, where slave culture lived on far longer than elsewhere, was truer still of those parts of the South in which the culture of the larger society was even more accessible.

The difficulty white contemporaries and folklorists frequently had in perceiving the coherent structure and grammar of Gullah and other black dialects was inevitably communicated to the blacks themselves. Shortly after the Civil War "a highly educated colored woman" told Elizabeth Kilham: "I won't go to the colored churches, for I'm only disgusted with bad grammar and worse pronunciation, and their horrible absurdities."[32] This defensiveness long outlived the freedmen's generation. In describing his first appearance with Joe Oliver's band in Chicago's Lincoln Gardens in 1922, Louis Armstrong wrote of King Jones, who was the master of ceremonies: "He acted as though he was not a colored fellow, but his real bad English gave him away." In another part of his autobiography Armstrong observed of a young black from Louisiana: "You could tell he was a real country boy by the way he murdered the King's English."[33]

Migration to northern urban centers intensified these attitudes, particularly the equation of southern country speech and incorrect speech. In her study of the language behavior of working class Negroes in Oakland, California, in the mid 1960s, Claudia Mitchell-Kernan found the southern black dialect referred to commonly as "country," "flat" or "bad" English, the opposite of "proper" or "good" English. Among Oakland blacks the least prestigious speech was that defined as "southern" and the most common linguistic insecurity stemmed from the knowledge that black English was looked down upon by the society at large. "Within the area of language," she writes, "the Black community exhibits its link with the wider American community by granting, at least for some purposes, prestige status to the code defined by the majority culture as superior. . . . Within the Black community as well as without, some aspects of Black speech carry the stigma of illiterate and uneducated and enjoy low prestige in this connection. Informants characteristically affirm a positive valuation of proper, good English."[34] Similarly, William Labov found that during the same period in New York City Negroes had a higher opinion of northern dialects and a more negative attitude toward southern speech patterns, which they identified as "rough" "uneducated" "bad" speech, than did New York whites.[35]

Sensitivity about "country" speech was part of a reaction toward "country" or traditional manners and behavior in general. At the turn of the century, didactic tales, such as this one from Elizabeth County, Virginia, stressed gentility and sophistication:

It was once a boy. Had been out to seek his wife. So he met three daughters, and he loved them all, but he didn't know which one to take. So his mother told him to invite them all to his house and give them each some cheese. The first one ate the cheese with the skin and all. The second cut the skin off, and took half the cheese with it. The last one did not cut too much nor too little. So that was the one he chose for his wife.[36]

Whites were frequently held up as models for proper conduct. "Look at de white folks," Helen Ludlow heard a black Virginia preacher admonish his congregation in the 1870s. "D'ye ever see a *white* man want to marry a woman when he had a lawful wife a libing? Neber! I never heared ob sech a thing in all my life. A white man is 'structed [instructed]: he knows dat's agin de law and de gospil."[37] Daniel Webster Davis, a black graduate of Hampton Institute, published an article in 1899 discussing the games and amusements of the slaves and complained of how quickly they were disappearing: "The natural tendency of the day is to forget the black history of the past; and so the younger generation seldom speak of the days of yore, with all of their lights and shadows. It is surprising to know the difficulty I have experienced in gathering the facts of this article."[38] The slaves' John Canoe or John Kuners festival in eastern North Carolina, described in Chapter 1, continued to exist after freedom and reached its peak of popularity in the 1880s when it became an eagerly anticipated annual event for blacks in the region. By 1900 it seems to have disappeared because of the growing opposition of the Negro clergy who felt it was an undignified exhibition, and of a growing number of Negro residents, especially among the middle class, who were convinced that the event lowered their status in the eyes of the whites. The "kooner folk got dicty [snobbish, high class]," a local black observed. "Then dey gave up ruffian's ways. Dey got educated."[39] The same observer doubtless would have applied the term "dicty" to the address "Caste in Our Own Churches" in which the Reverend Paul Pollard told his fellow Negro

Baptists at a state convention in Richmond, Virginia, in 1904 that a class line should be drawn between those colored people who had raised themselves above the ordinary level and those who still remained on the same old plain.[40]

The intensification of intragroup divisions based upon economic, social, educational, occupational, and regional distinctions did not have to wait for the adoption of Pollard's proposal. Inexorably, the traditional Afro-American cultural nexus was being shattered and reshaped. The alterations were accompanied by a chorus of lamentations from folklorists. While he was compiling his important collection of southern Negro folk beliefs, Newbell Niles Puckett requested the aid of a professor at a Negro college and his students in collecting local black superstitions and was informed: "This year we have decided that it would not be wise to suggest an assignment such as you wish because of the intense race consciousness of the recent years which includes temporarily the desire to forget the past in pressing forward to the future." "Line by line," Puckett complained, "increasing knowledge and pride of race are erasing forever these records of folk-thought."[41]

If some white folklorists feared the disappearance of traditional Afro-American culture, some Negro leaders, like Judge George Ruffin of Massachusetts, welcomed the prospect. "The negro," Ruffin declared in 1885, "must go; his fate is sealed; he must be swallowed up and merged in the mass of Southern people. . . . the merging . . . is inevitable." Though Ruffin's plea was echoed by others in the black community, it never became a dominant note. Far more typical of Negro leadership in the late nineteenth century was what August Meier, in his important study of black thought during these years, has called "the ethnic dualism of American Negroes" which led to a simultaneous identification with race and with nation.[42] During the decades following the brief era of Reconstruction—decades marked by a rampant growth of white racist thought and legislation—W. E. B. Du Bois was led to formulate his classic statement on "two-ness" which appears on the title page of this chapter, and an increasing number of Negro voices were raised in warning against an excessive degree of assimilation. In 1899, during a discussion of Negro literature at Hampton Institute, a participant urged black writers to go to the Sea Islands of Georgia and South Carolina "where are to be found the last ship loads of Negroes brought from Africa—the link between the Africans and the Afro-Americans—living a life and speaking a dialect of their own.

There they could find material for stories that would make people lie awake nights. There they could study the Negro in his original purity." "Too many of us," she charged, "are Anglo-Saxon Africans."[43]

The Sea Island folk of whom she spoke had their own defenses against either excessive cultural assimilation or excessive disappointment from the increasingly hollow promises of the postbellum years. Even as their tales urged certain degrees of acculturation, they continued the slave practice of warning against too strong an identification with outsiders. In a typical story, Horse and Mule are playing in the field when Horse begins to make fun of his companion's tail, which was ugly and not tall or long enough to switch flies. "Me duh buckruh, you duh nigguh!" Horse brags. Mule, who had always been content with his tail, now becomes dissatisfied, and in his shame and concern he forgets that he has no need to switch flies since his skin is so thick they don't bother him. Going through a field to get at some corn, Horse's thick tail becomes full of burrs and every time he tries to switch the flies off he whips himself painfully. Observing Horse's dilemma, Mule thanks God for his thin, practical tail. The story ends with a familiar aphorism: "Low tree stan' high win'!"[44]

In the decades after emancipation—and the story was to be repeated in the years after World War I as well—the acculturative thrust among Negroes was modified by a combination of black racial pride and white racial prejudice. Freedom may have dissolved the homogeneity of slave culture, but it did not completely dissolve that culture itself. Many components of it lived on not only in the more isolated rural sections of the South but in northern urban centers as well. But they lived on as part of an increasingly complex, rapidly shifting, highly self-conscious, and often confusingly heterogeneous cultural framework that embraced Afro-Americans in the century after emancipation. Once again a brief look at what happened to black language will prove instructive.

Among the inner city black populations studied by Claudia Mitchell-Kernan and William Labov there was, as we have seen, a self-consciousness about speech and a tendency to identify black English with "bad" English. Yet this tendency did not lead, as one might suppose, to the inevitable destruction of black dialect patterns. Linguists have debated the extent to which black dialects have structurally interfered with the learning of Standard English.[45] But whether or not there have been structural barriers to the acquisition of Standard English, there can be no question of the existence of cultural barriers. Language groups, as Albert Guerard has pointed out, can be far more potent realities than political units; linguistic boundaries cannot be undone by the mere stroke of a pen, for language communities, even more certainly than political communities, imply a common world view and cultural heritage.[46] This enables us to understand the persistence of the black language community in the face of the strong urges toward linguistic amalgamation. Living in the midst of a hostile and repressive white society, black people found in language an important means of promoting and maintaining a sense of group unity and cohesion. Thus while the appropriateness and utility of speaking Standard English in certain situations was understood, within the group there were frequently pressures to speak the vernacular. In both New York and Oakland those who paid too great an adherence to Standard English were often referred to as "lames," a pejorative term applied to those members of the peer group who, for one reason or another, were outside the central culture of the group.[47] One of Mitchell-Kernan's informants said contemptuously of a friend who was "trying to talk proper": "She think she gon get time off for good behavior."[48] A New Yorker succinctly described to William Labov the tension many Negroes perceived between peer group allegiance and the demands of the outside society:

> When I was small and going to school, if you talked that way [Standard English], the kids would kid you, but we had a few kids that would do it, and we always kid them. . . . There was a girl who was always very proper . . . so, she'd always walk up and say, "Pardon me." We'd all laugh, we knew it was correct, but we'd still laugh. Today, she end up successful.[49]

As the outside culture became more visible and more accessible in the twentieth century, the dilemma grew. The *lames* might be laughed at within the group, but it was they who often had the better chance of mobility and success outside. Negro children were hardly socialized to the vernacular of their own group before they learned of its disadvantages and low status in the larger culture. Thus, for black Americans as for other minority groups in the society, the socialization process increasingly became a dual one: an attempt to learn to live both within and outside the group. In language as in so many other areas of black culture this has produced a broad and complex spectrum. At one end were the upwardly mobile whose speech had become Standard English and who, when they did desire to relate to the language of the group, had to do so not through grammar or phonetics but, as J. L. Dillard has shown, through ethnic slang.[50] At the other end was a continuously diminishing group whose dialect was basically unaltered by the outside society. The majority could be found somewhere between these two extremes.

It would be a mistake to conceive of movement along this spectrum as proceeding progressively and at an ever-accelerating rate from the pole of parochial dialect to that of Standard English. As the twentieth century progressed, a growing number of Negroes clustered somewhere in the middle, switching first to one speech mode and then to another as need and values dictated. Even in the relatively isolated Sea Islands, as the already cited work of Parsons in 1919, Kane in the 1920s, and Turner in the 1940s illustrated, Negroes had acquired the ability to alter their vocabulary and syntax quite dramatically depending on whether they were speaking to strangers or to their own people. Linguists who have studied urban black communities have found that black speech tends to be age-graded or age-related. That is, the use of black vernacular is strongest among children and teenagers; as individuals leave their adolescence their speech patterns shift in the direction of Standard English.[51] Thus it has been common to find individuals who could speak the vernacular dialect in their own group while outside it they spoke, if not Standard English then some gradation closer to it than the vernacular. Maya Angelou, who grew up in Arkansas and California during the 1920s and 1930s, has written of how different her education was from that of her white schoolmates:

> In the classroom we all learned past participles, but in the streets and in our homes the Blacks learned to drop *s*'s from plurals and suffixes from past-tense verbs. We were alert to the gap separating the written word from the colloquial. We learned to slide out of one language and into another without being conscious of the effort. At school, in a given situation, we might respond with "That's not unusual." But in the street, meeting the same situation, we easily said, "It be's like that sometimes."[52]

Whatever direction Afro-American language practices take in the future, the patterns of change since emancipation seem to suggest that the movement until now has been in the direction of diglossia or bi-dialectism, the use of different languages or dialects for different purposes, rather than toward the wholesale destruction of traditional dialects in favor of Standard English. This combination of acculturation and cultural exclusivity, this movement into the larger society and simultaneous maintenance of ties with the smaller community, can stand as an example of what was occurring in other areas of Afro-American culture after slavery. Emancipation brought educational, occupational, and spatial mobility and mobility enhanced acculturation. But underlying all the changes there persisted crucial residues of traditional culture which helped shape expression in every sphere of black life, as an examination of postbellum black religion will indicate.

THE FATE OF THE SACRED WORLD

On a December evening in 1862 Thomas Wentworth Higginson walked through his encampment observing his black soldiers sitting before the camp fires. Some smoked silently; some cleaned their guns; some sang or prayed; some told stories or traded jokes and anecdotes, filling the air with shouts of laughter, often at their officers' expense. One group sat listening intently to words being spelled from a primer. This simple act, Higginson noted in his camp diary, was a feat "which always commands all ears,—they rightly recognizing a mighty spell, equal to the overthrowing of monarchs, in the magic assonance of *cat, hat, pat, bat*, and the rest of it. . . . Their love of the spelling-book is perfectly inexhaustible,— they stumbling on by themselves, or the blind leading the blind, with the same pathetic patience which they carry into everything."[1] Along with spatial mobility, literacy was one of the chief symbols of the former slaves' new status; one of the manifest signs that they were no longer chattels. Elizabeth Botume has described the freedmen's excited exclamations of "Dar, da him," "Missus comes fur larn we," that greeted her when she first arrived at her school house. Men and women crowded in to get their names recorded on the school's registration lists before they went back to the fields to complete their chores. "Each one regarded it as an honor to be enrolled as a scholar. They all left with a new consciousness of their own individuality and personal dignity. I use this term advisedly. The poorest and most down-trodden of these people are self-respecting."[2] Lucy Chase spoke of her students' "greed for letters" and commented that every step of educational progress confirmed their faith in a "brilliant promise."[3]

For many the promise was religious. After the war a black preacher, holding a Bible aloft, told his congregation: "Breddern and sisters! I can't read more'n a werse or two of dis bressed Book, but de gospel it is here— de glad tidings it is here—oh teach your chill'en to read dis yar bressed

Book. It's de good news for we poor coloured folk."[4] In 1864 Lucy Chase heard Virginia freedmen sing:

> Oh happy is the child who learns to read
>   When I get over
> To read that blessed book indeed.
>
> When I get over, when I get over
> 'Twill take some time to study
> When I get over.[5]

In North Carolina a freedman told David Macrae: "if I could on'y read God's own write I tink it would be wurf more'n than everything."[6] On the Sea Islands Harriet Ware attended a funeral and saw a group of children, school books in their hands, standing around the grave singing their A, B, C over and over as they stood waiting for the preacher to arrive— "another proof," Ware felt, that the freedmen considered their lessons as some sort of religious exercise.[7] True to the slaves' religion the promise was also deeply rooted in this world. "They had profound respect for education," Elizabeth Botume noted, "and felt that if they could read they would come nearer to the white race, and could better compete with them; all of which was true."[8] Sidney Andrews observed that the ex-slaves were so eager to read because they were convinced literacy was the road to honor and happiness.[9] "Times is hard and we can't get along fast," a freedman in North Carolina exclaimed, "but we has homes of our own now, and we can't be druv away, and we can send our chill'en to school now, and get 'em teached like de white folks—praise de Lord!"[10]

Literacy was not a gift bestowed upon the freedmen overnight; it was a skill acquired gradually, often painfully. Progress, however, was steady and, considering the obstacles confronting the ex-slaves and their descendants, extremely impressive. At the time of emancipation at least 93 per cent of the adult Negroes in the United States were illiterate. In 1870 the number had been reduced to about 80 per cent; by 1890, 56 per cent; 1900, 44 per cent; 1910, 30 per cent; 1920, 23 per cent; 1930, 16 per cent; 1940, 11 per cent; 1950, 10 per cent. Thus in the eight decades following emancipation the figures were reversed. When freedom first came, more than nine out of ten blacks had been illiterate; by the mid-twentieth century, nine out of ten were literate.[11] Literacy brought no miraculous changes in the external situation of the ex-slaves, though it clearly did increase their options in the long run. The most important initial changes brought about by the advent of literacy were internal: changes in perception and world view. The massive discrimination against black students in school systems throughout the nation, and especially the South, undoubtedly kept a far larger percentage of blacks than whites from progressing much beyond the level of sheer literacy—the minimal ability to read and write. Yet that very change was to bring about a revolutionary shift in Afro-American consciousness.

The Africans from whom the slaves had descended lived in a world of sound; a world in which the spoken, chanted, sung, or shouted word was the primary form of communication. Mary Kingsley captured some of the essence of this world which still existed when she made her trips through West Africa in the 1890s:

> Woe to the man in Africa who cannot stand perpetual uproar! Few things surprised me more than the rarity of silence and the intensity of it when you did get it. . . . We will give Man the first place in the orchestra, he deserves it. I fancy the main body of the lower classes of Africa think externally instead of internally. You will hear them when they are engaged together on some job—each man issuing the fullest directions and prophecies concerning it, in shouts; . . . even when you are sitting alone in the forest you will hear a man or woman coming down the narrow bush path chattering away with such energy and expression that you can hardly believe your eyes when you learn from him that he has no companion.
>
> Some of this talking is, I fancy, an equivalent to our writing. I know many English people who, if they want to gather a clear conception of an affair, write it down; the African not having writing, first talks it out.[12]

J. C. Carothers has contrasted this world of sound with the world of vision characteristic of modern Western Europeans. When words are written, he argues, they become part of the visual world, lose the personal qualities and the dynamism of the spoken word, and become static things, "symbols without existence in their own right." Thus it is typically in literate societies that the concepts of freedom of thought and speech can develop for only literate societies believe that verbal thought is separable from action, that ideas are distinct from behavior, that ideation can be contained. In nonliterate societies such distinctions are not made. Ideas and words are seen as part of the same reality as the events to which they refer; words are powerful, often magical parts of the real world in their own right; ideation is as "behavioral" as any other form of action.[13] To cite merely one instance from African culture, among the Ashanti the man or woman who spoke openly about having had an adulterous dream was subject to the same penalties as one who actually committed adultery.[14] Within this context we may understand even better the importance of the socially sanctioned mechanisms, described in Chapter 1, which the Ashanti and other African peoples devised to allow occasions and outlets for the free and open expression of certain feelings and thoughts.

It is because they came from such societies and were not inducted into the literate world of their white masters that slaves invested their songs, tales, and the spoken word in general with such importance. Their world remained a world of sound in which words were actions. To speak or sing of the heroes and exploits of the Old Testament, to relate orally the events that occurred in dreams or visions, was to give them a substance, a reality, to make them literally come alive. Here the medium and the message intermeshed in crucial ways. The dynamic, living quality of the spoken word was conducive to the sense of sacred space and time characteristic of Africans and Afro-Americans in slavery. To learn of the past through the personally related spoken word was to give the past a contemporaneity and personal significance missing from the more highly segmented and compartmentalized sense of time characteristic of literate societies in which knowledge of the past is derived largely from the more abstracted and detached printed page. It is necessary to understand the intimate relationship between the world of sound and the world of sacred time and space in order to understand one of the chief effects of literacy upon the world view of black Americans after the Civil War. Since it is not coincidental that preliterate societies tend to develop sacred notions of time and space, the introduction of literacy inevitably dilutes the predominance of the oral tradition and just as inevitably produces important shifts in the *Weltanschauung* of the group. Thus although it happened neither suddenly nor completely, the sacred world view so central to black slaves was to be shattered in the twentieth century. An examination of the changes of consciousness in Negro religious music will make the process clear.

Much about postbellum black religion and religious song remained familiar. The war and emancipation, as I have attempted to show, initially tended to reaffirm the validity of the slaves' religion. For three quarters of a century after emancipation, folklorists, travelers, and local residents were to collect songs of the type the slaves had sung and to describe religious meetings which differed little from those the slaves had participated in. All of the traditional trappings were there: the ecstacy, the spirit possession, the shouts, the chanted sermons, the sacred sense of time and space, the immediacy, the feeling of familiarity with God and the ancient heroes, the communal setting in which songs were created and re-created.

Religion frequently remained a vital, living experience. In the late nine-teenth century Emily Austin witnessed a large audience at a black Meth-odist conference so moved at the story of Joseph meeting his aged father "that the tears and sobbing, the hand shaking and shouting were uncon-trollable, and it was hard to believe that the story was a familiar one heard dozens of times by every one present."[15] In 1912 Harris Barrett described religious meetings in which the minister failed in his attempt to arouse re-ligious enthusiasm. After he sat down, resigned to failure, a member of the congregation began a spiritual slowly and monotonously. Gradually the congregation became worked up from one degree of emotion to an-other "until, like a turbulent, angry sea, men and women, to the accom-paniment of the singing, and with shouting, moaning, and clapping of hands, surged and swayed to and fro. I have seen men and women at these times look and express themselves as if they were conversing with their Lord and Master, with their hands in His; and to those benighted souls it was as real as any experience of their lives."[16]

Musically, the spirituals continued to fill their collectors with a sense of awe. William Arms Fisher warned his readers that his attempts to repro-duce the music of the spirituals he heard in the 1920s could not capture "the slurring and sliding of the voices, the interjected turns and 'curls,' the groans and sighs, the use even of quarter-tones, the mixture of keys, and the subtle rhythms."[17] Capacity for improvisation remained great. At-tempting to note the melody of a spiritual, Fisher complained to the singer that he had not sung it that way the first time. "Oh, no," the latter replied, "that's the way we do. We don't sing it alike ev'ry time." Another black singer was asked by a collector for the Federal Writers' Project how many stanzas there were to his song and replied: "until you get tired."[18]

The content of the spirituals retained contemporary applicability. Thus twentieth-century Negroes, like their slave forbears, continued to find pleasure and significance in the words of Samson:

If I had my way,
O Lordy, Lordy,
If I had my way;
If I had my way;
I would tear this building down.[19]

Religion continued to be prized for the justice it brought to a world that lacked it. Throughout the first half of this century blacks continued to sing:

Ef salvation wuz a thing money could buy
Den de rich would live an' de po' would die.

But Ah'm so glad God fix it so,
Dat de rich mus' die jes' as well as de po'!

In 1916 Alabama blacks gave the song an even more contemporary twist:

If-a 'ligion wuz er thing that money could buy,
The rich would live and the po' would die.
I'm so glad things jes' like dis,
Dere's 'nother good chance for the po' coon yet.[20]

Latter day spirituals continued to be ridden with ambiguous meanings. What precisely have Negroes meant in their twentieth-century religious music when they complained continuously: "Why doan de debbil let-a me be?" or asked: "What makes ole Satan hate me so?" and answered: "Cause he got me once an' let me go," or boasted: "Ole Satan thought he had me fast, / Broke his chain an' I'm free at last," or observed:

Just let me tell you how this world is fixed:
Satan has got it so full of tricks,
You can go from place to place,
Everybody's runnin' down the colored race.[21]

In freedom as in slavery, the Devil—over whom blacks generally triumphed in their songs—often looked suspiciously like a surrogate for the white man. Similarly, while Negroes had long sung of "letters from the Lord" and "trains to glory," and while there can be no doubt that these phrases were frequently meant literally, during the late nineteenth- and early twentieth-century migrations of blacks from the South to the North, which many southern states desperately tried to stop, it is difficult to imagine that these metaphors did not assume contemporary connotations. One spiritual after another during these years contained such lines as: "I am huntin' fo' a city fo' to stay a while," "You better run to de City of Refuge, / You better run!"

Yes I 'bleeged to leave this world,
Yes I 'bleeged to leave this world,
Sister, I's bleeged to leave this world,
For it's a hell to me.

I'm runnin' for my life
I'm runnin' for my life
What's the matter with me
Just tell 'em I said
I'm runnin' for my life.[22]

Perhaps the most important continuation of all was that these were not just songs of worship; they remained songs for all occasions. Evelyn Macon, a laundry worker in New York City during the Great Depression, described the effects that spirituals had upon herself and her fellow workers:

> Before we unionized, I worked as a press operator. Slavery is the only word that could describe the condition under which we worked. It was at least fifty-four hours a week, speed up—speed up—eating lunch on the fly, perspiration dropping from every pore, for almost ten hours per day. . . .
> The girls who worked in the starching department used to sing spirituals to enable them to breathe standing ten hours and sticking their hands into almost boiling starch. . . . the starchers used to sing, "Go Down Moses," "Down By the Riverside," and God the feeling they put in their singing. As tired as we were those spirituals lifted up our spirits and we joind in sometimes. . . . While singing we would forget our miserable lot, . . .[23]

Even such workers as Rose Reed of the Bronx who performed isolated tasks had resort to the spirituals to aid them: "There was a time when I worked for low wages, the same as many other women who are employed as household servants. But while my back was almost breaking from the work, my heart was light and as I sang, 'I got to Get Rid of this Heavy Load,' or 'Go Down Moses,' I searched my brain for some salvation from that awful work."[24]

By now we have examined the folk process closely enough so that continuities should not surprise us. But neither should they be allowed to obscure the changes that were taking place. Postbellum spirituals continued the message, the ethos, the images, of slave songs and remained a vital force in many places during the twentieth century. Nevertheless, they no longer occupied the central position of the past. They were in a serious state of decline and with them the religious world view they represented. This decline was catalogued in a number of the songs of the black folk:

> I wonder what de matter wid Zion, O my Lord,
> I wonder what de matter wid Zion, good Lord,
>   Rolling in Zion, Jubalee!
>
> My preacher don' preach a like a used to, O my Lord, . . .
> My sister don' shout like she used to, O my Lord, . . .
> My mou'ner don' mou'n like a used to, O my Lord, . . .
> My leader don' lead like a used to, O my Lord, . . .
> My deacon don' pray like a used to, O my Lord, . . .[25]

Oh, the people don't sing like they used to sing,
The mourners don't moan like they used to moan,
The preachers don't pray like they used to pray,
That's what's the matter with the church today.[26]

Robert Russa Moton, who was to succeed Booker T. Washington as head of Tuskeegee Institute, entered Hampton Normal and Agricultural Institute in 1885 at the age of eighteen. Like Washington, who had attended Hampton from 1872 to 1875, Moton made great personal sacrifices to attend the Virginia institution in an effort to lift himself out of the rural poverty into which he had been born. Hampton was to be the beginning of a new life. Yet there were traces of the old life still thriving there which disturbed Moton. Together with some six hundred Negro and Indian students and about one hundred white visitors and faculty, Moton spent his first Sunday night at Hampton listening to the white chaplain deliver an inspiring prayer which was followed by the singing of spirituals. Though Moton had known these songs all of his life, they were so beautifully performed that he was deeply moved. He was also deeply disappointed to hear plantation songs sung by educated people in an educational institution: "I had come to school to learn to do things differently; to sing, to speak, and to use the language, and of course, the music, not of coloured people but of white people." After the meeting Moton shared his feelings with his peers and found that most of the entering students agreed with him. One or two older students argued that the music brought great enjoyment and should be sung. "The only reply I could give was that they were Negro songs and that we had come to Hampton to learn something better; and then, too, I objected to exhibiting the religious and emotional side of our people to white folks; for I supposed the latter listened to these songs simply for entertainment and perhaps amusement." Moton was to spend three years at Hampton before he was willing to sing Negro songs in the presence of whites. And then it was to be a white man, General Samuel Chapman Armstrong, the founder and head of Hampton, who was instrumental in convincing him that the spirituals were a "priceless legacy" which should be cherished.[27]

Moton's attitude typified that of many first- and second-generation freedmen who were determined to divest themselves of the behavioral patterns of a slave past. It is not surprising that the religious practices which had been so crucial to slave culture were often a prime target. Hardly had northern observers discovered the religious songs of the slaves and freedmen than they were lamenting their decline, and while some of this clearly emanated from the faulty perceptions and unconscious attitudes of the collectors, there is too much of this testimony to ignore. As early as 1867, in the first major collection of Negro songs, *Slave Songs of the United States*, the editors commented that it was frequently no easy matter to persuade the freedmen to sing their old songs "such is the sense of dignity that has come with freedom."[28] That same year Harriet Beecher Stowe wrote that the spirituals were often being superseded by a style of music which lacked what Mrs. Stowe called "soul" and was instead "solemn, dull and nasal, consisting in repeating two lines of a hymn and then singing it, and then two more, *ad infinitum*. . . . This style of proceeding they evidently consider the more dignified style of the two, as being a closer imitation of white, genteel worship."[29] Between 1868 and 1870 John Mason Brown, Elizabeth Kilham, and David Macrae all noted that the distinctive features of Negro sacred song were disappearing and attributed it to the education of the young. "With increasing knowledge," Kilham observed, "comes growing appreciation of fitness and propriety, in this, as in everything else; and already they have learned to ridicule the extravagant preaching, the meaningless hymns, and the noisy singing of their elders."[30] In his 1874 collection of plantation songs, Thomas Fenner noted it was important to publish slave music as quickly as possible, for "it is rapidly passing away. . . . the freedmen have an unfortunate inclination to despise it as a vestige of slavery."[31]

That these warnings and predictions were still being issued half a century later indicates that the old music did not die a sudden death—folklore invariably seems to decline more slowly than its collectors' jeremiads are issued—but there can be no doubt that the spirituals no longer occupied the position they had enjoyed in slavery. One observer after another attested to the fact that they were being displaced by standard hymns, Moody and Sankey revival songs, and other forms of religious music.[32]

There is an abundant folk testimony on this point as well. In 1899 an ex-slave from Charleston, who had moved North, complained: "De niggers heah ain't got no Holy Spirit and dey is singing no 'count songs—dese white songs from books." An ex-slave in the South made the same complaint about the younger generation: "Dese young heads ain't wuth killin', fur dey don't keer bout de Bible nor de ole hymns. . . . de big organ and de eddication has done took all de Holy Spirit out en 'em till dey ain't no better wid der dances and cuttin' up dan de white folks."[33] During the Depression, Lillie Knox of South Carolina observed: "The younger race coming, they going to all sing out th' book. Terreckly ain't

going to be no spiritual left."[34] Many former slaves agreed: "The young
people don't live close to God now as they did in them times. God lived
close to them, too." "Deze last few y'ars day hab got ter stylish ter shout."
"They have college preachers now. They don't have religion like they
used to."[35] These observations were not new. The Civil War was hardly
over when a recently emancipated woman denounced the changes taking
place in religious worship:

> I goes ter some churches, an' I sees all de folks settin' quiet an' still,
> like dey dunno what de Holy Sperit am. But I fin's in my Bible, that when
> a man or a 'ooman gets full ob de Holy Sperit, ef dey should hol' dar
> peace, de stones would cry out; an' ef de power ob God can make de
> stones cry out, how can it help makin' us poor creeturs cry out, who feels
> ter praise Him for His mercy. Not make a noise! Why we makes a noise
> 'bout ebery ting else; but dey tells us we mustn't make no noise ter praise
> de Lord. I don't want no sich 'ligion as dat ar. I wants ter go ter Heaben in
> de good ole way.[36]

Ninety years later the black comedian Moms Mabley issued a similar complaint: "It used to be when you went to church you enjoyed it. Now, you
go t' church and you don't hear a sound. If anybody gonna say 'Amen,'
they wanna' hit him in the mouth. . . . You don't see Sisters shoutin' like
they used ta'."[37]

As these remarks indicate, it was not merely the spirituals but the entire
network of slave religious practices that was undergoing the erosions of
change. The pressures upon traditional modes of Afro-American worship
came from whites and blacks, North and South. Following the Charleston
earthquake of 1886, homeless Negroes gathered within the city in tents
and temporary sheds and spoke to their God to whose wrath they attributed the disaster. Their audible prayers soon led the white pastor of St.
Mark's Church to appeal to his black colleagues through the newspapers:
"Do stop these repeated so-called religious scenes, singing and loud praying, and stentorian preaching. God is not deaf, and I don't suppose all the
congregations are, and need not be 'hollered' at so. . . . You will never
elevate your people thus, and you antagonize the two races. The average
white man . . . looks with contempt, and says, What is the use to try
to elevate those savages?"[38]

The way in which white condescension could be transformed into
black defensiveness is illustrated in the case of Peter Randolph, an ex-
slave who was minister of a Negro Baptist church in Boston after the
Civil War. Lacking a baptismal pool in his Concord Street Church, Ran-

dolph asked Dr. Gordon of the white Clarendon Street Baptist Church for permission to use his facilities. Directly after Gordon's sermon one Sunday morning, Randolph appeared with twenty-one baptismal candidates, whom he had already cautioned to "be as careful and calm as possible." Randolph's warning proved to be no match for the Holy Spirit. "The first one I immersed showed a little sign of excitement, and the second a little more, so the excitement increased gradually, till some got happy in the water, and so on." As the enthusiasm grew, Gordon dismissed his white parishioners remarking that it was better for their black brethren to be alone as they had some ways peculiar to themselves. Randolph was mortified: "Reverend Mr. Gordon deeply sympathized with me in my embarrassed condition, and I was so ashamed of the action of my people that I never went there to baptize again."[39]

The shout, which the slaves had used as an outlet for their physical and spiritual passions as well as to bridge the thin line between past and present, continued to exist well into the twentieth century, but more and more it was on the defensive.[40] On the Sea Islands both Elsie Clews Parsons and Lydia Parrish found the local residents reluctant to perform the shout because of the disapproval of their white teachers and their fear that they would be laughed at.[41] During his youth in Jacksonville, Florida, in the 1870s and 1880s, James Weldon Johnson saw the shout performed many times but remembered that it was looked upon as a very questionable form of worship. Whispered invitations would go around: "Stay after church; there's going to be a 'ring shout.' " As fast as they were able, the more educated ministers and members braved what Johnson called the "primitive element" in the churches and placed a ban on the shout.[42] One of the most eminent and powerful of these educated black ministers, Daniel A. Payne, had been a bishop in the African Methodist Episcopal Church since 1852. In 1878 Payne attended a camp meeting, witnessed a ring shout, and asked the local pastor to end it. At the latter's request the worshippers stopped their dancing and hand clapping but remained in a circle singing and rocking their bodies. Payne then went to their leader and requested him to desist, telling him that "it was a heathenish way to worship and disgraceful to themselves, the race, and the Christian name." The ring was finally broken and the singers walked sullenly away. Everywhere he traveled Payne endeavored to make such practices "disgusting." When local ministers countered that any attempt to curtail such folk religion would simply drive people away from the church, Payne concluded that if ex-communication was necessary it should be used: "The time is at

hand when the ministry of the A. M. E. Church must drive out this heathenish mode of worship or drive out all the intelligence, refinement, and
practical Christians who may be in her bosom."[43]

Alterations in the traditional religious framework emanated not only
from those who despised or were ashamed of the old ways but frequently
from those who wanted to preserve them. The fate of the spirituals af-
fords a good example. In the fall of 1871 George L. White, a white native
of Cadiz, New York, who was treasurer and instructor of vocal music at
Fisk University in Nashville, took nine black students North on a concert
tour to raise money for the new struggling Negro school. The achieve-
ments of these students, soon to be known as the Fisk Jubilee Singers, are
familiar enough: after a shaky beginning marked by sparse crowds and
discrimination which made it difficult to secure food and shelter, they began to concentrate on the singing of spirituals, eliminating many of the
ballads, sentimental songs, temperance and patriotic songs that had characterized their initial programs, and soon swept the Northeast, exciting audience after audience. In the years to come they were to repeat these triumphs throughout much of the United States, England, and the European
Continent. In the wake of Fisk's success, Hampton Institute established a
similar group in 1873, and the Fisk and Hampton Singers, together with
the many groups later patterned upon them, familiarized the world with
the black spirituals.[44]

But they were not quite the spirituals as the slaves had sung them. In the
process of transmission from the praise house to the concert hall the songs
were denatured into a form more compatible with Euro-American musical tastes. After listening to a concert of spirituals at Hampton, an ex-slave
exclaimed: "Dose are de same ole tunes, but some way dey do'n sound
right," and many years later another former slave complained: "I do not
like the way they have messed up our songs with classical music."[45] John
Wesley Work's description of George White's training procedures with
the original Fisk singers is instructive: "At designated intervals he would
gather his choir into a room, close the door and the windows as closely as
advisable, and rehearse in pianissimo tones, the song of the cabin and of
the field. The training of this company was a work of patience. Many
were the devices and methods to teach them the proper tone production.
The smoothing down of their voices was an accomplishment which came
after long and hard labor."[46]

White wanted to retain the spirit and feeling of the original songs, but
in "smoothing" the voices, altering the grammar, teaching "proper" tone,

he helped to transform folk music into concertized and Europeanized art songs. In actuality, of course, it was not the work of one man but an entire process of education that produced the changes. In 1893 F. G. Rathbun, Director of Music at Hampton, put the matter in perspective when he observed that the students' singing initially was marked by "quaint little turns in the melodies and odd pronunciation." After contact with music, singing, English, and elocution teachers, however, "something is missing from the songs, and this goes on as long as the student remains here. Corrected pronunciation and corrected singing make the difference. It is very difficult to teach an educated colored youth to render these songs in the old ways."[47]

It would be an error to conceive of the students as passive subjects in this transformation; many of them desired precisely the changes that were taking place. This desire was shaped and fed by the attitudes of their teachers. Rathbun's choice of words, for instance, reveals a condescension of which he himself may have been unaware but which his students certainly would not have missed. Few black college students in the late nineteenth century desired to sing songs which inspired such adjectives as "quaint" or which were marked by "odd pronunciation." The same tone generally characterized the utterances of even the staunchest champions of the traditional slave songs. Theodore F. Seward, in his enthusiastic preface to a collection of the songs of the Jubilee Singers, spoke of them as "the simple ecstatic utterances of wholly untutored minds," and thanked God for having bestowed His inspiration upon "The child-like, receptive minds of these unfortunates."[48] Similarly, General Armstrong of Hampton, in his struggle to keep the spirituals unadulterated, exclaimed: "The more civilized you make them the more valueless you make them."[49] This was exactly the crux of the problem for Armstrong's students: "civilization" after all was precisely what Hampton intended to teach its Negro and American Indian students to crave.

It should not surprise us, then, that in spite of the immense popularity and prestige which the Fisk and Hampton singers brought the spirituals, educated blacks, and especially college students, commonly remained ambivalent about them. Ten years after the Jubilee Singers' triumphant first tour, the Negro writer and critic James Trotter distinguished between that which is progressive in music and that which is the reverse. The spirituals fit into the latter category, since, "notwithstanding their great beauty of melody, and occasional words of elevated religious character," they were reminiscent of "a former life of enforced degradation."

Although they would have to give way to music befitting a new order of things, Trotter was reluctant to lose their "heartiness" and "soulfulness." His ambivalence ended in fantasy: "My mind goes a few years into the future. I attend a concert given by students or by graduates of Fisk University; I listen to music of the most classical order rendered in a manner that would satisfy the most exacting critic of the art; and at the same time I am pleasantly reminded of the famous 'Jubilee Singers' . . . by the peculiarly thrilling sweetness of voice, and by the charming simplicity and soulfulness of manner."[50] Civilization and innocence, mind and heart, would reside together in happy union. Even at the home of the original Jubilee Singers, the students remained wary. For years, John Wesley Work remarked in 1915, "one would be as likely to hear Negro Folk Songs in St. Peter's at Rome as in Fisk University."[51] From the late nineteenth century through the 1920s there were to be periodic student rebellions against singing spirituals at Hampton Institute and Fisk and Howard Universities and a continuing debate over the efforts of such young Negro musicians as Harry T. Burleigh, R. Nathaniel Dett, and Will Marion Cook to continue the process begun by the Fisk Jubilee Singers and to "develop" the spirituals as a conscious art form.[52]

All of this considerable controversy should not obscure the fact that by the twentieth century and especially during the years after World War I, when the black contribution to the war effort was rewarded by a wave of race riots and lynchings, the spirituals became an object of pride among the black intelligentsia. Alain Locke was typical in hailing them as "the most characteristic product of Negro genius to date," its "great folk-gift," which he urged black writers and artists to emulate in their own work. The road pioneered by Hampton Institute's journal *The Southern Workman*, which was an early champion of teaching black children the old plantation melodies, was now followed by such new journals as the NAACP's *Crisis* and the Urban League's *Opportunity*, which printed editorials eulogizing black spirituals and quoting Anton Dvorak's dictum that "The future music of America must be founded on what is called 'Negro melodies.' "[53]

Defensiveness, of course, remained and was fed by such painful incidents as the one which occurred during the centennial celebration of Columbus, Mississippi. A group of seventy-five black field hands from the neighboring cotton fields were invited to entertain by singing their plantation melodies. Wearing their work clothes, they stood on a bandstand on Main Street before a crowd of thousands and sang their "wild and original" songs which were greeted by genuine interest but by something else as well, as reported by a contemporary observer: "The humor of the words was often apparent to the audience and caused laughter, but the singers being wholly unconscious of their blundering version of the scriptures sang on seriously."[54] Such scenes undoubtedly had their effect upon black intellectuals. Even while he was writing poems celebrating the "black and unknown bards of long ago" and editing two volumes of spirituals, James Weldon Johnson informed his readers that though it was "pardonable to smile at the naïveté often exhibited in the words" of the spirituals it should be remembered that rarely was anything humorous intended. "When it came to the use of words, the maker of the song was struggling as best he could under his limitations in language and, perhaps, also under a misconstruction or misapprehension of the facts in his source material, generally the Bible." Johnson and other black interpreters of the spirituals were also too insistent upon validating the slave songs by elevating them to a point where their essence became distorted. They converted a body of songs, so many of which focused upon the Hebrews' military victories and the retribution of Revelations, into a wholly "noble" and exclusively "exalted" group of sentiments voicing "all the cardinal virtues of Christianity." "You sang not deeds of heroes or of kings," Johnson wrote in one of his poems, "No chant of bloody war, no exulting paean / Of arms-won triumphs; but your humble strings / You touched in chord with music empyrean." "You may search the entire collection of Aframerican religious folk songs extant," the Negro singer Roland Hayes wrote, "and you will not find one word of hate or malice anywhere expressed in them."[55]

This defensiveness aside, there was an increasing acceptance of spirituals throughout the black community. Negro churches featured spirituals in their services and special programs; choirs were established and contests held to perpetuate the old songs; individuals like Edward Boatner and Tim Dennison, the founder of the Association for the Preservation and Development of the American Negro Spiritual, worked to bring about a renaissance of spiritual singing.[56] The eagerness with which black students during the civil rights movement of the 1950s and 1960s turned to the spirituals as the source of their freedom songs was both an effect and an integral part of this many-faceted movement to keep the spirituals alive.[57] And certainly they did remain alive, but more as a historical legacy, a proud heritage, than as a living expression of twentieth-century black consciousness.

The black folk did not follow the pattern I have been describing. Among them spirituals did not suffer a rapid eclipse and then a gradual rebirth. They continued to sing them in the decades following the Civil War, but less and less did the songs of their forbears express their own world view, and in the way of the folk they altered, supplemented, and replaced them by adaptation and adoption of new forms of religious song.[58] In addition to the declining spirituals, Negro religious music in the twentieth century included the old Watts hymns, surge songs, and lining hymns which went back to the colonial period and antedated the spirituals, Moody and Sankey revival songs of the late nineteenth century, and the newer standard hymns of white and black composition. In the 1920s, for instance, the Negro minister Charles P. Jones of Christ Church, Jackson, Mississippi, wrote the following hymn for his parishioners:

> Reap what we sow! Oh, solemn thought,
> With what an awful meaning fraught!
> Yet surely we to judgment go
> To reap just what in life we sow.[59]

While such songs show amalgamation of white and black religious practices and sensibilities, changes in black religious consciousness are better approached by concentrating on two more distinctive forms of religious music: religious disaster songs and gospel music.

Given their sacred mentality, the line between purely religious and purely secular songs was not clear to the slaves, and some of this blurring remained well after freedom. Guy Johnson's request for spirituals from school children on the Sea Islands frequently brought him such songs as *The Green Grass Grew All Around* and *Johnny's So Long at the Fair*.[60] Many songs, such as this one collected in Burnside, Kentucky, in 1912, began with a secular motif: "I got a yellow gal, / She is my honey, / She's a workin-woman, / Gibs me money," and ended on a religious note: "Gabriel, Gabriel, oil you horn, / Get yoursef ready fur de Reserection Morn. / Great day comin', / Comin' soon."[61] A graphic example of the mixture of the sacred and secular can be found on the Library of Congress recording of a work song Texas prisoners sang in 1934 celebrating the exploits of the legendary figure, Long John, who outwitted the sheriff and all of his deputies and bloodhounds and escaped to freedom. The song began with a description of Long John's escape:

> It's a *long* John,
> He's a *long* gone,

Like a *turkey* through the corn,
Through the *long* corn.

and then, without warning, transformed Long John into the Biblical evangelist John:

Well, my John said,
In the ten chap ten [tenth chapter, tenth verse],
"If a man die,
He will live again."
Well, they crucified Jesus
And they nailed him to the cross;
Sister Mary cried,
"My child is lost!"

With equal abruptness, the song leader and the axemen he was directing moved the song back to the story of Long John's escape:

Says-uh: "Come on, gal,
And-uh shut that do',"
Says, "The dogs is comin'
And I've got to go."[62]

The structure, form, and tone of religious songs could be used to speak of secular events. A young girl, standing with her parents as their house burned to the ground, spontaneously sang of her grief much as she might have in church:

Oh Lawd, Papa had some matches,
Took an' lef' 'em in de closet, Lawd,
Rat chawed de matches, Lawd,
Cotch'd all de clothes on fiah, Lawd.
Us throwed on watah, Lawd,
Couldn't put hit out, Lawd, couldn't put hit out!
An' all Papa's things done burned![63]

This tendency helped to create the religious disaster song which became an increasingly common feature of twentieth-century Negro sacred music. These songs were usually composed by an individual who had the lyrics printed on sheets of paper and sold them for five cents each. They were circulated by the composer, by itinerant street singers, and from the 1920s on by recordings which became an important means of preserving and disseminating religious songs of all kinds. From 1909 until he was interviewed in Coahoma County, Mississippi, in 1942, Charles Haffer, Jr., though himself illiterate, wrote over one hundred songs and supported himself by selling them personally. Following his first disaster songs about the *Titanic* in 1912, which sold three thousand copies, Haffer wrote songs about both world wars, hurricanes, storms, fires, and in all of them one theme predominated: the Hand of God was evident in all events. "Now Christians let's be careful," he wrote after a storm in 1942, "He can send a storm at any time and take us all away."[64] No event was too small to be memorialized in song. A windstorm in Terrebonne Parish, Louisiana, led an anonymous composer to create this song:

> In the last day of September
> In the year 1909
> God Almighty rose in the weather
> And that troubled everybody's mind. . . .
>
> God he is in the wind storm and rain
> And everybody ought to mind.[65]

Songs like these often followed the events they described with bewildering speed. Exactly one week after the *Titanic* sunk, A. E. Perkins boarded a train and found a blind black preacher selling a ballad he had composed explaining the significance of the event: "God Almighty talked like a natural man, / Spoke so the people could understand."[66] No other contemporary event was as celebrated in Negro religious song. The destruction of the *Titanic*, with the loss of 1500 lives, allowed comments on the meanness and inhumanity of the "millionaires and captains and mighty men of wealth" who had "put the poor below so they would be the first to go"; the justice of God who took the wealthy along with the poor:

> Well, that Jacob Nash was a millionaire,
> Lawd, he had plenty of money to spare;
> When the great Titanic was sinkin' down,
> Well, he could not pay his fare.

and the meaninglessness of Man's petty knowledge and possessions:

> And when they were a-building,
> They declared what they could do:
> They could build a ship that water couldn't go through;
> But God with his power in hand
> Showed to the world it could not stand.
> Wasn't it sad when that great ship went down?[67]

Disaster songs allowed the impact of an event to live on. In 1937 Chlotilde Martin of Beaufort County, South Carolina, was still singing of the storm of 1893 in a manner which brought it back to life:

It was on the 27th of August
Eighteen-ninety and three,
A cyclone begin ragin'
En' de people begin to pray
Islant [islands] around us did suffer
And we tremble' here een our home
And when we recognize een it
'Twas de wonderful power of Gawd.

De tin from de roof were taken
Great tree was deah lie low
De houses was broken een pieces
By de wonderful power of Gawd.

Preachers were preaching Gawd gospel,
En' de ooman [women] was singing His praise
All were pleadin' for sentence
An' beggin' Him to be saved.[68]

A sense of protest could be incorporated within the numerous interpretations of the meaning of events, as in this song collected in Columbia, South Carolina, shortly after World War I:

Reason why war did last so long,
So many people was livin' wrong,
Jes' goin' round runnin' down colors and race
An' oughter been beggin' fer little mo' grace.[69]

In a song he composed in May 1941, Charles Haffer had to search no farther than his Bible for the meaning of World War II:

Now brother these must be the days that Daniel spoke about. . . .
Maybe these are the Unclean Spirits that John spoke about. . . .
Causing us to make war.[70]

As late as 1959 Robert Pete Williams was pondering the meaning of a jet crash which took thirty-one lives:

Oh, Lord, oh Lord, I wonder,
I wonder who was in 'em,
Was it childs of God? . . .
Man, I could see when they was fallin' through the air,
Lord, have mercy on the poor people's soul.[71]

During the same decade a black street singer in New Orleans sensed potential disaster in the Soviet Union's attempts to send rockets to the moon:

Oh Russia, let that moon alone!
God told you go till the earth,

God didn't tell you to till the moon! . . .
You can't get God's moon!
Let God's moon alone![72]

The disaster songs resembled the traditional religious mentality in finding patterns of meaning in worldly events and in depicting an active deity
involved in the lives of human beings. But while the spirituals had easily
and naturally assumed the existence of God in every aspect of Man's life,
the newer songs seemed more strident, perhaps less secure, in their need
to prove God's being in the tragedies which everywhere beset humanity.
They appeared to be less certain of the presence of the kind of community
of belief into which the spirituals had fit. Unlike the spirituals the disaster
songs no longer freely negotiated between time dimensions. The omnipotence and omnipresence of God were usually documented not through
the precedents and promises of the past which continued into the present
and created an image of the future, but almost exclusively through the
events of one's own lifetime. The liberating amalgam of time and space
was missing; the focus was insistently, rigidly, upon the present generation.

THE DEVELOPMENT OF GOSPEL SONG

Changes in religious consciousness and world view are more clearly delineated in the gospel songs, which from the 1930s on displaced the spirituals as the most important single body of black religious music. There
were, to be sure, a number of important points of continuity in the consciousness of the gospel songs and the spirituals. In both, God was an
immediate, intimate, living presence. Such gospel titles as *I am Walking
With My Jesus, I Had a Talk With Jesus, I Know God, He's Holding
My Hand, He Has Never Left Me Alone, He Answers Me, Jesus Is Real
to Me, I Want Jesus to Walk With Me, I'm Going to Move in the Room
With the Lord*, abounded.[1] Like the spirituals the gospel songs were songs
of hope and affirmation. Explaining why she refused to give up gospel
music for blues, Mahalia Jackson exclaimed: "Blues are the songs of despair, but gospel songs are the songs of hope. When you sing them you
are delivered of your burden. You have a feeling that here is a cure for
what's wrong. It always gives me joy to sing gospel songs. I get to sing

and I feel better right away."[2] In song after song the singers affirmed: "There's a crown at the end of your road," "Going to live with God," "I've got a home, a home in heaven, I've got a home," "Some day I'm goin'. to see my Jesus," "There'll be joy on tomorrow . . . When my work on earth is through," "I've got heaven in my view Hallelujah."

> I can sing I can shout I can work joyfully
> I can pray I can smile I can feel Christ in me
> I can love I can live I can die peacefully
> For Jesus lives in me.[3]

As important as these similarities are, they are overshadowed by the differences. The overriding thrust of the gospel songs was otherworldly. Emphasis was almost wholly upon God with whom Man's relationship was one of total dependence. These typical gospel titles set the tone: *He's Everything to Me, Only God, He's Everything You Need, He's Got Everything You Need, Give God the Credit, He'll Fill Every Space in Your Life, I Don't Care What the World May Do, The Lord Will Provide, He'll Fix it All, The Lord Will Make a Way Some How.*

> I don't know what I'd do without the Lawd,
> I don't know what I'd do without the Lawd,
> When I look around and see
> What the Lawd has done for me,
> I don't know what I'd do without the Lawd.[4]

> I'm not worried about lov'd ones
> I'm not worried about friends
> Because He makes all my decisions for me;
> Yes, for me.
> He's a mighty good doctor
> I'm so glad that He's a lawyer
> Because He makes all my decisions for me.[5]

Jesus rather than the Hebrew Children dominated the gospel songs. And it was not the warrior Jesus of the spirituals but a benevolent spirit who promised His children rest and peace and justice in the hereafter. Again, titles are instructive: *The Lord Jesus is My All and All, Christ is All, Jesus is All, Jesus Knows and Will Supply My Every Need, Jesus, the Perfect Answer, More of Jesus and Less of Me, Wait on Jesus, I'm Goin' to Bury Myself in Jesus' Arms, Jesus is the Answer to Every Problem, I Live for Jesus, Jesus Will Make it Alright.* The focus was upon heaven, and in the gospel songs, unlike the spirituals, the concept of heaven remained firmly in the future, largely distinct from Man's present situation: "I'm not working for earthly fame / My deeds are not for material gain / . . . in heaven I'll find my reward."[6] There was, asserted one of the songs sung by the Golden Gaters and other gospel quartets in the 1940s, *No Segregation in Heaven.*[7] Where the spirituals proved their point by analogy, precedent, and concrete example, the gospel ethos was largely one of pure faith:

> The Lord will provide,
> The Lord will provide,
> Sometimes another, the Lord will provide.
>
> It may not be in my time;
> It may not be in yours,
> But sometimes another, the Lord will provide.[8]

> I don't know why I have to cry sometime
> I don't know why I have to sigh sometime
> It would be a perfect day but there's trouble in the way
> I don't know why but I'll know by in by.[9]

The religion of the gospel songs remained a sustaining, encouraging, enveloping creed. Nevertheless, it differed markedly from the beliefs of the spirituals. Certainly it recognized and discussed the troubles, sorrows, and burdens of everyday existence but its immediate solutions tended to be a mixture of Christian faith and one variety or another of positive thinking. Touches of American popular culture were increasingly evident: "The best things in life are free," "Just look around and take what God is giving you," "Life can be beautiful."

> If we put away our worries
> And think of good along the way
> Just take the whole world as you find it
> And try to live one day each day
> Life can be beautiful if you live it right today.[10]

In terms of long-range solutions for Man's problems, the gulf between this world and the next had grown wider. There were few songs about the Old Testament heroes, few songs portraying victory in this world. Ultimate change when it came took place in the future in an otherworldly context. Christ, with His promise of a better tomorrow "sometime, somewhere, someday, somehow," was the dominating figure upon whom Man was almost wholly dependent. No longer were temporal and spatial barriers transcended. This world had to be suffered; one had to take comfort from the blessings one had and from the assurances of the Almighty. The world had become increasingly compartmentalized. Thomas Wentworth Higginson's dictum that black religion exhibited "nothing but patience for this life,—nothing but triumph in the next," was far truer of the gospel songs than it had ever been of the spirituals. The sacred world of the antebellum slaves had been diluted if not dissolved. The literacy, the education, the conditions of the outside world had brought with them a cosmology more familiar to modern Western culture.

Gospel songs, of course, no less than the spirituals that preceded them, were more than collections of verbalized ideas and attitudes. As important as the lyrics were, to leave our discussion there without some consideration of the nature of the music and the mode of performance would lose the essence and distort the experience of gospel song. Consideration of these matters necessitates a brief discussion of the relationship between sacred and secular music after slavery. Though the slaves' blurred lines between sacred and secular song persisted after emancipation, as I have shown, the decline of the sacred world view inevitably created increasingly rigid distinctions among large numbers of black religious folk. In the early 1870s Helen Ludlow asked Harry Jarvis, a forty-year-old ex-slave and one-armed veteran of the Civil War, if he would sing some songs other than spirituals—songs he had used to accompany himself at work. His reply was to become familiar to scores of folklorists in the ensuing decades: "Not o' dem corn shuckin' songs, madam. Neber sung none o' dem sence I 'sperienced religion. Dem's wickid songs. . . . Nuffin's good dat ain't religious, madam. Nobody sings dem cornshuckin' songs arter dey's done got religion."[11]

The young William Handy discovered the force of these distinctions in the 1880s when he saved his money and bought himself a cheap guitar. Though his father, an Alabama minister, had sent him for organ lessons, his tolerance ended at the sight of the stringed instrument. "A box," he roared. "A guitar! One of the devil's playthings. Take it away. Take it away, I tell you. Get it out of your hands. Whatever possessed you to bring a sinful thing like that into our Christian home? Take it back where it came from." Handy's ambitions were similarly dampened at school when he told his teacher he wanted to be a musician. Musicians, the latter informed him coldly, were idlers, dissipated characters, whisky drinkers, rounders, social pariahs. Southern white gentlemen—who should serve as the youngster's models—looked upon music as a parlor accomplishment, not as a way of life. That evening his father told him: "Son, I'd rather see you in a hearse. I'd rather follow you to the graveyard than to hear that you had become a musician." When he arrived to sing with the church choir with his violin or cornet under his arm, Handy was convinced he heard one of the old sisters whisper: "Yonder goes de devil."[12]

This combination of religious and social resistance was to plague another black youngster, William Henry Joseph Bonaparte Bertholoff Smith, who, as Willie the Lion Smith, was to become an important jazz pianist. Smith had first learned music at the turn of the century by hearing his mother play the piano and organ in church and then broadened his education by listening to streetcorner quartets and frequenting the local saloons, dance halls, and theaters. When his mother finally bought a piano so her son could practice, he attempted to amalgamate the two styles. After listening to his mother play the familiar hymns he would tell her: "That's all right, but it can be beautified," and then would sit down and play *Sweet and Low* to a ragtime beat: "She actually would run me away from the piano when I'd play a blues or make the tunes she enjoyed playing into ragtime," Smith recalled.

> Back in those early days churchgoing Negro people would not stand for ragtime playing; they considered it to be sinful. Part of that feeling was due to the fact that the popular songs you heard played around in the saloons had bawdy lyrics and when you played in a raggy style, folks would right away think of the bad words and all the hell-raising they heard, or had heard about, in the red-light district.
>
> Yeah, in the front parlor, where the neighbors could hear your playing, you had to sing the proper religious words and keep that lilting tempo down![13]

These attitudes lived on well into the twentieth century. In 1933 John Lomax asked a cotton picker in Texas to sing the ballad of the boll weevil and was told: "Boss, dat a reel. If you wants to get dat song sung, you'll have to git one of dese worl'ly niggers to sing it. I belongs to de church." Lomax was in a better position to get his way when he asked a prisoner in the Nashville State Penitentiary to sing a levee camp holler. The prisoner, known as Black Samson, refused, explaining that as a Hard-Shell Baptist he would be in danger of hell-fire if he sang such a song. With the insensitivity that too frequently characterized the folklorists of the period, Lomax persisted, but the prisoner continued to refuse even when the white chaplain promised he would make it all right with the Lord. He gave in only when the warden, in Lomax's words, "especially urged him to sing." Even then he manifested his uneasiness by prefacing the song he sang into

Lomax's recording equipment with a protest: "It's sho hard lines dat a poor nigger's got to sing a wor'ly song, when he's tryin' to be sancrified; but de warden's ast me, so I guess I'll have to."[14] As late as 1937 when the Reverend Zema Hill of Nashville's Primitive Baptist Church organized a choir and added to it a "rhythmic piano" he was accused of heresy.[15]

It was within this context of a sharpening dichotomy between sacred and secular music that black gospel song developed. No matter how seriously many church folk took the distinctions between these two large genres of black song, the barriers were never complete. One has only to examine the recorded music of the 1920s and 1930s to see how permeable they were in terms of musical style. It was not uncommon during these decades for such blues singers as Charley Patton, Blind Willie McTell, Barbecue Bob, and Blind Lemon Jefferson to record religious songs as well as blues. Thus Patton did not find it incongruous to record blues with such suggestive lines as:

> You can shake it, you can break it, you can hang it on the wall,
> Throw it out the winder, catch it 'fore it falls, . . .
> My jelly, my roll, sweet mama don't you let it fall.

at the same time that he recorded fourteen sides of such religious songs as:

> Some day, some happy day, crying praise, praise be.
> I'll live with Christ for ages, some day.[16]

Accompanying themselves on the guitar, the style these singers brought to both types of music was often indistinguishable. Conversely, the recordings of such sacred singers as Arizona Dranes and Blind Willie Johnson and such groups as the Cotton Top Mountain Sanctified Singers and the Memphis Sanctified Singers were commonly marked by the rocking, driving beat that characterized the blues and jazz of the period. Recording for a black audience, they made no concessions to the "developed" singing of the jubilee songs as they cried out in harsh, urgent, unpolished tones: "Sweet Heaven is my home," "Trouble will soon be over," "I know I got religion and I ain't ashamed," "God don't never change," "I know His blood can make me whole," "Ain't it grand to be a Christian," incorporating all of the musical influences and sounds they had grown up with.[17]

Within the church these amalgamated sounds first became prominent in the Holiness and Spiritualist sects that developed at the turn of the century. While many churches within the black community sought respectability by turning their backs on the past, banning the shout, discouraging

enthusiastic religion, and adopting more sedate hymns and refined, concertized versions of the spirituals, the Holiness churches constituted a
revitalization movement with their emphasis upon healing, gifts of
prophecy, speaking in tongues, spirit possession, and religious dance. Musically, they reached back to the traditions of the slave past and out to the
rhythms of the secular black musical world around them. They brought
into the church not only the sounds of ragtime, blues, and jazz but also
the instruments. They accompanied the singing which played a central
role in their services with drums, tambourines, triangles, guitars, double
basses, saxophones, trumpets, trombones, and whatever else seemed musically appropriate. The spirit of their music was summed up years later
by a church patriarch who paraphrased Martin Luther: "The devil should
not be allowed to keep all this good rhythm."[18]

That the Devil was not allowed to is attested to by many contemporary
black observers. In Chicago around the time of World War I, Langston
Hughes, then still in his teens, encountered the music of the Holiness
churches for the first time: "I was entranced by their stepped-up rhythms,
tambourines, hand clapping, and uninhibited dynamics, rivaled only by
Ma Rainey singing the blues at the old Monogram Theater. . . . The
music of these less formal Negro churches early took hold of me, moved
me and thrilled me."[19] The jazz bassist Pops Foster found musical inspiration in the Holiness churches: "Their music was something. They'd clap
their hands and bang a tambourine and sing. Sometimes they had a piano
player, and he'd really play a whole lot of jazz. . . . The first time I heard
one of their bands was about 1930 in Washington, D.C. We used to hurry
to finish our theater job so we could go listen to them play. They really
played some great jazz on those hymns they played."[20] The blues singer
T-Bone Walker had a similar experience: "The first time I ever heard a
boogie-woogie piano was the first time I went to church. That was the
Holy Ghost Church in Dallas, Texas. That boogie-woogie was a kind of
blues, I guess. Then the preacher used to preach in a bluesy tone sometimes. You even got the congregation yelling 'Amen' all the time when
his preaching would stir them up—his preaching and his bluesy tone."[21]
During the 1930s Zora Neale Hurston, collecting folklore for the WPA in
Florida, reported: "In Jacksonville there is a jazz pianist who seldom has a
free night; nearly as much of his business comes from playing for 'Sanctified' church services as for parties. Standing outside of the church, it is
difficult to determine just which kind of engagement he is filling at the
moment."[22] The clarinetist Garvin Bushell, speaking of the jazz scene in

New York City when he arrived there in 1919, also testified to the musical interaction with the church: "They sang the blues in church; the words were religious, but it was the blues. They often had a drummer and a trumpet player."[23]

Indeed, some of the songs collected in Holiness churches were blues in everything but content:

> I woke up this mornin',
>   My mind staid on Jesus.
> I woke up this mornin',
>   My mind on the Lord.
> I woke up this mornin',
>   My mind staid on Jesus.
>   Hallelu, hallelu, halleluia.[24]

The music of the early Holiness churches comprised a wide variety of traditional and newly created songs, including a group of songs written by a Philadelphia Methodist, C. H. Tindley, during the first decade of this century. Neither spirituals nor hymns, Tindley's creations were prototypes of the gospel songs of the post-World War I years:

> When the storms of life are raging, stand by me,
> When the storms of life are raging, stand by me,
> When the world is tossing me,
> Like a ship upon the sea,
> Thou who rulest wind and water, stand by me.[25]

The music of the Holiness churches first penetrated the established denominations through the storefront Baptist and Methodist churches that grew rapidly in the urban centers whose black migrants found the older and larger churches unresponsive to their needs. The development of black gospel music can be understood by looking briefly at the careers of two of its leading early practitioners: Thomas A. Dorsey and Mahalia Jackson.

The son of a Baptist minister, Thomas A. Dorsey was born in Georgia in 1899. Musically precocious, he mastered several instruments by the time he was in his teens and played and sang in the dance halls, theaters, and house parties in and around Atlanta as well as in the church. After World War I he migrated North, settling eventually in Chicago, which he was to help make the mecca of gospel music. Inspired by Tindley's music, he began to write gospel songs early in the 1920s, but throughout that decade he pursued a successful career as a blues musician as well. Known as "Georgia Tom," he was the piano accompanist for the Classic Blues singer

Ma Rainey for several years and wrote, according to his own account, some two hundred blues and other secular songs. In 1928, just two years after composing what was to become his first successful gospel song, *If You See My Saviour, Tell Him That You Saw Me*, he wrote his most popular and lucrative secular song. Together with Tampa Red, he published and recorded *It's Tight Like That*, a song whose sexually charged lyrics helped to sell almost a million recordings and were to return to haunt Dorsey in his later years:

> Now the girl I love is long and slim,
> When she gets it it's too bad, Jim.
> It's tight like that, beedle um bum,
> It's tight like that, beedle um bum,
> Hear me talkin' to you, it's tight like that.

Dorsey's success in the church took a bit longer. For years he printed his religious songs on single sheets in the traditional manner and sold them himself for fifteen cents a copy in the face of a church leadership which found his style of music anathema. "Many are the times I walked from church to church seeking a chance to introduce my songs, my feet soaked from snow, sleet and rain." His first breakthrough came at the National (Negro) Baptist Convention in 1930. His gospel song, *If You See My Saviour*, was performed and swept the convention leading to orders from black Baptist churches throughout the nation. From that time Dorsey devoted himself to gospel music, composing over four hundred songs. So prolific was he that among church people gospel songs were often referred to as "Dorseys." He solidified his success in 1932 with his most famous gospel song, *Precious Lord*, which ultimately was translated into thirty-two languages. Dorsey's description of how he composed that song is similar to the slaves' insistence that their spirituals were inspired by visions: "De Holy Spirit done revealed 'em." A week after the death of his wife and infant son, he sat before a piano seeking consolation: "There in my solitude, I began to browse over the keys like a gentle herd pasturing on tender turf. Something happened to me there. I had a strange feeling inside. A sudden calm—a quiet stillness. As my fingers began to manipulate over keys, words began to fall in place on the melody like drops of water falling from the crevices of a rock:

> Precious Lord take my hand,
> Lead me on, let me stand,
> I am tired, I am weak, I am worn.
> Through the storm, through the night,

Lead me on to the light,
Take my hand precious Lord, lead me home."

Though Dorsey abandoned the world of blues after 1929, the blues did not abandon him, as he admitted in later years: "Blues is a part of me, the way I play piano, the way I write." "I was a blues singer, and I carried that with me into the gospel songs." "I started putting a little of the beat into gospel that we had in jazz. I also put in what we called the riff, or repetitive (rhythmic) phrases. These songs sold three times as fast as those that went straight along on the paper without riffs or repetition." If his music came from the entire black world around him, his lyrics came from the hope of the Christian message, and it is not a coincidence that his first great successes came during the Great Depression. "I wrote to give them something to lift them out of that Depression. They could sing at church but the singing had no life, no spirit. . . . We intended gospel to strike a happy medium for the downtrodden. This music lifted people out of the muck and mire of poverty and loneliness, of being broke, and gave them some kind of hope anyway. Make it anything but good news, it ceases to be gospel."[26]

What Dorsey was to gospel composition Mahalia Jackson was to its performance. Born into a devout Baptist family in 1911, she spent the first sixteen years of her life in New Orleans absorbing the musical sounds of her family's church, the local brass bands, Dixieland jazz, and the blues—especially the records of Bessie Smith, which her worldly cousin Fred brought into the house and which she listened to when no one was at home. She was particularly impressed by the music of the Sanctified church next door to her home, which she contrasted with the "sweet" singing of her own Baptist church: "Those people had no choir and no organ. They used the drum, the cymbal, the tambourine, and the steel triangle. Everybody in there sang and they clapped and stomped their feet and sang with their whole bodies. They had a beat, a powerful beat, a rhythm we held on to from slavery days, and their music was so strong and expressive it used to bring the tears to my eyes." All of these sounds blended into the music she brought with her when she migrated to Chicago in 1928. She experienced the same opposition to her style of gospel singing that Dorsey had: "In those days the big colored churches didn't want me and they didn't let me in. I had to make it my business to pack the little basement-hall congregations and store-front churches and get their respect that way. When they began to see the crowds I drew, the big churches began to sit up and take notice."

Again and again Jackson had to resist attempts to change her singing style. In 1932 a Negro music teacher she consulted stopped her in the midst of her rendition of the spiritual *Standing in the Need of Prayer* and told her to stop hollering: "The way you sing is not a credit to the Negro race. You've got to learn to sing songs so that white people can understand them." Thirty years later she still recalled her reaction vividly: "I felt all mixed up. How could I sing songs for white people to understand when I was colored myself? It didn't seem to make any sense. It was a battle within me to sing a song in a formal way. I felt it was too polished and I didn't feel good about it. I handed over my four dollars to the Professor and left." It was her first and last music lesson. But it was hardly her last criticism. On one occasion a minister rose after she had finished singing and denounced her from the pulpit for lacking dignity. Her response to denunciations of her rocking, swaying rhythm, her shouting, her use of her hands, her feet, her hips, her entire body while singing was always the same: "I had been reading the Bible every day most of my life and there was a Psalm that said: 'Oh, clap your hands, all ye people! Shout unto the Lord with the voice of a trumpet!' If it was undignified, it was what the Bible told me to do. . . . How can you sing of Amazing Grace? How can you sing prayerfully of heaven and earth and all God's wonders without using your hands? I want my hands, . . . my feet . . . my whole body to say all that is in me. I say, 'Don't let the devil steal the beat from the Lord! The Lord doesn't like us to act dead. If you feel it, tap your feet a little—dance to the glory of the Lord.' "[27]

It was a reaction common to the gospel singers of the period. "I'll sing with my hands, with my feet," Willie Mae Ford Smith declared, "—when I got saved, my feet got saved too—I believe we should use everything we got."[28] "Don't let the movement go out of the music," Thomas A. Dorsey warned. "Black music calls for movement! It calls for feeling. Don't let it get away."[29] Many black churchgoers agreed with these exhortations. Anna Wilson of Rosedale, Mississippi, was convinced that only a shouting religion could command the attention of the Lord: "Ef you doan' stamp in de 'ligion hit woan' git no further dan de ceilin'."[30] For many it was this quality that marked the difference between black religion and the more staid practices of the whites. "I stays independent of what white folks tells me when I shouts," Anderson Jackson of South Carolina affirmed. "De Spirit moves me every day, dat's how I stays in. White folks don't feel sich as I does."[31]

Members of the Sanctified churches in Florida felt that whites were ridiculous figures in church, Zora Neale Hurston reported in the 1930s. Negro ministers who emulated the pulpit style of their white colleagues were the objects of derision: "Why he don't preach at all. He just lectures." "Why, he sound like a white man preaching."[32] The superiority of black religious practices was underscored in a number of jokes. One told of a black man on his death bed who, although he had never been a churchgoer, requests that a preacher be sent for. His wife who was a Catholic calls in her priest. Focusing on the white skin of the cleric as he enters the room, the sick man cries out in anguish: "I don't want him. I need a real preacher, honey. I'm dying."[33] The white evangelist Sam Jones was the subject of a widely told anecdote that made the same point. After delivering a sermon to a large gathering of Negroes, Jones was approached by an old woman, who shook his hand vigorously and exclaimed: "Gawd bless you, Brudder Jones. You is everybody's preacher, black as well as white! You may have a white skin, Brudder, but you is sho got a black heart."[34] From the time it was first collected in 1909, through the Great Depression, Negroes in the South sang variants of the lines:

> White man go tuh meetin'.
>   Can't get up a smile;
> Nigger go tuh meetin',
>   Boys, yuh hyeuh him shout a mile.[35]

Mahalia Jackson's insistence upon uninhibited religion, then, reflected a commonly held attitude among the black folk. Jackson's un-self-conscious musical and kinetic style, her interpolated cries of "Lord," "Lord have mercy," "My Lord," "Well, well, well," "Yeah, yeah, yeah," her interaction with her audiences—"sometimes I get right down off the stage on my knees and sing with the folks"—prompted Robert Anderson, one of her fellow gospel singers, to comment: "Mahalia took the people back to slavery times."[36] Dorsey, Jackson, and the many talented gospel singers and composers around them revitalized black religious music by extending the developments that had taken place within the Holiness churches to the more established Negro denominations. They helped bring back into black church music the sounds and the structure of the folk spirituals, work songs, and nineteenth-century cries and hollers; they borrowed freely from the ragtime, blues, and jazz of the secular black world; they helped to keep alive the stylistic continuum that has characterized Afro-American music in the United States. Put simply, the antebellum songs of the praise house and field strongly influenced the work songs, blues, and jazz of the postbellum years which were incorporated into the gospel song that in turn helped to shape the secular rhythm and blues, jazz, and soul music of the post World War II era. All of the developments that have marked black music since the antebellum era took place within the context of a traditional Afro-American musical matrix. Increasingly, as John Szwed has suggested, social function alone became the primary means of distinguishing one black musical genre from another.[37]

To say this is not to deny that black gospel style and performance differed in important ways from that of the slave spirituals. There was, to begin with, the matter of composition. Where spirituals were created and disseminated in folk fashion, gospel music was composed, published, copyrighted, and sold by professionals. Nevertheless, improvisation remained central to gospel music. One has only to listen to the recorded repertory of gospel song to realize that gospel singers rarely sang a song precisely the same way twice and never sang it according to its exact musical notation. Each rendition was a new creation. Gospel singers produced what jazz musicians referred to as "head arrangements" proceeding from their own feelings, from the way in which "the spirit" moved them at the time. This improvisatory element was reflected in the manner in which gospel music was published. In 1956 Kenneth Morris, one of the leading composers and publishers of black gospel music, told an interviewer:

> We don't write it too difficult by including all of the harmony. The people who play it are not interested in harmony. There is no attempt to include perfect cadences and the like. It's not written for trained musicians. . . . A musician is a slave to notes. It's not written for that kind of person. It's written for a person who can get the melody and words and interpret the song for himself. We give only the basic idea and the person suits his own concept. If it were written correctly, we would go out of business. They wouldn't buy it.[38]

Black gospel composers scored the music intended for white consumption fully, indicating the various vocal parts—soprano, alto, tenor, and bass— and the accompaniment, while the music produced for the Negro market included only the minimum ingredients of a vocal line and piano accompaniment. Dorsey estimated that some 60 per cent of his sheet music was purchased by whites. "Negroes don't buy much music," he explained. "A white chorus of one hundred voices will buy one hundred copies of a song. A Negro chorus of the same size will buy two. One for the director and one for the pianist."[39] Most of Dorsey's published sheet music includes the admonition: "Do not print ballads of these songs—Penalty," reflecting the fact that formal publishing and copyrights did not end the Negro practice of circulating new songs in cheaply printed single-sheet versions. That these sheets or "ballits" included only the words and not the music is a further indication of the improvisation characterizing black gospel singing.

A more important distinction between gospel music and spirituals is that the former increased the distance between performer and audience. Where slave spirituals were almost always performed antiphonally by the entire congregation, gospel music was frequently marked by solo and choir singing with the majority of the congregation in the role of audience—a role that did not really exist in slave religious music. This development is undeniably important and again manifests a strong degree of acculturation, yet it needs to be examined more closely. Even in the setting which most clearly distinguished between the singers and their audience—that of the gospel concert in a theater—the audience participated in the music in terms of motor behavior—nodding, tapping, clapping, bodily movement, and dancing in the aisles—and commonly shouted assents and comments. In both the theater and the church, gospel singers reached out to their listeners in a dialogue that embraced familiar topics of concern and reminded everyone present of their roots. Thus the lead singer for the Pilgrim Jubilee Singers would tell his listeners between numbers: "You know I didn't always come from Chicago. Didn't always have it easy. My brothers and I grew up in a little three-room shack in Houston, Mississippi. We didn't have much back then, church, but we had a family altar. Aw, you all don't know what I'm talking about. . . ." The latter phrase, commonly used in sermons by black preachers, was, of course, a signal to the audience to demonstrate that indeed they did know. Similarly, Sister Rosetta Tharpe would introduce her songs by speaking of her youth in Cotton Plant, Arkansas: "I remember when I was a girl, how much love we had. Why, I used to be busy all day, carrying Aunt Lucy and Aunt Jane some po'k chops. You can't get them fresh no more, now they put them in the deep freeze and *embalm* them for months and months. Seems to me, church, the sweetness has gone out of the land."

This dialogue often included specific remembrances of baptisms and conversions—"I got my religion one Tuesday evening in the clay hills of Alabama,"—and such nostalgic songs as Rosetta Tharpe's *Bring Back those Happy Days:*

We healed the sick, we cared for the poor,
  And we even raised the dead

> We greeted each other with a holy kiss,
> Lord bring back those happy days.

In this manner gospel singers invoked a strong sense of communality and helped to perpetuate tradition among a people who had recently uprooted themselves in pursuit of a dream which, in the disillusioning years of post-World War I race riots, lynchings, and discrimination and the poverty of the Great Depression, seemed increasingly hollow.[40]

Just as there was no single black church so there was no uniform performance of gospel song. Again the increasing heterogeneity of Afro-American culture after slavery is crucial to an understanding of black consciousness. Religious affiliation became the most important variable in determining the style of musical performance. In the Negro Presbyterian, Congregational, and Episcopal churches, attended for the most part by upper- and upper-middle-class blacks, singing generally was confined to congregational or choral performances of standard hymns or selected spirituals or "anthems." Many of the larger Baptist and Methodist churches featured a more varied musical fare, often employing two choirs, one of which sang hymns in the Euro-American tradition and the other of which sang black gospel songs. In the Holiness and Spiritualist churches and the smaller or storefront Baptist and Methodist churches, attended by the mass of lower-middle-class and lower-class blacks, the singing of contemporary gospel songs, old hymns, and songs from the spiritual tradition by the congregation and by a choir, where one existed, predominated. But even when a choir was present the performance was marked by enthusiastic congregational participation. In his description of a service at the Bible Way Church of Jesus Christ Our Lord in Washington, D.C., in 1969, Donald Smith has described how the gospel choir and the congregation often became one. Late in the service the choir sang the gospel song

> Guide me gently Jesus as I go-o
> Guide me as I travel to and fro-o
> Lead me if I stray . . .
> Oh guide me!

As they repeated the line "Oh guide me!" over and over, "The members of the choir have melted into the congregation and still the music goes on; the two groups are one writhing, hand-clapping, thigh-slapping, glory-shouting company, passing into various shades of unconsciousness. . . . The rhythm is still going, except it has been taken over by everybody."

In these churches music often dominated the services to such an extent that it was not uncommon for the pastor to remind his flock that "singing won't get you into heaven," or that "you can't be saved just by singing." Nevertheless, black ministers appreciated the importance of religious singing and the rituals that accompanied it. Thus one minister invited his congregation to attend the regular Sunday evening service by telling them: "Bring along your dancing shoes, because the Spirit is going to come for sure, and he gets in your feet and you run." Vattel Elbert Daniel's notes on the congregations' reactions to sermons, prayers, and singing in urban Negro Baptist, Methodist, and Holiness churches, of what he termed "semidemonstrative" or "ecstatic" persuasion as opposed to the larger and more formal "liturgical" or "deliberative" churches, indicates how many elements of antebellum religious ritual and style lived on among large numbers of the black folk: "Assents and shouts of approval . . . running, dancing, and swooning . . . crying . . . rapid and rhythmic movements . . . yelling, tapping, stamping, shouting, and, in some instances, running and jumping . . . loud praying while standing with hands uplifted . . . rhythmic hand-clapping and foot-patting."[41]

To compare the words, the overt consciousness, of gospel songs with their style and performance is to reveal what appears to be a conundrum. While the message of black gospel music manifested the dissolution of the traditional sacred world and a high degree of acculturation to a modern religious consciousness, its style and performance were being revitalized by an intensified connection with the roots of traditional Afro-American religion and the sounds and styles of the twentieth-century secular music of the black community. This apparent paradox can serve as a model for the type of acculturation that has characterized black America in the twentieth century. Negro acculturation has often taken place within and been facilitated by a communal milieu. It has not been a simple one-dimensional process of switching allegiances or identities or life styles. It has been a complex process of shifting emphases and reaffirmations: of permitting certain new traits to permeate but of simultaneously re-emphasizing specific traditional loyalties and characteristics. Acculturation as symbolized by developments in language, religion, and, as the next chapter will demonstrate, secular song, saw not merely the emergence of the new but the revitalization of the old. It has been a dual process of creation and re-creation, of affirmation and reaffirmation, of looking both without and within the black community for the means of sustenance and identity and survival.

4

THE
RISE
OF
SECULAR
SONG

Me, I want to explain myself so bad. I want to have myself understood. And the music, it can do that. The music, it's my whole story.

Sidney Bechet[1]

. . . you can tell it to the public as a song, in a song. . . . You express yourself in a song like that. Now this particular thing reach others because they have experienced the same condition in life so naturally they feel what you are sayin' because it happened to them. It's a sort of thing that you kinda like to hold to yourself, yet you want somebody to know it. I don't know how you say that two ways: you like somebody to know it, yet you hold it to yourself. . . . but there's some things that have happened to me that I wouldn't dare tell, . . . but I would sing about them. Because people in general they takes the song as an explanation for themselves—they believe this song is expressing their feelin's instead of the one that singin' it. They feel that maybe I have just hit upon somethin' that's in their lives, and yet at the same time it was some of the things that went wrong with me too.

Henry Townsend[2]

If during slavery it was the secular songs that were occasional and the religious songs that represented the ethos of the black folk, in freedom the situation began to reverse itself. Secular song became increasingly important in black folk culture in the decades following freedom. Negroes were thrust into the larger world, and their response to their experience was couched more and more in explicitly worldly terms. The sacred world was not shattered immediately and decisively for all Negroes in the period after the Civil War; it continued, with different degrees of intensity and pervasiveness, to inform the consciousness and world view of large numbers of blacks both North and South. But never again was it to occupy the central position of the antebellum years. The aesthetics and forms of Afro-American slave folk culture remained fundamentally important throughout the years of freedom, but their content was reshaped by the experiences of the new existence and the new imperatives.

THE SHAPING OF BLACK SECULAR MUSIC

By now it should be evident that there were no cataclysmic demarcation points in Afro-American history which marked the absolute decline of one form of folk expression and the rise of another. There were rough watersheds, of course: the forced transportation of Africans from their homeland to the New World, the conversion of slaves to Christianity, the abolition of slavery, the large-scale migration of blacks from the country to the city and from the South to the North. But these—even emancipation itself in terms of its effects—were cumulative changes spread over an extensive time period and allowing for a gradual admixture of various styles and influences. Just as the sacred world of black slaves did not disappear all at once to be replaced by a new consciousness, so too the secular forms of folk expression that arose and became central after emancipation were the product of many years and diverse influences.

Not the least of these was the influence of slavery itself. The experiences, expressions, and musical styles of the slaves lived on long after slavery. The white song collector, Mina Monroe, who grew up on the Labranche Plantation in St. Charles Parish, Louisiana, in the late nineteenth century, recalled vividly the songs of the black workers:

> They were songs of long ago, the same songs my grandmother had heard, from much the same people, in her childhood, folk-songs that had com-

posed themselves as incidents occurred; . . . The old mammy rocked us
to sleep, gave us our meals, even bathed us, to the tune of these songs;
. . . When asked where they came from she would insist that they had
always existed; that her mother's mother had taught them to her as she
had been taught before.[1]

It is impossible to read through a collection of black work or social songs
collected in the late nineteenth or early twentieth centuries and not be
struck by the presence of antebellum elements. "Juba dis and Juba dat /
And Juba killed de yaller cat. / Juba! Juba!" remained popular well into
this century, as did "Run, nigger, run, de patter-roller get you, / Run,
nigger run, it's almost day," and these variants of a lyric first reported
by Frederick Douglass in slavery:

> She sift de meal, she gimme de dust,
> She bake de bread, she gimme de crust,
> She eat de meat, she gimme de skin,
> An' dat's de way she tuck me in.[2]

In the early 1830s Thomas D. Rice heard an old Louisville Negro, Jim
Crow, sing the refrain

> Wheel about, turn about, do jus' so,
> And ebry time I wheel about, I jump Jim Crow.

which Rice appropriated and transformed into one of the earliest and most
popular minstrel songs. In this way Rice helped to inaugurate the para-
doxical practice by which white minstrels frequently made stage hits out
of bits of black songs, spreading them through the South where they were
heard for the first time by other slaves who in their turn appropriated
them and reintegrated them into the black tradition. Thus in 1915 North
Carolina Negroes shucking corn sang a song virtually identical to the one
Rice had heard more than eighty years earlier.

> Fust upon yo' heel-top,
> Den upon yo' toe,
> Ev'ry time I turn aroun'
> I jump Jim Crow.[3]

Many other antebellum minstrel songs retained a place in black song
throughout the early decades of the twentieth century. In every section of
the South, Negroes continued to sing of the master or mistress who reneged on their promise of freedom:

> My ole Missis promise me
> When she died she'd set me free;

> Now ole Missis dead an' gone,
> She lef' ole Sambo hillin' up corn.

Other verses could be more ominous:

> Yes, my ole Mosser promise me;
> But "his papers" didn' leave me free.
> A dose of pizen he'ped 'im along.
> May de Devil preach 'is funer'l song.

During the Great Depression blacks in rural Louisiana could still be heard singing:

> My ole mistress promised me
> Before she died she would set me free. . . .
> Now she's dead and gone to hell,
> I hope the devil will burn her well.

The song remained a fixture of the oral tradition. Folklorists in Coahoma County, Mississippi, were able to collect versions of it in the early 1940s, and as late as the mid-1960s Bruce Jackson heard it being sung as a work song in the Texas prisons.[4] Equally popular was the old minstrel song dating from the 1850s relating the experiences of a slave owner and his light-skinned female slave:

> Old master had a yellow gal,
> He brought her from the south;
> Her hair was wropped so close an' tight,
> She couldn't shet her mouf. . . .
>
> Her head looked like a coffee pot,
> Her nose looked like the spout,
> Her mouf looked like the fireplace
> With the ashes taken out.[5]

Newman White has argued that songs like these—and there were many of them—"testify to the conservatism which is one of the chief traits of the folk-Negro,"[6] and doubtless he is correct. Yet they are a testament to much more. The themes common to so many of these antebellum songs make it clear that their continued popularity after slavery was only partly related to the strong ties of tradition. It is significant that a high proportion of the pre- and post-Civil War minstrel songs that lived on among black folk revolved around grievances against the master class. Songs like the ones just quoted complained about white duplicity and parodied the sexual relations between white masters and mulatto slaves. Others, such as the popular *Blue Tail Fly*, took only slightly disguised pleasure in the death of a master:

> Ole Massa gone, now let 'im rest;
> Dey say all t'ings am for de best.
> I nebber forget till de day I die,
> Ole Massa an' dat blue-tail fly.
>
> Jim crack corn, I don't care,
> Jim crack corn, I don't care,
> Jim crack corn, I don't care,
> Ole Massa's gone away.[7]

In general, the minstrel tunes that made their way firmly into the black repertory looked back on slavery and slaveowners with something less than reverence. Thus a song which won "everlasting shouts of applause" for the white minstrel Dan Emmett when he performed it in the 1840s was still being sung by blacks in Jackson County, Alabama, in 1916:

> Ol marster was a stingy man
> And everybody know'd it;
> Kept good likker in his house
> And never said here goes it.[8]

Antebellum white Southerners may have delighted in such songs as harmless and amusing burlesques and found in them relief for any repressed feelings of guilt and ambivalence they might have had concerning slavery. For the blacks who sang them, they were clearly outlets for a quite different complex of emotions. Just as the slaves found that they could most easily articulate their longing for freedom by projecting it into the future world, thus legitimizing it through their spirituals, so their descendants living in the repressive atmosphere of the turn-of-the-century South could most safely vent their complaints against the whites and the social system by projecting them back into the past and giving them the appearance of nostalgia and not protest. They were able to utilize the commonplaces of the minstrel idiom to criticize, parody, and sharply comment on their society and their situation.

The mixture of diverse elements that made up black secular music is well illustrated by the influence of minstrel songs but was not confined to them. After slavery Negroes were more subject to musical influences of all kinds than ever before. The rigid walls of segregation erected in every southern state at the turn of the century proved to be no more effective in preventing the relatively free trade of musical ideas and forms than the structure of antebellum slavery itself had been. In the late nineteenth and early twentieth centuries, southern whites and blacks shared a large common stock of folk songs. Such ballads as *Jesse James, Casey Jones, Joe Turner, John Henry, Brady, Railroad Bill, Delia, Lilly, Frankie and Johnnie*, and scores of others were widely known and sung by both groups. One has only to compare the many folk song collections compiled in this period or the records made by white and black country singers in the 1920s and 1930s to understand the deep pool of shared traditions.[9] Nor was black-white musical admixture limited to folk song; it was perpetuated and enhanced by vaudeville, phonograph records, movies, and the radio. Derrick Stewart-Baxter has shown the influence that the heterogeneous musical styles of vaudeville, the music halls, the tent shows, and the black variety circuit had upon almost every one of the Classic Blues singers of the 1920s. Ma Rainey was a good example. While traveling through the South with the Rabbit Foot Minstrels during the first two decades of this century, she sang a combination of minstrel songs, popular vaudeville and burlesque tunes, folk ballads, and traditional blues. She, and the Classic Blues singers who followed her, were to add what Paul Oliver has called a "conscious artistry" to the blues, even while they were imbuing popular songs from the American stage with the expressive qualities of the blues.[10] This eclecticism was not confined to professional singers. Edmond Souchon of New Orleans remembered the singing of the black nursemaid who used to care for him in 1901 and 1902: "Her songs were an admixture of Creole folk songs, church hymns, and up-to-date hits of the late '90s or early 1900s."[11] In 1911 Howard Odum commented upon the popularity of modern "coon-songs," "ragtimes," and the "latest hits" among blacks: "Young negroes pride themselves on the number of such songs they can sing, at the same time that they resent a request to sing the older melodies. Very small boys and girls sing the difficult airs of the new songs with surprising skill, until one wonders when and how they learned so many words and tunes."[12]

What is significant in all this is that in spite of their greater exposure to the musical styles of the larger society, in spite of the fact that as the century progressed larger and larger numbers of Negroes could listen freely to—indeed, could hardly escape—the music of the white majority, Afro-American music remained distinctive. In part, of course, this was because a large body of the white music they heard had already been profoundly influenced by black musical styles and thus could be reintegrated into the black tradition with little strain, and in part it was because black Americans have always had a penchant for refashioning the music they borrowed to fit their own aesthetic priorities and social needs. This latter phenomenon impressed all of the major collectors of black music. "The notes to the songs in my whole collection," Newman White wrote, "show nothing so clearly as the tendency of Negro folk-song to pick up material from any source and, by changing it or using it in all sorts of combinations, to make it definitely its own." Similarly, Odum and Johnson commented on "the facility of the Negroes in producing their own songs from material of any sort." Thus despite "the negro's fondness for the new and popular coon-songs," Odum observed, "these songs often lose their original words and take on words of negro origin."[13]

Many examples could be given of the ways in which Negroes altered the folk and popular songs they were exposed to, but a few will suffice. In 1909 country whites in Mississippi sang this version of a folk song common throughout the South:

> I wouldn't marry a preacher
>   I'll tell you the reason why:
> He goes all over the country,
>   And eats all the chicken pie.
>
> I wouldn't marry a widow,
>   I'll tell you the reason why:
> She's got so many children,
>   They'd make the biscuits fly.

In that same year, Mississippi Negroes sang the identical song with their own distinctive lyrics:

> I wouldn't marry a yaller gal;
> I'll tell you the reason why:
> She's all the time sitting in another man's lap
> And telling her husband lies.
>
> I wouldn't marry a black gal;
> I'll tell you the reason why:
> Her nose is always snotty,
> And her lips is never dry.[14]

During World War I the white folklorist John Jacob Niles set out to collect the songs of American soldiers in France. To his disappointment he found that among white troops original songs were rare: "They went to Broadway for their music, contenting themselves with the ready-made rhymes and tunes of the professional song-writers." He was about to abandon his project when he encountered Negro troops. At last, he exulted, "I had discovered something original—a kind of folk music brought up to date and adapted to the war situations—at the same time savoring of the haunting melodic value found in the Negro music I had known as a boy in Kentucky." Time and again he was struck by the Negro's unwillingness to accept the stock soldier songs:

> He'll remanufacture something he can understand . . . he'll make it over to suit his own personal immediate needs. Servitude to . . . established opinion, or to the followers of standardized forms would be a kind of mental slavery that the Negro would not endure. He has sung his songs the way he has because they pleased him that way. . . . The songs sent out by a so-called "Entertainment Board" operating from Tin Pan Alley, New York, got nowhere with the Negro soldiers. The white soldier sang these flag-waving monstrosities; but the black soldier did things like this . . .

> What do the Generals and the Colonels do,
>   I'll tell you—I'll tell you,
> Figure out just how the privates ought to do
>   The dirty little jobs for Jesus.

> Fifty thousand privates died for Democracy,
>   Dirty little job for Jesus,
> Twenty Major Generals got the D.S.C.,
>   Another dirty little job for Jesus.

The songs Niles heard were sung in the traditional communal style and consisted of sharp comments on the current situation:

> Jined de army fur to git free clothes—
> Lordy, turn your face on me—
> What we're fightin' 'bout, nobody knows—
> Lordy, turn your face on me.

Black troops even turned the one song universally known to British and American troops to their own purposes:

> Mademoiselle from Armentiers, parlez-vous,
> Mademoiselle from Armentiers, parlez-vous,
> I wouldn't give my high-brown belle,
> For every mademoiselle dis side o' hell—
> Inky Dinky, parlez-vous.[15]

A generation later, another folklorist, Leah Yoffie, was to discover among Negroes the same penchant for originality and innovation in song. Investigating the singing of play songs among kindergarten and elementary school children in St. Louis in 1944, Yoffie found that children in the white playgrounds were still singing and moving to such songs as *Sally Waters* in exactly the same fashion as she and her friends had in the 1890s:

> Little Sally Water,
> Sitting in a saucer,
> Weeping and crying for some one to love her.
> Rise, Sally, rise,
> Wipe off your eyes;
> Turn to the east,
> Turn to the west,
> Turn to the one that you love the best.

Young black children, however, sang their own version:

> Little Sally Walker,
> Sitting in a saucer,
> Weeping and crying for a nice young man.
> Rise, Sally, Rise;
> Wipe your weeping eyes.
> Put your hand on your hip,
> Let your backbone slip;
> Shake it to the east, O baby;
> Shake it to the west;
> Shake it to the one you love the best.

Not only the words but the gestures accompanying these play songs differed from those of the white children: "They have syncopated the rhythm, and they accompany the hand-clapping with a 'jazz' and 'swing' rhythm of the body."[16]

Throughout the twentieth century, then, Negroes felt free to transform whatever song traditions they were exposed to into entities of their own creation for their own use. During the Great Depression, Clyde (Kingfish) Smith, a black fish peddler in Harlem, found a direct relationship between his sales and the originality of his cries. Sometimes his songs were completely his own compositions:

> Yo, Ho, Ho, Fish Man!
> Bring down your dishpan!
> Fish ain't but five cents a pound.
> So come on down,
> And gather around,
> I got the best fish
> That's in this town.

More often his songs were his own versions of such currently popular hits as *Stormy Weather*

> I can't go home
> Till all my fish is gone.
> Stormy weather.
> I can't keep my fish together,
> Sellin' 'em all the time.

Minnie the Moocher, Tisket a Tasket, or the Yiddish tune, *Bei Mir Bist Du Shon,* which the Andrews Sisters had made popular throughout the nation:

> Bei mir bist du shon,
> I got big brudder fish again.
> Bei mir bist du shon,
> I think they're grand.
> I could say bello bello,
> And even voom de vah.
> That would only tell you,
> How grand they are.
> Bei mir bist du shon,
> I got flounders again.
> Bei mir bist du shon,
> I know they're grand.

"This," Smith commented, "goes over good in either Jewish or colored neighborhoods, but I have to swing it up in the colored neighborhoods."[17]

The eclecticism of black secular song was composed not merely of the mixture of white and black components but also of a combination of the varied and diverse styles common to Afro-American culture. As Charles Keil has pointed out, "The Afro-American tradition represents not only a variety of mixtures between European and African elements but a series of blendings within itself."[18] The cross-fertilization between sacred and secular black music has already been discussed in Chapter 3. There was, of course, resistance to this interaction, as the young William Handy and Willie the Lion Smith discovered so graphically. But in spite of their difficulties, in spite of all the angry verbiage about "devil songs," Handy and Smith and a significant proportion of other black youngsters imbibed and reflected the musical idioms of both the church and the secular world. Nor was there any necessary inner tension in the amalgamation. In any case, as Smith liked to point out, "All the different forms can be traced back to Negro church music."[19] Almost two generations after Handy and

Smith were raised, the black singer Nina Simone experienced similar difficulties and came to precisely the same conclusions: "Mama and them were so religious that they wouldn't allow you to play boogie-woogie in the house, but would allow you to use the same boogie-woogie *beat* to play a gospel tune. I just don't agree with this attitude because our music *crosses* all those lines. Negro music has *always* crossed all those lines."[20] In other homes the lines were crossed with less difficulty. Percy Heath, the bass player who was born in 1923 in Wilmington, North Carolina, and who grew up in Philadelphia, has described the heterogeneity of his musical background:

> Pop was an automobile mechanic. He was a wild little guy, a great guy, and sharp and handsome. He played clarinet with the Elks. . . . He had Bessie Smith records, and every once in a while he'd pull out his clarinet and do Ted Lewis or his own Silas Green routine—Silas Green from New Orleans. . . . My mother was a hairdresser. She was a choir singer, and her mother before her, in the Baptist church, where I spent a lot of time when I was growing up. Those old sisters screaming and falling out in church, you felt something going through you when you watched them. We had a family quartet. My grandmother sang alto and my mother soprano. I used to sing on a sepia kiddie hour on the radio, and the kids who made it on the show got special passes to the Lincoln Theatre, where we would get to go backstage and shake hands with Fats Waller and Louis Armstrong and Duke Ellington.[21]

Bessie Smith . . . Ted Lewis . . . Silas Green . . . the Baptist Church . . . Fats Waller . . . Louis Armstrong . . . Duke Ellington. From this musical crucible emerged not merely a syncretism of the sacred and the secular but of the many varied components of black secular music as well. Jelly Roll Morton (Ferdinand Joseph La Menthe), the New Orleans jazz pianist, has testified that around 1902 the bars in which he played catered to no single exclusive group. Men of all kinds rubbed elbows and styles: "St. Charles millionaires . . . longshoremen and the illiterate screwsmens from down on the river." In the midst of this environment, young urban jazzmen like the teen-aged Morton absorbed the music and the images of black workers as readily as they learned to imitate the elegant life styles of the millionaires.[22]

The interchange could be complex and it could involve dance as well as song. Shortly before World War I, Willie the Lion Smith was playing the piano in a New York bar which was frequented by Gullah and Geechee Negroes from the Carolina and Georgia Sea Islands who worked on the ships and the docks of the nearby West Sixties piers. "Those

Geechies really went for our style of playing," Smith remembered. "Our soft, slow, four-o'clock-in-the-morning music got to those folks from the South. . . . by this time we had learned to play the natural twelve-bar blues that evolved from the spirituals." The evening began with the dancing of two-steps, waltzes, and schottisches and ended in wild improvisation. "It was from the improvised dance steps that the Charleston dance originated. . . . all it really amounted to was a variation of a cotillion step brought to the North by the Geechies. There were many variations danced at the Casino and this usually caused the piano player to make up his own musical variation to fit the dancing."[23]

Thus the music and dance of the country and city, of white and black, of the folk and the commercial music hall, of the church and the street corner, met and amalgamated. At first the musical variations were shuttled back and forth from North to South and city to country by the migratory patterns of so many southern blacks; ultimately the phonograph and the radio played central roles in the constant process of syncretization. The result was that black music had no single locus; it existed wherever Negroes did. The career of Willie the Lion Smith is instructive in this respect. Although he was born in Goshen, New York, in 1897 and raised in Newark, New Jersey, where he was taken at the age of four, his musical education was strikingly similar to those of the New Orleans jazzmen:

> I first heard the blues sung while I was still a barefoot boy out of New Jersey. It was up around Haverstraw, New York, where they had around thirty-five brickyards. The yards employed Negroes to load and unload the millions of bricks, and when you got anywhere near to that town, you could hear the workers chanting and singing. Many of the songs you heard had things in them you read about in the Bible, or were familiar melodies from the church songs. They sang them in the style that is known as spiritual, or blues, today.

This authentic black jazz musician served his musical apprenticeship on the river boats not of the Mississippi but of the Hudson; he learned his style as a boy in the churches not of the rural South but the urban North, and by doing odd jobs in the dives and bars not of New Orleans but of the black tenderloin district in Newark.[24]

Similarly, the black clarinetist, Garvin Bushell, was well versed in traditional and contemporary Afro-American music by the time he arrived in New York City in 1919, although he had lived his entire seventeen years in Springfield, Ohio.

> I started on the piano when I was six . . . and *Maple Leaf Rag* was one
> of the first things I heard. People then were also playing the fast western,
> what later came to be called boogie woogie. It meant a fast bass, and it was
> said to have come out of Texas.
>
> We first heard instrumental ragtime in the circus bands which usually
> had about fourteen men—brass, clarinets and rhythm. They were Negro
> bands; the players improvised; and they played blues. They traveled all
> over the country, but the men in the band were mostly from Florida,
> Georgia, Tennessee, Louisiana.[25]

Young Northerners like Bushell were influenced as well by a series of
bands sent out by the Jenkins Orphanage of Charleston, South Carolina,
in the early twentieth century. These black youngsters, in their nonde-
script uniforms, would gather in a circle on the street corners of cities as
far north as New York playing what Leonard De Paur, who as a boy heard
them in Trenton, New Jersey, called "the most positive ragtime you ever
heard," improvising dance steps to their own rhythms, passing the hat,
and spreading the word.[26]

The career of Leadbelly (Huddie Ledbetter) is also revealing. Although he matured in the Deep South and in the isolation of southern prisons, his subsequent career in the North exposed him to a wide variety of
musical styles which he assimilated easily. His recorded output included
a fascinating blend of work songs, the songs of black prisoners, children's
ditties, spirituals, folk blues, bar-room ballads, pop songs from Tin Pan
Alley, and propagandistic pseudo-folk songs. He sang them all with equal
seriousness. "As he was a folksinger, not a folklorist," Daniel Hoffman has
observed, "all of these are equally admissible to his canon."[27] And they
were equally admissible to the canon of the larger community of blacks
who fashioned a music that knew neither rigid geographic nor stylistic
boundaries but that remained nonetheless their own cultural creation.

SECULAR MUSIC AND THE BLACK
COMMUNITY: WORK SONGS

In exasperation with those folklorists who insisted that a true folk song
had to be of unknown authorship and be transmitted through the oral tradition, the blues singer Big Bill Broonzy once remarked: "I guess all songs

is folk songs. I never heard no horse sing 'em."[1] While his interpretation of folk music may have been too all-inclusive, Broonzy was reflecting the fact that for Negroes, probably more than for any other group in the United States, music was, and remained, a *participant* activity rather than primarily a performer-audience phenomenon. In freedom as in slavery, this folk quality of black music is precisely what makes it such an important medium for getting at the thought, spirit, and history of the very segment of the Negro community that historians have rendered inarticulate through their neglect. This is evident in the recollections of Muddy Waters (McKinley Morganfield) concerning his boyhood in Clarksdale, Mississippi, during the 1920s:

> I was just a boy and they put me to workin' right along side the men. I handled the plough, chopped cotton, did all of them things. Every man would be hollerin' but you don't pay that no mind. Yeah, course I'd holler too. You might call them blues but they was just made-up things. Like a feller be workin' or most likely some gal be workin' near and you want to say somethin' to 'em. So you holler it. Sing it. Or maybe to your mule or something or it's gettin' late and you wanna go home. I remember I was always singin', "I cain't be satisfied, I be all troubled in mind." Seems to me like I was always singin' that, because I was always singin' jest the way I felt, and maybe I didn't exactly *know* it, but I jest didn't like the way things were down there—in Mississippi.[2]

Lydia Parrish has observed that by the late 1880s the blacks in her southern New Jersey neighborhood—many of whom were escaped slaves or their descendants—"began to pattern their behavior after that of the silent white folk, and from that time on, little of their singing was heard." In 1901 Georgia Bryan Conrad, who grew up in the South, lamented that while in her youth "the Negroes were always singing. . . . Nothing is in greater contrast to that time than the quietness of the Negroes now."[3] I have already noted the persistent tendency to write premature obituaries for Afro-American folk music. Still, complaints like these cannot be dismissed lightly. Silence was unquestionably one of the fruits of acculturation. The whites whom many blacks were being taught to emulate did not accompany their everyday tasks with song, and the modern society to which they were being acclimated was less conducive to un-self-conscious vocalization than the agricultural milieu that had enveloped them so exclusively before emancipation. And yet music remained an integral part of black communities and culture, especially when they are contrasted to neighboring racial and ethnic groups.

For many Negro youngsters growing up at the turn of the century, music seemed to be everywhere—in the fields, in the towns, in the cities. Danny Barker, the jazz guitarist and banjo player, has testified that the streets of New Orleans were filled with musical sounds:

> One of my pleasantest memories . . . was how a bunch of us kids, playing, would suddenly hear sounds. It was like a phenomenon, like the Aurora Borealis—maybe. The sounds of men playing would be so clear, but we wouldn't be sure where they were coming from. So we'd start trotting, start running—"It's this way!" "It's that way!"—And sometimes, after running for a while, you'd find you'd be nowhere near that music. But that music could come on you any time like that.[4]

Jelly Roll Morton, recalling the tenderloin district of New Orleans around 1902, agreed: "Music was pouring into the streets from every house. . . . I'd go to sleep to the sound of the mechanical piano playing ragtime tunes, and when I woke up in the morning it would still be playing. . . . Little boys and grown-ups would walk along the avenues, swaying and whistling jazz tunes."[5] W. C. Handy, roaming through the Mississippi Delta in the late 1890s and early 1900s, found that southern Negroes sang about everything: "Trains, steamboats, steam whistles, sledge hammers, fast women, mean bosses, stubborn mules—all become subjects for their songs. They accompany themselves on anything from which they can extract a musical sound or rhythmical effect, anything from a harmonica to a washboard."[6] This was still true during World War I. Arthur Little, a white officer with the black 15th New York Volunteer Infantry, reported from France: "Our men sang while they marched; they sang while they cooked; they sang while they washed their clothes and while they dug their ditches."[7]

In the early 1900s Louis Armstrong worked on a junk wagon for a dealer named Lorenzo and found himself learning more about music than about the junk business as he listened to his employer call people out of their houses by blowing on the type of tin horn normally used to celebrate with on New Year's Eve: "The things he said about music held me spellbound, and he blew that old, beat-up tin horn with such warmth that I felt as though I was sitting with a good cornet player." Young Armstrong's musical education included a pie man named Santiago who blew a bugle to attract customers, a banana man whose musical cries advertised the virtues of his ripe yellow fruit, a waffle man whose customers enjoyed his mess call as much as his waffles, and the barroom quartets "who hung around the saloons with a cold can of beer in their hands, singing up a breeze while they passed the can around. I thought I was really somebody when I got so I could hang around with those fellows—sing and drink out of the can with them."[8]

Charles Peabody, who undertook the excavation of a mound in Coahoma County, Mississippi, for Harvard University in 1901 and 1902, was so impressed by the quality and ubiquity of the music of the local Negroes he hired to dig for him that he found himself supplementing his archeological research with the collection of folklore: "Our ears were beset with an abundance of ethnological material in song—words and music. . . . The volume of song is . . . large and its variety not spare; it is in sharp contrast to the lack of music among the white dwellers of the district."[9] Growing up in Harlem during the 1930s, William Dixon recalled that "music was plentiful. . . . What was it that Bessie Smith said about Saturday night? It was music, dancing, dancing and music. Not that that was *all* there was to life. But, to face reality, who could view *only* the bad and sometimes terrible things and injustices twenty-four hours a day, seven days a week, three hundred and sixty-five days a year?"[10]

The music that abounded included the wide variety of styles and types already reviewed. "Our men had equal penchants for hymns and 'ragtime,'" Peabody reported, but in fact the music he collected embraced minstrel songs, ballads, blues, and popular tunes as well. These songs, whatever their source, were rarely completely formalized—handed down from generation to generation with no changes—or wholly spontaneous. Most often they were products of the process of "communal re-creation" which has already been discussed with reference to slave songs. The sociologist and song collector Howard Odum, hearing the singing of a Negro road gang working in front of his Georgia home, promptly sat on a rock wall nearby in an effort to record the lyrics of their songs. When he finally made out the words, they were:

> White man settin' on wall,
> White man settin' on wall,
> White man settin' on wall all day long,
> Wastin' his time, wastin' his time.[11]

Similarly, Peabody recorded that his black workers, deep in the trenches they were digging, used their music to convey their feelings to their white employers above: "One Saturday, a half-holiday, a sing-song came out of the trench,

> Mighty long half day, Capta-i-n,

and one evening when my companion and I were playing a game of mumble-the-peg, our final occupation before closing work, our choragus shouted for us to hear,

> I'm so tired I'm almost dead,
> Sittin' up there playing mumblely-peg."[12]

Utilizing a familiar structure and probably also a familiar tune, these black workers left themselves ample scope to improvise new words that fit their surroundings and their mood. Another good example of this process has been provided by the blues and jazz pianist Sam Price in relating an incident from his Texas boyhood in the second decade of this century:

> I'll never forget the first song I ever heard to remember. A man had been lynched near my home in a town called Robinson, Texas. And at that time we were living in Waco, Texas—my mother, brother and myself. And they made a parody of this song and the words were something like this:
>
> > I never have, and I never will
> > Pick no more cotton in Robinsonville,
> > > Tell me how long will I have to wait,
> > > Can I get you now or must I hesitate?[13]

The process that had structured black music in the antebellum South continued to operate in the twentieth century and continued to allow for simultaneous individual and communal spontaneity. "I can make up blues faster than I can sing them," T-Bone Walker told an interviewer. "I could sing the blues for you for a whole day and never repeat a verse."[14] He could, since the songs he sang were an integral part of the folk tradition in which he grew up. Simply because it remained closer to its folk roots than other forms of American music in the twentieth century, Afro-American song retained a high degree of redundancy in both its musical structure and its stock of poetic forms.[15] Hundreds of familiar phrases and images existed, and were continually added to, from among which black singers could pick and choose, arrange in novel combinations, and intersperse with their own individual comments. Many pages could be filled with familiar floating lines like these which appeared in different arrangements and contexts in song after song:

> I'm worried now but I won't be worried long.
> Got de blues but too damn mean to cry.
> Out in dis wide worl' alone.
> Brown-skin woman, she's chocolate to de bone.
> I got de blues an' can't be satisfied.
> I got a rainbow tied 'round my shoulder.

You don't know my mind.
I'm laughin' to keep from cryin'.
Woke up this mornin', blues all around my bed.
Look down that lonesome road.
I been down so long, it seems like up to me.
If you don't think I'm sinking look what a hole I'm in.

Wholly spontaneous and original song did exist, of course, for black music remained creatively dynamic. But insofar as these creations became part of the communal tradition, they took their place within the large reservoir of musical imagery which belonged to the community at large and which its members felt was at their disposal to do with what they liked.

The improvisation which was facilitated by this substantial body of shared expression made it possible for song to become a personal reflector of everyday experience. The songs his mother used to sing, Walker remembered, "were always homey things or things that were troubling her. She might sing about the dinner burning or anything like that."[16] The process by which original lines reflecting everyday events could be integrated with familiar lines or even whole verses from other songs to form a new creation is illustrated by the following song. Its first two stanzas recount a personal experience, ending in each case with a variation of the common phrase, "This mornin', this evenin', so soon," and its final stanza is borrowed from a well-known children's rhyme:

I went up Zion Hill this mornin' on a wagon,
I went on a wagon up Zion's Hill this mornin';
The durn ole mule stop right still,
This mornin', this mornin', so soon.

I got out an' went 'round to his head this mornin',
I got out an' went 'round to his head this mornin';
The durn old mule was standin' there dead,
This mornin', this mornin', so soon.

Yes, I hollow at the mule, an' the mule would not gee, this mornin',
Yes, I hollow at the mule, an' the mule would not gee;
An' I hit him on the head with the single-tree,
This mornin', this mornin', so soon.[17]

In this way, songs could be sung within a traditional communal context and still be regarded as deeply personal expressions. "Look-a-heah, man," a Negro in rural Mississippi told someone who questioned whether he was singing his song correctly, "dis yere *mah song*, en I'll sing it howsoevah I pleases."[18]

The clearest example of the communal nature of black secular music can be found in those songs used to accompany work. Afro-Americans in the United States may have forgotten the commonplace Nigerian proverb, "If the trees are to be cut, you must sing. Without song the bush knife is dull," but they constantly applied its message. Almost as if to explicate the proverb, a black prisoner from Texas in the mid-1960s described the essential role music played in the hazardous occupation of felling trees:

> When you're swinging that diamond [axe] you got to have somebody who knows how to handle a diamond and knows the song where he can push for it. When you're working with that diamond you got eight or twelve men on a tree with the axes and all of them swinging in union, in rhythm. They got to have rhythm and everybody got to know what they're doing. So generally, when a good group works together, maybe seven or eight or ten, they work together all the time. And they keep singing together. So it's just regular harmony.[19]

From the time of slavery until well into the twentieth century, black laborers wielded axes, sledge hammers, spades, and hoes, loaded and unloaded ships, rowed boats, dug ditches, husked grain, picked crops, and lined track to the accompaniment of song. And they did so long after their white counterparts performed similar tasks in silence.[20] So valuable was singing in the lives of black workers that the role of song leader assumed great importance in setting the work pace, supplying instructions, and providing diversion. "I'se de tune setter, and dey all work as I set de tune fur em," Bradley Eberhart, a track liner on the Florida railroads, testified in 1940:

> Now de hans, dey all ready on de track wif de bars under de line, and dey line on de rhyme. . . . On de fust line de boys got de bars under de line, de rail, I means, by we calls hit de line. Den on de second line ob de song dey come down hard, sit down on the bars we calls hit, and on the words what rhyme dey jerk de bars up and dat straightens de track.

> Hey, Hey, sit down boys
> I tole ol Bob to he face
> I buy my whiskey at another place.

> When I sung, "Hey, Hey, sit down boys" de hans got ready to go down hard on de bars, den jerk up on de words "face" and "place" and dat straighten de line ob de track. . . . Dem boys, dey just caint line track ifen a song aint set fur em.[21]

Songs like these were sung wherever the work called for closely coordinated group effort. A gang of Louisiana railroad workers, dragging out old wooden crossties and putting new ones under the rails, tugged at the new crosstie at the end of each line of their leader's song:

Come on cross tie-(*umph*)
Git yo' place-(*umph*)
Train be comin'-(*umph*)
By-an'-by-(*umph*)
Lay down easy-(*umph*)
On de groun'-(*umph*)
Y'ain' no longuh-(*umph*)
A growin' tree-(*umph*)
Come on cross-tie-(*umph*)
Slip along-(*umph*)
Yuh ain't nothin' now-(*umph*)
But a heavy log-(*umph*).[22]

Metrically timed work songs could be, as in the preceding example, all call and no response. The lead singer called and the others pulled, or shoved, or cut, at the appropriate interval. The antiphony in these songs consisted of the words of the lead singer and the grunts of the workers or the sounds of their tools. Easily as typical were songs in which the workers responded to their leader's lines with words of their own. In the following spading song the group's part is indicated in capital letters:

I need some water, LORDY NOW, WO,
I NEED SOME WATER, WO LORD.

I need a doctor, LORDY NOW, WO,
I NEED A DOCTOR, WO LORD.

My heart is aching, LORDY NOW, WO,
MY HEART IS ACHING, WO LORD.

Boss say I'm faking, LORDY NOW, WO
BOSS SAY I'M FAKING, WO LORD.

What I'm gonna do, man, LORDY NOW, WO,
WHAT I'M GONNA DO, MAN, WO LORD.[23]

Interaction between the workers and the song leader was not limited to singing. As they did in church, so too on the job, blacks would punctuate the songs with shouted exclamations: "Talk it to time, now!" "It's hard, boys, it's hard." "Tell 'em about it!" "Explain it to 'em!" "Dat's all right, now!"[24]

Singing could provide an immense stimulus to work. While he was excavating in Mississippi, Charles Peabody heard of a famous song leader who was begged by his co-workers not to sing a particular song which made them work too hard.[25] On a Texas prison farm in 1918, Leadbelly punished his fellow inmates, who had attempted to deprive him of his position as song leader, by brutally quickening the work pace:

> Man' I'd have 'em pantin' all day long, never would let 'em down. Niggers be fallin' out all over de fiel', an' I'd be feelin' jes' right. Den dey'd be sorry for tryin' to tes' me, an' they'd say, "Please, . . . you gonna kill us all. Please . . . give us a rest. We won' do it no mo'." I'd tell 'em, "I'm gonna learn you so good you won' do it no second time. You hadn' oughta been so big de fus' time." Den I'd fly on away, holl'in' an' singin', an' carry 'em dat way till sundown.[26]

However, a good song leader—and Leadbelly when he was not being vindictive was a very good one—was universally appreciated. John W. Work has related the story of the Reverend Israel Golphin, who was turned down for a job with a gang laying railroad tracks in Arkansas. As he walked away, he noticed that the song leader was inexperienced and the men were grumbling at his inept timing. Golphin offered to call for them, and his ability was so admired that the workers successfully requested he be hired.[27] In 1903 the *Baltimore Sun* reported that the white boss of a Negro grading crew on a Maryland railroad made the mistake of discharging a worker who appeared to be singing harder than he worked. At once the men became dispirited and inefficient and complained that they wanted the singer back. "Inquiry made known the fact this so-called 'singer' led them as they sang at their work. The singer was taken back and the men worked with renewed energy and good cheer."[28]

John Lomax has given us an excellent portrait of Henry Truvillion, a Texas track liner, who was paid more than his fellow workers since his songs greatly enhanced their efficiency. Stooped over, squinting down the rail that his men were straightening, Truvillion would chant directions:

> Now, wait a minute, you stop right there,
> Now put yo' guns on yo' shoulders
> An' come walkin' back.
> Go on to the nex' one now an' jes' barely move it.
> I want you to jes' barely touch it.
> Touch it jes' a little bit,
> Jes' somethin' or 'nother like a fraction.[29]

A Library of Congress recording made in 1940 allows us to listen to Truvillion's rapid but precise chant as he guided workers loading and unloading three thousand pound, thirty-three foot rails between the ground and a flat-car:

Walk humble and don't you stumble,
And don't you hurt nobody.
Walk to the car and steady yourself.
Stand a minute.
Head high!
Good-by rail!
Good iron!
I heard it ring-nng. . . .
Go back and get another one.[30]

Big Bill Broonzy, who worked in Mississippi as a track liner from 1912 to 1915, has spoken of the importance and omnipresence of the work rhythms created by Sleepy John Estes, who was himself to become a noted blues singer. Estes called the men to work in the morning by crying out:

Every morning every motherchild grab a bar and follow me.

They walked the half mile between the gang cars where they ate and slept and the work site to the accompaniment of Estes' singing. When they arrived, Estes gathered them around by hollering:

Gang around me, boys, like flies around sugar.

He would then give them the signal to place the six and a half foot bars they were carrying under the rails, singing:

All men to their places like horses to their traces.
Is every motherchild got a hold? If not get one and a good one.

Everything they did during the day was done to the rhythm of Estes' singing:

If we wanted to go to the toilet during work time we would tell John Estes and he would sing it to the boss. When he would get the sign from the boss he would sing to us:
"Everybody lay their bar down, it's one to go."
Of course there was no toilet, we just stooped behind a bush or a tree, and when the one that went off comes back he would holler:
"All men to their places like horses to their traces."[31]

Although a song leader spent much of his time issuing directions or giving work cues, he remained at one with his men. At points in the work pattern, for instance, Henry Truvillion would shout out, "All right now, boys, let me tell you what I had for breakfast now," and both leader and gang would complain together:

Little *rice*, little *beans*,
No *meat* to be *seen*.

Hard *work* ain't *easy*,
Dry *bread* ain't *greasy*. . . .

Yeah—
In the *mornin'* when you *rise*,
Pick an' *shevil* by yo' *side*.

In the *mornin'* when you *rise*,
Got a *pain* in yo' *side*.[32]

Creating a rhythm for work—issuing instructions which helped laborers to synchronize their efforts, supplying a beat which timed work and controlled body movements—was only one of the functions of song. Work songs flourished also in those occupations such as cotton-picking, cane-cutting, corn-husking, where group timing was not crucial. Work songs accompanied jobs of every conceivable nature because they provided psychic benefits which were no less important than the physical stabilization they afforded. Again and again, black workers have testified to the importance of song in relieving the tedium of work and making the time pass. When Howard Odum asked laborers if their singing didn't hinder them in their work, he was invariably met with a look of surprise and then an outburst of laughter. "Cap'n," one worker told him, "dat's whut makes us work so much better, an' it nuthin' else but." "I's not a singin'," another responded. "I's jes a hollerin' to he'p me wid my wu'k."[33] Houston Bacon, a black worker in Mississippi, maintained that there was hardly a day when "we ain't got nothin' to say to one another. Boss don't mind cause he knows the gang would have no spirit and wouldn't get no work done. When the boss is pleasant he gets three times as much work done. A mean, cussin' boss causes men to become sullen and do less work." Especially important, according to Bacon, were stories and songs which caused the men to laugh. As they worked, they would sing over and over and laugh uproariously at such lines as:

Dat old black gal
Pissed in the coffee, buddy,
Pissed in the tea, boy.
If I hadn't been a hustler,
She'd uv pissed on me, buddy,
She'd a pissed on me.[34]

In the decades after emancipation, secular rather than religious songs became the staples of workers. Still, the function of the work song remained what it had been in slavery. Secular work songs resembled the spirituals in that their endless rhythmic and verbal repetitions could transport the singers beyond time, make them oblivious of their immediate surroundings, and create a state of what Wilfrid Mellers has referred to as "ritualistic hypnosis"[35] which made it possible to persevere under the least favorable circumstances. "You sing this when you pickin' cotton, pullin' corn, where you don't need a heavy beat," David Tippett, a black prisoner in Texas, said of his version of *John Henry*. "You know, you just sing it mostly as a mind reliever." Many of his fellow inmates agreed that this was one of the prime functions of song. Singing, they testified, relieved the tension, made time pass quickly, allowed them to find relief from the enormity of the problems facing them and the tedium of the tasks they were forced to do, and enabled them to work in harmony.[36]

Work songs may not have been able to change the external conditions under which black laborers worked, but they did help them survive those conditions both physically and psychically. Working as a water boy in the rock quarry near Muscle Shoals, Alabama, in the late nineteenth century, W. C. Handy observed that the sweat-drenched black steel-drivers found relief by singing:

Oh, baby, 'member las' winter?
Wasn't it cold-hunh?
Wasn't it cold-hunh?[37]

Years later, on a hundred-degree July day, Howard Odum heard a group of black diggers sustaining themselves with the same image, now projected into the future:

Oh, next winter gonna be so cold,
Oh, next winter gonna be so cold,
Oh, next winter gonna be so cold,
Fire can't warm you, be so cold.[38]

Working in the ice, sleet, and cold of winter, black workers reversed the image:

Oh, nex' summer be so hot
Fan can't cool you;
Lawd, fan can't cool you.[39]

In songs like these, workers sought a shared remedy for a common plight. They comforted each other and themselves by memories of the past or projections of the future. Together, they transcended the present, however briefly. But though escape from the present was a common theme, it was not the dominant one. If songs could be utilized to deny the effects of the burning sun, they were as commonly used to picture them graphically. "I don't see no fiah / But I sho' is burnin' down," black workers in a northern Alabama sawmill sang in 1915, and two decades later farmers in Florida complained: "Look over yonder at de hot boiling sun rolling over, wont go down, / Lord, Lord, wont go down."[40] Black workers and prisoners often spoke of the sun directly, addressing it as "Old Hannah."

> Oh go down Old Hannah, well well well,
> Don't you rise no more, don't you rise no more,
> Why don't you go down Old Hannah, don't you rise no more.[41]

James (Iron Head) Baker of Texas recalled first singing *Old Hannah* in 1908 on hot summer afternoons when the sun appeared to stand still and "just hang" in the sky.[42] Leadbelly and his fellow inmates in the Texas prison system sang of the effects of the relentless heat and the brutal prison regimen:

> You oughta been on de Brazis [Brazos River] in nineteen and ten;
> Dey was workin' de women, like dey drove de men.
>
> You oughta been here in nineteen an' ten,
> The mens was fallin'—a reg'lar haulin' in.
>
> The sun was shinin', the mens was flyin',
> The cap'n was holl'in', we wuz almos' dyin'.[43]

Work songs, and black secular songs in general, were characteristically marked by a realistic depiction of the workers' situation. In this way too they provided relief by underlining the truth that the individual worker did not suffer an individual fate. His problems were shared and understood by his fellows to whom he could be frank, with whom he could communicate in detail. Work songs became popular when, as one singer put it, they "would touch so close that everybody would take a liking to them and then repeat them."[44]

Not only could Negroes realistically describe their condition in their work songs, they could depict the foibles of the whites around them with a frankness that simply would not have been allowed expression in any other form. "The blues is mostly revenge," a Memphis Negro reflected:

> You want to say something (and you know how we was situated so we couldn't say or do a lot of things we wanted to), and so you sing it. Like a friend of mine. He was workin' down on a railroad section gang a long

time ago. I don't remember when it was. Anyhow, this friend of mine looked at the boss lyin' up in the shade sleepin' while him an' his buddies was out there shakin' those ties. He wanted to say something about it, but he couldn't you know. So that give him the blues and he sung a little number about—

> Ratty [lazy, idle], ratty section,
> Ratty, ratty crew,
> The captain's gettin' ratty, boys,
> I b'lieve I'm gonna rat some, too.

Meanin' that he was signifying and getting his revenge through songs.[45]

Just as the white scholars Howard Odum and Charles Peabody learned that the black workers they were studying could use their songs to communicate with them, so too innumerable white bosses found the black workers they employed using song to make comments, articulate complaints, and issue warnings which otherwise they could not have verbalized safely:

> Naw I don't, don't, don't, naw I don't
> I don't like no red head boss man, naw I don't.
>
> Captain, O captain, you must be cross,
> It's six o'clock an' you won't "knock-off!"
>
> Captain, O captain, you must be blin'
> You keep hollerin' "hurry" an' I'm darn nigh flyin'.
>
> Cap'n did you heah 'bout all yo' men goin' leave you
> Jes because you make yo' day so long.[46]

In both form and function, then, the work song was a communal instrument. It allowed the workers to blend their physical movements and psychic needs with those of other workers; it provided important outlets for communication, commiseration, and expression; and, as Bruce Jackson has suggested, it well may have affected subtle shifts in the meaning of the work experience itself: "The songs change the nature of the work by putting the work into the worker's framework," Jackson has hypothesized. ". . . By incorporating the work with their song, by in effect, co-opting something they are forced to do anyway, they make it *theirs* in a way it otherwise is not."[47]

By the beginning of the twentieth century, folklorists and song collectors increasingly recognized the centrality of the work song and began to pay as much attention to what Negroes were singing in the fields, on the docks, along the roads and railroad tracks as they had to what was being sung in black churches and praise houses. At the very time that consciousness of the importance of work songs was growing, the songs themselves, which had in various forms existed as long as Negroes had been in the United States, were beginning a long, gradual decline. Urbanization, the changing social and economic situation of Negroes, the shift in the nature of the work experience, and growing mechanization combined to diminish the importance and frequency of work songs. "There ain't nothing about a tractor that makes a man want to sing," a young black farm worker in Mississippi said in the 1940s. "The thing keeps so much noise, and you so far away from the other folks. There ain't a thing to do but sit up there and drive."[48] The decline of these songs needs to be understood in a very relative sense. Black workers continued to sing throughout the century, and work songs remained more important among them than among any other group in the United States. In 1926 Odum and Johnson published a volume containing more than 250 Negro work songs which they had collected in North Carolina, South Carolina, Tennessee, and Georgia during the two preceding years. They found the work song tradition very much alive.[49] A decade later, Zora Neale Hurston, collecting folklore in her native Florida, found that although "conditions of work and an increasing complexity in the problem of living have taken away much of the colorful singing and play during worktime of the Negro laborers in Florida," the traditional singing still could be heard—especially among waterfront laborers, sawmill and log-chopping gangs, turpentine crews in the woods, road repairing crews, and farm laborers.[50]

Nevertheless, from John and Alan Lomax in the 1930s to Bruce Jackson in the 1960s, folklorists in search of work songs in their pristine form found it increasingly fruitful to visit southern prisons, which maintained many of those work conditions—gang labor, hand tools, closely coordinated group tasks calling for metrical stabilization—that were conducive to perpetuating work songs. And not even southern prisons were to remain unchanged. Visiting Texas prisons in the 1960s, Bruce Jackson was amazed at the richness of the folk traditions still there. However, his best sources turned out to be older prisoners and, in spite of the very impressive array of black work songs he was able to collect, he concluded that the songs were dying. "Very seldom do they use the worksongs now," one of the inmates told him. "They don't use the worksongs in the fields chopping because they don't chop, they don't work the fields now like they used to work. They have tractors now to do the work we did with hoes."[51]

The shifting patterns of black secular music in the twentieth century cannot be attributed exclusively to changing work conditions. Jackson found that many of the younger prisoners refused to sing work songs because they considered them to be "oldtimeyniggerstuff."[52] Revisiting the Mississippi State Penitentiary at Parchman in 1947, Alan Lomax discovered that most of the young black prisoners regarded the practice of work song singing as "old fogeyism."[53] In the 1940s and 1950s, Big Bill Broonzy often found blacks in his audiences disturbed by his music. "This ain't slavery no more," he was told, "so why don't you learn to play something else? . . . the way you play and sing about mules, cotton, corn, levee camps and gang songs. Them days, Big Bill, is gone for ever."[54] Just as the shift in religious music was related to changes in black thought and life style, so too were the transitions in secular music reflective of alterations in black consciousness and culture. Basic changes took place not only in the content of songs but in their very structure.

However great the differences between Afro-American religious and secular songs in the late nineteenth and early twentieth centuries, they shared a number of overriding similarities. In both the temple and the field, black song was for the most part communal song. Negroes sang in groups surrounded by and responding to other singers, melding their individual consciousness into the group consciousness. The most frequently pictured context for black song in this period was a serious, purposeful one: at work or at prayer. After World War I the images surrounding black music began to change. The work-prayer context seemed to give way to the leisure setting. The communal context faded into the background to be replaced by the image of an isolated individual with a guitar. The figure of the blues singer giving vent to his or her own emotions without the necessity of an audience, singing for the song's sake alone, without a shred of the Protestant ethos or the work ethic supplying a rationale for song, rose to eclipse the older and more familiar nineteenth-century figures.

SECULAR MUSIC AND THE BLACK COMMUNITY: THE BLUES

Individual voices had been prominent in Afro-American music before the rise of blues. In both church music and secular work songs, song leaders were important, but in both cases their contributions blended into an antiphonal communal situation. In church music the song leader was invariably answered by the group, and this was usually the case in secular work songs as well. In all cases the songs were sung in communal settings. Solo music, of course, existed among the slaves and freedmen. Almost any song could be sung as a solo piece by an individual working alone. The two chief forms of solo music that existed among nineteenth-century blacks—lullabies and field hollers—both arose out of situations of physical or social distance. Lullabies were addressed to infants or children too young to respond, while field hollers arose out of spatial isolation.[1] With the end of slavery, the percentage of Negroes who worked alone or in very small groups increased and the use of field hollers unquestionably increased as well.

Lydia Parrish remembered how the black farm workers in southern New Jersey in the 1870s and 1880s would holler to each other across wide fields: "The call was peculiar, and I always wondered how they came by such a strange form of vocal gymnastics, since I never heard a white person do anything like it."[2] Thomas Talley, a black scholar from Fisk University, recalled the field hollers he had heard as a youngster in Tennessee during the late nineteenth century. Often these hollers would be wordless:

> Hoo wee hoo wee hoo wee hoo!
> Hoo wee hoo wee hoo wee hoo!

Sometimes they would include words:

> I hears you holler "Eh hoo hoo wee!"

At other times they would articulate attitudes:

> I wants a piece a hoecake I wants a piece o' bread.
> Well, Ise so tired an' hongry dat Ise almos' dead.[3]

Field hollers often consisted of the isolated statements of one individual. Lewis Bell in Coahoma County, Mississippi, would moan to his draft animal:

> O-O-O, This donkey won't drink water.
> I'll knock him in the collar till he go stone blind.

And to himself:

> The gal I'm lovin' she can't be found.[4]

In the spring, when the doors and windows of the Tennessee Valley
school he attended were opened, W. C. Handy heard the cry of a black
plowman working half a mile away:

A-o,——oo A-o,——
I wouldn't live in Cai-ro-oo;
A-o,—oo A-o-oo.[5]

When other workers were present, field hollers found responses. Samuel
Brooks has described the "quitting time" hollers of black plantation workers near Edwards, Mississippi: "They sing it late in the evening. About the
time they quit, they generally feel good and they like to sing this kind of
thing. . . . If one man starts, well, across maybe another field close by,
why, they sing that same tune back to him. . . . Then maybe another
man may answer him another tune.

Ooooh, the sun going down,
And I won't be here long,
Ooooh, the sun going down,
And I won't be here long.
Ooooh, then I be going home.
Ooooh, I can't let this dark cloud catch me here.
Ooooooh, I can't stay here long,
Oooooooooooh, I be at home."[6]

Harold Courlander has divided hollers into two categories: calls and
cries. The former were used to communicate messages—to call people to
work or to attract the attention of others. The latter were a form of self-
expression, the cry of an individual attempting to verbalize, or, more
properly, vocalize his feelings.[7] Both forms existed in slavery. In 1853 the
northern traveler Frederick Olmsted was awakened by the laughter of a
group of South Carolina slaves and recorded his impressions of first a cry
and then a call:

Suddenly one raised such a sound as I had never heard before; a long,
loud, musical shout, rising, and falling, and breaking into falsetto, his voice
ringing through the woods in the clear, frosty night air, like a bugle-call.
As he finished, the melody was caught up by another, and then, another,
and then by several in chorus. . . .
    After a few minutes I could hear one urging the rest to come to work
again, and soon he stepped towards the cotton bales, saying, "Come, bred-
eren, come; let's go at it; come now, eoho! roll away! eeoho-eeoho-
weeioho-i!"[8]

Field hollers tended to stay in the fields, but Negroes who left the farms and plantations to go to the cities of first the South and then the North were soon chanting the structurally similar work calls. In antebellum New Orleans, for instance, the streets were alive with black vegetable vendors, cruller sellers, fish peddlers, shoeshine boys, girls balancing rice cakes on their heads—each offering their wares and services in their own individualized tune and rhythm.[9] Henry Ravenel described an old black peddler in antebellum Charleston who enlivened his cries by interspersing the Latin mottoes of the state of South Carolina and other fragments of learning: "Here goes ripe watermeelions!—mushmeelions!—green corn! *Dum spiro, spero!*—watermeelions!—mushmeelions!—ripe mushmeelions! *Animis opibusque parati!*—coucumbers!—coucumbers! *Ego sum stultus!* watermeelions!—mushmeelions!—spruce beer!—sassafac beer! manufactured by Shakespeare—bottled by Molière, and retailed by Voltaire!"[10] One hundred years later, streets in black neighborhoods in such northern cities as Chicago and New York were filled with foods, smells, and sounds that nineteenth-century urban blacks from the South would have found familiar. By the 1920s and 1930s migrants from the South could stroll through the markets on Fifth, Eighth, and Park avenues in Harlem and find chitterlings, yams, greens, rice and beans, cornpone, pork chops, hog maw—almost any traditional food or herb they desired—being offered in a manner that was equally familiar to them:

Don' yo' love 'em
Don' yo' love 'em
Greasy greens, Lawd, Greasy greens!

Er-beh e yah
Er-beh e yah
Wid alle erbs,
Wid alle erbs,
Erbs e' de ting
Erbs mek e sing,
Erbs 'e will bring
Ease to yo' pain
Ease to yo' pain.

Watah-ah-ah, mil—yon!
Watah-ah-ah, mil—yon!
She's sweet an' juicy,
She's ripe an' red!

Wake up lady,
Git out yo' bed!
Watah-ah-ah, mil—yon![11]

In certain forms of the holler, the cry, the call, slaves and freedmen had
the ingredients for a highly personalized, solo music. But while this individualized song may have been utilized frequently, it never became characteristic of nineteenth century Afro-American music, in which individualized solo songs remained atypical. Certainly, early examples of the
blues existed in the last half of the nineteenth century and possibly even
during slavery, but it was not until the twentieth century that it became
one of the dominant forms of black song. The rise of the blues did not call
for the invention of wholly new musical forms. The same musical repertory and traditions out of which black spirituals, work songs, and hollers
were forged was sufficient to structure the blues as well. What were necessary were not new types of music but new forms of self-conception.
The blues was the most highly personalized, indeed, the first almost completely personalized music that Afro-Americans developed. It was the
first important form of Afro-American music in the United States to lack
the kind of antiphony that had marked other black musical forms. The
call and response form remained, but in blues it was the singer who responded to himself or herself either verbally or on an accompanying instrument. In all these respects blues was the most typically American
music Afro-Americans had yet created and represented a major degree of
acculturation to the individualized ethos of the larger society—an ethos
which, as LeRoi Jones has argued so persuasively, was alien to the African
slaves brought to this continent and which remained one of the chief
sources of difference between black and white Americans throughout the
nineteenth century.[12]

The precise time and manner of the emergence of the blues are lost in
the irrecoverable past. For our purposes it is not crucial whether blues
songs were known to slaves or were created only after emancipation;
whether they evolved from the field hollers and work songs or, as is more
likely, grew up alongside of them, carved out of the same matrix of Afro-
American musical style. When the blues was created is less important
than when it became a dominant musical form among Negroes throughout
the country; when it can be taken as expressing the consciousness, the
attitudes, the experiences of large numbers of Negroes in America. By the
last decades of the nineteenth century, blues songs were increasingly com-

mon. Many black musicians born in this period—Big Bill Broonzy, Zutty Singleton, Jelly Roll Morton, Baby Dodds, George Morrison, and Bunk Johnson—have reported some familiarity with the blues in their youth.[13] W. C. Handy, who began publishing blues or, more accurately, blues-derived songs in 1912, claimed only the melodies as his own invention, the rest belonged and had belonged for some time to the folk: "the twelve-bar, three-line form of the first and last strains, with its three-chord basic harmonic structure (tonic, subdominant, dominant seventh) was that already used by Negro roustabouts, honky-tonk piano players, wanderers and others of their underprivileged but undaunted class from Missouri to the Gulf, and had become a common medium through which any such individual might express his personal feeling in a sort of musical soliloquy."[14] Collecting black songs in Mississippi and Georgia between 1905 and 1908, Howard Odum found that blues, in various stages of development, were "common property among the Negroes of the lower class."[15]

Although folk blues always retained a flexible style and structure, there was a tendency toward the form that was to become their most familiar characteristic: the twelve-bar, three-line stanza with an AAB pattern—a first statement repeated in the second line (sometimes with slight variations), followed by a new statement in the third line that developed or supplemented the first, as in the *Green River Blues* by Charley Patton:

> Some people say the Green River blues ain't bad.
> Some people say the Green River blues ain't bad.
> Then it must not have been the Green River blues I had.
>
> It was late one night, everything was still.
> It was late one night, Baby, everything was still.
> I could see my Baby upon a lonesome hill.
>
> How long, evening train been gone?
> How long, Baby, that evening train been gone?
> Yes, I'm worried now but I won't be worried long.[16]

Whatever structural variations were to take place, the blues from the very beginning was marked by what Abbe Niles referred to as "the element of pure *self*."[17] The blues were solo music not only in performance but in content. The persona of the individual performer entirely dominated the song which centered upon the singer's own feelings, experiences, fears, dreams, acquaintances, idiosyncrasies.

It was not coincidental that a new emphasis upon the individual and individual expression was taking hold in black song at the very time that

Booker T. Washington's philosophy was taking hold among black intellectuals and the black middle class. The individualist ethos, always strong in the United States, was perhaps ideologically most persuasive in the decades before and after the Civil War. In the latter period especially, the nation was imbued with the notion that Man could progress according to the Horatio Alger model, that the individual molds his own destiny. Freedmen had this message thrust upon them by the Yankee school teachers who flocked South to create institutions of education, by the black school teachers produced by such new institutions as Hampton and Tuskeegee, by the popular press, and by the endless oratory of black and white politicians, preachers, businessmen, and "leaders" of every sort. This is not to suggest that the blues mirrored the moral and economic lessons of the Alger message; the opposite would be closer to the truth. But there was a direct relationship between the national ideological emphasis upon the individual, the popularity of Booker T. Washington's teachings, and the rise of the blues. Psychologically, socially, and economically, Negroes were being acculturated in a way that would have been impossible during slavery, and it is hardly surprising that their secular music reflected this as much as their religious music did.

If blues singing signalled the rise of a more personalized, individual-oriented ethos among Negroes at the turn of the century, did it also testify to the decline of that sense of communality which was so characteristic of both the structure and content of nineteenth-century songs? Here the answer must be sought on several levels. The rise of the blues embodies much of the complexity for the cultural historian that the rise of gospel music does. Gospel song was a musical and structural return to African and slave music and away from Western hymnology, even while its lyrics —its message—evidenced an abandonment of the sacred universe of the African and slave past and an adjustment to modern religious consciousness. The development of blues poses some of these same paradoxes. The personalized, solo elements of the blues style may indicate a decisive move into twentieth-century American consciousness, but the musical style of the blues indicates a holding on to the old roots at the very time when the dispersion of Negroes throughout the country and the rise of the radio and the phonograph could have spelled the demise of a distinctive Afro-American musical style. While it is undoubtedly true that work songs and field hollers were closer to the West African musical archetype, so much of which had survived the centuries of slavery, blues with its emphasis upon improvisation, its retention of the call and response pattern,

its polyrhythmic effects, and its methods of vocal production which included slides, slurs, vocal leaps, and the use of falsetto, was a definite
assertion of central elements of the traditional communal musical style.

Throughout the early decades of the twentieth century there are indications that the black migrants who made their way to the cities of the
North were determined to hold on to the musical patterns that had been
familiar to them in their former environments. James P. Johnson, who
played piano in a Manhattan dance hall in 1913, recalled the insistence of
the Negro patrons on traditional dances and music:

> These Charleston people and the other Southerners had just come to New
> York. They were country people and they felt homesick. When they got
> tired of two-steps and schottisches (which they danced with a lot of
> spieling), they'd yell: "Let's go back home!" . . . "Let's do a set!" . . .
> or, "Now, put us in the alley!" I did my *Mule Walk* or *Gut Stomp* for
> these country dances.[18]

In 1909 the Lincoln Theatre, the first black theater in Harlem, opened at
58 West 135th Street and began to feature the blues singers and other
acts that were staples of the southern theater circuit. Three years later
the Lafayette Theatre opened just a few blocks away but with a policy
far removed: white entertainers and segregated seating. The courts soon
prohibited the seating arrangements. More significantly, the local black
residents, by their refusal to attend, forced the management to feature
Negro musicians and performers.[19] The record companies were to learn
the same lesson: the black masses, North and South, wanted black music.

In 1902 the Victor Talking Machine Company released six sides of religious songs by the Dinwiddie Colored Quartet whose renditions lacked
the doctoring of other recorded black religious music in the early twentieth century. It was to be some two decades before records featuring
black secular music of equal authenticity appeared.[20] In 1919 Perry Bradford, a black pianist and composer, spent a good deal of his time urging
recording companies to cut some records of his tunes by a black female
singer. "I'd walked out two pairs of shoes going from one studio to another, and my friends were begging and pleading with me to give up my
fantastic dream," Bradford has written. His argument never varied:
"There's fourteen million Negroes in our great country and they will buy
records if recorded by one of their own."[21] During these years W. C.
Handy was attempting the same thing with the same results: "I tried to
introduce colored girls for recording our blues. In every case the man-
agers quickly turned thumbs down. 'Their voices were not suitable.'

'Their diction was different from white girls.' 'They couldn't possibly fill the bill.' "[22] Finally, early in 1920, a new company, Okeh Records, agreed to record two of Bradford's songs as sung by Mamie Smith, a young black singer who had been featuring Bradford's material on the theater circuit for some time. When the recording session was held on a snowy morning in February 1920, Bradford wanted to jump up and yell "Hallelujah, it's done!" His joy was justified.

That first Mamie Smith record was a cautious affair, using a white musical group and sounding far from authentic black song. But it featured a black singing in a style familiar enough so that although the advertising was as circumspect as the recording, enough copies were sold in black neighborhoods to encourage Okeh to try again and emboldened Bradford and Smith to insist that this time Bradford's *Crazy Blues* be featured and that a black band be used. "Mamie could now for a releasing moment rejoin that part of ourselves which we have sacrificed to civilization," Bradford wrote.[23] There was some hyperbole here. Mamie Smith's *Crazy Blues*, like so much of the deceptively named "Classic Blues" of the 1920s, was hardly blues as millions of Negroes knew it. One critic has suggested that this style would more appropriately be called "jazz singing," and another has argued that it should be called "vaudeville blues" since it was so deeply influenced by the American music hall and vaudeville stage.[24] Whatever the style is called, it was closer to traditional blues than anything else on records, it fit in with the eclecticism so characteristic of black music, and it obviously had great appeal to Negroes, North and South. Within a year of its release, Mamie Smith's second recording, although it was substantially priced at one dollar, sold more copies than anyone had imagined possible—some estimates going as high as one million.[25] The record companies no longer had to be convinced; there was a market for black music and they lost no time supplying it.

This is not the place to rehearse the important story of the rise of what quickly became known as "race records" in the 1920s. Some aspects of that story, however, are central to the question of to what extent blues remained communal music. First, the sale of Mamie Smith's second record was not an aberration. Blues continued to be immensely popular throughout the 1920s and after. In 1926 Odum and Johnson calculated that the three largest companies issuing blues recordings sold five to six million copies of blues records every year—a phenomenal figure considering that the entire black population in the United States in the 1920s numbered no more than fifteen million. Between 1920 and 1942, some 5500 different blues records were issued involving over a thousand Negro musicians.[26] Bradford's dream had succeeded beyond his own imagination. Three years after the advent of Mamie Smith, Bessie Smith, who was to become the most popular and successful of the Classic Blues singers, cut her first record, *Down Hearted Blues*. Although this number had already been recorded by every major female blues singer, Bessie Smith's version sold three-quarters of a million copies before the year was over. From that point on any record she made was assured of success. Before her active recording career ended in the early years of the Depression, Bessie Smith's recordings alone had sold somewhere between six and ten million copies.[27]

The issuance of new blues records created a sense of excitement. Clarence Williams, the black pianist and composer who accompanied Bessie Smith on her first records, owned a record shop in Chicago's South Side and reported that "Colored people would form a line twice around the block when the latest record of Bessie or Ma [Rainey] or Clara [Smith] or Mamie come in. . . . sometimes these records they was bootlegged, sold in the alley for four or five dollars apiece. . . . nobody never asked for Paul Whiteman; I doubt if they ever knew about him." Pullman porters would buy up dozens of copies of hit records and sell them in rural districts for a profit.[28] When small towns had their own record shops, the excitement was as great as in the large cities. "Every payday we'd bottle up the home brew we'd been getting ready and Mama would send us kids down to the store to get the latest blues records," a resident of a West Virginia coal-mining town during the 1920s told Phyl Garland. "Everybody else we knew would be there too and we'd carry those records home, stacked in our arms. All the Negroes lived together in that 'company' town and you could go from street to street and hear those blues records blasting out from the open doors. I'll never forget it."[29]

The second point to be made about recorded blues derives from these observations: their market remained almost exclusively black throughout the 1920s and 1930s. The record companies aimed their race records entirely at the Negro community. "The World's Greatest Race Artists on the World's Greatest Race Records," Okeh Records advertised from 1923 on, and Black Swan Records, the Negro-owned company, asserted in all its ads: "The Only Genuine Colored Record. Others Are Only Passing for Colored."[30] These were not tactics designed to win white purchasers. Nor were the distribution patterns. Blues records were listed in the "Colored" or "Race" catalogues and were available only in stores in Negro neighborhoods. When the young John Hammond returned from England in 1923, he tried to purchase blues records in downtown Manhattan shops only to find that he had to go to Harlem to buy or listen to such records.[31] Another early white devotee of black music, the jazz historian Ross Russell, learned a similar lesson in his career as a collector of old jazz and blues records during the 1930s, first on the West Coast and then in Chicago. After a period of unrewarding searching in white neighborhoods, where he found not "a single bar of collectible jazz or blues," he concentrated on Negro neighborhoods exclusively. "Here the phonographs were poor and the records badly used, indicating they had been played often, but their musical riches were wonderful."[32]

The phonograph quickly became an important feature in rural and urban Negro homes. Zora Neale Hurston spent most of 1927 in the South collecting Negro material for her graduate work in anthropology at Columbia University. "The bulk of the population," she reported to Professor Franz Boas, "now spends its leisure in the motion picture theatres or with the phonograph."[33] Even Mahalia Jackson, who received an extremely strict religious upbringing in New Orleans, could not be sheltered from the influence of the recorded blues:

> Everybody was buying phonographs—the kind you wound up on the side by hand—just the way people have television sets today—and everybody had records of all the Negro blues singers—Bessie Smith . . . Ma Rainey . . . Mamie Smith . . . all the rest.
> The famous white singers like Caruso—you might hear them when you went by a white folks' house, but in a colored house you heard blues. You couldn't help but hear blues—all through the thin partitions of the houses—through the open windows—up and down the street in the colored neighborhoods—everybody played it real loud.[34]

Nor—to make the final point about the recorded blues—was this large black audience merely passive, accepting whatever the recording companies sent their way. As the competition for blues singers increased, the companies began to heed the letters flooding in from southern customers recommending local singers. In 1925 Paramount Records, a small company whose extensive mail order sales gave them a large number of rural customers, responded to some of these suggestions and brought Blind Lemon Jefferson, a rough, authentic, itinerant blues singer and guitar player from Texas to Chicago to record. In 1926 eight of his records were released and were so successful that Paramount followed quickly with recordings by other southern bluesmen: Blind Blake from Jacksonville, Florida, Charley Patton, Sam Collins, and Son House from Mississippi.

Soon a new talent hunt was on. Okeh Records, Columbia Records, Victor, and other companies began to send recording crews directly into the South to search for and record local favorites. Farmers, sharecroppers, street singers, honky-tonk entertainers were auditioned. A new host of rural bluesmen, accompanying themselves on guitar or banjo, began to fill the pages of the race catalogues. The hybrid blues of the female Classic Blues singers were supplemented by the more traditional sounds of a steady stream of bluesmen whose regional styles were given wide exposure for the first time.

The Negro market not only existed, it was able to impose its own tastes upon the businessmen who ran the record companies and who understood the music they were recording imperfectly enough so that they extended a great deal of freedom to the singers they were recording. Son House, who recorded for Paramount Records, told John Fahey that the recording engineers exercised no control over what he recorded and that the same was true of Charley Patton, Louise Johnson, and Willie Brown whose recording sessions he attended. Skip James, who also recorded for Paramount, corroborated this. Different takes of a number were made, they insisted, only when they themselves were dissatisfied with their first performance. This non-directive policy was typical. There was probably never a period in which it was easier for singers to get auditions. Both Fahey and Samuel Charters have demonstrated that in the late 1920s almost any black blues singers could get a test. "By 1931," Fahey has concluded, "the companies had been performing for three or four years the function of passively allowing hundreds of Southern Negroes to sit in their studios and record the songs which they had been singing for decades."[35]

We have become so accustomed to what appears to be the imposition of culture upon passive people by modern media that it is difficult to perceive variations in the pattern. In the case of blues at least (and I suspect that subsequent studies will prove this to be true of many other categories of popular entertainment as well), the imposition of taste and standards was by no means a one-way process. Unfortunately, we have been slow in recognizing this. Samuel Adams, in a valuable study of one hundred black sharecropper families on the King and Anderson plantation in the Mississippi Delta in the 1940s, has shown the impact of modernity. Fifty of the families had radios; thirty subscribed to urban newspapers; twenty-eight had some member who went to the nearest city, Clarksdale, at least once every two weeks; thirty had automobiles; and almost all frequented the movies, the juke joints where they danced to recorded or live music, and other "urban" events. Changes seemed most pronounced in musical tastes. Of the songs preferred by the older generation, 54 per cent were religious, 14 per cent were blues, 29 per cent were other types of "popular song," and 2 per cent were lullabies and work songs. Among the younger generation, only 30 per cent were religious songs, 30 per cent were blues, 28 per cent were other popular songs, and 2 per cent were work songs.[36] Adams' assertion that these findings showed the growth of urban cultural tastes and acculturation among rural blacks is unexceptionable. His further conclusion that "the present-day Negroes on the King and Anderson plantation are ceasing to be a folk people" is more problematical since it rigidly equates the concept of "folk" with rural and it overlooks the interaction that went on between the black folk and commercially recorded and performed black music.

While it is essential to note the differences and changes implicit in the rise of the blues, it would be a distortion to overlook how similar they were to the other types of Afro-American music already discussed. Blues too drew upon a large reservoir of phrases and expressions which were there to be used by all and to be added to constantly. No more than any other form of black music were blues meant to be repeated in a frozen form. Black singers felt absolutely free to take blues sung by others—friends, professional performers, singers on records—and alter them in any way they liked. Though blues became part of the commercial world of the entertainer and the recording industry, they remained communal property and were vehicles for individual and group expression. No single person "owned" a blues song. Ma Rainey expressed this well in her *Last Minute Blues:*

> If anybody ask you who wrote this lonesome song
> Tell 'em you don't know the writer, but Ma Rainey put it on.[37]

In 1926 Odum and Johnson published the following revealing list:[38]

LINES AND TITLES OF SONGS COLLECTED TWENTY YEARS AGO	LINES AND TITLES OF RECENT POPULAR BLUES
Laid in jail, back to the wall.	Thirty days in jail with my back turned to the wall.
Jailer, won't you put 'nother man in my stall?	Look here, mister jailer, put another gal in my stall.

Baby, won't you please come home?	Baby, won't you please come home?
I'll see her when her trouble's like mine.	I'm gonna see you when your troubles are just like mine.
I'm on my las' go-'round.	Last go-'round blues.

Without much difficulty this list could be extended by many pages. Utilizing many traditional and familiar phrases, recorded blues were worked on by the folk process which has already been described. In this way they re-entered the folk tradition and became the basis for future commercial blues which in their turn, if they became popular, were re-worked by the folk and reintegrated into the oral tradition. This constant process can be illustrated by the following example. The slave spiritual

> I am a-trouble in de mind,
> O I am a-trouble in de mind;
> I ask my Lord what shall I do,
> I am a-trouble in de mind.[39]

put the title phrase firmly in the folk repertory where it was commonly used in both religious and secular songs. In 1926 Richard M. Jones incorporated it and such other familiar folk expressions as "When you see me laughin' / I'm laughin' to keep from cryin'," and "The sun's gonna shine in my back door some day," into a formal song that was to become extremely popular:

> Trouble in mind, I'm blue,
> But I won't be blue always,
> For the sun will shine in my back door some-day.
>
> Trouble in mind, that's true,
> I have almost lost my mind,
> Life ain't worth livin'—feel like I could die.
>
> I'm gonna lay my head on some lonesome railroad line,
> Let the two nineteen train ease my troubled mind.
>
> Well, trouble, oh, trouble,
> Trouble on my worried mind,
> When you see me laughin',
> I'm laughin' just to keep from cryin'.[40]

In this form the song was recorded by Chippie Hill that same year and by more than fifty other singers in the years to come. In the late 1930s railroad workers in Palatka, Florida, heard the song on a juke box and had no difficulty reintegrating its familiar lines into their work song tradition:

Mama, I sure am blue;
Seems like I'm gonna lose my mind,
Sometimes I feel like laughing
Other times I feel like dying.

I'm gonna lay my head
Out yonder on that railroad line,
Just to feel that Special
Runnin' 'cross my mind.[41]

The effects of the phonograph upon black folksong are not easily summed up. Recordings unquestionably had a disrupting effect on many local styles and traditions. Zora Neale Hurston found that when what she called "the mechanical, nickel phonograph" made its way into the remote turpentine, logging, phosphate, and other work camps of rural Florida there was an immediate change in the songs of the section. Songs that had been peculiar to a particular region began to give way to such recorded blues as *Pine-top's Boogie-Woogie* and *Mistreating Blues*. "The song on the phonograph record soon becomes the music of the work-crew," Hurston concluded, "but with this interesting change: the original words and music are changed to satisfy the taste of the community's own singers."[42] In this way local styles were certainly diluted and influenced by commercial recordings. However, what was taking place was not a total erosion of regional styles in favor of some standard product, but rather a blending process. The eclectic flexibility so characteristic of black secular music was enhanced by the phonograph. Local traditions could now become quickly known to Negroes in every section of the country; the developments in the new urban centers could be spread throughout the South even while the traditions of the South could be perpetuated and strengthened among the recent urban migrants. Negroes living far apart could now share not only styles but experiences, attitudes, folk wisdom, expressions, in a way that was simply not possible before the advent of the phonograph. In this sense records can be seen as bearers and preservers rather than primarily destroyers of folk traditions.

Recordings, of course, did have their negative effects: they could stultify originality, corrupt discrete styles, force songs to conform to the limiting medium of two- or three-minute renditions per record side and thereby artificially shorten texts and garble content. But their most important effect was to allow millions to continue to possess and millions more to repossess a body of tradition and expression which otherwise must surely have perished in the conditions of modern industrial life. Commentators like Adams, though they correctly perceived the new trends, were premature in proclaiming the end of the folk. The process of cross-fertilization in Afro-American music, dating back to the interaction of African and Euro-American musical styles in the colonial period and the camp meetings of the late eighteenth and early nineteenth centuries, was vastly accelerated in the 1920s and 1930s by the introduction of such mass media as radio, movies, and, especially, records. It is crucial that we understand that it remained a process of *cross*-fertilization, rather than one in which the urban and the commercial demolished all before them. Commercial recordings deeply influenced black folk music but also remained dependent upon folk music as a source. The new urban forms that influenced the country were, after all, constructed out of country traditions in the first place and continued to be profoundly shaped by those traditions.[43]

The folk process may have been altered by the mass migrations to the cities and by the advent of mass media and commercialization, but it remained a central ingredient in Afro-American music. This can be demonstrated further by an examination of the Negro audience. Black music was a participant activity not only for those who hollered in the fields, sang in the churches, or picked a guitar at home, but also for those who went out to listen and respond to professional entertainers. Norman Mason, a trumpet player who backed up such Classic Blues singers as Ida Cox, Mamie Smith, and Ma Rainey, has testified that he liked the blues "because it do express the feeling of people and when we used to play around through Mississippi in those cotton sections of the country we had the people *with* us! They hadn't much outlet for their enjoyment and they get together in those honkeytonks and you should hear them. That's where they let out their suppressed desires, and the more suppressed the better the blues they put out, seems to me."[44]

As a young man, the black poet and scholar Sterling Brown attended some of Ma Rainey's performances and still spoke of their impact years later: "She wouldn't have to sing any words; she would moan, and the audience would moan with her. . . . Ma really *knew* these people; she was a person of the folk; she was very simple and direct."[45] Ethel Waters, who began her career in 1917, did not sing before a northern white audience until the 1920s, and the sharp difference in audience reactions confused her and led her to conclude that she had been rebuffed when in fact she had scored a great success. "You know we took the flop of our lives just now," she told her partner, Earl Dancer. "Those people out front applauded us only because they wanted to be polite. Nobody stomped as they always do in colored theaters when I finish my act. Nobody screamed or jumped up and down. Nobody howled with joy." Later in her long career her attitude had completely reversed, but the differences in audiences obviously remained the same: "After years in white theaters I dreaded working with the unit in colored houses. The noise, the stomping, whistling, and cheering that hadn't annoyed me when I was young was now something I dreaded. There was also the familiarity of the colored audience to contend with."[46]

In New Orleans, as bands paraded through the streets, black youth, not content to merely watch and listen, would form what was called a "second line" and march alongside the musicians. "They had to make their own parade with broomsticks, kerchiefs, tin pans, any old damn' thing," Sidney Bechet recalled. "And they'd take off shouting, singing, following along the sidewalk. . . . When I was just a kid I used to get in on a lot of those second lines, singing, dancing, hollering—oh, it just couldn't be stopped." Even those who didn't second line had a chance to participate. In the frequent "bucking contests" that took place between bands, it was the crowds of onlookers that decided when one band had fallen noticeably behind the other in quality. When that happened the people watching would crowd around the victorious musicians cheering and encouraging them to go on. The process by which the audiences determined which band was superior intrigued Bechet. He concluded that it had to do with the fact that the audience was more than an audience, it was also participating: "how it was they could tell—that was the music too. It was what they had of the music inside themselves." It was always the people who made the decision: "You was always being judged."[47]

Many black musicians have echoed Bechet on this latter point. Negro audiences were much tougher than white ones, Willie the Lion Smith maintained, and the blues singer Memphis Slim agreed that white audiences were easier to win over than black ones "because you can't fool a colored audience! They're quite hard to please because *all* black Americans can sing the blues or play something and you've really got to be playing something *hard* or something different to move them."[48] These "bucking" or "cutting" contests, in which the audience determined musical quality and superiority, were not limited to the South. Garvin Bushell recalled working in a New York club named Leroy's on 135th Street and

Fifth Avenue in 1922 where such pianists as Willie the Lion Smith, James P. Johnson, Fats Waller, and Willie Gant would engage in battles of skill that would last for three or four hours. "There'd be more controversy among the listeners than the participants. There was betting and people were ready to fight about who'd won."[49]

Within Afro-American culture, then, the relationship of performers to their audience retained many of the traditional participatory elements, the give-and-take that was so familiar to nineteenth-century black storytellers and their audiences. The analogy is a particularly apt one since the performer and audience were frequently having an extended and complex conversation. Phyl Garland's description of a B. B. King performance at the Apollo Theatre in Harlem illustrates this clearly:

> he moves on into one of his most popular numbers, *You Done Lost Your Good Thing Now*, and is instantly transformed from a performer on the stage into a down-hearted man pouring out his pain to a woman who has walked all over his heart. . . . he wails out his mournful ballad of misbegotten love in a musical style that simulates all the inflections of a spoken monologue torn from the depths of the soul.
>
> He begins . . . turning his head to the side, shaking it in disbelief and grimacing at the ingratitude of this invisible woman. Squeals of delight at recognition of this common human plight issue from the audience as he repeats the statement in slightly altered form, building up to a tortured confession.
>
> Women shout out, "No! No! Don't *do* it B.B.!" Men, seeming to identify completely with the situation, vocally nod their agreement, "Man, do your *thing*, B.B.! All *right!*"[50]

Scenes like this have prompted Charles Keil to suggest that much of what appears on the surface to be mere popular entertainment in fact has a ritual significance; that such black performers as singers, musicians, comedians, disc jockeys, and even some athletes share the expressive role occupied by the preacher. The kind of blues gathering described above has definite sacred overtones in that it combines the elements of charisma, catharsis, and solidarity in the same manner a church service does: common problems are enunciated, understood, shared, and frequently the seeds of a solution to them are suggested. Similarly, John Szwed has argued that the bluesman is something of a shaman: "He presents difficult experiences for the group, and the effectiveness of his performance depends upon a mutual sharing of experience. . . . Church music is directed collectively to God; blues are directed individually to the collective. Both perform similar cathartic functions but within different frameworks." The performance of blues singer Bobby Bland at the Ashland Auditorium in Chicago is a good example. Singing of familiar human situations and dilemmas, Bland often addressed his audience much as a minister would. "Do I have a witness out there?" he would call out, to be answered by phrases common to any church goer: "Tell it like it is," "Lord, have mercy," "All right, brother."[51] Viewed in this light, blues performed some of the functions for the secularized masses that religion did: it spoke out of a group experience; it made many individual problems—dislocation, loneliness, broken families, economic difficulties—seem more common and converted them into shared experiences.

The religious analogy is borne out by many other descriptions of blues and jazz performances. In the late nineteenth century W. C. Handy and his band were playing at a black dance in the South. At certain points in the music a roar of voices came from the dance floor crying, "Set in it!" "Set *in* it!" Confused by this, Handy turned to his Creole trombone player, George Williams, who shouted "Didn' ya heah 'em?" "Sure," Handy responded, "I heard. But what do they mean? Set in *what?*" "Mon," Williams answered, "What do de jigwalk [Negroes] do wen de preacher make 'em happy, eh? Don't dey say 'hallelu' or 'glory be'? Well, dot piece make dem happy, too."[52] Toward the close of Thanksgiving Day, 1925, the white novelist Carl Van Vechten crossed the Hudson River and visited the Orpheum Theatre in Newark to hear Bessie Smith perform before an almost exclusively black audience. "Never before had I seen such an audience save at a typical Negro camp-meeting in the far South," Van Vechten wrote. As Smith sang her blues, cries of "That's right," and "Lawdy, Lawdy!" punctuated her phrases: "the crowd burst into hysterical shrieks of sorrow and lamentation. Amens rent the air."[53] Her blues, the drummer Zutty Singleton has said, "seemed almost like hymns."[54] Danny Barker, the black guitarist, has confirmed these impressions. He was convinced that Smith's performance "had a church deal mixed up in it."[55] Bessie Smith made this process of sacralizing the secular overt in her 1927 recording, *Preachin' the Blues:*

Preach them blues
Sing them blues
They certainly sound good to me. . . .

Moan them blues.
Holler them blues.
Let me convert your soul. . . .

I ain't here to try to save your soul,
Just want to teach you how to save your good Jelly Roll. . . .

Read on down to Chapter Nine,
Women must learn how to take their time.

Read on down to Chapter Ten,
Taking other women's men, you are doing a sin.

Sing 'em, sing 'em, sing them blues
Let me convert your soul.[56]

During the Great Depression an observer from the Federal Writers' Project left a memoir of a dance at the Savoy Ballroom which evoked the mood of a religious service:

> [Louis] Armstrong took up a trumpet solo, rising clear and solid above the ensemble. It seemed like a terrible weight was on him and he was lifting it higher and higher. . . . Heads shook reverently. . . .
>
> A girl had her eyes half closed. . . . Her face was a tortured inland lake in a strong wind. The song came out of her throat in a boom from deep within her bosom. There were no words: her voice, and other vibrating voices, was just a part of the inflecting band that gave Armstrong the base to improvise. . . .
>
> Nobody was alone. Each spine passed on its . . . feeling to another.[57]

Observers so frequently saw black musical performances in these terms, I suspect, because the performers themselves saw things that way. When Charlie Parker responded to a question about his religious affiliation with the seemingly flippant remark, "I am a devout musician,"[58] he was not merely signifying but testifying. That is, he was not merely putting his questioner down but stating a truth in his own cryptic way. Too many black blues singers and musicians have spoken of the sacred elements of their craft for us to ignore it. Many of T-Bone Walker's friends were convinced that he would become a preacher when he stopped singing because of the way he sang the blues. "They say it sounds like a sermon."[59] The blues singer Alberta Hunter testified that to her the blues were "almost religious. They're like a chant. The blues are like spirituals, almost sacred."[60] Frequently while he watched his fellow blues singers on stage, B. B. King maintained, "I feel like I'm in church and even want to shout."[61] A blues musician was simply telling people "what it was all about," Willie the Lion Smith was convinced, "just like a blood and thunder Baptist preacher sounding off."[62] For Sidney Bechet both the spirituals and the blues were prayers: "One was praying to God and the other was praying to what's human. It's like one was saying, 'Oh, God, let me go,' and the other was saying, 'Oh, Mister, let me be.' And they were both the same thing in a way; they were both my people's way of praying to be themselves, praying to be let alone so they could be human."[63]

Thus although blues songs were individual expression they were meant to be shared, they were meant to evoke experiences common to the group, they were meant to provide relief and release for all involved. And, the point is, all present *were* involved for black musical performances properly speaking had no audience, just participants. It was precisely these qualities that made the blues anathema to so many of the religiously committed. Lil Son Jackson, who abandoned the blues for religious singing, expressed these objections well:

> If a man feel hurt within side and he sing a church song then he's askin' God for help. . . . if a man sing the blues it's more or less out of himself. . . . He's not askin' no one for help. And he's not really clingin' to no-one. But he's expressin' how he feel. He's expressin' it to someone and that fact makes it a sin you know. . . . you're tryin' to get your feelin's over to the next person through the blues, and that's what makes it a sin.[64]

The blues was threatening not primarily because it was secular; other forms of secular music were objected to less strenuously and often not at all. Blues was threatening because its spokesmen and its ritual too frequently provided the expressive communal channels of relief that had been largely the province of religion in the past. Blues successfully blended the sacred and the secular. Like the folktales of the nineteenth century they had no beginning or end. One blues song took up where another left off; blues singer followed blues singer in a never-ending repetition that expressed the permanence of the forces that beset the individual and the group. Like the spirituals of the nineteenth century the blues was a cry for release, an ode to movement and mobility, a blend of despair and hope. Like both the spirituals and folktales blues was an expression of experiences and feelings common to the group.

"It's not only what happened to you," John Lee Hooker has said, "it's what happened to your foreparents and other people. And that's what makes the blues."[65] During the first decade of this century a young Sidney Bechet was imprisoned for the crime of being found walking in the wrong neighborhood in Galveston, Texas. While in the Galveston jail he heard a blues he was never able to forget. The black prisoner who sang it "was more than just a man. He was like every man that's been done a wrong. Inside him he'd got the memory of all the wrong that's been done to all my people. That's what the memory is . . . when I remember that man,

I'm remembering myself, a feeling I've always had. When a blues is good, that kind of memory just grows up inside it."[66] The blues allowed individuals greater voice for their individuality than any previous form of Afro-American song but kept them still members of the group, still on familiar ground, still in touch with their peers and their roots. It was a song style created by generations in the flux of change who desired and needed to meet the future without losing the past, who needed to stand alone and yet remain part of the group, who craved communication with and reassurance from members of the group as they ventured into unfamiliar territories and ways.

Although I have made no attempt to deal in detail with music that was largely instrumental and non-verbal, I should add parenthetically that in a number of respects jazz represented much the same phenomenon as blues. That is, it manifested the simultaneous acculturation to the outside society and inward-looking, group orientation that was so characteristic of black culture in the twentieth century. In terms of the growing importance of the solo instrument and of the improvised solo, jazz showed the same individualized emphasis—an emphasis essentially new to black music—as did the blues. But, like the blues, jazz too remained a communal music. In explaining his role, the great New Orleans drummer Baby Dodds illustrated the respect black jazz musicians had for the individual identities and styles of their peers even as he stressed the dependence every one of them still had upon the group:

> I feel them all out. I work with all of them because they all belong to me. I feel I'm the key man in that band. In drumming you have got to pay attention to each, everyone. You must *hear* that person distinctly, and what he wants. You got to give it to him. . . . You must study a guy's human nature, study about what he will take, or see about what he will go for. And that's in a drum, and that's why all guys are not drummers that's drumming. . . . *drumming is spirit.* You got to have that in your body, in your soul. . . . you've got to keep a spirit up. And it's a drummer's job because he's playing nothing. . . . His place it to help the other fellow, not make him play himself to death. . . . Without a drummer that knows how to *help*, there's no band.[67]

During the years of transitions from slavery to freedom, from rural to urban, from South to North, from self-containment to greater exposure to the larger society, black secular music became an increasingly dominant expressive mode reflecting inevitably the decay of the sacred universe. Secular music was not a homogeneous force; it was composed of distinct and varied elements and it underwent constant change, just as black people themselves did. But within all the varied components of black music and throughout all the changes it underwent, it remained a group-oriented means of communication and expression. Acculturation to the tastes and standards of the larger society was undeniably taking place but the continued existence of a flexible, creative, and distinct Afro-American expressive culture indicated that the group itself remained alive, creative, and distinctive. An understanding of its values and attitudes requires an examination of the content of the black secular music we have been discussing.

SECULAR SONG AND PROTEST

To argue that Negro secular song has functioned primarily or even largely as a medium of protest would distort black music and black culture. Blacks have not spent all of their time reacting to whites and their songs are filled with comments on all aspects of life. But it would be an even greater distortion to assume that a people occupying the position that Negroes have in this society could produce a music so rich and varied with few allusions to their situation or only slight indications of their reactions to the treatment they were accorded. While black secular song is not dominated by such reactions, it is a rich repository of them and offers a new window onto the lives and into the minds of a large segment of the black population.

For millions of Negroes during the century after emancipation, the normal outlets for protest remained closed. They were denied the right of political expression and active demonstration. To understand their reaction to the system under which they lived, it is necessary to broaden our definition of protest and resistance, to make it less restrictive and more realistic. This is particularly important because so much of the recent discussion has been concerned with the effects of American racial patterns upon Negro psychic and emotional development. There has been an unfortunate if understandable tendency in our political age to conceive of protest in almost exclusively political and institutional terms. Thus group consciousness and a firm sense of the self have been confused with political consciousness and organization, "manhood" has been equated with armed rebellion, and resistance with the building of a revolutionary tradition. To state that black song constituted a form of black protest and resistance does not mean that it necessarily led to or even called for any tangible and specific actions, but rather that it served as a mechanism by which Negroes could be relatively candid in a society that rarely accorded them that privilege, could communicate this candor to others whom they would in no other way be able to reach, and, in the face of the sanctions of the white majority, could assert their own individuality, aspirations, and sense of being. Certainly, if nothing else, black song makes it difficult to believe that Negroes internalized their situation so completely, accepted the values of the larger society so totally, or manifested so pervasive an apathy as we have been led to believe.

What Harold Courlander has argued for blues and religious songs applies to most forms of black song: they generally are not vehicles for the telling of explicit, chronological, developed stories. They more often embody personal comment and reaction and put their message across through innuendo, repetition, hints, and allusion.[1] As Bruce Jackson has maintained, the structural units in Negro folksongs are typically the metaphor and line rather than the plot; Negro songs don't tend to weave narrative elements together to create a story but instead accumulate images to create a feeling.[2] These characteristics have made black song an especially effective medium for complaint, protest, and the venting of frustrations. These same qualities, of course, also make it difficult to interpret the meaning of many black songs.

A number of twentieth-century secular songs continued the covert symbolic practices of nineteenth-century slave lore. The most common of these were the ballads of the boll weevil—an insect which first made its way from Mexico to Texas in the 1890s and by the mid-1920s had inundated the cotton South. In 1921 the weevil damaged more than 30 per cent of the cotton crop. Many areas were totally devastated. Greene County, Georgia, fell from a high of 20,039 bales of cotton ginned in 1919 to 333 bales ginned in 1922.[3] Negro farmers and sharecroppers were badly hurt by the activities of the boll weevil, yet the chief sentiment expressed in black song was one of admiration for the tiny creatures' ability to withstand all that civilization could do to them:

I found a little boll weevil,
An' put 'im on de ice.
Thought dat dat 'ud kill him,
But he say, "Oh ain't dat nice
  Dis is mah home, dis is mah home!"

Found anodder little weevil,
Put 'im in de sand.
Thought dat sure would kill 'im,
But he stood hit lack a man.
    Dat was his home, dat was his home![4]

There were inevitable complaints about the weevil:

Don't you see how them creeturs
Now have done me wrong?
Boll weevil's got my cotton
And the merchant's got my corn.
What shall I do? What shall I do?

But in the same song in which this lament occurs, there is obvious vicarious pleasure derived from the weevil's success in humbling one pillar of society after another:

Boll weevil said to the merchant,
"Better drink you cold lemonade;
When I git thru with you
Gwine drag you out o' the shade—
I have a home! I have a home!"

Boll weevil said to the doctor,
"Better po' out all them pills;
When I get through with the farmer
He can't pay no doctor's bills—
I have a home! I have a home!"[5]

In her autobiography Mahalia Jackson made this sense of satisfaction even more explicit:

They were a proud and selfish people, those plantation owners, and I believe . . . that God finally sent the boll weevil to jumble them. When the boll weevil came, it ate right through thousands of fields of cotton and most of those big plantations went bankrupt. That part of the South went down and it has never come back up. Thanks to the boll weevil, a lot of those thieving plantation people died out, too.[6]

In Texas, Negroes sang of an equally indomitable gray goose who was shot while in flight and took six weeks to fall, six weeks to be plucked, six weeks to boil, and then neither fork nor knife could penetrate his skin.

So they throwed him in the hog pen, Lawd, Lawd, Lawd,
He broke ol' Jerry's jawbone, Lawd, Lawd, Lawd.
So they taken him to the sawmill, Lawd, Lawd, Lawd.
He broke the saw's teeth out, Lawd, Lawd, Lawd.

Well, the last time I seed him, Lawd, Lawd, Lawd.
He was flyin' across the ocean, Lawd, Lawd, Lawd.
With a long string of goslins, Lawd, Lawd, Lawd.
All gwine quink-quank, Lawd, Lawd, Lawd.

Leadbelly, who sang *Gray Goose* as a prisoner in Texas, maintained that the song was used by the convicts to express defiance of their jailers and admiration of their fellows who could withstand the inhumanities of prison life.[7]

The existence of double meaning in black folk songs has long been recognized. Howard Odum, for example, reflected upon the "paradoxes and contradictions" contained in the songs he collected, admitted that "the negro is very secretive," and spoke of "the resourcefulness and adaptability of the negro" and of "his hypocrisy and two-faced survival mechanisms."[8] The only instance in which this phenomenon was studied in any detail by the early-twentieth-century collectors, however, focused upon sexual relations. In 1927 Guy Johnson pointed out that when black songs depict men stealing, cheating, and dying for a piece of their woman's jelly roll, angel food cake, or shortening bread, it is difficult to believe that these terms refer to food.

Dupree was a bandit,
He was brave an' bol',
He stole that diamon' ring
For some of Betty's jelly roll.

Johnson found that words like "cabbage," "keyhole," "cookie," and "cake," were frequently used as symbols for the female sexual organs.[9]

Johnson's list of sexual metaphors just began to touch the surface of the rich sexual imagery that filled the blues recordings of the 1920s and 1930s. The bluesman of the period could refer to his penis in the imaginative terms of Blind Lemon Jefferson:

Um-um, black snake crawling in my room.
Um-um, black snake crawling in my room.
Yes, some pretty mama better get this black snake soon.[10]

Or the more open lines of Bo Carter:

I come over here, sweet baby, just to get my ashes hauled,
Lord, the women at the other place goin' to let my ashes spoil,
Won't you draw on my cigaret, smoke it there all night long,
Just draw on my cigaret, baby, until you make my good ashes come.[11]

With the adaptability so typical of black music, the blues' sexual imagery reflected the technology of the period. Thus Memphis Minnie pleaded:

> Won't you be my chauffeur, won't you be my chauffeur?
> I want someone to drive me, I want someone to drive me downtown.
> Baby drives so easy I can't turn him down.[12]

And, in the most popular record he made, Robert Johnson sang more enigmatically:

> I said I flashed your light, mama, your horn won't even blow.
> I even flashed my light, mama, this horn won't even blow.
> There's a short in this connection way down below. . . .
>
> I'm going to get deep down in this connection, keep on tangling with your wires.
> I'm going to get deep down in this connection, keep on tangling with your wires.
> And when I mash down on your starter, then your spark plugs will give me fire.[13]

On record after record, blues singers boasted: "My daddy rocks me with one steady roll," exclaimed jubilantly: "It's tight like that," sang of their "easy rider," and their "ramrod daddy," pleaded: "Let me in your saddle," warned: "You sure won't miss your jelly, till your jelly roller's gone," and complained: "My pencil won't write no more."[14]

A number of students of blues have rather defensively attributed what they call "the unbelievable horrors of bad taste," the "degrading material," and the "cheap vulgarity" of many of these blues to the recording companies' desire for profits. Certainly commercialization may have stimulated the use of thinly veiled sexual metaphors, though this was a two-edged sword since the public nature of the recording industry also led to some censorship and suppression of this material. But it is essential to remember that the recording companies, however they may have encouraged the use of metaphor and innuendo, did not create the practice. They were tapping a deep wellspring of tradition. At the turn of the century Negro workers digging railroad tunnels in the South would sing over and over:

> O my baby, my honey gal—
>   Driving hard,—huh. [This follows each line.]
> Hard to please, never done—
> Just one inch, was the bargain—
> Wants another, and another—
> I told her, "Bargain's a bargain"—

Done no good, not a bit—
Change her mind, right away—
Wants a yard, foot ain't enough—
Wants my hammer, handle too—
Says, "Be a man, like your old dad—
Drive her home, my honey boy"—[15]

Working in noisy seclusion with no women and few outsiders around, these tunnel gangs used sexual indirection and metaphor not because they had to but because they wanted to, because they found its use challenging, aesthetically pleasing, and humorous. Circumlocution and indirection were not merely tactics to evade censorship or glean profits but deeply satisfying folk devices which can be traced directly back to African tradition, though certainly they had their analogues in Euro-American folk practices as well.

Songs of sexual circumlocution, then, long antedated the recording industry, remain in the folk tradition to this day, and make it clear just how common the technique of indirection remained in twentieth-century black song.[16] Guy Johnson never claimed that all double meanings in Negro music were of a sexual nature, and in a footnote he indicated: "There are, for example, many hidden references to the white man in the Negro's songs. This is an interesting field of research in which little has been done."[17] But it was doubtless easier for Johnson and many of his colleagues to admit the existence of double meaning in sexual relations, since that merely confirmed their image of the low moral state of the Negro. They were less ready to analyze double meaning that reflected lack of contentment or anything less than total adjustment. Once the door is opened, however, it is difficult to close again. Once the existence of *double entendre* and veiled meaning is admitted in one area, it is hard to rule it out in others.

We have seen that in their religious music blacks continued the nineteenth-century practices of meanings within meanings: the Devil and the Old Testament figures could be surrogates for contemporaries; "letters from the Lord," and "trains to glory" could refer to the migrations that were altering the face of American life. Secular work songs and blues tended to be more direct and open, but this was by no means invariable. Even in songs as familiar as the John Henry work songs, ambiguities were not uncommon:

This old hammer killed John Henry
But it can't kill me.

Take this hammer, take it to the Captain,
Tell him I'm gone, babe, tell him I'm gone.[18]

The possible meanings of the following lyrics from another song are also intriguing:

Niggers gettin' mo' like white fo'ks,
Mo' like white fo'ks eve'y day.
Niggers learnin' Greek an' Latin,
Niggers wearin' silk an' satin,
Niggers gettin' mo' like white fo'ks eve'y day.[19]

In 1917 John Lomax interpreted those lines as presenting "the cheerful side of improving social conditions." But they could as easily, and perhaps more meaningfully, be seen as an example of lower-class black satire and anger directed at those Negroes who were trying to become culturally "white." An even greater interpretative challenge is presented by these lyrics sung by a black Georgia worker in the 1920s:

Ever see bear cat
Turn to lion,
Lawd, Lawd,
Down in Georgia?

My ol' bear cat,
My ol' bear cat
Turn to lion,
Lawd, Lawd, Lawd. . . .[20]

The most ostensibly innocent and lighthearted song could suddenly be transformed by the injection of one or two lines. This Sea Island jingle, the chorus of which went, "Ding dang me one / Ding Dang. / Ding dang me two / Ding dang," and so on, is a good example:

Once I went out huntin'
I heard de possum sneeze
I holler back to Susan
Put on de pot o' peas.

CHORUS

I went down to Missy house
    Missy was in bed
I took de marrow bone
    An' beat her in de head.

CHORUS.[21]

"Snappo-snap-peter, snap-nany goat eater, snap-po," a Negro in Auburn, Alabama, sang and suddenly followed these apparently nonsense syllables with the sober observation: "I'm gwine away and never come back no more."[22]

Recalling her youth in Philadelphia where she lived in a three-room shanty in an alley in the heart of the red-light district, Ethel Waters described how she and other black children would act as lookouts for the prostitutes. Whenever they would spot a stranger who had the appearance of a plain-clothes policeman, they would sing a prearranged children's song, such as:

King William was King James's son,
Upon his breast he wore a star, . . .

"The other kids, even those who weren't lookouts, would innocently imitate us, and in no time at all the whole neighborhood would be alerted. The street women would disappear, the lights would go out, and the doors would be locked in the sporting houses."[23]

The number of songs containing ambiguous metaphors and intriguing but obscure symbolism could be extended indefinitely. Still, there are hollers, work songs, and blues whose meaning is not subject to a great deal of interpretation. A large body of songs from the first four or five decades of this century make it unmistakably clear that Negro music has been a crucial and perhaps central vehicle for the expression of discontent and protest. There were constant complaints about the white "captain," working conditions, the unfairness of the sharecropping system, long hours, low pay. Often, fear of the white boss drove these attitudes completely underground. As one Memphis worker put it:

I've knowed guys that wanted to cuss out the boss and was afraid to go up to his face and tell him what they wanted to tell him. And I've heered a guy sing those things to the boss when he were out behind a wagon, hookin' up the horses. He'd make out like a horse stepped on his foot and he'd say, "Get off my foot, goddam!"—saying just what he wanted to say to his boss, only talkin' to the horse—"You got no business doin' me like that! Get offa my foot!"[24]

Sometimes these attitudes were expressed satirically:

Reason I love my captain so,
'Cause I ast him for a dollah,
Lawd, he give me fo'.[25]

But more often twentieth-century work songs described working conditions and feelings with a jarring candor and realism which give substance to Alan Merriam's generalization that "song texts provide a framework for permissive language behavior." The African tradition of being able to verbalize publicly in song what could not be said to a person's face, not only lived on among Afro-Americans throughout slavery but continued to be a central feature of black expressive culture in freedom.[26]

In the fall of 1965, Bruce Jackson recorded a group of black prisoners in Texas singing a work song which called the prison captain a devil, held him responsible for the birth of a blue-eyed baby by one of the prisoner's women, and in the process played with the word "rider," which in black song normally means sexual partner but in this song refers as well to the mounted prison guards:

> Carrie got a baby, Carrie got a baby OH YEAH.
> It's got blue eyes, sir, It's got blue eyes, sir, OH YEAH.
> Blue eyes like the rider, WO, blue eyes like the rider, WO MY LORD.
> He was always there, sir, always there, sir, OH YEAH.
> Looka looka yonder, looka looka yonder, OH YEAH.
> I believe I spy the devil, WO, I believe I spy the devil, WO MY LORD.
> Who is that devil? Who is that devil? OH YEAH.
> Captain McGaughey, Captain McGaughey, OH YEAH.
> He's the devil in the bottom, WO, he's the devil in the bottom, WO MY LORD.

The next year Jackson heard a work gang in another prison sing:

> I see the Captain sittin' in the shade
> YEAH, YEAH, YEAH, YEAH,
> He don't do nothin' but a he gets paid,
> YEAH, YEAH, YEAH, YEAH.

"In the river songs you tell the truth about how you feel, you know, but you can't express it, see, to the boss," one of the prisoners told him. "They really be singing about the way they feel inside. Since they can't say it to nobody they sing a song about it."[27]

In their willingness to criticize the white boss openly through song, these contemporary prisoners were following a tradition established by black laborers long before. Negro work songs published by Howard Odum in 1911 were filled with complaints and even threats:

> Well, captain, captain, how can it be?
> Whistles keep a-blowin', you keep a-workin' me.

> Well, if I had my weight in lime,
> I'd whip my captain till I went stone-blind.
>
> Well, cap'n, cap'n, didn't you say
> You wouldn't work me in rain all day?
>
> Well, you can't do me like you do po' Shine,
> You take Shine's money, but you can't take mine.

One black worker let his boss know he resented the treatment he had been given: "You hurt my feelin's, but I won't let on," while another asserted his independence from the white man's domination:

> If you don't like the way I work, jus' pay me off;
>   I want to speak one luvin' word before I go;
> I know you think I'm pow'ful easy, but I ain't so sof',
>   I can git another job an' be my boss.[28]

Throughout the 1920s black laborers continued to point out the discrepancies between themselves and their employers:

> White man in starched shirt settin' in shade,
> Laziest man that God ever made,
>   Baby, baby.[29]

These comments intensified during the Great Depression. "The Boss-man he is evil, the job is hard as hell, / But I'm gonna stay here with it on account of my big brown gal," Florida phosphate miners sang.[30] Again and again black workers commented upon the heartlessness of the whites:

> I ask my cap'n,
> "Cap'n won't you have a little mercy."
> I ask my cap'n,
> "Cap'n won't you have a little mercy
> Upon a man,
> Oh my Lord, upon a man."
>
> My cap'n cried out,
> "Lordy we don' have no mercy."
> My cap'n cried out,
> "Lordy we don' have no mercy
> On no one man,
> On no one man."[31]

Black sharecroppers in the Mississippi Delta in the 1940s continued the tradition:

> Old Capt. Quinn I most all forgot
> He's the meanest old white man we had in the lot

For $5.00 he'd run you right well
For $25.00 he'd run you to hell
Hard times, po' boy
Hard times, po' boy.[32]

If black workers suffered, then, they hardly suffered in silence; their feelings about the white men who employed them and supervised their labors were articulated frequently and publicly. These songs constituted more than conventional griping. Throughout them there ran a deep feeling of injustice and an enduring sense of being used unfairly. A number of songs expressing these sentiments dated from at least the nineteenth century and lived on well into the twentieth. In 1853 the fugitive slave William Wells Brown printed this slave song:

The big bee flies high,
The little bee makes the honey;
The black folks makes the cotton
And the white folks gets the money.[33]

In 1880 Joel Chandler Harris printed this little rhyme in his original Uncle Remus volume:

De ole bee make de honey-comb,
    De young bee make de honey,
De niggers make de cotton en co'n,
    En de w'ite folks gits de money.[34]

In 1914 on a plantation in Scotland County, North Carolina, Negro share-croppers sang:

The old bee makes de honey-comb,
The young bee makes de honey;
Colored folks plant de cotton and corn,
And de white folks gits de money.[35]

During the Great Depression Negro farm workers sang the closely related lines:

Niggers plant cotton,
Niggers pick it out,
White man pockets money,
Nigger does without.[36]

Other songs of discontent had similar longevity. In 1891 Gates Thomas collected a song that was to become one of the most ubiquitous songs of injustice among twentieth-century blacks:

> Nought's a nought, figger's a figger,
> Figger for the white man, nought for the nigger.
> Nigger and a white man playin' seven up,
> Nigger won the money but was feard to pick it up.[37]

The song proved adaptable to the varied situations Negroes found themselves in. Twenty-five years later, for instance, black workers at a dolomite quarry in Ketona, Alabama, sang:

> Aught is an aught
> And figger is a figger
> All for the company
> And none for the nigger.[38]

In 1895 Thomas collected another song that was to be sung throughout the South in the twentieth century:

> White man goes to college,
> Nigger to the field;
> White man learns to read and write;
> Poor Nigger learns to steal, Honey Babe,
> Poor Nigger learns to steal.[39]

The central feeling of all these songs was expressed in still another well-known song first collected by Howard Odum in Newton County, Georgia, in 1909:

> Ain't it hard, ain't it hard,
> Ain't it hard to be a nigger, nigger, nigger?
> Ain't it hard, ain't it hard,
> For you can't git yo' money when it's due.[40]

Long hours of hard labor, low wages, and a system which kept most of the capital and land in the control of whites were the chief grievances of black song. There was, one singer admitted, "Plenty to eat, / Place to sleep," but "nothin' fer a feller, / Lawd, nothin' fer / A feller to keep."[41] Black roustabouts loading and unloading the steamboats, used one phrase to describe both the load on their shoulders and their entire social situation:

> Oh Lawd, I didn't know
> I had to bow so low.[42]

A female cotton picker on the Sea Islands complained of conditions which made it impossible for her to meet her daily quota of one hundred pounds of cotton:

> Black man beat me—white man cheat me
> Won' get my hundud all day.[43]

"Po' farmer, po' farmer," a Negro sharecropper on the Smithers Plantation in Huntsville, Texas, chanted in 1934, "Dey git all de farmer make." The hard work and small return were universal complaints: "Fer a nickel's worth of crackers and a dime's worth of cheese, . . . Dey treat him like a dog and do him like dey please." "Work all week in the noonday sun;/ Fifteen cents when Sat'day come."[44]

Next to the arbitrary boss, the low pay, and the poor working conditions, the chief grievance was the lack of legal justice. In 1915 blacks in Auburn, Alabama, sang:

> If a white man kills a negro, they hardly carry it to court,
> If a negro kills a white man, they hang him like a goat.[45]

During the Great Depression blacks in Atlanta complained: "Niggers ain't got no justice in Atlanta, / Lockin' up nigger, letting the white folks go."[46] New York City Negroes felt no less vulnerable:

> Here's a little something what you should all know
> They always pinch the nigger and let the white folks go.[47]

In his *Death Cell Blues*, Blind Willie McTell used phrases common to many black songs concerning justice: "They got me killed for murder, and I haven't even harmed a man. . . . They have me charged for burglarin', I haven't even raised my hand. . . . They got me 'cused for forging, and I can't even write my name."[48] The charge of police harassment was common throughout the South and North:

> Walked down the avenue
> Who should I meet
> Forty leven 'liceman
> Coming down the street
> Well I ain't done nothing
> What they foller after me
> I ain't done nothing
> Can't they let me be?[49]

No lines more graphically described the feelings of many blacks about the justice they received than these:

> White folks and nigger in great Co't house
> Like Cat down Celler wit' no-hole mouse.[50]

For many Negroes the Depression merely intensified an unjust economic situation that was already prevalent. "De raggedy man see de hahd time, . . . When his money is gone," black workers in the South sang,

"Now you an' me see de hahd time, . . . Sence we wuz bawn."[51] Although there were quite a few songs praising Roosevelt and the agencies he established to alleviate the worst effects of the Depression, there were no illusions about the New Deal and its racial attitudes. "I gave up my room 'cause I couldn't pay rent," a New Orleans black sang, "I went to the Welfare, they wouldn't give me a cent."[52] The experience was echoed in a New York song:

> Woke up this morning about half past four
> To wait on line down the welfare store
> No-lunch noon afore I get into that place
> Man look at my face
> Nothing for you
> Cause done close your case.[53]

This situation produced Big Bill Broonzy's *Black, Brown and White:*

> I went to an employment office
> Got a number and I got in line
> They called everybody's number
> But they never did call mine.
>
> They say if you's white, should be all right
> If you's brown, stick around
> But as you're black
> Mmm, Mmm, Brother, git back, git back, git back.[54]

This sense of injustice, which embodied no illusions about the realities of the American racial situation or the Negro's place in it, was often accompanied by a great deal of anger and aggression:

> I asked that boss-man for to gimme my time;
> Sez he, "Ole Nigger, you're a day behin'."
>
> I asked him once, I asked him twaist;
> Ef I ask him again, I'll take his life.[55]

Lines like "I didn't come here to be nobody's dog," "Ain't let nobody treat me dis way," "Ain't gonna be bossed aroun' no mo'," "Ain't gwine let you humbug me," "I ain't gonna be your old work ox no more, / You can never tell what your old work ox gwine do," "Get away all you white folks, stop worrying me," "I ain't gonna let nobody, / Nobody make a fool out o' me," were common.[56]

Often this anger took the form not of overt expressions of aggression so much as of refusing to play the game by the white man's rules: "Cap'n says hurry, I say take my time," "Dere ain't no use in my workin' so hard," "When you think I'm workin', I ain't doin' a thing."[57] In spite of the pervasiveness of the Alger message among spokesmen, both black and white, it was becoming increasingly clear to black workers that the American success ethos was not designed to include them. As workers in Georgia in the early years of the century put it:

> If you work all the week,
>   An' work all the time,
> White man sho' to bring
>   Nigger out behin'.[58]

This sentiment was a common one. In 1905 blacks in Texas made it clear that they understood they were condemned no matter what their actions:

> Well, they call me a rounder if I stay in town, and they say
>   I'm a rounder if I roam aroun';
> I got it writ on the tail of my shirt: "I'm a nachel-bo'n
>   rounder and don't need to work."
> And so I ain't bothered; no, I ain't bothered.[59]

Three decades later, depression-ridden Negroes in New York agreed:

> 'Cause white folks expect nigger to be lazy
> Ain't no cause to worry
> I wouldn't disappoints him for the world
> That's why I never hurry.[60]

In 1939 a Harlem prostitute told a WPA interviewer: "They says this is a rich country. I ain' seen it nevva. I don't expects t' see it nevva. I almos' give up hope fur anythin' except this here so n' so business. Whut else is there, huh? Nothing."[61] At approximately the same time Gracie Turner, a North Carolina sharecropper, told an interviewer for the Federal Writers' Project: " 'Tain't no while to say dis is de hardest year we's ever had. Every year's been hard, de forty-nine years I been here. Dat's all dey is to expect—work hard and go hongry part time—long as we lives on de other man's land. Dey ain't nothin' in sharecroppin', not de way it's run."[62] In the early 1950s James Cotton, born and raised in the farm country around Tunica, Mississippi, recorded his *Cotton Crop Blues* with its familiar theme:

> Ain't gonna raise no mo' cotton, I'll tell you the reason why I says so,
> Ain't gonna raise no mo' cotton, tell you the reason why I says so,
> Well you don't get nothin' for your cotton and your seed's so dog-gone
>   low. . . .

> I've ploughed so hard baby, till corns have got all over my hands,
> I ploughed so hard baby till I got corns all over my hands,
> I wanna tell you people it ain't nothin' for a poor farmin' man.[63]

The lesson was learned anew generation after generation. During the 1960s a black prisoner told Bruce Jackson how he used to work hard picking cotton in order to win the prize for the most cotton picked. Finally the grand moment came: "The captain called us up to the picket. He said, 'Give me my three best cotton pickers here.' Me and Willie Lawrence and old Foots, we all went up there. 'Seein' the way you picked, I'm gonna give you all the prize.' He say, 'You all split this.' He gave us a quarter. After that I never picked for no prize, that broke it up."[64]

These lyrics and attitudes are important because they not only indicate a rather precise understanding of the way in which the American economic system operated for most black farmers and workers, but because they are an assertion of a break with a number of the idealized values and mores of American society. Few songs articulated this disillusionment with the American mythos more clearly than one heard by Walter Prescott Webb in Gatesville, Texas, after World War I:

> Geo'ge Washin'ton, I hate to say you nevah tole a lie,
> I wish there wuz no Washin'ton, I do, I hope I die.
> When I wuz a little boy some white man felt o' my haid,
> Said, "Some day you may be president,"—some day I nevah see.
> Somebody lie, dat's sho as you born, somebody lie on me.[65]

Independence of judgment, refusal to blindly accept the prevalent stereotypes about blacks and whites, marked many black songs: "Cap'n called me . . . 'a nappy-headed devil,' / That ain't my name, that ain't my name." "Captain called me lazy, but I am a working man." "White man think he smart, / Niggers thinks he's dumb." "White folks he ain't Jesus, he jes' a man, grabbin' biscuit out of poor nigger's hand."

> Think something of yourself you crazy dunce
> No matter if you was a slave once
> Every nation done been a slave once
> They didn't draw up and act a dunce
> Think because you a nigger
> You just can't get no bigger.[66]

Of course there was some tension between the boast in one song, "I'm de lazies' Nigger sho' as yo' born," and the admonition in another, "Think because you a nigger / You just can't get no bigger." The tension was inherent in the black situation: a need to role play—to use the stereotypes of the larger society to one's own advantage—and a need to make sure the role was not internalized, that the stereotype did not become real. The importance of Negro folk culture is that it afforded the opportunity to talk about these problems, to share them, to convince blacks and warn whites that the situation which produced these tensions was not impervious to change. Black secular song, no less than black religious song, contained assurances of change and retribution. Many of the captain songs warned him that his power was ephemeral: "Oh listen, Cap'n, want you to know, you got to reap jes' what you sow." "Some of these days, you gwine get your due."[67]

In a commonly sung work song, black prisoners in 1934 openly promised their jailers retribution:

Oh well, you kicked and stomped and beat me,
Oh well, you kicked and stomped and beat me,
Oh Captain, and you called it fun, O Lord,
O Lordy Lord.

Well, I may meet you over in Memphis,
Well, I may meet you over in Memphis,
O Captain, we're going t' have a little run, O Lord,
O Lordy Lord.[68]

Occasionally, there was even a sense of the possibility of turning the tables completely, as in this early twentieth-century song:

Well, I'm goin' to buy me a little railroad of my own,
Ain't goin' to let nobody ride but the chocolate to the bone.

Well, I goin' to buy me a hotel of my own,
Ain't goin' to let nobody eat but the chocolate to the bone.[69]

This kind of cataclysmic change was pictured less frequently in secular than in religious song. More common were simple demands for a change in the way Negroes were treated. Thus in the early years of the Great Depression a gang of black workers in the Craggy Mountains of North Carolina sang:

If you treat me right,
I'd sooner work than play;
If you treat me mean,
I won't do neither way.[70]

Twentieth-century black secular songs pictured the condition and problems of black Americans with such detailed realism that they were often accompanied by a deadening sense of despair. Indeed, one of the most popular forms of black secular song, the blues, became synonymous with trouble. As folk blues singers in Alabama in 1915 and 1916 defined them: "Blues ain't nothin' but a good man feeling bad."[71] The mood described in this definition probably has been overemphasized and has tended to distort the image of the blues and, by extension, of all black secular music. It is a necessary corrective to agree with Richard Wright's depiction of the blues as "sad-happy songs that laugh and weep all in one breath," and with Ortiz Walton's more recent assertion that the blues embodied "the seemingly contradictory elements of rapture and melancholy."[72] Blues, and other forms of twentieth-century black secular music, attempted to portray the entire spectrum of black experiences and reactions. Still, as varied as this spectrum may have been, it did contain a substantial amount of articulated troubles and misery.

"There's lots of trouble here, and more on down the road, / You will always find trouble, no matter where you go," Floyd Canada of Beeville, Texas, sang in 1915.[73] "Talk about trouble," Negroes in North Carolina agreed, "That's all I've ever known."[74] "I'm goin' crazy, I'm goin' crazy, . . . I don't know what to do," black pick and shovel workers sang around 1909.[75] Loading and unloading the steamboats on southern rivers, black roustabouts sang over and over:

> Don' know what in this worl' I'm goin' to do, oh Baby,
> Don' know what in this worl' I'm goin' to do, oh Baby,
> Don' know what in this worl' I'm goin' to do.[76]

The pain that filled so many southern black songs was echoed in the songs of northern migrants. The following examples were collected from New York City Negroes in the 1930s:

> Bad luck started with me when I was born
> Leastwise so the old folks say
> That same hard luck's been closer to me than a friend
> To this very day.

> If you don't believe I'm sinking
> Just look at the hole I'm in
> If you don't believe I'm bound up in trouble
> Just look at the color of my skin.[77]

J. B. Smith, a prisoner in Texas, summed up the essence of many black songs when he sang: "Life's been a long lone gamble, I just can't seem to win."[78]

Blues and other forms of secular song were not only ways of articulating troubles, they were also a means of exorcising them, or at least their effects. This has been testified to by one black singer after another. Lil Son Jackson recalled the massive burden of economic and social injustice his sharecropper father labored under: "That was the onliest way he could get relief from it, by singin' them blues. Just like me or anybody. I can get vexed up or somethin' or I have a sad feelin'; seems like to me that if I can sing, I feel better." "I tell you," Henry Townsend agreed, "in most cases the way I feel, the song will come to you when you are really depressed you know. I mean, words'll come to you and you feel them and you decide you'll do something about it, so the thing that you do about it is more or less to put it in rhymes and words and make them come out. It give you relief—it kinda helps somehow, I don't know—it kinda helps."[79] "I've had sad feelings to come on me," Robert Pete Williams has testified. "Know what I mean by sad feelings? It's something like the whole world's kinda like against you or down on you. I've walked along with a sad feeling and cried to myself. I have. . . . But I go ahead and sing the blues 'til I kinda get eased. When I get eased, well, it look like things kinda lighten up off of me, you know? That's right."[80]

The fact that song could be utilized to expunge difficulties may well help to account for the strong tradition of disaster songs in black music. The prolific body of song describing natural and man-made calamities was one of the few types of Afro-American song that came close to being a historical record. The periodic financial crises that marked the American economic system were caught in black song. Years after the Panic of 1907, southern Negroes were still describing it in song:

> A nickel worth of meal and a dime of lard
> Will do while the panic's on.
> Save up yo' money,
> Don' you buy no corn
> Cause de panic's on.
> I wear shoes made of all kinds of leather,
> I wear clothes made for all kinds of weather
> Cause de panic's on.[81]

A few decades later descriptions of the Great Depression became common:

> Well, look down the country! It almost make you cry.
> Well, look down the country! It almost make you cry.
> *Spoken:* My God, children.
> Women and children flagging freight trains for rides.[82]

Financial disaster, already so well interwoven into black song, was less central in disaster songs than other types of calamity. In 1911 a special train carrying 912 Negro passengers pulled out of Durham, North Carolina, on the annual excursion of the St. Joseph's African Methodist Episcopal Sunday School. Outside Hamlet, North Carolina, the excursion special collided with a freight train, leaving scores of passengers dead and injured. Decades later North Carolina blacks were still singing of the tragedy:

> Now, colored people, I will tell you to your face,
> The train that left Durham was loaded with our race,
> And some did not think of dying
> When they rode down the line.
> So many have lost their lives.[83]

One year later another dramatic wreck, that of the *Titanic*, captured the imagination of Negroes throughout the country. The last chapter illustrated the ways in which disasters such as the *Titanic* were used to strengthen belief in God. But there were secular versions and secular functions as well. They shared with the religious renditions satisfaction that the rich were treated no differently than the poor; the version learned and perpetuated by Leadbelly derived pleasure from the fact that the disaster was an all-white affair and made much of the report that the black heavyweight champion of the world, Jack Johnson, had been refused passage on the doomed voyage:

> Jack Johnson wanted to get on boa'd;
> Captain Smith hollered, "I ain't haulin' no coal."
> Cryin', "Fare thee, *Titanic*, fare thee well!"
>
> Jack Johnson heard the mighty shock,
> Might' a seen the black rascal doin' the Eagle Rock.
> Cryin', "Fare thee, *Titanic*, fare thee well!"
>
> Black man oughta shout for joy,
> Never lost a girl or either a boy.
> Cryin', "Fare thee, *Titanic*, fare thee well!" ©[84]

Natural calamities, which proved to be the most common focus of disaster songs, were often the subject of the race records of the 1920s and 1930s. The Mississippi floods of 1927, which left over a half million people homeless and destitute, were described by one blues singer after another. Charley Patton cried out:

> Ohhhhh-aah, the water was rising, and we're sinking down.
> Then, the water was rising, at places all around.

Spoken: Boy they's all around.
It was fifty men and children, tumble in, sink, and drown.

Ohhhhh, Lordy, women and grown men down.
Ohhhhh, women and children sinking down.
Spoken: Lord have mercy.
I couldn't see nobody home, and wasn't no one to be found.[85]

Bessie Smith echoed his anguish:

Ma and Pa got drownded, Mississippi you to blame,
My Ma and Pa got drownded, Mississippi you to blame,
Mississippi River, I can't bear to hear your name.[86]

The drought that began in 1930 and destroyed crops and parched fields throughout the Southwest and Lower Mississippi Valley quickly became an important topic of song. "I ain't got no money and I sure ain't got no home, / The old weather done come in, parched up all the cotton and corn," Charley Patton lamented.[87] "I stood in my back yard, I wrung my hands and screamed," Son House sang. "And I couldn't see nothing, couldn't see nothing green."[88] Recordings made it possible to spread the news of local calamities throughout the Afro-American world. In 1940 Gene Gilmore reported a fire in the Natchez Rhythm Club which killed two hundred people gathered there for a dance:

Lord, I know, I know—how you Natchez people feel to-day;
  (twice)
Some of them thinking of the fire that took their children's
  lives away. . . .

Lord, it was sad and misery when the high flames began to roll,
  (twice)
There was over two hundred dead and gone, Lord, and they
  can't come here no more.[89]

Fire and flood, wind and drought, crashes of trains, ships, and stock markets; songs about these and similar calamities constituted another example in black song of the need to seek strength in the group by reaching out with tales of grief and woe, to share them with others who could understand. They also may have functioned as a kind of secular ceremonial incantation against the repetition of such disasters by assuring oneself and the group that once having happened they were not likely to happen again. This tradition has endured in black song. In 1967 George Coleman (Bongo Joe), a forty-four-year-old street singer in Galveston, Houston, and San Antonio, included in his repertory songs about such disasters as race riots, the assassination of John F. Kennedy, and the administration of Lyndon Johnson.[90]

As common as the elements of trouble, despair, and hopelessness were in black song, they were leavened by the element of humor that was such a powerful motif in all black lore. Singers could evoke sympathy and laughter at the same time:

> I can't make a nickel, I'm flat as I can be [twice],
> Some people say money is talking, but it won't say a word
>   to me.

> I had a big check when the Devil was a boy [twice],
> If I got a real job, I'd pass out with joy.[91]

"Ef trouble was money," a woman on the Brazos River sang, "I'd be a milioneer."[92] In the commonly sung *Match Box Blues*, Blind Lemon Jefferson used a comic image to describe his real plight:

> I'm sittin' here wonderin' would a match box hold my clothes,
> I'm sittin' here wonderin' would a match box hold my clothes,
> I ain't got so many matches but I got so far to go.[93]

Even the desperation of suicide could be dealt with humorously:

> Want to lay my head on de railroad line,
> Let the train come along and pacify my mind.[94]

The same elements of pathos and humor were present in what was perhaps the most familiar line in all of the blues:

> Oh, I got the blues, but I'm too damn mean to cry.[95]

The ability to laugh was itself conditioned by perspective—by the refusal to see anything as inexorable or unchanging. Big Maceo was typical in his tendency to balance his anguish with hope:

> Everything I do, it looks like I do it wrong,
> Sometime I hate the day that I ever was born—
> I'm so disgusted, I ain't got no place to go.
> But if I ever get lucky,
> I won't be a biggy fool no more.[96]

Even amidst the almost total despair of Robert Pete Williams' prison blues, the possibility of change could be interjected suddenly:

> Lord, my worry sho' carryin' me down
> Lord, my worry sho' is carryin' me down.
> Sometimes I feel like, baby, commitin' suicide.

I got the nerve if I just had anythin' to do it with.
I'm goin' down slow, somethin' wrong with me.
Yes, I'm goin' down slow, somethin' wrong with me,
I've got to make a change while that I'm still young
If I don't, I won't never get old.[97]

However slim at times, a note of hope echoed consistently through black secular song. "Lawd, I'm worried now, Lawd, / But I won't be worried long," black workers sang, and throughout the country other workers agreed:

If I make this day, huh,
I'll make tomorrow flyin', huh.
If I make this day, huh,
I'll make tomorrow flyin'.[98]

Prisoners in the Jefferson County, Alabama, jail, commonly known as Big Rock, sang: "Nine mo' months an' two mo' days, Gonna leave Big Rock behind. / An' when I leave this jail I'm gonna mend my ways, Gonna leave Big Rock behind."[99] "Trouble, trouble, I've had it all my days," Bessie Smith sang in 1923, on her first record, "It seem like trouble going to follow me to my grave." Before *Down Hearted Blues* had finished, however, her mood had changed:

I've got the world in a jug, the stopper's in my hand
I've got the world in a jug, the stopper's in my hand.
I'm gonna hold it until you come under my command.[100]

The use of black song as a vehicle for the expression of trouble and woe was common in the nineteenth as well as the twentieth century. In both centuries this mood was modified by a characteristic optimism which was based upon the strong sense of imminent change that pervaded black thought. In slavery this hope was stimulated by the sacred quality of black culture—by the religious faith in transformation and transcendence. This sacred trust did not disappear after emancipation but it was soon matched, if not eclipsed, by a new foundation for the belief in change: the freedom of movement that was increasingly possible.

The theme of mobility pervaded black music from the minstrel-like lines sung by Negro farmers in Alabama early in the century:

Over der fence and through de pasture
White man run, but de nigger run faster.[101]

to Robert Johnson's intense blues of the late 1930s:

I got to keep moving, I got to keep moving,
Blues falling down like hail, blues falling down like hail.
UmmmmUmmmmUmmmm, blues falling down like hail, blues falling
   down like hail.
And I can't keep no money with a hellhound on my trail,
Hellhound on my trail, hellhound on my trail.[102]

As important as spatial mobility has been throughout American history for all segments of the population, it was a particularly crucial symbol for Afro-Americans to whom it had been denied throughout the long years of slavery. Freedom of movement, as Howard Thurman has argued, was for Negroes the "most psychologically dramatic of all manifestations of freedom."[103] The need to move, the existence of places to go, and the ability to get there, constituted central motifs in black song after emancipation: "I jest came here to stay a little while," "Gwine whar' I never been befo'," "Oh, goin' down dat lonesome road," "I'm gonna row here few days longer, / Then, Lawd, I'm goin' on," "Gone away, never come back no more," "I'm Alabama bound," "I'm on my way, / O Lawd, I'm on my way," "I'm goin' up country," "My home ain't yere, / It's further down de road," "I got up this morning and I wash my face, / Goin' to eat breakfast in a bran' new place."[104] The railroad snaked its way through black song becoming a persistent image of change, transcendence, and the possibilities of beginning again. Generations of Negroes repeated variants of the lines sung by black ditch diggers in Andalusia, Alabama, in 1915:

When a woman takes the blues,
She tucks her head and cries;
But when a man catches the blues,
He catches er freight and rides.[105]

One of the most common hopes enunciated by black rousters on the steamships, sharecroppers in the fields, gang laborers on the railroad tracks —workers of every sort—was contained in these lines:

One a these mornin's
And it won't be long
The cap'n gonna call me
An' buddy I'm gonna be gone.[106]

The emphasis upon movement in black song reflected the currents that helped to shape Afro-American history in the United States after emancipation. There has been an unfortunate tendency to equate Negro migrations with the Great Migration to the North during the World War I period. In fact, significant movement of Negroes began as soon as freedom made it possible. Unsettled conditions after the Civil War, the novelty of freedom, economic and political repression, a quest for change and improvement, and acculturation to the American way in which movement was so important—all stimulated the migratory urge during the postbellum decades. Some of this consisted of aimless wandering as an assertion of the new freedom, but much of it was a purposeful movement to places with better economic or social conditions.

Even those who would not or could not leave their homes permanently, manifested the need to take advantage of one of the chief fruits of freedom, and railway excursions became an important part of black social life. "The Negroes are literally crazy about travelling," a white South Carolinian wrote in 1877. "The railway officials are continually importuned by them to run extra trains, excursion trains, and so on, on all sorts of occasions: holidays, picnics, Sunday-school celebrations, church dedications, funerals of their prominent men, circuses, public executions. . . . They attract whole counties of negroes."[107] The wonder and excitement of the freedom of movement was still fresh to an ex-slave sixty-five years after emancipation. Rising to terminate an interview, she remarked: "I can go when I please and come back when I please. I'll come to see you, I must go home now. I am a free rooster. I got nobody to tell me nothin."[108]

During the two and a half decades following the Civil War, then, tens of thousands of Negroes were on the move—from town to town, plantation to plantation, state to state, region to region. These migratory patterns intensified with the beginning of large-scale emigration to northern cities after 1890. The raw statistics of black migration North only begin to give a sense of the movement involved, since so much of this was secondary migration. The route from the southern farm to the northern city was not necessarily direct but frequently was preceded by migration to a southern town or city. A large percentage of the migrants from the Sea Islands, for example, got their first taste of urban life not in New York or Boston but in Savannah.[109] Even after the migration North there remained a great deal of shuttling back and forth. Thus significant demographic shifts marked the lives of large numbers of Negroes from emancipation on. When black turpentine crews in the Florida woods sang

When I left de State of old Virginia,
I left in de winter time;
Where you guin Nigger?
I'se guin to Florida, I'se guin to Florida,
Guin to Florida to work in de turpentine.

they were reciting history. And when black sawmill gangs in the same
state paced their work by shouting

> OH-HO-In the morning;
> OH-HO-In the evening;
> OH-HO-Hallelujah!
> Ain't gonna be here all my days.[110]

they were reflecting not a fantasy of escape but a possibility that was
enough of a reality so that it operated as a safety valve for millions of Negroes who without the alternative of migration would have felt trapped
and hopeless. The *idea* of emigration could be as important psychologically as the *fact* of emigration itself. One fed the other, of course. The
images of movement that informed so many black songs not only mirrored what was taking place but helped to encourage and perpetuate it—
helped to make movement an enduring part of black reality.

Black songs make it clear that economic privation was an important
stimulus to migration. Blacks in Mississippi in 1909 sang a verse which
was to be repeated many times in many parts of the country in the coming
years:

> Times is gittin' might ha'd,
> Money gittin' might scace;
> Soon's I sell my cot'n 'n co'n,
> I'se gwine tuh leave dis place.[111]

Four decades later, in 1950, Enoch Brown of Livingston, Alabama, was
singing:

> Oh the times don't get no better here
> I'm goin' down the road
> I'm goin' a-way to leave you. . . .
> If the times don't get no better,
> If the times don't get no better
> Down the road I'm gone.[112]

As indisputably important as the economic motive was, it is possible to
overstress it so that the black migration is converted into an inexorable
force and Negroes are seen once again not as actors capable of affecting
at least some part of their destinies, but primarily as beings who are acted
upon—southern leaves blown North by the winds of destitution. Those
unfortunate enough not to have left the proper records behind often become converted into anonymous beings transformed by forces larger than

themselves. This problem, of course, is not limited to Negroes but extends
to that large shapeless majority that we tend to refer to as "the masses."
Within this amorphous group there are many shapes and elements which
might make the whole more meaningful if we took the time and effort to
discern them. It is clear, for instance, that often those blacks who had the
best economic reasons for leaving were unable to, shackled as they were
by virtual peonage. "I have knowed lots of people in Mississippi who
cain't leave," Robert Curtis Smith, a sharecropper, has said. "Because if
you make a crop and don't clear nothin' and you still wound up owin' on
your sharecrop and on your furnish' and you try to move, well the police
be after you then all right. But if you're clear well mostly, you can't go
too far because of the money. . . . if they like the way you work they
make you pay somethin' just for holdin' the house up. If after you pay
that you want to move, well . . . you cain't go too far, because you ain't
got enough in hand to go that far."[113]

Large numbers of those Negroes who left the South did so not because
they had no economic alternatives but because they made a decision to
leave; a decision typically based upon a complex of motives. Northern
black newspapers like the *Chicago Defender,* which played so important
a role in urging southern blacks to migrate in the early twentieth century,
called the North the "Promised Land" and made it clear that the promise
was only partly economic opportunity. The *Defender* emphasized the injustices, the outrages, the denial of rights that occurred in the South and
insisted that when the segregation laws were repealed, when Jim Crow
cars were abandoned, when courts dispensed justice, when black women
were no longer abused, then and only then should Negroes remain in the
South. The same varied motives are revealed in the letters the prospective
migrants wrote the *Defender* seeking help in leaving:

> I has heard so much talk about the north and how much better the colard
> people are treated up there than they are down here. . . . I sure am
> ancious to make it in the north because these southern white people are so
> mean and they seems to be getting worse and I wants to get away. . . .
> We collord people are almost afraid to walke the streets after night.

> O please help me to get out of this low down county i am counted no
> more thin a dog.

> I want a job in a small town some where in the north where I can receive
> verry good wages and where I can educate my 3 little girls and demand
> respect of intelegence.

My children I wished to be educated in a different community than here. Where the school facilities are better and less prejudice shown and in fact where advantages are better for our people in all respect.[114]

Black songs too make it clear that migration was more than the product of pure economic forces. "Oh, I'm leaving if I never come back," North Carolina Negroes sang, "And I ain't gonna be treated this-a way."[115] Black workers in the Deep South emphasized this point:

> Lord, I rather be in Mobile in a hollow log
> Than to be here treated like a dog.[116]

In their songs, blacks continually reminded whites that they had the alternative of leaving if conditions did not improve:

> My home ain't here, captain,
> An' I ain't got to stay.[117]

Mississippi Negroes in the early years of this century made it as clear as possible that migration could be a weapon:

> The time is coming and it won't be long,
> You'll get up some morning, and you'll find me gone.
> So treat me right and jolly me along
> If you want this nigger to sing the old home song.[118]

Mobility in America has always had two meanings: lateral movement to and from places, and movement upward socially and economically. These rather distinct meanings have become so frequently confused, so tightly interwoven, that movement per se commonly came to be equated with progress. "In our lexicon, movement means improvement," George Pierson has noted. "In other words, lateral movement implied vertical movement, too."[119] This was certainly true of black Americans for whom pure physical movement between places was often the only avenue, the sole hope, of progress.

> I been down so long, being down do not worry me no more,
> I been down so long, being down do not worry me no more,
> I'm goin' pack my suitcase, an' cross the way you know, I'll go.[120]

There seemed to be a new self-consciousness about movement and a need to distinguish it from mere running away. In *John Henry*, and similar works songs, the request to "Take my hammer . . . to my captain, / Tell him I'm gone," was accompanied frequently by the admonition:

> If he ask you was I running,
> Tell him no,

shal in the Odd Fellows parade. I was very proud to see him in his uniform and his high hat with the beautiful streamer hanging down by his
side. Yes, he was a fine figure of a man, my dad. Or at least that is the way
he seemed to me as a kid when he strutted by like a peacock at the head
of the Odd Fellows parade."[125]

There was a similar structural relationship between the blues and the
situation of the people who sang them. Within the brutal racial repression
following World War I, the rise of a music that stressed the individual
personality and focused upon the individual problems of the singer, constituted in and of itself, regardless of the verbal content of the songs, a social message of importance. For many Negroes World War I seemed a
perfect test for proving their worth to the nation. Here was a situation
made to order for the Alger philosophy whose heroes had always proved
their worth through inspired acts of heroism and devotion. "We believe
that our second emancipation will be the outcome of this war," the Texas
Grand Master of the Negro Masons announced in 1918.[126] This loyalty
and hope was rewarded by inferior treatment for black troops, by a hard-
ening of the lines of discrimination, by increased humiliation, and by the
bloody summer of 1919 which saw major race riots in city after city.

Blacks had played the game by the rules and discovered definitively
that the rules simply did not apply to them. The anxiety that accompanied
this discovery was marked by the dramatic rise of a series of revitalization
movements: Marcus Garvey's United Negro Improvement Association,
with its insistence upon race history, race pride, and an autonomous race
development; the Harlem Renaissance, whose poets and artists explored
the roots of Afro-American culture and flirted with the dream of Africa
and a separate Negro people; the uninhibited growth of a series of cities
within cities which were increasingly separate culturally and socially; the
spread of traditional black religious practices from the Holiness churches
to the larger denominations and the subsequent popularity of the culturally mixed gospel music; the rise of the blues which, like all of these
other developments, embodied so much of the complexity that witnessed
the simultaneous intensification of acculturation and cultural exclusivity
among American blacks.

The blues insisted that the fate of the individual black man or woman,
what happened in their everyday "trivial" affairs, what took place within
them—their yearnings, their problems, their frustrations, their dreams—
were important, were worth taking note of and sharing in song. Stressing
individual expression and group coherence at one and the same time, the

blues was an inward-looking music which insisted upon the meaningfulness of black lives. In these respects it was not only the more obviously angry work songs but the blues as well, that were subversive of the American racial order and proved to be an important portent of what was to come in a very few decades.

SECULAR SONG AND CULTURAL VALUES—BLACK AND WHITE

Inquiring into the fate of the English and Scottish ballad in the United States, Stanley Edgar Hyman has asserted, "it has become inadequate narrative, aborted drama, happy-ending tragedy, corrupt and meaningless verbiage, and bad poetry in general. Some of this may be the effect of transmission in time, which seems to degenerate and deteriorate folk literature wherever we can observe its effects. Some of it, however, is certainly the effect of the American ethos, with its denial of death, its resistance to the tragic experience, its deep repression of sexuality, its overriding pieties, and its frantic emphasis on the rationalistic, the inconsequential, and the optimistic." In those British ballads that survived transplantation to the United States, Hyman argues, magic and the supernatural were dropped or diminished, extrahuman beings such as demons, ghosts, elves, and mermaids were rationalized or humanized, sex was repressed, and such unpleasant human acts as incest and kin-murder were expunged or played down.[1] After many years of collecting folk songs in both Great Britain and the United States, Alan Lomax was impressed by the differences he encountered. The "paganism," the "easy and natural acceptance of the pleasures of the flesh and the bed," which he found in British song, were foreign to American folklore. "The British song-tradition in America has been censored, both conscientiously and consciously." The mass of "gently erotic ditties" which in England and Scotland were still common and widely heard, were in America relegated to the "nether world" of dirty songs and were replaced by ballads and love songs "shrouded in gloom, drowned in melancholy, and poisoned by sado-masochism."[2]

The same process of denial, dilution, repression, sentimentalization, and trivialization that Hyman and Lomax described has been particularly evident in American popular music. S. I. Hayakawa in his revealing article,

"Popular Songs vs. the Facts of Life," maintained that the lyrics of popular songs "tend towards wishful thinking, dreamy and ineffectual nostalgia, unrealistic fantasy, self-pity, and sentimental clichés masquerading as emotion." Focusing upon the love songs of the 1920s, 1930s, and 1940s, Hayakawa in his brief analysis demonstrated how the idealization so omnipresent in these songs, by creating impossible demands and dreams, led first to frustration and ultimately to demoralization.[3] My own careful reading of those love songs popular on the American musical stage, in the movies, and on the radio and records during this period supports Hayakawa's analysis. The titles alone indicate how important the elements of idealistic, dreamlike, magical love were in the hit tunes from 1920 to 1950. The following are typical: *Love Will Find A Way, Angel Child, I'll Build A Stairway To Paradise, Don't Wake Me Up Let Me Dream, Looking At The World Thru Rose Colored Glasses, My Blue Heaven, Dream Lover, You're My Everything, Did You Ever See A Dream Walking? (Well I Did), A Star Fell Out of Heaven, I Married An Angel, You Stepped Out Of A Dream, You're Nobody 'Til Somebody Loves You.* Frustration and disillusionment were only slightly less common: *I Lost The Best Pal That I Had, All Alone, Oh, How I Miss You Tonight, Broken Hearted, Lover Come Back To Me, You Took Advantage Of Me, Why Was I Born, Dancing With Tears In My Eyes, When Your Lover Has Gone, Say It Isn't So, Somebody Else Is Taking My Place, I'll Never Smile Again, You Always Hurt The One You Love.*[4]

Though unhappiness was often the result, the frustrated lover—like the dupe in the slaves' trickster tales—kept returning for more, unable to alter the course of events, unable to resist fate.

> That old black magic has me in its spell.
> That old black magic that you weave so well. . . .
> I should stay away but what can I do
> I hear your name and I'm aflame,
> Aflame with such a burning desire
> That only your kiss can put out the fire.[5]

As these lines indicate, an overarching fatalism needs to be added to those characteristics of American love songs discussed by Hayakawa. These songs could be cathartic in providing an expressive outlet for suffering lovers and a reminder that one was not suffering alone, but they were rarely didactic; they offered no help in finding a mate. Love remained a magical process which simply happened:

Blue Moon
You saw me standing alone.
Without a dream in my heart,
Without a love of my own. . . .
And then there suddenly appeared before me
The only one my arms will ever hold.
I heard somebody whisper, "Please adore me,"
And when I looked, the moon had turned to gold![6]

The qualities necessary for the successful lover seemed to be primarily faith and patience:

After waiting so long for the right time,
After reaching so long for a star,
All at once, from the long and lonely night time
And despite time,
Here you are.[7]

When the right mate miraculously appeared, there was nothing for the patient lover to do but passively surrender no matter how poor the chances for a happy culmination:

Alone from night to night, you'll find me,
Too weak to break the chains that bind me;
I need no shackles to remind me,
I'm just a pris'ner of love.[8]

The failed lover—and a high proportion of the lovers in American popular songs did fail—had no recourse but self-pity and escape in memories. In spite of all the painful experience lovers in these songs amassed, love was portrayed in a large number of the songs as a permanent, undying relationship. George and Ira Gershwin put it as well as anyone:

It's very clear
Our love is here to stay;
Not for a year
But ever and a day. . . .
In time the Rockies may crumble, Gibraltar may tumble,
They're only made of clay,
But our love is here to stay.[9]

To say only this about the popular songs of the period is not to say enough, of course. There were many innovative composers and lyricists—Cole Porter, George and Ira Gershwin, Richard Rodgers, Jerome Kern, Lorenz Hart, Oscar Hammerstein, and others—who brought imagination and wit to popular music. Their skillful and sensitive use of language occasionally allowed them to deal with normally forbidden topics, as in Cole Porter's treatment of prostitution in his 1930 hit, *Love For Sale*. For all their considerable insight and refreshing tongue-in-cheek quality, even the most talented creators of America's popular songs paid obeisance to the prevailing norms and reflected the central needs and myths of their society. However deeply their wit could cut through the sentimentality that marked most popular music, their songs have endured with the generations that grew up with them because they reinforced deeply inculcated dreams and ideals in a world which daily disproved them. In a period when divorce rates were rising, family stability declining, pastoral life styles disappearing, bureaucratic impersonality and organization increasing, popular music constructed a universe in which adolescent innocence and naïveté became a permanent state. Men and women (often referred to in the songs as boys and girls) dreamed pure dreams, hopefully waited for an ideal love to appear (the gift of some beneficent power that remained undefined and unnamed), and built not castles but bungalows in the air complete with birds, brooks, blossoms, and babies.

Adults were being socialized to a world constructed out of childhood fantasies or, more accurately, adult views of childhood fantasies:

> You're right out of a book,
> The fairy tale I read when I was so high.
> No armored knight out of a book,
> Was more enchanted by a Lorelei than I.[10]

As in the fairy tales, so too in popular songs, life was not purely idyllic. Reality was allowed to intrude: often lovers were faithless, promises broken, hopes unfulfilled. But the reality proved as insubstantial as the dream. Tears were shed and self-pity expressed, yet little was learned and less resolved. Fatalism prevailed and the fantasies went on and on.

In the movies they saw, the radio programs they listened to, and, to a much lesser extent, the records they heard, black Americans were exposed to and affected by American popular music. As Americans, Negroes shared many of the assumptions and dreams of popular music. But they had recourse to another music which differed markedly from the larger society's popular songs. Negroes were not the only group in the society to have alternatives to American popular music. Eastern European Jewish immigrants, Scandinavian, Irish, Mexican, Puerto Rican-Americans as well as many other ethnic minorities kept aspects of their old music alive in their homes, churches, and fraternal organizations and often constituted markets for phonograph records, foreign-language radio programs, ethnic theater, and show performances which also featured music that differed from the songs of the Hit Parade variety. Alternatives existed not only for ethnic groups but for those whose tastes and values were represented in country-western music which, like the black music that profoundly influenced it, also dealt much more explicitly with such subjects as sex, divorce, drink, and what one of its songs called *The Cold Hard Facts of Life* than did American popular music. Until a greater understanding is gained of what was happening within the thought and culture of the sub-groups that made up the United States, our view of American culture must remain a partial one.[11]

In his study, *Jazz and the White Americans*, Neil Leonard has argued that toward the close of the 1920s a change took place in what he somewhat vaguely calls "jazz lyrics." Before then jazz lyrics were frank, uninhibited, realistic, reflective of the life of the Negro subculture. After 1928 they tended to mirror the shallow idealism, escapism, superficial philosophizing, and mawkish clichés of Tin Pan Alley.[12] Leonard's entire thesis is based upon a comparative analysis of a random sample of the lyrics of Louis Armstrong's recordings from 1925 to 1927 with his recordings from 1929 to 1931, and of Bessie Smith's records from 1923 to 1925 with those of Billie Holiday from 1936 to 1939. The problem with this sample is that it does not reflect what Leonard wants it to. In the 1930s and after, both Armstrong and Holiday, though they retained a jazz oriented musical style, sang popular American tunes to audiences that often contained large numbers of whites. They were expressing the values of American popular songs simply because their repertory now consisted of large numbers of those songs. Of course, the fact that Negro entertainers like Armstrong and Holiday could reach so far outside the Negro market while retaining enough elements of Afro-American musical style to appeal to that market as well, was a significant development and was still one more channel through which Negroes could absorb the values of American popular music. But to generalize from this sample about black music while ignoring the blues would be like judging Negro music in the 1950s and 1960s from the jazz singer Ella Fitzgerald's successful and popular recordings of the songs of the Gershwins, Cole Porter, Irving Berlin, and Rodgers and Hart while ignoring the rhythm and blues and what eventually came to be called Soul music.

The recorded blues was largely a music by and for Negroes. Throughout the 1920s Negroes bought blues recordings in large numbers and while this activity diminished considerably during the depths of the Depression, by the late 1930s the black demand for blues recordings was renewed. Zora Neale Hurston and other investigators for the Federal Writers' Project in the 1930s have testified that blues recordings dominated the selections in juke boxes in Negro dance halls, and Muriel Davis Longini, collecting Negro folk songs in Chicago during the Depression, found that "the blues comprise the greater portion of the songs."[13] Blues, then, was the closest Negro equivalent to American popular music and no comparison between white and black song lyrics can ignore them. Any such comparison shows important and revealing differences. While both blues and popular music were dominated by lyrics concerning love, black consciousness of and attitudes toward this relationship differed considerably from those of the larger society.

The blues was far less pervaded by the self-pity, the profound fatalism, and the very real disillusionment that marked American popular music. Bessie Smith's *Young Woman's Blues* is an excellent example of the differences. Recorded in 1926, when Smith was at the height of her powers and popularity, her blues opens with a lament:

> Woke up this mornin', when chickens were crowin' for day.
> And on the right side of my pillow, my man had gone away.
>
> By his pillow he left a note, readin' "I'm sorry Jane you got my goat.
> No time to marry, no time to settle down."

Although the mention of "pillow" indicated an aspect of love generally missing from popular American music, the lament was characteristic of both black and white music. Negro lovers as well as white ones complained often and bitterly of infidelity and disappointment. What was different was Smith's reaction:

> I'm a young woman and ain't done runnin' 'roun';
> I'm a young woman and ain't done runnin' 'roun'.
>
> Some people call me a hobo, some call me a bum.
> Nobody knows my name, nobody knows what I've done.
>
> I'm as good as any woman in your town.
> I ain't no high yella, I'm a deep yella brown. . . .
>
> See that long, lonesome road? Lord, you know it's gotta end.
> And I'm a good woman, and I can get plenty men.[14]

Here was a sense of self-pride and worth and a confidence in alternative possibilities largely missing from popular music. This is not to argue that self-pity was absent from the blues. Indeed, folk definitions of the blues equated them with disappointment in love:

> Dem blues ain't nothin'
> But a woman lost her man.

> De blues ain't nothing
> But a poor man's heart disease.[15]

Blues are filled with the self-pitying cries of grieving lovers. "I don't feel welcome and I don't care where I go, / The woman I love she drove me from her door," Blind Lemon Jefferson complained.[16] "You don't miss your water, till your well goes dry," Leadbelly moaned. "You don't miss your mama, till she shakes your hand goodby."[17] It was not uncommon for aggrieved lovers in the blues to even threaten suicide:

> Gonna build me a scaffold, I'm gonna hang myself.
> Cain't get the man I love, don't want nobody else.[18]

For all this pathos, the blues was never pervaded by the kind of self-conscious, fatalistic self-pity that characterized American popular song. In part the blues was saved from this by the strong sense of humor and proportion which frequently prevented even the most pitiable lover from posturing:

> Gwine lay my head right on de railroad track,
> Gwine lay my head right on de railroad track,
> 'Cause my baby, she won't take me back.

> Gwine lay my head right on de railroad track,
> Gwine lay my head right on de railroad track,
> If de train come 'long, I'm gwine to snatch it back.[19]

Equally important was the context; no matter how aggrieved the lover, his or her laments generally took place within an ethos resembling life. Even in his most love-struck and submissive mood, Blind Lemon Jefferson made it clear that he knew what he was doing and had few illusions:

> Mmmmmmm, hitch me to your buggy, mama, drive me like a mule
> Hitch me to your buggy and drive me like a mule
> Reason I'm going home with you, sugar, I ain't much hard to be fooled.[20]

In the blues, love seldom resembled the ethereal, ideal relationship so often pictured in popular songs. Love was depicted as a fragile, often ambivalent human relationship between imperfect beings. "Sometimes I say I need you," Charley Patton sang, "then again I don't. . . . Sometimes I think I'll quit you, then again I won't."[21] Rabbit Brown shared the ambiva-

lence: "Sometime I think that you too sweet to die, . . . And another
time I think you ought to be buried alive."[22] Although love was not seen
in magical, deterministic terms, there was room in the blues for complete
faithfulness and permanence in love: "I'll love my baby till the sea runs
dry." "I love my good girl no matter what she do." "Now the love I have
for you woman / God knows it can't be turned around."[23] But undying,
untroubled love was seldom held up as the norm which one should expect
to experience. Peetie Wheatstraw, in his *Hearse Man Blues*, expressed a
thought more commonly felt than articulated:

> I went around the casket and looked down in my baby's face [twice]
> Then I was soon wonderin' what good woman will take her place.[24]

As in the folk tales, romantic sentimentality was rarely indulged in. Blues
singers could pledge their love to mates whose faults they recognized, in
the spirit of the workers who sang: "My black baby, you got no wings,/
But, my black baby, you got better things."[25]

The blues were filled with descriptions of imperfect mates. "I love you,
baby," Big Bill Broonzy sang, "but I hate your dirty ways."[26] Bessie Smith
complained continually of her men and with her characteristic independence she laid down an ultimatum:

> I've had a man for fifteen years,
> Give him his room and board.
> Once he was like a Cadillac,
> Now he's like a old worn-out Ford.
> He never brought me a lousy dime
> And put it in my hand.
> So there'll be some changes from now on
> Accordin' to my plan:
> He's got to get it, bring it, and put it right here
> O' else he's gonna keep it out there.[27]

Other women blues singers issued similar complaints and similar warnings.
"I been your dog, been your dog all of my days," Jenny Pope lamented
and then announced: "The reason I'm leavin' you, I don't like your dog-
ging ways."[28] "I'm through with these no good trifling men," Ma Rainey
swore:

> My daddy come home this mornin' drunk as he could be.
> My daddy come home this mornin' drunk as he could be.
> I knowed by that, he's done got bad on me.
>
> He used to stay out late, now he don't come home at all.
> He used to stay out late, now he don't come home at all.

Spoken: No kidding either.
I know there's another mule been kickin' in my stall.

If you don't like my ocean, don't fish in my sea.
Don't like my ocean, don't fish in my sea.
Stay out of my valley and let my mountain be.[29]

The bluesmen replied in kind. Big Bill Broonzy observed that his father would always remind him that he was thirty minutes younger than his twin sister, the point being "You came into this world behind a woman and you'll always be behind them."[30] This was the spirit of many of the male blues. "Woman rocks the cradle and I declare she rules her home,/ Many man rocks some other man's baby and the fool thinks he's rocking his own," Blind Lemon Jefferson observed. "Brownskin girl is 'ceitful," Jefferson sang in another blues, "till she gets you all worn down. . . . She get all your pocket change, she gonna drive you from her town."[31] These themes were repeated endlessly. "Mmmm, Lord, oh, Lord, oh Lord, oh Lord, oh Lord," Ishman Bracey moaned, "Now the woman I'm loving, she treat me like a mangy dog."[32] "Some of these women sure do make me tired," Sleepy John Estes sang, "Got a handful of 'gimme' and a mouthful of 'much obliged.' "[33] Rabbit Brown articulated a common complaint: "Cause I was born in the country she thinks I'm easy to rule / She tried to hitch me to her wagon: she wanta drive me like a mule."[34] These singers continued on records a debate that had long pervaded black folk song. Early in the century W. C. Handy overheard a woman in the South singing: "The man I'll marry ain't born yet—an' his mamy's dead," and recorded this cry from a Memphis mule-driver:

G'wan, mule!
Don't you want to wuhk?
Hadn't ought t'been a mule.
Ought t'been a woman.
Then I'd be workin' fo' you.
G'wan, mule![35]

The blues functioned not merely as a mechanism for individual catharsis but also as a vehicle for passing on group knowledge. The blues that dealt with love were filled with aphoristic messages based upon folk experience:

When you love a man, he treats you lak a dog.
But when you don't love him, he'll hop aroun' you lak a frog.[36]

My mama told me,
Never love a woman like she can't love you.[37]

You can always tell when your woman got another man,
You can always tell when your woman got another man,
Your meals ain't regular and your house ain't never clean.[38]

The blues singer Henry Townsend remembered that as a teen-age boy he learned a great deal from the blues singing of Lonnie Johnson: "He used to explain himself very distinct to me, and—this will embarrass me but I'm going to have to say it—at that time I was trying life too, and I run into the same things he was running into; so I gathered what he was saying had to be true."[39] The young Townsend could learn from the blues because the world they described was the one the singers and their audiences inhabited. The rich sexual imagery that filled the blues has been discussed in another context and need not be re-introduced here. But it is important to reiterate that the physical side of love which, aside from some tepid hand holding and lip pecking, was largely missing from popular music, was strongly felt in the blues. In the early years of the century, black miners and railroad gangs near Lineville, Alabama, made fun of the different white and black depictions of love:

White folks on the sofa
Niggers on the grass
White man is talking low
Nigger is getting ass.[40]

Black song depicted sex freely as a natural and expected part of life:

Nobody's business wen a good feelin' feller takes a hard workin' lady from
　a lonesome home,
'Cause yo' mind an' yo' heart an' yo' whole body tell you 'tain' right for
　a natchal man to live alone.[41]

Precisely because love was portrayed realistically as a multidimensional experience, there was, in spite of all the disappointment and complaints, less demoralization in the blues than in popular music. If love was not an ideal, magical phenomenon which settled every problem, then a failed relationship, for all the pain it entailed, was not a final experience. There were alternatives and these bred an independence and confidence largely missing from American popular song. Pride was expressed in one of the more common lines in black secular song:

I told my baby, like the Dago told the Jew,
If you don't want me, cinch I don't want you.[42]

Few lovers in black song were ideal and fewer still were irreplaceable.
In 1905 Gates Thomas heard these lines in Texas:

I got a wife and a woman still; if my wife don't do right my woman will;
And so, ole Nigger, you ought to be like me; instead o' one woman, get
you two or three.[43]

A few years later Howard Odum published a female variant: "I got a husband, a sweetheart, too, . . . Husband don't love me, sweetheart do."[44]
"If you go fishin'," a black woman in Texas sang to her man, "I'm a-goin'
a-fishin' too, / You bet yo life yo sweet little wife can catch as many fish
as you."[45] The recorded blues in the 1920s and 1930s continued to express
these themes. "Just as sure as the winter follows the fall," Charley Patton
sang, "There ain't no one woman got it all."[46] Edith Johnson agreed:
"Now if you get loaded, baby, and think you want to go, . . . Remember, baby, you ain't no better than the man I had before."[47] And Ma
Rainey shared the good news given her by a fortune teller: "He said,
'You'll get a man anywhere you go.' "[48]

Black secular song dealt with an entire range of love relationships ignored in the music of the larger society. On his record, *When You Fall
For Someone That's Not Your Own*, Lonnie Johnson treated sensitively
the problem of falling in love with a married woman:

Blues and trouble, they walk hand in hand.
(repeat)
But you never had no trouble, 'til you fall for the wife of
another man.

When it begins raining, you're looking out your window pane.
(repeat)
Thinking of that other man's wife, it's enough to drive you
insane. . . .

A married woman is sweet, the sweetest woman ever was born.
(repeat)
Only thing wrong with her, every time she has to go back home.[49]

Texas workers in 1890 sang of prostitution:

Well, Baby, your house rent's due, Baby, your house rent's due;
Just put on your bustle and make a little rustle,
And bring in a dollar or two.[50]

Charley Patton, after singing of being rejected by his woman, referred to the prostitutes to whom he could now turn: "There's a house over yonder painted all over green. . . . Some of the finest young women, Lord, man most ever seen."[51]

There was discussion of homosexuality and lesbianism:

> Ketch two women runnin' togedder long,
> Ketch two women runnin' togedder long,
> You can bet yo' life dere's somethin' gwine wrong.[52]

On her 1926 recording, *Sissy Blues*, Ma Rainey complained:

> I dreamed last night I was far from harm,
> Woke up and found my man in a sissy's arms. . . .
>
> Now all the people ask me why I'm all alone,
> A sissy shook that thing and took my man from home.[53]

On his 1938 recording, *Sissy Man Blues*, Kokomo Arnold pleaded humorously: "If you can't send me no woman, please send me a sissy man."[54] Whatever the attitude toward homosexuality, and it was usually negative, it was recognized as a part of life. In his *Freakish Blues*, George Hannah attempted to deny his homosexual proclivities but ended by admitting them:

> Had a strange feeling this morning, I've had it all day,
>   (*twice*)
> I wake up one of these mornings, that feeling will be here to stay.[55]

Even masturbation was not beyond mention. "I woke up this mornin' with my pork-grinder in my hand," Kokomo Arnold sang, and Whistling Rufus Bridey left only a little more to the imagination, allowing his guitar rather than his voice to speak the final word:

> In Dixieland I'll make my stand,
> Can't get the woman I want I'm gonna use my——.[56]

To make comparisons like these between the blues and popular song is not for the purpose of engaging in some mystique about the superiority of black music or black sensibilities over those of the rest of society. The point is to indicate important cultural divergences. Negro song aimed at a Negro audience could take cognizance of and deal with certain realities largely ignored by the popular culture of the society as a whole and was free of a number of the myths and fantasies that marked popular music written for a predominantly white audience. It may be argued that the differences between the blues and popular music merely reflected the different sexual behavior patterns separating the mass of Negroes and other Americans. I have no intention of adding to the under-researched guess work, the projections, the stereotypes, the fantasizing that have dominated this question. More than song lyrics are needed to re-create the sociology and history of black and white male-female relations and familial patterns—subjects which scholars still have not dealt with adequately. Nevertheless, one thing is clear: differences in Negro and white sexual patterns cannot account for the complete absence of physical love from popular song. However much American popular culture might have eschewed sex, Americans themselves did not. The Kinsey reports published after World War II showed that American men and women of all colors and creeds went to bed with one another regularly, engaged in pre- and extra-marital sexual liaisons, and to a surprising extent indulged in sexual practices which the society officially branded as deviant.[57]

Without denying the obvious truth that there were significant variations in the sexual practices of different groups within American society, the varying pictures that emerge from a study of popular music and the blues are due at least as much to attitudinal as to behavioral differences. In their folk and popular culture, Negroes were able to discuss the male-female relationship with a realism, candor, and freedom absent in the larger society. In this area, at least, Negro children were not being socialized to an ideal that bore little resemblance to what actually existed. Instead of being filled with the kind of unreal expectations that led inevitably to very real feelings of guilt, inadequacy, and failure, they were being given what Kenneth Burke has argued good poetry always gives: "equipment for living." If the knowledge they derived from secular song did not necessarily enable them to change the environment they inhabited, it allowed them to understand and cope with it and in the process perhaps to understand themselves and their drives as well. It provided still another layer of insulation against some of those outside standards and expectations which, even when they were not positively dysfunctional, had only peripheral meaning for their lives.

For so long black song had been the outlet for expressing deeply held attitudes concerning justice, whites, working conditions, and other primary concerns, it is not surprising that it continued to be a channel for articulating truth in the affairs of personal life. Afro-Americans were often freer to express these truths for the simple reason that they had less stake in the preservation of the sexual myths of the larger society. Having on the one hand been denied full participation in American society and on the other having resisted complete acculturation, Negroes had not succumbed to many of the society's central projections and dreams. This pattern of denial and resistance increased black separateness and autonomy. Lee Rainwater has argued that for lower-class groups on the whole, the failure of the social system to meet their needs produces a relatively high degree of functional autonomy. "In general the fewer the rewards a society offers members of a particular group in the society, the more autonomous will that group prove to be with reference to the norms of the society."[58] The illusions and self-deceptions of white people, Clyde Taylor has asserted, "are simply not allowable to Black people, if they are to keep sane and whole."[59]

The rootlessness and alienation which were so well articulated in the blues and work songs were not solely the reflection of Afro-American culture but of the larger society as well, which was at its heart rootless and deeply afraid of the rapid changes that were transforming it. Living on the periphery of American society materially and spiritually, imperfectly acculturated and rejected Negroes had less need to nourish and preserve the society's dreams and myths and were thus more able to accept the fact of their alienation, their isolation, their fears, and give unambiguous voice to the anguish of modern Man. This truth is important but care must be taken not to put it too starkly. Social and economic background and aspiration shaped the attitudes of Negroes as well as of other groups in the society. These intragroup differences produced a kaleidoscope of black behavioral and attitudinal patterns, many of them in agreement with the larger society. Even among the Negro lower classes there was no single homogeneous response to the norms officially endorsed by the outside society. But for large numbers of Negroes, the bulk of them on the lower end of the social and economic scale, it was possible and necessary to speak openly about a number of realities that American popular culture needed to repress.

Not only with regard to sex but such problems as alcoholism, gambling, and drug addiction, black secular music reflected aspects of the world that popular music ignored. Charley Patton needed alcohol to withstand the pressures in his life—"It take boozy booze, Lord, to carry me through"—while black workers in Scotland County, North Carolina, longed for marijuana—"I's gwina save all of my nickels and dimes / To buy me a Mary Jane."[60] Other black workers sang of more serious dependencies: "I had a good woman / But she took morphine and died." "Well, the cocaine habit is might' bad, / It kill ev-ybody I know it to have had."

Coke I love, coke I buy,
I'm gonna sniff my coke till I die.
Hey honey take a whiff on me.[61]

Even the desperate drinking of Sterno was memorialized in Tommy Johnson's tortured recording of *Canned Heat Blues:*

Cryin' canned, canned heat, mama,
Cryin' sure enough killing me, . . .
Cryin' ma, mama, mama,
Know canned heat killin' me.
Canned heat, Lord, killin' me.[62]

Although these were intragroup songs, there was a certain amount of defiance in their singing; a recognition that the practices they described thwarted the mores of the society. On one of her early recordings, Bessie Smith made this clear in her version of a widely known folk song:

If I go to church on Sunday
Then just shimmy down on Monday,
Tain't nobody's business if I do.
    If I do. . . .

I swear I won't call no copper
If I'm beat up by my papa.
Tain't nobody's business if I do.
    If I do.[63]

Thus though the songs reflected important aspects of reality, they were also often statements of independence which characterized black secular song throughout the century. "Lord, my mother tole me, my father tole me too," Leon Strickland sang in the 1950s:

Lord my mother have tole me, an' my father tole me too,
Hey, Leon, some brownskin woman gone be the death o' you.

Lord, I looks at my mother, swear begin to smile,
Eeh, I looks at my mother, swear begin to smile,
I say, "(If) good time kill me, Mama, please, Mama, let me die."[64]

The same independence from some of the central values of the outside society can be seen with regard to color. After the Spanish-American War, when black troops were receiving high praise for gallantry in action, Negro orators would proclaim: "It always was true that *fast black never runs!*"[65] Negro troops in France during World War I often were heard singing: "It takes a long, tall, slim, black man to make a German lay his rifle down." And when a group of black soldiers put on a show at Orly Flying Field in France in 1918, they sang to their white compatriots:

> Goin' to git myself a French gal wid nice smooth flanks,
> An' tell her de blacks is de best o' de Yanks.[66]

Certainly, Negro songs were often marked by the color preferences of white American society. In 1942 Will Starks could still sing a "coon song" which he had heard in a minstrel show around 1914:

> Coon, coon, coon, I wish my color would fade;
> Coon, coon, coon, I'd like a different shade.
> Coon, coon, coon, from mornin', night, and noon;
> I wish I was a white man instead of a coon.[67]

Every collection of early twentieth-century Negro songs included at least several with this theme:

> Stan' back, black man,
> You cain't shine;
> Yo' lips is too thick,
> An' you hain't my kin'.[68]

Frequently, frustration with the configurations of blackness focused upon women. In 1919 a Negro on a freight train in North Carolina sang: "I don't want no jet black woman for my regular."[69] A decade earlier black children in the Deep South sang: "I marry black gal, she was black, you know. / For when I went to see her, she look like a crow-ow / She look like a crow-ow-ow."[70] Frederick Ramsey, Jr., collecting in Mississippi in the 1950s, and Harry Oster collecting in Louisiana a decade later, both found a series of traditional songs which dismissed black women as evil. The most commonly repeated warning was:

> Woh, I don't want no black woman, babe, to bake no bread for me,
> Lord, I don't want no black woman, yeah, to bake no bread for me,
> Because black is evil, Lord, I'm 'fraid that she might poison me.[71]

As important as these persistent sentiments are, Negro attitudes toward color cannot be summed up this simply. It is hardly surprising that the deeply ingrained prejudices of American society should have affected some of its victims to the point where they turned the hatred upon themselves and their peers. What has been neglected is how much color pride managed to exist in such unpromising circumstances. Black song and black culture did not envision color as a simple polarity between white and black. A number of quite distinct shades were recognized: deep black, ashy black, pale black, dead black, chocolate-brown, coffee, sealskin-brown, deep brown, dark brown, reddish brown, deep yella brown, chocolate, high-brown, low-brown, velvet brown, bronze, gingerbread, fair light brown, tan, olive, copper, pink, banana, cream, brightskin, high yaller, lemon. But the three colors most commonly referred to in the songs were black, brown, and yellow. Not infrequently the latter was favored. In eastern Tennessee around 1913 Negroes sang:

> Yonder come a yaller gal,
> All dressed up in red—
> Well, I wish my wife was dead,
> Well, I wish my wife was dead.[72]

"Brownskin women are evil, black women are evil too," Texas Alexander sang in 1927, "I'm gonna get myself a yeller gal, see what she will do."[73]

Choice of the lightest skinned possibility (excluding white, which never seemed to be a preferred choice) was not the most common, however. Quite frequently both yellow and black were specifically rejected in favor of brown which proved to be without exception the most favored color in every collection of twentieth-century black song. "Some say give me a high yaller," workers in the 1920s sang,

> I say give me a teasin' brown,
> For it takes a teasin' brown
> To satisfy my soul.
>
> I don't want no coal-black woman for my regular,
> Give me brown, Lawd, Lawd, give me brown.[74]

A decade later workers in the Deep South articulated the commonly sung reasons for the preference of brown over black or yellow:

> I don't want no jet black woman for my regular,
> O give me brown, and oh my Lord, give me brown.
> For black is evil, evil, yella so low down,
> When you git in trouble, and oh my Lord, yella can't be found.[75]

The reasons were aesthetic as well as practical: "Brownskin woman like something fit to eat," Charley Patton sang, while Texas Alexander, Wright Holmes, and other bluesmen saw them as part of Paradise:

> I'm gonna build me a Heaven, have a kingdom of my own,
>   (twice)
> Where these brownskin women can cluster round my throne.[76]

Brown was held up as the ideal in so many songs that it, rather than lighter shades, may well have been the goal of many of those who used skin lighteners. Leadbelly referred to this in the spoken monologue with which he accompanied his song *Roberta*. Roberta's man is searching for her and asks the police for help:

> When he got de police station, de police ask him how they gonna know Roberta from any other brown-skin. All of 'em is brown-skin now, an' all got black wavy hair. You take a black woman, she . . . jus' like a teasin' brown. She got so much powder on her face—high brown powder—you cain' tell whether she brown or black.[77]

The admiration for brown-skinned women and men was widespread but there were numerous dissenting voices. Black skin was the choice of a significant number of songs. In 1915 and 1916 Negro women in Auburn, Alabama, sang:

> Ain't crazy 'bout no high yellows, worried about no brown,
> Come to picking my choice, gimme
> The blackest man in town.[78]

"A yellow girl I do despise, / But a jut black girl I can't denies," Negroes in Mississippi sang around 1910, and more than a decade later workers in the Upper South continued the refrain: "You take yaller, / I take de black."[79]

There was a certain defensiveness in the celebration of blackness. A popular folk song with an almost endless series of stanzas stood up for the "black gal" against her more well-endowed competitors:

> Brown gal she dress like Paris,
> Yellow gal she do de same;
> Old black gal wears a burlap sack,
> But that's dressin' jus' de same.[80]

At times the defensiveness became more overt, as in the folk rhyme collected by Talley:

> Nev' min' if my nose are flat,
> An' my face are black an' sooty;
> De jaybird hain't so big in song,
> An' de Bullfrog hain't no beauty.

or in Sara Martin's 1928 recording:

> Now my hair is nappy and I don't wear no clothes of silk
>   (*twice*)
> But the cow that's black and ugly, has often got the sweetest milk.[81]

The aesthetics of the outside society were often countered by the use of
folk proverbs in song to proclaim the virtues of black men and women:

> The blacker the berry the sweeter the juice
> I wants a real black woman for my special use.[82]

If there was some defensiveness about the aesthetics of blackness, there
was a repeatedly expressed conviction that in general dark skin could be
trusted more than lighter complexions:

> Gonna git me a black woman,
> Play safe all the time.
> For your brown skin woman
> Keep you in trouble all the time.

> Yaller gal's yourn
> An de black gal's mine,
> You never can tell
> When de yaller gal's lyin'.[83]

The full meaning of these songs would be enhanced by a better understanding of their dynamics. Big Bill Broonzy, for instance, has suggested
that songs making color comparisons could not be sung indiscriminately.
A "light-brown-skinned Negro" might sing "The blacker the berry the
sweeter the juice / I want a real black woman for my special use," but only
a "real black Negro" could sing "Don't want no black woman to bake no
bread for me / Because she's black and evil and might poison me." "If a
half-white Negro sings either one of the songs," Broonzy wrote, "he will
be beaten up by the black women or men."[84] Another problem is just how
literally these color distinctions are to be taken. Did the many songs ex-
tolling the virtues of brown men and women and boasting of being
"Chocolate to de bone," mean to exclude those of darker complexion or
were they aimed more directly, as I suspect they were, at lighter-skinned
Negroes? Certainly a number of songs explicitly joined dark-skinned Negroes against those of lighter shades. The *Poor Stranger Blues*, which was
a favorite in the southern juke joints during the 1930s, is an example:

> Some people like high yellers,
> But gimme my black and brown.[85]

Whatever ambivalence and defensiveness there was concerning blackness, the real animus of the songs was reserved for lighter skin and especially whites, as in the well known folk rhyme:

My name's Ran, I wuks in de san';
But I'd druther be a Nigger dan a po' white man. . . .

I'd druther be a Nigger, an' plow ole Beck
Dan a white Hill Billy wid his long red neck.[86]

"When he gits old, old and gray," an early twentieth-century song from Mississippi asserted, "Then white folk looks like monkeys, / When dey gits old, old an' gray." In 1909 Negroes from the same state made it clear that they would "As soon kiss a monkey as a poor white man."[87] Whites were almost never mentioned in any love song except to warn blacks away from having affairs with them:

Quit lookin' at de mens an' leave 'em be, ole sugar babe
    (twice)
I mean quit lookin' at de white mens an' leave 'em be,
If you got to have a man can't you look at me
'Cause you black as I is fur as I see,
Ole sugar babe.[88]

Ridicule of blacks trying to pass as white was particularly common in Creole songs from Louisiana:

Look at that mulatto, li'l Mister Banjo,
See how he struts so proud!
Hat cock'd on one side, Mister Banjo,
Brandishing his stick,
Puffing such a big cigar, Mister Banjo,
Shiny boots that clack and click!
Yet he's but a half-caste, li'l Mister Banjo,
Although he struts so proud![89]

The haughtiness and pretensions exhibited by the mulatto targets in the Creole songs were really not necessary to generate antipathy. Light skin, in and of itself, was often provocation enough. Dora Franks of Mississippi, whose mother was a slave and whose father was her white master, grew up as the only light child in a family of "coal black" children. "Lord, it's been to my sorrow many a time, 'cause de chillen used to chase me round and holler at me, 'Old yellow nigger.' Dey didn't treat me good, neither."[90] During her sojourn on the Georgia Sea Islands, Lydia Parrish asked one of the islanders why she tended to have more trouble with light than with dark Negroes: "he explained with a wide grin: 'High yalla pizens the stream.' "[91] Ethel Waters, who grew up in and around Philadelphia, recalled the hatred she had for whites and Negroes with light skins: "I made life a nightmare for my step-sister Genevieve, who was lighter in color than I and was treated much better by my mother. 'Yaller dog' and 'yaller puppy' were my favorite names for Genevieve."[92] As a schoolgirl Lena Horne, who had been born in Brooklyn, went to live in Fort Valley, Georgia, bearing the double burden of her accent and her color: "There, as elsewhere, my speech was made fun of, my color was made fun of and I was often called a little yellow bastard because I had no visible, immediate family. I was always being asked why I was so light, why my uncle was so light. To some Negroes light color is far from being a status symbol; in fact it's quite the opposite. It is evidence that your lineage has been corrupted by the white people." Reflecting on her problems many years later, Horne saw them as ironic: "On the one hand much money was spent on hair-straighteners and skin-lighteners, on the other you were put down for being naturally closer to the prevailing ideal of beauty. I did not know whether I was supposed to be proud of my color or ashamed of it."[93]

This irony and confusion were not confined to the black world. At the very time twentieth-century American society insisted upon racial purity and upon the natural superiority of white over black, it was also increasingly indulging in a fetish for dark skin. Much has been made of the fact that Negro newspapers carried advertisements for skin lighteners and hair straighteners, but almost no notice has been given to the presence in American popular media of advertisements for a wide array of skin darkeners: sun tan lotions and oils for the summer, and for colder seasons sun tan lamps and ultimately chemicals that did their work without recourse to the sun at all. Cultural historians have not yet explored the meaning of the change in twentieth-century Western European and American aesthetics from a preference for a pallid complexion to one for suntanned skin.[94] The signals that black and white Americans received vis-à-vis the aesthetics of color were never unambiguous. It would be inaccurate to speak of a monolithic American ideology concerning color. There was never a total consensus, not merely because racism negated so many things Americans liked to think about themselves, but equally because, for all the denigration of Africans, "swarthy" Mediterranean types, and Asians, dark skin color symbolized a number of traits twentieth-century Americans found attractive: closeness to nature, lack of inhibitions, freedom from the restraints of civilization. Thus Americans spoke of Nordic superiority at the same time they spoke of being "tall, *dark*, and handsome"; they restricted southern European immigration but elevated Rudolph Valentino with his "Latin" mystique to the status of a sex god; they dismissed Negroes as uncultured even as they adopted black dances, imitated black music, read novels and attended plays and musicals about Negroes, made superstars out of black-face entertainers like Al Jolson and Eddie Cantor, and made a vogue of Harlem.

On the subjects of race and culture, twentieth-century Negroes were surrounded by cultural and ideological confusion and ambiguity rivaling that which had plagued their slave forebears. In both nineteenth- and twentieth-century America we have evidence of the validity of James Fernandez's observation that there is "nothing intrinsically good about the end of any continuum. No culture is so unambiguous about its choices that a clever man cannot turn a continuum to his advantage. In a culture that lauds whiteness there is yet an attraction and an energy to blackness. In a competitive culture the last shall yet be first."[95] We have been led to believe that, in the midst of this ambiguity, blacks wanted nothing more than to be white. But even if everything in the culture around them had been conducive to creating this desire, the impossible wish itself ran directly counter to the realistic, practical thrust so prominent in black consciousness. Black songs indicate that attitudes toward color were complex and not easily characterized without oversimplification. If one overriding color preference did emerge, it was certainly not white but brown.

This is not to maintain that the aesthetics of American society did not filter down and often become internalized. Of course they did. But they were not blindly adopted nor did they easily become dominant. When Malcolm X was a young man in New York he followed the practice of many lower-class Negroes and black entertainers and "conked" or straightened his hair through the painful process of applying lye. In his autobiography he wrote that he engaged in this "self-degradation" in order to make his hair look like a white man's: "I had joined that multitude of Negro men and women in America who are brainwashed into believing that the black people are 'inferior'—and white people 'superior'—that they will even violate and mutilate their God-created bodies to try to look 'pretty' by white standards." The problem with this interpretation is that nothing else Malcolm X did during those years was designed to win the approval of whites. He lived almost entirely within a black world conforming to the standards of his particular peer group of gamblers, pimps, musicians. He earned his living peddling marijuana on the streets of Harlem. He was a hipster and a hustler. If he painfully straightened his hair in order to conform with white standards of beauty, he did not give up his cultural independence in other areas. For instance, he certainly did not choose his clothing with mainstream America in mind: "I studied carefully everything in my size on the racks. And finally I picked out my second zoot. It was a sharkskin gray, with a big, long coat, and pants ballooning out at the knees and then tapering down to cuffs so narrow that I had to take off my shoes to get them on and off. With the salesman urging me on I got another shirt, and a hat, and new shoes—the kind that were just coming into hipster style; dark orange colored, with paper-thin soles and knob style toes."[96]

According to the pianist James P. Johnson, conking the hair dates back to an early twentieth-century New York City barber named Hart who invented a hair preparation named Kink-No-More which was called "Conk" for short. "His preparation," Johnson has testified, was "used by all musicians—the whole Clef Club used him. You'd get your hair washed, dyed and straightened; then trimmed. It would last about a month."[97] Whatever the original motives for conking, and certainly white standards may have played a prominent role, by the time the young Malcolm did it in the 1940s it had become an in-group phenomenon among certain strata of blacks and it is clear from the evidence of his own autobiography that, whatever he thought of his motives later, at the time his standard of reference was a black peer group not the white world. This was true of color in general. Like many immigrant groups, blacks lived in a society where the mass media helped to glorify standards and aesthetic preferences which were not only alien but often impossible to emulate. If European immigrants had it easier in this respect than Negroes and nonwhite immigrants, they had their difficulties nonetheless. Names could be changed but skin shades, hair color and texture, and stereotypical physical features presented greater problems. Philip Roth's Alexander Portnoy, a mixed product of ethnicity and American popular culture, tried desperately to force his protruding nose back into its infantile snubness in order to conform to the standards of male beauty set by Hollywood and Madison Avenue, and lusted after the blond-haired *shickses* his Jewish heritage denied him.[98]

These inevitable tensions and frustrations, which afflicted all peripheral groups in America to varying degrees, and which surely affected many individual lives, were not strong enough to lead to the wholesale substitution of the fantasies of the outside society for a group's own traditional aesthetic standards. Black color preferences, like black music, were deeply influenced by contact with the larger society but remained apart from and independent of outside groups. Indeed, black color and black music, as part of the same cultural complex, often reinforced each other. In the 1940s Sue Flowers, a young woman living on a Mississippi Delta plantation, made the connections clear: "I like Negro music best. Heard that before I ever heard any other, and I'm used to it and can enjoy it the best. It seems to me like praising God through my own color, and I loves my color and I'll go further to praise them than whites. Ain't nothing no white man do sincere."[99]

In *Toward the African Revolution*, Frantz Fanon wrote that without oppression and racism there could have been no blues and predicted that the end of racism "would sound the knell of great Negro music." Ortiz Walton has given an appropriate response to this argument: "The Blues cannot be reduced to a reaction against what white people do and have done; rather they would be more accurately conceived of as a positive form that affirms and preserves Afro-American culture."[100] Several decades earlier Ralph Ellison had responded similarly in his review of Gunnar Myrdal's *An American Dilemma:* "can a people . . . live and develop for over three hundred years simply by *reacting?* Are American Negroes simply the creation of white men, or have they at least helped to create themselves out of what they found around them? Men have made a way of life in caves and upon cliffs, why cannot Negroes have made a life upon the horns of the white man's dilemma?"[101] The blues with its individualized tone, its transitional musical style, its inward-looking, communally oriented ethos, its independent voice, is a testament to the validity of these responses. But black song was not the only form of Afro-American music able to go beyond the repressions, myths, and traditions of American society and carve out independent values and standards. While the social implications and importance of instrumental black music have not yet been accorded the scholarly attention they deserve, it is clear that for both its partisans and its detractors, jazz came to symbolize many of the very qualities we have found central to the blues.

The work of such scholars as Morroe Berger, Aaron Esman, Norman Margolis, and Neil Leonard has shown that jazz was seen by many contemporaries as a cultural form independent of a number of the basic central beliefs of bourgeois society, free of its repressions, in rebellion against many of its grosser stereotypes. Jazz became associated with what Esman has called the "vital libidinal impulses . . . precisely the id drives that the superego of the bourgeois culture sought to repress." By threatening to expose and return what was repressed, jazz quickly won the enmity of the respectable arbiters of the society's culture and of segments of the Negro middle and professional classes who desired to become part of mainstream America and found jazz an anachronistic embarrassment. Jazz was denounced as barbaric, sensuous, jungle music which assaulted the senses and the sensibilities, diluted reason, led to the abandonment of decency and decorum, undermined dignity, and destroyed order and self-control.[102]

Jazz won the allegiance of members of those segments of the society—intellectuals, adolescents, and, of course, many Negroes—who felt themselves marginal to the central framework and alienated from many of its conventional values. Many of those whites who found jazz and blues stimulating and attractive in the 1920s and 1930s did so because these musical forms seemed to promise them greater freedom of expression, both artistically and personally. This was especially true of young people whom Louis Armstrong observed were among the most numerous and avid followers of the bands he played with.[103] In the early 1920s a group of young whites who were born or raised in and around Chicago and who were to become well-known jazz musicians—Benny Goodman, Bud Freeman, Dave Tough, Eddie Condon, Milton "Mezz" Mezzrow, Gene Krupa, Muggsy Spanier, Jimmy McPartland, Frank Teschemacher, Joe Sullivan, George Wettling—were stunned by the music of such black jazzmen as Joe Oliver, Jimmie Noone, Johnny and Baby Dodds, and Louis Armstrong, all of whom were then playing in clubs on Chicago's Southside. These white youngsters spoke about jazz, Condon recalled, "as if it were a new religion just come from Jerusalem."[104]

The analogy was not far-fetched: in their autobiographies these musicians often described what amounted to conversion experiences. In the summer of 1923 two white musicians associated with the Chicago group, Hoagy Carmichael from Indiana and Bix Beiderbecke from Iowa, along with some of their friends, went to a club where Oliver's band was playing and for the first time they encountered the sounds of the young Louis Armstrong. Carmichael recorded their reaction: "I dropped my cigarette and gulped my drink. Bix was on his feet, his eyes popping. . . . Bob Gillette slid off his chair and under the table. He was excitable that way. 'Why,' I moaned, 'why isn't everybody in the world here to hear that?' "[105] A year later Eddie Condon, Jimmy McPartland, and Bud Freeman dropped in to hear Oliver's group, with the same results: "Oliver lifted his horn and the first blast of Canal Street Blues hit me," Condon has written. "It was hypnosis at first hearing. Everyone was playing what he wanted to play and it was all mixed together as if someone had planned it with a set of micrometer calipers; notes I had never heard were peeling off the edges and dropping through the middle; there was a tone from the trumpets like warm rain on a cold day. Freeman and MacPartland [*sic*] and I were immobilized; the music poured into us like daylight running down a dark hole."[106]

From these encounters the young white musicians absorbed a new means of expressing their musical individuality. Growing up in Indianapolis, Carmichael spent much of his time listening to the music of Reggie Duval, a local black pianist. The excitement of what he was learning still comes through Carmichael's memoirs: "He hit keys where they shouldn't quite be hit, but it came out right. . . . I would sit there absorbed, watching the flighty movements of his brown wonderful hands." Duval reiterated one precept to his young admirer: "Never play anything that ain't *right*. You may not make any money, but you'll never get hostile with yourself."[107] Jazz was teaching these youngsters to break away from what Mezz Mezzrow called the "handcuff-and-straight-jacket discipline of the classical school," to speak out in their own "honest and self-inspired language."[108]

It was not just the musical but the cultural freedom—the ability to be and express themselves, the sense of being natural—which they associated with jazz, that many of these young white musicians found attractive. World War I was over, Carmichael recalled, but the rebellion against "the accepted, the proper and the old" was just beginning. "And for us jazz articulated. . . . It said what we wanted to say though what that was we might not know."[109] Mezzrow called his fellow musicians in the Chicago group "teenage refugees from the sunny suburbs," and characterized their determination to learn and emulate the expressive modes of black jazz as "a collectively improvised nose-thumbing at all pillars of all communities, one big syncopated Bronx cheer for the righteous squares everywhere. Jazz was the only language they could find to preach their fire-eating message." Working on one of his first jobs as a pit musician in Minsky's burlesque house on New York's Lower East Side, Mezzrow was repelled by the heavy-footed, graceless burlesque queens and even more appalled at the audiences that came to ogle them: "those rows of heated-up faces and frustrated maniac grins and bulging eyeballs every time the strip-teaser heaved her middle." He contrasted this "culture where all your dreams dangle from a G-string . . . a culture of mastubators," with his sense of black culture where people "led full and functioning lives, no matter how heavy a ball of oppression they carried around their necks, so they weren't walking skinfuls of repressions. . . . Up in Harlem a dancer had to have real talent, make wonderful graceful steps with her feet and do delicate things with her body, really express something, before anybody applauded. Tongues didn't hang out at the sight of a torso with the palsy."[110]

This sense of artistic and cultural difference set Mezzrow and his colleagues back upon themselves and created a developing *Gemeinschaft*. Benny Goodman has written that "musicians who played hot were pretty much of a clique by themselves. They hung around in the same places, made the same spots after work, drank together whenever they had the chance. . . . None of us had much use for what was known then and probably always will be as 'commercial' musicians. . . . we didn't pay much attention to them."[111] There was a direct line between this group of white jazz musicians in the 1920s and the alienated youth of the 1950s and 1960s whose rebellion owed so much, directly and indirectly, to aspects of Afro-American culture, particularly its music. It was the cultural rebels of the 1950s whom Norman Mailer characterized as "urban adventurers who drifted out at night looking for action with a black man's code to fit their facts. The hipster had absorbed the existentialist synapses of the Negro, and for practical purposes could be considered a white Negro."[112]

Even this cursory look at the symbolic meanings of jazz, and of blues as well, indicates that the numerous differences in the aesthetics and values between Negro folk culture and the larger society are not a retrospective figment of the historical imagination. These differences were recognized persistently throughout the twentieth century by contemporaries, some of whom abhorred what they saw, some of whom were frightened by it since cultural differences worn naturally are always potentially threatening, and some of whom—especially an increasing number of white youth—were excited by what they perceived to be new possibilities and alternatives. In these responses there was some prejudice, some ignorance, and some romanticism. But in them also the historian may find additional evidence of the truth that Negro folk culture cannot be viewed accurately as predominantly a reaction to oppression and hardship. It was that, of course, but it was also far more, and its constant interaction with and influence upon American culture are still imperfectly understood.

Inevitably, even in a chapter as long as this one, many things about black music have to be left unsaid. Enough has been said to indicate the continuing importance of song in the Afro-American oral tradition and the continuing centrality of that tradition itself. There were numerous changes in the consciousness manifested in the secular songs of the twentieth century when compared to the sacred songs that both antedated and paralleled them. But one function at least remained the same: secular songs like sacred ones were designed to give a sense of direction and meaning in a world that often seemed anarchic. In his autobiography Sidney Bechet recalled an incident when a white brakeman caught him riding the rails and was about to throw him off the speeding train. Inexplicably, he changed his mind, treated Bechet with kindness, and informed him that the train was heading for his exact destination. Reflecting on this youthful experience many years later, Bechet mused: "That kind of changing around, the way luck goes faster than you can figure it, it just won't be understood. You start doing a thing and sometimes there's nothing happens, and sometimes there's trouble busting faster than you know it, and sometimes it's luck comes busting. It's nothing you can figure. The onliest thing I've ever been sure of how it was going is the music; that's something a man can make himself if he has the feeling.[113] In the 1930s a young William Dixon looked around his neighborhood and concluded that even in Harlem whites were everywhere in control, from the schoolhouse to the butcher shop, from the police station to the gas station: "it did seem, to a little boy, that these white people *really* owned everything. But that wasn't entirely true. They didn't own the music that I heard played."[114]

This is, perhaps, the final thing to be said about the music: it gave a sense of power, of control. If it did not affect the material being of its creators, it certainly did have an impact upon their psychic state and emotional health. It allowed them to assert themselves and their feelings and their values, to communicate continuously with themselves and their peers and their oppressors as well. Here was an area in which they could at least partly drop the masks and the pretense and say what they felt, articulate what was brimming up within them and what they desperately needed to express. Black secular song, along with other forms of the oral tradition, allowed them to express themselves communally and individually, to derive great aesthetic pleasure, to perpetuate traditions, to keep values from eroding, and to begin to create new expressive modes. Black secular song revealed a culture which kept large elements of its own autonomous standards alive, which continued a rich internal life, which interacted with a larger society that deeply affected it but to which it did not completely succumb.

5

BLACK
LAUGHTER

He remembered once the melancholy-comic notes of a "Blues" rising out of a Harlem basement before dawn. . . . melancholy-
comic. That was the key to himself and to his race. . . . No
wonder the whites, after five centuries of contact, could not
understand his race. . . . No wonder they hated them, when out of their
melancholy environment the blacks could create mad, contagious music
and high laughter.

Claude McKay[1]

In the early 1890s James Weldon Johnson spent three months teaching in
the backwoods of Georgia—an assignment that brought him closer to the
rural black folk than he had been before. Years later he summed up his
experience in the form of a conundrum: "The situation in which they
were might have seemed hopeless, but they themselves were not without
hope. The patent proof of this was their ability to sing and to laugh. I
know something about the philosophy of song; I wish I knew as much
about the philosophy of laughter. Their deep genuine laughter often puzzled and irritated me. Why *did* they laugh so? How *could* they laugh so?
Was this rolling, pealing laughter merely echoes from a mental vacuity or
did it spring from an innate power to rise above the ironies of life? Or
were they, in the language of a line from one of the blues, 'Laughing to

keep from crying'? Were they laughing because they were only thought-
less? Were they laughing at themselves? Were they laughing at the white
man? I found no complete answer to these questions."[1] In *Negro Dancers*
the black poet Claude McKay expressed the same perplexity:

> And yet they are the outcasts of the earth,
> A race oppressed and scorned by ruling man;
> How can they thus consent to joy and mirth
> Who live beneath a world-eternal ban?[2]

These questions were genuine; yet they were also rhetorical. On one
level or another both writers understood the needs and uses of black
laughter. "It seems to me," Johnson wrote in his autobiography, "that for
the grim white man in the backwoods of the South this deep laughter of
the Negro should be the most ominous sound that reaches his ears."[3]
Earlier, in his 1912 novel, *The Autobiography of an Ex-Coloured Man*,
Johnson had the narrator say more positively, "I have since learned that
this ability to laugh heartily is, in part, the salvation of the American
Negro; it does much to keep him from going the way of the Indian."[4]
McKay agreed:

> The laughter gay like sounding silver ringing,
> That fills the whole wide room from floor to ceiling,—
> A rush of rapture to my tried soul bringing—
> The deathless spirit of a race revealing.[5]

Throughout the twentieth century many black writers and intellectuals
joined Johnson and McKay in stressing the positive aspects of Negro humor. In her contribution to Alain Locke's *The New Negro*, Jessie Fauset
spoke of "the gift of laughter" which Negroes brought to America. It was
a gift that arose "from the very woes which beset us." Laughter was a
compensating mechanism which enabled blacks to confront oppression
and hardship: "It is our emotional salvation."[6] In his collection of Negro
folk rhymes, Thomas Talley asserted that what had enabled blacks to
come into prolonged and intimate contact with white civilization without
being annihilated and to emerge from slavery in a comparatively strong
state was their "power to muster wit and humor on all occasions, and even
to laugh in the face of adversity."[7] The race, W. E. B. Du Bois wrote in
1940, possessed the greatest of the gifts of God, laughter: "If you will hear
men laugh, go to Guinea, 'Black Bottom,' 'Niggertown,' Harlem. If you
want to feel humor too exquisite and subtle for translation, sit invisibly

among a gang of Negro workers. . . . We are the supermen who sit idly by and laugh and look at civilization."[8] These attitudes were not universal. For many the sights and sounds of black laughter verged too near the vacuous, happy-go-lucky, Sambo image; black people needed to confront their problems not grin at them. "We laugh too much," the *Chicago Defender* complained in the midst of the Great Depression. "There is nothing to laugh at, except our condition, and it's too serious to be funny. There is nothing funny about a group of people who cannot find a grocery store in the community in which they live owned by them."[9]

Whatever the causes of black laughter, whatever its effects, whether it was celebrated or lamented, the degree of attention Negro intellectuals accorded it was a manifest sign of its pervasiveness. Laughter, of course, springs from many sources. Central among them is the desire to place the situation in which we find ourselves into perspective; to exert some degree of control over our environment. The need to laugh at our enemies, our situation, ourselves, is a common one, but it often exists the most urgently in those who exert the least power over their immediate environment; in those who have the most objective reasons for feelings of hopelessness. It is this that gives meaning to the proverb of East European Jews who lived on such intimate terms with poverty, prejudice, and pogroms: "Suffering makes you laugh too."[10] No inquiry into the consciousness and inner resources of black Americans can ignore the content and structure of Afro-American humor.

LAUGHING AT THE MAN

In his important analysis, *Laughter*, Henri Bergson specified what he called "inversion" as one of the prime comic methods: "Picture to yourself certain characters in a certain situation: if you reverse the situation and invert the roles, you obtain a comic scene. . . . Thus, we laugh at the prisoner at the bar lecturing the magistrate; at a child presuming to teach its parents; in a word at everything that comes under the heading of 'topsyturvydom.' "[1] Other students of humor have called this comic principle by other names: "universe-changing," "deviations from institutionalized meaning structures," and perhaps most commonly, "incongruity." All describe the same process: the trivialization or degradation of ideas or personages normally held to be lofty or noble, and the advancement of those normally consigned to an inferior or inconsequential position.[2]

The British actor and comedian John Bernard, who lived in the United States between 1797 and 1819, would have found these analyses particularly applicable to the slaves in whose culture he was so interested. After calling the slaves "the great humorists of the Union," Bernard characterized their humor as that "which lowered the most dignified subjects into ludicrous lights and elevated the most trivial into importance."[3] We have already observed this element at work in the slave trickster tales which induced laughter through a sudden reversal of roles or fortunes. However temporarily, the venerated were vanquished or at least made to look foolish by the lowly. Reversal of roles remained one of the chief mechanisms of black laughter long after slavery, not only in the trickster tales which continued to be popular but in the entire body of jokes which the freedmen and their descendants told one another.

One of the oldest and most persistent cycles of jokes in Afro-American lore focused upon the numskull doings of immigrant Irishmen. Jokes ridiculing the Irish became popular in the United States following the large-scale migrations from Ireland in the mid-nineteenth century. Negroes, who came into hostile contact with the Irish immigrants in the South and the North, learned the current anecdotes and undoubtedly created many of their own. These jokes were probably known to the slaves and were certainly widely disseminated among the freedmen. They were collected as early as the 1870s; Joel Chandler Harris included one in the first volume of his Uncle Remus tales; and by the end of the century they had become so ubiquitous that the *Southern Workman* noted in 1899, "Irishmen stories form as widespread a part of the American Negro folk-lore as do the animal stories."[4] The jokes were evidently told with great style. In 1876 Lafcadio Hearn noted that the Negro stevedores along the Cincinnati levee "can mimic the Irish accent to a degree of perfection which an American, Englishman or German could not hope to acquire."[5]

The Irishman remained a central butt of black humor throughout the twentieth century. In her 1917 collection of black lore from Guilford County, North Carolina, Elsie Clews Parsons reported that "Anecdotes about Irishmen have a distinct vogue. Indeed, the Archman [Irishman] has become as much of a stock character as Rabbit or Hant."[6] In 1923 the Negro folklorist Arthur Huff Fauset collected jokes about the Irish from Philadelphia blacks and two years later, after ranging widely through Alabama, Mississippi, and Louisiana, he concluded that left to themselves Negroes were even more apt to relate a story about the Irish than about Brer Rabbit: "It is curious to hear a native-born southern Negro, nearly full-blooded, telling a story about Pat and Mike with all the spirit and even the inflection of voice that one might expect of an Irishman."[7] A generation later Richard Dorson found jokes and anecdotes ridiculing the Irish still quite common, South and North.[8]

Jokes at the expense of the immigrant Irish who were themselves at the lower reaches of the American society and economy may hardly seem a good example of incongruity in black humor. Yet I think they are. Humor about the Irish functioned in several ways. Most obviously, these jokes allowed Negroes to join the white majority in looking down upon and feeling superior to the strange folkways of an alien group. For once black Americans could feel part of the mainstream as they ridiculed the awkward actions of unassimilated immigrants. (Just as for their part European immigrants could quickly feel at one with their new country by identifying themselves with the white majority.) Thus on the one hand these jokes permitted a reversal of roles by elevating blacks and allowing them to identify with and share the superior feelings of the groups at the center of American society. But they also reversed roles in the more traditional sense, for no matter how marginal the Irish may have been, they remained white, and as part of the racial majority they had made the Negro suffer at their hands, as in the New York Draft Riots in 1863. Irish jokes became a means of taking revenge upon these newcomers who had learned to hate Negroes so quickly and efficiently. Perhaps more importantly, they allowed Negroes to openly ridicule and express contempt for white people. The Irish characters of black jokelore became surrogates for all the other whites against whom it could be dangerous to speak openly. This may well account for the ease with which folklorists were able to collect these anecdotes and for the fact that they remained a central part of Afro-American expressive culture for at least a century.

The tone of most of these jokes was captured in the nineteenth-century story of the visitor to Hell who saw Germans, English, Japanese, and Negroes burning in torment, but no Irish. When he asked why, the Devil took him into a warm room filled with Irish. "We are just drying them here," the Devil informed his guest, "they are too green to burn now."[9] Irishmen in Afro-American lore were pictured as the quintessential greenhorn immigrants bumbling their way through an environment with which they were in no way prepared to cope. Discovering pumpkins for the first time, an Irishman is told they are mule's eggs. He pays an exhorbitant price for one, tries to hatch it by sitting on it, and when it rolls out from under him into the brush below frightening a rabbit which scampers off, he is convinced his egg has hatched and runs after the rabbit calling, "Koop Colie! Koop Colie! Here's your mammy."[10] Buying their first watermelon, two Irishmen give the heart of it away to some nearby Negroes and keep only the rind for themselves saying, "Guts is good enough for Naygurs."[11] The Irish that march through these anecdotes mistake turtles for pocket watches, wear them between their breeches, and respond to queries about the time by saying things like, "eleven-thirty, and scratching like hell for twelve"; they mistake mosquitoes for squirrels, frogs for deer, deer for railroad trains, a black slave for the Devil and his fiddle for a squalling baby. One Irishman finds a pocket watch, listens to it go "tick, tick," is convinced that it is the mother of all the ticks in the world, and smashes it with a club; others do the same thing when they mistake a watch for a rattlesnake.[12] Pat and Mike see a gun for the first time, buy it from its black owner, and Mike immediately kills Pat by trying to shoot a grasshopper off his chest.[13] Death by drowning is the fate of two Irishmen who decide that the water in which they have dropped their watch is shallow enough to wade into when they hear some frogs singing what sounds like "Knee deep, knee deep, knee deep."[14] Asked which way a road goes, an Irishman answers, "Faith, I've been living here twenty years, and it's never gone anywhere yet."[15]

Nor were the Irishmen in these tales going anywhere, hampered as they were by their great disabilities. The Irish immigrants with whom Negroes often came into economic competition were pictured in black humor as invariably incompetent and lazy. In one anecdote a recent Irish migrant gets a job as a hod carrier and writes to his brother in the Old Country, "Come at once, I've got a good easy job, a dollar and nine cents an hour carrying brick and mortar on the second floor. The other fellow does all the work, so come at once. Your brother Pat."[16] In a nineteenth-century anecdote an Irish orator cries out, "Who puts up all the fine buildings?—The Irish. And who puts up the court-houses?—The Irish. And who builds the State penitentiaries?—The Irish. And who fills them?—The Irish, be-gobs!"[17] When they became tired of lampooning Irish stupidity, indolence, and dishonesty, black storytellers could and did turn to Irish religion. Walking through the woods Pat comes across a panther, kills it with a club, and then continues to beat it into a bloody pulp. A passer-by asks him why he is doing that, "Can't you see it's dead?" "Yes," responds Pat. "But I want to show him that there's punishment after death."[18] Two

Irishmen in a boat are caught in rough seas and conclude, "Be fait' an' be Chris'! I believe we better pray." Pat prays, "O Gawd, Gawd! if you help me across dis time, I'll give you a big pertater. De 'tater will be as big as a peck tub." His partner remonstrates, "You know you ain't got no 'tater like dat." Pat responds, "Hush, hush, hush! I jes' foolin' him. I jes' want him to get me 'cross de river." In an identical situation, another Irishman prays vulgarly, "O Gawd, Gawd! If you help me cross dis bloody river, I wouldn't worry you no damn mo'. "[19]

Black attitudes toward the Irish were not as unambiguous as the general tone of these jokes implies. No matter how great the animosity between the two groups, they shared a lowly position in American society which created a certain empathy among Negroes for their Irish protagonists. This sympathy was manifest in the commonly told story of the Irishman and Englishman who go hunting and kill a turkey and a turkey buzzard: "When the hunt was over, of course the Englishman thought he was the smartest man. He suggested how the game ought to be divided. He said, 'Pat, I killed both the real turkey and the buzzard; but you may take the turkey-buzzard, and I the turkey; or I'll take the turkey, and you the buzzard.'—'Say that again,' said Pat to Joe; and he said it again the same way. 'You haven't said turkey to me the first nor the last, now I'll take the real turkey,' said Pat to Joe, and leave the smart Englishman very sorrowful."[20] In another joke a sea captain has some fun with one of his Irish sailors by telling him he might marry the most beautiful of his daughters if he can find three ends to a piece of rope. Pat studies the problem for several days and finally calls the captain over to the ship's side. He shows the captain both ends of the rope and then throws it overboard, saying, "Faith, and there's the other end!"[21] In a South Carolina story an Irishman is condemned to be hung alongside a black man and a Dutchman. Allowed to pick the tree they would be hung on, the black chooses an oak, the Dutchman a pine tree, and the Irishman a gooseberry bush. Informed it would not be large enough, the latter replies, "By Jesus! Me will wait till it grow."[22] The sensitive identification that occasionally marked Irish stories was reflected too in the strangely moving anecdote concerning three Irish greenhorns who knew only three phrases in English. Through a series of comic misadventures these three expressions lead them to confess to a murder they did not commit. "They knew too much after all," the storyteller concluded. "They knew just enough about America to get hung."[23]

The ambivalence noticeable in black attitudes toward Irish Americans was evident in their approach to other minority groups as well. The anti-Semitism of nineteenth- and twentieth-century America functioned precisely the same way for Negroes as did nativistic anti-Catholicism: it allowed them to feel part of the larger fabric by distinguishing themselves from a despised group on the periphery, and it again permitted them to openly ridicule white people with impunity. Still, as with the Irish, the fact that Jews were not just white Americans but were themselves excluded and discriminated against tempered black feelings toward them. Seth Scheiner, who has studied black attitudes toward Jews in New York City at the turn of the century, has shown how philo-Semitic and anti-Semitic attitudes could be entertained simultaneously. The Negro newspaper *New York Age* was not atypical in denouncing Jews as "a peculiar race . . . parasitical and predatory . . . preying upon and devouring the substance of others rather than creating and devouring the substance of itself," even while it urged its readers to emulate the business acumen of the Jews, to teach their girls to copy the "almost universal chastity" of Jewish girls, to educate their children with the same zeal the Jews showed, and to "cultivate a lofty pride of race," comparable to that of the Jewish people.[24]

The traditional stereotype of the Jew as a money-grubbing materialist was prominent in Negro humor. North Carolina Negroes told the story of Jim Johnson who bought a suit at Mr. Rubenstein's store. The first time he wore it he was caught in the rain, and the suit shrunk so badly the pants came up almost to his knees and the coat wouldn't button. Wearing the ill-fitting suit, he returns to the store and asks the owner, "Mr. Rubenstein, does you remember me, Jim?" "Sho, I remembers you," Rubenstein responds and then looking at the suit he exclaims, "but my! how you has growed!"[25] More common still was the joke concerning four friends—a colored man, a Jew, an Italian, and a white man—who agree to contribute five dollars each to the first one that dies so that he might carry some money with him across the Jordan. A few months later the Italian dies, and his friends line up at his coffin to fulfill their promise. The white man drops a five dollar bill in. The black man follows suit. Finally the Jew goes to the coffin, removes the cash and writes the departed Italian a check for fifteen dollars.[26] A similar joke concerned a black man who buried his savings in a graveyard and put a tombstone at the head reading, "Dead and Buried." A Jew who witnessed the act snuck in, dug up the money, and replaced the tombstone with one that read, "Rose and Gone to Glory."[27]

A striking characteristic of black humor concerning Jews was how often it played on not merely the Jewish stereotypes but the Negro stereotypes as well. Although these jokes repeatedly pictured Jews taking advantage of blacks, there seems to have been an unstated bond of empathy between the two caricatured groups, who, along with other minorities that happened to be pictured, were always carefully distinguished from the "white man." In one of the oldest and most popular of these jokes, a white man, a colored man, and a Jew die and go to Hell at a time when the Devil is inundated with souls. He offers to let them go if they pay him five dollars apiece. The white man does so immediately and returns to the world. When he is asked what happened to his companions, he explains, "When I left the Jew was offering him $4.98 and the colored man said he would pay him on Saturday."[28] Another anecdote which retained its popularity through most of this century told of the time, during the Creation, when the various races were asked what talents and possessions they desired. The Anglo-Saxon asked for political domination, the Chinese asked for peace and isolation, the American Indian asked for a happy hunting ground, the Negro asked for a million dollars, and the Jew asked for the Negro's address.[29] During the Depression, Harlem Negroes regaled themselves with the caustic but still warmly humorous story of Mr. Ginsberg, who came into their neighborhood to recruit a crew for his ship, *Rebecca*, bound for Georgia to pick up a cargo of watermelons. On its return trip the ship is trailed by a huge whale. Fearful that the creature will overturn the small ship, watermelons are thrown to it. Swallowing them, the whale continues his pursuit. In the hope that it might like dark meat, Ginsberg has some members of the crew thrown overboard. The whale swallows them and continues to trail the ship. Finally mutiny ensues and Ginsberg himself is thrown into the yawning mouth of the whale. In desperation the remaining crew harpoon their pursuer and tow it back to New York. Setting anchor in the Harlem River, the crew tell their tale to an excited crowd and then cut the whale open to prove that the events really had taken place. "And, lo and behold, there was Ginsberg selling watermelons to the crew on a ten-payment plan."[30]

Irishmen and Jews had no monopoly on the ethnic humor of black Americans. Italians, Mexicans, American Indians, and Chinese also figured—though less prominently—in the rich and active vein of Negro humor concerning other ethnic groups in the United States. Negroes utilized stereotyped accents, character types, and situations in ways which allowed them both to identify with and to ridicule white America, but

which also exhibited a certain understanding of and frequently an empathy for the position of these other minorities.

Poor southern whites, whom Negroes had looked upon with contempt and hostility since the days of slavery, were another marginal group at whose expense black people laughed. After collecting black folklore in North Carolina, J. Mason Brewer concluded that the North Carolina Negro "thinks himself better and more intelligent than mountain whites and poor 'city whites,' and takes great delight in spinning yarns about their stupidity, imitativeness, and other bad qualities he claims they possess."[31] Moonshine, old-fashioned rifles, even more old-fashioned mores, and a general lack of sophistication dominated these stories. Thinking the first motorcycle he has ever seen is a wild animal, a mountain white shoots it causing it to spin around and its rider to fall off. "Did you kill it," his wife asks. "No, I didn't kill it, but I sho made it turn that man loose."[32] In Coahoma County, Mississippi, at the close of the Depression, Will Starks parodied poor whites in a bit of doggerel:

Doggone luck! Doggone luck!
I don't know ought from a figger.
But I got so much good blood,
I can't associate with a nigger.[33]

The most obvious examples of inversion or incongruity in black humor focused upon situations in which the normal relationships between southern whites and blacks were suddenly reversed. South Carolina Negroes in the 1940s were still telling the story of the supposed exchange between the racist politician Ben Tillman and a Negro delegate during the state Constitutional Convention of 1890. Tillman had delivered a speech in which he disparaged South Carolina's black population. The Negro delegate arose and denounced Tillman, who the next day responded in an even stronger speech during which he roared, "Why, you dirty black rascal, I'll swallow you alive." "If you do," his black antagonist shouted back, "you'll have more brains in your belly than you've got in your head."[34] A similar example of one-upmanship is recorded in a widely told joke in which a Negro is brought into court for kicking a white man. He responds to the judge's query concerning his motive by asking, "Well, Capum, what would you do if someone called you a black son of a bitch?" "That," the judge answers superciliously, "would hardly be likely to happen." "Well, Capum," the black defendant persists, "spose they call you the kind of a son of a bitch you is?"[35] A reversal of the usual stereotypes occurs also in the joke about the black maid and her white employer who become pregnant and give birth at the same time. One day the white woman runs into the kitchen crying out in delight, "Oh, my baby said his first word today." The black baby, in his basket on the kitchen floor, looks up and asks, "He did, wha' 'id 'e say?"[36]

Perhaps the most widely disseminated joke of this type concerns a northern Negro, traveling through the South in a luxury automobile, who asks for service at a gas station without displaying the usual deference demanded of southern blacks. The white attendant pulls out a gun and performs some act of remarkable markmanship, such as putting five holes through a dime he throws high in the air. "Now you look that over and think about it," he says menacingly. The black man responds by throwing an apple into the air, whipping out a knife and making a few passes in the air so that when the apple lands it is peeled, cored, and quartered. The attendant studies the apple for a long while and then asks, "How many gallons of gas did you want, Mister?"[37] A similar joke told of a white man who asks a black farmer riding his mule whether the animal could dance. When the farmer replies, "I don't know, Mr. White man," the latter proceeds to empty his revolver at the feet of the mule which responded predictably, badly frightening its rider and almost throwing him to the ground. When the white man has emptied his gun, "the nigger reached in his jacket and pulled out his forty-five and the nigger say, 'Is you ever kissed a mule's ass?' and the white man say, 'No Sir, Mr. Nigger, but I always wanted to.' "[38]

Reversal of roles through direct confrontation with mainstream whites rather than through trickery or the use of surrogate ethnic groups seems to be a more recent development in black humor, but the technique itself is a traditional one dating back to slavery. A very large category of humor, of course, involves some degree of inversion or reversal. The very act of ridiculing individuals, groups, ideas, or institutions easily creates feelings of superiority on the part of the joke-tellers. But unless reversal of roles is used in this all-inclusive sense, it was only one of the humorous devices employed by Negroes. Much black humor was sycophantish and manipulative: Negroes played up to and attempted to control whites through laughter. This type of laughter had been a crucial weapon in the slaves' arsenal, and it remained central in the century following emancipation. Driving through Tennessee and Kentucky during the Depression, the black writer J. Saunders Redding gave a ride to Bill Perry, an itinerant black singer and guitarist. Together they drove through a succession of half-deserted, heavily patrolled mining towns. In one of them they were stopped by a guard with an automatic rifle:

> He wanted to know where we "boys" were going. Before I could answer, Bill Perry broke in:
>
> "Cap'n, we'se goin' to Kintucky. See all dat stuff back dere, Cap'n? Well, dat stuff 'longs ter Mista Rob French, an' he sho' will raise hell ef we don' git it to him," Bill lied convincingly.
>
> "That gittar too?" the guard questioned, already softened to a joke.
>
> Bill grinned. "No, suh, Cap'n. Dis yere box is mine. Dis yere's ma sweetheart! If we-all hed time an' you hed time, I'd beat one out fer you," Bill said.
>
> "G'on. But don' stop nowheres. Don' even breathe hard," the guard said grinning.
>
> "No, suh, Cap'n. I ain't much of a breever noway. Jus' 'nough ter live on. No, suh. I don' want no mo' o' white folks' air den I jus' got ter have."
>
> We drove on. Bill Perry doubled with laughter, his narrow, slanting shoulders almost touching his knees.
>
> "I kin lie when I has ter."
>
> "I see you can."
>
> "Man, dat gun was 'bout de mos' uglies' thing I ever seen."
>
> "What do you suppose the trouble is, Bill?"
>
> " 'Deed, I ain't got no notion. But hits white folks' trouble, an' dat's 'nough fer me," Bill said. "Peckerwoods is allus got some trouble. Near 'bout all de trouble dey is is white folks' trouble. Be a reg'lar ol' levee jubilee if som'pin was to blow de white folks all up. Ain't no sense to deir trouble neither. Peckerwoods kin't live less'n dey messed up wid som'pin."[39]

The scene enacted in that small Tennessee town had occurred and would be repeated countless times, South and North. If it demeaned all who participated in it, it also revealed the vein of contempt for and ridicule of the white man that underlay so much of black humor. We have seen this motif dominating the wit of the human trickster tales told during and after slavery. The white man's pretensions, hypocrisies, fragilities were revealed and mocked. Indeed, nothing more effectively burlesqued the entire notion of ownership in human beings than the incessantly told story of the slave who was caught killing and eating one of his master's pigs and who mockingly rationalized his act by arguing that since both the animal and the slave were the master's possessions nothing was lost: "Yes, suh, Massa, you got less pig now but you sho' got more nigger." In this popular joke we can see a paradigm for an entire strain of Afro-American humor which produced laughter by carrying the whites' claims to their logical and absurd conclusion. Thus the slave's assertion that consuming the master's pig was merely an enhancement of the owner's property, and Bill Perry's pledge, "I don' want no mo' o' white folks' air den I jus' got ter have," were funny for identical reasons: without warning they stripped the actors bare revealing the ludicrousness of the white man's puffery and the black man's situation. It was on this plane of absurdity that much of Afro-American humor took place.

The humor of absurdity worked through a straight-faced assumption of the rationality of the system and the belief structure upon which it rested. Events could then be unfolded which exposed the system and its underlying beliefs by accepting them with complete and faithful literalness. No institution or custom, South or North, lent itself better to this humor than segregation, and the amount of wit devoted to it is difficult to assimilate no less summarize. Black jokes about segregation were as old as the practice itself. Mrs. Hannah Prosser, who was born a slave in Maryland in 1812, purchased her freedom along with that of her husband in 1841, and moved to Columbia, Pennsylvania, where she lived the remaining fifty-four years of her life, told of her response to an instance of segregation in the pre-Civil War North:

> Yes, honey, sometimes you fin's de right wo'd jes like as ef it was lef' on yo' tongue a pupp'ose. Dar was de time I was gwine to Media [Media, Pennsylvania] long befo' de wah. De cyars dem days had de stoves in de middle, an' up over de do' was a signbo'd wid writin' on it: "Cullud people will take de reah end of de passenger cyar, ur de fo'ard end ob de baggage cyar." Hit wur mighty col', so I sot down by de stove, like as ef dar wa'n't no signbo'd on top dat do'. D'rec'ly come a sassy little Jack-sparrer of a newsboy, an' he hollers at me, flingin' his imperdence 'bout cullud people, but I don' nuvver pay no 'tention to w'ite trash. Atter w'ile de conductor-man, he come in an' he pint up to de signbo'd over de do', an' says he, "Don' you see dat?" den, mighty cross, "Whar you gwine?" "Media, sir," says I. "All right," says he, "you mus' take de reah end o' de passenger cyar ur de fo'ard end ob de baggage cyar." I jumps right up an' collec's my basket jes as quick as I kin, an' I tole dat conductor-man I'm 'bleeged fer his kin'ness in warnin' me. I tol' him I done s'posed bot ends ob de cyar wen' to Media, but ef its only de reah end, in co'se I'll take it.[40]

The note of absurdity struck by Mrs. Prosser remained the chief thrust of black humor concerning American racial codes. Throughout the century blacks told one comic anecdote after another about being punished if they whipped their white horses and of being forced to address their light-skinned draft animals with respect—"you say, 'Mr. Mule'; don't you come callin' no white mule just another mule!"; of having to ask for a can of "*Mr.* Prince Albert" tobacco in little country stores because there was a picture of a white man on the cans; of having to call a Ford automobile "Mister Ford," because it bore the name of a white man; of not being allowed to wear white shoes, drink white milk, or sing *White Christmas;* of having to wear colored shirts and collars, except for Negro ministers who were allowed to wear white collars—on the condition that the collars were dirty; of developing a taste for black-eyed peas and red beans due to a fear of ordering white beans—"Here you are up North ordering *white* bean soup. Man, I know you are really free, now."[41] The logical culmination of these endless anecdotes was the Memphis story of Mr. White who refused to allow Negroes on his huge plantation. He surrounded his land with white fences, painted all of his trees white as high as he could reach, and made certain that all of his cattle, sheep, goats, hogs, mules, horses, and chickens were white: "Anytime one of his animals have a black calf or a black goat—whatsonever it was—Mister White give it to the niggers. Even down to the chickens. He had all white chickens, too. And when a chicken would hatch off some black chickens, he'd say, 'Take those chickens out and find a nigger and give 'em to him. Get rid of 'em. I won't have no nigger chickens on this plantation!' "[42]

These jokes acknowledged black fear and subservience even as they stressed the inanity and fantasy nature of the system which bound them. One anecdote told of a northern black visitor in a small Georgia town who sang the popular song:

> Just Mollie and me
> And baby makes three.
> We're happy
> In my blue heaven.

Interrupted by a local white who yelled, "What did you say, nigger?" the black man immediately changed the words:

> Just Molly and you-all
> No niggers at all.
> You-all happy as you-all
> In you-all's blue heaven.[43]

The salient function of these jokes was to rob the American racial system of any legitimacy long before the courts and the government began that still uncompleted task. The absurdity of the system in every area it touched was driven home. A white deacon in Mississippi walks into his church and finds a Negro standing there. "Boy," he calls out. "What you doin' in here? Don't you know this is a white church?" "Boss, I only just got sent here to mop up the floor," the black man informs him. "Well, that's all right then," the deacon responds. "But don't let me catch you prayin'."[44] A light-skinned Negro college student in an Eastern college has an affair with a local white girl. He is drafted and returns a year later to find that she has become the mother of his child. He protests that if she had told him he would have come home and married her. "I know," she says, "but I talked it over with my family and they decided they'd rather have an illegitimate child in the family than a nigger."[45] During the influx of southern Negroes to the North during and after World War I, the story circulated through black communities that the Biblical prophet must have been referring to a black man moving into a white neighborhood in a northern city when he predicted that one "shall chase a thousand" and that two shall "put ten thousand to flight."[46] A Negro chauffeur driving a movie magnate through Alabama on their way to Florida develops a terrible toothache. They stop at the next small town where the local dentist tells him it will cost $500 to have the tooth pulled. The employer asks how much it would cost to have his tooth pulled and is told $20. Incredulous at the disparity, he demands an explanation. "Well, it's a major operation, for here in Alabama a Negro doesn't dare open his mouth to a white man, so we have to pull it out his anus."[47] Few jokes on the subject of segregation were more prevalent than the story of the elderly black man who successfully talks his way out of a traffic ticket by telling the judge, "Lord, boss, I sho' thought them green lights was for the white folks and the red lights was for us cullud folks."[48]

   The tendency of black wit to focus upon the absurdity inherent in the subjects it treated has long been recognized. In 1870 N. S. Dodge characterized the language of the freedmen as "abundantly humorous. . . . There is either no patois so capable of expressing the ludicrous, or no people using a patois so alive to the ridiculous. Nothing was more manifest during the rebellion [Civil War]. The keenest wit, the sharpest retorts, severest satire, and most amusing repartees came from the negro."[49] Closely related to the humor of absurdity, and often having the same effects, was humor which revealed the gap between appearance and actuality and performed what Anton Zijderveld has called "unmasking functions."[50] Dodge told of an elderly freedman whose cabin, along with those of his neighbors, was appropriated for Union Army use by a quartermaster named Worms. When asked by a Methodist class-leader if it was not time at his age to be preparing for another world, the freedman answered,

"Yes, Massa, tink it is time, for Cap'n Worms gwying to hab *all dere is in dis world!*"[51] In a few humorous and incisive words the uniformed saviours of the North, as a local group of freedmen experienced them, were revealed as potential new oppressors.

Humor of this sort often proves elusive to those outside the group. Newbell Niles Puckett attributed the failure of the simple, spare jokes of the Negro "to nourish a commonplace grin on the face" of whites to the whites' lack of imagination, while John Dollard explained it by black secretiveness. "White informants frequently comment on the unaccountable manner in which Negroes laugh," Dollard wrote in his study of race relations in Indianola, Mississippi, during the 1930s. "Very often when whites suddenly come upon Negroes laughing and the Negro refuses to explain, it is not because he cannot give a reason or that he is a mere idiot laughing at nothing, but rather that the joke is on the white man and an explanation would be tactless."[52] This, of course, supplies only a partial explanation. A substantial percentage of Negro humor, even had it been revealed to whites, would simply not have struck them as funny. The experiences, the perspective, and the needs of many black Americans so often diverged from those of the majority of white Americans that their humor with its incisive commentary upon reality from the vantage point of black consciousness was not easily comprehensible to whites. Dollard relates a good example told to him by a black resident of Indianola. A Negro named George goes into a white store to purchase a hat. The clerk asks, "Well, *Bill*, what will you have?" The black man replies that he doesn't want anything, and leaves. He enters a second store, where he is greeted, "Well, *son*, what will you have?" Again he leaves without making a purchase. So it continues from store to store where he is greeted by a variety of names, "Uncle," "Mose," and the like, until he comes to a store in which the clerk says, "Well, *George*, what will you have?" "A hat," he replies and buys one. This fragile joke about a proud black man who refused to respond to any of the stock names whites used for Negroes until he was called one which happened to coincide with his own, revealed the meanness of the white custom and the agonizing difficulty of the black's situation in a way which many white contemporaries would have found difficult to fathom, or at least difficult to fathom *as humor*. Certainly this is what Dollard was expressing when he commented, "Negro humor is often so delicate that it is hard to locate, and one comes off with the baffled general feeling that the whites have been lampooned without knowing quite how."[53]

In 1919 the sociologist Robert E. Park unwittingly supplied an example of what Dollard has called the "delicate suppressed quality" of Negro humor when he wrote of his interview with an old man who had been part of the cargo of one of the last ships to land slaves successfully from Africa in the United States just on the eve of the Civil War. "The old man," Park wrote, "remembered Africa and gave me a very interesting account of the way in which he was captured and brought to America." Park asked him if he had ever wished to return, and he replied that he and many of the others he had been brought over with had been visited by a missionary who knew their country and their language. The missionary offered to send them back to Africa. "I told him," said the old man, "I crossed the ocean once, but I made up my mind then never to trust myself in a boat with a white man again." Park missed, as he probably was meant to miss, the humorous thrust of this remark and saw in it only somber evidence that "the slave had in fact very little desire to return to his native land."[54] Following the Detroit race riot of 1943, a black newspaper printed a cartoon, the reaction to which also illustrated the propensity of outsiders to see only a painful message where blacks could also see humor. The cartoon pictured the den of a sportsman in which the head of a Negro was hung next to the mounted heads of wild animals. One of the two little white boys who were shown looking at the trophies points to the stuffed Negro head and tells his friend, "My daddy got that one in Detroit last week." Langston Hughes has written that Harlemites thought this cartoon "highly, if wryly, hilarious. But no white person to whom I have ever shown it even cracks a smile, let alone laughs aloud."[55]

The oblique jokes of southern blacks were able to draw humor from the most painful situation. In Memphis during the 1940s, Alan Lomax had an extended conversation with three black workers named Natchez, Leroy, and Sib. At one point they discussed the hardships of life in the work camps along the roads, levees, and rock quarries of the South:

> Natchez went on, forcing us to savor the dirt, see the hoggish way the men had to live. "They'd just go out in those big truck gardens and pull up greens by the sackful, take 'em down to some lake or creek, sort of shake 'em off in the water, and cook 'em, roots, stalk, and all, in one of them big fifty-two gallon pots."
>
> Leroy, beginning to laugh his big laugh again, broke in. "And if you found a worm in your greens and say, 'Captain, I found a worm here,' he'd say, 'What the hell you expect for nothing?' "
>
> Natchez and Sib burst out in great yells of laughter, as Leroy hurried on to top his own story: "And then some fellow over 'long the table would holler, 'Gimme that piece of meat!' "

"Yeah, I've heard that—'Gimme that piece of meat! Don't throw it away!'" Natchez gasped out between the gusts of laughter that were shaking his whole body. Sib couldn't sit still any longer; his laughter was riding him too hard. . . .

When we had recovered from this healing laughter, Leroy added thoughtfully, "Those guys seemed to get a kick out of the whole thing."[56]

Langston Hughes has described a Negro college president who would convulse his black audiences by telling of a time when he was descending the train steps at the station in Atlanta and heard a scream behind him. A white woman had caught her heel and was falling head first down the steps. Instinctively he raised his arms to catch her when he remembered where he was and quickly dropped them to his sides allowing her to fall and be injured badly, a victim not of misfortune alone but of laws and customs she herself probably approved of.[57] One of the most popular comic anecdotes of the black folk similarly emphasized the manner in which southern racial codes forced their black victims to reverse their instincts. A black man, either falling accidentally or jumping suicidally from a height, suddenly realizes that he is going to land on top of a white woman. He stops in mid-air, forces himself to reverse direction, and lands again in his original position.[58] Blacks in North Carolina, Arkansas, and Texas were able to joke about the way in which their white landlords cheated them. In a North Carolina story a black sharecropper, tired of doing nothing better than breaking even year after year, decides to report only ten of the twelve bales of cotton he raises one exceptionally good year. After elaborate figuring, his white landlord informs him, "Well, well, you done putty good dis year too, Fred. You broke dead even." "Well, dat's good," the sharecropper replies, "but dere's two mo' bales I didn't tell you 'bout." "The hell you did," the white man screams as he tears up the paper on which he had been figuring. "Don't you never do nothin' like dat again, nigger. Have me refigurin' yo' crop all over so you can come out dead even."[59]

Not surprisingly, one of the prime foci of black unmasking humor was the South and white southerners. Joke after joke attempted to expose aspects of reality that lay beneath the surface. One of the favorite themes was white preoccupation with and dependence upon blacks. A joke in circulation at the turn of the century told of an old black man in a small southern town wandering into an immigration meeting. He listened to the rhetoric for a while and then asked a nearby white, "Boss, who is dis here emmygration man and what is dis here emmygration?" When it was explained that the speaker was an agent of the railroad company trying to find ways of inducing more whites to migrate to the South, the old man shook his head in instant disagreement and commented, "But Cap'n, us niggers has got mo' white folks around here now dan us kin take kere of."[60] Another joke popular during the same period told of a young boy who went to work as a butler's assistant in the home of a prominent family in Atlanta. His relatives were curious about what went on in the white man's house and asked him, "What do they talk about when they're eating?" The boy thought for a while and replied, "Mostly they discusses us culled folks."[61] During the early years of World War II Gunnar Myrdal reported a bit of comic dialogue that was making the rounds of black communities:

> "It says in the white folks' newspapers that our women are trying to ruin the white folks' homes by quitting their jobs as maids."
> "Yeah. A whole lot of white women are mad because they have to bring up their own children."[62]

In a more recent example, told by a sixty-five-year-old woman, two old ladies are talking about white folks running everywhere trying to escape from blacks. "Honey," one says, "I think the only reason the white folks want to go to the moon is so they can get rid of us and everytime they look up there we is. If we come in their neighborhoods they run, we done even run them out of their churches. I know once they get to the moon they ain't going allow us niggers up there." Her friend rocks and thinks for a time before responding: "Don't worry none honey, they going to get up to the moon and find out they don't know how to wash and iron, then they'll send for us."[63] The situation of many domestic workers in white families was handled succinctly in the joke concerning the black cook who informed her white employer she was quitting her job. "Well, I don't understand it," the white woman remonstrates. "Haven't we always treated you like one of the family?" "Yes, you have," the cook agrees, "and I've put up with it just as long as I'm going to."[64]

Many jokes were used to ridicule the claim that southern whites understood and were concerned for the welfare of their black neighbors. The difficulty whites often boasted of having in distinguishing one black from another was lampooned in the popular joke about two black men in a car with a stolen hog. Stopped by a policeman they quickly disguise the animal in a coat and hat and seat it between them. The policeman speaks to them for a while and lets them go, commenting, "You two boys is all right but that Negro in the middle, the grunting Negro, he's about the ugliest Negro I've ever seen in my life."[65] Widespread black attitudes toward white generosity were summed up in the story, told throughout the century, of the white man who gave his black employee a cheap bottle of liquor. When the latter was asked how it was, he replied, "Just right, boss, just right. . . . if it had been any better you wouldn't have give it to me, and if it had been any worse I couldn't have drunk it."[66] Black migrant farmers in New York State told of the starving Negro in Georgia who had had nothing to eat for three days. He saw a white woman come out on her porch and said to himself, "I bet if I go up there and start eating the grass she'll give me something to eat." The woman immediately exclaimed, "Oh my God, look at that poor nigger out there eating the grass," and hailed him. He looked up expectantly, "Maam?" "When you finish with that short grass there," she called out, "there is some longer grass in the back if you want it."[67]

Whites at all levels of the social spectrum were the targets of black humor. A traditional joke depicts two "crackers" named Reuben and Maggie in bed on their wedding day. "Reuben," Maggie moans happily, "does niggers do this, Reuben?" "I reckon they does, honey. Reckon they does." "Well," Maggie complains, "they hadn't oughta let 'em. Hit's too good for 'em."[68] At the other end of the social scale, a wealthy white North Carolinian, who prides himself on being a practicing Christian, picks up a black hitchhiker on the road to Raleigh. He makes his passenger sit in front next to him and says, "You're as good as I am." When he stops to have a drink from his thermos of ice water he urges the black man to drink from the same thermos, assuring him again, "You're as good as I am." A bit later one of the tires blows out and the driver pulls the car to the side of the road where both men sit silently until the black hitchhiker exclaims, "Ain't it awful the fix we is in; just have to sit here and look at one 'nother, 'cause they ain't a nigger nowheres 'round to change this tire."[69]

Black jokes were by no means invariably oblique or guarded. The anger and aggression that had to be swallowed and hidden normally could surface in jokes. A smile, a guffaw, permitted things to be called by their right name. A widely disseminated story told of a black preacher who did not believe in the existence of Hell and who proved his point by telling his flock, "Oh, no my friends! The Lord would not repeat himself by making a place called Hell when we already have a place called Georgia!"[70] During the Depression, Negroes in Jacksonville, Florida, joked about a young boy who took his piece of bread and went out to play with some white children in the street. "Hey, Willie," his mother calls after him, "you come back heah dis instant, and quit playin wid dem white chilluns. You knows dey'll jus lick all de syrup off your bread, and then call you niggah."[71] One of the most popular black jokes, North and South, told of a black sharecropper in the Deep South who has to accompany his landlord to a radio station where he is to tell the rest of the nation how well colored people are treated in his state:

> "Now there's the microphone, Sam. Jes' talk into it."
> "This the microphone, boss?"
> "That's right, Sam."
> "And when I talk into it, the whole world can hear me?"
> "That's right, Sam."
> "Outside of Mississippi? All over the world?"
> "Sure enough, Sam. Jes' you go ahead and tell 'em."
> So Sam walked over to the microphone, grabbed on to it with both hands and hollered:
> "HE-E-E-E-ELP!"[72]

Such venerable institutions as southern justice and southern education were constant subjects of black humor. As he is leaving the railroad depot with a northern visitor, a southern white man spies two Negroes, one asleep and the other reading a newspaper. He kicks the latter. "Would you please explain that?" the northerner asks. "I don't understand it. I would think that if you were going to kick one you would kick the lazy one who's sleeping." "That's not the one we're worried about," the southerner replies.[73] The Brown decision of 1954 spawned a cycle of jokes about discrimination in education. During the summer of 1956, Raven McDavid was told at least half a dozen times about the two South Carolina Negroes who made a lot of money and went to Washington, D.C., to celebrate. Checking in at the Willard Hotel, they ordered several bottles of good whiskey and asked the bell captain to send up a couple of women. A few minutes later two white women appear at their door. "Man," one of the men cries out, "we are sure in trouble now!" "Shut your mouth, man!" his companion calls back. "We ain't trying to go to school with them."[74]

Favorite joking situations concerning the legal system centered upon cases where innocent blacks were arrested while guilty whites went free. A white man driving a convertible in Mississippi runs into two Negroes, hitting them so hard that they fly straight up into the air. One lands in the back seat of the convertible and is charged with illegal entry, while the other lands about 150 feet down the road and is charged with leaving the scene of a crime.[75] The attitude toward southern justice found most frequently in black humor is well summarized by the popular joke concerning the judge who interrupts a lynch mob and pleads, "We've always been considered a progressive community and I think we're progressive enough so's we can give this boy a fair trial and then lynch him."[76] Perhaps the most widely told joke about discrimination in the South was the tale of the black man who tries to register to vote. After he more than fulfills the literacy requirements, panicky registrars confer and then confront him with a headline in a Chinese newspaper and ask him if he knows what it means. "Yeah, I know what it means," he replies. "It means that niggers don't vote in Mississippi again this year."[77] In a variant of this joke, a black attempting to register to vote is ordered to recite the United States Constitution, word for word. Without hesitation he begins, "Four-score and seven years ago," and makes his way verbatim through the Gettysburg Address, finishing with Lincoln's peroration, "that government of the people, by the people, and for the people shall not perish from the earth." The white registrar slowly shakes his head, whistles in astonishment, and mutters, "I didn't think you could do it. I didn't think *any* nigger could do it."[78]

Unmasking humor was not confined to segregation; it could be aimed at integration as well. Perhaps the oldest joke of this kind was the commonly told story of the elderly black man who has been trying for years to become a member of a white church in the South. Finally the minister tells him to take his request to the Lord. Some time later he returns to the minister and reports, "I ax the Lord if'n He wouldn't pervide a way fer dis ole nigger to be 'mitted. . . . The Lord say, 'go on nigger! I'se been trying to get in there *myself* for twenty-five years and I ain't made it yet!' "[79] More recent examples include the anecdote about the old black lady who observes a group of disheveled white and black teenagers walking together arm in arm and comments, "Lord, honey, integration is fine. But sometimes I wish they had integrated with us rather than us with them."[80] The most common joke of this kind tells of a Negro who decides to test the new integration by eating in a plush restaurant. Greeted politely by the headwaiter, she orders pigtails and black-eyed peas only to be told they are not on the menu. She then requests chitterlings, rutabagas, and corn bread and is again met with a negative response. "Then I know you got ham hocks and collard greens," she says finally. "Regrettably, no," the waiter replies. "Honey," the old lady tells him as she rises to leave, "I knowed you-all wasn't ready for integration."[81]

Black humor provided splendid and important opportunities to laugh at the whites who so profoundly affected the quality of the life black Americans lived, and it is not surprising that a substantial percentage of it focused upon white people and their ways. But whites dominated black laughter no more than they dominated any other form of Afro-American verbal expression. Whether employing the techniques of inversion, absurdity, or unmasking, the intent of Negro humor was broader than merely taking a few swipes at white people. To relate the joke concerning a segregationist leader, like Orville Faubus of Arkansas or George Wallace of Alabama, dying, going to Heaven, and knocking at the Pearly Gates where he is greeted by the voice of the Lord or St. Peter asking, "Who dat?" was not to laugh exclusively at whites but at the precariousness of the entire human state and the fruits of human conceit.[82] This had been the effect of black wit from the trickster tales of the slaves to the most modern post-World War II jokes about integration. Black laughter provided a sense of the total black condition not only by putting whites and their racial system in perspective but also by supplying an important degree of self and group knowledge. To comprehend this more fully it is necessary to take a closer look at the manner in which the mechanism of humor allowed Negroes to evaluate and comment upon a wider range of subjects and concerns than perhaps any other medium in their expressive culture.

THE ECONOMY OF LAUGHTER

"Under the mask of humor," Gershon Legman has observed, "our society allows infinite aggressions, by everyone and against everyone."[1] The process by which the aggression embodied in humor brought so much pleasure to so many people intrigued Freud, who attempted to explain it through what he called "the principle of economy." By "economy" Freud meant more than the familiar joking technique of condensing meaning into a relatively few words, a technique that was certainly characteristic of Afro-American humor.[2] The verbal shorthand entailed in joking worked to facilitate the expression of hostility—and a wide range of other feelings for that matter—but there was another and more important process of economy at work as well. Assuming that for the erection of a psychic inhibition some expenditure of psychic energy is necessary, Freud reasoned that jokes brought pleasure by disguising aggression sufficiently to get it past both external and internal censors, thus relieving the joke-teller and his audience of the need to expend this inhibiting energy. Humor allowed economy in the expenditure of that energy used for the purposes of inhibition or suppression by liberating feelings which normally had to be contained. This liberation brought with it immense feelings of relief and pleasure, a fact that certainly helps to explain why an active humor has been so notably present among people who seem to outsiders to have so little to laugh about. Freud used the term "tendentious" to characterize those jokes which accomplished this end: "tendentious jokes are especially favoured in order to make aggressiveness or criticism possible against persons in exalted positions who claim to exercise authority. The joke then represents a rebellion against that authority, a liberation from its pressure."[3]

Freud's analysis describes with great precision the humor concerning whites discussed in the first section of this chapter. The substantial quantity of aggression and criticism in black humor, however, was not reserved for white people. The repressed feelings liberated by tendentious humor, as Freud himself knew quite well, could concern oneself and one's immediate group as well as those outside. A crucial aspect of black humor can be grasped by noting Kenneth Burke's observation that "the comic frame should enable people *to be observers of themselves while acting*. Its ultimate would not be *passiveness*, but *maximum consciousness*. One would 'transcend' himself by noting his own foibles."[4] The critical thrust of Negro humor was aimed inward as well as outward, at blacks as well as whites.

The rubes, hicks, and clowns who stumbled their way through black jokes were not exclusively Irish greenhorns or poor southern white nincompoops. "You better go back to the country. . . . I'm tired of hearin' you hollerin' City Lights ain't no good," Jazz Gillum sang in his recording of Washboard Sam's ferociously funny blues take-off on the black hegira to the big city:

You want the finest house in town for two or three dollars a month,
You seem to think it's alright for you to go out in the park and hunt. . . .

You wants a whole lot of credit to pay off once a year,
But you owe the salary you make for just liquor and beer, . . .

You decorate the window with your great big rusty feet,
You want hogs in your front yard so you can have plenty of meat.
You better go back to the country,
Way back out in the woods.
Plant you forty acres of cotton,
And try to do yourself some good.[5]

This captures the tone of much of the intragroup humor concerning the rural black. Throughout the century Negro jokes were peopled with black characters like the country types who, when they see their first railroad train sitting in the station dripping water and emitting steam, say, "Po thing, I know she's tired," and begin to fan it with their hats; or Grandma Wicks, who is asked by the postal clerk what denomination of stamps she wants and replies, "Same ez me, Baptis' "; or Honest Anna, who on filling out her first job application hesitates when she comes to the line marked "Sex," bites her lip, and then quickly writes, "Just once. . . ."[6] Inevitably there were people like John the Numbskull, a black hired hand whose white employer's wife rides with him deep into the forest, gets off her horse, and tells him, "Do everything that I do." She takes off all of her clothes and John does the same. Then she lies back on the ground and says, "Allright, big boy, get in the saddle and go to town!" whereupon John jumps onto the horse and rides into town stark naked.[7]

The main thrust of black on black humor was hardly this benign. To laugh at the rural ethos that had enveloped most of the race at the beginning of the century accomplished several ends. Obviously it was a way of denying the immediate southern rural past and of encouraging acculturation to northern and urban life styles. It was also a way of laughing at oneself and one's peers, but it was a comparatively easy way. There were more complex and meaningful techniques of accomplishing the serious and necessary end of gaining perspective on oneself and one's situation, and black humor utilized all of them.

Humor allowed black people to laugh at their entire situation in the United States. A black man talking to the Lord asked Him why He had given the Negro such dark skin, nappy hair, and long legs. The Lord answered each question quite specifically. Black skin was to protect against the African sun; nappy hair to cushion the skull against things falling from the trees; long legs to make jumping over the African bush easier. "O. K. Lord I dig all that shit, but answer me one more thing," the black man responds, "what in the fuck am I doing in Baltimore?"[8] The same tone was achieved when the greeting "What's new?" was met with the standard joking response, "White folks still in the lead."[9]

Humor allowed laughter at the idiosyncrasies of behavior often produced by mobility and the transitions between South and North. A black man moved away from the Mississippi plantation on which he had lived all of his life. Some time later he wrote to the plantation owners, "Dear Mr. John and Miss Mary, Ah'm doin' fine. Ah made uh good crop an' Ah bought me uh house." After even greater prosperity he wrote, "Dear John and Mary, Ah'm doin' fine. Ah made a big crop and Ah bought me uh car." A year later he decided to send a telegram, "Dear John and Mary, I'm doin' fine. I made a big crop and I got some money in the bank." The telegrapher asked him if he wanted to send the telegram to Mississippi and he replied, " 'Missi' nothin'—jes' 'Sippi.' "[10] Another black man on a rail trip from the Deep South to the North experiences the usual humiliations and discriminations, especially from the conductor, who continually calls him "boy." He endures it all with patience, merely asking the conductor to tell him when they have crossed the Mason-Dixon Line into the North. When the conductor does so, the black jumps up, grabs him by the collar, and hollers, "Who are you callin' Boy?"[11] Two Mississippi-born brothers, who had been living in New York City for a decade, reluctantly head home when they are informed of their mother's death. One drives their car while the other sits with a shotgun in his lap. They arrive in Mississippi without any problems, and once the funeral is over they drive back, again with one of them riding shotgun. Only when they are through Central Park and onto Lenox Avenue in Harlem do they shout out their relief and joy. A Negro policeman, hearing their roars of laughter, halts their car and arrests them both for possession of a concealed weapon.[12]

The limits of northern deliverance were the subject also of a story about a young black man who came to Chicago because he heard that there all men were created equal. After three months he loses his job and is reduced to begging. He knocks on the door of a house, where he is treated with great respect, "Good morning, sir. Something I can do for you?" but is denied help. Finally he makes his way south into Tennessee, where he knocks on the door of the first house he comes to and is greeted by a fat white man:

"What can I do for you, nigger?"
"Boss-man, I'm hongry."

"Bring your black self to the back door and I'll give you something to eat."

"Thanks God, I'm back home."[13]

The propensity of proud northern blacks to revert to their old behavior patterns once they returned to the South was the subject of many jokes. A northern Negro decided to drive "down home" to Mississippi for an annual reunion, and he wanted to return in style. He bought a Cadillac with all the accessories, loaded it with all of his fancy clothes, and began his trip. "As he drove through Kentucky with his shades on, everything was cool. But when he got on the other side of Nashville going into Memphis, he started thinking about Mississippi. And the closer he got to Memphis, the scareder he got. So when he got to Memphis, he parked his Cadillac and caught a bus into Mississippi."[14]

Humor allowed the black folk to laugh at and thereby gain some perspective upon their own anger. A number of these jokes date from the great increase in black mobility at the turn of the century. A black woman in Georgia walked up to the ticket window in the railroad station and asked for a ticket. "Where to?" the clerk inquired, "where you going?" "None yo' bizness whar I'se *gwine!*" she replied. "Dat's whut's de matter now: white fokes wants to know too much 'bout cullud fokes's bizness. —You jes' gimme a ticket."[15] In a South Carolina story an old man realized his lifelong ambition to take a train trip to New York City. All went well until Washington, D.C., when he was transferred to an integrated train. A white man sitting beside him, noticing two bed bugs crawl out of his shirt collar, picked them off and threw them on the floor. "What did you pick off me?" the black farmer asked. "Why, two bed bugs," the white replied. "Put mah bug right back," the farmer insisted, "white people ain't war [want to] see cullud man wid nuttin'."[16] An old washerwoman in Alabama, informed by a white census taker that he has come "to take your census, that's all," explodes, "Dat's all. . . . 'Fore de Gawd o' Jacob, whut mo' could you do nex' after dat? You done made dem radios jes so you kin hear evahthing de Negro say,—you done made dem airy-planes jes' so you kin watch de Negro all de time,—you done made dem 'lect'ic lights jes' so you kin see de Negro as good in de night as you kin in de daytime an' now, 'fore de Lawd, hyeah you come to take de Negro's senses 'way from him!"[17]

Jokes like these make it clear that there was an awareness that American race prejudice could divest the victims as well as the prejudiced of a sense of reality. Blacks were one of the ethnic groups that told the story of the young man (in this version, of course, black) who auditions for a job as a radio announcer. When a friend inquires if he got the job, he shakes his head sadly. "Why did they turn you down?" the friend asks and he replies, "S-s-s-same old th-th-th-thing. P-p-p-pure p-p-p-prejudice."[18] There was understanding too that prejudice could erode the ability of its victims to see the victimizing group as individuals. A commonly told joke pictured two neighbors, one white and one black, talking. The white man complains of his massive problems: his house has just burned down without insurance coverage, his wife has taken his automobile on which he still owes ten payments and run away with his best friend, his doctor has informed him that he needs a serious operation immediately. The black man looks at him impassively and remarks, "What you kicking about? You white, ain't you?"[19]

Humor allowed laughter at the expense of those members of the community who thought too highly of white skin and white ways. Throughout the century blacks told of a speech Frederick Douglass made in Dublin that filled his Irish listeners with great admiration. When one of them learned that Douglass was only "half-Negro" he exclaimed, "Faith, an' if half a Naigar can make a speech like that, whut could a whole Naigar do?"[20] A seven-year-old black boy helping a neighbor paint his fence gets so covered with whitewash that the neighbor tells him jokingly, "You look jus' like a white boy." Delighted with his new identity he rushes home to show his family, each one of whom is unimpressed and orders him to clean himself immediately. Disheartened by this indifference, he mutters, "I ain't been white but ten minutes an' I'm already plum wore out with these collud people."[21] A similar put-down of color pretensions occurs in the popular joke in which a mother, hearing her lightest child lording it over his darker siblings, yells at him, "Shut your mouth, you half white rascal. If I hadn't got behind in my insurance you would have been as black as the rest of um."[22] There was related laughter at those blacks whose desire to assimilate was a bit too avid. The most popular of these jokes described a black man who boards a commuter bus or train in his Brooks Brothers suit, homburg, gray gloves, and begins to read his *Wall Street Journal*. When a white passenger leans over and shouts, "Nigger!" he jumps and calls out in alarm, "Where? Where? Where?"[23]

Just as there were jokes about country blacks and country ways, so, too, there were satirical thrusts at the conceit of northern Negroes. A widely distributed example concerned a young man who had made good in the city and returned to his small North Carolina town to visit his parents.

Attending church with them he listens to a long debate on whether the congregation's funds should be used to buy a piano or a chandelier. A member suggests they solicit the opinion of their visitor "what done been up de country and done come to be a knowledge man." Accordingly, the young man rises, pokes his chest out, and exclaims, "If'n I was y'all I believe I'd buy a piano wid de money, 'cause as far back as y'all is in de woods I don't believe you gonna find nobody out here can play no chandelier."[24]

The decline of the sacred world view was reflected throughout the twentieth century in the proliferation of jokes at the expense of religion. Black preachers became a favorite target of black humor. The nature of these jokes was summed up in the Arkansas anecdote of a young couple who are killed on their way to get married. Upon arriving in Heaven they find their desire to be wed is again frustrated because no preacher has been admitted through the Pearly Gates for twenty-five years.[25] The substantial anger blacks felt at the hypocrisy and dishonesty of the "respectable" world around them was projected onto the figure of the black minister, whose lofty pretensions were constantly pictured as being undermined by his compulsive lust for chicken, liquor, money, and women. "Chicken wid a preacher don't stand no show," black workers in the 1920s sang, "When the preacher is about chicken gotta go."[26] "Religion is something for your soul / But preacher's belly done get it all," Negroes in New York City sang during the Great Depression.[27] Louisiana blacks added their own humorous verses to the theme:

> I wouldn't trust a preacher out o' my sight,
> Say I wouldn't trust a preacher out o' my sight,
> 'Cause they believes in doin' too many things far in de night.[28]

The bluesman Frank Stokes used humor to begin his portrait of the preacher:

> Well some folks say 'bout a preacher wouldn't steal
> I caught about eleven in the watermelon field

and then turned more serious as he catalogued the salient sins of the stereotyped Men of God:

> I don't like 'em
> They'll rob you
> Steal your daughter
> Take your wife from you
>   Yeah

Eat your chicken
Take your money
    Yeah.[29]

These portraits were elaborated upon in scores of Negro jokes. In Mississippi, Ulysses Jefferson told the story of the parishioner who suspected his minister of having an affair with his wife. He tells the minister that he is going away on a trip and asks him to look after his wife. That evening the preacher sneaks into the house, gets undressed, and crawls into bed only to find himself lying next to the husband. "I knew it was a trap," the preacher cries out. "Anytime you set a trap and bait it with pussy you catch me."[30] After twenty years of carrying on with the wives of his fellow Baptists, a Deacon in Texas decides to mend his ways and rises in church one Sunday to confess his excesses. As he describes one of his conquests after another, an elderly church member calls out: "Brothuh Wright, is you testifyin', o' is you braggin'?"[31]

The black preachers that paraded through these anecdotes not only lacked restraint, they lacked faith. Walking through the woods one day, a preacher and his son are attacked by a bear. As they run for their lives, the son asks his father to pray. "Son," the preacher responds, "prayers is all right in prayer meetin' but they ain't no good in bear meetin'."[32] One of the most commonly told jokes of this type pictured a preacher who was in the habit of rising in church every Sunday to invite Gabriel to blow his horn. One Sunday two boys climbed into the attic and punctuated the minister's habitual invitation by blowing a horn. Panicking, the congregation fled the church. The minister followed them, but as he went through the exit he caught his coat on the door knob. "Gabriel," he cried out, "leave off holdin' onto mah coat. You know I was only playin'. Whut's de matter with you fool angels? Can't you take a joke?"[33]

The thrust of Negro humor was not confined to black preachers but focused upon the entire spectrum of black religion. One anecdote, indeed, hinted that black parishioners often got the kind of preachers they deserved. A minister asked a colleague what his church paid him. "Oh, they pay me molasses and corn and sometimes a little money." "Isn't that kind of poor pay?" the first minister inquired. "Yes, it is," the second responded, "but it's damn poor preachin' they get, too."[34] The hypocrisy of black congregants was portrayed as frequently matching that of their preachers. Two old sisters sat in church one Sunday crying out, "Amen!" to each of the sins their minister eloquently denounced from the pulpit. When he reached their own favorite vice—snuff dipping—they lost their enthusiasm and exclaimed: "He done quit preachin' now and gone to med-dlin'."[35] South Carolina Negroes related the story of Sister Rosie, a pious but poor woman who told her minister, "Ah don't have nothin' to give, Revun, but if I had a thousand dollars ah sho would give it to the church." Two weeks later her house burned down, and she collected a thousand dollars insurance. When the minister came to collect it she told him, "Well, Revun, ah tells yuh, when ah was tellin' yuh 'bout it ah had de will but ah didn't have de money, an' now ah's got de money, but ah ain't got de will."[36] Throughout the twentieth century blacks told the story, which probably dated back to the antebellum period, of the slave who continu-ously and loudly announced that he was tired of living and prayed to the Lord to come and take him to Heaven. Weary of his pronouncements, his master disguised himself, knocked on the slave's cabin door, and pro-claimed: "It's the Lord. I come to take you away." The slave responded predictably, either running away or pleading: "No, no I ain't ready yet. I ain't ready to meet you. I don't want to die."[37]

Inevitably, humor was used as a weapon in interdenominational rivalry. In Mississippi, Bill Baker told of three ministers who were forced to spend the night in a haunted house. When the ghosts began to assemble, the Baptist preacher sang holy songs, but the more he sang the more the ghosts came in. The Presbyterian preacher then began to pray, but the more he prayed the quicker the ghosts came in. In desperation the two ministers turned to their Methodist colleague, who announced: "Let's take up a collection," and the ghosts began to leave.[38] Alabama Methodists told of the Baptist missionary in Africa whose conversion efforts were so suc-cessful that the Emperor passed an edict making the preaching of Chris-tianity punishable by death. The minister was arrested and pleaded inno-cent. "Ain't you a Christian?" he was asked. "No," he responded, "I'se a *Baptist*."[39]

Twentieth-century black humor did not aim its sharp criticism at any single denomination, however, but at the very message and efficacy of reli-gion itself. Walking home from church one cold Sunday morning, a young boy is filled with the inspiration of his minister's sermon concerning love for all of God's creatures. Finding a frozen rattlesnake, he put it in his bosom to warm it up. When the snake thawed out it announced: "Nigguh, Ah'm gonna bite de hell outen you!" "Mistuh Snake," the boy asked, "you mean to tell me you gonna bite me attuh Ah done what de preachuh say do an' teck you in mah bosom . . . ?" "Hell, yeah, Nigguh," the snake replied, "you knowed Ah was a snake when you picked me up, didn't you?"[40] During his visit to the farm of one of his church members, a Negro minister remarked several times: "You and the Lord have certainly done a fine job out here." "Yes, Parson," the farmer responded. "What you say is true. But I just wish you could have seen this here farm about five years ago, when the Lord had it all by Himself."[41] The limits of the Lord's aid were stressed too in the story of the northern black student who was searching for his mission in life and was awakened in the middle of the night by a voice which proclaimed: "Go to Mississippi! Go to Mississippi!" "All by myself?" the frightened student inquired. "Have no fear," the voice reassured him. "I'll be with you—as far as Memphis."[42]

In one of the most commonly told stories of this century, a black man and a white man go to Heaven, where they are informed that only mounted riders are allowed in. They walk away dejected until the white thinks of a plan: he will mount the Negro and in this way both of them will get through the gates. When they approach for the second time, the angel asks: "You ridin', you walkin'?" "I'm ridin'," the white man responds. "Well, hitch yer horse on de outside, an' you come in," the angel instructs him.[43] A more recent joke made the point still more explicit. Two Negroes escape from a road gang. After running a long distance, one stops to pray. "Oh man, come on here," his partner exclaims. "Don't you know God is white folks, too."[44] The message was emphasized in a bit of doggerel recited by Negroes in New York City during the Great Depression:

> Two niggers
> Ninety-nine years in jail
> Waiting for Jesus
> To go their bail.[45]

Blacks from Bastrop County, Texas, agreed:

> White man got de money an' education,
> De Nigguh got Gawd an' conjuration.[46]

No matter how negative its tone might become, Negro humor concerning preachers and religion, by its very ubiquity, indicated that they remained a force in Afro-American life. We have scant cause to laugh at those matters which no longer affect us. But the laughter contained other meanings as well. There was still affect and indeed there was still affection, but there was also increasing distance and growing perspective.

Black humor reinforces the conclusions arrived at in earlier chapters: the church and its leaders were becoming a distinct area increasingly apart from the regular ebb and flow of life.

Humor allowed the articulation of criticism concerning characteristics of the race that troubled and often shamed certain members. One of the most frequent subjects of these jokes was the alleged inability of Negroes to cooperate and help one another. A South Carolina anecdote told of a test instituted by God for those who sought admission to Heaven: they could enter only if they asked God a question He could not answer. Several whites tried and failed, and then a black man gained entry to Paradise by asking the one question the Lord could not answer: "When will Negroes get together?"[47] There were many variations on this theme. In a joke dating back to the early years of the century, a clown, after asking ten black men to stand behind a curtain, announced to the audience: "Now, ladies and gentlemen, when I withdraw the curtain, you will see something the like of which you have never seen before. It is the hitherto impossible,—the Eighth Wonder of the World." Withdrawing the curtain he revealed the ten black men all tugging on a rope securely tied to a post, "all pulling *together* and *in the same direction*."[48] A far more bitter approach to the same theme pictured a monkey begging in the road. A white man riding along stopped and put a dime in the monkey's paw. "Suddenly, lickety-split down the road came a horse and wagon driven by a Negro. Before the monkey could move or say a word, the Negro drove right over him. Then the wagon stopped. The monkey groaned and thought to himself: 'This brother isn't too bad. He's coming back to help me.' The Negro stooped over the poor monkey, saw the dime still clutched in his paw, snatched it away, and then drove off. Said the monkey sadly shaking his head, 'Our race won't do.' "[49] The alleged reluctance of black people to patronize businessmen of their own race was the target of the joke about a black ice dealer who had built up a good business in a small southern community among both whites and blacks. When a white competitor came into town, one Negro lady immediately began to buy from him. "Now why did you stop buying from John?" her white neighbor asked, "he was so courteous and nice, and we did business with him a long time." "Well I tell you truth Miz George, I tell you just why I changed," the black woman replied, "that white man's ice is just colder than that nigger's ice."[50]

The negative images in intragroup black humor were not all internal or necessarily self-generated. A number of them paralleled stereotypes widely held in the society as a whole. North Carolina blacks told of the little white boy who informed his father that he wanted to be a nigger. "Why do you want to be a nigger, son?" asked his father. "So I can buy me a Cadillac," the boy replied. This was presumably the same boy who went to a country fair and began to drink one coke after another. Every time he bought a coke he took a penny out of his pocket and threw it away. Observing this behavior, his father asked him what he was doing. "I'm acting like a nigger, daddy. . . . Drinkin' too much, and throwin' money away."[51] A cycle of jokes focused upon the maladroitness of stereotypical blacks in Paradise. In one of them a recent arrival in Heaven is being shown around by God. He observes a number of different groups: Swedes, Irish, English, Mexicans, Germans. Finally he sees a group of people in a far corner sleeping and asks the Lord who they are. "Sh-h-h," God replies. "Those are the colored people. For heaven's sake don't wake them up. If you does, they'll break up heaven."[52] God's fears come true in another very popular joke picturing a black angel who uses his wings to cut up in Heaven and Earth doing aerial acrobatics which endanger everyone in sight. God finally demands the wings back. "But you know one thing, God," the ex-angel says as he hands back the battered wings, "I was a flying black bastard while I did have them."[53] Hell itself was not safe from the raucous doings of unrestrained blacks. The first Negro sent to Hell grabbed the Devil's daughter and ruined her. Ten minutes later he lured the Devil's wife behind a rock and ruined her. Next he grabbed the Devil's mother and ruined her. Trembling, Satan dropped to his knees and entreated God, "Lord *please*, take this Negro out of here before he ruins me!"[54]

A great many jokes focused upon purported black laziness or tardiness —often referred to in intragroup humor as CPT (Colored People's Time). This theme stretches through black humor from Creation to Judgment. At the time the world was made, according to black jokes, people were allowed to select their own skin color and hair texture and style. Negro people, arriving late, as usual, had to take what was left. In another popular joke a man walking along a southern road passed a white congregation's church and heard the people singing, "I'll Be There When You Open Those Gates." Then he walked past a black church and heard the people singing, "Don't Close Those Gates 'Till I Get There." The message was reiterated in another joke which asserted that when the trumpet blew announcing Judgment Day the white people left their graves and immediately went to Heaven. Two days later angels noticed dense black clouds arising in the West and immediately gave the alarm that a great storm was coming. "Oh, no," St. Peter assured them. "That's only the colored people coming to Judgment."[55] No aspect of the stereotype eluded black humor: stealing, lying, excessive drinking, even smell, were all joked about freely:

> A Negro, an Indian and a white man were trying to get a goat out of the barn. The white man went in and came out holding his nose. The Indian went in and came out holding his nose. The Negro said, "Wait. Damn if I can't get him." He went in and the goat came out holding his nose.[56]

No part of the traditional stereotype of the Negro was more commonly played with and joked about in black expressive culture than the element of sex. There were, of course, many sexual jokes that were totally independent of the stereotyped images. There were didactic parables which made the point that experience and technique could be as important as youth and vigor. Two bulls standing on a hill looked down upon a field of cows. Young Bull, hardly able to contain himself, cried out, "Look here, old bull, let's run down in the valley and fuck a few of those cows." Old Bull looked at him and replied, "Son, if you take your time, we *walk* down, we might fuck 'em all."[57] There were jokes that seemed simultaneously to be making fun of traditional sexual standards and at those who broke them. A Negro maid on her day off is pushing a baby carriage with twins in it and meets her employer. When the latter is informed that the babies are her maid's she exclaims, "I thought you were an old maid." "Well, ma'am, I is," the black woman responds. "But I ain't a fussy old maid."[58] Similarly, a black woman informs her neighbors that she is going to have a baby. When the local preacher remonstrates, "How kin dat be? Yo' husban' he bin daid fo' mo'n a yeah," she counters, "You fuhgittin' somethin', Revun'. *He's* the one what's daid—not *me!*"[59] Typical of black jokes concerning sex were those which laughed at the ludicrous situations created by attempts to circumvent the sexual mores, such as this one collected by Elsie Clews Parsons in North Carolina in 1917:

> Man was jealous of his wife, an' he come in one day an' ask her who had been there. An' she said, "No one." But he said, "Yes, there have, an' I'm goin' to beat you." She said, "Well, you can, but there's a man above knows all things." And the man above said, "Yes, an' there's a man under the bed knows as much as I do."[60]

Inevitably, there were jokes touching on the theme of incest. A young country boy, still a virgin, is given a turkey by his father and told to take it to town and offer it to a woman in return for sexual intercourse. He stops at his grandmother's house on the way and tells her of his mission. She sees no reason to waste a good turkey on a stranger and offers to initiate him herself. When his father hears of it he screams, "Goddamn your soul. You mean you fucked my mama?" "You're damn right," the boy replies. "You fucked mine, didn't you?"[61]

No motif was more prominent in black sexual humor than the stereotyped one of extraordinary black sexual prowess and superiority. Popular anecdotes were told about male slaves who were used as "stud niggers" on the plantations of the Old South. A slave named Jim, who was supposed to be chiefly responsible for the ratio of three Negroes to one white in the Alabama Black Belt, was so renowned that his master was approached by a planter from Louisiana who wanted to rent Jim to increase the population of his plantation. Jim's owner had no objection if Jim was willing:

> "How fur is it, boss," said Jim, "to down aroun' New Orleans?"
> " 'Bout five hundred miles, Jim."
> "An' how fur is it back?"
> "Just about the same."
> "An' how many gals you got down there on your plantation?"
> " 'Bout two hundred."
> "Well, boss," said Jim, "I'll go. But it seems a mighty fur piece for just a few days' work."[62]

In the 1920s and 1930s blacks told a joke about a Negro who was able to have intercourse thirty times a night. On the night his friends bet on him against unbelieving skeptics, however, he was able to perform only twenty-six times. "I can't understand it," he remarked later. "It went perfect at the rehearsal this afternoon."[63] The same theme was stressed in a more recent example from North Carolina. A white man promised his daughter that when she turned sixteen he would have her satisfied. After sending her several men who proved unsatisfactory, he finally sent up a black man who stayed and stayed. At midnight, while the father waited anxiously on the corner, his little son came down and cried out, "daddy, daddy, you know that black man you sent home, well, he done satisfied sister, sister sue, mary lou, he done packed me [had anal intercourse] and he waitin' on you, so get yo ass on down there."[64] An extremely popular joke depicted a white man who came home one cold winter night and discovered his wife on the living room divan in the arms of a black man. Astonished, the man stood in the open doorway and, thinking his wife was being raped, he cried, "Darling, what shall I do to this Negro?" Looking up with a sigh she said, "Just shut the door so he won't catch cold."[65]

A common context for jokes of this type was a contest between blacks and whites, with the former clearly demonstrating their sexual superiority. The whites hanging around the general store in a small southern town decide to try out the storekeeper's new scales by having a penis-weighing contest. Each man antes up one dollar, and they begin the contest. John the lover wins easily, weighing in at fourteen pounds. Before he can collect, the white men realize they had forgotten to include the black employee, Sam the sweeper. The reluctant black man is forced to enter the contest, and the weight of his penis breaks the scale. When he explains to his wife how he won all the money he brings home, she exclaims in astonishment, "you mean you done won all this money showin' yo dick?" "HUH," he responds, "I only showed half of it."[66]

Blacks, according to these jokes, not only had superior equipment, they were better at using it. A Negro, a white man, and an Italian agree to reveal how many times they had intercourse during the night by saying the word "morning" for each time. At breakfast the next day the white man appears and says, "Good morning." Then the Italian comes in and says, "Good morning, this morning." Finally the black man enters and calls out, "Good mornin this mornin'! How's everything this mornin'? If this mornin' was as good as tomorrow mornin', I'll be back the next mornin'!"[67] Black women were also featured in these contest situations. Three little girls in school were asked by their teacher to spell "Peter." The little white girl tried first, "P . . . , P-e . . . , teacher, that's too long." Next the little Spanish girl attempted it, "P . . . , P-e . . . , teacher that's too hard." Finally, the teacher asked the little Negro girl who answered without hesitation, "P-e-t-e-r, they don't come too long and hard for me."[68] The message of these jokes was articulated explicitly in an Oakland toast:

> Now, ladies and gentlemen,
> It has come to the test
> To see what nation
> Can fuck the best
> Get back white folks
> Get in your class.[69]

Instances of a marginal group envisioning itself partially in terms of the stereotyped images fashioned by the majority are not unusual, but they do remain perplexing. The causative factors underlying this phenomenon are generally seen in terms of pathology. In addition to the inevitable speculation that jokes about genital size and potency betray fears of impotence or emasculation and evidence homosexual interests, it has been argued that Negro jokes which reflect aspects of the general American stereotypes of blacks reveal a lack of ego identification, self-hatred, a need to compensate for failure in the goal of "being white," and a strong "mechanism of identification with the aggressor."[70] Once again it is necessary to observe that without absolutely denying elements of validity in these interpretations they remain a sterile approach to black humor as they do to black consciousness in general. Black people built a life style on the jagged ground of American racism and, while it may prove to contain more than its share of self-destructive elements, it cannot be understood by focusing exclusively upon these aspects as so many students have done.

Central to the question of this type of humor is how prevalent it would appear to be among other marginal groups. American Jews, for instance, not only possessed an abundance of jokes which seemed to confirm the outside world's stereotype of Jews, they even had a joke about these jokes: One member of a group of Jewish friends rose one day to complain that the telling of Jewish jokes ought to be stopped. When Jews told these stereotyped stories, he argued, they seemed to be identifying with their enemies into whose hands they were delivering fresh anti-Semitic material. His companions remained thoughtfully silent for a time, and then one of them began to tell a new joke with the words, "Two Chinamen came out of a synagogue on their way to a Bar Mitzvah—."[71] The point is clear: these jokes had to be told, and they made sense only when they featured members of the group. But why did they have to be told? Why the urge to embrace the stereotype? Certainly, self-degradation, masochism, an urge to accept the majority group's negative image, cannot be ruled out as motives, but in themselves they constitute too pat and simple an explanation for a complex phenomenon.

First of all, it is obvious that black humor as a whole did not tend to reaffirm the outside world's opinion of blacks. On the contrary, no other mechanism in Afro-American expressive culture was more effective than humor in exposing the absurdity of the American racial system and in releasing pent-up black aggression toward it. This has been too easily ignored in the discussions of the meaning of stereotyped humor among Negroes. Still, the question itself is a valid one demanding an answer. A clue to the most obvious explanation is contained in Julius Lester's discussion of the blacks' use of the word "nigger": "The slave owner profaned the Portuguese word for black, 'Negro,' and made it 'nigger.' It was a brutal, violent word that stung the soul of the slave more than the whip did his back. But the slaves took this ugly word and, like the white man's religion, made it their own. In their mouths it became an affectionate, endearing word. As much as was possible they robbed it of its ability to spiritually maim them."[72] What Martin Grotjahn has written of Jewish humor applies to Negro humor as well:

> The Jewish joke is only a masochistic mask; it is by no means a sign of a masochistic perversion. The Jewish joke constitutes victory by defeat. . . . one can almost see how a witty Jewish man carefully and cautiously takes a sharp dagger out of his enemy's hands, sharpens it so that it can split a hair in mid-air, polishes it so that it shines brightly, stabs himself with it, then returns it gallantly to the anti-Semite with the silent reproach: Now see whether you can do half so well. . . . It is as if the Jew tells his enemies: You do not need to attack us. We can do that ourselves—and even better. But we can take it and we will come out all right.[73]

Undoubtedly, there was a greater degree of ambivalence in the use of these negative images and terms than the statements of either Lester or Grotjahn indicate. Nevertheless, their approach remains a fruitful one. Marginal groups often embraced the stereotype of themselves in a manner designed not to assimilate it but to smother it. Consciously or unconsciously, blacks used the majority's stereotypes in their humor in order to rob them of their power to hurt and humiliate. To tell jokes containing the stereotype was not invariably to accept it but frequently to laugh at it, to strip it naked, to expose it to scrutiny.

What has too often been lost in analyses of Negro reaction to American racism is that there has rarely been one monolithic image of black people. Blacks, for instance, have been pictured as senselessly violent and dangerous even while they were also depicted as docile, passive, and obedient. Caught in the pincers of this dual image, if Negroes reacted to the American system with force they were living up to a stereotype, and if they did not they were also living up to a stereotype. Similarly, Negroes have been pictured at one and the same time as compliant, brute-like workers and idle, easy-going hedonists. Antithetical aphorisms such as "to work like a nigger," and "lazy as a nigger," had them conforming to a stereotype if they worked hard or if they did not. For any period of American history, assiduous scholars have been able to show black people conforming to an ingeniously malleable set of images. The same flexibility and shifting standards have existed with regard to the characteristics of most marginal groups in America, who were denounced not only if they deviated from the majority group's ideals but also if they conformed to them. The sociologist Robert Merton has captured brilliantly this cruel paradox by which the in-group transmutes its own virtues into the out-group's vices:

> We are prepared to observe how the very same behavior undergoes a complete change of evaluation in its transition from the in-group Abe Lincoln to the out-group Abe Cohen or Abe Kurokawa. We proceed systematically. Did Lincoln work far into the night? This testifies that he was industrious, resolute, perseverant, and eager to realize his capacities to the full. Do the out-group Jews or Japanese keep these same hours? This only bears witness to their sweatshop mentality, their ruthless undercutting of American standards, their unfair competitive practices. Is the in-group hero frugal, thrifty, and sparing? Then the out-group villain is stingy, miserly and penny-pinching. All honor is due the in-group Abe for his having been smart, shrewd, and intelligent and, by the same token, all contempt is owing the out-group Abes for their being sharp, cunning, crafty, and too clever by far. . . .

"The moral virtues remain virtues only so long as they are jealously confined to the proper in-group," Merton has concluded. "The right activity by the wrong people becomes a thing of contempt, not of honor."[74]

The plasticity of standards with regard to minority groups in the United States was a wondrous thing to behold, particularly in the late nineteenth and early twentieth centuries. When American Indians and Negroes scored higher than whites on a test designed to measure quickness of sensory perception, the results were interpreted to prove the superiority of whites whose reactions were slower because they belonged to a more deliberate and reflective race. When a test administered to five hundred white and five hundred black children in 1897 indicated that the Negro youngsters scored higher in memory ability than the whites, the results again were taken as a sign of white superiority since memory was a "mechanical" process requiring no extensive "cerebration." As E. L. Thorndike was to put it in later years, "the apparent mental attainments of children of inferior races may be due to lack of inhibition and so witness precisely to a deficiency in mental growth."[75] The numerous and intricate traps fashioned for marginal groups have permitted American society to view their every activity and trait, even when they paralleled precisely those of the majority, in negative terms indicating inferiority or degeneracy, and American scholarship to view almost any action of marginal groups—and particularly those of black people—as signs of pathological striving to conform to other people's standards, other people's images, other people's goals. In this area as in so many others, black Americans have been treated as passive subjects reacting in an almost classic Pavlovian manner to external stimuli, rather than as people with a point of view and a cultural frame of reference who were able to respond with some degree of selectivity and intelligence to their environment. Certainly, it would be unrealistic to argue that Negroes were not affected, often profoundly, by the conflicting sets of stereotypes and the malleable standards and evaluations which made it difficult for them to win—in the eyes of the majority at least—no matter what they did. But it would be equally myopic to maintain that they were not aware of the traps that surrounded them. Indeed, the humor that they utilized to turn American racism on its head, to emphasize its absurdities, to unmask its hypocrisies and double standards, to play with its stereotypes, indicates that they understood with great precision the intricacies and perversions of the system in which they lived.

It has been a consistent theme of this study that such understanding was conceived of, from the time of slavery on, as essential to black survival and the maintenance of group sanity and integrity. This understanding included not only a perception of the shifting, malleable nature of the American stereotypes of blacks but also of the ambivalences contained in those stereotypes. Black humor reflected an awareness that the pervasive stereotype of Negroes as oversexed, hyper-virile, and uninhibitedly promiscuous was not purely a negative image; that it contained envy as well as disdain, that it was a projection of desire as well as fear. This was clear in the many contest jokes in which blacks emerged as sexually superior to whites and other groups. It was clear, too, in the jokes that changed the emphasis and quite explicitly laughed at white sexual inferiority:

> Three men were sent to court: a white, a Negro and a Mexican. They got to court and the judge said, "If you have fifteen inches of length between you, I'll let you go." The judge called for the bailiff to measure the penises. So he measured the Negro's and it was seven and one-half inches long. Then he measured the Mexican's and it was five and one-half inches long. Next he measured the white man's and it was two inches long. That was fifteen inches. Therefore they were set free. When they got outside the court, they all started laughing and bragging. The Negro said, "You'd better be glad mine was seven and a half inches." The Mexican said, "You'd better be glad mine was five and a half inches." The white man looked at them and said, "Both of you better be glad that I was on hard."[76]

The tendency to seize upon the ambivalences in the negative image and use them to turn it into something positive is illustrated in the widespread group of jokes about the black man who was arrested every Saturday night. One day in court the judge asks him why he is jailed every week-end, and he replies, "Judge, you jest ought to be a nigger one Sadday night. You wouldn't ever want to be a white man no mo."[77]

There has been a tendency to perceive American blacks as an undiffer-entiated, homogeneous group. In this way, any joke told by a Negro re-flecting a negative image of blacks can be taken as an attack upon the entire group as well as upon the person telling the joke itself. This proce-dure, though it has been widely indulged in, is no more valid for blacks than for whites. Understanding black humor requires some comprehen-sion of the intragroup tensions and differences existing among Negroes in the United States. A study conducted by Russell Middleton has shown a greater disparity of response to humor between middle- and lower-class blacks than among middle- and lower-class whites. Middleton found that middle-class blacks responded more favorably than lower-class blacks to anti-Negro jokes, a fact which Middleton interprets, correctly I think, as indicating that the middle classes conceive of anti-Negro jokes "as di-rected not at Negroes in general but at the behavior of lower class Ne-groes."[78] The validity of this argument becomes clear when one looks at the stereotypes in the anti-Negro jokes Middleton used: inordinate love of chicken, sexual laxity, dishonesty, laziness—traits which middle-class blacks did not associate with themselves and which they were eager to identify as marking themselves off from the lower classes. In another study, Middleton and John Moland found that Negro college students in the South tended to tell more anti-Negro jokes than did white southern college students.[79] Again, the fact that these jokes were not merely an exercise in self-deprecation but a class phenomenon and, as the authors suggest, perhaps an attempt at social control as well, is indicated by the nature of the stereotypes contained in what was called anti-Negro humor: uninhibited sexual behavior, cowardice, the tendency to fight with knives and razors, dishonesty, verbal difficulties, and deviant behavior in general. These largely middle-class students were not laughing at themselves or at "Negroes" but rather they were laughing at, as well as preaching to, lower-class Negroes.

For their part, the latter had jokes aimed at the middle classes and "up-ward strivers" who tried in their language, behavior, and self-conceptions to place too much distance between themselves and the black masses. There were, in addition, regional differences manifest in Negro humor. Northern blacks, as we have seen, told jokes at the expense of the "country" speech, mannerisms, dress, and general lack of sophistication of their southern brethren, who retaliated by aiming their wit at the uppitiness and pretensions of the northerners. The biases could be much more specific. J. Mason Brewer found that North Carolina Negroes laughed at the stupidity and ignorance of South Carolina and Georgia Negroes and told what he called "migrant tales" which stressed the sad plight of Negroes from North Carolina who had made the mistake of going "up the road" or "up the country" to New York City to live.[80] An understanding of these internal tensions and of this group diversity does not negate the fact that stereotyped humor among blacks often indicated an acceptance of the whites' view of the Negro, but it does offer the opportunity of a more subtle and accurate appraisal of black humor and black consciousness.

Finally, with regard to stereotyping in black humor, it is important to remember the degree of negative stereotyping of whites that existed among Negroes. If the black students in Middleton and Moland's study told more anti-Negro jokes than their white counterparts, they also told more anti-white jokes. As section one of this chapter makes clear, the image of white people in black humor was a decidedly negative one. Thus Negroes could tell jokes about their own smell even while, as Roger Abrahams has shown, they held the belief that whites smelled like goats or dogs with wet hair.[81] In his autobiography, Richard Wright related the following streetcorner dialogue among black youth shortly after World War I:

> "Man, what makes white folks so mean?"
> "Whenever I see one I spit."
> "Man, ain't they ugly?"
> "Man, you ever get right close to a white man, close enough to smell 'im?"
> "They say we stink. But my ma says white folks smell like dead folks."
> "Niggers smell from sweat. But white folks smell *all* the time."[82]

Similarly, Negroes could relate jokes about the black tendency to steal, lie, and commit sexual excesses even while often believing that whites were less honest, less trustworthy, and dirtier in sexual morals than blacks. Hylan Lewis, in his study of the black community in a small South Carolina city in the heart of the Piedmont South after World War II, was told again and again of the low state of white people:

> White man'll take it all. A Negro'll take a little bit for himself and leave you a little bit. A Negro ain't like a peckerwood.

Ain't white folks dirty? A Negro ain't as dirty as a white man.

Ain't it a damn shame that white woman doing like that—betraying her country. There ain't never been a Negro was a traitor to his country. And yet a foreigner can come here and be anything he want and a poor Negro can't get nothing.

One black resident carried Erskine Caldwell's novel *Tobacco Road* almost everywhere she went, having read it several times and seen the movie six times. When she was asked why she admired the book so, she replied, "I just likes to have white folks see how bad some white folks live. . . . I just likes that book." "Reports from Negro servants and workers as to the sex and drinking behavior of whites are common," Lewis concluded. "They are usually told with an air of amused superiority, with emphasis upon the low-down or dirty aspects of the behavior."[83] The process of stereotyping, like the process of human thought itself, is marked by intricacies and contradictions that do not lend themselves easily to facile generalizations.

The principle of economy allowed jokes to explore not only the stereotypes which affected Negroes but a whole array of subjects usually ignored in other areas of black expressive culture. The taboo subject of miscegenation is a perfect example of the liberty afforded by humor. A number of jokes played with the image of black men desiring white women and generally seemed to discourage the practice. Two black soldiers sitting on the dock at Brest at the end of the First World War spoke of what they would do when they were shipped home. One said that he would take a lesson from the French, who had no race feelings and drew no color line. On arriving in their home town he would buy a white suit, white tie, white straw hat, and white shoes. "An' I goin' put 'em on an' den I'm goin' invite some w'ite gal to jine me an' wid her on my arm I'm gwine walk slow down de street bound fur de ice-cream parlor. Whut does you aim to do w'en you gits back?" His companion replied, "I 'spects to act diffe'nt frum you, an' yet, in a way, similar. I'm goin' git me a black suit, black frum haid to foot, and black shoes, an' I'm gwine walk slow down de street, jes' behin' you—bound fur de cemetery!"[84] An extremely popular joke told of a black man on the street who sees a white woman pass and says, "Lawd, will I ever?" A white man who hears him says, "No, nigger, never." The black man responds, "Where there's life there's hope." And the white man ends the dialogue by saying, "Where there's a nigger there's a rope."[85]

Far more common were jokes about white men and black women. In a take-off on the sexual proclivities of respectable white southerners, one joke depicted a southern mayor in Washington, D.C., on official business who seeks out a black tavern in which to while away his evening hours. The next morning he awakes in a hotel room with a black woman lying next to him. He quickly offers her twenty dollars to forget the whole thing. When he opens his wallet, however, he finds it empty, and she comments, "Oh, don't you remember? You gave it all away last night—to our bridesmaids!"[86] A southern plantation owner who lived with an attractive black woman was accused by his fellow planters of believing in racial equality. "That's a damn lie," he protested. "It's true I stay with that girl a plenty, but I'll be damned if I let her sit at the table with me!"[87] The most telling joke on this subject was about a Negro sharecropper whose wife gives birth to a light-skinned child. Convinced that the white land-owner must be responsible, the sharecropper becomes hostile to him. When the landowner asks him what's wrong, he says, "Well, you know all my thirteen children are of the same color, and the fourteenth child came up half white." The white man quickly assures him he has nothing to worry about; such is the way of nature. Pointing to his sheep he comments, "They all are supposed to be white, but every now and then one comes up black. But I don't worry about it." The sharecropper thinks this over and replies, "If you stay out of my house, I'll stay out of your pasture."[88]

No subject was excluded from the province of humor which allowed black people to express their feelings on the whole range of American violence from rape to legalized capital punishment to extra-legal race murder. Negroes in the early twentieth century told of a black man who was sentenced to be hanged publicly. Whites and blacks from the area gathered for the spectacle, and the condemned man stepped forward to say the customary final words: "Ladies an' gents, I can't make no speech, but I wants to say something: trouble wid me wuz, nobody couldn't never *teach* me nuthin'. My mother tried to teach me somethin', an' couldn't. My father tried to teach me somethin', and couldn't. De preacher and de teacher—*nobody* couldn't teach me *nuthin'*. But I wants to say to you, ladies an' gents, dat at las' I done changed, an' whut's gwine to happen hyeah to-day *suttinly is gwine to be one good lesson to me!*"[89] Getting off a bus in a strange Mississippi town, a Negro visitor saw no members of the race around and asked a white man, "Where do the colored folks hang out here?" Pointing to a large tree in the public square, the white man replied, "Do you see that limb?"[90] In his study of Indianola,

Mississippi, in the 1930s, John Dollard heard the following joke told at a public meeting by a Negro speaker: A black man was lynched in Texas and while he was still hanging a sign reading "In statu co" was attached to his neck. The Negroes in town were frightened and wanted to know what the sign meant. They called in the preacher, but he said the words were not in the Bible and thus he could not be expected to know. They called on various other leaders, but they too were unable to decipher the strange message. Finally they asked the " 'fessor," who was equally helpless but since he was the learned man of the community he felt he was expected to know, and he explained, "Well, I can't tell you *exactly* what the words mean, but in general they mean that this man is in a hell of a fix."[91]

"To take cheerfully a matter of such terrible moment is really to turn the joke back on the white man," Dollard concluded. Jokes about lynching and other forms of racial violence illustrate still one more function of humor, referred to by Freud as "the triumph of narcissism." Humor, according to this view, is not resigned; it is rebellious and signifies the victory of the ego which refuses to be hurt by the arrows of adversity and instead attempts to become impervious to the wounds dealt it by the outside world. Freud illustrated this process by relating the joke about a condemned man going to the gallows on a Monday morning and commenting as he walked his last steps, "Well, this is a good beginning to the week." Jokes like these, Freud insisted, seemed to be saying, "Look here! This is all that this seemingly dangerous world amounts to. Child's play— the very thing to jest about." In telling such jokes the humorist was adopting the attitude of an adult toward a child "recognizing and smiling at the triviality of the interests and sufferings which seem to the child so big. Thus the humorist acquires his superiority by assuming the role of the grown-up, . . . while he reduces the other people to the position of children."[92]

A good deal of twentieth-century Negro humor, then, continued the process familiar to us from the trickster tales: the outer world was reduced to pygmy proportions; the situation was dwarfed; and the joke-tellers and their audiences were allowed to set aside, or at least to minimize, the pain and defeat imposed upon them by the external world. Thus blacks told many jokes directly analogous to the one related by Freud. A Negro got off a bus in the South, penniless, hungry, and lonely. The first person he saw was a white policeman, whom he approached politely and asked what time it was. The policeman hit him twice with his club and said, "Two o'clock, nigger. Why?" "Nothing, capum," he answered. "I'se just glad it ain't twelve."[93] An old Negro, making his way home at night, stumbled across a lynching party and hid until the mob finished its work. As it was dispersing, the old man was discovered and dragged into the middle of the road. Waving a pistol in his face, the mob leader warned him that if he ever said a word about what he saw they would kill him the same way. "Besides," the leader added, "you know damn well that black rascal yonder got what he deserved, don't you!" The old man looked again at the dangling body and replied, "Appears to me like he got off mighty light, boss."[94]

No more than any other form of black expressive culture, did humor change external realities, but it did alter their perception and their impact. Humor was one of the mechanisms Negroes in the United States devised not only to understand the situations they faced but also to mute their effect, to release suppressed feelings, to minimize suffering, to assert the invincibility of their own persona against the world, and to accomplish all of this, as Freud put it, "without quitting the ground of mental sanity." The chain gang remained the chain gang and black prisoners remained prisoners, yet the humor expressed in such prison songs as the following allowed inmates to step outside and above a situation designed to reduce them to malleable things:

Cawn pone, fat meat,
All I gits to eat—
Better'n I has at home,
Better'n I has at home.

Cotton socks, striped clothes,
No Sunday glad rags at all—
Better'n I gits at home,
Better'n I gits at home.

Rings on my arms,
Bracelets on my feet—
Stronger'n I has at home,
Stronger'n I has at home.[95]

THE RITUAL OF INSULT

Growing up in St. Louis during the Depression and World War II, the black comedian Dick Gregory often found himself the butt of jokes cen-

tering upon the extreme poverty of his family and the absence of his
father:

> "Hey, Gregory."
> "Yeah."
> "Get your ass over here, I want to look at that shirt you're wearing."
> "Well, uh, Herman, I got to . . ."
> "What do you think of that shirt he's wearing', York?"
> "That's no shirt, Herman, that's a tent for a picnic."
> "That your Daddy's shirt, Gregory?"
> "Well, uh, . . ."
> "He ain't got no Daddy, Herman, that's a three-man shirt."
> "Three-man shirt?"
> "Him 'n' Garland 'n' Presley [Gregory's brothers] supposed to wear
> that shirt together."

This barrage of abuse often sent Gregory home crying but taught him the
power of humor. Soon he learned that if he anticipated his attackers, if he
expropriated their lines, they would be laughing with him rather than at
him:

> "Hey, Gregory, get your ass over here. Want you to tell me and
> Herman how many kids sleep in your bed."
> "Googobs of kids in my bed, man, when I get up to pee in the middle
> of the night gotta leave a bookmark so I don't lose my place."
> Before they could get going, I'd knock it out first, fast, knock out those
> jokes so they wouldn't have time to set and climb all over me.
> "Other night I crawled through one of them rat holes in the kitchen,
> would you believe it them rats were sleeping six to a bed just like us."

In time he had gained the facility to turn his wit on his adversaries:

> "Hey, Gregory, where's your Daddy these days?
> "Sure glad that mother-fucker's out the house, got a little peace and
> quiet. Not like your house, York."
> "What you say?"
> "Yeah, man, what a free show I had last night, better than the Muni,
> laying in bed with the window open, listening to your Daddy whop your
> Mommy. That was your Daddy, York, wasn't it?"

Soon he had a reputation, and youngsters came from other neighborhoods
to challenge him. Always he would try to score first:

> "You Richard Gregory?"
> "Yeah."
> "I'm George. . . ."
> "You're midnight, blackest cat I ever saw, bet your Mammy fed you
> buttermilk just so you wouldn't pee ink."[1]

Gregory was learning, as generations of black children before him had, the central importance of verbal art. More specifically, he was being initiated into the verbal dueling that played so crucial a role in large segments of Afro-American culture. H. Rap Brown, born a decade after Gregory, learned the same lessons:

> The street is where young bloods get their education. I learned how to talk in the street, not from reading about Dick and Jane going to the zoo and all that simple shit. The teacher would test our vocabulary each week, but we knew the vocabulary we needed. They'd give us arithmetic to exercise our minds. Hell, we exercised our minds by playing the Dozens.
>
>> I fucked your mama
>> Till she went blind.
>> Her breath smells bad,
>> But she sure can grind.
>>
>> I fucked your mama
>> For a solid hour.
>> Baby came out
>> Screaming, Black Power.
>>
>> Elephant and the Baboon
>> Learning to screw.
>> Baby came out looking
>> Like Spiro Agnew.
>
> And the teacher expected me to sit up in class and study poetry after I could run down shit like that. If anybody needed to study poetry, she needed to study mine. We played the Dozens for recreation, like white folks play Scrabble.[2]

The Dozens was the most common name for the verbal dueling described by Gregory and Brown, though its precise name differed from community to community. In Baton Rouge where Brown grew up, for instance, the Dozens referred only to verbal contests which focused on the adversary's mother; Signifying was the term describing contests where the adversaries themselves were the subjects of verbal abuse. In Chicago, as Claudia Mitchell-Kernan recalled it, games of verbal insult were called Sounding in general, while the Dozens was a specific variety which involved broadening the target from the adversary to his or her ancestors, relatives, and, especially, mother. Sounding and the Dozens could consist of either direct insults, "sounds," or indirect insults, "signifying." In Oakland, California, the game was known as Sounding or Woofing, in Philadelphia as the Dozens, Sounding, or Woofing, in Washington, D.C., as

Joning, in Harrisburg, Pennsylvania, as Screaming, in parts of the West Coast as Cutting or Chopping, and these terms do not begin to exhaust the list.[3]

Wherever they existed and whatever they were called, these verbal contests—referred to here collectively as the Dozens, which seems to be their oldest known name—involved symmetrical joking relationships in which two or more people were free to insult each other and each other's ancestors and relatives either directly or indirectly. The mother was a favorite though not an invariable target. A group of onlookers was generally present, audibly commenting upon the performances of each player, judging their relative abilities, inciting them, and urging them on:

He's talking about YOUR mother so bad
He's making ME mad.[4]

Within the permitted boundaries of the Dozens such ritual insults as:

Your mother so old she fart dust.

Your father drawers have so many holes in them that when he walk they whistle.

Your mother raised you on ugly milk.

I fucked your mother on an electric wire.
I made her pussy rise higher and higher.

Your house is so small the roaches walk single file.

Your family is so poor the rats and roaches eat lunch out.

and such counter-insults as:

At least my mother ain't no cake—everybody get a piece.

At least my mother ain't no doorknob—everybody gets a turn.

Least my father ain't tall as a pine tree, black as coal, talk more shit than the radio.

Least my mother ain't no railroad track, lay all around the country.

Least my brother ain't no store; he takes meat in the back.[5]

were challenges not to one's honor but to one's humor and verbal ingenuity.

Though the Dozens could end in physical violence, it was not the planned or even the preferred climax. The Dozens was an oral contest, a joking relationship, a ritual of permitted disrespect in which the winner was recognized on the basis of verbal facility, originality, ingenuity, and humor. The relative absence of violence can be explained by understanding that the Dozens and its analogues were, as William Labov and his associates have put it, a speech event with a well articulated structure. Ritual insult was countered by ritual insult, as in this example from the streets of New York City:

David: So then I say, "Your father got brick teeth."
Boot: Aw your father got teeth growing out his behind. [Money, Ricky, Roger laugh].
David: Yeah, your father, y- got, your father grow, uh, uh, grow hair from, from between his, y'know. [Money laughs].
Boot: Your father got calluses growin' up his ass, and comin' through his mouth. [Boot, Money and Ricky laugh].

In this instance, however, the losing player breaks the pattern and moves from ritual insult to personal insult by commenting on the tendencies of his opponent's father to stutter:

David: At least my —— at least my father don't be up there talking uh-uh-uh-uh-uh-uh.

This interrupts the controlled counterpoint of ritualized insult and first leads to denial, then to more personal insult, and finally to excited argument rather than disciplined word play:

Boot: Uh-so my father talks stutter talk what it mean? . . . At least my father ain't got a gray head! His father got a big bald spot with a gray head right down there, and one long string . . .
David: Because he's old, he's old, that's why! He's old, that's why! . . .
Boot: . . . and one long string, that covers his whole head, one, one long string, about that high, covers his whole head. [Roger: ho lord, one string! Money, Boot laugh].
David: You lyin' Boo! . . . You know 'cause he old, tha's why!
Ricky: Aw man, cut it out.[6]

Here is a perfect example of what Huizinga meant when he wrote of the "profound affinity between play and order" and observed that play "creates order, *is* order. Into an imperfect world and into the confusion of life it brings a temporary, a limited perfection. Play demands order absolute and supreme. The least deviation from it 'spoils the game,' robs it of its character and makes it worth less."[7] The Dozens, then, was a speech act with clearly understood governing principles. They could be violated, of course, but the cost of deviating from the normal pattern was anger, loss of control, and confusion.

The Dozens constitutes still further proof of how highly verbal ability was regarded by the black folk. The man of words, Roger Abrahams observed in his study of black folklore in Philadelphia, was an important member of the male group whose ability with words was as highly valued as physical strength.[8] This pattern emerges from every study of black urban communities and oral culture. "Concern with verbal art," Claudia Mitchell-Kernan concluded in her analysis of black speech behavior in Oakland, "is a dominant theme in Black culture."[9] Duke Ellington recalled that in the early 1920s the drummer Sonny Greer came from New York to join a band in Washington, D.C., where Ellington himself was then holding forth. Greer arrived with a reputation as a fast and ecstatic drummer and being from New York City put him already one step ahead of most of his fellow musicians. They watched his first performance in the pits closely: he was flashy and knew many tricks, but still their minds were not made up, as Ellington reports:

> We decided to give him the works and find out just what sort of a guy he was, maybe he hadn't done any more than just pass through New York. We stood on the street corner and waited for him. Everybody used to stand on street corners then and try to look big-time. Here comes Sonny. 'Watcha say?' we ask him. I take the lead in the conversation because I'm sure that I'm a killer with my new shepherd plaid suit, bought on time. Sonny comes back with a line of jive that lays us low. We decide he's O.K.[10]

Similarly, no small part of the fascination of a figure like the heavyweight champion boxer Muhammad Ali (Cassius Clay) was that in addition to his boxing skills he was a man of words who began to work on his adversaries long before he walked into the ring with them, predicting the round in which he would win, ridiculing his opponent, describing in advance the events to come, as in this toast concerning a fight with one of his potential challengers, Ernie Terrell:

> Clay swings with a left, Clay swings with a right.
> Just look at young Cassius carry the fight.
> Terrell keeps backing but there's not enough room.
> It's a matter of time until Clay lowers the boom.
> Then Clay lands with a right—what a beautiful swing.
> And the punch raised Terrell clear out of the ring. . . .
> Who on earth thought when they came to the fight
> That they would witness the launching of a human satellite?

He concluded a similar ode to a forthcoming fight with Sonny Liston with the lines:

Yes, the crowd did not dream when they laid down their money
That they would see a total eclipse of the Sonny.[11]

The Dozens was clearly one of the whetstones on which Clay honed his
oral style. Verbal art was central in black culture, and the formalized joking relationships so popular with black youth functioned as one of its
primary training grounds.

In 1939, when he published his pioneer essay on the Dozens, John Dollard judged it impossible to say whether the Dozens was borrowed from
Western European culture and refashioned by Negroes in the New
World, whether it was adapted from the native African heritage, or
whether it was independently invented by American Negroes.[12] Today,
as then, the origins and development of the game remain obscure. Still,
there is no question that institutionalized ritual insult was well known
and widely practiced in the African cultures from which the slaves came.
Although such insults were most frequently characterized by indirection,
allusion, and metaphor, direct insult was certainly not unknown. During
the annual eight-day *Apo* ceremony, R. S. Rattray heard the populace
openly ridicule an Ashanti king and his officials:

Your head is very large,
And we are taking the victory from out your hands.
O King, you are a fool.
We are taking the victory from out your hands.
O King, you are impotent.
We are taking the victory from out your hands.

Similarly, during the *avogan* ceremony in Dahomey, Melville and Frances
Herskovits heard citizens of Abomey ridiculing each other in songs like
the following:

Woman, thy soul is misshapen.
In haste was it made, in haste.
So fleshless a face speaks, telling
Thy soul was formed without care.
The ancestral clay for thy making
Was moulded in haste, in haste.
A thing of no beauty art thou,
Thy face unsuited to be a face,
Thy feet unsuited for feet.[13]

Other analogues exist in the joking relationships which were common
in both West and East Africa and which among the Gusii included such

insults as "Eat your mother's anus!" and "copulate with your mother!" and in the curses, stereotyped sarcasm, and retorts to curses which were widely practiced and which embraced such statements as "you flatulate in the market," "child of mixed sperm," "look at your mother with three corns in her vagina," "It is your mother you abuse and not me."[14] In 1856 the Reverend Leighton Wilson reported from West Africa that "More fights are occasioned among boys by hearing something said in disparagement of their mothers than all other causes put together."[15] Institutionalized insults and ancestor derision, then, were well known in Africa as they were in many cultures including those of Europe. Huizinga has noted that contests in which individuals praised their own virtues were transformed almost naturally into contests in which they heaped contumely upon their adversaries. "It is remarkable," he has written, "how large a place these bragging and scoffing matches occupy in the most diverse civilizations."[16] Here again is an example of a cultural practice with which African slaves were familiar and which was so widely diffused that it easily could have been reinforced by their contact with other cultures in the New World.

This was true also of the rhetoric of exaggeration so necessary to the Dozens. Exaggeration was a characteristic of early nineteenth-century American folklore, and long after the heroes of those tales had waned as central folk figures the hyperbole which had characterized them lived on, especially in the South and Southwest, where such proverbial statements as "I'm so hungry I could eat the ass of a skunk and never hold my nose," "This place is so dead that it would make a morgue look like a merry-go-round," "She is so skinny she could swallow a prune and look pregnant," "So low he could walk under a snakes' belly with a top hat on," were common.[17] This pattern was well represented in black folklore, as in these humorous riddles from South Carolina children:

Question: What is de tallest man you ever see?
Answer: De tallest man ah ever seen was gittin' a hair cut in Heaven and a shoe shine in Hell.

Question: What de shortest man you done seen?
Answer: The shortest man ah done seen took a ladder to climb a grain o' sand.

Question: What de fattest woman you done see?
Answer: De fattest woman ah done see—her husban' have to hug her on de installment plan.

Question: What de blackest man you done see?
Answer: De blackest man ah ever done saw, de chickens go in de chicken house, think hit sundown.[18]

The close parallels between this kind of humor and the Dozens are evident:

Now dig. Your house is so small, the roaches have to walk sideways through the hallways.

Your mother is so small she can do chin-ups on the curb.

If electricity was black, your mother would be a walking powerhouse.

Your mother so old she got spider webs under her arms.

Your mother's so skinny . . . she can get in a Cheerioat and say "Hula hoop, hula hoop!"

Your mother so low, got to look down to look up.

Your mother so black, she sweat chocolate.[19]

Thus all of the ingredients of the Dozens, if not the actual game itself, were present in the heritage and environment of the American slaves. But though it is not unlikely that slaves played some equivalent of the Dozens, there is no evidence that they did. The earliest documentation of the Dozens seems to be in a Texas song collected in 1891:

Talk about one thing, talk about another;
But ef you talk about me, I'm gwain to talk about your mother.[20]

Song remained an important vehicle for ritual insult throughout the twentieth century. During his trip collecting folk song in Mississippi and Georgia from 1905 to 1908, Howard Odum found lyrics identical to those above.[21] A decade later Newman White was sent these lyrics from Auburn, Alabama:

I don't play the dozen
And don't you ease me in.[22]

Protestations about not playing the Dozens were not to be taken literally, as Little Hat Jones of Texas demonstrated on a recording he made some years later:

Well, I don't play the dozen and neither the ten
'Cause you keep on talking I'll ease you in
Well, you keep on talking till you make me mad
Gonna tell you 'bout the mothers that your father had
'Cause I don't play the dozen, I declare, man, and neither the ten.[23]

During the 1920s Speckled Red (Rufus Perryman) sang authentic Dozens songs in the rough turpentine and sawmill juke joints of the South:

> Fucked your mammy, fucked your sister too,
> Would've fucked your daddy but the sonofabitch flew,
> Your pa wants a wash, you mother turns tricks.
> Your sister loves to fuck and your brother sucks dick, . . .[24]

In 1929 he recorded a version of *The Dirty Dozens* which sold well enough to justify recording a second version a year later. As he put it, "I had to clean it up for the record but it meaned the same thing but it was a different attitude."

> Now, you naughty mistreater, robber and a cheater,
> I'll slip you in the dozens,
> Your pappy is your cousin,
> Your mama does she Lordy, Lord!"[25]

The success of Perryman's recording led to recordings of similar versions of the Dozens by Leroy Carr, Tampa Red, Ben Curry, Victoria Spivey, Kokomo Arnold, George Noble, and others.[26] The interactive process between commercial recordings and folk songs, discussed in Chapter 4, led to the incorporation, or reincorporation, of Perryman's verses into the folk tradition. Members of the Louisiana Writers' Project noted that the following "little mocking song" was popular among Louisiana children during the Great Depression:

> You dirty mistreater,
> You robber and cheater,
> I'll put you in the dozen,
> Your mammy and your cousin,
> Your pappy do the lordy lord.[27]

As late as 1962 black prisoners in Louisiana were singing:

> Dirty mistreater, robber an' a cheater,
> Sister an' yo' dozens, mama an' you' cousins,
> Dozens an' dozens, Lawdy, mama,
> Doin' the Lawdy Lawd.[28]

Perryman's version, for all its popularity, did not totally dominate the recorded Dozens. Leadbelly, in his 1935 recording of *Kansas City*, for instance, was clearly treating his listeners to a session of the game:

> You keep on talking 'till you make me think
> Your daddy was a bulldog, your mammy was a mink. . . .

You keep on talking till you make me mad
I'll tell you 'bout the troubles that your sister had.[29]

These recordings attest to the popularity of the Dozens and indicate that although contemporary collectors have found the Dozens concentrated among adolescents, they were an adult phenomenon as well during the first half of the century. Speaking of the jazz musicians Frankie Dusen, Buddy Bolden, and Lorenzo Stall, who played together in the 1890s in New Orleans, Dude Bottley recalled, "When they arrived on the bandstand they greeted each other with such nasty talk as, 'Is your mother still in the district catchin' tricks?' 'They say your sister had a baby for a dog.' 'Don't worry about the rent—I saw your mother under the shack with the landlord.' These three men could go on insulting you for hours if you played 'the dozens.' "[30] Nor was the Dozens confined to boys and men, as some studies seem to indicate. There were, of course, a number of inhibiting factors, as these lines from a Mississippi toast in 1941 indicate:

All you gals better take a walk,
Cause me and my pal gonna start some dirty talk.[31]

In his Philadelphia study Roger Abrahams found these taboos strong enough to prevent boys from regularly playing the Dozens in the presence of girls.[32] As real as these inhibitions could be, they did not prevent women blues singers like Lucille Bogan and Memphis Minnie from singing raw and earthy lyrics in their personal appearances and on their records, and they did not prevent women and girls from playing the Dozens.[33]

In the 1930s a number of Dollard's informants told him that "girls put one another in the Dozens as well as boys, and that the game may be played between girls and girls, and girls and boys."[34] Writing of his youth in Baton Rouge in the 1940s and 1950s, H. Rap Brown recalled, "Some of the best Dozens players were girls."[35] Among women as among men the practice of ritual insult was learned early. In her study of black women, Joyce Ladner has written of Kim, a ten year old living in a St. Louis housing project. "Although Kim was a charming and well-mannered child, she often engaged in 'grown-up' activities with her peers. She 'played house,' played the 'dirty dozens,' cursed and occasionally imitated sex play with her twelve-year-old boyfriend."[36] Even before she was old enough to attend school, Nikki Giovanni and her sister Gary, who was then in elementary school, engaged in a bout of Dozens-like verbal insult with a group of young girls who surrounded them on the streets of Knoxville, Tennessee, and chanted: "Look at the stuck-up boobsie twins," "They walk alike, talk alike and roll on their bellies like a reptile." Gary Giovanni offered to fight their tormentors, and the following exchange took place:

> You and what army, 'ho'?
> Me and yo' mama's army.
> You talking 'bout my mama?
> I would but the whole town is so I can't add nothing.
> You take it back, Gary.
> Yo' mama's so ugly she went to the zoo and the gorilla paid to see her.
> You take that back!
> Yo' mama's such a 'ho' she went to visit a farm and they dug a whole field before they knew it was her.[37]

This particular encounter ended in a fight. The game was in better control among youngsters in a Washington, D.C., housing project, where two girls aged six and twelve exchanged the following rhymed insults, with the six year old, whose contribution comes first, clearly getting the better of her older opponent:

> I hate to talk about your Mama
> She's a sweet old soul.
> She's got a rap-pa-tap-pa tap dick
> And a pussy hole.
> Listen Mother Fucker
> You a two-timing bitch
> You got a ring around your pussy
> Make an old man rich.
>
> Your mama don't wear no drawers
> She wash'm in alcohol
> She put 'em on a clothesline
> The sun refused to shine
> She put 'm in a garbage can
> They scared old garbage man
> She put 'em on the railroad track
> The train went back and back.
> She put 'em in the midnight train
> They scared old Jesse James.[38]

The existence of such joking relationships as the Dozens was neither random nor accidental. Their longevity and pervasiveness in black American culture were related to the importance of the functions they performed. As all play does, the Dozens entertained; as much play does, it had a number of latent functions as well. It was, as I have noted, an important training ground for the development of verbal facility in a group in which oral culture played a central role and which consequently held verbal ability in high regard. This function may help to explain part of the popularity of the Dozens, but it does not really explain its specific contours or content. It is possible to have verbal contests and joking relationships without the ritual of insult so central to the Dozens. Among black youth in Philadelphia, for example, an exaggerated complaint could be converted into a battle of wits devoid of ritual insult:

I'm so broke, I couldn't buy a crippled crab a crutch if I had a forest of small trees.

Oh man, I'm so broke, I couldn't buy a dick a derby, and that's a small fit.

Yeah, well I'm so broke, I couldn't buy a mosquito a wrestling jacket, and that's a small fit.

My soles are so thin that if I stepped on a dime I could tell whether it's heads or tails.[39]

To explain the peculiar function of the Dozens it is necessary to explain the mechanism of interactive insult at its very core. John Dollard made the first attempt at such an explanation. Emphasizing that the dialectic of insult characterizing the Dozens was confined strictly within the group, Dollard reasoned that the Dozens was a vehicle for deflecting aggression away from the white world, where it was dangerous, into a permissive channel within the black world where it would have few serious consequences. The Dozens was "a valve for aggression in a depressed group."[40] It is difficult to take exception to Dollard's analysis simply because it contains a great deal of truth. The practice of ritual insult was a perfect channel for anger which was either unfocused or which could not be aimed at its appropriate target. It is not coincidence that during the Great Depression, when the American people had a substantial amount of anger of this sort, ritual insult flourished in popular humor: Jack Benny vs. Fred Allen, Bobe Hope vs. Bing Crosby, Edgar Bergen vs. Charlie McCarthy, the Marx Brothers vs. each other and anyone else available, W. C. Fields vs. the world. The problem with Dollard's thesis, as Roger Abrahams has noted, is that *any* aggression committed within a marginal or oppressed group can be written off as "substitute aggression." Dollard's hypothesis, then, explains both too much and too little.

Abrahams himself, in searching for a more culturally specific explanation, focused upon what he considered to be the intense Oedipal and identity problems of black adolescents who, having matured in a strongly matrifocal system, needed to find some means of exorcising the influence of the mother. In this quest, the adolescent "creates a playground which enables him to attack some other person's mother, in full knowledge that that person must come back and insult his own. Thus someone else is doing the job for him, and between them they are castigating all that is feminine, frail, unmanly."[41] Even if one does not agree—as I do not—with this strong emphasis on the black male's identity crisis, it is difficult to categorically dismiss this interpretation because the theme of maternal sexuality and the use of the mother as a target figured so prominently in black ritual insults. Black adolescents, no less than adolescents from many other groups in Western society, do have needs that undoubtedly help to explain the popularity of games like the Dozens among them. This adolescent syndrome helps to account for the appearance of games of ritual insult among white youth in the United States as well.[42]

The difficulty with Abrahams' emphasis upon explanations featuring matriarchy and identity crisis among adolescent black males is that it leaves too much unexplained: Why the Dozens has been so popular among girls and women who seem to attack the mother figure with as much enthusiasm as do boys and men. Why, if the primary purpose of the Dozens is the exorcism of maternal influence, such male figures as fathers and brothers are also so often the subjects of abuse. And, finally, why throughout most of its history the Dozens has been popular, both in its contest form and its sung versions, with adults as well as adolescents. There are, of course, dangers in searching for any overarching explanation of a cultural phenomenon. William Labov and his associates have shown how pointedly specific the purposes of the Dozens could be: to remind someone of their social place within the peer group; to relieve tension by transforming a personal conflict into a ritual one.[43] Ulf Hannerz in his study of Washington, D.C., has demonstrated that while some of the youngsters who played the Dozens may have had sex identity problems, others engaged in the ritual because it was an important part of peer group culture and had to be mastered as a prerequisite for personal success in the group.[44]

Whatever the specific manifest purposes served by the ritual of insult, it is possible to identify two overriding functions: The first—training in verbal facility—has been mentioned often. The second—training in self-discipline—has been too widely neglected. Almost every student of the Dozens has commented upon the fact that resort to physical reprisal was a sharp break with the rules governing the ritual and was considered to be the mark of a loser who had exhausted his or her verbal skills and lost control.[45] From the time of slavery, self-control in certain situations, the ability to "take it" when necessary, have been highly praised virtues. Jesus served as an exemplar in one of the slaves' most striking portraits of the Crucifixion:

> They crucified my Lord, an' He never said a mumbalin' word;
> They crucified my Lord, an' He never said a mumbalin' word.
> Not a word, not a word, not a word.
>
> They nailed him to the tree, an' He never said a mumbalin' word . . .
>
> They pierced him in the side, an' He never said a mumbalin' word . . .
>
> The blood came twinklin' down, an' He never said a mumbalin' word . . .
>
> He bowed his head an' died, an' He never said a mumbalin' word . . .
> Not a word, not a word, not a word.[46]

The inculcation of this kind of discipline was one of the central objects of the ritual of insult. Developed at a time when black Americans were especially subject to insults and assaults upon their dignity to which they could not safely respond, the Dozens served as a mechanism for teaching and sharpening the ability to control emotions and anger; an ability which was often necessary for survival. If, as the evidence seems to indicate, the Dozens has become more exclusively a vehicle for adolescents and juveniles in the past few decades, this development certainly is more than casually related to the expansion of opportunities for black adults to express their discontent more openly in a variety of ways. Throughout much of Afro-American history, however, joking relationships featuring ritual insult seem to have been common to all age groups, both sexes, and a variety of social and economic groups within the black community because they related to a situation which deeply affected the majority of black people in American society.

THE COMMUNITY OF LAUGHTER

Humor is an eminently social phenomenon. The natural environment of laughter, Henri Bergson noted, is society: "You would hardly appreciate the comic if you felt yourself isolated from others. Laughter appears to stand in need of an echo. . . . It must have a *social* signification."[1] Humor is primarily an interactive process among those who share a sense of commonality of experience and situation. This sense pervaded the jokes heard by Rose Laub Coser in her study of hospital humor. Shortly after eating, a patient complained to Coser, "Dinner was not good, what I cook is better." Ten minutes later, surrounded by her fellow patients, she transformed the complaint into a joke: " 'Those hamburgers today were as hard as rocks, if I'd bounced them against the wall they'd come right back' (breaks out in laughter about her own good joke and other patients join in)." The complaint which was related to Coser—an outsider—as a personal experience was related to other patients—insiders—as a general experience in which all shared. Favorite jokes among the patients revolved around such common phenomena as the difficulty of getting rest:

> At 6 o'clock they wake you up. So I thought I'll sleep after breakfast. I dozed off, and there I hear the doctor: "Are you sleeping?" Of course I said, "Not anymore." I went to sleep after they left, so the nurse comes up with a pill.

This ironic complaint was accompanied by expansive laughter from fellow patients who shared the experience and the sense of annoyance and rebellion against the routine which it aroused.[2]

The relevance of Coser's findings is obvious. Black humor, too, presupposed a common experience between the joke-teller and the audience. Black humor, too, transformed personal expression into collective expression. Black humor, too, functioned to foster a sense of particularity and group identification by widening the gap between those within and those outside of the circle of laughter. In none of these characteristics was black humor or hospital humor necessarily unique. As Bergson observed, "laughter always implies a kind of secret freemasonry, or even complicity, with other laughers, real or imaginary."[3] Laughter, then, not only helps to strengthen a sense of group cohesion, it assumes the presence of at least the rudiments of an already existing sense of identification. The widespread existence of laughter throughout Afro-American history is in itself evidence of the retention and development of forms of communal consciousness and solidarity among a group that too often and too easily has been pictured as persistently and almost totally demoralized and atomized.

In a number of the characteristics just discussed, the contours and functions of black laughter resembled those of black music, especially the blues, for which a sense of community was also fundamental. In laughter as in blues the line between the commercial and the folk is not easily delineated because of the close interaction and the bonds of identity between professional entertainers and their audiences. Black comedians, no less than blues singers, were reflectors as well as creators; they not only developed new material within the boundaries of folk expression, they also disseminated, perpetuated, and reaffirmed traditional forms of style and content. They spoke for as well as to their audiences. In one of the skits they performed at the Apollo Theater in Harlem in the 1930s, the comedy dancing team of Stump (James Cross) and Stumpy (Harold Cromer) gave voice to the bitter lessons learned by their migrant audiences who just a few years before had seen the North as a Mecca containing the answer to their problems:

> Both dark-skinned, they are seated happily in a night club "up North." Behind Stump and out of his sight stands a light-skinned and threatening bouncer-waiter, a napkin over his arm. His glowering presence sobers Stumpy, who is facing him. Stump, unaware of the threat, tries to cheer up his buddy: "Whatsa matter, man? You up No'th now, let's have a ball!" He is convinced that his troubles are over since he has left the South. Stumpy, watching the bouncer, tries to hush Stump, who is becoming noisier and noisier. "You up No'th, man!" Stump cries.
>
> At last Stumpy catches Stump's eye and nods fearfully at the bouncer. Stump turns around, puzzled at first by the figure towering above him. For a moment his newly won confidence does not falter. He pulls his buddy's coat, points wildly at the bouncer and commands: "Straighten that fool *out*, man, straighten that fool *out!*" Whereupon the bouncer picks him up, and as the audience screams with laughter, thrashes him unmercifully.[4]

In satire ostensibly aimed at the naïve black rustic migrant, Stump and Stumpy enabled their audiences to laugh at themselves, their fragile hopes, and the absurdities of the American racial situation.

Earlier in the century the great Negro comedian Bert Williams, whose career stretched from 1892 to 1922, also produced laughter out of pain. He would tell his audiences a story in the first person of a young black boy who supported his family by catching and selling fish. One day he took his catch up a mountain lined with the houses of white people. Rebuffed again and again, he finally made his way to the top, where he found a small white man standing in the doorway of a house. "I walks up to him and I bows low to him, ver' polite, and I sez to him I sez: 'Mister, does you want some fresh feesh?' And he sez to me, he sez: 'No, we don't want no feesh to-day.' " Making his way down the mountain the boy is overtaken by a landslide which carried him painfully to its foot. Digging his way out he looked up and saw at the top the little man beckoning him. "So I sez to myself: 'Praise God, that w'ite man is done changed his mind.' So I climbs back again up the mountain, seven thousand feet high, till I comes to the plum top and w'en I gits there the little w'ite man is still standin' there waitin' fur me. He waits till I'm right close to him befo' he speaks. Then he clears his throat and he sez to me, he sez: 'And we don't want none to-morrow neither.' "[5]

Unmasking jokes were an important element in Williams' humor. A black man, brought before a white judge for stealing chickens, is asked how he was able to steal the chickens with dogs present in the yard. The old man responds, "Hit wouldn't be of no use, judge, to try to explain things to you all, if you was to try it you would as like as not get your hide full of shot an' get no chickens either. If you want to engage in any rascality, judge, you bettah stick to de bench whar you am familiar."[6] The sense of a common fate, which so often informed his jokes, was sometimes made quite explicit by Williams, as in his story about an unemployed man who finds work with a circus posing as a lion. In his first appearance he is forced into a cage with a ferocious Bengal tiger. Trying unsuccessfully to escape, he drops to his knees and begins to pray. "And this big Bengal tagger leaped toward me and jus' as my heart was gettin' ready to stop for good, that tagger took and leaned over and I heard him whisper right in my ear, 'Don't be skeered, pal. I'm colored same as you.' "[7]

The sense of commonality which allowed Negroes to laugh at themselves and their plight characterized black comedians throughout the century, including those who spent much, or even all, of their time entertaining whites. Thus Redd Foxx would confide to his audiences, "It's tough coming from mixed parents. You wake up in the morning with a taste for pheasant and black-eyed peas, or filet mignon with biscuits," admonish them, when their response to his jokes was inadequate, "Laugh out loud will ya. Y'all up North now," and confess that "Negroes have fooled whites for years with that 'Boss' stuff. . . . 'Boss' spelled backwards is double SOB."[8] With some accuracy, Dick Gregory marveled, "I'm getting $5,000 a week—for saying the same things out loud I used to say under my breath." Before black and white audiences he continued the traditional humor of absurdity and exposure, describing a Mississippi survival kit as "Ten 'Yassuh, bosses,' and a shuffle," asserting, "There is no truth to the rumor that Georgia is passing a law banning mixed drinks," complaining that he offered $40,000 dollars for a $23,000 house in a white neighborhood and was turned down "cause you'd be lowering the realty values," and commenting on the conceit of the white race: "Who else could go to a small island in the South Pacific where there's no poverty, no crime, no unemployment, no war and no worry—and call it a 'primitive society'?"[9] Godfrey Cambridge was equally effective turning the focus of his humor on whites—"Do you realize the amount of havoc a Negro couple can cause just by walking down the street on a Sunday morning with a copy of the *New York Times* real-estate section under the man's arm?"—and on blacks. He laughed at faddish color consciousness: "My wife was on a back-to-Africa kick. She did the bedroom in brown, the whole thing, drapes, ceiling, carpet, spread, pillow. One day she took a bath, came into the room, and it took me three hours to find her." He laughed at racial hypersensitivity: "Conversation between a policeman and a Muslim, 'Sir, may I see your license, please,' says the policeman. 'What did you call me?' shouts the black, 'We're not in Alabama, you know!' " He laughed at the self-consciousness of a Negro on the rise who points to a watermelon and tells a grocery clerk, "That big squash over there. Wrap it up."[10]

The role of black comedians in both fostering and reflecting a sense of community is well illustrated in the career of Jackie "Moms" Mabley which spanned most of this century. Born Loretta Mary Aiken in North Carolina around the turn of the century, Moms Mabley began her career at the age of fourteen as a performer on the black vaudeville circuit. In 1923 she went to Harlem, where she appeared for several years at Connie's Inn and then spent the remainder of the 1920s and the following decades touring Negro theaters in black urban centers. In the late 1950s and 1960s she was at the peak of her career; a career which, despite performances at Playboy Clubs and on television, was still largely confined to black audiences. The extent of her popularity in the black community can be gauged by the fact that during the 1960s seventeen albums of her comedy routines were recorded and at least two of them sold more than a million copies each.[11] The black comedian Bill Cosby has testified that as a youngster in Philadelphia he went to the Uptown Theatre to see Moms Mabley whenever he could afford it, sometimes sitting through four shows: "It was over for me the minute she ambled on stage in her chic, early American cast-off outfit. And when she started talking about her young men, I knew she was peeping at me. But I was cool. Then she would go into that weird 'Moms Shuffle' and that was it. I was hers forever."[12]

The appeal of Mabley's humor was precisely its degree of folkishness. Her antique clothing, her easy manner, her sense of kinship with her audiences—marked by her references to them as her "children"—her lack of pretentiousness, the easy familiarity of her language, her movements, her dialogue, were at the core of her vast popularity. Sitting on a chair onstage, she would often begin her routine saying confidentially and conversationally, "I got somethin' to tell you!" In most of her appearances she lost no time establishing bonds of identity with her listeners. "Thank you, thank you, children, and home folks, and kin folks," she greeted an audience in Washington, D.C., assuring them, "I'm telling you I'm glad to be at *home*. And I had my first real meal in months [laughter]. My niece cooked me some hog *mawwws* [laughter], and some cracklin' corn *b-r-e-a-d* [laughter], and a few greens on the side [laughter]. *Thank* the Lord I'm talking to people that know what I'm talking *about* [prolonged laughter and applause]."[13] Traditional foods were often the vehicle she chose to create an air of community and familiarity. She told a Philadelphia audience that her folks down South had sent her something during hog-killing time: "They shipped me some of that meat, you understand what I me-e-ean. They shipped me some of them back bones with a whole lot of meat on it. Not like these neck bones you get up here. When they say neck bone, they mean neck *bones* . . . Nothin' on 'em but the *bones*. Baby, I had the meat on, I put it on with a pot of cabba-a-age . . . And I made some cracklin' bread . . . Went down to the board and got me two quarts of buttermil-l-lk . . . Then I cooked me some gre-e-ens, you understand what I me-e-ean . . . and corn on the cob."[14]

"For years, we Negro comics only worked the Negro ghetto theaters and night clubs," Godfrey Cambridge has observed, "and told the Negro audiences what they already knew. They laughed out of recognition."[15] Recognition was the focal point of Moms Mabley's humor. Many of her jokes were familiar. In her routines a widow again reminds those who criticize her for having a fifteen-year-old child when her husband has been dead for twenty years that *"He's* dead, *I* ain't." A southern sheriff again assures his black prisoner, "I'm gonna get you a good lawyer and see that you get a fair trial. And then I'm gonna hang you." A black customer again demonstrates his prowess with a switch blade knife, peeling and coring an apple in mid air forcing a southern white gas station attendant to treat him with respect and call him "mister." An old lady (in this case Moms Mabley herself) again responds to the question of what denomination she wants her stamps or traveler's checks in by saying, "Baptist." An expectant Negro voter in the South is again confronted with a "literacy test" consisting of a headline in a Chinese newspaper.[16]

As important as the retelling of traditional jokes was, the familiarity of Moms Mabley's humor consisted not in its material—the bulk of which was original and topical—but in its style and intent. Her jokes were her own, but the contours of her humor were so traditional that it was probably indistinguishable from folk humor to her audiences.

Reversal of roles played an important part in her humor. Throughout her topical jokes she pictured herself attending important conferences, giving advice to the rulers of the world, addressing Dwight Eisenhower, John F. Kennedy, and Lyndon Johnson as "boy," ordering the latter to get a colored astronaut up in space, calling the Secretary of State "son," crying out to Mamie Eisenhower, "Listen Mame," and having her respond, "Yes Mrs. Mabley," addressing Jacqueline Kennedy as "girl," talking of "Me and Eleanor [Roosevelt]," telling Fidel Castro he is a fool and advising Nikita Khrushchev, "You ain't nothin' but a little sawed-off, bald-headed FBI—Fat, Bald, and Impossible."[17] White southerners were a particular target of her humor. In her comic poem, "The Dream of a Southern Governer," she would delight her audiences by describing the anguish of a bigoted politician who dreams that Martin Luther King has been elected President, that all of Congress was colored, that Negroes have taken over the government, and that the tables are now turned:

> I rushed over to the Capitol
> And this is an honest fact:
> I started in the front door
> And Roy Wilkens made me go around to the back.[18]

Her attitude toward the South mirrored the ambivalence of her audiences. She referred to the South as "down home," the place which harbored so many relatives and friends and which was still symbolic of much of Afro-American culture. Yet more often the South was spoken of as something exotic, aberrant, and dangerous which was better left behind. She referred to it as "down there," "behind the scorched curtain," and "no man's land number two." In one of her imaginary dialogues with Khrushchev, she told him she would meet him in "Alabama, Mississippi, or any other foreign country you want to fight in." "Oh, I'm telling you, I meet so many foreigners in my travelling," she informed her northern black listeners. "I just been down and met some foreign people. Some Georgionians . . . and Alabamians . . . and Mississippians . . . And Texasseses." She refused an offer to go South, she told a Chicago audience, "because I just bought me a brand new white car, you know, and I didn't want to paint it all up. Cause you know you have to be the same color your car is down there. And I thought a brown car with black-wall tires would look terrible."[19]

Though she was openly and frequently appreciative of the North—"A million thankful kisses I'll deliver / Just as soon as I see that good old Hudson River"—she was not unaware of its limitations. She told a Philadelphia audience that she walked into a fancy restaurant and was immediately stared at by the white patrons and staff. "I don't want to go to school with you," she assured them. "I just want a piece of cheese cake."[20] The humor of exposure and absurdity, as these examples attest, figured prominently in her repertory. She told an audience at the Apollo Theatre in Harlem of two men, one white and one black, who robbed a bank, killed three tellers, two policemen, wounded a bystander, and were sentenced to be hung. In their cell awaiting their fate, the white man cries out, "I don't wanna be hung. I don't wanna be hung." His black partner tells him, "Oh, man, we done killed up all them people and you talk bout you don't wanna be hung. . . . They gonna hang us so why don't you face it like a man." "That's easy for you to say," the white responds, "cause you used to it."[21] She would convulse her listeners and herself with laughter while recounting one of Redd Foxx's comments on the ludicrousness of race relations in the United States: "Folks, you colored folks, my friends, don't get mad when you pass through a suburban town and see those beautiful split-level houses with the little black iron man standing out in the front yard. Don't get mad. Get you some money. Build you a split-level house. And put a little white boy out in front."[22]

The ritual of insult was an important element in Moms Mabley's humor. Whether engaging in verbal battle with her pianist—"One of my thoughts would bust your head wide open," or attacking her *bête noire*, old men—"Old man can't do nothin' for me but bring me a message from a young one"—she utilized the folk technique superbly, as in her signifying against the old man she claimed her father made her marry when she was just a teen-ager:

> This O–L–D . . . dead . . . puny . . . moanin' man. I mean an O—L—D man. Santa Claus looked like his son. He was older than his mother . . . The nearest thing to death you've ever seen in your life. His shadow weighed more than he did. He got out of breath threading a needle. And U–G–L–Y! He was so ugly he hurt my feelings. He was so ugly he had to tip on a glass to get a drink of water. . . .[23]

Folk rituals helped to structure her humor, as did the folk practice of utilizing long-standing stereotypes both as a fact of life and an object of ridicule. "We women of America can whip your women," she warned Khrushchev as the women in her audience shouted their agreement. "Cause the women over there don't know anything about no razor blades. And throwin' that can of lye."[24] She told her audiences of the sign in Harlem Hospital: "Do your cuttin' on Tuesday, Wednesday, and Thursday and avoid the weekend rush."[25]

Moms Mabley's humor, like the folk humor out of which it came, was broader than the white South or American racial hatreds. Her target was often the human condition: "Little boy walking down the street cryin'. *Old* man walked up to him, said, 'Little boy why do you cry?' Little boy say, 'Cause I can't do what the big boys do.' Old man cried too."[26] She told jokes about the relationships between men and women, children and adults; about everyday black people in small southern towns and large northern cities; about hipsters and homosexuals, winos and drug addicts; about the churches and the bars, the bookie joints and the schools, the streets and the homes of black America. The one element common to all her humor was that it dealt almost exclusively with black people in their dealings with whites and with each other. It was the type of humor that black people told each other, the type of humor that was an end in itself but also was interlarded with folkish wisdom and advice.

My slogan is: by all means do *what you want to do*. [Voices of assent]. But *know what you're doin'* [Assent and laughter].[27]

Stop sitting down telling these children about the good old days. What good old days?—When?—I was here. Where was they at?[28]

The next time a child gets big enough to ask you something, you be big enough to tell 'em the truth about it.[29]

Don't make sense to tell children lies and then call them delinquents.[30]

She dealt with her audiences not as a professional entertainer but as a member of their community. "But listen children, I want to give you a piece of advice. If you got an idea you're goin' down home to see the folks. Be careful, darlin' goin' thru' them little small towns."[31] And her audiences responded as participants—laughing, commenting, urging her on to speak for them all in the cathartic, integrative ritual of laughter.

6

A
PANTHEON
OF
HEROES

One thing you left with us, Jack Johnson.
One thing before they got you.

      You used to stand there like a man,
Taking punishment
With a golden, spacious grin;
Confident.
Inviting big Jim Jeffries, who was boring in:
"Heah ah is, big boy; yuh sees whah Ise at.
Come on in. . . ."

Thanks, Jack, for that.

John Henry, with your hammer;
John Henry, with your steel driver's pride,
You taught us that a man could go down like a man,
Sticking to your hammer till you died.
Sticking to your hammer till you died.

Brother,
When, beneath the burning sun
The sweat poured down and the breath came thick,

And the loaded hammer swung like a ton
And the heart grew sick;
You had what we need now, John Henry.
Help us get it.

So if we go down
Have to go down
We go like you, brother,
'Nachal' men. . . .

Sterling Brown, "Strange Legacies"[1]

The legends and stories of antebellum blacks lived on well past their generation. They were to be found throughout the twentieth-century South and North—wherever Negroes were. Black storytellers still told and black audiences still relished supernatural tales, moral and didactic tales, human and animal trickster tales, tales centering on both real and apocryphal personal experiences—indeed, the entire range of tales that slaves had told and retold. The art of story telling retained its importance and continued for many to be a prime means of entertainment.

Ralph Ellison, who grew up in Oklahoma City during the 1920s, recalled that every fall, during the cotton-picking season, a number of his classmates left school and went with their parents to work in the cotton fields. Most of the local black parents tried to protect their children from the experience of working in the cotton patch—an aspect of the Old South which they had gone west to escape. But Ellison envied the children who had to make the annual migration because "the kids came back with such wonderful stories. And it wasn't the hard work which they stressed, but the communion, the playing, the eating, the dancing and the singing. And they brought back jokes, *our* Negro jokes—not those told about Negroes by whites—and they always returned with Negro folk stories which I'd never heard before and which couldn't be found in any books I knew about. This was something to affirm and I felt there was a richness in it. . . . It seemed much more real than the Negro middle-class values which were taught in school." Ellison absorbed black folklore not only from his peers but from his elders as well. He has described the drugstore he worked in after school "where on days of bad weather the older men would sit with their pipes and tell tall tales, hunting yarns and homely versions of the classics." In this setting he heard tales of adventure, ghost stories, legends of slaves and black outlaws. "There was both truth and fantasy in this, intermingled in the mysterious fashion of literature."[1]

"Yes I can remember them old times," a farmer in the Mississippi Delta said in the 1940s. "We just stayed around home sitting by the fireside telling them old tales, and then that was just about all."[2] By the 1940s such alternative means of entertainment as the phonograph, the radio, the movie theater had penetrated even the Mississippi Delta, yet blacks continued to tell tales. "Telling tales while working helps the work and makes time pass," Houston Bacon, a worker in the Delta, testified in 1942. "When it's real hot, no stories—but otherwise we're laughin' and tellin' stories all day long."[3] Tales were perpetuated because they were entertaining and brought relief from tedious and difficult tasks. But they lived also because they were bearers of tradition and of group memory. "My story goes a long way back," Sidney Bechet has written. "It goes further back than I had anything to do with. . . . the stories my father gave down to me. . . . those stories are all I know about some of the things bringing me to where I am."[4] "The tales that we trade on the corners are taken seriously," the contemporary poet Nikki Giovanni has insisted. "Lives have been lost over one version or another, and it's not because Niggers just like to kill Niggers but because we have a duty—call it a religious calling—to record and pass on orally."[5]

For these reasons among others, Afro-American folk tales have had an impressive longevity. Sitting in a barber shop in Mound Bayou, Mississippi, in the 1950s, Richard Dorson listened to an elderly minister, J. H. Lee, and a nineteen-year-old bellhop, Billy Jack Tyler, match tales. "Watching the septuagenarian and the stripling exchange variants, I appreciated the tenacity of Southern Negro folk tradition, that embraces the aged and the young with so firm a hold."[6] Roger Abrahams' important collections of Negro folklore in the 1950s and 1960s also indicate that while a substantial portion of the traditional tales had disappeared, many of them continued to flourish in both the South and the North.[7] Thus the repertory the slaves and freedmen had known endured, but it endured with important alterations and a good deal of expansion. The new mobility, the new possibilities, the new experiences following emancipation that broadened the scope and variety of Afro-American music and religion had a similar effect upon other aspects of black expressive culture.

The changes that freedom wrought are made particularly clear by focusing upon the figures who dominated black lore. The relatively narrow range of secular heroes celebrated by the slaves in their tales underwent considerable transformation during the years of freedom: new figures appeared and old ones were frequently altered in aspect or significance. There were, of course, close correspondences between all black hero figures, the most obvious one being the common needs that called them into being. If emancipation brought Negroes new freedom, it also continued many of their old frustrations. The enduring plight of black Americans produced a continuing need for a folklore which would permit them to express their hostilities and aspirations and for folk heroes whose exploits would allow them to transcend their situation. Thus it might be argued that all Afro-American folk heroes sprang from the same causes and reflected identical needs; that they constituted, in Joseph Campbell's phrase, a "hero with a thousand faces." Nevertheless, the specific ways in which hostilities are expressed and transcendence symbolized are revealing; the face a hero assumes is crucial. The appearance of new heroes, the alteration of old ones, and the blending of the new and the old that went on continually have a great deal to say about the changes in black situation and consciousness that were occurring. The heroes about whom nineteenth- and twentieth-century Negroes sang and told stories reveal much about their creators' state of mind. Neither the heroes nor the consciousness that molded them remained static in the century following emancipation.

THE FATE OF THE TRICKSTER

It is not possible to draw a hard and fast line between the prime of the slave trickster in slavery and his decline in the twentieth century. Continued Negro vulnerability—the lack of independent political and economic power bases and protracted dependence upon whites and the institutions they controlled—prolonged the need for tricksters and the lessons they had to impart. Despite changing conditions, neither the trickster figure nor its creators were completely able to forget their exposed position. In a tale told by Rich Knox of South Carolina in the 1930s, Rabbit goes to a meeting and to his dismay finds himself sitting next to a hound dog. "Hound wasn't payin' no 'tention to Budder Rabbit at the time.—But Budder Rabbit payin' 'tention to the hound!"[1] Another meeting which Rabbit attends in a Florida tale results in the momentous declaration that dogs would no longer hunt rabbits. In spite of this great reform, Rabbit declines Brer Dog's dinner invitation, telling him, "some of dese fool dogs ain't got no better sense than to run all over dat law and break it up. De rabbits didn't go to school much and he didn't learn but three letter, and that's trust no mistake. Run every time de bush shake."[2] Richard Smith of Texas stressed the same cautionary message in his introduction to a tale in which Wolf unsuccessfully tries to capture Rabbit by pretending to be dead:

> Onct upon a time they was a wolf and a rabbit . . . they was friends all right, but the wolf was more friend to the rabbit more so because he wanted to get a chance to eat the rabbit up, but the rabbit was watchable, and the rabbit thought that that was what he wanted, but he always watched Mr. Wolf and Mr. Wolf he jest tried every way he could to make friends with Mr. Rabbit so Mr. Rabbit would trust him, you know, but Mr. Rabbit never would trust him 'cause he jest always felt that that was what Mr. Wolf wanted to do to him.[3]

Thus the trickster, and the need for the trickster, endured long past slavery. With few exceptions, every trickster tale related in Chapter 2 continued to exist, usually in at least several versions, well into the twentieth century. Occasionally the animals were pictured in more modern garb: "Brother Rabbit was sitting up on the porch, smoking a cigar with his legs crossed, his derby on. (He was a hard sport.)"[4] If Rabbit's outer trappings were subject to change, his basic nature remained stable. In an Arkansas tale collected in the 1950s, John Courtney told the familiar tale of Rabbit stealing the butter with the less familiar ending picturing Rabbit being caught and trapped in a log. Every day Bear and Fox go back and call Rabbit's name, and every day his answer is fainter, until there is no answer at all. Anticipating a fine meal, they open the log, and Rabbit, still very much alive, escapes crying out: "Oh yes, you son of bitches think you're smart. I can be your schoolteacher yet."[5] And he could, as John Kendry pointed out in a toast:

> You know—you see, the raccoon, you know, he was an engineer
> And the possum, he always tend to the switch,
> Old rabbit didn't have no job at all
> But he was a running son-of-a-bitch.[6]

In 1920 youngsters in Aiken, South Carolina, told and retold animal trickster tales, putting the language of their own day into Rabbit's mouth but keeping his character intact. "Ah tell yer, big boy," Rabbit informs Wolf in one of these stories, "you can't foller me, 'cause Ah'm a rounder to dis

worl'.'" Another Aiken school child, Lendy Hutto, repeated the message
in a symbolically arresting story: Wolf and Rabbit let a dove fly in the
parlor, and it picks Rabbit's eyes out. Rabbit offers Wolf $5000 to lead
him, and Wolf does—directly into the fire where Rabbit is fried and eaten
by his friend. In Wolf's stomach, Rabbit begins to speak, and Wolf
belches him up piece by piece: "He said, 'O Lord! Buh Wolf, Ah'm
trouble in dis worl'.' Said, 'When you got me, you got it all, 'cause Ah'm
trouble in this worl'.' So he jumped out, went runnin' off. He was sayin',
'Hippity hoppity, hippity hop! 'Cause when you got me, you got it all!'
You never hear Buh Rabbit get killed."[7]

Throughout these tales Rabbit continued the work that had occupied
him during the years of slavery. He protected himself against the murderous designs of the more powerful; he outwitted and humiliated Fox, Bear,
and Wolf; he taught Alligator the meaning of trouble; he performed impossible tasks in quest of an elusive prize; he extricated himself from one
difficult situation after another, often at the expense of other animals; he
used his considerable wit to win the food and claim the women. His actions could be defensive or offensive, they could be tinged with malice or
merely marked by mischief. Consistently he acted against the powerful,
the pompous, the hypocritical, not for higher social purposes but in the
name of survival and for the sheer joy he derived from it. Constantly his
actions underlined the need for caution and for keeping one's own counsel.
During a great revival meeting all of the preachers get together, and
Preacher Coon addresses his colleagues: "Brothers, all night long we been
preachin' about sin and human weakness." Then in an act of contrition he
confesses his own: he steals apples and grapes from other people's gardens.
A veritable orgy of confession follows. Preacher Dog admits he steals
meat; Preacher Rooster that he chases chickens; Preacher Fox that he
drinks corn liquor. All confess but Preacher Rabbit. "He just set there.
They asks Buh Rabbit if he didn't have no weaknesses. He say, 'Brothers,
I got a human weakness too. It's a real terrible human weakness. It's so
bad I just hate to tell you about it. My weakness is gossip; can't never
keep anything to myself, and I just can't wait to get out of here!' And
BAM! He was gone."[8] As late as the 1950s and 1960s, Roger Abrahams
was able to collect cautionary proverbs which paralleled exactly those the
slaves had told: "That's why a dog has so many friends—he wags his tail
and keeps his mouth shut." "A fish would never get caught if he kept his
mouth shut."[9]

A number of the old slave tales took on the trappings of the postbellum era and reflected the current concerns of the storytellers. Thus the traditional tops and bottoms tale was recast in a Texas version into a tale concerning a landowner, Bear, who tries to trick his sharecropper, Rabbit, but is undone by him instead. The entire plot is summed up in Bear's troubled musings at the end of the tale:

> "De fust year I rents to de ole Rabbit, I makes de tops my sheer, en ole Rabbit planted 'taters; so I gits nothin' but vines. Den I rents ergin, en der Rabbit is to hab de tops, en I de bottoms, en ole Rabbit plants oats; so I gits nothin' but straw. But I sho is got dat ole Rabbit dis time. I gits both de tops en de bottoms, en de ole Rabbit gits only de middles. I'se bound ter git 'im dis time."
>
> Jes' den de old Bear come ter de field. He stopped. He look at hit. He shet up his fist. He cuss en he say, "Dat derned little scoundrel! He done went en planted dat fiel' in corn."[10]

In one respect the stock of trickster figures expanded in the twentieth century. The traditional African trickster, Anansi the spider, assumed new importance because of the large West Indian migration and occasionally replaced Rabbit in such common tales as Tar-Baby.[11]

There can be no question that the animal trickster tale remained amazingly enduring, though folklorists continued to speak of its demise. In the introduction to her 1917 collection of Negro tales from Guilford County, North Carolina, Elsie Clews Parsons wrote that "here we see the art of the folk-tale in its last stage of disintegration. The tale is cut down or badly told or half forgotten." One narrator told her, "Lor', my gran'-daddy tol' me that tale, but I hasn' thought of it for thirty years. I'se been working too hard." Other storytellers told what Parsons called "popular anecdotes" rather than "true tales." Still others admitted that they had learned their stories directly or indirectly from a literary source—"Several of my younger informants stated that they had read 'Tar-Baby' in a book"—which disturbed Mrs. Parsons as much as the knowledge that some blacks were learning blues from phonograph records disturbed the song collectors of the time.[12] The situation was not quite so bleak, as Parsons herself was to prove in subsequent work. In 1919 she spent a month on the South Carolina Sea Islands and came away with a major collection of folktales. And among her best informants were schoolchildren as conversant with traditional tales as they were with more contemporary ones. A year later Parsons was gathering tales among the school children of Aiken, South Carolina, and again she discovered impressive familiarity with the old tales of tricksters, animal and human.[13] Precisely the same was true of the stories collected from Negro students in Tuskegee Institute in Alabama, the Georgia State College in Savannah, and Penn School in St. Helena, South Carolina.[14] Collecting tales on St. Helena Island in the 1920s, Guy Johnson found that Negro children were deeply steeped in the tale traditions and related them with a blend of naïveté and skill. "On the way to school, at recess time, at parties, at home around the fireside, or at work, the young folk tell stories and riddles."[15] Nor was this true only of black youngsters along the Carolina and Georgia coasts. In 1923 Arthur Huff Fauset collected numerous traditional trickster tales in Philadelphia, many of them from young people in their teens and twenties. Two years later Fauset collected tales in Alabama, Mississippi, Louisiana, and Tennessee and found that while adults often exhibited "a reticence and apology about telling stories of Rabbit and Fox," among the children "these stories develop freely."[16] The fact that children knew these old stories as well as they did indicates that while older Negroes may have been reticent in front of outsiders, they were not hesitant before their own children to whom they were obviously relating the old tales, thus assuring their longevity.

This is not to imply that the old animal tales were being handed down in a frozen state. In the manner of the oral tradition, the black youngsters from whom folklorists were learning so much had no interest in preserving any given story or cycle of stories intact as they had learned them. "They may deviate from the traditional version of a tale," Guy Johnson noted, "but they are good at supplying new incidents and at combining several stories to make a new one."[17] This was true of black storytellers in general, regardless of age. They made no special effort to keep the old tales alive. Those that continued to reflect their interests, needs, and aesthetic sensibilities survived. Those that did not had to give way or undergo alteration, often beyond recognition. What Mrs. Parsons in her Guilford County study called disintegration would be more accurately described as transformation. Animal and human trickster tales continued to exist, and not merely as vestiges to be dredged up from the past for curious folklorists. They endured, but they underwent continuous change reflective of the changes taking place in Afro-American consciousness.

The long-standing ambivalence toward the animal trickster, described in Chapter 2, was heightened in the twentieth century: there were increasing doubts about the appropriateness or efficacy of the trickster's approach. In the 1950s, the sixty-five-year-old William Willis Greenleaf of Texas told a story that showed that "hits de lazy ones what allus gits de whole bunch in trouble." Rabbit wants to cross the swamp, but there is no bridge in sight. He hails an alligator and bets him that there are more rabbits in the world than alligators. Alligator calls up all of his brethren, and they form a line from one side of the river to the other. Rabbit jumps from one back to another, ostensibly counting but really using them as a bridge. When he finished, Alligator asks him to call all the rabbits so they may be counted. "De swamp rabbit jes' crack his sides a-laffin' an' say, 'Ah don' in no wise hab no intention of callin' out de rabbits—Ah jes' wanted to git 'cross de rivuh.' " In fury, Alligator bites off the end of Rabbit's tail, "an' dats why all rabbits . . . hab a short tail rat today. All of 'em got to suffer for what dat no-good triflin' ole swamp rabbit done did."[18] During the same decade J. D. Suggs told the tale of Deer's plunder of a pea patch owned by Rabbit and Fox. Eventually Deer is caught and put in a pen to await execution. He sings a song so beautiful that Fox begs him to sing again. He refuses until Fox lowers the pen's rail so that he can sing right in Fox's ears. When the fence is short enough, Deer jumps over and escapes, calling out, "My song is in the woods." Rabbit executes Fox for letting Deer escape. Suggs evinced little empathy for Deer: "There's people just like that, these confidence men. You start talking to them, and draw all your money out of the bank, and give it to them before you know what's going on. Didn't you read in the papers about that old man, seventy years old, who confidented all those women out of their money? There's a lesson in all those stories."[19]

Arthur Huff Fauset was correct in perceiving an enhanced self-consciousness among those who related the animal trickster tales. During the Depression Leman Jones, who was born in North Carolina in 1916, spent five years riding the freights and living in hobo camps in Georgia and the Carolinas. Spending many of his evenings sitting around the campfires with his fellow hoboes "drinkin' and tellin' lies," Jones built up an impressive repertory of traditional tales. In 1970 in Baltimore, where Jones had been living for the past twenty years, Michael Quitt collected some of his tales but found Jones a reluctant and defensive informant. Whenever anyone entered the room he would break off his tale on the grounds that he no longer recalled the rest, only to recover his memory instantaneously when the intruders departed. Quitt was convinced that Jones "obviously felt himself open to ridicule" when he told traditional animal tales. Whatever defensiveness or ambivalence Jones might have felt about the tales, he still had command of them and related them superbly: "Each tale is brought to life by Leman's use of hand gestures, facial contortions, and voice modulations. He imitates dogs and hunting horns, as well as characters in his narratives. To watch him is to witness a raconteur who acts out and virtually lives his tales."[20]

Other recent folklorists have had varying experiences. Richard Dorson, collecting in the South and North in the 1950s, found much less reticence and self-consciousness and compiled a wealth of traditional tales from a number of first-rate storytellers, the most important of whom was James Douglas Suggs. Born in 1887 in Kosciusko, Mississippi, Suggs led an extraordinarily varied life which took him through thirty-nine states. He was respectively a prison guard in Mississippi, a singer and dancer with the Rabbit Foot Minstrel Show which toured from New Mexico to North Dakota, a professional baseball player in Mississippi, North Carolina, Tennessee, and Arkansas, a brakeman in Memphis, a sandhog on the Mississippi River, a cook and nurse in Mississippi, a soldier in France during World War I, a boatman in Missouri, a laborer in Arkansas, a steelworker in Missouri, a "sport" in Chicago, a farmer, hunter, and cook in Arkansas, an assistant in his brother's rooming house in Chicago, and finally a laborer in Calvin, Michigan, where he died in 1955 at the age of sixty-eight. Suggs' kaleidoscopic experiences brought him an easy familiarity with the entire range of black folklore. When he met Dorson in 1952, he was still in command of 175 representative tales which he related with neither self-consciousness nor ambivalence.[21] Collecting folklore during the same decade as Dorson, Roger Abrahams found open hostility for the traditional trickster among young blacks in Philadelphia.[22] Obviously there was a range of attitudes that makes it impossible to write any definitive obituaries for the slaves' favorite trickster figure. But it is equally obvious that the events and developments of the twentieth century had substantially eroded the animal trickster's central importance in black lore.

Changes in the place the animal trickster occupied in black lore were manifest not only in attitudes the storytellers expressed about him but also in the fate that befell him in an increasing number of tales, especially those told by younger people. In an early twentieth-century tale from South Carolina, Cat catches Mouse and is about to devour him when Mouse says, "You have no manners: you should wash your face and hands before you eat." Cat begins to lick her paws and rub them on her face, giving Mouse the chance to escape. "Ever since that time, the cat eats first and washes afterwards."[23] The implication at the end of the story that Cat, unlike the perennial dupes of the slave tales, had learned something from her experience was verified in a Florida tale collected during the Depression. Sis Cat catches Rat and is tricked in precisely the same way. Soon thereafter she catches another rat who immediately exclaims: "Where's yo' manners at, Sis Cat? You going set up to de table and eat 'thout washing yo' face and hands?" "Oh, Ah got plenty manners," Cat replies. "But Ah eats mah dinner and washes mah face and uses mah manners afterwards."[24]

In the tales Parsons collected on the Sea Islands in 1919 the defeat of the trickster was a recurrent theme. The traditional tale in which Rabbit cheats his partner out of their jointly owned butter and then tricks him into thinking he had eaten it himself was often told in the customary manner by both old and young Sea Islanders, but quite a few versions deprived Rabbit of his normal victory. Maggie Powell, aged twenty-five, had Rabbit and Fox lie in the sun to see who the guilty party was. The butter melted out of Rabbit, but this time Fox remained awake and Rabbit was not able to work his usual deception. "Ber Rabbit, you eat de butter," Fox cries out as Coon carries Rabbit to the block and cuts his head off. "Ber Rabbit said, 'Bing! Bing! God damn! Butter has brought me to dis.' And de story is en'." Theodore Roosevelt Younge, a pupil in Port Royal Industrial and Agricultural School, told a version in which the guilty Rabbit smears Alligator's face while he sleeps in the sun and then calls out, "Ha, ha, ha! Brother Gater eat the butter." But Alligator remains unconvinced. "Brother Gater went to work and run Brother Rabbit down an' grind up his bones. That was the last of Brother Rabbit." In another tale told by a young pupil, Rabbit accompanies Alligator to church every Sunday. Just before arriving, Rabbit excuses himself saying he must go back for something, runs to Alligator's house and eats his Sunday food. Alligator finally catches him and beats him half to death. In still other tales, Rabbit is caught stealing Wolf's hog, and his ruse of pretending he is dead in order to avoid punishment fails; he tricks Man's daughter into letting him into the garden where he has a feast, but he is caught by Man and beaten to death; he is killed by Brer Tiger whose wife he attempts to steal.[25] In versions of the traditional race between Terrapin and Deer, collected in Guilford County, North Carolina, in 1917, Chatham County, North Carolina, in the 1920s, and Bolivar County, Mississippi, in the 1950s, Terrapin wins the race as usual by placing friends along the course, but Deer no longer plays the role of docile dupe. "An' de deer, bein' so outrun by de tarpin, he runs to de tarpin, an' he jus' stomps de tarpin all to pieces. From that day to this a deer has no use for a tarpin."[26] That the slippery qualities of a trickster had their limits seemed to be the burden of a tale told by Suggs:

A Crane has just one straight gut. He was fishing, and he seed an Eel, and swallowed it. Then he turned around and the Eel had slipped out his backside. So he swallowed him again, and he slipped out again. The Crane goes over and sits on a dead log. "I got the dead wood on you this time." He had him till he died.[27]

These limitations were made particularly clear in the saga of the Signifying Monkey, which was generally related in the long oral narrative poems known as "toasts" in Afro-American culture. As a form of black expressive art, the toast was largely ignored by folklorists until Roger Abrahams' study of black Philadelphia. In the 1950s and after, the story of the Signifying Monkey was collected not only in Philadelphia but in New York City and State, Michigan, New Jersey, Indiana, Kentucky, and Texas, though it probably had been in circulation well before that.[28] The story revolves around a plot common to a number of black tales: a weak animal uses indirection to create difficulties between two stronger animals and enjoys the ensuing conflict.[29] In some versions Monkey's motive is revenge:

> Down in the jungle near a dried-up creek
> The signifying monkey hadn't slept for a week
> Remembering the ass-kicking he had got in the past
> He had to find somebody to kick the lion's ass.

In others it is malice and boredom:

> Deep down in the jungle so they say
> There's a signifying motherfucker down the way.
> There hadn't been no disturbin' in the jungle for quite a bit,
> For up jumped the monkey in the tree one day and laughed,
> "I guess I'll start some shit."

He sets Lion against Elephant by reporting a fictional conversation:

> He said, "Mr. Lion," he said, "A bad-assed motherfucker down your way."
> He said, "Yeah! The way he talks about your folks is a certain shame.
> I even heard him curse when he mentioned your grandmother's name."
> The lion's tail shot back like a forty-four,
> When he went down the jungle in all uproar.

Lion challenges Elephant, who almost destroys him, and Monkey literally adds insult to injury, calling down from the safety of his tree: "Shut up motherfucker, you better not roar / 'Cause I'll come down there and kick your ass some more." Delighted at what he has wrought, Monkey jumps up and down in the branches above and slips. Lion is upon him immediately. Monkey's plea for his life is both craven—"Please, Mr. Lion, I apologize"—and bold—"You lemme get my head out the sand / Ass out the grass, I'll fight you like a natural man." A surprised Lion accepts the challenge and steps back ready to fight. Monkey leaps up to the security of the treetops from where he continues his merciless verbal assault. This is commonly where the story ends. In a Harlem version a frustrated Lion shouts: "You and all your signifying children / Better stay up in them trees," which leads the storyteller to conclude in the old style of the didactic tales:

> Which is why today
> Monkey does his signifying
> *A-way-up* out of the way.

In several versions collected in Philadelphia and Texas, however, there are very different resolutions to the conflict between the weak and the strong. In them, Monkey is captured again by Lion and this time finds no way to talk himself out of difficulty:

> Lion said, "Ain't gonna be no apologizing.
> I'ma put an end to his motherfucking signifying."
> Now when you go through the jungle, there's a tombstone so they say,
> "Here the Signifying Monkey lay,
> Who got kicked in the nose, fucked-up in the eyes,
> Stomped in the ribs, kicked in the face,
> Drove backwards to his ass-hole, knocked his neck out of place."

An ignoble end to a career that increasing numbers of Negroes throughout the twentieth century were beginning to find ignoble. The manner in which tales such as the *Signifying Monkey* could be used to socialize children is revealed by Claudia Mitchell-Kernan, who first heard the story as a child of seven or eight in Chicago:

> I was sitting on the stoop of a neighbor who was telling me about his adventures as a big game hunter in Africa, a favorite tall-tale topic, unrecognized by me as tall-tale at the time. A neighboring woman called to me from her porch and asked me to go to the store for her. I refused, saying that my mother had told me not to, a lie which Mr. Waters recognized and asked me about. Rather than simply saying I wanted to listen to his stories, I replied that I had refused to go because I hated the woman. Being pressured for a reason for my dislike, and sensing Mr. Waters' disapproval, I countered with another lie, "I hate her because she say you were lazy," attempting, I suppose, to regain his favor by arousing ire toward someone else. Although I had heard someone say that he was lazy, it had not been this woman. He explained to me that he was not lazy and that he didn't work because he had been laid-off from his job and couldn't

find work elsewhere, and that if the lady had said what I reported, she had not done so out of meanness but because she didn't understand. Guilt-ridden, I went to fetch the can of Milnot milk. Upon returning, the tale of the "Signifying Monkey" was told to me, a censored prose version in which the monkey is rather brutally beaten by the lion after having suffered a similar fate in the hands of the elephant. I liked the story very much and righteously approved of its ending, not realizing at the time that he was *signifying* at me. Mr. Waters reacted to my response with a great deal of amusement. It was several days later in the context of re-telling the tale to another child that I understood its timely telling. My apology and admission of lying were met by affectionate humor, and I was told that I was finally getting to the age where I could "hold a conversation," i.e., understand and appreciate implications.[30]

Once again the transformation I am describing was a relative one. Throughout the century of freedom, guile and wit remained necessary and ubiquitous tools with which to confront the dominant culture. Seventy years after emancipation, Duncan Heyward of South Carolina wrote: "Having been thrown much of my life with Gullah Negroes and knowing their natures fairly well, I have wondered if they had not inherited from their ancestors a trait often noticed—that of pretending to misunderstand what was said to them when it suited their purpose to do so." He then related the story of a white traveler who knocked at the house of a Negro one night to see if he could get someone to row him several miles up the river in the face of a strong tide. Waking the Negro, the traveler asked him if he could row. The former replied that he could not. The traveler hired him to accompany him anyway, hoping he might make himself useful in other ways. Thus the difficult and tiring trip up river was made entirely under the white man's power. The harder he rowed the angrier he became at the Negro who was sitting comfortably in the stern of the boat. When the trip ended he finally exclaimed: "Why in the devil, living right on a river, can't you row a boat?" "I kin row boat, Boss," the black man replied. "When you come to my house an' call an' ax me if I could row, I t'ought you mean if I could roar like a lion, an' I tell you 'No, Sir.' Me no know it was row boat you mean."[31] In the 1930s a story was told of a white northerner who came South to speculate, found a rich plantation, and was on the verge of buying it when he met an old Negro sharecropper, with whom he had the following conversation:

Do you live on this farm?
Yes Sir.

How long?
All my life, Sir.
Will this farm make good crops?
Yes, make anything, if you can keep the ducks off.
What do you mean to say? Will the ducks eat up the crop after it is made?

The northerner calls the sale off, and the landowner berates the old Negro, who replies: "Well, now, Boss, you see he did not understand what I meant. I meant this, that when the crop is gathered, you ducks [deducts] for this, and ducks for that, and when you get through ducking, it's all gone."[32]

During the Depression, Negro prisoners in Florida told tales of Daddy Mention, who many insisted was a real figure with whom they had served time. Their favorite exploit seemed to be the tale of how Daddy Mention escaped from the jail just outside of Lakeland in Polk County. He worked harder than anyone else in the gang and would chop a tree down by himself and carry it alone to the pile. The white captain soon was winning money betting that Daddy could lift and carry away any tree anyone cut down. It became a common sight to see him walking around the jail yard carrying a big tree in his arms. One evening after dinner he left the dining room, went to the yard, picked up a huge log and walked right out of the prison gates with it. "None of the guards didn't bother him, because who ever saw a man escape with a pine butt on his shoulder?" The tale ends with the storyteller asking Daddy Mention how he made out once he left the prison: "I didn't have no trouble," he told him later. "I just kept that log on my shoulder and everybody I passed thought it had fell off a truck, and I was carrying it back. They knew nobody wouldn't have nerve enough to steal a good pine log like that and walk along the highway with it. . . . But soon as I got to Plant City, though, I took my log to a little woodyard and sold it. Then I had enough money to RIDE to Tampa. They ain't goin' to catch me in Polk County no more."[33]

Tactics like these have lived on. The Texas prisoners whom Bruce Jackson interviewed in the 1960s told him of stuffing their cotton sacks with rocks, dogs, even a jackrabbit, in order to make their weight. They sang of the exploits of Crooked-Foot John, who escaped by using the ruse of a double-heeled pair of shoes which confused his trackers.[34] Nor was the modern trickster confined to the anachronistic conditions of the southern prison camp. In the 1950s, J. D. Suggs told this story:

The revenue man in prohibiting days was out trying to catch a bootlegger. So, Sam (I know his right name but I won't call his name personally) was coming down Lawton Street; and the revenue man, the agent, we'll say, he was on the corner, looking shabby. "Say, boy," the agent called to Sam, "come here." Sam goes over to him and the agent flashes a ten-dollar bill. He says, "I'll give you this if you get me a quart of whiskey." Sam says, "Yessir, but a quart will cost you forty dollars." So he gives Sam forty dollars. Sam has a shoebox under his arm. He asks the agent, "Will you hold this shoebox till I go around the corner? I'll be right back." So the law he taken the box and held it for Sam, while Sam went to get the whiskey. Sam stayed so long, he said, "I'm going to see what's in this box." So there was his quart of whiskey. He had his quart of whiskey, Sam had his forty dollars, but the law hasn't got his man yet.

That's true, sure enough; that happened in St. Louis.[35]

In the 1960s, Big Bill, a resident of Washington, D.C., related the following incident:

Let me tell you fellows, I've been arrested for drunkenness more than two hundred times over the last few years, and I've used every name in the book. I remember once I told them I was Jasper Gonzales and then I forgot what I had told them, you know. So I was sitting there waiting, and they came in and called Jasper Gonzales, and nobody answered. I had forgotten that's what I said, and to tell you the truth, I didn't know how to spell it. So anyway, nobody answered and they were calling 'Jasper Gonzales! Jasper Gonzales!' So I thought that must be me, so I answered. But they had been calling a lot of times before that. So the judge said, 'Mr. Gonzales, are you of Spanish descent?' And I said, 'Yes, your honor, I came to this country thirty-four years ago!' And of course I was only thirty-five, but you see I had this beard then, and I looked pretty bad, dirty and everything you know, so I looked like sixty. And so he said, 'We don't have a record on you. This is the first time you have been arrested?' So I said, 'Yes, your honor, nothing like this happened to me before. But my wife was sick and then I lost my job, you know, and I felt kind of bad. But it's the first time I ever got drunk.' So he said, 'Well, Mr. Gonzales, I'll let you go, 'cause you are not like the rest of them here. But let this be a warning to you.' So I said, 'Yes, your honor. Thank you, your honor.' And then I went out, and so I said to myself, 'I'll have to celebrate this.' So I went across the street from the court, and you know there are four liquor stores there and I got a pint of wine and the next thing I was drunk as a pig.[36]

The traits of the trickster are important also in the considerable number of toasts centering on pimps and whores.[37] In their study of black pimps in San Francisco, Christina and Richard Milner concluded that the pimp's attraction as a hero stems from the fact that he is a trickster: "By the use of wit and guile he earns a rich living and maintains aristocratic tastes without having to resort either to violence or to physical labor. As a trickster, this modern Br'er Rabbit must learn the ways of the Fox, his cunning adversary. He must be able to observe the society around him with honesty and awareness. . . . pimps and hustlers depend for their livelihood on an awareness of social forces and an understanding of the human psyche."[38] The very language of pimps suggests the importance of trickery. The term *trick* refers to a prostitute's customer; the phrase *to turn a trick* means to perform a sex act for money, as does the term *tricking*. Thus the power of the pimp derives from the fact that he gets his women to give him the money they earn by tricking their tricks. "The men give my girls lollipops and I end up with the lollipops," a twenty-five-year-old black pimp told an interviewer. "That makes me very different from other men. I've learned to control a woman. Other men are tricks. They'll be driving along and see a cute little piece of ass on the corner. They can't resist, stop, and pay her money. But she gives the money to me, because I am the master. I cannot be tricked. . . . I make more money than the President and I haven't even begun in this life."[39]

The wiles of the trickster have remained important, then, but throughout the twentieth century black folklore has made it abundantly clear that they no longer proved sufficient; the central trickster figures increasingly found themselves forced to supplement their traditional tactics. Antebellum animal tricksters had never been beyond murder to accomplish their ends, but they had almost always murdered through trickery. Now they frequently did so in direct confrontation with their more powerful adversaries. In a tale told by a youngster in Aiken, South Carolina, in 1920, Rabbit tries his usual tactics to convince Fox that he and not Rabbit had eaten the butter, but Fox is not to be outsmarted: "Brother Fox . . . went back to eat up Brother Rabbit. Brother Rabbit hit him one side, an' drove de nail right in his head. Dat killed him dead."[40] In some tales it is the stronger animal who is depicted as the trickster against whom the weaker animal employs sheer force. In a Georgia tale collected in 1900, Brer Bear knocks on the door of Brer Coon and Sis Coon every day when they are away at work, frightens their children by pretending to be a spectre, and eats their food. Brer Coon tries to stop him, but he proves too timorous and ends up in hiding with his children. The plundering Bear is finally stopped by a terrified Sis Coon who accomplishes the task not through counter trickery but by taking an axe and splitting Bear's head open.[41] The woman is the powerful trickster's downfall again in a 1918 West Virginia tale. Craving Rabbit's tender young children, Brer Wolf has a blacksmith put a red-hot poker down his throat to alter his voice so that it will sound like Rabbit's. In this way he gains entry to Rabbit's house and is prevented from devouring the helpless children only when Mis' Rabbit plunges a knife into his side.[42] Buzzard is still up to his old tricks in the 1950s, inviting animals to go for a ride on his back and then dropping them to their deaths and eating them. Monkey ends Buzzard's career by wrapping his tail around Buzzard's neck, forcing him to land peacefully:

> The buzzard took the monkey for a ride in the air.
> The monkey thought that everything was on the square.
> The buzzard tried to throw the monkey off his back.
> The monkey grabbed his neck and said,
> "Now listen Jack,
> Straighten up and fly right."[43]

The most graphic example of this transformation can be seen in Roger Abrahams' comparison of a nineteenth-century Brer Rabbit tale published in the second volume of Joel Chandler Harris' Remus tales in 1883, and the same tale collected some seventy-five years later by Abrahams in Philadelphia. In the older version Fox invites all the animals but Rabbit to his house for a party. While the party is taking place and the animals are drinking Fox's good liquor, Rabbit begins to beat a small drum in the forest while walking toward Fox's house: *"Diddybum, diddybum, diddybum-bum-bum-bum—diddybum!"* As he gets closer, the animals become more nervous and soon flee the party with Fox in the lead. Rabbit saunters in, takes a chair, puts his feet up on the sofa, spits on the floor, and helps himself to the liquid refreshment.[44] The newer version begins in much the same way. Fox and Bear have a party to which all the animals in the forest except Rabbit are invited. "He'll be so embarrassed and hurt that he won't want to live and he'll give himself up. And we'll have rabbit stew before the week is up," Fox reasons. Rabbit's initial reaction confirms Fox's prediction: "the Rabbit turned away with his head turned down. He feeling sad, downhearted, tears in his eyes. Felt like he was alone in the world." In the twentieth century as in the nineteenth, Rabbit decides not to take this insult passively. He remains aggressive, but the nature of his aggression changes:

> He said, "I know what I'll do." He went home and shined his shoes, and got his shotgun and went back and kicked the door open. "Don't a motherfucker move." He walked over the table, got all he wanted to eat. Walked over to the bar and got himself all he wanted to drink. He reached over and he grabbed the lion's wife and he dance with her.

Grabbed the ape's wife and did it to her. Then he shit in the middle of the floor and he walked out.[45]

The attitudes underlying this transformation were articulated succinctly in a tie-tamping chant sung by Negro railroad workers during the 1930s. The workers began by boasting of the tactics that allowed them to outsmart the white overseer:

> Oh, de cap'n done learnt me how to make a day—
> Jes' rap on de railin' an' pass de time away.
>
> I got a new way o' tampin' dat de cap'n don' lak,
> I kin tamp 'em up solid an' never ben' my back.

In the very next stanza of their song, however, the workers indicated their recognition of the limitations of their trickery:

> You fool de cap'n, an' I fool de straw [straw boss],
> But de gen'l road manager, he gonna fool us all.

In the long run, they realized, it was the strong and not the weak who were in the best position to triumph through the use of guile and deceit:

> I look at de sun an' de sun look high,
> I look down on de boss-man an' he look so sly.
>
> "Boss man, boss man, cain' you gimme one dime?"
> An' de boss man say, "One dime behin'."
>
> Ask Cap'n George did his money come,
> Said, "De river too foggy, de boat won't run."

Thus a song which began with the boasts of the trickster ended with the promise of violent and direct retribution:

> Well, if I had my weight in lime,
> I'd whip my cap'n till he wen' stone blin'.[46]

Direct confrontation was not a quality totally unknown to the heroes of antebellum slaves. The Biblical figures that played so important a role in slave mythology were anything but tricksters: David confronted Goliath, Moses the Pharaoh, Samson the Philistines, Jesus the religious and secular authorities of his time. These figures retained importance in the twentieth century, but the weakening of the sacred universe rendered them less immediate and potent. The crucial change marking black folklore after emancipation was the development of a group of heroes who confronted power and authority directly, without guile and tricks, and who functioned on a secular level. It is to the nature and extent of this development that the remainder of this chapter will be devoted.

THE SLAVE AS HERO

St. Elmo Bland, born in Coffeeville, Mississippi, in 1895, a migrant to Chicago in 1917 and to Calvin, Michigan, after World War II, told Richard Dorson in the 1950s: "It seems to me I've lived pretty close to slavery."[1] Although Bland may have been referring primarily to the injustices and hardships he had known, there is another level of meaning in his statement which supplies insight into black consciousness during the past century. Long after emancipation many Negroes may be said to have lived "pretty close to slavery" in that they kept slave memories and traditions alive in their stories, their anecdotes, their reminiscences. For some, of course, slavery was an embarrassing legacy which was better forgotten as soon as possible. Lena Horne, born into an upper-middle-class Brooklyn black family in 1917, experienced this attitude: "My grandmother, Cora Calhoun Horne, was an ardent fighter for Negro Causes, but even she, the direct issue of a slave-owner, never talked to me about the central issue of Negro history, which is slavery. She dismissed it, by force of will, I think, from her consciousness."[2] Others were unable or unwilling to erase the slave past from their minds, although many were openly ashamed of what they considered the inaction of their ancestors. In relating the story of how her pregnant grandmother was brutally whipped for working inefficiently, Mary Richardson commented: "I wouldn't took all they took. I'd a took the grave."[3] Robert Falls, an ex-slave, was apologetic in discussing his past: "If I had my life to live over . . . I would die fighting rather than be a slave again. . . . But in dem days, us niggers didn't know no better. All we knowed was work and hard work."[4] Robert Williams found it difficult to speak of his slave past. After describing slave auctions in which mothers were often separated from their children, he commented: "Lord, Lord, chile, I don't like to recollec' dose days!"[5]

However embarrassing or painful the legacy of slavery may have been, it was passed on, learned, and repeated. During the Depression, Ella Johnson illustrated the manner in which stories of the slave era were handed down to children by still being able to re-create vividly her mother's feelings at the time of emancipation: "When my mother was a little girl and freedom had just been declared, she was dancing up and down and making a big noise outside in the yard. Her madam came to the door and said, 'What is the matter with you Helen? Are you crazy?' Mother said, 'No, I'm not crazy. I'm free, bless God, I'm free at last.' "⁶ Betty Jones told of her grandmother's reaction to the news of liberation: "she dropped her hoe an' run all de way to de Thacker's place—seben miles it was—an' run to ole Missus an' looked at her real hard. Den she yelled, 'I'se free! Yes, I'se free! Ain't got to work fo' you no mo'. You can't put me in yo' pocket now!' " "Gramma used to tell dis story to ev'ybody dat would lissen," Jones commented, "An' I spec' I heered it a hundred times."⁷ Billie Holiday, as a young girl in Baltimore in the early 1920s, learned of the slave past from her great-grandmother, whom she used to take care of. "She really loved me and I was crazy about her. She had been a slave on a big plantation in Virginia and she used to tell me all about it. . . . We used to talk about life. And she used to tell me how it felt to be a slave, to be owned body and soul by a white man who was the father of her children."⁸

Significant numbers of Negroes throughout the twentieth century talked about slavery and their slave ancestors not with defensiveness and shame but eagerly and often with pride. During her Sea Islands sojourn in 1917, Elsie Clews Parsons found the ex-slaves frequently more eager to speak about their past than to recount the tales she was seeking: "To the drama of 'Rebel time' the talk of the elder people readily turns. From the whippings and the excessive labors, the lack of holidays and the skimped and niggardly funerals, of those days, I had difficulty to divert Toby Byas, for one, to riddle or tale—he could not 'get his mind togeder.' "⁹ That the stories which Mrs. Parsons heard with ill-concealed impatience were listened to with more interest by the young children, is shown by the fact that more than thirty to forty years after Mrs. Parsons' interviews such folklorists as Richard Dorson and J. Mason Brewer were still discovering abundant stories of slave experiences, real and imagined. "On my first meeting with E. L. Smith," Dorson has written, "he recited the superman adventures of his maternal grandfather, Romey Howard, in escaping from the patterollers and bloodhounds that pursued runaway slaves. These wonderful exploits sounded like fiction, but Mr. Smith told them for literal truth, having them firsthand from his grandfather, a self-made folk hero, who thwarted and rendered ridiculous the white oppressor. Katy Pointer began relating the escape of her father from slavery within five minutes of our acquaintance, and her familiarity with every detail of the harrowing flight revealed plainly enough how often she had listened to and later repeated the saga."[10]

For generations of Negroes, slavery refused to fade into a historical abstraction. It remained alive on a number of levels. Emotionally it continued to evoke feelings of anger and compassion. "I so often think of de hard times my parents had in their slave days," Mary Bell testified in the 1930s.[11] Speaking of her father's tribulations in slavery, Katy Pointer exclaimed in the 1950s: "You know sometimes when I think about it I want to cry, a human being getting treated that way."[12] Kathryn Morgan's great-grandmother would show her children and grandchildren the marks that the cat-o'-nine-tails had left on her back. "They were thumb deep, but she didn't want them to forget what slavery was like." Mrs. Morgan, who never saw them herself, was told about them so that she, too, would not forget.[13]

Slavery remained alive, too, in the specific details and descriptions embodied within the stories of the slave past. The narratives of ex-slaves and the stories, anecdotes, and legends of their descendants are filled with information about the everyday conduct and culture of slaves and the mechanics of the slave system. In the important autobiography which he dictated in the 1950s, Sidney Bechet devoted an entire chapter to his slave grandfather, Omar, whose story duplicates almost precisely the New Orleans legend of Bras Coupé.[14] Regardless of how fanciful Bechet's picture of his grandfather may have been—and it is likely that he or his family consciously or unconsciously borrowed from local legend in constructing it—his narrative is filled with accurate details about numerous aspects of nineteenth-century black culture: the place of music and dance in slave life, the nature of slave folk beliefs, the role of superstitions and occult beliefs in slave consciousness. In his description of a voodoo rite in which his grandfather participated, for instance, Bechet reflects comprehension of the intimate relationship between Christian and non-Christian elements in slave religion. In the midst of the ceremonies a potion thrown into the fire by an old crone explodes: "And it was a sign to them, and they set to clapping and shouting. Everyone came up to my grandfather and wanted to touch him to get a hold of some of the power that was going to work for him. And then they started singing a praise [spiritual]." The same verity marks Bechet's account of the impact of emancipation as his father described it to him: "There was all that excitement, and then the settling down. Even with Emancipation people had their living to get done. A lot of the Negroes were taking off, moving around, trying to find a new way. Others just stayed where they were, doing what they were used to doing, not knowing any other thing to do. A lot of people found Emancipation day hadn't made much change."[15] In the 1950s, J. D. Suggs introduced a traditional slave tale with this accurate explanation of an important aspect of slavery: "The slaves would slip out from one plantation to another when they wanted to go to prayer meeting. They could get passes from Old Marster to visit, but not to go to meeting. If they got caught by the padderolls without a pass they got a beating. (The padderolls were poor white folk who didn't farm, and that was the only way they had to make money.) When they had the meeting they would turn the iron pot over to keep the sound in."[16]

Historians have much to learn from these prolific reminiscences not merely because they are so often accurate but also because they are so often legendary; because they blend and interweave myth with fact. The folk are not historians; they are simultaneously the products and creators of a culture, and that culture includes a collective memory. If we probe that memory it becomes clear that, as B. A. Botkin maintained years ago, "ex-slaves have kept alive their own tradition of slavery to match the white plantation tradition."[17] It is a tradition that until recently has largely been ignored by scholars but not by the children, grandchildren, and great-grandchildren of the slaves who have repeated, embellished, and perpetuated it throughout the century of freedom. Historians have debated and will continue to debate the exact amount of resistance that occurred during slavery, and for an understanding of the slaves this debate is crucial. For an understanding of the post-slave generations, the history of slave resistance is less important than the legends concerning it, though the two by no means invariably contradict each other. Looking back upon the past, ex-slaves and their descendants painted a picture not of a cowed and timorous black mass but of a people who, however circumscribed by misfortune and oppression, were never without their means of resistance and never lacked the inner resources to oppose the master class, however extreme the price they had to pay.

The slave trickster continued to play an important role in this tradition of resistance. As was the case with animal tricksters, slave tricksters, too, lived on long after the institution that had helped to mold them was abolished—and they lived on for the same reasons: because they continued to mirror the plight and reflect the needs of Afro-Americans. "John was an old man in slavery time," David Edwards said in 1942. "He was smart enough to get out of everything."[18] The stories focusing upon the slave John were frequently told as true, beginning with such phrases as "Old man told me a tale about slavery times," or "My grandfather told this from slavery times, he said it was a fact." In them John was depicted as still existing in quiet but determined tension with the system he was forced to live under. Using his wits and his nerve, he carved out his own little world of knowledge and privileges. He outwitted his master, kept a step ahead of the "padderollers," frequently escaped the punishment he seemed destined to receive, proved to be a master thief capable of stealing the very ring off his mistress' finger, the clothes off his master's back, or the sheets off his owner's bed at night; and he continued to take advantage of every weakness and blindness of those around him.[19]

Slave trickster tales did not seem to create the same self-consciousness and ambivalence in modern storytellers that animal trickster tales frequently did. As recently as 1965 Negro storytellers were delighting audiences with the escapades of the slave trickster. Arlette Jones of Houston, Texas, for instance, told of a slave named Tom whose master sells him and warns the new owner never to make a bet with him. The new master responds: "Oh, I'm smarter than a nigger anyday." Tom soon bets his master a thousand dollars that the white man will be constipated by twelve o'clock. At the appointed hour Tom returns and explains that he will have to put his finger up his master's rectum in order to see if he is constipated. After doing so, Tom admits that the white man is not constipated. "Well, I guess that means you owe me a thousand dollars," the master says as he goes to tell a friend how he triumphed over his uppity slave. "What?" the friend exclaims. "Man, Tom had bet me *two* thousand dollars that by twelve o'clock today he'd have his finger up your ass."[20]

Although the slave trickster's tactics continued to work well enough, there are instances in which he was made to supplement them with direct confrontation. In a Mississippi tale related by the teen-aged Billy Jack Tyler, Old Master sends John to the barn to harness the mules. When John stays away a long time, Master goes to see where he is. John insists he is cold and needs to rest before continuing his work. He is ordered again to harness the mules to the wagon and get some firewood, and he again complains that it is too cold at the present time to do anything. "Don't be so sassy old nigger," Master warns him, "because if I had my pistol I would blow your brains out." John replies, "Oh Master, you don't have your pistol? I'm going whip you this morning."[21] In a tale told by Jeff Alexander of Benton Harbor, Michigan, John is caught shooting squirrels on his master's land and is warned against any more hunting. The next morning John goes out and shoots a crow and is caught. Old Master asks to see John's gun, and when John gives it to him, Master points it at John, orders him to pick the feathers off the crow, halfway down. "Now start at his head, John, and eat the crow up to where you stopped picking the feathers at." When John finishes eating half of the raw bird, Master gives him his gun back and tells him not to be caught hunting any more. John begins to walk away, then stops, levels the gun at Master, throws him the half-eaten crow and says, "Lookee here, Old Marster. I want you to start at his ass and eat all the way, and don't let a feather fly from your mouth."[22] In a familiar Virginia tale, John becomes a spokesman for justice. Caught stealing a chicken, John is brought before his master, who asks him, "John, what did you steal my chicken fo'?" John replies, "Mahster, let me tell you dishyere one t'ing. I done saw in de Bible dat de man had to reab whey he labor. Mahster, I done labor raisin' dose chickens."[23]

It was not necessary to transform the traditional slave trickster in order to produce situations in which slaves directly confronted their masters. Black lore is filled with hundreds of stories, anecdotes, and reminiscences which relate with admiration and pride instances of slaves standing up to the whites, insisting upon their rights, utilizing force, dying, if necessary, to protect their family and friends. Though the memories of slavery are filled with pain and anguish, a significant number of them are also filled with pride: "My grandfather was a slave," Sidney Bechet has written.

> But he was a man who could do anything. He could sing; he danced, he was a leader. It was natural to him; and everyone followed him.
> Sundays when the slaves would meet—that was their free day—he beat out rhythms on drums at the Square—Congo Square they called it—and they'd all be gathered there around him. Everyone loved him. They waited for him to start things: dances, shouts, moods even. Anything he wanted to do, he'd lead them. He had a power. He was a strong man. His name was Omar.[24]

This positive image was not unusual. "I loved my father," an ex-slave testified. "He was such a good man. He was a good carpenter and could do anything. My mother just rejoiced in him."[25] "My mother was the smartest black woman in Eden [Tennessee]," another former slave recalled. "She was as quick as a flash of lightning, and whatever she did could not be done better. She could do anything. She cooked, washed, ironed, spun, nursed and labored in the field. She made as good a field hand as she did a cook. . . . With all her ability for work, she did not make a good slave.

She was too high-spirited and independent. I tell you, she was a captain." She pictured her father as less independent but no less talented: "Pa was also a sower of all seeds. He was a yardman, houseman, plowman, gardner, blacksmith, carpenter, keysmith, and anything else they chose him to be."[26] "Father's name was John Jones Littleton," Cornelia Carney told an interviewer. "Had a long thin nose like a white man, and had the loveliest white teeth and the prettiest mouth, but his back was a sight. It was scarred up an' brittled fum shoulder to shoulder." Tired of being beaten, her father escaped to the woods and visited his family on Saturday nights and Sundays. "Father wasn't the only one hiding in the woods. There was his cousin, Gabriel, that was hiding and a man named Charlie. Niggers was too sharp for white folks."[27]

The personal element in these stories was crucial. Kathryn Morgan, who grew up in a black middle-class family in Philadelphia, recalled that of all the stories of slavery she heard as a youngster the most important were those concerning her great-grandmother, Caroline Gordon, who was known as Caddy. "The other narratives, along with the Negro spirituals, finally belonged to the world but Caddy was ours." These Caddy legends were consciously used in Mrs. Morgan's family as buffers against the stereotypes, the anxiety, the anger that black people had to struggle with. Sitting in the kitchen while her mother prepared meals, or trailing after her mother while she performed her household chores, she heard stories of Caddy's great beauty, which caused white women to envy her and white men to lust after her, and of Caddy's fierce independence, which led her to run away time and again, only to be caught and beaten. "Do you think she'd cry when they whipped her with a cat-o-nine-tails? Not Caddy. It would take more than a cat-o-nine-tails to make Caddy cry in front of white trash." The following story is typical of those that Mrs. Morgan heard from her mother before she was old enough to go to school and later passed on to her own daughter, Susan, who by the age of ten knew them well enough to tell them to her younger cousins:

Caddy had been sold to a man in Goodman, Mississippi. It was terrible to be sold in Mississippi. In fact, it was terrible to be sold anywhere. She had been put to work in the fields for running away again. She was hoeing a crop when she heard the General Lee had surrendered. Do you know who General Lee was? He was the man who was working for the South in the Civil War. When General Lee surrendered that meant that all the colored people were free! Caddy threw down that hoe, she marched herself up to the big house, then, she looked around and found the mistress. She went over to the mistress, she flipped up her dress and told the white woman to do something. She said it mean and ugly. This is what she said: *Kiss my ass!*

Of the many tales she heard about her great-grandmother, this remained Kathryn Morgan's favorite. She and her siblings would beg their mother to repeat over and over again the part where Caddy flipped up her dress. In the seclusion of her room, Morgan would stand in front of a mirror and practice flipping up her dress while exclaiming: "kiss my ass." "As a teenager I remember how wonderful I thought it would be to be able to tell the whole white world to 'kiss my ass.' "[28]

The salient source of admiration in most of these tales was the slave ancestor's opposition to the power of the whites. A former slave told an interviewer of how an overseer approached his father and informed him that he was going to beat him. "Daddy said, 'I ain't done nothing,' and he said, 'I know it, I'm gonna whip you to keep you from doing nothing,' and he hit him with that cowhide . . . and daddy was chopping cotton, so he just took up his hoe and chopped right down on that man's head and knocked his brains out. Yes'm it killed him, but they didn't put colored folks in jail then, so when old Charlie Merrill, the nigger trader, come along they sold my daddy to him, and he carried him way down in Mississippi."[29] "My mother wouldn't let nobody whip her," another ex-slave testified. "Old mistress couldn't do nothing with her. She would have the men to tie her, and after she was tied they was 'fraid to whip her."[30] Kiziah Love of Oklahoma told the story of his Uncle Bill, who was ordered to hitch up the overseer's team before doing his own. His uncle replied that he didn't have time and besides it was the custom for every man to catch his own team. "Of course this made the overseer mad and he grabbed a stick and started cussing and run at Uncle Bill. Old Bill grabbed a single-tree and went meeting him. Dat white man all on a sudden turned round and run for dear life and I tell you, he fairly bust old Red River wide open getting away from there and nobody never did see hide nor hair of him round to this day."[31] Ellen Cragin of Mississippi told of her mother, who worked so hard at the loom that she frequently fell asleep. Her master's young son observed this, informed on her, and was told to whip her. He began to whip her while she slept. Awakening, she took a pole out of the loom and beat him nearly to death with it. "She said, 'I'm going to kill you. These black titties sucked you, and then you come out here to beat me.' And when she left him, he wasn't able to walk."[32] Wiley Childress of Tennessee was told by his parents of a slave named Fedd who "wuz de strongest man neah dat part ob de kuntry" and wouldn't allow anybody to whip him. Once his master brought several men to help him whip Fedd, who immediately "struck one ob de mans so hahd dey had ter hab de doctuh. De Marster said let 'im 'lone he's too strong ter be whup'd."[33] Dave Lawson of North Carolina perpetuated the story of his grandparents, Cleve and Lissa, who found out that their master planned to sell Lissa to Alabama or Georgia. They begged him not to do so, but he was insistent. Finally they captured him and poured boiling water down his throat in an attempt to force him to change his mind. He died refusing. The sheriff found Lissa and Cleve sitting in front of their cabin holding hands and hung them on the spot.[34]

Generally these stories of slave opposition clustered around three themes. The first of these was escaping the slave system entirely by running away. "Talking about niggers running away," Harriet Robinson said, "didn't my step-pappy run away? Didn't my Uncle Gabe run away? The frost would just bite they toes most nigh off, too, whiles they was gone. They put Uncle Isom, my step-pappy, in jail and while's he was in there he killed a white guardsman. . . . He was a double-strengthed man, he was so strong. He'd run off, so help you God. They had the bloodhounds after him once and he caught the hound what was leading and beat the rest of the dogs. The white folks run up on him before he knowed it and made them dogs eat his ear plumb out. But don't you know he got away anyhow."[35] In the 1950s E. L. Smith spoke of his grandfather, who roamed around at will: "He could outrun bloodhounds, till they were too tired to jump over the fence. . . . Four patterols died owing him a whipping." In the same decade Katy Pointer spoke in admiration of how her father, Isaac Berry, ran away from slavery in 1859.[36] A former slave told of the constant attempts of his brother to escape bondage: "They nearly whipped him to death but it didn't take the starch out of him for as soon as he got well and felt able, he began to talk about going again. And he did go. But it was not until the war that he got away for good."[37]

These stories were related with pride, as were the ubiquitous accounts of slaves successfully confronting the authority of overseers and masters, which constituted the second major theme. "Old Master taught us to never answer back to no white folks," Mittie Freeman testified. "But one day that overseer had my pappy whipped for somethin' he never done, and Pappy hit him."[38] Slaves in these accounts often went much further.

Anthony Abercrombie told of "one mighty bad overseer" who was killed down on the bank of the creek one night. "Dey never did find out who killed him, but Marse Jim always b'lieved de field han's done it."[39] John Henry Kemp told of an old lady plowing a field when an overseer reprimanded her for working slowly. She answered angrily and the overseer began to lash her. "The woman became sore and took her hoe and chopped him right across his head, and child, you should have seen how she chopped this man to a bloody stump."[40] Masters too were not immune from the wrath of their slaves, as Lucretia Anderson made clear: "You know in slave times, sometimes when a master would get too bad, the niggers would kill him—took him off out in the woods somewheres and get rid of him. Two or three of them would get together and scheme it out, and then two or three of them would get him way out and kill him." She spoke also of her father who was sold five times. "Wouldn't take nothin'. So they sold him. They beat him and knocked him about. They put him on the block and they sold him about beatin' up his master."[41]

Though the price for such resistance was high, that made the act all the more admirable and the stories celebrating it all the more important. Susan Snow told of a white man who earned money hunting runaway slaves. "His own niggers kilt him. Dey hung 'em for it."[42] Fanny Cannady spoke with some awe of two brothers, Leonard and Burrus Allen: "Dem niggahs wuzn' skeered of nothin'. If de debil hese'f had come an' shook er stick at dem dey'd hit him back. Leonard wuz er big black buck niggah; he wuz de bigges niggah I ever seed, an' Burrus wuz neer 'bout as big, an' dey 'spized Marse Jordan wus'n pizen." During the Civil War the master's son, Gregory, came home on furlough and Leonard Allen said: "Look at that goddam soldier. He fighting to keep us niggers from being free." The master got his gun: "He leveled it on Leonard an' tole him to pull his shirt open. Leonard opened his shirt an' stood dare big as er black giant sneerin' at Ole Marse." The white man "shot er hole in Leonard's ches' big as yo fis'. . . . I could see Leonard layin' on de groun' wid dat bloody hole in his ches' an' dat sneer on his black mouf."[43] Anne Clark recalled the similar murder of her father: "My papa was strong. He never had a licking in his life. He helped the master, but one day the master says, 'Si, you got to have a whopping,' and my papa says, 'I never had a whopping and you can't whop me.' And the master says, 'But I can kill you,' and he shot my papa down. My mama took him in the cabin and put him on a pallet. He died."[44]

The final prominent theme in tales of slave opposition centered upon the protection slaves gave or tried to give those they loved. At the turn of the century, Virginia Negroes told the story of a slave family that stole and slaughtered their master's hogs. Every time he killed one, they did the same. Finally they were caught, and the master picked up his switch and began to beat the young son first while his father stood by calling out words of defiant encouragement: "Stand to it, my son! stand to it! . . . Stand to it, my son! Neber fail. Stand to it!"[45] Several decades later, Fannie Moore of North Carolina spoke with gratitude of her mother's protection: "I never see how my mammy stand such hard work. She stand up for her children though. The old overseer he hate my mammy, 'cause she fight him for beating her children. Why, she git more whuppings for that than anything else."[46] J. T. Tims of Mississippi told of how his family stood together against the family of Blount Steward, his master. One day during the Civil War, when Tims was just a boy, his mistress tried to give him a beating:

> I was at the back steps playin' and she decided to whip me. I told her I hadn't done nothin', but she put my head between her legs and started to beatin' me. And I bit her legs. She let me loose and hollered.
>
> Then she called for William to come and beat me. William was one of the colored slaves. William come to do it. Ma had been peeping out from the kitchen watchin' the whole thing. When William come up to beat me, she come out with a big carving knife and told him, "That's my child and if you hit him, I'll kill you."
>
> Then she sent for Tully to come and whip me, I mean to whip my mother. Tully was my young master. Tully come and said to my mother, "I know you ain't done nothin' nor your child neither, but I'll have to hit you a few light licks to satisfy Ma." Blount [his master] come the next day and went down to where Pa was making shoes. He said, "Daniel, you're looking mighty glum." Pa said, "You'd be lookin' glum too if your wife and child had done been beat up for nothin'."
>
> When he said that, Blount got mad. He snatched up a shoe hammer and hit Pa up side the head with it. Pa said, "By God, don't you try it again!" Blount didn't hit him again. Pa was ready to fight, and he wasn't sure that he could whip him. Pa said, "You won't hit me no more."[47]

Here is a very different picture of slavery and of slaves than the one which, until very recently at least, was traditionally accepted by popular culture and by many scholars as well. This was not the sole image of slavery created by blacks, of course. There were other slave types as well, and black folklore has not neglected them: the craven, the sycophants, the foolish, the ruthless who preyed upon their own group. But slavery also produced heroic figures who have long occupied an important place in Negro thought. I have only begun to touch upon the reservoir of tales and reminiscences which stress slave courage, self-respect, sacrifice, and boldness. The accuracy of this picture is less important for our purposes than its existence. These stories were told and accepted as true—a fact of crucial importance for any understanding of post-slavery Afro-American consciousness. Once again a vibrant and central body of black thought has been ignored while learned discussions of the lack of positive reference group figures among Negroes, the absence of any pride in the Afro-American past, the complete ignorance Negroes have concerning their own history, have gone on and on. The concept of Negro history was not invented by modern educators. Black men and women dwelt upon their past and filled their lore with stories of slaves who, regardless of their condition, retained a sense of dignity and group pride. Family legends of slave ancestors were cherished and handed down from generation to generation. Postbellum Negroes told each other of fathers and mothers, relatives and friends who committed sacrifices worth remembering, who performed deeds worth celebrating, and who endured hardships that have not been forgotten.

THE MODERNIZATION OF THE BLACK HERO

Black folklore did not confine tales of direct confrontation to slave heroes. The freedmen and their twentieth-century descendants figured prominently in such tales as well. During the Depression, Anne Ulrich Evans of Alabama told of how her husband and friends resisted the violence of the Ku Klux Klan during Reconstruction: "One night dey come to our house after my husband to kill him, and my husband had a dream dey's coming to kill him. So he had a lot of colored men friends to be at our house with guns dat night, and time dey seed dem Ku Klux coming over de hill dey started shooting just up in de air and shout, and dem Ku Klux never did bother our house no more."[1] Amidst the tales of Klan atrocity, intimidation, and murder, stories of courageous resistance came through again and again. Pierce Harper of North Carolina told of how the freedmen in Greene County armed themselves against the Klan: "They got together and organized the militia and had leaders like regular soldiers. They didn't meet 'cept when they heared the Ku Kluxes was coming to get some colored folks. Then they was ready for 'em. They'd hide in the cabins, and then's when they found out who a lot of them Ku Kluxes was, 'cause a lot of 'em was kilt."[2] Anderson Bates of South Carolina related the story of Dick James, who was warned by the Klan that they were coming to get him. James armed himself with a shotgun. When the pair of Klansmen, who turned out to be two local whites named Bishop and Fitzgerald, arrived, "Uncle Dick open the door, slap that gun to his shoulder, and pull the trigger. That man Bishop hollers: 'Oh, Lordy.' He drop dead and lay there till the coroner come. Fitzgerald leap 'way. They bring Dick to jail, . . . the judge tell the jurymen that Dick had a right to protect his home and hisself and to kill that white man, and to turn him loose. That was the end of the Ku Kluxes in Fairfield."[3]

Narrative tales of blacks fighting for their rights featured twentieth-century Negroes as well. J. D. Suggs had a number of such tales in his comprehensive repertory. He related the story of Will Kimbro, who taught Suggs in a Mississippi school in the early twentieth century. Kimbro taught school during the winter and rented land on which he raised cotton and corn the rest of the year. His troubles began when he helped his mother-in-law, who also rented land to farm, prove that her landlord had cheated her out of sixty dollars. He was given ten days to leave the county. Aided by two white merchants, who told him, "You furnish the grit and we'll furnish the guns and ammunition," Kimbro almost single-handedly held off some three hundred white attackers, killing fifteen of them. He was arrested, tried, acquitted, and the next fall was back in Suggs' classroom. "He was about thirty then," Suggs remembered. "He was a brownskinned man, about a hundred and seventy-five pounds, about five foot nine. He didn't look hard at all. He ended up as a United States detective." The other heroes of whom Suggs spoke also seemed to be simple, outwardly unremarkable people into whose shoes any other ordinary person could step. In 1914, for instance, Jack Farmer was doing what he had done for most of his life: farming on someone else's land in Sunflower County, Mississippi. When his landlord, Mr. Casey, whipped his daughter for taking time off from work to go to the doctor, Farmer's life changed suddenly: "he just picked up his shotgun and called Mr. Casey to the door and killed him." Suggs related in detail how Farmer eluded a posse of three to four hundred men with the help of his father, "who was a hoodoo," and told of the bravery of Farmer's brother and sister-in-law, who in spite of being badly beaten refused to give him away. Confrontation tales could be less grim. Suggs claimed the following incident took place in Morehouse, Missouri, in 1924. Every time a Negro came through Morehouse, a group of young whites would force him to dance and then run him out of town. "These two colored boys come along, and they made them dance, and then chuck rocks at 'em and run 'em out of town." Six months later the two blacks returned carrying suitcases, and were forced to dance again. After a while one of them asked: "Did you ever see that step, Get Your Gun?" When the whites shook their heads, he said, "If we had our light shoes on we'd show you something. That beats any step we know." They were urged to get their shoes on. They went to the suitcases, unlocked them, reached in, brought out guns, and said, "Now let's see you all dance." The whites proved to be terrible dancers and, after making them jump up and down for forty minutes, the two blacks picked up their suitcases, said, "That's pretty good, boys," and walked off.[4]

Suggs' stories were not unique; tales like them continued to be an important element in black lore throughout the twentieth century. Kathryn Morgan, for instance, told of how her Uncle William was forced by his grandmother, Caddy, and his mother, Kate, to confront directly the white boys who were chasing him home from school in Lynchburg, Virginia: "Kate beat him for running. Then Caddy beat him again. Caddy told him if he ever ran away from trash again she was going to beat his ass every day and that's what happened. William would run and Caddy would beat him—every day for about a week." Finally, William stood up to his tormentors and triumphed. When he arrived home that day his mother and grandmother praised him and gave him an extra piece of hoe cake. "Then Caddy went to get the shotguns. She and Kate took turns sitting at the kitchen window with the shotguns all that day and all night. . . . Caddy sent for all the boy cousins. Cousin Dave's younger children and all the children had to walk back and forth from school together for a long time. Nothing happened, but Kate and Caddy sat up a whole week all night and all day taking turns—just in case. Kate said nothing happened because we were respected and Caddy said it didn't hurt to be respected by high and low alike."[5] In the 1940s, a Memphis Negro named Natchez told of his uncle:

> My uncle was a man that, if he worked, he wanted his pay. And he could figger as good as a white man. Fact of the matter, he had a better education than some of them and they would go to him for advice.

One day his white boss come to his house and told him, say, "Sam, I want you to git that woman of yours out of the house and put her to work." Say, "It's no woman on this plantation sits up in the shade and don't work but Mizz Anne."

An' my uncle say, "Well, who is Mizz Anne?"

The white man tell him, "Mizz Anne is my wife."

My uncle say, "Well, I'm sorry, Mister Crowther, but my wife is named Anne, too, and she sets up in the shade and she don't come out in the field and work!"

The man say, "She got to come out there."

My uncle look at him. "There's one Mizz Anne that's a Negro and she ain't gonna work in the field."

The white man jumps off his horse and my uncle whipped him and run him and his horse off his place. So the white man rode to town and he got him a gang and come back after my uncle. My uncle shot four or five of them, but they finally caught him and hung him. . . .

Fifty or sixty of them come out there and killed him. That was on account of him trying to protect his own wife. Because he didn't want his own wife to work out on the farm when she had a new baby there at the house an' was expecting another one pretty soon![6]

These hero figures were important. They symbolized the strength, dignity, and courage many Negroes were able to manifest in spite of their confined situation. Yet, however different their tactics and approach were from those of the slave trickster, they did share one important characteristic: they too are circumscribed by the limits of reality. The sweet taste of vengeance was usually their greatest victory, and they often paid for that with their lives. Like the human trickster, they generally counted themselves fortunate when they were able to hold their own. After slavery Afro-American folklore began to feature other types of heroes as well: secular, human heroes who were not to be contained by the limits of the actual.

In Chapter 2 I argued that the primary difference between the central secular hero figures of the slaves and of the whites around them was that the former continued the African patterns of manipulating the strong and reversing as far as possible the normal structure of power and prestige, while the heroes who dominated white American folklore in the first half of the nineteenth century were those expanded figures who grew in proportion to the problems they faced: the Paul Bunyans, Mike Finks, Davy Crocketts, whose magnified images were not constrained by the bounds of the possible or the plausible. Secular slave heroes operated by eroding and nullifying the powers of the strong; by reducing the powerful to their own level. Central white folklore heroes triumphed through an expansion of the self—by inflating the individual rather than deflating the antagonistic forces he faced. The cultural self-containment and imperfect acculturation characteristic of nineteenth-century slaves made the adoption of such exaggerated heroes by the slaves unlikely because the secular, individualistic orientation of post-Enlightenment Western culture was still foreign to them. Among themselves, slaves undoubtedly told stories of direct confrontation with the master class, though such tales proliferated after emancipation in proportion to the actual development of new and varied alternatives and possibilities. There is, however, no evidence that tales of exaggeration were common to slaves. The creation of these kinds of heroes required the growth of a more pronounced Western orientation, the decline of the sacred universe, and the growth of the individualist ethos among black Americans. All of these developments accompanied freedom. It is not surprising, then, that only with freedom did Negroes fashion their own equivalents of the Gargantuan figures that strode through nineteenth-century American folklore. Indeed, the presence of such figures in black folklore was, along with the decline of an all-encompassing religiosity and the rise of the blues, another major sign of cultural change among the freedmen.

The spirit of many of the tales of exaggeration was summed up in a toast and a tale collected by Richard Dorson. Lying on the surface of the bayou one day, Alligator is enjoying the scenery when some boatloads of oil come in from the Mississippi River. He watches the slaves unload the boats and hears one referred to as a "Nigger." "So that's what he is," he thinks to himself and swims to the bottom to urge his wife to go up and take a look at the Niggers. While she observes the scene, a slave strikes a match on the seat of his pants, lights his cigarette, and throws the match into the water where some oil that had leaked from one of the drums ignites, covering the water. Quickly swimming to the bottom, she is asked by her husband, "Well honey did you see them Niggers?" and she replies, "Yes honey, I saw them. That Nigger's a bitch. He strike his ass and set the world on fire."[7] The spirit was expressed also in a song of the 1920s:

I'm de hot stuff man
Frum de devil's lan'.
Go on, nigger,
Don't you try to buck me,
I'm de hot stuff man
Frum de devil's lan'.

I'm a greasy streak o' lightnin',
Don't you see?[8]

Some years later Willie George King of Louisiana sent this song, written
in her own hand, to Alan Lomax:

There is nothing in the jungle is any bader than me.
I am the badest woman ever come out Tenisee;
I sleep with a panther till the break of day;
I caught a tiger-cat in the collar and i ask him what he had to say;
And i wore a rattlesnake for my chain,
And a Negro man for my fob, . . .

When John Lomax visited her she described her upbringing in song:

Borned by a p'ickly pear,
Suckled by a grizzly bear,
Rocked in a cradle with butcher knives, . . .[9]

Here was language reminiscent of that used to describe the American
heroes of the nineteenth century. The heroes themselves were often quite
similar. J. D. Suggs told of Brother Bill, a Negro cowboy in El Paso, Texas,
whose story he first heard in 1908:

I looked down the road and see Brother Bill coming down on a bobcat.
He had two guns, one on each side; he had barbed wire for his bridle
reins (on his naked hands too) and a live rattlesnake, a diamond-back
rattlesnake for a riding whip (that's the baddest snake we got in the
United States). He run up to the drugstore, and jumped down and ran inside to the pharmacy. Told the man to give him a big glass of glycerine
mixed with twenty sticks of dynamite. Pharmacist he made it and handed
it to him. Bill turns it up and drinks it down, all in one gulp. Reaches on
each side and gets his two guns. Went a walking down the street yelling,
"I'm a bad man." Killed him twenty men. Came back and got on his bobcat. He left town, and I haven't heard from my brother Bill since.[10]

This rhetoric was often transformed into the idiom of the city streets
of the South and North. In his autobiography, H. Rap Brown, who grew
up in the 1940s and 1950s in Baton Rouge, Louisiana, gave an example of
the line that earned him his nickname—Rap:

Man, you must don't know who I am.
I'm sweet peeter jeeter the womb beater
The baby maker the cradle shaker
The deerslayer the buckbinder the women finder
Known from the Gold Coast to the rocky shores of Maine
Rap is my name and love is my game. . . .

I'm the man who walked the water and tied the whale's tail in a knot
Taught the little fishes how to swim
Crossed the burning sands and shook the devil's hand
Rode round the world on the back of a snail carrying a sack saying
   AIR MAIL.
Walked 49 miles of barbwire and used a Cobra snake for a necktie
And got a brand new house on the roadside made from a cracker's hide,
Got a brand new chimney setting on top made from the cracker's skull
Took a hammer and nail and built the world and calls it "THE
   BUCKET OF BLOOD." . . .
I might not be the best in the world, but I'm in the top two and my
   brother's getting old.[11]

The heroes emerging from these tales were gifted with extraordinary, often extrahuman powers. Jacksonville Negroes spoke at length about Henry Peterson, familiarly known as Old Pete, who had prodigious strength when he was young, at the turn of the century. For a nickel he allowed coconuts to be broken open on his skull, and for fifty cents he had butting contests with billy goats, whom he invariably bested. Even during the early 1930s, when he was in his seventies, he was willing to break one-by-ten-inch boards in two by butting his head against them for ten cents. A freight train was supposed to have run over his head while he was sleeping on the tracks, and it was the train that was damaged. He once used a ship's anchor for a pickaxe, lifted a derailed locomotive back onto the track, swam out and pushed a grounded ship off the bar into the channel, uprooted a bee tree with his hands and toted it home on his shoulder to get the honey out of it, stopped a runaway freight train by the sheer strength of his body, subdued an alligator, which he saddled and bridled and rode into Fort Myers, and in his spare time fathered fifty-six children.

Other Florida heroes included Old Doc, who was capable of superhuman feats of strength, Big Sixteen, and High John de Conqueror, who bested the Devil. High John eloped with the Devil's daughter. The Devil pursued them and, when they met, High John tore off one of the Devil's arms and almost beat him to death with it. Before he left Hell he passed out ice water to everyone and turned the dampers down so that when he returned to visit his in-laws the place wouldn't be so hot.[12] The exploits of the exaggerated hero could be less exotic though no less fantastic. K. Leroy Irvis, born and raised in the Catskill Mountains of New York State, related a story he had learned from his mother. A black cook named Tom was hired as chef on a ship because he boasted he was fast. He proved it by cooking a meal for the entire ship's company in one minute: Beginning at one minute before noon, "He killed, drew, and roasted a pig, mashed potatoes, canned some pickles, caught, scaled and washed some fish, added all the trimmings, besides setting the table for forty men, and then served dinner at twelve o'clock sharp." The surprised captain complained that he was too fast, whereupon he jumped into the sea and when the ship docked in its Chinese port Tom was waiting on the dock calling, "Have you changed your mind, captain?"[13]

The qualities of the exaggerated hero could be found in almost any type of twentieth-century black tale. The trickster John could suddenly manifest super powers and be transformed into superblack. In a tale which began traditionally with John cheating Master and getting caught, John evades punishment by turning himself into a rabbit and calling out, "Massa, Ah's a rabbit in de fiel'." Master calls back, "Ah's a houn' on de groun' rat attuh you!" They run until they come to the Gulf of Mexico and John jumps in calling out, "Massa, Ah's a fish in de sea," and Master calls back, "Ah's a shark in de sea rat attuh you!" and continues the pursuit. John then turns into a bird, "Ah's a bird in de air, Massa," and flies high in the air to which the white man replies, "Ah's a hawk in de sky rat attuh you!" They fly so high " 'till dey fin'ly rech de moon, an' his ole massa comed to be de man in de moon." John falls back to earth safe from his pursuer.[14] John Courtney related a widely known tale about John in freedom. John goes to Alabama for a vacation and while there tells his friends how in Arkansas the colored were treated better. A white man hears this and asks John where he's from. John tells him he wasn't speaking to him. The white knocks John down, but John fights back. "So they seed John was going to win that fight. Up came the laws. They arrested John. Then they carried him to the place to punish. Buried him in the ground up to his shoulder. Got two bulldogs and turned them loose on John. John was nodding his head so fast they stopped those dogs, called John, told John to fight those two bulldogs fair." In a similar tale, John uses his incredible speed and ability to dodge to prevent Bob Fitzsimmons, former world heavyweight champion, from laying a glove on him.[15]

In other tales extrahuman speed allowed blacks who had retaliated against whites to elude their pursuers. Running abreast of a deer, the fugitive would normally call out: "Mr. Deer, you must have killed one [white] too." In some stories the hero outruns a Cadillac and a train, and in tales which Suggs found common in Alabama, Mississippi, and Arkansas, a black fugitive from the police "just spread his arms and sailed right on off. And they never did catch him. Said he was faster than the planes."[16] Not even the minstrel-derived, stereotyped "coon" figure was immune from transformation into a hero with superhuman attributes. A song popular in the 1920s featured a "travellin' man" from Tennessee who wandered around "stealin' chickens, / An' anything he could see." He commits crime after crime with impunity, once outrunning a police car for more than thirteen hours:

> The coon ran so bloomin' fast
> That fire come from his heels;
> He scorched the cotton an' burnt the corn
> An' cut a road through the farmer's fields.

At another point the police shoot him through the head, but to no avail:

> They sent down South for his mother,
> She was grieved and moved with tears,
> Then she open the coffin to see her son,
> An' the fool had disappeared.

Finally he is caught but not even the gallows can contain him:

> They put the coon on the gallows
> An' told him he would die;
> He crossed his legs an' winked his eye
> And sailed up in the sky.[17]

In 1939, collecting folklore in Harlem for the Federal Writers' Project, Ralph Ellison was told a tale by Leo Gurley which embodies the salient features of its genre and which, because it has to my knowledge never been published, deserves to be included here in full:

> I hope to God to kill me if this aint the truth. All you got to do is go down to Florence, South Carolina and ask most anybody you meet and they'll tell you its the truth.
> Florence is one of these hard towns on colored folks. You have to stay out of the white folks way; all but Sweet. That the fellow I'm fixing to tell you about. His name was Sweet-the-monkey. I done forgot his real name, I caint remember it. But that was what everybody called him. He wasn't no big guy. He was just bad. My mother and grandmother used to say he was wicked. He was bad allright. He was one sucker who didn't give a dam bout the crackers. Fact is, they got so they stayed out of *his* way. I caint never remember hear tell of any them crackers bothering *that* guy. He used to give em trouble all over the place and all they could do about it was to give the rest of us hell.
> It was this way: Sweet could make hisself invisible. You don't believe it? Well here's how he done it. Sweet-the-monkey cut open a black cat and

took out its heart. Climbed up a tree backwards and cursed God. After that he could do anything. The white folks would wake up in the morning and find their stuff gone. He cleaned out the stores. He cleaned up the houses. Hell, he even cleaned out the dam bank! He was the boldest *black* sonofabitch ever been down that way. And couldn't nobody do nothing to him. Be-*cause* they couldn't never see im when he done it. He didn't need the money. Fact is, most of the time he broke into places he wouldn't take nothing. Lots a times he just did it to show 'em he could. Hell, he had everybody in that lil old town scaird as hell; black folks and white folks.

The white folks started trying to catch Sweet. Well, they didn't have no luck. Theyd catch 'im standing in front of the eating joints and put the handcuffs on im and take im down to the jail. You know what that sucker would do? The police would come up and say: "Come on Sweet" and he'd say "You all want me?" and they'd put the handcuffs on im and start lead- ing im away. He'd go with em a little piece; sho, just like he was going. Then all of a sudden he would turn hissself invisible and disappear. The police wouldn't have nothing but the handcuffs. They couldn't do a thing with that Sweet-the-monkey. Just before I come up this way they was all trying to trap im. They didn't have much luck. Once they found a place he'd looted with footprints leading away from it and they decided to try and trap im. This was bout sun up and they followed his footprints all that day. They followed them till sundown when he come partly visible. It was red and the sun was shining on the trees and they waited till they saw his shadow. That was the last of Sweet-the-monkey. They never did find his body and right after that I come up here. That was bout five years ago. My brother was down there last year and they said they think Sweet done come back. But they caint be sho because he wont let hisself be seen.[18]

Gurley not only told this as a true story but, through the operation of what Roger Abrahams has called the "intrusive I,"[19] he managed to continually bring himself and members of his family into the tale. Thus even when the storytellers were not themselves actors in the tales they told, they managed to make themselves—and probably their audiences as well—participants and by so doing brought even the most fantastic tales within the orbit of reality. This was accomplished as well by incorporat- ing into the genre well-known personalities who by assuming some of the attributes of exaggerated heroes rendered them more meaningful, if not more believable. This anecdote from the 1960s illustrates the point:

Two Negroes meet on a street corner in Atlanta, Georgia, and strike up a conversation.

First speaker. Boy, did you hear 'bout dey gonna move de Rock o' Gibraltar?

Second speaker. Man, is you done loose you' mind? You know dey ain't nobody can move de Rock o' Gibraltar but God.
First speaker. Yeah, dey is gonna move it, too.
Second speaker. Well, who gonna move it?
First speaker. Martin Luther King, dat's who.
Second speaker. Where he gonna put it?[20]

Like the blues and the gospel songs, the significance of the tales I have been describing cannot be summed up simply. They can be seen as indications of acculturation to a Western Euro-American ethos in which the individual was at the center of his universe. At the same time they give evidence of the continued existence and vitality of a separate Afro-American culture. Like the nineteenth-century tall tales they so closely resembled, they stressed an approach to problems which in good American fashion placed emphasis upon the growth of individual powers. Here were the elements of the extended man, the superman, who has been so central in both the rustic and the industrial folklore of modern America, from tales to comic books. But if black and white fantasies came closer together in the twentieth century, they were still separated by varying sets of priorities, needs, pressures, and styles. In the exaggerated hero, black folk created secular, human figures who could contravene the established mores and standards of the society; figures who could pursue an independent course and look within themselves for the necessary strength. The form such heroes took varied considerably, but it is possible to focus upon two predominant types: the badman who transgressed totally all of the moral and legal bounds of society and the strong, self-contained hero who violated not the laws or the moral code but the stereotyped roles set aside for black people in a white society. To comprehend the contours of black consciousness in the twentieth century, it is necessary to examine in detail the role of these new heroes in providing occasions for the release of hostilities, the transmission of observations concerning power, and the celebration of black culture.

BAD MEN AND BANDITS

From the late nineteenth century black lore was filled with tales, toasts, and songs of hard, merciless toughs and killers confronting and generally vanquishing their adversaries without hesitation and without remorse. As animal tricksters waned, black bad men and bandits became increasingly omnipresent and important. Postbellum black songs are studded with boasting, threats, and the language of violence:

> I went down town de yudder night,
> A-raisin' san' an' a-wantin' a fight.
> Had a forty dollar razzer, an' a gatlin' gun,
> Fer to shoot dem Niggers down one by one.[1]

> I'm de bad nigger,
> If you wants to know;
> Look at dem rounders
> In de cemetery row.
>
> Shoot, nigger,
> Shoot to kill, . . .[2]

> I'm so bad, I don't ever want to be good, uh, huh;
> I'm going to de devil and I wouldn't go to heaven, uh, huh,
> No I wouldn't go to heaven if I could.[3]

Cheating at love was one of the more common catalysts for violence, or the threat of it, in black songs. *Frankie and Albert* (also commonly known as *Frankie and Johnny*) originated some time between 1850 and the turn of the century and was easily the most long-lived and the most popular song of this type, being as widely diffused among whites as blacks. The classic story of the loyal woman whose lover betrayed her was sung in hundreds of variants, each of them containing a dramatic death scene:

> First time she shot him, he staggered,
> Next time she shot him, he fell,
> Third time she shot him O Lawdy,
> There was a new man's face in hell.
>   She killed her man,
>   For doing her wrong.[4]

Like Frankie, other women resorted to violence in order to keep or to punish their lovers. In 1928, Bessie Tucker moaned:

> I got cut all to pieces, aah-aah . . . about a man I love,
> I'm gonna get that a-woman, just as sho' as the sky's above.[5]

In another blues she warned her man what would happen if he kept "pallin' " around with other women:

I love you, hey, but you won't behave.
I love you, hey, but you won't behave.
You going to keep on a pallin', going to wake up in your grave.[6]

In 1941 Merline Johnson employed the humor of understatement to issue similar threats:

I've got a two-by-four, and it just fits my hand, (twice)
I'm goin' ta stop all you women from runnin' around with my man.

I don't want to hurt that man, just going to kill him dead, (twice)
I'll knock him to his knees, go back to the man I once have had.[7]

More typically, it was the man not the woman who acted as avenger in black songs. In 1895 a Texas singer warned:

If you don't quit monkeyin' with my luluh, tell you what I'll do:
I'll feel aroun' your heart with my razor, and I'll cut you half in two,
Nigger man, I'll cut you half in two.[8]

Two decades later black miners in Birmingham sang:

Gona get me a pistol with a shiny barrel
Gona kill the first fellow
Fooling with my long-haired girl.[9]

The bluesmen of the 1920s, 30s, and 40s continued the theme. "Dam you, I'm going to shoot you," Lonnie Johnson warned his "careless love." "Shoot you four or five times. / Then stand over you until you finish dying."[10] Big Maceo explained how he spent all night, a pistol in his hand, trailing his woman and found her with another man:

I ain't,no bully an' I don't go for the baddest man in town, (twice)
When I catch a man with my woman I usually tear his playhouse down.[11]

A number of bluesmen issued similar threats:

I'm a hard working man and, baby, I don't mind trying,
I'm a hard working man and, baby, I don't mind trying,
I catch you cheating on me, then, baby, you don't mind dying.[12]

From his cell in the Louisiana State Penitentiary, Otis Webster explained why he was jailed for attempted murder:

You take a no good woman, don't mean no good,
She'll put you in a place, man, in your neighborhood,
I wouldn'ta been here, baby, it hadn'ta been for you,
I thought you loved me, honey, you wasn't even true. . . .

I mess up your ears,
I mess up your face,
I leave you with both your legs outa place,
So evil, evil as a man can be,
I'm a hoochie coochie man,
Don't nobody mess with me.[13]

The amount of violence and the number of hard men pictured in the context of male-female conflict cannot be minimized, but it was the bandit and not the vengeful, frustrated lover who emerged as the chief bad man in black lore. The folklore of black outlaws was often based upon the exploits of real men. Perhaps the best known of these was John Hardy, a black West Virginia steel-driver, who killed a man in a crap game during a dispute and was hung for it in January 1894. This simple incident became deeply embedded in the oral tradition and, while songs about Hardy were to become more familiar to whites than blacks, he remains typical of the outlaw figures pictured in Negro folklore: hard, unyielding, remorseless:

John Hardy married a loving wife,
    And children he had three:
He cared no more for his wife and child
    Than the rocks in the bottom of the sea, poor boy!
    Than the rocks in the bottom of the sea.

Standing on the scaffold in the last moments of his life, he is asked if he wants to pray and replies: "Just give me time to kill another man, Lord, Lord, / Just give me time to kill another man." In another version, as the blue cap is placed over his face, he boasts: "Hand me down my blue-steel gun / And the men will all leave this place."[14]

More interesting than Hardy, and certainly more important in Negro lore, was Railroad Bill, a figure based upon the exploits of Morris Slater. In 1893, Slater, a black turpentine worker in the pine woods of Escambia County, Alabama, shot and killed a policeman during an argument and escaped on a freight train. For the next three years freight trains were to be his means of sustenance. He robbed trains throughout southwest Alabama, stealing canned food and selling it to the poor Negroes who lived in shacks along the rails, threatening their lives if they refused. In a gun battle on July 3, 1895, he shot and killed Sheriff E. S. McMillan who had been devoting himself to Slater's capture. Less than a year later Slater's career came to an abrupt end. As he entered Tidmore's Store in Atmore, Alabama, in March 1896, his head was almost blown off by two men who ambushed him for the $1250 reward. The known facts of Slater's life were embellished by legend. He was reported to have successfully robbed a train which he knew carried a posse sent to hunt him down. Numerous stories insisted that he had been able to elude his pursuers for three years because he was a conjure man and could transform himself when threatened by the law. With posses close behind him, he would turn himself into a sheep, a brown dog, a red fox and watch them ride by. Even after he was killed there were those who, in the tradition of outlaw legends, refused to believe that he was dead; he merely had transformed himself once again and was still watching his pursuers with amusement.[15] The widely known songs about his career are filled with ambivalence: admiration for his daring and censure for his preying upon his own people:

> Railroad Bill cut a mighty big dash;
> Killed McMillan like a lightnin'-flash.
>> En he'll lay you po body down.

> Railroad Bill was a desprit sport,
> Shot all those buttons off that head brakeman's coat.
> Ain't it sad!

> Railroad Bill so mean an' so bad,
> Till he tuk ev'ything that farmer had,
>> It's that bad Railroad Bill.

> Railroad Bill so desp'rate an' so bad,
> He take ev'ything po' womens had,
>> An' it's that bad Railroad Bill.[16]

Throughout the black world there were local bad men who shared the qualities of Railroad Bill. Jelly Roll Morton recalled several figures like these from his youth in New Orleans:

> men like Chicken Dick, who had shoulders and arms on him much more stronger-looking than Joe Louis—and Toodlum and Toodoo Parker, guys you couldn't afford to bother with—and Sheep Eye (I was raised with him), he was real loud-mouthed and, if he could bluff you, he might murder you. Sheep Eye was a raider around these little Cotch games and when he would walk in, everybody would quit—
> "Cash in my checks here, I've got to go."
> And Sheep Eye would holler, "You gonna play! Sheep Eye's here and I'm the baddest sonofabitch that ever moved. Set down there and play. If you don't, I'm taking this pot."
> Of course, it made no difference whether Sheep Eye won or lost. He'd take all the money anyway. Curse you, kick you, and slap you cross the head with a pistol. He was the toughest guy in the world until Aaron

Harris showed up, but, when Aaron entered, Sheep Eye would become the nicest little boy anywhere—just lovely.

Aaron Harris was one of the few members of this group of New Orleans toughs whose reputation outlived him:

Aaron Harris was a bad, bad man,
Baddest man ever was in this land.

Killed his sweet little sister and his brother-in-law,
About a cup of coffee, he killed his sister and his brother-in-law.

He got out of jail every time he would make his kill,
He had a hoodoo woman, all he had to do was pay the bill.

Harris combined features of Hardy and Slater but was more ruthless than either. Born in New Orleans between 1875 and 1880, he became famous as a young man for his feats of strength. His first killings took place during brewery crap games when he would kill players who won money from him. After killing some eight people this way, he became a big-time gambler and killed an additional twelve men and four or five women, including his own sister. One tale described how he murdered two policemen before witnesses. "He was a big man and a real bully," Johnny St. Cyr remembered, "stood six feet, weighed two hundred pounds and would draw a knife on a police officer. He was a bad, bad actor—killed his brother-in-law, and then beat the rap. I heard—I don't know it to be a fact, but I heard that he had some protection from a hoodoo woman." Sexually attractive and virile, Harris had a string of prostitutes among his admirers who gave him their love and their money. He killed two of these for withholding money from him and is supposed to have strangled a third in front of witnesses just for sport. This hard, silent (he was reputed to have had a vocabulary of only one hundred words), moody man finally met his end on July 14, 1915, when he was ambushed by another tough, George Robertson (Boar Hog):

Aaron pawned his pistol one night to play in a gambling game,
He pawned his pistol one night to play in a gambling game,
Then old Boar Hog shot him and blotted out his name.[17]

The actual careers of men like Slater and Harris served as models for a host of legendary bad men figures in black lore: Po' Lazarus, Billy Bob Russell, Dupree, Bolin Jones, Snow James, Roscoe Bill, Shootin' Bill, Slim Jim, Eddy Jones, Brady, Bad-Lan' Stone, Bill Martin, Bad Lee Brown, Devil Winston, Dolomite, the Great MacDaddy, Toledo Slim.[18] In these figures the classic qualities of the black bad man were preserved. Bad Lee Brown, for instance, coolly described the murder of his wife:

> Late las' night I was a-makin' my rounds,
> Met my woman an' I blowed her down,
> Went on home an' I went to bed,
> Put my hand cannon right under my head.

He escapes to Mexico but is caught, tried, and sentenced to ninety-nine years of hard labor. He ends his story with regrets but little sense of remorse:

> Here I is, bowed down in shame,
> I got a number instead of a name.
> Here for de res' of my nachul life,
> An' all I ever done is kill my wife.[19]

A ballad collected in Texas in 1892 told of Billy Gelef, who "had got so bad he was skeered of hisself."[20] One of the most recent creations in this genre, the Great MacDaddy, whose story Roger Abrahams encountered in Philadelphia during the 1950s, remains wholly within the tradition. Arrested and brought to trial, his badness impresses even the judge who tells him: "You're the last of the bad. / Now Dillinger, Slick Willie Sutton, all them fellows is gone, / Left you, the Great MacDaddy to carry on." Although he treats his sister-in-law and mother-in-law with open contempt, they pass him two guns which enable him to escape. Finally he is shot in the back by a policeman, but to the end he typifies the totally hard man:

> I've got a tombstone disposition, graveyard mind.
> I know I'm a bad motherfucker, that's why I don't mind dying.[21]

The legendary prototype for many of these figures, the most important and longest-lived bad man in black lore, was Stagolee, who was known also as Stackolee, Stackerlee, Stackalee, Stacker Lee, and Staggerlee. Charles Haffer of Coahoma County, Mississippi, remembered first singing of Stagolee's exploits in 1895, while Will Starks, also a resident of the Mississippi Delta, initially heard the Stagolee saga in 1897 from a man who had learned it in the labor camps near St. Louis.[22] In the first decade of the 1900s, Howard Odum found that songs of Stagolee were common throughout Mississippi, Louisiana, Tennessee, Alabama, and Georgia, "besides being sung by the negro vagrants all over the country."[23] Half a century later, in the 1950s and 1960s, toasts, songs, and tales of Stagolee were still in the active oral tradition in Michigan, Philadelphia, New York, Chicago, and Texas.[24]

In whatever period and whatever form he was encountered, Stagolee was pure trouble:

> Stagolee was a bully man, an' ev'y body knowed,
> When dey seed Stagolee comin', to give Stagolee de road,
> O dat man, bad man, Stagolee done come.[25]

> Stagolee, he went a-walkin' with his .40 gun in his hand;
> He said, "I feel mistreated this mornin', I could kill most any man."[26]

> Stacker Lee's Mamma said, "Stacker Lee wuz the wurst she evuh nursed,
> Stacker Lee wuz a bad boy, he wuz a bully frum his birth,"
> Stacker, Stacker Lee.[27]

> Back in '32 when the times was hard
> I carried a sawed-off shotgun and a crooked deck of cards.
> Wore blue-suede shoes and carried a diamond cane;
> Had a six inch peck with a be-bop chain.
> Had a one button robe and a lap-down hat;
> And ever'time you saw me I looked just like that. . . .
> I'm that mean son-of-a-bitch they call "Stackolee."[28]

The central event in every version is a gun battle between Stagolee and another hard man, Billy (or Bully) Lyons, arising from Stagolee's anger at losing his Stetson hat while gambling. Billy Lyons is soon at Stagolee's mercy and begs: "Boy please don' take ma life, / For I got three little chillun, an' a poor little helpless wife."[29] Stagolee's responses vary but they are all characterized by a complete lack of compassion:

> What do I care fo' yo' children, what do I care fo' yo' wife,
> You taken my new Stetson hat, an' I'm goin' to take yo' life.[30]

The law is at first reluctant to pursue him:

> The high sheriff said, "Go bring me dat bad man Staggerlee here."
> The deputy pulled off his pistols and he laid them on the shelf
> And said, "If you want dat bad man you got to go 'rest him by yo'self."[31]

Ultimately Stagolee is captured and, while in one version he is tortured by nightmares of his deed and in another he pleads for his life,[32] more typically he is hard and arrogant to the end. When the judge sentences him to ninety-nine years, he replies contemptuously: "Judge, ninety-nine ain't no goddam time. / My father's in Sing Sing doing two-ninety-nine." In another rendition the judge is afraid to sentence him:

> Judge said, "well, I'm gonna have to let you go, Stack,
> 'Cause I don't want to wake up with a knife in my back."[33]

In some renditions Stagolee proves as difficult to kill as he was to live with:

> De hangman put de mask on, tied his han's behin' his back,
> Spring de trap on Stagolee, but his neck refused to crack.

> Hangman, he got frightened, he said: "Chief, you see how it be,
> I cain' hang this man, you better let him go free."[34]

In others he is killed and sent to Hell, where he begins his career anew, as in this version from Texas and Louisiana in the 1930s:

> When de devil wife see Stack comin' she got up in a quirl,—
> "Here come dat bad nigger an' he's jus' from de udder worl'. "

> All de devil' little chillun went sc'amblin' up de wall,
> Say, "Catch him, pappa, befo' he kill us all." . . .

> Stagolee took de pitchfork an' he laid it on de shelf—
> "Stand back, Tom Devil, I'm gonna rule Hell by myself."[35]

In a number of recent variants Stagolee's saga ends not with his imprisonment or death but with his intimidation of his victim's gang in a boast that typifies his entire career:

> "So when I come in here, I'm no stranger,
> 'Cause when I leave my ass-hole print leaves 'danger.' "[36]

"Danger" was an accurate epithet for almost every bad man in black lore; they seemed to leave behind them no other legacy. Obviously Negro singers, storytellers, and audiences derived certain rewards and benefits from their bad men and bandits or such figures would not have lived so long or been so ubiquitous in postbellum black lore. But whatever needs bad men filled, black folk refused to romantically embellish or sentimentalize them. Missing entirely from black lore was the Robin Hood figure so familiar in the folklore of other Americans and other cultures. The "good bad man," the "noble robber," the "gentleman killer," the "social bandit," who dominated the outlaw legends of the United States and of many of the European countries from which American immigrants came, shared characteristics which black outlaws generally lacked: Such romanticized bad men turn to lives of crime only under the most extreme provocation, often to avenge a wrong by the authorities. Their crimes are selective, aimed against those with economic or political power. Robbing from the rich and giving to the poor, they become, consciously or inadvertently, public benefactors: the friends and champions of the oppressed. They kill primarily in self-defense and almost never harass the unarmed or the weak.

On the contrary, they usually treat the latter, and especially women, with courtesy and chivalry. Robin Hood never interfered with yeomen, women, or with honest monks. As an early popular ballad put it: "So curteyse an outlawe as he was one / Was never none yfounde." Jesse James was equally circumspect. In one tale he returned valuables to a man of the cloth, explaining that "we never take from preachers, widows, or orphans." In another tale he returned the money he had taken from a one-armed man when he learned that the man's arm was lost fighting for the Confederacy. And he not only returned the $70 he had taken from a sobbing widow whose husband's corpse was in the baggage car of the train James was robbing but added an additional $120 as a gift. Billy the Kid nursed an old blind prospector back to health and then put a rope in his hand on the other end of which was a fully provisioned pack mule. "A kinder-hearted feller," the ballad of the bandit Sam Bass asserted, "you'll seldom ever see." Operating within familiar territory, the noble outlaws were admired and supported by the plain, decent people of the community who, after the outlaw is led to his death through foul treachery, mourn him and perpetuate his good deeds and acute social conscience in their ballads and stories.[37]

Thus the balladeers sang of Jesse James:

O Jesse was a man and friend to the poor,
He would never see a man suffer pain. . . .
He robbed from the rich and he gave to the poor,
He'd a hand and a heart and a brain.[38]

Similarly they sang of the guerrilla leader Quantrill:

Oh, Quantrell's a fighter, a bold-hearted boy,
A brave man or woman he'll never annoy,
He'd take from the wealthy and give to the poor,
For brave men there's never a bolt to his door.[39]

In his ballad of Pretty Boy Floyd, Woodie Guthrie caught the spirit of the legends that had grown up around this Depression bank robber in Oklahoma and the Southwest:

There's many a starving farmer
The same old story told,
How the outlaw paid their mortgage
And saved their little home.

Others tell you 'bout a stranger
That come to beg a meal

And underneath his napkin
Left a thousand dollar bill.[40]

Black and white bandits did share important qualities. Aaron Harris,
Railroad Bill, Stagolee, along with Jesse James, Sam Bass, Billy the Kid,
were men apart—loners. They came, as the ballad of Jesse James put it,
"from a solitary race." In his role as the solitary individual, the outlaw,
black or white, symbolized antagonism toward the settled order. The outlaw was in constant conflict with and continually asserted his freedom
from organized society. He was not only a man apart but a man above:
above the statutory law, above the judicial process, above the normal restrictions and expectations that fashion the lives of modern men and
women. It was this solitariness and superiority that destined bad men, in
the legends that were woven about them, to celebration and destruction.
The bandit's insistence on individual autonomy both appealed and repelled, and the folk ritually paid homage to the nascent nihilism of the
bandit even as they punished it by making certain that the outlaw was
destroyed at the end of his saga. In these respects black and white bandits
were similar, as in all probability they were, too, in the actual contours of
their careers. White bandits no less than black ones were ruthless, de-
structive, selfish, asocial. What is culturally revealing is not the differences in their careers but the divergences in the legends that grew up
about them.

The Negro folk could never pray for their fallen outlaws as did the
Calabrian women of San Stefano for the early twentieth-century brigand,
Musolino:

Musolino is innocent
They have condemned him unjustly;
Oh Madonna, oh Saint Joseph,
Let him always be under your protection. . . .
Oh Jesus, oh my Madonna,
Keep him from all harm
Now and forever, so let it be.[41]

This kind of wailing was precluded because black bandits, no matter how
appealing many of their actions and qualities may have been, were never
pictured as either innocent or good. Black legend did not portray good
bad men or noble outlaws. The brutality of Negro bad men was allowed
to speak for itself without extenuation. Their badness was described without the excuse of socially redeeming qualities. They preyed upon the weak
as well as the strong, women as well as men. They killed not merely in

self-defense but from sadistic need and sheer joy. They fit the description of what Eric Hobsbawm in his study of bandits has called "the avengers" —bandits whose reputations are built not upon justice but terror. "They are heroes not in spite of the fear and horror their actions inspire, but in some ways because of them. They are not so much men who right wrongs, but avengers, and exerters of power . . . who prove that even the poor and weak can be terrible." Coming from the depths of the society, representing the most oppressed and deprived strata, these bandits are manifestations of the feeling that, within the circumstances in which they operate, to assert any power at all is a triumph.[42]

They are manifestations of much more than this, of course. They express the profound anger festering and smoldering among the oppressed— anger that we have seen expressed in myriad ways in black lore; anger that could suddenly burst forth in the song of a Memphis black:

I feel my hell a-risin', a-risin' every day;
I feel my hell a-risin', a-risin' every day;
Someday it'll bust this levee and wash the whole wide world away.[43]

It was present in the blues fantasies of Furry Lewis:

I believe I'll buy me a graveyard of my own, (twice)
I'm gon' kill everybody that have done me wrong.

and in the fantasies of Violet Mills:

Want to set this world on fire, that is my mad desire,
I'm the devil in disguise, got murder in my eyes.

Now if I could see blood runnin' through the streets, (twice)
Could see everybody lying dead right at my feet.

Give me gunpowder, give me dynamite, (twice)
Yes, I'm gonna wreck the city, gonna blow it up to-night.[44]

For those students of black culture who seem destined to find pathology wherever they look, black banditry is a simple phenomenon. Here are the sick and bloody anti-social fantasies of the repressed and alienated. The sadism of the black bandit can be seen as "a defense against castration fears. . . . What might happen to the subject passively is done actively to others." The hypervirility of the bandit becomes a projection of the severely restricted masculine instincts and the "severely dislocated ego" of the black male. The self-destructiveness of the bandit relieves the guilt which his creators feel at the lengths to which their needs have driven their fantasies. But it is all worth it since the bandit creations help the

Negro male achieve "self respect."[45] It is not necessary to deny elements of truth in these interpretations in order to insist that they are too limited and explain too little. It is possible, after all, to make many of the same assertions about the bandit heroes of all cultures. Those who are satisfied with their lot, who possess a sense of power, who share a feeling of integration with their society are not generally those from whom the lore of banditry emanates. The prerequisite for the creation of such figures in white as well as black society has been a sense of frustration and powerlessness. The "sicknesses," the anxieties, the tensions, the profound feeling of social and cultural dislocation that are inherent in bandit lore are shared, to one extent or another, in the folklore of both whites and blacks. It must be reiterated that the crucial cultural difference in these folk figures is that whites have tended to sanitize and civilize them, to make them benefactors who dispense social justice to the entire group, while Negroes have refrained almost entirely from this form of ritual. If a sense of realism and perspective are signs of "health," then the usual interpretations of the meaning of black bad men should at least be balanced by the observation that black bandits, instead of being rendered more appealing by romantic sentimentality, were portrayed with the kind of unadorned realism generally lacking in white bandit lore.

Black bandits may have provided catharsis but, characteristic of black lore, they also furnished some hard lessons. Their careers made it clear that the wages of the kind of intragroup violence they practiced were death and the results were anti-social. They were hard men, but the world in which they lived, and perished, was harder. Eric Hobsbawm has asserted that insofar as social bandits have a program it is the defense or restoration of the traditional order of things: the reassertion of life as it was or is believed to have been in the past.[46] This hypothesis would help to explain why in the United States we have had the efflorescence of both real and mythic bandits in periods of great social stress when new forces and new institutions were visibly changing the patterns of life: the 1880s and 1890s, when bandits waged war on the railroads; the 1920s, when they undermined the enforcement of prohibition; and the Great Depression, when they attacked the banks. It would explain also why legendary social bandits as they were known among white Americans and in other societies were generally missing from Afro-American lore. The situation of Negroes in the United States was too complex for nostalgia. The simple restoration of things as they had been held no allurement. Society had to be unhinged, undone, made over. That certainly is a clue to the total anarchy and lawlessness of black bandits, and to their total hopelessness as well. They never really tried to change anything. They were pure force, pure vengeance; explosions of fury and futility. They were not given any socially redeeming characteristics simply because in them there was no hope of social redemption. Black singers, storytellers, and audiences might temporarily and vicariously live through the exploits of their bandit heroes, but they were not beguiled into looking to these asocial, self-centered, and futile figures for any permanent remedies.

Many of the qualities which white Americans invested in their bandit heroes were reserved in Negro lore for another kind of hero who by transcending society's restrictions and stereotypes could directly confront it on its own terms and emerge victorious.

THE HERO VS. SOCIETY: JOHN HENRY TO JOE LOUIS

In black parlance the adjective *bad* does not invariably have negative connotations. The term can be one of approbation, especially when the *a* is prolonged and the word changed into something approaching *baaad*. Thus transformed, the term has been used to describe those who were admired because they had the strength, courage, and ability to flout the limitations imposed by white society. In this form the word could, and frequently did, apply to black bandits.[1] But it was used to describe another hero figure as well: the moral hard man. The morality of these heroes did not derive from their necessary acceptance of the society's official moral code relating to such things as sexual conduct and personal behavior. Two of these heroes—John Henry and Joe Louis—did tend to operate within this code, while two others—Shine and Jack Johnson—did not. Their morality stemmed rather from the two characteristics that typified their lives: they never preyed upon their own people and they won their victories within the confines of the legal system in which they lived. They defeated white society on *its* own territory and by *its* own rules. They triumphed not by breaking the laws of the larger society but by smashing its expectations and stereotypes, by insisting that their lives transcend the traditional models and roles established for them and their people by the white majority. They were moral figures, too, in the sense that their lives provided more than vehicles for momentary escape; they provided models of action and emulation for other black people.

John Henry was probably the first and without question the most long-lived hero figure of this type. In their studies of John Henry, Guy Johnson and Louis Chappell found that songs celebrating his exploits were already widespread in the early 1880s. By the time they conducted their research in the 1920s each scholar found that the John Henry legend was diffused throughout the country, that among black workers John Henry was perhaps the best known Negro personage, and that in most cases his story was accepted as fact. "Whether John Henry was a flesh-and-blood man or not," Johnson wrote in 1929, "there are thousands of Negroes who believe that he was, and many of them can give the intimate details of his career. . . . His fame is sung in every nook and corner of the United States where Negroes live, sung oftenest by wanderers and laborers who could tell three times as much about John Henry as they could about Booker T. Washington."[2] The advent of the phonograph and mass media only tended to enhance and diffuse the popularity of the black steel-driver's epic. By the early 1960s there were some fifty recorded versions of *John Henry* available, and more than one hundred songs about him had been copyrighted.[3]

It seems likely that the John Henry legend had its origins in the building of the Chesapeake and Ohio Railroad in West Virginia in the 1870s. The progress of the C & O line through the mountainous terrain depended upon the construction of a series of tunnels, the most important of which was the Big Bend Tunnel which upon its completion in June 1872 was a mile and a quarter long, then the longest tunnel in the United States. During the two and a half years of Big Bend's construction, more than one thousand workers, most of them Negroes, labored under inferno-like conditions. Working in oppressive heat and dim light, breathing in thin and foul air, enduring shattering noise and thick yellow smoke from the constant dynamite blasts, facing the omnipresent threat of death or disablement from falling rock or tunnel sickness, semi- or wholly naked workers, called turners or shakers, squatted with long steel drills between their knees, steadying and turning the drills while steel-drivers like John Henry stood over them with great hammers pounding the drills into the rock to create holes into which explosives were inserted.

> John Henry said to his shaker,
> "Shaker, you better pray,
> For if I miss that little piece of steel

Tomorrow'll be your buryin' day, O Lord,
Tomorrow'll be your buryin' day."[4]

The songs sung by these workers reflected the conditions under which they operated. The ubiquitous *John Henry* work songs often expressed the loneliness of the tunnel crews and their concern with what was happening to their wives and children from whom they were forced to be apart for prolonged periods:

I told Hattie,—huh,
To whip-a those children,—huh;
I told Hattie,—huh,
To whip-a those children,—huh;
I told Hattie,—huh,
To whip-a those children,—huh;
Make 'em mind,—huh.

'Cause the penitentiary,—huh,
Is full o' people,—huh;
'Cause the penitentiary,—huh,
Is full o' people,—huh;
'Cause the penitentiary,—huh,
Is full o' people,—huh;
Won't raised right,—huh.

I told Hattie,—huh,
To make her dress a little longer,—huh;
I told Hattie,—huh,
To make her dress a little longer,—huh;
I told Hattie,—huh,
To make her dress a little longer,—huh;
A-showin' of her laig,—huh.

Relief from oppressive working conditions and aching loneliness could be found in song—particularly bawdy, suggestive songs which often produced warm waves of convulsive laughter. Thus, as I indicated in Chapter 4, sexual innuendo and metaphor were constantly present in the songs of tunnel gangs, and *John Henry* was no exception. More than one version suggests that the steel-driver's demise resulted not from too much work but from too many women. At the beginning of his saga the young John Henry is frequently pictured contemplating his future profession in terms which could easily be references to the sexual organs of the adults in whose laps he sits:

When John Henry was a little boy,
Sitting on his papa's knee,

Looking down at a piece of steel,
Says "A steel-driving man I will be."

When John Henry was a little boy,
Sitting on his mama's knee,
Says, "Big Bend Tunnel on the C and O Road
Is going to be the death of me."

Sexual implications become clearer in stanzas describing John Henry as an adult:

He placed his drill on the top of a rock,
The steam drill standing close at hand.
He beat it down an inch and a half,
He laid down his hammer like a man,
He laid down his hammer like a man.

John Henry hammered in the mountains
Way in the north end of town.
The womans all laid their heads in the windows
When he laid his hammer down.

In versions of *John Henry* collected from young men in Philadelphia in the late 1950s and from Texas prisoners a few years later, the sexual content had become overt:

When John Henry was a baby,
You could hold him in the palm of your hand.
But when he got nineteen years old,
He could stand that pussy like a man.

Now when John Henry died
They say he died from shock.
But if you want to know the truth
He died from too much cock.
Yes the boy died from too much cock.[5]

Everybody in a-Houston, Texas,
Thought little John Henry was dead.
Well he was layin' at home with a big hard-on,
With his shirt-tail over his head, Lord, Lord,
With his shirt-tail over his head.[6]

Growing awareness of the sexual implications of the John Henry legend need not divert our attention from its other central meanings. No more than any other epic hero should John Henry be converted into a narrow one-dimensional figure whose significance has to be measured within the framework of any single interpretive device. Fundamental to

an understanding of John Henry's significance is the economic plight of
black workers who in the late nineteenth and early twentieth centuries
faced competition both from the millions of new European immigrants
and the growing mechanization symbolized in *John Henry* by the steam
drill, which was introduced into railroad construction after the Civil War.
The continued displacement of black workers and farmers by machines
throughout the twentieth century accounts in part for the continued popularity and relevance of the John Henry saga.

> Old John Henry
> Got to find a job,
> Old John Henry
> Got to find a job,
> Dat steam driller's here,
> Here a good man to rob.
>
> Lordy, Lord,
> Why did you send dat steam?
> Lordy, lord,
> Why did you send dat steam?
> It's caused de boss man to run me,
> Run me like a oxyen team. . . .
>
> Got a wife and a child
> Waiting for me at de fire.
> Got a wife and a child
> Waiting for me at de fire.
> If I don't work
> Ain't no way dey can smile.
>
> Tomorrow at sunrise
> I am goin' be a natural man.
> Tomorrow at sunrise
> I am goin' be a natural man.
> Goin' take dat hammer, drive dat
> Spike de fastest in de land.

This determination to be a "natural man," to stand up to the machine
and, by extension, to the dehumanizing modern civilization which created
it, accounts for the grandeur of John Henry, who was celebrated because
he refused to bow to the power of organized society:

> John Henry said to the captain,
> "A man ain't nothing but a man.
> And before I'll be governed by this old steam drill,
> Lawd, I'll die with the hammer in my hand,
> Lawd, I'll die with the hammer in my hand."

"It was de flesh ag'in' de steam," George White of the Sea Islands emphasized during his narrative version of *John Henry*. "De flesh ag'in' de steam." And the flesh, weak as it was, won:

> The man that invented that steam drill
> He thought he was mighty fine.
> John Henry sunk the steel fourteen feet
> While the steam drill only made nine, O Lord,
> While the steam drill only made nine.[7]

While in virtually every version John Henry dies of over-exertion, it is the glory of his victory not the tragedy of his demise that dominates the songs. In the fashion of so many legendary heroes, John Henry is occasionally pictured as having survived his own death and continues to inhabit Big Bend Tunnel and the surrounding mountains:

> Up on the mountain,
> Up on the mountain,
> Well, up on the mountain,
> Heard John Henry cryin'. . . .
> "An' I won't come down."[8]

More than any other figure in black folklore John Henry fits the description of the epic hero. He comes into the world fully conscious of his fate. He informs his parents of it while still very young and reiterates his prediction when full grown:

> "Oh, look away over yonder, captain,
> You can't see like me."
> He hollered out in a lonesome cry,
> "A hammer be the death of me."

From the beginning he was pictured as a man of uncommon powers. The force of his hammer made the mountain shake; the example of his skill filled others with awe:

> If I could hammer
> Like John Henry,
> If I could hammer
> Like John Henry,
> Lawd, I'd be a man,
> Lawd, I'd be a man.

An elderly Alabama steel-driver, F. P. Barker, and others like him who claimed to have known John Henry, perpetuated the stories of his prowess: "I could drive from both shoulders myself, and I was as far behind

John Henry as the moon is behind the sun. The world has not yet produced a man to whip steel like John Henry."[9] For all his skill and confidence, his knowledge of his own destiny produces momentary despair:

> John Henry went up on the mountain,
> He came down on the side;
> The rock was so tall, John Henry was so small,
> That he laid down his hammer and he cried, "Lawd, Lawd."

In the end, he does what he has to do and he dies enveloped in the same
morality and sense of purpose that characterize him throughout most of
the songs and tales:

> John Henry told the captain
> Just before he died,
> "Only one favor I ask of you:
> Take care of my wife and child
> Take care of my wife and child."

The contrast with the trickster hero could not be greater. Confronting
his adversary directly, John Henry is contemptuous of guile and indirection:

> John Henry told the people,
> "You know that I am a man.
> I can beat all the traps that have ever been made,
> Or I'll die with a hammer in my hand,
> Die with a hammer in my hand."

There was similar contrast with the bandit hero over whom John Henry's
superiority is clearly affirmed, as in this chant-fable from Rappahannock
County, Virginia:

> John Henry met Stackolee one time. Both of them were very good friends.
> Stackolee was goin' with John Henry's Old Lady. Jus' tryin' to cut in on
> John Henry. At that time they were down on the Mississippi River. Now
> John Henry met Stackolee down on the river. Stackolee was just a little
> short fellow. About so tall and John Henry was a great big man. Stacko-
> lee and John Henry got into a great big argument. John Henry started to
> hit Stackolee. Stackolee shot the ties off John Henry's shoes. He shot the
> buttons off his shirt. He shot the shirt off his collar. Then John Henry
> turned around and smack Stackolee right down in the river. Then he run
> way down the Mississippi River and smack Stackolee out again. Smacked
> him clean out the river. That's John Henry.[10]

Like the bad man, John Henry is a contest hero—he is placed in the
position of defeating rivals and does so, directly and publicly. But John

Henry is a much more fully developed hero figure than the bad man. In many ways he is a secular version of the Biblical heroes who were traditionally so important in black thought. He is bestowed with extraordinary powers, forced to undergo a superhuman test, is momentarily plagued by doubt, and then faces his ordeal and ultimate martyrdom stoically and with complete faith. Above all, he is a culture hero. The bad man's contests tend to be individual; they are *his*. While the folk may derive vicarious rewards from his direct, violent approach, they remain separated from his life, in which they are often his victims, and detached from his death which they greet with no particular dismay. John Henry's epic contest is never purely individual. He is a representative figure whose life and struggle are symbolic of the struggle of worker against machine, individual against society, the lowly against the powerful, black against white. His victory is shared and his demise is mourned. "Lord," his wife cries out when she learns of his fate, "there is one more good man done fell dead."

> John Henry was buried,
> He was buried with each hammer in his hand.
> It was written on his tomb just as solid as a doom,
> "Here lies our steel-driving man."

It is this representative quality that gives his struggle epic proportions and makes John Henry the most important folk hero in Afro-American lore.

Though the popularity and importance of John Henry were without parallel, he was not an aberration; there were analogous heroes celebrated by the black folk. The sinking of the *Titanic* in 1912 was used for a number of purposes in Negro thought as we have seen: to reaffirm the powers of the Almighty; to proclaim the futility of earthly grandeur and riches; to taunt the whites for excluding blacks from the vessel. In no instance was it used to greater advantage than as a setting for the legendary confrontation between a black worker and the white world.

There *was*, this myth insisted, a Negro aboard the *Titanic:* the lowly black stoker, Shine. It is Shine who emerges from the bowels of the vessel time after time to warn the captain that the water level below is rising dangerously, only to be told time after time to get his "black ass" below where it belongs. Finally perceiving the danger in spite of the captain's blindness, Shine jumps overboard, withstands a series of temptations and threats, and with superhuman skill swims to shore, the ship's only survivor. In its barest outlines the tale seems to have been anticipated by the quasi-minstrel song, *The Travelling Coon,* which I discussed in another context earlier in this chapter. In one of his many fantastic escapes from the police, the Travelling Coon hides out on the *Titanic*. When he spies the iceberg he jumps overboard and swims to shore:

> The people standin' aroun',
> Said that nigger was sure a fool,
> But when the Titanic ship went down,
> He was shootin' craps in Liverpool.[11]

The more complex and interesting story of Shine and the *Titanic* was first collected in songs and toasts in Louisiana and Mississippi in the 1930s and early 1940s, though there are indications that it is older than this. By the end of World War II it emerged as one of the three most popular Negro toasts throughout the South and North.[12]

The allegorical qualities of *Shine* are striking. Like John Henry, Shine is a representative figure. His very name has generic overtones stemming from the term "Shine" in black slang which was used to refer to a very dark-skinned person, as in "He's so black he shines!"[13] If Shine's name describes his racial attributes, his situation is symbolic of that of his people. Trapped in lowly service deep within the interior of a white vessel, he is the first to understand the imminent danger and tries to warn the captain who ignores him and places blind confidence in his machines, assuring Shine: "Shine, Shine, have no doubt. / I told you we got ninety-nine pumps to pump the water out." At first obeying the captain's orders to return to his post, Shine finally allows his common sense to overcome his faith in modern technology and tells the captain:

> Your words sound happy and your words sound true,
> But this is one time, Cap, your words won't do.
> I don't like chicken and I don't like ham—
> And I don't believe your pumps is worth a damn!

In a more recent version he counters the captain's assurances by exclaiming: "Your shittin' is good and your shittin' is fine, / But there's one time you white folks ain't gonna shit on Shine." Jumping overboard, Shine swims away with powerful strokes. The ship's plight now becomes apparent to the whites, who place several temptations in Shine's way. The captain cries out: "Shine, Shine, save poor me, / I'll give you more money than any black man see." But Shine understands the emptiness of material rewards in his present situation. "Money is good on land or sea," he taunts the captain. "Take off your shirt and swim like me." He is tempted by a "big fat banker" who offers him "a thousand shares of T and T," to which Shine casually replies: "More stocks on land than there is on sea." He tells a "big man" from Wall Street, "You don't like my color and you down on my race, / Get your ass overboard and give these sharks a chase." The women prove no more successful in tempting Shine. The captain's daughter, his wife, and in one instance "Jay Gould's millionary daughter" run up to the railing in various stages of undress, crying out: "Shine, Shine, save poor me. / Give you more pussy than any black man see." Shine responds: "Pussy on land, there's pussy on the sea, / But the pussy on land's the pussy for me." In one version he tells the captain's daughter: "One thing about you white folks I couldn't understand: / You all wouldn't offer me that pussy when we was all on land."

Abandoning the whites to their fate, Shine exhibits latent powers in the water which previously he was unable to use. He is stopped by a shark, who warns him: "Shine, Shine, can't you see. / When you jump in these waters you belongs to me." Shine replies: "I know you outswim the barracuda, outsmart every fish in the sea, / But you gotta be a stroking motherfucker to outswim me." Similarly threatened by a whale, Shine exclaims: "You swallowed old Jonah and spit him on dry land, / But you'll never swallow me 'cause I'm a hell of a man." In a final act of irreverence, Shine is on shore in the process of getting drunk when news arrives that the *Titanic* has sunk:

> When all them white folks went to heaven,
> Shine was in Sugar Ray's Bar drinking Seagrams Seven.

Shine, like John Henry, is an epic figure, a culture hero whose exploits are performed in the name of the entire race. He breaks all precedents and all stereotypes; he defies white society and its technology and he triumphs.

Such figures were not confined to the deeds of men like John Henry, who once may have lived but had quickly become legends, or men like Shine, who were wholly mythic. They were inspired, too, by the acts of a number of living figures, the most important of whom in the first half of the twentieth century were the first two modern black heavyweight boxing champions of the world: Jack Johnson and Joe Louis.

Standing on a street in Chapel Hill, North Carolina, in 1927, listening to a broadcast of the Dempsey-Sharkey fight, Guy Johnson heard a black man express his displeasure with Dempsey's performance: "If they'd put old Jack Johnson in there, he'd lay that Sharkey man out." At the end of the round he added: "I'll tell you another colored man would've made a real prize fighter—that's John Henry. Yessir, anybody that could handle a thirty-pound hammer like that man could would make a sure-'nough fighter."[14] This coupling of John Henry and Jack Johnson was not surprising. The two shared some obvious traits, the most important being that they were both representative figures. From the beginning, Jack Johnson's career was profoundly shaped by the fact that he was not merely a fighter but a symbol.[15]

Like a number of black heavyweights before him, Johnson had difficulty getting a championship fight. After two years of constant pressure, Johnson was able to force the champion, Tommy Burns, to recognize his clear superiority to any other challenger. The resulting match, which took place in Australia at the end of 1908, was a rout. Before the fight Burns had accused the challenger of being yellow. In the ring Johnson threw the accusation back at the champion, dropping his hands to his side and extending his chest and chin, inviting Burns to hit him and sneering: "Find that yellow streak . . . uncover it." When at the beginning of the twelfth round of the twenty-round fight a bookie called out: "Even money Burns is there at the finish!" Johnson yelled back: "A hundred to one he don't black my eye!" In the fourteenth round the officials stopped the fight, saving the badly hurt and defenseless champion from more punishment. Johnson had not just defeated Burns, he had toyed with him, humiliated him. It was not a fight, Jack London wrote in the *New York Herald*, it was an "Armenian massacre," a mismatch "between a pygmy and a colossus . . . a playful Ethiopian at loggerheads with a small white man . . . a grown man cuffing a naughty child . . . a dewdrop had more chance in hell than he [Burns] with the Giant Ethiopian." London inaugurated the call for Jim Jeffries, the former champion who had retired undefeated, to re-enter the ring and "remove the golden smile from Jack Johnson's face."

Only after more than a year had passed and Johnson had beaten a string of white challengers did Jeffries heed the call and emerge to represent, as he put it, "That portion of the white race that has been looking to me to defend its athletic superiority." Everywhere the white press hailed him as "the hope of the white race." One journal assured Jeffries that the moment he looked Johnson directly in the eye the fight would be over, since Jeffries had Runnymede and Agincourt behind him, while his black opponent had nothing but the jungle.[16] The *San Francisco Examiner* insisted that the "spirit of Caesar in Jeff ought to whip the Barbarian."[17] The *Chicago Defender* warned its black readers that Johnson would not be battling merely Jeffries but "Race Hatred," "Prejudice," and "Negro

Persecution." "He will have them all to beat," they asserted. "The future welfare of his people forms a part of the stake." Other Negro spokesmen echoed this message. In a widely read sermon, the Reverend Reverdy Ransom predicted that black musicians, poets, artists, scholars would "keep the white race busy for the next few hundred years . . . in defending the interests of white supremacy. . . . What Jack Johnson seeks to do to Jeffries in the roped arena will be more the ambition of Negroes in every domain of human endeavor."[18] Johnson, who was not prone to see himself as a representative of any larger cause, was inevitably affected by the clamor. In his autobiography he wrote that he had not looked upon his defeat of Burns as a "racial triumph," but by the Jeffries fight he realized that not just the championship was at stake: "it was my own honor, and in a degree the honor of my race."

Johnson upheld both with superb skill, defeating Jeffries on July 4, 1910, as easily as he had Burns. "Hardly had a blow been struck when I knew that I was Jeff's master," Johnson later wrote. "Come on now, Mr. Jeff," he called out as they faced each other in the ring. "Let me see what you got. *Do* something, man. This is for the cham*peenship*." Not content with humiliating one former white champion, he shouted over to another ex-champion, Jim Corbett, who sat in Jeffries' corner: "Watch this one, Jim. . . . How did you like that?" He invited Corbett to come into the ring and promised to take him on too. Hitting Jeffries almost at will, he boasted: "I can go on like this all afternoon, Mr. Jeff." Jeffries, however, could not. Once the pattern of the fight became set, there were shouts from the largely white crowd: "Stop it! Stop it! Don't let him be knocked out!" It was not the referee but Johnson who ended the fight in the fifteenth round, knocking Jeffries half out of the ring in the process. "That Mr. Johnson should so lightly and carelessly punch the head off Mr. Jeffries," the *New York World* observed, "must have come as a shock to every devoted believer in the supremacy of the Anglo-Saxon race."[19]

The shock had its reverberations. On the day of Johnson's victory, Louis Armstrong, then just ten years old, was walking through the streets of New Orleans on his way to collect the newspapers for his delivery route. On Canal Street he met a group of black youngsters running toward him. "You better get started, black boy," one of them shouted at Armstrong. "Jack Johnson has just knocked out Jim Jeffries. The white boys are sore about it and they're going to take it out on us." The young Armstrong heeded the advice and ran home.[20] Many other Negroes were less fortunate or less cautious. Throughout the afternoon and evening deaths and injuries from racial conflict were reported in every state in the South as well as in New York, Massachusetts, Ohio, Missouri, Oklahoma, Colorado, and Washington, D.C.[21] The very extent of white anger and frustration made Johnson's victory sweeter. In Brooklyn a fight began when a black man, Edward Coleman, called to a dog, "Lie down there, Jeffries." He was immediately confronted by three whites who demanded: "Why don't you call it Johnson?" "Because," Coleman replied, "Johnson is black and this dog is yellow."[22] In Monroe, North Carolina, a blind black man walked down the street singing:

Jack Johnson be de champion of de worl',
Jack Johnson be de champion of de worl',
Jack Johnson be de champion, Jack Johnson be de champion,
Jack Johnson be de champion of de worl'.

Other North Carolina Negroes sang:

Amaze an' Grace, how sweet it sounds,
Jack Johnson knocked Jim Jeffries down.
Jim Jeffries jumped up an' hit Jack on the chin,
An' then Jack knocked him down agin.

The Yankees hold the play,
The white man pulls the trigger;
But it make no difference what the white man say,
The world champion's still a nigger.[23]

It was not Johnson's physical prowess alone that infuriated whites; it was his entire life style: his fast cars, fancy clothes, ready tongue, white wife (the first of three white women he married), and white mistresses. Johnson ruptured role after role set aside for Negroes in American society, and, despite the criminal charges which forced him into exile from his own country for seven years, he made the whites accept it. Long after Jess Willard took Johnson's championship away by knocking him out in the twenty-sixth round of their 1915 fight in Cuba, stories of his physical strength, his great speed, his habit of publicly predicting with some precision the outcomes of his fights, and above all his ability to humble his white opponents and thwart American society still circulated in the black community. When Johnson and Tommy Burns met in the center of the ring just before their championship fight in 1908, a favorite Negro anecdote asserted, the white champion warned: "Boy, I'm gonna whip you good. I was *born* with boxing gloves on." Johnson replied with a grin: "I have news for you, white man. You're about to die the same way!"[24] Half a century after Johnson first entered the consciousness of black America by wresting the championship from Burns, William Wiggins was told the following story by his father:

> It was on a hot day in Georgia when Jack Johnson drove into town. He was really flying: Zoooom! Behind his fine car was a cloud of red Georgia dust as far as the eye could see. The sheriff flagged him down and said, "Where do you think you're going, boy, speeding like that? That'll cost you $50.00!" Jack Johnson never looked up; he just reached in his pocket and handed the sheriff a $100.00 bill and started to gun the motor: ruuummm, ruuummm. Just before Jack pulled off the sheriff shouted, "Don't you want your change?" And Jack replied, "Keep it, 'cause I'm coming back the same way I'm going!" Zooooooom.[25]

Twenty-two years were to pass between Johnson's loss of the heavyweight crown to Willard and Joe Louis' victory over James J. Braddock on June 22, 1937, to become the second Negro heavyweight champion of the world. Louis' remark that he was pleased he was able to knock Braddock out cleanly and quickly since "Braddock was one of the gamest men I ever fought. I didn't want to hurt him any more than I had to," is a good indication of the differences between the new champion and his black predecessor. Johnson was a manipulator of words, a master of the verbal assault; Louis was quiet, in public almost inarticulate, a man who could say with little exaggeration: "I always believed in letting my fists talk for me."[26] Johnson lived a public life, defying the larger society at almost every turn. Louis lived a relatively private, controlled life, speaking continually of how much he owed his mother, his friends, his country; emerging as the epitome of decency and respectability. Yet this paragon must take his place in the pantheon of folk heroes alongside other "hard" men because, however quietly and with whatever degree of humility he did it, Joe Louis, like Jack Johnson before him, stood as a black man in the midst of a white society and beat representatives of the dominant group to their knees. In this sense no degree of respectability could prevent Louis from becoming a breaker of stereotypes and a destroyer of norms. He literally did allow his fists to talk for him, and they spoke so eloquently that no other contemporary member of the group was celebrated more fully and identified with more intensely by the black folk.

In our own day when heavyweight boxing, along with many other sports, is dominated by Negro athletes, it requires an act of historical empathy to comprehend fully the importance of Louis' career and image. A year before he defeated Braddock for the championship, Louis was knocked out in twelve rounds by the German fighter and ex-champion Max Schmeling. While Louis was losing in Yankee Stadium, Lena Horne was singing with Noble Sissle's black band in Cincinnati's Moonlight Gardens. "Until that night," she has written, "I had no idea of the strength of my identification with Joe Louis."

> We had the radio on behind the bandstand and during the breaks we crowded around it to hear the fight. I was near hysteria toward the end of the fight when he was being so badly beaten and some of the men in the band were crying. . . . Joe was the one invincible Negro, the one who stood up to the white man and beat him down with his fists. He in a sense carried so many of our hopes, maybe even dreams of vengeance. But this night he was just another Negro getting beaten by a white man, . . . My mother was furious with me for getting hysterical. "How dare you?" she screamed. "You have a performance. The show must go on. Why, you don't even know this man."
> "I don't care, I don't care," I yelled back. "He belongs to us."[27]

Five years later, on June 18, 1941, Louis almost lost his championship to Billy Conn, whom he finally knocked out in the thirteenth round. According to Roi Ottley, during the first twelve rounds, when it looked as if Louis would lose, Negroes in Harlem listening to the fight broadcast were anxious and extremely tense. "As the fight progressed, there were ominous grumblings, with some near hysteria. The cheers of fifty-five thousand white people in the Polo Grounds, which echoed down the streets of Harlem, heightened the distress." Evidently the reaction was similar in other cities, for the next day the editor of the black *Pittsburgh Courier* felt it necessary to brace his readers for the inevitable:

> Can Negro America "take it"? Frankly I don't believe they can. And if they can't take it, I'm preparing them right now for something—which might happen at any time. . . .
> We've built out of the mists a "superfighter"—a man who just can't be beaten. We've been selfish in the perpetuation of an ideal which few of us would be willing to live up to. . . .
> If—and when—he loses, Joe will take his defeat in his stride!
> So will we!
> And so must you![28]

For the most part, of course, Louis' career before he joined the army in World War II created jubilation, not distress. His victories were occasions for street celebrations, with tens of thousands of black residents of northern cities parading, singing, dancing, deriving all the joy possible from this collective victory of the race. A quarter of a century after Louis' defeat of Braddock for the championship, Malcolm X still recalled the reaction of blacks in Lansing, Michigan: "all the Negroes in Lansing, like Negroes everywhere, went wildly happy with the greatest celebration of race pride our generation had ever known."[29]

In small southern towns the celebrations were more subdued but no less important. Maya Angelou has described the scene in her grandmother's general store on the night of a Louis fight. The black farmers and workers in and around Stamps, Arkansas, would gather to listen to the fight on the store's radio. The adults filled the rows of chairs, stools, and upturned wooden boxes that had been set up for the occasion, and stood tightly packed against the walls of the store; the children overflowed onto the porch. The air was alive with hopeful predictions: "I ain't worried 'bout this fight. Joe's gonna whip that cracker like it's open season." "He gonna whip him till that white boy call him Momma." When the white fighter sought relief from Louis' massive attack by forcing himself into a clinch, the auditors' joy was punctuated by biting humor: "That white man don't mind hugging that niggah now, I betcha." When Louis' opponent rallied, forced the Brown Bomber against the ropes, and seemed on the verge of victory, all noise and movement in the little store stopped. It wasn't just one black man in trouble, Angelou recalled in a passage that captures the symbolic importance of the event, "It was our people falling. It was another lynching, yet another Black man hanging on a tree. One more woman ambushed and raped. A Black boy whipped and maimed. It was hounds on the trail of a man running through slimy swamps. It was a white woman slapping her maid for being forgetful. . . . We didn't breathe. We didn't hope. We waited." And when the waiting was rewarded by the increasingly familiar announcement: "The winnah, and still heavyweight champeen of the world . . . Joe Louis," there was quiet jubilation:

> Then even the old Christian ladies who taught their children and tried themselves to practice turning the other cheek would buy soft drinks, and if the Brown Bomber's victory was a particularly bloody one they would order peanut patties and Baby Ruths also. . . .
>
> Champion of the world. A Black boy. Some Black mother's son. He was the strongest man in the world. People drank Coca-Colas like ambrosia and ate candy bars like Christmas. Some of the men went behind the Store and poured white lightning in their soft-drink bottles, and a few of the bigger boys followed them. . . .
>
> It would take an hour or more before the people would leave the Store and head for home. Those who lived too far had made arrangements to

stay in town. It wouldn't do for a Black man and his family to be caught on a lonely country road on a night when Joe Louis had proved that we were the strongest people in the world.[30]

Figures like Joe Louis were so important because they were never perceived as isolated men but rather as an integral part of the entire network of black culture. Claude Brown has described a dialogue in which he participated on a Harlem streetcorner in 1951:

> I remember getting high on the corner with a bunch of guys and watching the chicks go by, fine little girls, and saying, "Man, colored people must be somethin' else!"
> Somebody'd say, "Yeah. How about that? All those years, man, we was down on the plantation in those shacks, eating just potatoes and fatback and chitterlin's and greens, and look at what happened. We had Joe Louises and Jack Johnsons and Sugar Ray Robinsons and Henry Armstrongs, all that sort of thing."
> Somebody'd say, "Yeah, man. Niggers must be some real strong people who just can't be kept down. When you think about it, that's really something great. Fatback, chitterlin's, greens, and Joe Louis. Negroes are some beautiful people. Uh-huh. Fatback, chitterlin's, greens, and Joe Louis . . . and beautiful black bitches."[31]

Because he was enshrined as a culture hero, everything Joe Louis did was seen in symbolic terms. His 1935 knock-out of the Italian heavyweight Primo Carnera was more than a victory over Carnera, it was a triumph over the Italian oppressor whose invasion and bombing of Ethiopia had stirred deep anger throughout black America. His first round knock-out of Max Schmeling in their second fight was interpreted as a blow against Nazi racial theories. And the meaning of every victory over every white opponent was obvious. Negro children on 135th Street and Lenox Avenue in Harlem sang, after Louis' defeat of Bob Pastor in 1939:

Bob Pastor was on his knees
Said, "Joe,
Don't hit me please,
Just go trucking out of the ring."

On West 63rd Street black children bounced their balls and jumped rope while celebrating another Louis victory:

I went down town last Tuesday night
To see Joe Louis and Max Baer fight.
When Joe Louis socked, Max Baer rocked.
Dream of a viper,

Yeah man, Tee man,
Dream of a viper.[32]

As they unloaded ships on the wharves of Fernandina, Florida, black dock workers rehearsed Louis' triumph over the white heavyweight champion over and over:

Joe Louis hit him so hard he turn roun and roun,
He thought he was Alabama bound. Ah, Ah,
He made an effort to rise agin,
But Joe Louis' right cut him on the chin, Ah, Ah,
Weak on his knees and tried to rise,
Went down crying to the crowd's surprise, Ah, Ah.[33]

On record after record, blues singers helped their audiences relive Louis' triumphs over his white opponents. Following Louis' defeat of Carnera, Joe Pullum of Houston, Texas, celebrated Louis' stature as a boxer and a man:

Joe Louis is a battlin' man,
The people think his fame will always stand.
He's the brown bomber of this land,
He's supposed to whop 'most any man. . . .
I said Joe is the battlin' man,
Bought his mother a brand new home and some brand new land.
You can gather his intentions must be good,
'Cause he's doing the things for his mother a boy really should.
He's makin' real good money and it doesn't swell his head,
He throws his fist like a 45 throwin' lead.
He throws them heavy and he throws them slow,
Then you know it's powerful Joe,
And boy if he hits you, you sure bound to hit the floor.

The image of white fighters on their knees before the black champion was a recurring one:

I came all the way from Chicago to see Joe Louis and Max Schmeling fight, (2)
Schmeling went down like the *Titanic* when Joe gave him just one hard right. . . .

It was only two minutes and four seconds poor Schmeling was down on his knees, (2)
He looked like he was praying to the Good Lord to have "Mercy on me please."[34]

Trickster figures operated from within black society. They might have made forays into the white world to win victories and score points but ultimately their only safety was in retreat. The Signifying Monkey might humble the Lion but only from the security of his tree top. When he met Lion on the latter's ground he was destroyed. Black bandits, too, operated almost solely within their own territory. They broke restrictions and stereotypes but although they did battle with the impersonal forces of white law, their major contests were generally with other blacks. John Henry and Shine, Jack Johnson and Joe Louis were major departures. They could stand within the very center of white society, and they could stand there as black men operating victoriously on their own terms.

In their study of black Chicago, Drake and Cayton have shown that "Beating the white man at his own game" was often a powerful motivation for achievement among Negroes in the period between the first and second world wars.[35] This was what the moral hard men did particularly well, and they made it possible for others to dream of doing it also. In a reminiscence of Joe Louis' impact, which certainly can be projected beyond the black community in Lansing, Michigan, Malcolm X recalled that "Every Negro boy old enough to walk wanted to be the next Brown Bomber." This included Malcolm's brother Philbert and ultimately Malcolm himself. In 1938 the example of Joe Louis propelled the thirteen-year-old Malcolm into the ring for his first amateur fight against a white boy named Bill Peterson, who defeated him decisively. "He did such a job on my reputation in the Negro neighborhood that I practically went into hiding. A Negro just can't be whipped by somebody white and return with his head up to the neighborhood, especially in those days, when sports and, to a lesser extent show business, were the only fields open to Negroes, and when the ring was the only place a Negro could whip a white man and not be lynched."[36] For the young Malcolm X and his peers the career of Joe Louis was a testament to the fact that defeat at the hands of the white man was no longer to be taken for granted. Similarly, black workers saw in the death of John Henry not a defeat but a challenge:

This old hammer
Killed John Henry,
Can't kill me, Lord,
Can't kill me.

The changes taking place in black folklore, then, were occurring in black life as well, for the symbolic figures I have been discussing reflected rather than created the mood of increasing numbers of Negro Americans.

These changes were evident in many areas of Negro life. The changing pattern of race riots in America is a particularly good example. What were referred to as race riots in the last half of the nineteenth century and the early years of the twentieth would be more accurately described as pogroms. Whites attacked, murdered, and pillaged blacks. Of course there were important exceptions, such as the Atlanta riot of 1906, but it was not until the twenty-five riots of 1919 that a new pattern of reaction to white violence was definitely established. During the Washington, D.C., riot in July 1919, for instance, the local black community exhibited a major commitment to challenge the assumption of their own subordination. Washington Negroes armed themselves, the NAACP helped to defend them, and many black papers urged them to fight back. "As the police have failed to protect the Negroes of the capital," the *New York Commoner* wrote, "there is but one course open. Let every Negro arm himself and swear to die fighting in defense of his home, his rights and his person." The *Pittsburgh Courier* asserted that Negroes had learned that "a bullet in Washington has no more terrors than . . . in the Argonne." James Weldon Johnson, who visited Washington during the riot, expected to find his people "excited and perhaps panicky." Instead he found them "calm and determined, unterrified and unafraid. . . . they had reached the determination that they would defend and protect themselves and their homes at the cost of their lives, if necessary and that determination rendered them calm." The same reaction occurred in city after city and was defended not only by civil rights leaders and the Negro press but by many black church and fraternal leaders. One Negro bishop urged his people to "protect their homes at any cost," while another counseled that they should first practice the Christian virtues. If these failed then the black man should do "what self respecting people should do—namely use his gun with effect and impose respect." In California a Negro Masonic leader concluded that the battlefield had shifted from Europe to America: "If the Negro could afford to . . . die . . . to liberate the serfs of Europe . . . can he afford to do less to protect his own home and loved ones from the insults and rages of the brute force of the degenerates of America." In the Harlem riot of 1935, the Detroit and Harlem riots of 1943, and the riots of the 1960s, black action took still another turn and shifted from defense to offense, from reaction to instigation.[37]

It is evident that the folk heroes of black Americans were not merely mechanisms of escape or fantasies that brought relief from a difficult world. They were also mirrors of reality. They paralleled and reflected the changing situation of Negro Americans in the century after emancipation: their ability to publicly express attitudes which for too long had been bottled up within the individual or the group, their lessened faith in orderly progress through the American system, and their heightened dependence upon themselves and their people. The situation still necessitated surreptitiousness, guile, and the skills of the trickster and these abilities continued to be cultivated. But the ambivalence that had always surrounded them was increasingly evident, and criticism of such tactics and the limited goals they pursued grew throughout the years of freedom. New heroes took their place alongside the trickster: slave ancestors who had dared defy the system in defense of their dignity, their rights, their family and friends; exaggerated heroes who symbolized a growing belief in the ability of the individual to cope with the exigencies that faced him; bad men and bandits who could act out the fury and anger felt by so many; moral hard men who broke the molds that Negroes were supposed to conform to and created new roles and new possibilities. In the twentieth century the pantheon of heroes became more varied and versatile, reflecting the greater diversity and heterogeneity that were the fruits of freedom, mobility, and urbanization. The cultural containment that had characterized slaves was forever eradicated, and yet the imperatives of American racism continually reminded black Americans that despite the new social, economic, and cultural diversity that marked them they were bound together by a common identity and a shared heritage. John Henry, Shine, Jack Johnson, and Joe Louis were important folk figures because they signified the growing Negro insistence, borne of black culture and white oppression, that they be accepted in American society not merely as Americans but as black Americans, not merely as individuals but as a people.

EPILOGUE

We are practical beings, each of us with limited functions and duties to perform. Each is bound to feel intensely the importance of his own duties and the significance of the situations that call these forth. But this feeling is in each of us a vital secret, for sympathy with which we vainly look to others. The others are too much absorbed in their own vital secrets to take an interest in ours. Hence the stupidity and injustice of our opinions, so far as they deal with the significance of alien lives. Hence the falsity of our judgments, so far as they presume to decide in an absolute way on the value of other persons' conditions or ideals.

William James, "On A Certain
Blindness in Human Beings"[1]

These thoughts of William James' were stirred by Robert Louis Stevenson's essay, "The Lantern-Bearers," in which Stevenson described how he and his schoolmates used to place a bulls-eye lantern under their coats, its presence unknown to all but one other. Thus equipped, each boy would walk through the night "a mere pillar of darkness" to ordinary eyes, but each exulting in the knowledge that he had a hidden lantern shining at his belt. For Stevenson, as for James after him, this scene of boyhood bliss became a paradigm for the human condition. A good part of reality, Stevenson asserted, "runs underground. The observer (poor soul, with his documents!) is all abroad. For to look at the man is but to court deception. . . . To one who has not the secret of the lanterns, the scene upon the links is meaningless. And hence the haunting and truly spectral unreality of realistic books."[2]

This "secret of the lanterns" remains to plague those who would comprehend the history of the human condition. Stevenson's anecdote has its parallels in the American past. The black folk are only one of the groups of people who have walked through American history with their cultural lanterns obscured from the unknowing and unseeing eyes of outside observers. Abram Kardiner and Lionel Ovesey wrote in 1951 that at the time of emancipation the freedman "had no culture, and he was quite green in his semi-acculturated state in the new one. He did not know his way about and had no intrapsychic defenses—no pride, no group solidarity, no tradition. This was enough to cause panic. The marks of his previous status were still upon him—socially, psychologically, and emotionally. And from these he has never since freed himself."[3] Similarly, in 1962 another social scientist, in explaining why Negroes were still only in the process of becoming an ethnic group, characterized the freedmen as "a collection of unrelated individuals . . . without the community of tradition, sentiment, and so forth, that has marked other populations and given rise to ethnic groups such as the Italian immigrants."[4]

The assumption that the African slaves had been wholly denuded of their traditional culture and emerged from bondage in an almost cultureless state, led to the easy conclusion that during the century of freedom the Negro had become what Horace Mann Bond called a "quintessential American" and what Gunnar Myrdal and his associates termed an "exaggerated American." Examining Negro life in the United States, Myrdal found it characterized not by any degree of cultural distinctiveness, but by unhealthy deviance. "The instability of the Negro family, . . . the emotionalism in the Negro church, the insufficiency and unwholesomeness of Negro recreational activity, the plethora of Negro sociable organizations, the narrowness of interests of the average Negro, the provincialism of his political speculation, the high Negro crime rate, the cultivation of the arts to the neglect of other fields, superstition, personality difficulties"— all of these "characteristic traits" converged to create Myrdal's italicized assertion: "*In practically all its divergences, American Negro culture is not something independent of general American culture. It is a distorted development, or a pathological condition, of the general American culture.*"[5]

Myrdal's conclusion embodied the attitudes that have tended to dominate the work of social scientists. E. Franklin Frazier summed up much of his research by concluding in 1957 that "unlike any other racial or cultural minority, the Negro is not distinguished by culture from the dominant group. Having completely lost his ancestral culture, he speaks the same language, practices the same religion, and accepts the same values and political ideals as the dominant group."[6] "The key to much in the Negro world," Nathan Glazer and Daniel Moynihan maintained in their 1963 study of ethnic groups in New York City, is that "the Negro is only an American, and nothing else. He has no values and culture to guard and protect."[7] As late as 1970, someone as conversant with Afro-American culture as Roger Abrahams could question whether Negroes should be considered a minority group in the sense that Jewish, Italian, and Mexican-Americans were. While these latter groups had a sense of identity apart from that of the dominant culture, and felt their cultural distinctiveness threatened by the possibility of acculturation into the American mainstream, black Americans "in accepting the white stereotype and the American dream, commonly see themselves as outsiders waiting to get in."[8] Even more recently, Stanford Lyman, in his assessment of the sociological treatment of American blacks, compared Negroes to people living in a wilderness from which there were no roads going either forward or backward: "The black has been deprived of his history, and with this deprivation not only the past but also the future is wiped out: He has neither known predecessors to provide tradition nor unambiguously defined successors to instill promise. . . . Such is the conscious world of the Negro."[9]

It is obvious that what James referred to as the "vital secret" is no easier to penetrate in our day than it was in his. We have discovered no formula for uncovering "the personal poetry, the enchanted atmosphere, the rainbow work of fancy" that Stevenson insisted lay hidden within every human being. But to say that there is no easy access to the inner core of a person or a people, is not to say there is no access at all. "In all the books that you have studied you never have studied Negro history have you?" an ex-slave asked an interviewer from Fisk University. "If you want Negro history," he insisted, "you will have to get [it] from somebody who wore the shoe, and by and by from one to the other you will get a book."[10] Of course many different kinds of black people "wore the shoe" during and after slavery and no one body of sources could speak for them all. Nevertheless, the materials of Afro-American oral expressive culture give voice to that very large segment of the black community about whom we have known the least.[11] Careful study of oral culture reveals the multi-dimensioned complexity of the black American past and helps us to progress beyond a number of assumptions that have been accepted uncritically for too long: that African culture disappeared quickly and almost completely under the rigors of North American slavery and in the face of the yawning and unbridgeable gulf between African and European culture; that most manifestations of Negro American culture were taken over wholesale from the whites; that black Americans had little sense of group cohesion, group pride, or group history, and few if any group models for their young to pattern themselves upon; that blacks yearned hungrily and unhesitatingly to adopt the culture of the majority and that their acculturation, while gradual, was taking place progressively and irreversibly. Black folk thought suggests a series of quite divergent pictures.

From the first African captives, through the years of slavery, and into the present century black Americans kept alive important strands of African consciousness and verbal art in their humor, songs, dance, speech, tales, games, folk beliefs, and aphorisms. They were able to do this because these areas of culture are often the most persistent, because whites tended not to interfere with many of these culture patterns which quickly became associated in the white mind with Negro inferiority or at least peculiar Negro racial traits, and because in a number of areas there were important cultural parallels and thus wide room for syncretism between Africans and Europeans.

Cultural diffusion between whites and blacks was by no means a one-way street with blacks the invariable beneficiaries. Afro-American impact upon wide areas of American expressive culture has become increasingly obvious, though it has not yet been adequately assessed.

Black relationship to the larger culture was complex and multi-dimensional. Again and again oral expressive culture reveals a pattern of simultaneous acculturation and revitalization; a pattern which suggests that the old notions of acculturation may need further modification. Blacks shared with a number of other ethnic minorities a deep ambivalence concerning the degree to which they desired to enter the mainstream of white American culture because they shared with these other groups a strong centripetal urge which continually drew them back to central aspects of their traditions even as they were surging outward into the larger society. It was precisely because periods of increased opportunity and mobility posed the greatest threats to whole layers of black cultural tradition that such periods often witnessed important manifestations of cultural revitalization. The black experience may well help us to further re-evaluate the entire image and theory of the melting pot. It may help us to understand the process by which many different groups in the United States have managed to maintain a remarkably independent though only partially separate existence.

Black verbal art makes it clear that a people is, in Ralph Ellison's phrase, "more than the sum of its brutalization."[12] "We had joys back there in St. Louis," Dick Gregory remembered in his account of his poverty-stricken youth, "joys that made us want to live just as surely as the pains taught us how to live."[13] The historical use of folklore helps us to recapture the joys as well as the pains, to gain some sense of a people's angle of vision and world view, to better understand the inner dynamics of the group and the attitudes its members had toward each other as well as toward the outside world, to comprehend the mechanisms members of the group erected to guard their values, maintain their sense of worth, and retain their sanity. It allows us, finally, to respond to Ralph Ellison's eloquent and urgent challenge: "Everybody wants to tell us what a Negro is. . . . But if you would tell me who I am, at least take the trouble to discover what I have been."[14]

NOTES

CHAPTER 1: THE SACRED WORLD OF BLACK SLAVES

EPIGRAPH

1. Mary A. Livermore, *The Story of My Life* (Hartford, Conn., 1897), 306-7.

INTRODUCTION

1. Robert E. Park, "The Conflict and Fusion of Cultures with Special Reference to the Negro," JNH, 4 (1919), 116-18.

2. Robert Redfield, *The Primitive World and Its Transformations* (Ithaca, 1953), 51-53. Richard Hoggart has illustrated this same point with reference to the British and Italian working classes in *The Uses of Literacy* (Harmondsworth, 1958), 104-5.
3. VèVè Clark, public lecture, Berkeley, Calif., fall 1973.

THE CONTOURS OF SLAVE SONG

1. Thomas Jefferson, *Notes on the State of Virginia*, William Peden, ed. (Chapel Hill, 1955), 140; Frederick Law Olmsted, *A Journey in the Back Country* (New York, 1863), 146; "Songs of the Blacks," *Dwight's Journal of Music*, 9 (1856), 51-52; Fisk University, *Unwritten History of Slavery: Autobiographical Accounts of Negro Ex-Slaves*, Ophelia Settle Egypt, J. Masuoka, and Charles S. Johnson, eds. (Nashville, 1945, unpublished typescript), 320.
2. Alan Lomax, "Folk Song Style," *American Anthropologist*, 61 (1959), 930.
3. Songs containing African words and phrases can be found in Nicholas Joseph Hutchinson Smith, "Six New Negro Folk-Songs with Music," *PTFS*, 7 (1928), 117; *Tennessee Folklore Society Bulletin*, 15 (1949), 17; Dorothy Scarborough, *On the Trail of Negro Folk-Songs* (Cambridge, Mass., 1925), 19; WPA, Savannah Unit, Georgia Writers' Project, *Drums and Shadows: Survival Studies Among the Georgia Coastal Negroes* (Athens, Ga., 1940), 54-55; Lydia Parrish, *Slave Songs of the Georgia Sea Islands* (1942; reprint ed., Hatboro, Pa., 1965), 45-53.
4. Fisk University, *Unwritten History*, 140.
5. J. K[innard], Jr., "Who Are Our National Poets?" *Knickerbocker Magazine*, 26 (1845), 338.
6. WPA Slave Narratives, microfilm ed. (Va.).
7. William Bosman, *A New and Accurate Description of the Coast of Guinea* (1704; reprint ed., New York, 1967), 158.
8. R. S. Rattray, *Ashanti* (London, 1923), Chap. 15; R. S. Rattray, *Akan-Ashanti Folk-Tales* (Oxford, 1930), xi-xii.
9. Melville J. and Frances S. Herskovits, *Dahomean Narrative* (Evanston, 1958), 61-62; Melville J. Herskovits, "Freudian Mechanisms in Primitive Negro Psychology," in Melville J. Herskovits, *The New World Negro* (Bloomington, 1966), 138-39.
10. Rattray, *Ashanti*, 153.
11. Alan P. Merriam, "Music and the Dance," in Robert Lystad, ed., *The African World: A Survey of Social Research* (New York, 1965), 452-68; William R. Bascom, "Folklore and Literature," *ibid.*, 469-88; Alan P. Merriam, "African Music," in William R. Bascom and Melville J. Herskovits, eds., *Continuity and Change in African Cultures* (Chicago, 1959), 49-86; Hugh Tracey, *Chopi Musicians* (London, 1948), Chaps. 1-2; Ruth Finnegan, *Oral Literature in Africa* (Oxford, 1970), Chap. 10.
12. WPA, *Drums and Shadows*, 154.
13. This song first appeared in "An Editorial Voyage to Edisto Island," in the Charleston magazine *Chicora*, 1 (1842), 47, 63, and was reprinted in Jay B. Hubbell, "Negro Boatmen's Songs," *SFQ*, 18 (1954), 244-45.
14. Solomon Northup, *Twelve Years a Slave* (1854; reprint ed., New York, 1970), 220.
15. Frances Anne Kemble, *Journal of a Residence on a Georgian Plantation in 1838-1839* (1863; Knopf reprint ed., New York, 1961), 163-64.

16. Chadwick Hansen, "Jenny's Toe: Negro Shaking Dances in America," *American Quarterly*, 19 (1967), 554-63.
17. Butler H. Waugh, "Negro Tales of John Kendry from Indianapolis," *MF*, 8 (1958), 132.
18. Caroline Howard Gilman, *Recollections of a Southern Matron* (1838; 2nd ed., New York, 1852), 76-77.
19. *The Journal of Nicholas Cresswell, 1774-1777* (London, 1925), 18-19.
20. Linda Brent [Harriet Brent Jacobs], *Incidents in the Life of a Slave Girl* (1861; reprint ed., New York, 1973), 122.
21. *Life and Times of Frederick Douglass* (revised ed., 1892; Collier reprint ed., New York, 1962), 146-47.
22. Dougald MacMillan, "John Kuners," *JAF*, 39 (1926), 53-57. The event was also celebrated in such other eastern North Carolina towns as Edenton, New Bern, Hillsboro, Hilton, Fayetteville, and Southport. See Ira de A. Reid, "The John Canoe Festival," *Phylon*, 3 (1942), 349-70.
23. WPA Slave Narratives (Ark.). The history of this song after emancipation is discussed below in Chap. 4.
24. John Lambert, *Travels Through Canada, and the United States of North America, in the Years 1806, 1807, & 1808* (3rd ed., London, 1816), II, 254.
25. *America of the Fifties: Letters of Fredrika Bremer*, Adolph B. Benson, ed. (New York, 1924), 262.
26. *SW*, 24 (1895), 31; WPA Slave Narratives, interviews with John C. Becton (N.C.), Ferebe Rogers and Callie Elder (Ga.).
27. Northup, *Twelve Years a Slave*, 322.
28. John Dixon Long, *Pictures of Slavery in Church and State* (1857; reprint ed., New York, 1969), 198.
29. William Cullen Bryant, "A Tour in the Old South," *Prose of William Cullen Bryant*, Parke Godwin, ed. (New York, 1884), VI, 32.
30. WPA Slave Narratives, (Ala.).
31. In an earlier article on slave songs (Lawrence W. Levine, "Slave Songs and Slave Consciousness," in Tamara Hareven, ed., *Anonymous Americans*, Englewood Cliffs, N.J., 1971, 99-130), I concluded that "our total stock of these [secular] songs is very small." Subsequent research convinces me that there is an abundant store of such songs in the sources mentioned above. This substantial number can be further expanded by following Constance Rourke's suggestion that we attempt to disentangle elements of Negro origin from those of white creation in the "Ethiopian melodies" of the white minstrel shows of the antebellum period. Rourke, *The Roots of American Culture and Other Essays* (New York, 1942), 262-74. This task is complicated by the probability that, as Newman White has argued, many minstrel songs were created by whites and that these songs made their way back to the plantations where they were integrated into the slaves' repertory. White, *American Negro Folk-Songs* (1928; reprint ed., Hatboro, Pa., 1965), 7-10 and Appendix IV. A similarly complex relationship between genuine Negro folk songs and their more commercialized versions was to take place in the twentieth century and will be discussed in subsequent chapters. Robert Toll, *Blacking Up: The Minstrel Show in Nineteenth-Century America* (New York, 1974), Chap. 2, contains a fine discussion of the relationship of minstrelsy to black song.
32. WPA, Workers of the Writers' Program in the State of Virginia, *The Negro in Virginia* (New York, 1940), 88.

33. Gene Bluestein, "America's Folk Instrument: Notes on the Five-String Banjo," *WF*, 23 (1964), 241-48; David Evans, "Afro-American One-Stringed Instruments," *WF*, 29 (1970), 229-45; Russell Roth, "On the Instrumental Origins of Jazz," *American Quarterly*, 4 (1952), 305-16.
34. WPA, *Negro in Virginia*, 35.
35. Northup, *Twelve Years a Slave*, 217.
36. John Bernard, *Retrospections of America, 1797-1811* (New York, 1887), 206.
37. WPA manuscripts, Florida File, Archive of Folk Song, Library of Congress.
38. Melville J. Herskovits, *The Myth of the Negro Past* (New York, 1958), 76.
39. This account of African dance characteristics is based upon Marshall and Jean Stearns, *Jazz Dance: The Story of American Vernacular Dance* (New York, 1968), Chaps. 2-4. The most complete study of Afro-American dance in the United States is Lynne Fauley Emery, *Black Dance in the United States from 1619 to 1970* (Palo Alto, 1972). Benjamin Henry Boneval Latrobe, *Impressions Respecting New Orleans: Diary & Sketches, 1818-1820* (New York, 1951), 49-51, and Henry William Ravenel, "Recollections of Southern Plantation Life," *Yale Review*, 25 (1936), 768-69, contain lengthy descriptions of slave dance by white contemporaries. The WPA Slave Narratives are filled with testimony concerning dance.
40. *South Carolina Gazette*, Sept. 17, 1772, reprinted in Hennig Cohen, "A Negro 'Folk Game' in Colonial South Carolina," *SFQ*, 16 (1952), 183-84.
41. *Prose of William Cullen Bryant*, VI, 33.
42. Stearns, *Jazz Dance*, 22.
43. Rudi Blesh and Harriet Janis, *They All Played Ragtime* (Oak Publications ed., New York, 1971), 96.
44. *Prose of William Cullen Bryant*, VI, 26.
45. James McKim, "Negro Songs," *Dwight's Journal of Music*, 21 (1862), 148.
46. Thomas Wentworth Higginson, *Army Life in a Black Regiment* (1869; Beacon Press ed., Boston, 1962), 220-21.
47. Norman R. Yetman, ed., *Life Under the "Peculiar Institution": Selections from the Slave Narrative Collection* (New York, 1970), 333.
48. Sir Charles Lyell, *A Second Visit to the United States of North America* (New York, 1849), I, 269-70.
49. Bremer, *America of the Fifties*, 105.
50. Charles C. Jones, *The Religious Instruction of the Negroes in the United States* (1842; reprint ed., New York, 1969), 266.
51. Ravenel, *Yale Review*, 25 (1936), 769.

A QUESTION OF ORIGINS

1. The contours of this debate are judiciously outlined in D. K. Wilgus, *Anglo-American Folksong Scholarship Since 1898* (New Brunswick, N.J., 1959), Appendix One.
2. Lucy McKim, "Songs of the Port Royal 'Contrabands,'" *Dwight's Journal of Music*, 22 (1862), 255.
3. W. F. Allen, "The Negro Dialect," *The Nation*, 1 (Dec. 14, 1865), 744-45.
4. See, for instance, Henry Edward Krehbiel, *Afro-American Folksongs* (1914; reprint ed., New York, 1963); John Wesley Work, *Folk Song of the American Negro* (Nashville, 1915); James Weldon Johnson, *The Book of American Negro*

Spirituals (New York, 1925), and *The Second Book of Negro Spirituals* (New York, 1926); Parrish, *Slave Songs;* LeRoi Jones, *Blues People* (New York, 1963); John Lovell, Jr., *Black Song: The Forge and the Flame* (New York, 1972).

5. White, *American Negro Folk-Songs;* Guy B. Johnson, *Folk Culture on St. Helena Island, South Carolina* (Chapel Hill, 1930); George Pullen Jackson, *White and Negro Spirituals* (New York, 1943).

6. Louise Pound, "The Ancestry of a 'Negro Spiritual,'" *Modern Language Notes,* 33 (1918), 442-44.

7. Frederick W. Root, "Folk-Music," *International Folk-Lore Congress of the World's Columbian Exposition, Chicago, 1893,* I, 424-25. Even the contemporary proponents of the African derivation school were affected by the belief in an evolutionary process. In 1915 the black scholar John Wesley Work in describing the "evolution" of African song in America wrote: "In proportion as the life of the New World was above that of Africa, in proportion as the light of this New World was brighter than the dim haziness of the dark continent, in that same proportion is this new song brighter and more spiritual" (*Folk Song of the American Negro,* 18).

8. C. C. Jones, *Religious Instruction,* 36-38; Joseph B. Earnest, Jr., *The Religious Development of the Negro in Virginia* (Charlottesville, 1914), 41-42.

9. Lucius Bellinger, *Stray Leaves from the Port-Folio of a Methodist Local Preacher* (Macon, Ga., 1870), 17.

10. Don Yoder, *Pennsylvania Spirituals* (Lancaster, Pa., 1961), 24.

11. Bremer, *America of the Fifties,* 115.

12. D. R. Hundley, *Social Relations in Our Southern States* (New York, 1860), 348.

13. Fisk University, *Unwritten History,* 282.

14. The question of racial separation at camp meetings is treated in Dickson D. Bruce, Jr., *And They All Sang Hallelujah: Plain-Folk Camp-Meeting Religion, 1800-1845* (Knoxville, Tenn., 1974), 73, 86, 89, and Charles A. Johnson, *The Frontier Camp Meeting* (Dallas, 1955), 46, 114-15.

15. Earnest, *Religious Development of the Negro in Virginia,* 48.

16. White, *American Negro Folk-Songs,* 11-13.

17. Dickson Bruce has shown that the revivals of the first half of the nineteenth century appealed most to the plain-folk "at the margin of antebellum Southern society. Not really poor, they were nevertheless outside the major political and economic processes of the South" (*And They All Sang Hallelujah,* 123); John Boles has argued that nineteenth-century southern evangelism was most attractive to those "with little education, wealth, or pretensions" (*The Great Revival, 1787-1805,* Lexington, Ky., 1972, 45); and Don Yoder in his examination of the related "Bush-Meeting" revivalism of the Pennsylvania Dutch country found its strength among those groups which for various reasons felt themselves disinherited and persecuted (*Pennsylvania Spirituals,* 100-106).

18. George Pullen Jackson, "The Genesis of the Negro Spiritual," *The American Mercury,* 26 (1932), 248.

19. Jackson, *White and Negro Spirituals,* Chap. 15.

20. Richard Alan Waterman, "African Influence on the Music of the Americas," in Sol Tax, ed., *Acculturation in the Americas* (Chicago, 1952), 207-18; Wilgus, *Anglo-American Folksong Scholarship,* 363-64; Merriam, "African Music," in Bascom and Herskovits, eds., *Continuity and Change in African Cultures,* 76-80; Gilbert Chase, *America's Music* (New York, 1966), Chaps. 4, 12; Bruno Nettl, *Music in Primitive Culture* (Cambridge, Mass., 1956), Chap. 9.

21. White, *American Negro Folk-Songs*, 29, 55.
22. Jackson, *White and Negro Spirituals*, 266-67.
23. McKim, *Dwight's Journal of Music*, 21 (1862), 149.
24. Higginson, *Army Life*, 218-19.
25. Chase, *America's Music*, 235-36.
26. Jeannette Robinson Murphy, "The Survival of African Music in America," *Popular Science Monthly*, 55 (1899), 662.
27. Natalie Curtis Burlin, "Negro Music at Birth," *Musical Quarterly*, 5 (1919), 88.
28. Clifton Joseph Furness, "Communal Music Among Arabians and Negroes," *Musical Quarterly*, 16 (1930), 49-51. Similar accounts of black religious meetings include Lucille Price Turner, "Negro Spirituals in the Making," *Musical Quarterly*, 17 (1931), 480-85; Marion Alexander Haskell, "Negro 'Spirituals,'" *Century Magazine*, 58 (1899), 578; *SW*, 22 (1893), 163; *SW*, 28 (1899), 151-54; *SW*, 41 (1912), 240.
29. Olmsted, *Back Country*, 189.
30. Nehemiah Adams, *A South-Side View of Slavery; Or, Three Months at the South in 1854* (Boston, 1854), 57-58.
31. Mary Boykin Chesnut, *A Diary from Dixie*, Ben Ames Williams, ed. (Boston, 1949), 148-49.
32. Elizabeth Kilham, "Sketches in Color: Fourth," *Putnam's Magazine*, 5 (1870), 308-9.
33. John Mason Brown, "Songs of the Slaves," *Lippincott's Magazine*, 2 (1868), 618.
34. W. E. B. Du Bois, *The Souls of Black Folk* (1903; Premier Edition, New York, 1961), 140-41.
35. Bruno Nettl, "Stylistic Change in Folk Music," *SFQ*, 17 (1953), 216-20, and *Folk and Traditional Music of the Western Continents* (Englewood Cliffs, N.J., 1965), 4-6; Phillips Barry, "The Transmission of Folk Song," *JAF*, 27 (1914), 67-76, and "American Folk Music," *SFQ*, 1 (1937), 29-47.
36. J. K[innard], *Knickerbocker Magazine*, 26 (1845), 336.
37. Kilham, *Putnam's Magazine*, 5 (1870), 306, 309.
38. White, *American Negro Folk-Songs*, 57.

THE QUEST FOR CERTAINTY: SLAVE SPIRITUALS

1. Lyell, *Second Visit*, I, 244-45.
2. Mary Dickson Arrowood and Thomas Hoffman Hamilton, "Nine Negro Spirituals, 1850-61," *JAF*, 41 (1928), 582, 584.
3. Lucy McKim, *Dwight's Journal of Music*, 21 (1862), 255.
4. Mircea Eliade, *The Sacred and the Profane* (New York, 1961), Chaps. 2, 4, and *passim*. For the similarity of Eliade's concept to the world view of West Africa, see W. E. Abraham, *The Mind of Africa* (London, 1962), Chap. 2; R. S. Rattray, *Religion and Art in Ashanti* (Oxford, 1927); and John S. Mbiti, *African Religions and Philosophies* (Garden City, N.Y., 1969), especially Chap. 3.
5. Claude Lévi-Strauss, *Triste Tropiques* (New York, 1964), 215.
6. William Francis Allen, Charles Pickard Ware, and Lucy McKim Garrison, *Slave Songs of the United States* (1867; reprint ed., New York, 1951), 27-28; William E. Barton, *Old Plantation Hymns: A Collection of Hitherto Unpublished Melodies of the Slave and the Freedmen* (Boston, 1899), 9.

7. Paul Radin, "Status, Phantasy, and the Christian Dogma," in Fisk University, *God Struck Me Dead: Religious Conversion Experiences and Autobiographies of Negro Ex-Slaves*, A. P. Watson, Paul Radin, and Charles S. Johnson, eds. (Nashville, 1945, unpublished typescript).

8. Lines like these could be quoted endlessly. For the specific ones cited, see Higginson, *Army Life*, 206, 216-17; Allen *et al.*, *Slave Songs*, 7, 13, 58, 77, 104; Thomas P. Fenner, *Religious Folk Songs of the Negro as Sung on the Plantations* (1874; revised ed., Hampton, Va., 1909), 10-11, 48; J. B. T. Marsh, *The Story of the Jubilee Singers; With Their Songs* (Boston, 1880), 136, 167, 178.

9. Quoted in J. L. Dillard, *Black English* (New York, 1972), 103.

10. Douglass, *Life and Times*, 41.

11. *SW*, 26 (1897), 210.

12. Charles Ball, *Fifty Years in Chains* (1837; reprint ed., New York, 1970), 220-22.

13. Fisk University, *God Struck Me Dead*, 215.

14. Fisk University, *Unwritten History*, 118.

15. *Ibid.*, 134, 136.

16. B. A. Botkin, ed., *Lay My Burden Down: A Folk History of Slavery* (Chicago, 1945), 121.

17. *Ibid.*, 18.

18. *Narrative of Lewis Clarke*, in *Interesting Memoirs and Documents Relating to American Slavery* (London, 1846), 87, 91.

19. Stanley Elkins, *Slavery* (Chicago, 1959), 136.

20. Allen *et al.*, *Slave Songs*, 2, 7, 15, 97-98; Barton, *Old Plantation Hymns*, 19, 30; Marsh, *Jubilee Singers*, 132.

21. "The Religious Life of the Negro Slave [Second Paper]," *Harper's New Monthly Magazine*, 27 (1863), 681.

22. Fisk University, *God Struck Me Dead*, 61.

23. Bremer, *America of the Fifties*, 277-79.

24. Fisk University, *God Struck Me Dead*, 4, 20, 30, 96, 101, 102, 154.

25. Fenner, *Religious Folk Songs*, 162; E. A. McIlhenny, *Befo' De War Spirituals* (Boston, 1933), 39.

26. Yoder, *Pennsylvania Spirituals*, 54-55.

27. There are numerous descriptions of the ring shout in the WPA Slave Narratives. Contemporary white descriptions include Lyell, *Second Visit*, I, 269-70; Bremer, *America of the Fifties*, 119; Long, *Pictures of Slavery*, 383; H. G. Spaulding, "Under the Palmetto," *Continental Monthly*, 4 (1863), 196-200; Abigail M. Holmes Christensen, "Spirituals and 'Shouts' of Southern Negroes," *JAF*, 7 (1894), 154-55; *The Nation*, May 30, 1867, 432-33. The Library of Congress recorded a superb example of the shout in 1934 which may be heard on its record, AAFS L3, *Afro-American Spirituals, Work Songs, and Ballads*.

28. Fenner, *Religious Folk Songs*, 8, 63-65; Marsh, *Jubilee Singers*, 240-41; Higginson, *Army Life*, 205; Allen *et al.*, *Slave Songs*, 46, 53; Natalie Curtis Burlin, *Negro Folk-Songs* (New York, 1918-19), I, 37-42.

29. Allen *et al.*, *Slave Songs*, 6.

30. *Ibid.*, 5; Burlin, *Negro Folk-Songs*, II, 8-9; Fenner, *Religious Folk Songs*, 12.

31. Allen *et al.*, *Slave Songs*, 75; Fenner, *Religious Folk Songs*, 127; Barton, *Old Plantation Hymns*, 26. The deep internalization of many of these spirituals is illustrated in the slaves' conversion experiences in which such lines as those above were incorporated verbatim into the slaves' own accounts of their conversions. See Fisk University, *God Struck Me Dead*, 24, 54, 87.

32. Boles, *The Great Revival*, Chap. 9; Charles Johnson, *The Frontier Camp Meeting*, Chap. 9; William G. McLoughlin, Jr., *Modern Revivalism* (New York, 1959), Chaps. 1-2.
33. Fenner, *Religious Folk Songs*, 10; Theodore F. Seward, *Jubilee Songs* (New York, 1872), 48; Emily Hallowell, *Calhoun Plantation Songs* (Boston, 1901), 40.
34. Allen *et al.*, *Slave Songs*, 30-31, 55, 94; Barton, *Old Plantation Hymns*, 9, 17-18, 24; Marsh, *Jubilee Singers*, 133, 167.
35. Allen *et al.*, *Slave Songs*, 55; Mary Allen Grissom, *The Negro Sings a New Heaven* (Chapel Hill, 1930), 73.
36. Allen *et al.*, *Slave Songs*, 107-8.
37. *Ibid.*, 12.
38. Jacobs, *Incidents in the Life of a Slave Girl*, 73.
39. Marsh, *Jubilee Singers*, 179, 186; Allen *et al.*, *Slave Songs*, 10-11, 13, 93; Barton, *Old Plantation Hymns*, 30.
40. McIlhenny, *Befo' De War Spirituals*, 31.
41. *Gumbo Ya-Ya: A Collection of Louisiana Folk Tales*, compiled by Lyle Saxon, Edward Dreyer, and Robert Tallant from materials gathered by workers of the WPA, Louisiana Writers' Project (Boston, 1945), 242.
42. WPA Slave Narratives, interviews with Amanda McCray (Fla.) and Andrew Moss (Tenn.).
43. WPA, *Negro in Virginia*, 110, 146.
44. John B. Cade, "Out of the Mouths of Ex-Slaves," *JNH*, 20 (1935), 330-31.
45. Descriptions of the turned-down pot can be found in all the testimony of ex-slaves. See, for instance, Fisk University, *Unwritten History*, 35, 44, 53, 98, 173, 193, 222, 300; Fisk University, *God Struck Me Dead*, 147, 156; WPA Slave Narratives, interviews with Oliver Bell (Ala.), Henry Bobbitt (N.C.), Mary Gladdy (Ga.), Anne Matthews (Tenn.), Charles Hinton (Ark.).
46. Fisk University, *God Struck Me Dead*, 171-72.
47. Bremer, *America of the Fifties*, 150.
48. Fisk University, *God Struck Me Dead*, 153.
49. Olmsted, *Back Country*, 187-96.
50. WPA, *Negro in Virginia*, 108.
51. Allen *et al.*, *Slave Songs*, 10-11, 40, 51; Marsh, *Jubilee Singers*, 168, 203; Burlin, *Negro Folk-Songs*, II, 8-9.
52. Howard Thurman, *Deep River* (New York, 1945), 16-17.
53. Higginson, *Army Life*, 221.
54. Quoted in Dena J. Epstein, "Slave Music in the United States Before 1860: A Survey of Sources," *Music Library Association Notes*, 20 (1963), 205.
55. WPA, *Negro in Virginia*, 108-9.
56. Peter Randolph, *From Slave Cabin to the Pulpit: The Autobiography of Rev. Peter Randolph* (Boston, 1893), 196-97, 200-201. Pages 145-220 of this volume contains Randolph's earlier autobiography.
57. A. F. Dickson, *Plantation Sermons, or Plain and Familiar Discourses for the Instruction of the Unlearned* (Philadelphia, 1856).
58. Ralph Thomas Parkinson, *The Religious Instruction of Slaves, 1820-1860* (unpublished M.A. thesis, University of North Carolina, 1948), 81; C. C. Jones, *Religious Instruction*, 198-201.
59. Donald Matthews, *Slavery and Methodism* (Princeton, 1965), 87.
60. James Redpath, *The Roving Editor: or, Talks with Slaves in the Southern States* (1859; reprint ed., New York, 1968), 19.

61. Botkin, ed., *Lay My Burden Down*, 25-26.
62. WPA, *Negro in Virginia*, 109.
63. Frederick Law Olmsted, *A Journey in the Seaboard Slave States* (1856; reprint ed., New York, 1969), 118-19; Parkinson, *Religious Instruction of Slaves*, 78.
64. Long, *Pictures of Slavery*, 227-29, 269-70.
65. William W. Freehling, *Prelude to Civil War: The Nullification Controversy in South Carolina* (New York, 1966), 335.
66. Eugene D. Genovese, *Roll, Jordan, Roll: The World the Slaves Made* (New York, 1974), 255-79; Henry Mitchell, *Black Preaching* (Philadelphia, 1970), Chap. 3; Charles V. Hamilton, *The Black Preacher in America* (New York, 1972), Chap. 2.
67. Quoted in Herbert S. Klein, "Anglicanism, Catholicism, and the Negro Slave," in Anne Lane, ed., *The Debate Over Slavery* (Urbana, Ill., 1971), 179-80.
68. Lyell, *Second Visit*, II, 72.
69. Olmsted, *Seaboard*, 450.
70. Ravenel, *Yale Review*, 25 (1936), 766.
71. WPA Slave Narratives (Fla.).
72. Spaulding, *Continental Monthly*, 4 (1863), 195-97.
73. Yetman, ed., *Life Under the "Peculiar Institution,"* 95.
74. Fisk University, *Unwritten History*, 259-60.
75. Cade, *JNH*, 20 (1935), 329.
76. Mrs. M. F. Armstrong and Helen W. Ludlow, *Hampton and Its Students* (New York, 1874), 102.
77. Botkin, ed., *Lay My Burden Down*, 26.
78. "The Religious Life of the Negro Slave," *Harper's New Monthly Magazine*, 27 (1863), 482-83, 677.
79. Bremer, *America of the Fifties*, 132-33.
80. Karl Mannheim, *Ideology and Utopia* (New York, 1936).
81. Higginson, *Army Life*, 27, 205.
82. Spaulding, *Continental Monthly*, 4 (1863), 195-96.
83. Quoted in Peter Kolchin, *First Freedom: The Responses of Alabama's Blacks to Emancipation and Reconstruction* (Westport, Conn., 1972), 118.
84. Allen *et al.*, *Slave Songs*, 94; Fenner, *Religious Folk Songs*, 21; Marsh, *Jubilee Singers*, 134-35; McIlhenny, *Befo' De War Spirituals*, 248-49; *SW*, 41 (1912), 241.
85. Hallowell, *Calhoun Plantation Songs*, 30; Yetman, ed., *Life Under the "Peculiar Institution,"* 112.
86. Douglass, *Life and Times*, 159-60.
87. Higginson, *Army Life*, 217.
88. *Ibid.*; Fisk University, *Unwritten History*, 124-25.
89. Parrish, *Slave Songs*, 247.
90. "Actually, not one spiritual in its primary form reflected interest in anything other than a full life here and now" (Fisher, *Negro Slave Songs in the United States*, New York, 1963, 137).
91. Barton, *Old Plantation Hymns*, 25; Allen *et al.*, *Slave Songs*, 48; James McKim, *Dwight's Journal of Music*, 21 (1862), 149.
92. Higginson, *Army Life*, 201-2, 211-12.
93. Elkins, *Slavery*, Chap. 2; Frank Tannenbaum, *Slave and Citizen* (New York, 1946).
94. WPA, *Negro in Virginia*, 110, 146.
95. E. J. Hobsbawm, *Primitive Rebels* (New York, 1959), Chap. 1.
96. C. M. Bowra, *Primitive Song* (London, 1962), 285-86.

456/ Notes for pages 55-63

THE QUEST FOR CONTROL: SLAVE FOLK BELIEFS

1. Anthony F. C. Wallace, *Religion: An Anthropological View* (New York, 1966), 5.
2. Quoted in Alan Dundes, "Brown County Superstitions," *MF*, 11 (1961), 26.
3. Quoted in Gustav Jahoda, *The Psychology of Superstition* (Harmondsworth, 1970), 1.
4. WPA Slave Narratives (Ala.).
5. WPA Slave Narratives (Ga.).
6. Yetman, ed., *Life Under the "Peculiar Institution,"* 95.
7. WPA Slave Narratives (Ala.).
8. WPA, *Drums and Shadows*, 28.
9. WPA Slave Narratives, interview with Mary Gladdy (Ga.); Allen *et al.*, *Slave Songs*, 108; Barton, *Old Plantation Hymns*, 11.
10. Livermore, *The Story of My Life*, 255.
11. Du Bois, *Souls of Black Folk*, 144; Du Bois, *The Negro Church* (Atlanta, 1903), 5.
12. Mary H. Kingsley, *West African Studies* (1899; 3rd ed., London, 1964), 53, 98, 105-10, 168-69, 178, 394.
13. In addition to the studies of African culture and religion already cited in this chapter, my understanding of African cosmology was informed by the following: Melville and Frances Herskovits, *An Outline of Dahomean Religious Belief* (Memoirs of the American Anthropological Association, No. 41, 1933); Daryll Forde, ed., *African Worlds: Studies in the Cosmological Ideas and Social Values of African Peoples* (London, 1954); Meyer Fortes, *Oedipus and Job in West African Religion* (Cambridge, 1959); Geoffrey Parrinder, *African Traditional Religion* (Westport, Conn., 1954); William Bascom, *Ifa Divination: Communication Between Gods and Men in West Africa* (Bloomington, 1969); E. E. Evans-Pritchard, *Witchcraft, Oracles, and Magic Among the Azande* (Oxford, 1937).
14. Keith Thomas, *Religion and the Decline of Magic* (New York, 1971), *passim*.
15. For an application of this argument in the area of material culture, see Henry Glassie, *Pattern in the Material Folk Culture of the Eastern United States* (Philadelphia, 1968), 115-17.
16. Newbell Niles Puckett, *Folk Beliefs of the Southern Negro* (1926; reprint ed., New York, 1969), vii, 20-21, 583-84.
17. We still need to uncover the extent to which African folk beliefs influenced those of the Europeans in the New World; the prevailing assumption that the flow of influence was almost entirely from white to black is no more tenable with folk beliefs than with music.
18. Quoted in Marcus W. Jernegan, "Slavery and Conversion in the American Colonies," *American Historical Review*, 21 (1916), 523-26.
19. C. C. Jones, *Religious Instruction*, 127-28; Olmsted, *Seaboard*, 114-15.
20. Peter H. Wood, *Black Majority: Negroes in Colonial South Carolina* (New York, 1974), 55-62, 119-24. As Wood demonstrates, American Indians too passed on their knowledge of the environment to both whites and blacks.
21. Bronislaw Malinowski, *Magic, Science, and Religion and Other Essays* (Garden City, N.Y., 1954), 17-92, 138-43.
22. Samuel A. Stouffer *et al.*, *The American Soldier* (New York, 1965), II, 188.
23. George Gmelch, "Baseball Magic," *Transaction*, 8 (1971), 39-41, 54.

24. WPA Slave Narratives, interview with Callie Elder (Ga.). Slaves often had reason for their lack of trust both because in many areas of medicine white knowledge and remedies were egregiously faulty and because there is evidence that some white doctors used ailing slaves for experimental purposes. See Kenneth M. Stampp, *The Peculiar Institution* (New York, 1956), 307-14, and Walter Fisher, "Physicians and Slavery in the Antebellum Southern Medical Journal," in August Meier and Elliott Rudwick, eds., *The Making of Black America* (New York, 1969), I, 153-64.

25. Quoted in Ulrich B. Phillips, *American Negro Slavery* (1918; paperback ed., Baton Rouge, 1966), 323.

26. Ravenel, *Yale Review*, 25 (1936), 767.

27. WPA Slave Narratives (Fla.).

28. WPA, *Drums and Shadows*, 65.

29. Phillips, *American Negro Slavery*, 322-23; Mrs. F. W. Crandall and Lois Gannett, "Folk Cures of New York State," *NYFQ*, 1 (1945), 178-80; Eston Everett Ericson, "Folklore and Folkway in the Tarboro (North Carolina) Free Press (1824-1850)," *SFQ*, 5 (1941), 123.

30. Thomas, *Religion and the Decline of Magic*, 12.

31. Fisk University, *Unwritten History*, 180, 38.

32. Yetman, ed., *Life Under the "Peculiar Institution,"* 202.

33. WPA Slave Narratives, interviews with Cheney Cross, William Henry Towns, Carrie Davis, Emma Jones (Ala.), Charlette Raines, Will Sheets, Callie Elder (Ga.); Fisk University, *Unwritten History*, 223; *SW*, 23 (1891), 66; Mrs. L. H. C. Packwood, "Cure for an Aching Tooth," *JAF*, 13 (1900), 66; Roland Steiner, "Sol Lockheart's Call," *ibid.*, 67.

34. WPA, *Drums and Shadows*, 144-45, 68-69.

35. Elizabeth Kilham, "Sketches in Color: First," *Putnam's Monthly*, 4 (1869), 741.

36. WPA Slave Narratives, interviews with Susie Johnson, Robert Heard, Marshal Butler, Julia Bunch (Ga.), Tines Kendricks, Mary Jane Hardrige (Ark.), Lula Flannigan (Ala.), Susan Kelley (Va.), Scott Martin, Measy Hudson, Emma Grisham (Tenn.); Fisk University, *Unwritten History*, 167-68, 212-13, 302, 316-17; *SW*, 25 (1896), 16; *SW*, 41 (1912), 246-48.

37. Fisk University, *God Struck Me Dead*, 159.

38. WPA Slave Narratives, interviews with Minnie Green (Ga.), Simon Stokes (Va.), Scott Martin (Tenn.), Casie Jones Brown, Clark Hill (Ark.); *SW*, 23 (1894), 16, 46-47; *SW*, 25 (1896), 16; Puckett, *Folk Beliefs*, 276, 318, 449.

39. WPA Slave Narratives (Miss.).

40. Margaret Jackson, "Folklore in Slave Narratives Before the Civil War," *NYFQ*, 11 (1955), 5-6, 12.

41. Douglass, *Life and Times*, 160-72.

42. Clarke, *Narrative* in *Interesting Memoirs and Documents Relating to American Slavery*, 27-28.

43. Douglass, *Life and Times*, 163-64.

44. *Ibid.*, 115-44.

45. William Wells Brown, *My Southern Home* (1880; reprint ed., Upper Saddle River, N.J., 1968), 70.

46. Quoted in Genovese, *Roll, Jordan, Roll*, 216.

47. Jackson, *NYFQ*, 11 (1955), 8.

48. *Narrative of the Life and Adventures of Henry Bibb, An American Slave* (New York, 1850), 25-31.

49. Elsie Clews Parsons, *Folk-Lore of the Sea Islands, South Carolina* (*MAFS*, XVI, 1923), 61-62.
50. *SW*, 26 (1897), 37-38.
51. Roland Steiner, "The Practice of Conjuring in Georgia," *JAF*, 14 (1901), 177.
52. WPA Slave Narratives (Ala.).
53. WPA Slave Narratives, interviews with Henry Green (Ark.), Annie Huff (Ga.); *SW*, 23 (1894), 46-47.
54. WPA Slave Narratives, interviews with Amanda Syles (Ga.), Eda Harper (Ark.); Yetman, ed., *Life Under the "Peculiar Institution,"* 201; *SW*, 23 (1894), 46-47.
55. Louis Hughes, *Thirty Years a Slave* (1897; reprint ed., New York, 1969), 108.
56. Fisk University, *Unwritten History*, 139.
57. *Ibid.*, 100. Also Steiner, *JAF*, 14 (1901), 178. For similar testimony from other slaves and for another interpretation of this evidence, see Genovese, *Roll, Jordan, Roll*, 222-23.
58. Livermore, *The Story of My Life*, 306-7; Yetman, ed., *Life Under the "Peculiar Institution,"* 201.
59. *SW*, 26 (1897), 38; Leonora Herron, "Conjuring and Conjure-Doctors," *SW*, 24 (1895), 118.
60. Yetman, ed., *Life Under the "Peculiar Institution,"* 290.
61. Brown, *My Southern Home*, 70-81.
62. Thaddeus Norris, "Negro Superstitions," *Lippincott's Magazine*, 6 (1870), 95.
63. C. C. Jones, *Religious Instruction*, 128.
64. Gerald Mullin, *Flight and Rebellion: Slave Resistance in Eighteenth-Century Virginia* (New York, 1972), Chap. 5.
65. Kenneth Scott, "The Slave Insurrection in New York in 1712," *New York Historical Society Quarterly*, 45 (1961), 47.
66. Phillips, *American Negro Slavery*, 476.
67. Robert S. Starobin, ed., *Denmark Vesey* (Englewood Cliffs, N.J., 1970), 13-66; Robert S. Starobin, "Denmark Vesey's Slave Conspiracy of 1822," in John H. Bracey, Jr., *et al., American Slavery: The Question of Resistance* (Belmont, Calif., 1970), 142-57.
68. *The Confessions of Nat Turner . . . As Fully and Voluntarily Made to Thomas R. Gray* (reprint of 1861 ed., Miami, 1969).
69. Jacob Stroyer, *My Life in the South* (Salem, Mass., 1890), 57-59. Similar methods were used by blacks and poor whites in Virginia and North Carolina and had been widely used in sixteenth- and seventeenth-century England. See Sara M. Handy, "Negro Superstitions," *Lippincott's Magazine*, 48 (1891), 738, and Thomas, *Religion and the Decline of Magic*, 212-22. For instances of masters employing such means to detect thieves among their slaves, see Puckett, *Folk Beliefs*, 281-82, and A. M. Bacon and E. C. Parsons, "Folk-Lore from Elizabeth City County, Virginia," *JAF*, 35 (1922), 282.
70. WPA Slave Narratives (Ga.).
71. *Ibid.*; Herron, *SW*, 24 (1895), 118.
72. WPA Slave Narratives, interviews with Easter Huff, Jefferson Franklin Henry, Dosia Harris, Mary Colbert, Georgia Baker (Ga.), Ellen Crosley (Ark.), Frank Mehefee (Ala.), Jane Lassiter (N.C.), Florida Clayton (Fla.); Botkin, ed., *Lay My Burden Down*, 29.
73. WPA Slave Narratives (N.C.); Yetman, ed., *Life Under the "Peculiar Institution,"* 289.

74. WPA Slave Narratives (N.C.).
75. Yetman, ed., *Life Under the "Peculiar Institution,"* 57.
76. Clarke, "Questions and Answers," in *Interesting Memoirs and Documents Relating to American Slavery*, 87, 91.
77. Ball, *Fifty Years in Chains*, 260-62.
78. WPA Slave Narratives, interviews with Cheny Cross (Ala.), Josephine Anderson (Fla.); Yetman, ed., *Life Under the "Peculiar Institution,"* 57; Puckett, *Folk Beliefs*, 107-8; *SW*, 23 (1894), 26-27, 46-47; *SW*, 24 (1895), 49-50.

CHAPTER 2: THE MEANING OF SLAVE TALES

EPIGRAPH

1. Duncan Clinch Heyward, *Seed from Madagascar* (Chapel Hill, 1937), 165.
2. Fisk University, *God Struck Me Dead*, 161.

INTRODUCTION

1. Octave Thanet, "Folk-Lore in Arkansas," *JAF*, 5 (1892), 122.
2. The following African tale type and motif indices were used in this comparison: Erastus Ojo Arewa, *A Classification of the Folktales of the Northern East African Cattle Area by Types* (unpublished Ph.D. dissertation, University of California, Berkeley, 1966); Winifred Lambrecht, *A Tale Type Index for Central Africa* (unpublished Ph.D. dissertation, University of California, Berkeley, 1967); Kenneth Wendell Clarke, *Motif-Index of the Folk-Tales of Culture-Area V West Africa* (unpublished Ph.D. dissertation, Indiana University, 1958). See also William D. Pierson, "An African Background for American Negro Folktales?" *JAF*, 84 (1971), 204-14, and Alan Dundes, "African and Afro-American Tales," to be published in the 1976 issue of *Research in African Literatures*.
3. *Uncle Remus: His Songs and His Sayings* (New York, 1880); *Nights with Uncle Remus* (Boston, 1883); *Daddy Jake, the Runaway* (New York, 1889); *Uncle Remus and His Friends* (Boston, 1892); *Told by Uncle Remus* (New York, 1905); *The Tar-Baby and Other Rhymes of Uncle Remus* (New York, 1904); *Uncle Remus and Brer Rabbit* (New York, 1907); *Uncle Remus and the Little Boy* (Boston, 1910); *Uncle Remus Returns* (Boston, 1918); *Seven Tales of Uncle Remus* (Atlanta, 1948).
4. *Nights with Uncle Remus*, xli.

SLAVE TALES AS HISTORY

1. Malinowski, *Magic, Science and Religion*, 126. Scholars long accepted the widespread presence of such myths in Africa. More recently this view has undergone revision. See Finnegan, *Oral Literature in Africa*, 361-67, and Paul Radin, *African Folktales* (Princeton, 1970), 2.
2. WPA Slave Narratives (Ala.).
3. Ericson, *SFQ*, 5 (1941), 124.

4. Mary Walker Finley Speers, "Maryland and Virginia Folk-Lore," *JAF*, 25 (1912), 284.
5. A. F. Chamberlain, "Negro Creation Legend," *JAF*, 3 (1890), 302.
6. Speers, *JAF*, 25 (1912), 284.
7. James H. Penrod, "Folk Motifs in Old Southwestern Humor," *SFQ*, 19 (1955), 117-18; Harris, *Uncle Remus: His Songs and His Sayings*, 163-65. Motif A1614.2, Races dark-skinned from bathing after white man. In this and the following notes, the motif numbers listed are taken from Stith Thompson, *Motif-Index of Folk-Literature*, 6 vols. (Bloomington, Ind., 1955-58).
8. Harden E. Taliaferro, *Fisher's River (North Carolina) Scenes and Characters* (New York, 1859), 188-89.
9. Bernard, *Retrospections of America, 1797-1811*, 130; Ericson, *SFQ*, 5 (1941), 124; Fanny D. Bergen, *Animal and Plant Lore* (*MAFS*, I, 1899), 80; Puckett, *Folk Beliefs*, 4-5; William Pickens, *American Aesop: Negro and Other Humor* (1926; reprint ed., New York, 1969), 22-23.
10. Kingsley, *West African Studies*, 328. Also her *Travels in West Africa* (reprint of 1897 ed., London, 1965), 430-31.
11. Richard F. Burton, *Wit and Wisdom from West Africa* (London, 1865), 124.
12. Recently, Ruth Finnegan has raised some questions concerning how widespread historical narratives were in Africa itself (*Oral Literature in Africa*, 367-73).
13. Richard M. Dorson, *Negro Folktales in Michigan* (Cambridge, Mass., 1956), 84-85.
14. Ravenel, *Yale Review*, 25 (1936), 750.
15. A. M. H. Christensen, *Afro-American Folk Lore: Told Round Cabin Fires on the Sea Islands of South Carolina* (1892; reprint ed., New York, 1969), 4-5.
16. WPA Slave Narratives (Ga.).
17. WPA Slave Narratives (Ark.).
18. WPA Slave Narratives (Fla.).
19. Yetman, ed., *Life Under the "Peculiar Institution,"* 89.
20. WPA, *Drums and Shadows*, 20. Stories of flying Africans are one of the most common in this collection. Also John Bennett, *The Doctor to the Dead: Grotesque Legends & Folk Tales of Old Charleston* (New York, 1946), 139-42; Zora Neale Hurston, "High John De Conquer," *American Mercury*, 57 (1943), 450-58.
21. WPA, *Drums and Shadows*, 175-76; WPA Slave Narratives, interview with Mary Anngady (N.C.).
22. These stories of resistance will be examined in another context in Chapter 6.
23. *JAF*, 1 (1888), 164; WPA manuscripts, New York File, Archive of Folk Song.
24. Fisk University, *Unwritten History*, 84.
25. Yetman, ed., *Life Under the "Peculiar Institution,"* 73; Botkin, ed., *Lay My Burden Down*, 16-18; WPA Slave Narratives, interview with Mary Wallace Bowe (N.C.); WPA, *Negro in Virginia*, 194-95, 204.
26. Emma M. Backus, "Folk-Tales from Georgia," *JAF*, 13 (1900), 32.
27. Parsons, *Folk-Lore of the Sea Islands*, xx-xxi.
28. Dorson, *Negro Folktales in Michigan*, 24.
29. *Nights with Uncle Remus*, xv-xvi.
30. Parsons, *Folk-Lore of the Sea Islands*, xviii, 51; Alcée Fortier, *Louisiana Folk-Tales* (*MAFS*, II, 1895), 53, 61; Dorson, *Negro Folktales in Michigan*, 42; Richard M. Dorson, *Negro Tales from Pine Bluff, Arkansas, and Calvin, Michigan* (Bloomington, 1958), 254; Bennett, *Doctor to the Dead*, xiii.

OF MORALITY AND SURVIVAL

1. Bascom, "Folklore and Literature," in Lystad, *The African World*, 482; Melville J. and Frances S. Herskovits, *Suriname Folk-Lore* (New York, 1936), 141.
2. Richard M. Dorson, "Negro Tales of Mary Richardson," *MF*, 6 (1956), 5.
3. Examples of explanatory tales may be found in *SW*, 25 (1896), 82, 102; *SW*, 27 (1898), 36-37, 76; Charles C. Jones, Jr., *Negro Myths from the Georgia Coast* (Boston, 1888), 1-3, 90-93; Emma M. Backus, "Animal Tales from North Carolina," *JAF*, 11 (1898), 288-89; Bacon and Parsons, *JAF*, 35 (1922), 266-67; Parsons, *Folk-Lore of the Sea Islands*, 59-60. Zora Neale Hurston, *Mules and Men* (Philadelphia, 1935), contains a disproportionately high number of such tales.
4. Heli Chatelain, *Folk-Tales of Angola* (MAFS, I, 1894), 21.
5. Melville J. Herskovits, *Dahomey: An Ancient West African Kingdom* (Evanston, 1967), I, 35.
6. Parsons, *Folk-Lore of the Sea Islands*, 71. A-T tale type 1705, Talking Horse and Dog.
7. *SW*, 26 (1897), 229-30.
8. Dorson, *Negro Folktales in Michigan*, 166.
9. Elsie Clews Parsons, "Tales from Guilford County, North Carolina," *JAF*, 30 (1917), 185.
10. C. C. Jones, Jr., *Negro Myths*, 25-26.
11. Puckett, *Folk Beliefs*, 559.
12. Richard M. Dorson, "Negro Tales from Bolivar County, Mississippi," *SFQ*, 19 (1955), 107.
13. Parsons, *Folk-Lore of the Sea Islands*, 80.
14. C. C. Jones, Jr., *Negro Myths*, 33-34, 42-48.
15. Examples may be found in Portia Smiley, "Folk-Lore from Virginia, South Carolina, Georgia, Alabama, and Florida," *JAF*, 32 (1919), 360-65.
16. Parsons, *Folk-Lore of the Sea Islands*, 97.
17. C. C. Jones, Jr., *Negro Myths*, 57-58.
18. Parsons, *Folk-Lore of the Sea Islands*, 57; Smiley, *JAF*, 32 (1919), 378.
19. Parsons, *Folk-Lore of the Sea Islands*, xvi-xvii, 75-76. For similar African dilemma tales, see Finnegan, *Oral Literature in Africa*, 433, and William R. Bascom, *African Dilemma Tales* (The Hague, 1975), 42-52.
20. C. C. Jones, Jr., *Negro Myths*, 127.
21. Parsons, *JAF*, 30 (1917), 193-94.
22. *Ibid.*, 196-97; Edward A. Pollard, *Black Diamonds: Gathered in the Darkey Homes of the South* (New York, 1859), 76. A-T tale type 720, My Mother Slew Me; My Father Ate Me.
23. Parsons, *Folk-Lore of the Sea Islands*, 122.
24. *Ibid.*, 115-16.
25. Louis Pendleton, "Notes on Negro Folk-Lore and Witchcraft in the South," *JAF*, 3 (1890), 202-3.
26. Christensen, *Afro-American Folk Lore*, 10-14.
27. Backus, *JAF*, 11 (1898), 285-86.
28. Botkin, ed., *Lay My Burden Down*, 23.
29. Parsons, *Folk-Lore of the Sea Islands*, 109; Parsons, *JAF*, 30 (1917), 194; Smiley, *JAF*, 32 (1919), 365; Puckett, *Folk Beliefs*, 33.

30. Elsie Clews Parsons, "Folk-Lore From Aiken, S.C.," *JAF*, 34 (1921), 10.
31. Botkin, ed., *Lay My Burden Down*, 163.
32. J. Mason Brewer, "Juneteenth," *PTFS*, 10 (1932), 33-34.
33. Examples of Negro versions of such tales may be found in *SW*, 28 (1899), 232-33; Elsie Clews Parsons, "Tales from Maryland and Pennsylvania," *JAF*, 30 (1917), 210-13; Parsons, *Folk-Lore of the Sea Islands*, 23-24, 52-53, 80-88, 120-21; Arthur Huff Fauset, "Negro Folk Tales from the South (Alabama, Mississippi, Louisiana)," *JAF*, 40 (1927), 243-60; Arthur Huff Fauset, "Tales and Riddles Collected in Philadelphia," *JAF*, 41 (1928), 537-40.
34. Stith Thompson, *The Folktale* (New York, 1946), 7-8.
35. Radin, *African Folktales*, 5.
36. Brewer, *PTFS*, 10 (1932), 48-50; Parsons, *JAF*, 30 (1917), 176-177; Fauset, *JAF*, 41 (1928), 536-37; Dorson, *Negro Tales from Pine Bluff and Calvin*, 48-50. Motif B210.2, Talking animal or object refuses to talk on command.
37. Long, *Pictures of Slavery*, 196-98.
38. *Letters and Diary of Laura M. Towne: Written from the Sea Islands of South Carolina, 1862-1884*, Rupert Sargent Holland, ed. (Cambridge, Mass., 1912), 23, 42.
39. WPA Slave Narratives (N.C.).
40. *Uncle Remus: His Songs and His Sayings*, xiv; *Nights with Uncle Remus*, xiv-xvii.
41. Parsons, *Folk-Lore of the Sea Islands*, xiv.
42. Parrish, *Slave Songs*, 20-22.
43. J. A. Macon, *Uncle Gabe Tucker: or, Reflections, Song, and Sentiment in the Quarters* (Philadelphia, 1883), 131-32, 142; J. Mason Brewer, "Old-Time Negro Proverbs," *PTFS*, 11 (1933), 102; F. W. Bradley, "South Carolina Proverbs," *SFQ*, 1 (1937), 100; Guy Johnson, *Folk Culture on St. Helena Island*, 160.
44. C. C. Jones, *Religious Instruction*, 110-11.
45. Heyward, *Seed from Madagascar*, 162.

"SOME GO UP AND SOME GO DOWN": THE ANIMAL TRICKSTER

1. Rattray, *Akan-Ashanti Folk Tales*, x-xii.
2. Quoted in Janheinz Jahn, *Muntu: An Outline of the New African Culture* (New York, 1961), 221.
3. Rattray, *Akan-Ashanti Folk Tales*, xiii; Herskovits, *Suriname Folklore*, 138; *Standard Dictionary of Folklore, Mythology and Legend*, Maria Leach, ed. (New York, 1949-50), I, 52-53.
4. Other primary animal trickster figures in Africa whose geographical distribution is less clear cut include Antelope, Squirrel, Wren, Weasel, and Jackal. Finnegan, *Oral Literature in Africa*, 344-54; Richard A. Waterman and William R. Bascom, "African and New World Negro Folklore," *Standard Dictionary of Folklore, Mythology and Legend*, I, 18-24; A. B. Ellis, "Evolution in Folklore: Some West African Prototypes of the 'Uncle Remus' Stories," *Popular Science Monthly*, 48 (1895), 93-104. For a refutation of the once widely held thesis that the slaves' rabbit trickster was borrowed from the North American Indians, see Alan Dundes, "African Tales Among the North American Indians," *SFQ*, 29 (1965), 207-19.
5. Herskovits, *Dahomean Narrative*, 99-101.

6. Constance Rourke, *American Humor* (New York, 1931), Chaps. 1-2; Jesse Bier, *The Rise and Fall of American Humor* (New York, 1968), Chaps. 1-2; Richard M. Dorson, *American Folklore* (Chicago, 1959), Chap. 2; James T. Pearce, "Folk-Tales of the Southern Poor-White, 1820-1860," *JAF*, 63 (1950), 398-412.

7. Dorson, *American Folklore*, 185. In fact, as this chapter demonstrates, Anansi stories were present in the nineteenth-century United States in small numbers. Not until the twentieth-century influx of West Indians into the United States are Anansi tales found with any regularity. WPA manuscripts, New York File, Archive of Folk Song.

8. For an indication of the distribution of Anansi stories in South America, see Terrence Leslie Hansen, *The Types of the Folktale in Cuba, Puerto Rico, the Dominican Republic, and Spanish South America* (Berkeley, 1957).

9. The tar-baby story (A-T tale type 175), appears in virtually every collection of black tales in this period. For examples, see Norris, *Lippincott's Magazine*, 6 (1870), 94-95; William Owens, "Folk-Lore of the Southern Negroes," *ibid.*, 20 (1877), 750-51; C. C. Jones, Jr., *Negro Myths*, 7-11; Pendleton, *JAF*, 3 (1890), 201; *SW*, 23 (1894), 149-50; Christensen, *Afro-American Folk Lore*, 62-72.

10. Parsons, *Folk-Lore of the Sea Islands*, 78.

11. C. C. Jones, Jr., *Negro Myths*, 35. Motif K1723, Goat pretends to chew rock.

12. *SW*, 22 (1898), 125.

13. C. C. Jones, Jr., *Negro Myths*, 97-99.

14. WPA manuscripts, Mississippi File, Archive of Folk Song. This story (A-T tale type 32), remained in circulation throughout the twentieth century. For a version collected in Texas in 1965, see Roger D. Abrahams, *Positively Black* (Englewood Cliffs, N.J., 1970), 51-52.

15. Backus, *JAF*, 13 (1900), 22-24.

16. For examples of the many versions of this tale (A-T tale type 15, The Theft of Butter by Playing Godfather), see Christensen, *Afro-American Folk Lore*, 73-80; Guy Johnson, *Folk Culture on St. Helena Island*, 138-40; C. C. Jones, Jr., *Negro Myths*, 53-57; Bacon and Parsons, *JAF*, 35 (1922), 253-56.

17. Harris, *Uncle Remus: His Song and His Sayings*, 80-86; Parsons, *JAF*, 30 (1917), 192-93; Richard Smith, "Richard's Tales," recorded by John L. and Stella A. Sinclair, *PTFS*, 25 (1953), 220-24.

18. C. C. Jones, Jr., *Negro Myths*, 102-5; Parsons, *Folk-Lore of the Sea Islands*, 39. A-T tale type 1, The Theft of Fish.

19. *SW*, 25 (1896), 185-86, 205; Bacon and Parsons, *JAF*, 35 (1922), 277-78; C. C. Jones, Jr., *Negro Myths*, 49-53; Christensen, *Afro-American Folk Lore*, 73-80.

20. Christensen, *Afro-American Folk Lore*, 104-7; Parsons, *Folk-Lore of the Sea Islands*, 30-31; WPA Slave Narratives, interview with Cecelia Chappel (Tenn.).

21. Backus, *JAF*, 13 (1900), 25.

22. For examples, see Anne Virginia Culbertson, *At the Big House* (Indianapolis, 1904); Backus, *JAF*, 11 (1898), 288-89; Bacon and Parsons, *JAF*, 35 (1922), 266; Harris, *Seven Tales of Uncle Remus*, tale 7.

23. *SW*, 27 (1898), 76.

24. Backus, *JAF*, 13 (1900), 21-22.

25. Emma M. Backus, "Tales of the Rabbit from Georgia Negroes," *JAF*, 12 (1899), 113-14.

26. Various versions of this widely popular tale (A-T tale type 72, Rabbit Rides Fox A-Courting), can be found in Owens, *Lippincott's Magazine*, 20 (1877), 753; C. C. Jones, Jr., *Negro Myths*, 27-31; *SW*, 23 (1894), 149-50; Mrs. William Pres-

ton Johnston, "Two Negro Tales," *JAF*, 9 (1896), 194-96; Bacon and Parsons, *JAF*, 35 (1922), 265-66; Parsons, *Folk-Lore of the Sea Islands*, 53-55.

27. Christensen, *Afro-American Folk Lore*, 36-41; C. C. Jones, Jr., *Negro Myths*, 99-102; Parsons, *Folk-Lore of the Sea Islands*, 14-19. Motif H1154.4, Task: capturing elk.

28. *Nights with Uncle Remus*, 330; *Uncle Remus: His Songs and His Sayings*, xiv.

29. Christensen, *Afro-American Folk Lore*, ix-xiv.

30. Thanet, *JAF*, 5 (1892), 122.

31. See, for instance, John Stafford, "Patterns of Meaning in Nights with Uncle Remus," *American Literature*, 18 (1946), 89-108; Louise Dauner, *ibid.*, 20 (1948), 129-43; Bernard Wolfe, "Uncle Remus and the Malevolent Rabbit," *Commentary* (1949), 31-41; Marshall Fishwick, "Uncle Remus vs. John Henry," *WF*, 20 (1961), 77-85.

32. Christensen, *Afro-American Folk Lore*, 1-5.

33. J. Mason Brewer, *Dog Ghosts and Other Texas Negro Folk Tales* (Austin, 1958), 50.

34. Versions of this ubiquitous tale (A-T tale type 1074, Race Won by Deception: Relative Helpers), can be found in Owens, *Lippincott's Magazine*, 20 (1877), 751; Christensen, *Afro-American Folk Tales*, 79; Sadie E. Stewart, "Seven Folk-Tales From the Sea Islands, S.C.," *JAF*, 32 (1919), 394; C. C. Jones, Jr., *Negro Myths*, 5-6; Botkin, ed., *Lay My Burden Down*, 23; Backus, *JAF*, 11 (1898), 284-85; Parsons, *Folk-Lore of the Sea Islands*, 79.

35. C. C. Jones, Jr., *Negro Myths*, 105.

36. Christensen, *Afro-American Folk Lore*, 101-3.

37. Parsons, *Folk-Lore of the Sea Islands*, 44.

38. C. C. Jones, Jr., *Negro Myths*, 11-14.

39. Parsons, *Folk-Lore of the Sea Islands*, 66-67. A-T tale type 122D, Let Me Catch You Better Game.

40. Mrs. William Preston Johnson, *JAF*, 9 (1896), 196-98.

41. Christensen, *Afro-American Folk Lore*, 54-57; Hurston, *Mules and Men*, 141-42.

42. *SW*, 25 (1896), 82; Bacon and Parsons, *JAF*, 35 (1922), 252-53; C. C. Jones, Jr., *Negro Myths*, 73-81; Harris, *Nights with Uncle Remus*, 314-19.

43. Backus, *JAF*, 12 (1899), 111-12.

44. Christensen, *Afro-American Folk Lore*, 26-35.

45. Elsie Clews Parsons, "Folk-Tales Collected at Miami, Florida," *JAF*, 30 (1917), 226. Motif J2413.4.2, Fowl makes another animal believe that he has head cut off.

46. Backus, *JAF*, 11 (1898), 288-89.

47. C. C. Jones, Jr., *Negro Myths*, 91-93.

48. *SW*, 26 (1897), 58.

49. Wolfe, *Commentary* (1949), 36.

50. C. C. Jones, Jr., *Negro Myths*, 128-29.

51. Botkin, ed., *Lay My Burden Down*, 91.

52. Fisk University, *God Struck Me Dead*, 177. Also WPA Slave Narratives, interviews with Cecelia Chappel (Tenn.), Rivlana Boynton (Fla.).

53. Emma M. Backus and Ethel Hatton Leitner, "Negro Tales from Georgia," *JAF*, 25 (1912), 127-28; Owens, *Lippincott's Magazine*, 20 (1877), 752; Bacon and Parsons, *JAF*, 35 (1922), 262-64; Christensen, *Afro-American Folk Lore*, 19-22, 62-72; Backus, *JAF*, 13 (1900), 24-25; *SW*, 28 (1899), 113.

54. Dauner, *American Literature*, 20 (1948), 135.

THE SLAVE AS TRICKSTER

1. Long, *Pictures of Slavery*, 194-95.
2. Botkin, ed., *Lay My Burden Down*, 1-2; Macon, *Uncle Gabe Tucker*, 141-47; Bradley, *SFQ*, 1 (1937), 100; Brewer, *PTFS*, 11 (1933), 102.
3. Towne, *Letters and Diary*, 30.
4. A mass of evidence from plantation records concerning slave intransigence is presented in Stampp, *Peculiar Institution*, Chap. 3. Also John W. Blassingame, *The Slave Community* (New York, 1972), Chap. 7; Eugene D. Genovese, *The Political Economy of Slavery* (New York, 1965), Chaps. 2, 5; Freehling, *Prelude to Civil War*, 63; Redpath, *Roving Editor*, 88; Lyell, *Second Visit*, II, 72; James Stirling, *Letters from the Slave States* (London, 1857), 231-32; Fisk University, *Unwritten History*, 140.
5. Yetman, ed., *Life Under the "Peculiar Institution,"* 116.
6. Fisk University, *Unwritten History*, 148-49.
7. WPA Slave Narratives (Ala.).
8. Botkin, ed., *Lay My Burden Down*, 241; Dorson, *Negro Tales from Pine Bluff and Calvin*, 109.
9. Pickens, *American Aesop*, 26.
10. Gresham M. Sykes and David Matza, "Techniques of Neutralization: A Theory of Delinquency," *American Sociological Review*, 22 (1957), 664-70; David Matza, *Delinquency and Drift* (New York, 1964), 60-62 and *passim*.
11. WPA Slave Narratives (Ga.).
12. John G. Williams, *"De Ole Plantation"* (Charleston, 1895), 11.
13. Henry Lee Swint, *The Northern Teacher in the South, 1862-1870* (Nashville, 1941), 89.
14. Fisk University, *God Struck Me Dead*, 216.
15. Olmsted, *Seaboard*, 117.
16. Clarke, "Questions and Answers," in *Interesting Memoirs and Documents Relating to American Slavery*, 92.
17. Allen *et al.*, *Slave Songs*, 89; WPA Slave Narratives, interview with Jake Green (Ala.); Yetman, ed., *Life Under the "Peculiar Institution,"* 253.
18. *Ibid.*, 316.
19. *Ibid.*, 183.
20. Fisk University, *God Struck Me Dead*, 178.
21. Fisk University, *Unwritten History*, 134.
22. WPA, *Negro in Virginia*, 156.
23. Botkin, ed., *Lay My Burden Down*, 4-5.
24. John tales are collected in the following: John Q. Anderson, "Old John and the Master," *SFQ*, 25 (1961), 195-97; J. Mason Brewer, "John Tales," *PTFS*, 21 (1946), 81-104; Hurston, *American Mercury*, 57 (1943), 450-58; Harry Oster, "Negro Humor: John and Old Marster," *Journal of the Folklore Institute*, 5 (1968), 42-57; Richard M. Dorson, *American Negro Folktales* (Greenwich, Conn., 1967), 124-71.
25. C. C. Jones, Jr., *Negro Myths*, 89-90; Brewer, *PTFS*, 10 (1932), 24-25; Speers, *JAF*, 25 (1912), 284-85; Smiley, *JAF*, 32 (1919), 370. A-T tale type 1641, Dr. Know-All.

26. Botkin, ed., *Lay My Burden Down*, 3-4; Brewer, *PTFS*, 10 (1932), 10-11.
27. Henry D. Spalding, *Encyclopedia of Black Folklore and Humor* (Middle Village, N.Y., 1972), 35-37.
28.. WPA manuscripts, South Carolina File, Archive of Folk Song. A-T tale type 785A, The Goose with One Leg.
29. Bacon and Parsons, *JAF*, 35 (1922), 296. A-T tale type 1741, The Priest's Guests and the Eaten Chickens.
30. Parsons, *Folk-Lore of the Sea Islands*, 76-77; Dorson, *American Negro Folktales*, 151-52; Fauset, *JAF*, 40 (1927), 266-67.
31. Bacon and Parsons, *JAF*, 35 (1922), 293-94; WPA Slave Narratives, interview with Jake Green (Ala.).
32. R. R. Moton, "Sickness in Slavery Days," *SW*, 28 (1899), 75.
33. C. C. Jones, Jr., *Negro Myths*, 119-20; Brewer, *PTFS*, 10 (1932), 25-26.
34. C. C. Jones, Jr., *Negro Myths*, 115-16.
35. Brewer, *PTFS*, 10 (1932), 15-16; Parsons, *Folk-Lore of the Sea Islands*, 112-13.
36. *The Frank C. Brown Collection of North Carolina Folklore*, Newman I. White, ed. (7 volumes, Durham, 1952-62), I, 702.
37. Botkin, ed., *Lay My Burden Down*, 9; WPA Slave Narratives, interview with Julia Larkin (Ga.).
38. Macon, *Uncle Gabe Tucker*, 164-66.
39. *SW*, 26 (1897), 210.

SLAVE TALES AND THE SACRED UNIVERSE

1. On this point, see Herskovits, *Dahomean Narrative*, 44-45, and Hurston, *American Mercury*, 57 (1943), 455.
2. Claude Lévi-Strauss, "The Story of Asdiwal," in Edmund Leach, ed., *The Structural Study of Myth* (London, 1967), 1, 13-14, 17.

CHAPTER 3: FREEDOM, CULTURE, AND RELIGION

EPIGRAPH

1. W. E. B. Du Bois, *The Souls of Black Folk* (1903; Premier Edition, New York, 1961), 17.

INTRODUCTION

1. Quoted in Bell Irvin Wiley, *Southern Negroes, 1861-1865* (New Haven, 1965), 109.
2. Randolph, *Slave Cabin to Pulpit*, 59.
3. WPA, *Negro in Virginia*, 211-12.
4. Edmund L. Drago, *Black Georgia During Reconstruction* (unpublished Ph.D. dissertation, University of California, Berkeley, 1975), 6-7.
5. Fisk University, *Unwritten History*, 232; Yetman, ed., *Life Under the "Peculiar Institution,"* 113-14; Newman I. White mss., Houghton Library, Harvard University.
6. David Macrae, *The Americans at Home* (1870; reprint ed., New York, 1952), 210.

7. Towne, *Letters and Diary*, 162.
8. Yetman, ed., *Life Under the "Peculiar Institution*," 264.
9. Botkin, ed., *Lay My Burden Down*, 16.
10. *Ibid.*, 191.
11. WPA Slave Narratives (Va.).

THE LANGUAGE OF FREEDOM

1. For a useful discussion and summary of various theories of marginality, see H. F. Dickie-Carr, *The Marginal Situation: A Sociological Study of a Coloured Group* (London, 1966), Chap. 1.
2. Macrae, *Americans at Home*, 318.
3. State studies demonstrating some of these trends include, Peter Kolchin, *First Freedom: The Responses of Alabama's Blacks to Emancipation* (Westport, Conn., 1972), Chaps. 1, 4, 5; Joel Williamson, *After Slavery: The Negro in South Carolina During Reconstruction, 1861-1877* (Chapel Hill, 1965), Chaps. 7, 8, 11; George Tindall, *South Carolina Negroes, 1877-1900* (Baton Rouge, 1966), Chaps. 9, 10, 11; Vernon Lane Wharton, *The Negro in Mississippi, 1865-1900* (New York, 1965), Chaps. 7, 17, 18.
4. Swint, *Northern Teacher in the South*, 41.
5. Towne, *Letters and Diary*, 20.
6. Lucy Chase to her family, Jan. 15, 1863, March 4, 1863, July 1, 1864, in Henry L. Swint, ed., *Dear Ones at Home: Letters from Contraband Camps* (Nashville, 1966), 21-22, 58, 124-25.
7. Swint, *Northern Teacher in the South*, 41-42, 57-58, 66, 74; Towne, *Letters and Diary*, 20, 22.
8. Elizabeth Ware Pearson, ed., *Letters from Port Royal, 1862-1868* (1906; reprint ed., New York, 1969), 25.
9. Macrae, *Americans at Home*, 342-43. Lucy Chase wrote her family that "the habit of the Negro is to say whatever he thinks his interrogator wishes him to say" (Swint, ed., *Dear Ones at Home*, 22). This attitude was to long outlive the nineteenth century. During the Great Depression a black odd-job worker confided: "Now they's one thing you got to be mighty keerful about when you is doin' for white folks. Don't never tell them nothin' that they don't want to hear. . . . Let them find out they own bad news" (WPA, *These Are Our Lives*, 1939; reprint ed., New York, 1975, 358). In their study of speech patterns more than a decade later, Raven and Virginia McDavid found that blacks more than whites were willing "to accept as authentic the responses suggested by the field worker, no matter how deliberately far-fetched some of these suggestions might be" ("The Relationship of the Speech of American Negroes to the Speech of Whites," *American Speech*, 26 [1951], 8 n.).
10. The values in nineteenth-century schoolbooks are discussed in Ruth Miller Elson, *Guardians of Tradition* (Lincoln, Nebr. 1964).
11. Parrish, *Slave Songs*, 196; Grissom, *The Negro Sings a New Heaven*, 3.
12. For an excellent picture of some of these developments, see August Meier, *Negro Thought in America, 1880-1915* (Ann Arbor, 1963).
13. Parsons, *Folk-Lore of the Sea Islands*, xx.
14. Elisha K. Kane, "The Negro Dialects Along the Savannah River," *Dialect Notes*, 5 (1925), 354.

15. Towne, *Letters and Diary*, 6. Towne herself found the freedmen's speech "not very intelligible."

16. Allen *et al.*, *Slave Songs*, xxvii.

17. Elizabeth Hyde Botume, *First Days Amongst the Contrabands* (Boston, 1893), 45-46.

18. For discussions of slave speech and the continuing influence of African language upon it, see Lorenzo D. Turner, *Africanisms in the Gullah Dialect* (Chicago, 1949); Herskovits, *Myth of the Negro Past*, Chap. 8; William A. Stewart, "Sociolinguistic Factors in the History of American Negro Dialects," *The Florida FL Reporter*, 5 (1967); William A. Stewart, "Continuity and Change in American Negro Dialects," *The Florida FL Reporter*, 6 (1968); Dillard, *Black English*. Peter Wood, *Black Majority*, Chap. 6.

19. Botume, *First Days Amongst the Contrabands*, 222.

20. John Bennett, "Gullah: A Negro Patois," *South Atlantic Quarterly*, 7 (1908), 340.

21. Turner, *Africanisms in the Gullah Dialect*, 11-14; Turner, "Problems Confronting the Investigator of Gullah," *Publication of the American Dialect Society*, No. 9 (1947), 74-84.

22. Bennett, *South Atlantic Quarterly*, 7 (1908), 336, 338; *South Atlantic Quarterly*, 8 (1909), 40; Ambrose E. Gonzales, *The Black Border: Gullah Stories of the Carolina Coast* (Columbia, S.C., 1922), 10.

23. Pearson, ed., *Letters from Port Royal*, 217.

24. Botume, *First Days Amongst the Contrabands*, 223.

25. Puckett, *Folk Beliefs*, 28-29.

26. Parsons, *Folk-Lore of the Sea Islands*, 134.

27. Smiley, *JAF*, 32 (1919), 369.

28. Richard M. Dorson, "A Negro Storytelling Session on Tape," *MF*, 3 (1953), 206; Hurston, *Mules and Men*, 204-5.

29. Parsons, *Folk-Lore of the Sea Islands*, xx.

30. Parrish, *Slave Songs*, 10.

31. Parsons, *Folk-Lore of the Sea Islands*, 199-200.

32. Kilham, *Putnam's Magazine*, 5 (1870), 311.

33. Louis Armstrong, *Satchmo: My Life in New Orleans* (New York, 1955), 188, 38.

34. Claudia Mitchell-Kernan, *Language Behavior in a Black Urban Community* (Working Paper No. 23, Language-Behavior Research Laboratory, University of California, Berkeley, 1969), 42-48, 60-61, 65-66.

35. William Labov, *The Social Stratification of English in New York City* (Washington, D.C., 1966), 495-96; William Labov, "Stages in the Acquisition of Standard English," in Roger W. Shuy, ed., *Social Dialects and Language Learning* (Champaign, Ill., 1965), 96-97.

36. Bacon and Parsons, *JAF*, 35 (1922), 300.

37. Armstrong and Ludlow, *Hampton and Its Students*, 85.

38. Daniel Webster Davis, "Echoes from a Plantation Party," *SW*, 28 (1899), 54.

39. Ira De A. Reid, *Phylon*, 3 (1942), 351-52.

40. Richmond *Times-Dispatch*, Aug. 28, 1904, quoted in Earnest, *Religious Development of the Negro in Virginia*, 129 n.

41. Puckett, *Folk Beliefs*, 581-82; Puckett, "Race Pride and Folk-Lore," *Opportunity*, 4 (1926), 82-85.

42. Meier, *Negro Thought in America*, 55, 161-70.

43. *SW*, 28 (1899), 362.

44. Gonzales, *Black Border*, 219-20.

45. The linguistic features of Black English which structurally inhibit the acquisition of Standard English are described in William A. Stewart, "Facts and Issues Concerning Black Dialect," *The English Record*, 21 (1971), 121-35, as well as in his other works cited above. See also Dillard, *Black English*. William Labov, on the other hand, has argued that the main barrier to the acquisition of Standard English by Negroes has been the conflict of values and culture. See Labov, *Language in the Inner City: Studies in the Black English Vernacular* (Philadelphia, 1972), Chaps. 6-7.
46. Albert Guerard, *Literature and Society* (Boston, 1935), 38.
47. Labov, *Language in the Inner City*, Chap. 7; Mitchell-Kernan, *Language Behavior in a Black Urban Community*, 82.
48. *Ibid.*, 148-49.
49. Labov, *Social Stratification of English in New York City*, 494.
50. Dillard, *Black English*, 239.
51. Stewart, *Florida FL Reporter*, 6 (1968); Dillard, *Black English*, Chap. 6; Labov, *Language in the Inner City*, Chap. 7.
52. Maya Angelou, *I Know Why the Caged Bird Sings* (Bantam ed., 1971), 191.

THE FATE OF THE SACRED WORLD

1. Higginson, *Army Life*, 24-25.
2. Botume, *First Days Amongst the Contrabands*, 62.
3. Lucy Chase to her family, Feb. 7, 1863, Swint, ed., *Dear Ones at Home*, 41.
4. Macrae, *Americans at Home*, 368.
5. Lucy Chase to "My Dear Friends," July 1, 1864, Swint, ed., *Dear Ones at Home*, 125-26.
6. Macrae, *Americans at Home*, 370-74.
7. Pearson, ed., *Letters from Port Royal*, 65.
8. Botume, *First Days Amongst the Contrabands*, 221.
9. Sidney Andrews, *The South Since the War: As Shown by Fourteen Weeks of Travel and Observation in Georgia and the Carolinas* (Boston, 1866), 227.
10. Macrae, *Americans at Home*, 214.
11. U.S. Department of Commerce, *Negro Population, 1790-1915* (Washington, D.C., 1918), Chap. 16; U.S. Department of Commerce, *Historical Statistics of the United States, Colonial Times to 1957* (Washington, D.C., 1960), Chap. H; Horace Mann Bond, *The Education of the Negro in the American Social Order* (New York, 1934), Chap. 9.
12. Kingsley, *West African Studies*, 53-54.
13. J. C. Carothers, "Culture, Psychiatry, and the Written Word," *Psychiatry* (1959), 307-20. For further analysis of the effects of literacy, see Marshall McLuhan, *The Gutenberg Galaxy* (New York, 1962), and Jack Goody and Ian Watt, "The Consequences of Literacy," *Comparative Studies in Society and History*, 5 (1963), 304-45.
14. Rattray, *Religion and Art in Ashanti*, 93.
15. Emily Austin, "Reminiscences of Work Among the Freedmen," *SW*, 26 (1897), 129.
16. Harris Barrett, "Negro Folk Songs," *SW*, 41 (1912), 240.
17. William Arms Fisher, *Seventy Negro Spirituals* (Boston, 1926), xi-xii.
18. *Ibid.;* WPA manuscripts, Florida File, Archive of Folk Song.

19. R. Emmet Kennedy, *Mellows: A Chronicle of Unknown Singers* (New York, 1925), 13-17; John A. and Alan Lomax, *Our Singing Country: A Second Volume of American Ballads and Folk Songs* (New York, 1941), 6-8; Arthur P. Hudson, *Specimens of Mississippi Folk-Lore* (mimeographed collection, Mississippi Folk-Lore Society, 1928), 95-96.

20. John A. and Alan Lomax, *American Ballads and Folk Songs* (New York, 1934), 610; White, *American Negro Folk-Songs*, 380; Byron Arnold, *Folksongs of Alabama* (University, Ala., 1950), 173.

21. Howard W. Odum and Guy B. Johnson, *The Negro and His Songs* (1925; reprint ed., Hatboro, Pa., 1964), 41, 42, 124, 131.

22. Nicholas George Julius Ballanta, *Saint Helena Island Spirituals* (New York, 1924), 26, 48; Scarborough, *On the Trail*, 209; Odum and Johnson, *Negro and His Songs*, 116; Coahoma County, Mississippi, Tape (1942), Archive of Folk Song.

23. WPA manuscripts, interview with Evelyn Macon, Feb. 10, 1939, File 45-4, Archive of Folk Song.

24. WPA manuscripts, interview with Rose Reed, Feb. 3, 1939, File 45-4, Archive of Folk Song.

25. Hallowell, *Calhoun Plantation Songs*, 36.

26. Tony Heilbut, *The Gospel Sound* (New York, 1971), 20.

27. Robert Russa Moton, *Finding a Way Out: An Autobiography* (1920; reprint ed., New York, 1969), 56-61. Moton's later very positive attitude toward the spirituals is expressed in his article, "A Universal Language," *SW*, 56 (1927), 349-51.

28. Allen *et al.*, *Slave Songs*, x.

29. Harriet Beecher Stowe, *Watchman and Reflector*, April 1867, quoted in Allen *et al.*, *Slave Songs*, xx.

30. Brown, *Lippincott's Magazine*, 2 (1868), 617-18; Kilham, *Putnam's Magazine*, 5 (1870), 308; Macrae, *Americans at Home*, 365.

31. Fenner, *Religious Folk Songs*, iv.

32. The literature on this point is too large to cite in full. Some examples: William Wells Newell, "The Importance and Utility of the Collection of Negro Folk-Lore," *SW*, 23 (1894), 131-32; Booker T. Washington, Preface to Samuel Coleridge-Taylor, *Twenty-Four Negro Melodies Transcribed for the Piano* (Boston, 1905), viii-ix; Jeannette Robinson Murphy, "The True Negro Music and Its Decline," *The Independent*, 55 (1903), 1724, 1730; Parrish, *Slave Songs, passim.*

33. Murphy, *Popular Science Monthly*, 55 (1899), 662, 664.

34. WPA manuscripts, interview with Lillie Knox, South Carolina File, Archive of Folk Song.

35. Fisk University, *Unwritten History*, 46-47; WPA Slave Narratives, interviews with Frankie Goole (Tenn.), Arrie Binns (Ga.).

36. Kilham, *Putnam's Magazine*, 5 (1870), 306.

37. Barbara Walsh, "Moms Mabley, 'I Got Sumpin' to Tell Ya' " (unpublished seminar paper, University of California, Berkeley, 1967), 22.

38. Quoted in Tindall, *South Carolina Negroes*, 207-8.

39. Randolph, *Slave Cabin to Pulpit*, 112-13.

40. Descriptions of the latter-day shout can be found in Christensen, *JAF*, 7 (1894), 154-55; Parrish, *Slave Songs*, Chap. 3; WPA, "Negroes of New York City," microfilm in Schomburg Collection, New York Public Library. Excellent examples of the shout exist on Library of Congress recording AAFS L3, *Afro-American*

Spirituals, Work Songs, and Ballads, and on Atlantic recording, 1351, *Negro Church Music.*

41. Parsons, *Folk-Lore of the Sea Islands,* 206; Parrish, *Slave Songs,* 55.

42. James Weldon Johnson, *Book of Negro Spirituals,* 33-34.

43. Daniel A. Payne, *Recollections of Seventy Years* (reprint ed., New York, 1969), 253-57.

44. The work of the Jubilee Singers is described in Marsh, *Jubilee Singers;* John Wesley Work, *Folk Song of the American Negro,* Chap. 8; Lovell, *Black Song,* 402-22; and Arna Bontemps' novel, *Chariot in the Sky* (Philadelphia, 1951).

45. *SW,* 22 (1893), 174; WPA Slave Narratives, interview with Squire Dowd (N.C.). In *Black Song,* 422, Professor Lovell argues against the notion that the spirituals were adulterated by the Jubilee Singers.

46. John Wesley Work, *Folk Song of the American Negro,* 104.

47. F. G. Rathbun, "The Negro Music of the South," *SW,* 22 (1893), 174.

48. Seward, "Preface to the Music," in Marsh, *Jubilee Singers,* 121-22.

49. *SW,* 22 (1893), 174.

50. James M. Trotter, *Music and Some Highly Musical People* (Boston, 1881), 267-69.

51. John Wesley Work, *Folk Song of the American Negro,* 114.

52. Lovell, *Black Song,* Chap. 25; Zora Neale Hurston, "The Hue and Cry About Howard University," *The Messenger,* 7 (1925), 315; Raymond Wolters, *The New Negro on Campus: Black College Rebellions of the 1920s* (Princeton, 1975), 37-38, 75, 249-55; R. R. Moton, "Negro Folk Music," *SW,* 44 (1915), 329-33; Phyl Garland, *The Sound of Soul* (Chicago, 1969), 62-64.

53. Alain Locke, "Our Little Renaissance," in Charles S. Johnson, ed., *Ebony and Topaz: A Collectanea* (New York, 1927), 117-18; Alain Locke, *The Negro and His Music* (New York, 1936), Chap. 3; Alain Locke, "The Negro Spirituals," in *The New Negro* (New York, 1925); *Opportunity,* 3 (1925), 322-23. W. E. B. Du Bois, the editor of *Crisis,* was also an early advocate of the spirituals. See his essay, "The Sorrow Songs," in *Souls of Black Folk.*

54. Alice Graham, "Original Plantation Melodies as One Rarely Hears Them," *Etude,* 40 (1922), 127-28.

55. James Weldon Johnson, *Book of Negro Spirituals,* preface; Langston Hughes and Arna Bontemps, eds., *The Poetry of the Negro, 1746-1949: An Anthology* (Garden City, N.Y., 1949), 23-24; Roland Hayes, *My Songs* (Boston, 1948), 113.

56. WPA manuscripts, Chicago File, Archive of Folk Song, contain material on the use of spirituals in Chicago churches during the 1930s. Also Mabel Travis Wood, "Community Preservation of Negro Music," *SW,* 53 (1924), 60-62; "Negro Spiritual Contest in Columbia," *SW,* 55 (1926), 372-73; *New York Times,* Sept. 30, 1971; Tim Dennison, Sr., *The American Negro and His Amazing Music* (New York, 1963); Lovell, *Black Song,* Chap. 25.

57. For these songs, see Guy and Candie Carawan, *We Shall Overcome: Songs of the Southern Freedom Movement* (New York, 1963).

58. By 1947 Samuel Adams found that only 19 per cent of the songs in active use among the sharecroppers on a large Mississippi Delta plantation were spirituals. "The Acculturation of the Delta Negro," *Social Forces,* 26 (1947), 203-4. A decade later Harry Oster found that in Louisiana spirituals were "no longer a natural spontaneous part of the repertoire of most folk Negroes." Oster, notes to Arhoolie Records, 2013, *Angola Prison Spirituals.*

59. A. E. Perkins, "Negro Spirituals from the Far South," *JAF,* 35 (1922), 239-40.

60. Guy Johnson, *Folk Culture on St. Helena Island,* 67-68.
61. John J. Niles, *Seven Negro Exaltations* (New York, 1929), 10-11.
62. Library of Congress recording AAFS L3, *Afro-American Spirituals, Work Songs, and Ballads.*
63. Puckett, *Folk Beliefs,* 62-63.
64. Interview with Charles Haffer, Jr., Coahoma County, Mississippi, Tape, Archive of Folk Song.
65. Saxon *et al., Gumbo Ya-Ya,* 476-77.
66. Perkins, *JAF,* 35 (1922), 223.
67. Henry, *JAF,* 44 (1931), 111-12; Parsons, *Folk-Lore of the Sea Islands,* 191-92; John and Alan Lomax, *Our Singing Country,* 26-27; Newman White, ed., *Frank C. Brown Collection,* VII, 664-68; Harold Courlander, *Negro Folk Music, U.S.A.* (New York, 1963), 76-78; White, *American Negro Folk-Songs,* 347-48.
68. WPA manuscripts, South Carolina File, Archive of Folk Song.
69. Howard W. Odum and Guy B. Johnson, *Negro Workaday Songs* (1926; reprint ed., 1969), 169-70.
70. Coahoma County, Mississippi, Tape, Archive of Folk Song.
71. Arhoolie Records, 2013, *Angola Prison Spirituals.*
72. Courlander, *Negro Folk Music,* 78-79.

THE DEVELOPMENT OF GOSPEL SONG

1. Unless otherwise noted, the gospel music used in this discussion can be found in the extensive collection of gospel sheet music in the Music Division of the Library of Congress.
2. Mahalia Jackson, *Movin' On Up* (New York, 1966), 72.
3. Thomas Dorsey, *Jesus Lives in Me,* copyright 1937, Thomas Dorsey.
4. WPA manuscripts, South Carolina File, Archive of Folk Song.
5. Alex Bradford, *He Makes All My Decisions For Me,* copyright 1959, Martin and Morris.
6. Alex Bradford, *My Reward Is in Heaven,* copyright 1953, Martin and Morris.
7. Heilbut, *Gospel Sound,* 13, 323.
8. WPA manuscripts, Florida File, Archive of Folk Song.
9. Thomas Dorsey, *I Don't Know Why I Have To Cry Sometime,* copyright 1942, T. A. Dorsey Publishing Co.
10. Thomas A. Dorsey, *Life Can Be Beautiful,* copyright 1940, T. A. Dorsey Publishing Co.
11. Armstrong and Ludlow, *Hampton and Its Students,* 113.
12. W. C. Handy, *Father of the Blues: An Autobiography* (1941; Collier Book ed., 1970), 5, 9-13, 134.
13. Willie the Lion Smith, *Music on My Mind: The Memoirs of an American Pianist* (London, 1965), 25-26.
14. John A. Lomax, "Sinful Songs of the Southern Negro," *Musical Quarterly,* 20 (1934), 181; John and Alan Lomax, *American Ballads,* 49.
15. John W. Work, "Changing Patterns in Negro Folk Songs," *JAF,* 62 (1949), 138-39.
16. John Aloysius Fahey, *A Textual and Musicological Analysis of the Repertoire of Charley Patton* (unpublished M.A. thesis, University of California, Los An-

geles, 1966), 88, 148; Paul Oliver, *Aspects of the Blues Tradition* (New York, 1970), 199; Robert M. W. Dixon and John Godrich, *Recording the Blues* (New York, 1970), 57-58; Roots Recording, RL-304.

17. Examples of their music can be found on the following recordings: Roots, RL-304 and RL-328; Historical, HLP-34; RBF 10; Atlantic 1351.

18. Work, *JAF*, 62 (1949), 140.

19. Langston Hughes, "Gospel Singing," newspaper clipping dated Oct. 27, 1963, in Music Division, Library of Congress.

20. *Pops Foster: The Autobiography of a New Orleans Jazzman*, as told to Tom Stoddard (Berkeley, 1971), 20-21.

21. Nat Shapiro and Nat Hentoff, eds., *Hear Me Talkin' to Ya: The Story of Jazz by the Men Who Made It* (Penguin Books ed., 1962), 247.

22. WPA manuscripts, Florida File, Archive of Folk Song.

23. Nat Hentoff, "Jazz in the Twenties: Garvin Bushell," in Martin Williams, ed., *Jazz Panorama: From the Pages of the Jazz Review* (New York, 1964), 76.

24. Gertrude P. Kurath, "Syncopated Therapy: The Testifying Service," *MF*, 1 (1951), 185.

25. Heilbut, *Gospel Sound*, 60.

26. This account of Dorsey's career was derived from the following: Thomas A. Dorsey, "The Precious Lord Story and Gospel Songs," mimeographed ms. in Music Division, Library of Congress; Thomas A. Dorsey, "Gospel Music," in Dominique-René de Lerma, ed., *Reflections on Afro-American Music* (1973), 189-95; Hollie I. West, "The Man Who Started the Gospel Business," newspaper clipping dated Dec. 7, 1969, in Music Division, Library of Congress; Heilbut, *Gospel Sound*, Chap. 2; George Robinson Ricks, *Some Aspects of the Religious Music of the United States Negro: An Ethnomusicological Study with Special Emphasis on the Gospel Tradition* (unpublished Ph.D. dissertation, Northwestern University, 1960), Chap. 4; Eileen Southern, *The Music of Black Americans* (New York, 1971), 402-4; Samuel B. Charters, *The Country Blues* (London, 1960), 92-93. A conveniently available selection of Dorsey's gospel songs can be found on the recently released two-record album, Columbia KG 32151, *Precious Lord: New Recordings of the Great Gospel Songs of Thomas A. Dorsey.*

27. This account of Jackson's career is derived from her autobiography, *Movin' On Up, passim.* Also Heilbut, *Gospel Sound*, Chap. 4. Jackson's singing can be sampled on her many recordings including: Columbia CL 644, *World's Greatest Gospel Singer*; Columbia CL 1643, *Every Time I Feel the Spirit*; Kenwood 474, *In the Upper Room*; Kenwood 486, *Mahalia.*

28. Heilbut, *Gospel Sound*, 224-25.

29. Dorsey, "Gospel Music," in de Lerma, ed., *Reflections on Afro-American Music*, 190-91.

30. Newbell Niles Puckett, "Religious Beliefs of Whites and Negroes," *JNH*, 16 (1931), 26.

31. WPA Slave Narratives (S.C.).

32. WPA manuscripts, Florida File, Archive of Folk Song.

33. Langston Hughes, *The Book of Negro Humor* (New York, 1966), 264.

34. Sterling Brown, "Negro Jokes," unpublished ms.; Pickens, *American Aesop*, 33.

35. E. C. Perrow, "Songs and Rhymes From the South," *JAF*, 28 (1915), 140; Scarborough, *On the Trail*, 168; John A. and Alan Lomax, *Folk Song U.S.A.* (New York, 1947), 337.

36. Mahalia Jackson, *Movin' On Up,* 66; Heilbut, *Gospel Sound,* 94.
37. John F. Szwed, "Negro Music: Urban Renewal," in Tristram P. Coffin, ed., *Our Living Traditions* (New York, 1968), 282.
38. Kenneth Morris, interview with George Robinson Ricks, 1956, in Ricks, *Some Aspects of the Religious Music of the United States Negro,* 143.
39. Thomas A. Dorsey, interview with George Robinson Ricks, 1956, in *ibid.,* 143-44.
40. Heilbut, *Gospel Sound,* 19-20, 216, 231-32.
41. Ricks, *Some Aspects of the Religious Music of the United States Negro,* 123-26; Richard Alan Waterman, "Gospel Hymns of a Negro Church in Chicago," *International Folk Music Journal,* 3 (1951), 87-91; Vattel Elbert Daniel, "Ritual and Stratification in Chicago Negro Churches," *American Sociological Review,* 7 (1942), 352-61; Gertrude P. Kurath, "Afro-Wesleyan Liturgical Structures," *MF,* 13 (1963), 29-32; Melvyn D. Williams, *Community in a Black Pentecostal Church: An Anthropological Study* (Pittsburgh, 1974), 150; Donald Smith, "The Gospel Way," clipping from *Washington Star,* Jan. 26, 1969, in Music Division, Library of Congress.

CHAPTER 4: THE RISE OF SECULAR SONG

EPIGRAPH

1. Sidney Bechet, *Treat It Gentle* (New York, 1960), 218.
2. Paul Oliver, *Conversation with the Blues* (New York, 1965), 164-65.

THE SHAPING OF BLACK SECULAR SONG

1. Mina Monroe, *Bayou Ballads: Twelve Folk-Songs from Louisiana* (New York, 1921), iii.
2. Newman White, ed., *Frank C. Brown Collection,* III, 237; Scarborough, *On the Trail,* 12, 99.
3. White, *American Negro Folk-Songs,* 162-63. Twentieth-century versions of this song were also collected in Scarborough, *On the Trail,* 126-27; Talley, *Negro Folk Rhymes,* 13; Robert Duncan Bass, "Negro Songs from the Pedee Country," *JAF,* 44 (1931), 427-28.
4. Scarborough, *On the Trail,* 106, 165, 179, 194, 223-25; Talley, *Negro Folk Rhymes,* 25-26; White, *American Negro Folk-Songs,* 151-52; Odum and Johnson, *Negro Workaday Songs,* 173-76; Loraine Darby, "Ring-Games From Georgia," *JAF,* 30 (1917), 218-21; Saxon *et al., Gumbo Ya-Ya,* 447; Parrish, *Slave Songs,* 118, 121, 234; Perrow, *JAF,* 28 (1915), 138-39; Coahoma County, Mississippi, Tape, Archive of Folk Song; Bruce Jackson, *Wake Up Dead Man: Afro-American Worksongs from Texas Prisons* (Cambridge, 1972), 109-10.
5. White, *American Negro Folk-Songs,* 152-56. Newman White, ed., *Frank C. Brown Collection,* III, Chap. 12, contains many old minstrel songs which have passed into the oral tradition.
6. White, *American Negro Folk-Songs,* 150.
7. Scarborough, *On the Trail,* 201-3; Newman White, ed., *Frank C. Brown Collection,* III, 496-97.
8. White, *American Negro Folk-Songs,* 157.

9. For an explication of this point, see Tony Russell, *Blacks, Whites and Blues* (New York, 1970).
10. Paul Oliver, *Bessie Smith* (New York, 1961), 3-5; Derrick Stewart-Baxter, *Ma Rainey and the Classic Blues Singers* (New York, 1970), 18 and *passim.*
11. Edmond Souchon, "King Oliver: A Very Personal Memoir," in Martin Williams, ed., *Jazz Panorama: From the Pages of the Jazz Review* (New York, 1964), 22.
12. Howard W. Odum, "Folk-Song and Folk-Poetry as Found in the Secular Songs of the Southern Negroes," *JAF*, 24 (1911), 259.
13. White, *American Negro Folk-Songs*, 186; Odum and Johnson, *Negro and His Songs*, 149; Odum, *JAF*, 24 (1911), 374.
14. Perrow, *JAF*, 28 (1915), 136, 176.
15. John J. Niles, *Singing Soldiers* (New York, 1927), 50, 60-61, and *passim.* John J. Niles, "White Pioneers and Black," *Musical Quarterly*, 18 (1932), 69-70.
16. Leah Rachel Clara Yoffie, "Three Generations of Children's Singing Games in St. Louis," *JAF*, 60 (1947), 39-41.
17. Interview with Clyde (Kingfish) Smith, WPA manuscripts, Archive of Folk Song. Frank Byrd, "32 Negro Market Songs," August 1934, unpublished typescript in the New York Public Library, contains a good collection of the cries of Harlem peddlers during this period.
18. Charles Keil, *Urban Blues* (Chicago, 1966), 33.
19. Willie the Lion Smith, *Music On My Mind*, 3.
20. Phyl Garland, *The Sound of Soul* (Chicago, 1969), 184-86.
21. Whitney Balliett, "Profiles: Room to Live In," *New Yorker* (Nov. 20, 1971), 76.
22. Alan Lomax, *Mister Jelly Roll: The Fortunes of Jelly Roll Morton, New Orleans Creole and "Inventor of Jazz"* (New York, 1950), 49-50.
23. Willie the Lion Smith, *Music On My Mind*, 65-66.
24. *Ibid.*, Chaps. 1-4.
25. Nat Henthoff, "Jazz in the Twenties: Garvin Bushell," in Martin Williams, ed., *Jazz Panorama*, 72.
26. *Ibid.*, 77; Leonard Feather, *The Book of Jazz* (New York, 1965), 28.
27. Daniel Hoffman, "From Blues to Jazz: Recent Bibliographies and Recordings," *MF*, 5 (1955), 111-12.

SECULAR MUSIC AND THE BLACK COMMUNITY: WORK SONGS

1. "Folk Singing," *Time* (Nov. 23, 1962), 60.
2. Oliver, *Conversation*, 29-30.
3. Parrish, *Slave Songs*, 197.
4. Nat Shapiro and Nat Henthoff, eds., *Hear Me Talkin' to Ya: The Story of Jazz by the Men Who Made It* (Penguin Book ed., 1962), 19.
5. *Ibid.*, 22-23.
6. Handy, *Father of the Blues*, 78.
7. Arthur W. Little, *From Harlem to the Rhine: The Story of New York's Colored Volunteers* (New York, 1936), xii.
8. Louis Armstrong, *Satchmo: My Life in New Orleans* (New York, 1955), 85-86; Richard Meryman, "An Authentic American Genius: An Interview with Louis Armstrong," *Life* (April 15, 1966), 100.
9. Charles Peabody, "Notes on Negro Music," *JAF*, 16 (1903), 148-52.

10. William R. Dixon, "The Music of Harlem," in John Henrik Clarke, ed., *Harlem: A Community in Transition* (New York, 1964), 70.

11. Odum and Johnson, *Negro and His Songs*, 2-3. A visitor to Florida had an identical experience. When Negro workers in a lumber camp became aware that he was attempting to copy down their songs, they became silent for several minutes and then chanted these lines: "White man dar, settin' on de lawg / Wastin' his time, jes wastin' his time." Charles Richard Greene, "Three Florida Negro Tunes and Words," *SFQ*, 9 (1945), 105.

12. Peabody, *JAF*, 16 (1903), 150.

13. Oliver, *Conversation*, 34-35.

14. Shapiro and Henthoff, eds., *Hear Me Talkin' to Ya*, 245-47.

15. The functions of redundancy in folk song are discussed in Alan Lomax and Joan Halifax, "Folk Song Texts as Culture Indicators," in *Structural Analysis of Oral Tradition*, Pierre and Elli Maranda, eds. (Philadelphia, 1971), and Alan Lomax, "Special Features of the Sung Communication," in *Essays on the Verbal and Visual Arts*," June Helm, ed. (Seattle, 1967).

16. Shapiro and Henthoff, eds., *Hear Me Talkin' to Ya*, 247.

17. Odum and Johnson, *Negro and His Songs*, 154.

18. Puckett, *Folk Beliefs*, 64.

19. Bruce Jackson, *Wake Up Dead Man*, 22-23.

20. There is a great deal of testimony concerning the relative silence of whites as compared with blacks. See, for instance, Bruce Jackson's *Wake Up Dead Man*, xv, 18, 32; Peabody, *JAF*, 16 (1903), 152; Labov *et al.*, *Non-Standard English of Negro and Puerto Rican Speakers*, 46.

21. Interview with Bradley Eberhart, WPA manuscripts, Florida File, Archive of Folk Song.

22. R. Emmet Kennedy, *Mellows: A Chronicle of Unknown Singers* (New York, 1925), 26-27.

23. Bruce Jackson, *Wake Up Dead Man*, 216-17.

24. John and Alan Lomax, *American Ballads*, 57.

25. Peabody, *JAF*, 16 (1903), 148.

26. John and Alan Lomax, *Negro Folk Songs as Sung by Leadbelly* (New York, 1936), 17-18.

27. John W. Work, *American Negro Songs and Spirituals* (New York, 1940), 38.

28. Whitney and Bullock, *Folk-Lore from Maryland*, 165-66.

29. John A. Lomax, *Adventures of a Ballad Hunter* (New York, 1947), 253-62.

30. Library of Congress recording AAFS L8, *Negro Work Songs and Calls*.

31. Big Bill Broonzy, *Big Bill Blues: William Broonzy's Story*, as told to Yannick Bruynoghe (New York, 1964), 108-11.

32. John Lomax, *Adventures of a Ballad Hunter*, 258-59.

33. Odum and Johnson, *Negro Workaday Songs*, 52-53, *Negro and His Songs*, 1.

34. Interview with Houston Bacon, Coahoma County, Mississippi, Tape, Archive of Folk Song.

35. Wilfrid Mellers, *Music in a New Found Land* (New York, 1965), 264.

36. Bruce Jackson, *Wake Up Dead Man*, 233, 1-2, 17-19, 25-27.

37. Handy, *Father of the Blues*, 145.

38. Odum and Johnson, *Negro Workaday Songs*, 3.

39. Howard W. Odum, *Rainbow Round My Shoulder* (Indianapolis, 1928), 280.

40. White, *American Negro Folk-Songs*, 279; WPA manuscripts, Florida File, Archive of Folk Song.

41. Courlander, *Negro Folk Music, U.S.A.*, 142.
42. A good version of *Go Down Old Hannah*, sung by Baker and his fellow inmates, may be heard on Library of Congress recording AAFS L8, *Negro Work Songs and Calls*.
43. John and Alan Lomax, *Negro Songs as Sung by Leadbelly*, 118-20.
44. Bruce Jackson, *Wake Up Dead Man*, 17.
45. Alan Lomax, "I Got the Blues," *Common Ground*, 8 (1948), 42.
46. John W. Work, *American Negro Songs and Spirituals*, 237-39. Virtually every collection of black work songs includes lines like these.
47. Bruce Jackson, *Wake Up Dead Man*, 30. Robert Ladner has made a similar point in his argument that one of the latent functions of Negro work songs was "that of boundary-maintenance between the Negro laborers and their white overseers. Singing laborers would tend to isolate non-singing overseer, generating group cohesion and making the degradation of slavery or imprisonment perhaps a bit more bearable." Robert Ladner, Jr., "Folk Music, Pholk Music and the Angry Children of Malcolm X," *SFQ*, 34 (1970), 140-41.
48. Samuel Adams, "The Acculturation of the Delta Negro," *Social Forces*, 26 (1947), 203.
49. Odum and Johnson, *Negro Workaday Songs*, 14, 88-89, and *passim*.
50. Hurston, "Florida Folklore," in WPA manuscripts, Florida File, Archive of Folk Song.
51. Jackson, *Wake Up Dead Man*, xxi-xxii, 25-27.
52. *Ibid.*, xxi.
53. Notes to Traditions Records, TLP 1020, *Negro Prison Songs from the Mississippi State Penitentiary*.
54. Broonzy, *Big Bill Blues*, 30.

SECULAR MUSIC AND THE BLACK COMMUNITY: THE BLUES

1. John F. Szwed, "Musical Adaptation Among Afro-Americans," *JAF*, 82 (1969), 116.
2. Parrish, *Slave Songs*, 197.
3. Talley, *Negro Folk Rhymes*, 277-80.
4. Coahoma County, Mississippi, Tape, Archive of Folk Song. Many excellent examples of levee and cornfield hollers can be heard on these tapes.
5. Handy, *Father of the Blues*, 143.
6. Library of Congress Recording, AAFS L8, *Negro Work Songs and Calls*.
7. Courlander, *Negro Folk Music, U.S.A.*, 81-82. For a more complicated and comprehensive categorization, see Willis Laurence James, "The Romance of the Negro Folk Cry in America," *Phylon*, 26 (1955), 15-30.
8. Olmsted, *Seaboard*, 394-95.
9. Henry A. Kmen, *Music in New Orleans: The Formative Years, 1791-1841* (Baton Rouge, 1966), 237. Twentieth-century market songs in New Orleans may be heard on Folkways Records FA 2461, *The Music of New Orleans*, vol. 1.
10. Ravenel, *Yale Review*, 25 (1936), 773.
11. Frank Byrd, "32 Negro Market Songs," typescript in New York Public Library. The Frank Byrd folder of the WPA manuscripts in the Archive of Folk Song is filled with descriptions of Harlem markets and peddlers.
12. Jones, *Blues People, passim*, especially Chap. 1.

13. Gunther Schuller, *Early Jazz: Its Roots and Musical Development* (New York, 1968), 67, 359ff.; Marshall W. Stearns, *The Story of Jazz* (New York, 1956), 105; Feather, *Book of Jazz*, 147-48; John W. Work, *American Negro Songs*, 32; Broonzy, *Big Bill Blues*, 54.
14. Handy, *Father of the Blues*, 103.
15. Odum, *JAF*, 24 (1911), *passim*.
16. Origin Jazz Library recording, OJL-1, *The Immortal Charlie Patton*, no. 1. It is important to reiterate that this was a common but certainly not an inevitable blues form. For instance, Patton's *Green River Blues* contains one stanza in which the first statement is repeated three times (AAA) and another in which it is the second and not the first statement that is repeated (ABB). It also was not uncommon for blues to have four or six line stanzas and consist of eight, eleven, thirteen, fifteen, or even twenty-two bars.
17. Abbe Niles, "Blue Notes," *New Republic*, 45 (1926), 292.
18. Tom Davin, "Conversations with James P. Johnson," in Martin Williams, ed., *Jazz Panorama*, 49-50.
19. Samuel B. Charters and Leonard Kuhnstadt, *Jazz: A History of the New York Scene* (Garden City, N.Y., 1962), 111.
20. Robert M. W. Dixon and John Godrich, *Recording the Blues* (New York, 1970), 7; John Godrich and Robert M. W. Dixon, *Blues and Gospel Records, 1902-1942* (London, 1969), 10.
21. Perry Bradford, *Born with the Blues: Perry Bradford's Own Story* (New York, 1965), Chap. 10.
22. Handy, *Father of the Blues*, 207.
23. Bradford, *Born with the Blues*, 118-19.
24. George Hoefer notes to Columbia Records album, C3L 33, *Jazz Odyssey*, vol. III; Stewart-Baxter, *Ma Rainey*, 6-7, 98.
25. Charters and Kuhnstadt, *Jazz*, Chap. 7.
26. Odum and Johnson, *Negro Workaday Songs*, 34; Dixon and Godrich, *Recording the Blues*, 99.
27. Oliver, *Bessie Smith*, 17, 42; George Avakian, "Bessie Smith," in Martin Williams, ed., *The Art of Jazz* (New York, 1959), 79, 90; John Hammond, "An Experience in Jazz History," in Dominique-René de Lerma, ed., *Black Music in Our Culture* (Kent, Ohio, 1970), 59; Charters and Kuhnstadt, *Jazz*, 108.
28. Stearns, *Story of Jazz*, 167-68; Handy, *Father of the Blues*, 208; Bradford, *Born with the Blues*, 48.
29. Garland, *Sound of Soul*, 90.
30. Dixon and Godrich, *Recording the Blues*, 14-20.
31. Hammond in de Lerma, ed., *Black Music in Our Culture*, 44.
32. Ross Russell, *Jazz Style in Kansas City and the Southwest* (Berkeley, 1971), 39.
33. Robert Hemenway, "Zora Neale Hurston and the Eatonville Anthropology," in Arna Bontemps, ed., *Harlem Renaissance Remembered* (New York, 1972), 205.
34. Mahalia Jackson, *Movin' On Up*, 29-30.
35. Fahey, *Charley Patton*, 11-16; Charters, *Country Blues*, Chap. 6; Dixon and Godrich, *Recording the Blues*, 41-63. There was, of course, greater artistic flexibility for those singers who accompanied themselves than for those vocalists who had to blend in with a large group of background musicians. There is evidence that record companies did censor some songs they felt were too bawdy, but their policies were by no means consistent or predictable.

36. Samuel Adams, *Social Forces*, 26 (1947), *passim*.
37. Biograph Records, BLP-12032, *Gertrude 'Ma' Rainey Queen of the Blues*, vol. 3.
38. Odum and Johnson, *Negro Workaday Songs*, 24-25. The list printed here is an abbreviated version of theirs.
39. Allen *et al.*, *Slave Songs*, 30-31.
40. *The Book of the Blues*, edited by Kay Shirley, annotated by Frank Driggs, (New York, 1963), 192-93.
41. WPA manuscripts, Florida File, Archive of Folk Song.
42. *Ibid.*
43. Bertrand Harris Bronson, "Folk-Song and Live Recordings," in Bronson, *The Ballad as Song* (Berkeley, 1969), 202-10; John F. Szwed, "Negro Music: Urban Renewal," in Tristram P. Coffin, ed., *Our Living Traditions*, 272-78; John W. Work, *American Negro Songs*, 29; Odum and Johnson, *Negro Workaday Songs*, Chap. 2; Courlander, *Negro Folk Music, U.S.A.*, 10-11.
44. Oliver, *Conversation*, 121-23.
45. Stewart-Baxter, *Ma Rainey*, 42.
46. Ethel Waters (with Charles Samuels), *His Eye Is on the Sparrow: An Autobiography* (Garden City, N.Y., 1951), 175, 235.
47. Bechet, *Treat It Gentle*, 61-64. The second line tradition has continued in New Orleans to this day. See Jack V. Buerkle and Danny Barker, *Bourbon Street Black: The New Orleans Black Jazzman* (New York, 1973), 16, 50, Chap. 4.
48. Willie the Lion Smith, *Music on My Mind*, 197; Valerie Wilmer, "Memphis Slim's Parisian Love Affair," *Downbeat*, 37 (Aug. 6, 1970), 15, 32.
49. Henthoff, "Jazz in the Twenties: Garvin Bushell," in Martin Williams, ed., *Jazz Panorama*, 81.
50. Garland, *Sound of Soul*, 115-17.
51. Keil, *Urban Blues*, Chaps. 5-6 and *passim*; Szwed, *JAF*, 82 (1969), 116-17. See also the discussions of the blues as "secular spirituals" in James H. Cone, *The Spirituals and the Blues* (New York, 1972), Chap. 6, and of the blues singer as a "secular priest" in Richard Middleton, *Pop Music and the Blues* (London, 1972), 22-25.
52. Handy, *Father of the Blues*, 105-6.
53. Carl Van Vechten, "Negro 'Blues' Singers," *Vanity Fair* (March 25, 1926), 67, 106.
54. Chris Albertson, *Bessie* (New York, 1972), 130.
55. Shapiro and Henthoff, eds., *Hear Me Talkin' to Ya*, 240.
56. Columbia Records G31093, *Bessie Smith / Nobody's Blues But Mine*.
57. Sam Rose, "Savoy Ballroom," typescript in WPA manuscripts, Archive of Folk Song.
58. Ross Russell, *Bird Lives! The High Life and Hard Times of Charlie (Yardbird) Parker* (New York, 1973), 270.
59. Shapiro and Henthoff, eds., *Hear Me Talkin' to Ya*, 247.
60. *Ibid.*, 243.
61. Garland, *Sound of Soul*, 112.
62. Willie the Lion Smith, *Music on My Mind*, 129, 3-4.
63. Bechet, *Treat It Gentle*, 212-13.
64. Oliver, *Conversation*, 165.
65. *Ibid.*, 25.
66. Bechet, *Treat It Gentle*, 105-8.
67. Mellers, *Music in a New Found Land*, 301.

SECULAR SONG AND PROTEST

1. Courlander, *Negro Folk Music, U.S.A.*, 176-77.
2. Bruce Jackson, Foreword to the 1965 reprint edition of Newman White, *American Negro Folk-Songs*, xi.
3. George B. Tindall, *The Emergence of the New South, 1913-1945* (Baton Rouge, 1967), 121-22; Arthur F. Raper, *Preface to Peasantry* (Chapel Hill, 1936), Chap. 11.
4. Scarborough, *On the Trail*, 77-79. Gates Thomas first heard versions of *Boll Weevil* in Texas in 1897. Thomas, *PTFS*, 5 (1926), 173-75. The many recorded versions include: Biograph Records, BLP-12013, *Early Leadbelly, 1935-1940;* Yazoo Records, L1020, *Charley Patton;* Melodeon Records, MLP 7323, *Blind Willie McTell: 1940.*
5. Newman White, ed., *Frank C. Brown Collection*, III, 245-47.
6. Mahalia Jackson, *Movin' on Up*, 13-14.
7. John Greenway, "The Flight of the Gray Goose," *SFQ*, 18 (1954), 171-72; John and Alan Lomax, *Negro Songs as Sung by Leadbelly*, 108-10. Leadbelly's version has been recorded on Folkways Records, FP 2941, *Leadbelly's Last Sessions.* Another version by James "Iron Head" Baker can be heard on Library of Congress Recording, AAFS L3, *Afro-American Spirituals, Work Songs, and Ballads.* Bruce Jackson found the *Gray Goose* still in the active tradition in the Texas prisons in the 1960s. See *Wake Up Dead Man*, 95-97.
8. Howard W. Odum, "Religious Folk-songs of the Southern Negroes," *The American Journal of Religious Psychology and Education*, 3 (1909), 269; Odum and Johnson, *Negro and His Songs*, xvii, 9.
9. Guy B. Johnson, "Double Meaning in the Popular Negro Blues," *Journal of Abnormal Psychology*, 22 (1927), 12-20.
10. Samuel Charters, *The Poetry of the Blues* (New York, 1963), 89; Biograph Records, BLP 12015, *Blind Lemon Jefferson, 1926-29*, Vol. 2.
11. "Cigaret Blues" on Folkways Records, RBF 14, *Blues Roots / Mississippi.*
12. "Me and My Chauffeur Blues," on Blues Classics Records 1, *Blues Classics by Memphis Minnie.*
13. "Terraplane Blues," on Columbia Records, CL 1654, *Robert Johnson: King of the Delta Blues Singers.*
14. Sexual imagery in Negro blues is discussed in Charters, *Poetry of the Blues*, Chap. 7; Oliver, *Blues Tradition*, Chap. 6; Paul Oliver, *Blues Fell This Morning* (New York, 1960), Chap. 4.
15. Louis W. Chappell, *John Henry: A Folk-Lore Study* (Jena, 1933), 86-87.
16. Many such songs were collected during the past forty years. Muriel Davis Longini, "Folk Songs of Chicago Negroes," *JAF*, 52 (1939), 101, 105-106; Bass, *JAF*, 44 (1931), 421; Saxon *et al.*, *Gumbo Ya-Ya*, 457; WPA manuscripts, Archive of Folk Song; Coahoma County, Mississippi, Tape, Archive of Folk Song; Harry Oster, *Living Country Blues* (Detroit, 1969), 352-63; Bruce Jackson, *Wake Up Dead Man*, 277, 279.
17. Guy Johnson, *Journal of Abnormal Psychology*, 22 (1927), 13n.
18. Chappell, *John Henry, passim*; Guy B. Johnson, *John Henry: Tracking Down a Negro Legend* (Chapel Hill, 1929), *passim*.

19. John Lomax, *Nation*, 105 (Aug. 9, 1917), 144.
20. Odum and Johnson, *Negro Workaday Songs*, 121-22.
21. Parrish, *Slave Songs*, 120.
22. White, *American Negro Folk-Songs*, 159.
23. Waters, *His Eye Is on the Sparrow*, 16.
24. Alan Lomax, *Common Ground*, 8 (1948), 42.
25. Odum and Johnson, *Negro Workaday Songs*, 112.
26. This tradition was not exclusively African, of course, but existed in many cultures, especially preliterate ones, including those of the American Indians. See Alan P. Merriam, *The Anthropology of Music* (Evanston, 1964), Chap. 10.
27. Bruce Jackson, *Wake Up Dead Man*, 126-28, 172, 18. In the 1930s John and Alan Lomax collected this tie-tamping chant: "Mary got a baby, an' I know it ain' mine, / I b'lieve it is de cap'n's 'cause he goes dere all de time," *American Ballads*, 18.
28. Odum, *JAF*, 24 (1911), 381-82, 388.
29. Odum and Johnson, *Negro Workaday Songs*, 116.
30. WPA manuscripts, Florida File, Archive of Folk Song.
31. Timely Records, TI-112, *Collection of Lawrence Gellert*.
32. Adams, *Social Forces*, 26 (1947), 203.
33. William Wells Brown, *Clotel, or the President's Daughter* (1853; reprint ed., New York, 1969), 138.
34. Harris, *Uncle Remus, His Songs and Sayings*, 195.
35. White, *American Negro Folk-Songs*, 382.
36. Philip Schatz, "Songs of the Negro Worker," *New Masses*, 5 (May, 1930), 7. During the 1930's black turpentine workers in Florida shaped the song to their own purposes: "Niggers get de turpentine, / Niggers empty it out, / White man pockets the money, / Niggers does without." WPA manuscripts, Florida File, Archive of Folk Song.
37. Thomas, *PTFS*, 5 (1926), 172.
38. Newman White Papers, Houghton Library, Harvard University. Other twentieth-century versions are printed in Talley, *Negro Folk Rhymes*, 207; Puckett, *Folk Beliefs*, 73; Bass, *JAF*, 44 (1931), 432; Perrow, *JAF*, 28 (1915), 140; John and Alan Lomax, *American Ballads*, 234.
39. Thomas, *PTFS*, 5 (1926), 165. Twentieth-century versions are printed in Perrow, *JAF*, 28 (1915), 140; John Lomax, *Nation*, 105 (Aug. 9, 1917), 144; Newman White, ed., *Frank C. Brown Collection*, VIII, 53, 549; White, *American Negro Folk-Songs*, 381.
40. Odum, *JAF*, 24 (1911), 267. Also John Lomax, *Adventures of a Ballad Hunter*, 231.
41. Odum and Johnson, *Negro Workaday Songs*, 116.
42. Mary Wheeler, *Steamboatin' Days: Folk Songs of the River Packet Era* (Baton Rouge, 1944), 28.
43. Parrish, *Slave Songs*, 247.
44. John and Alan Lomax, *Our Singing Country*, 280-83.
45. White, *American Negro Folk-Songs*, 382. Also WPA manuscripts, Florida File, Archive of Folk Song.
46. Timely Records, TI-112, *Collection of Lawrence Gellert*.
47. WPA, "Negroes of New York City," microfilm in Schomburg Collection.
48. Folkways Records, RBF 15, *The Atlanta Blues*.

49. WPA, "Negroes of New York City," microfilm in Schomburg Collection.
50. Russell Ames, "Protest and Irony in Negro Folksong," *Science and Society,* 14 (1950), 210.
51. Gellert, *Negro Songs of Protest* (New York, 1936), 27-28.
52. Saxon *et al., Gumbo Ya-Ya,* 453.
53. WPA, "Negroes of New York City," microfilm in Schomburg Collection.
54. Broonzy, *Big Bill Blues,* 82-86. Broonzy sings this song and discusses its creation on Folkways Records, FG 3586, *Big Bill Broonzy Interviewed by Studs Terkel.*
55. Thomas, *PTFS,* 5 (1926), 168.
56. Odum and Johnson, *Negro and His Songs,* 171; Odum and Johnson, *Negro Workaday Songs,* 76, 128; White, *American Negro Folk-Songs,* 255, 258; Scarborough, *On the Trail,* 190; Lawrence Gellert, *"Me and My Captain": Chain Gang Songs of Protest* (New York, 1939), 7, 18.
57. White, *American Negro Folk-Songs,* 255, 302; Scarborough, *On the Trail,* 235; Odum and Johnson, *Negro and His Songs,* 163; Courlander, *Negro Folk Music, U.S.A.,* 106-7, 265-66; WPA Slave Narratives, interview with Ira Foster (Ark.).
58. Odum, *JAF,* 24 (1911), 267.
59. Thomas, *PTFS,* 5 (1926), 166.
60. WPA, "Negroes of New York City," microfilm in Schomburg Collection.
61. WPA manuscripts, Vivian Morris File, Archive of Folk Song.
62. WPA, *These Are Our Lives* (1939; reprint ed., New York, 1975), 20.
63. Oliver, *Conversation,* 156-57.
64. Bruce Jackson, *Wake Up Dead Man,* 10.
65. W. P. Webb, "Miscellany of Texas Folk-Lore," *PTFS,* 2 (1923), 47.
66. John and Alan Lomax, *Our Singing Country,* 380-81; WPA manuscripts, Florida File, Archive of Folk Song; Gellert, *Negro Songs of Protest,* 16-17; Adams, *Social Forces,* 26 (1947), 203.
67. Gellert, *"Me and My Captain,"* 19; WPA manuscripts, Florida File, Archive of Folk Song; Wheeler, *Steamboatin' Days,* 118.
68. "Jumpin' Judy" on Library of Congress Record AAFS L3, *Afro-American Spirituals, Work Songs, and Ballads.*
69. Odum, JAF, 24 (1911), 282; John Lomax, *Nation,* 105 (Aug. 9, 1917), 144; Newman White papers, Houghton Library, Harvard University.
70. Mellinger E. Henry, "More Songs From the Southern Highlands," JAF, 44 (1931), 80.
71. White, *American Negro Folk-Songs,* 395-96.
72. Richard Wright, *12 Million Black Voices* (New York, 1941), 128; Ortiz M. Walton, *Music: Black, White & Blue* (New York, 1972), 29.
73. Walter Prescott Webb, "Notes on Folk-Lore of Texas," JAF, 28 (1915), 295.
74. Newman White, ed., *Frank C. Brown Collection,* III, 564.
75. Odum, JAF, 24 (1911), 386.
76. Wheeler, *Steamboatin' Days,* 81.
77. WPA, "Negroes of New York City," microfilm in Schomburg Collection. Longini, JAF, 52 (1939), 96-111, contains similar songs from Chicago.
78. Bruce Jackson, *Wake Up Dead Man,* 158.
79. Oliver, *Conversation,* 33-34, 24.
80. Pete Welding, "Robert Pete Williams," *Downbeat,* 37 (August 6, 1970), 17.
81. White, *American Negro Folk-Songs,* 350-351.
82. Fahey, *Charley Patton,* 158-59.
83. Newman White, ed., *Frank C. Brown Collection,* VII, 674-76.

84. Huddie Ledbetter, *Leadbelly: A Collection of World-Famous Songs by Huddie Ledbetter* (New York, 1959), 49; John and Alan Lomax, *Negro Songs as Sung by Leadbelly*, 181-83; Folkways Records, FA 2941, *Leadbelly's Last Sessions*, vol. I.

85. "High Water Everywhere," on Origin Jazz Library Records, OJL-7, *The Immortal Charlie Patton*, No. 2.

86. "Homeless Blues," on Columbia Records, G30818, *Bessie Smith: The Empress*.

87. "Dry Well Blues," on Origin Jazz Library Records, OJL-7, *The Immortal Charlie Patton*, No. 2.

88. Biograph Records, BLP-12040, *Son House—Blind Lemon Jefferson*.

89. Oliver, *Blues Fell This Morning*, 248-49.

90. Patrick B. Mullen, "A Negro Street Performer: Tradition and Innovation," *WF*, 29 (1970), 91-103; Arhoolie Records, 1040, *George Coleman, "Bongo Joe."*

91. Oliver, "Blues to Drive the Blues Away," in Henthoff and McCarthy, eds., *Jazz*, 90-91.

92. John and Alan Lomax, *American Ballads*, 193.

93. Biograph Records, BLP-12000, *Blind Lemon Jefferson, 1926-1929*, Vol. I. Leadbelly's version of this popular blues is on Elektra Records, EKL-301/2, *Leadbelly: The Library of Congress Recordings*.

94. Sterling A. Brown, "The Blues as Folk Poetry," in Hughes and Bontemps, *Book of Negro Folklore*, 384.

95. Odum and Johnson, *Negro Workaday Songs*, 18; White, *American Negro Folk-Songs*, 393; Scarborough, *On the Trail*, 274.

96. Paul Oliver, "Big Maceo," in Martin Williams, ed., *Art of Jazz*, 113.

97. "Prisoner's Talking Blues," on Arhoolie Records, 2011, *Angola Prisoner's Blues*.

98. Odum and Johnson, *Negro Workaday Songs*, 38; WPA manuscripts, Florida File, Archive of Folk Song; Timely Records, TI-112, *Collection of Lawrence Gellert*.

99. John W. Work, *American Negro Songs*, 245.

100. Columbia Records, GP 33, *Bessie Smith: The World's Greatest Blues Singer*.

101. White, *American Negro Folk-Songs*, 285.

102. "Hellhound on My Trail," on Columbia Records, CL 1654, *Robert Johnson*.

103. Thurman, *Negro Spiritual Speaks of Life and Death*, 50.

104. Odum and Johnson, *Negro and His Songs*, 171, 176; Odum and Johnson, *Negro Workaday Songs*, 46, 112-13; White, *American Negro Folk-Songs*, 306-8.

105. White, *American Negro Folk-Songs*, 394. Walter Webb heard similar lines in Texas that same year: "When a woman's in trouble, she wring her hands and cry; / But when a man's in trouble, it's a long freight-train and ride." Webb, *JAF*, 28 (1915), 293.

106. Coahoma County, Mississippi, Tape, Archive of Folk Song; Wheeler, *Steamboatin' Days*, 96-97; Bass, *JAF*, 44 (1931), 424.

107. Tindall, *South Carolina Negroes*, 153.

108. Fisk University, *Unwritten History*, 37.

109. Clyde Vernon Kiser, *Sea Island to City* (New York, 1969), Chap. 6.

110. WPA manuscripts, Florida File, Archive of Folk Song.

111. Perrow, JAF, 27 (1915), 140.

112. Harold Courlander, *Negro Songs from Alabama* (second ed., New York, 1963), 91.

113. Oliver, *Conversation*, 72. See Pete Daniel, *The Shadow of Slavery: Peonage in the South, 1901-1969* (Urbana, 1972).

114. "Letters of Negro Migrants of 1916-1918," *JNH*, 4 (1919), 330, 332, 337; "Additional Letters of Negro Migrants of 1916-1918," *JNH*, 4 (1919), 436-43.
115. Newman White, ed., *Frank C. Brown Collection*, VIII, 524.
116. Timely Records, TI-112, *Collection of Lawrence Gellert*.
117. Odum and Johnson, *Negro Workaday Songs*, 45.
118. Perrow, *JAF*, 27 (1915), 189.
119. George W. Pierson, *The Moving American* (New York, 1973), 12.
120. Oliver, *Conversation*, 146.
121. White, *American Negro Folk-Songs*, 259.
122. Jones, *Blues People*, 96.
123. Charters, *Poetry of the Blues*, 67-68; Stewart-Baxter, *Ma Rainey*, 76; Fahey, *Charley Patton*, 132; "Poor Man's Blues," on Columbia Records, G30450, *Bessie Smith: Empty Bed Blues*; Eric Sackheim, *The Blues Line: A Collection of Blues Lyrics* (New York, 1969), 135; Oliver, *Blues Fell This Morning*, 51.
124. WPA manuscripts, Florida File, Archive of Folk Song.
125. Bechet, *Treat It Gentle*, 63; Armstrong, *Satchmo*, 177, 25.
126. William Alan Muraskin, *Middle-Class Blacks in a White Society: Prince Hall Freemasonry in America* (Berkeley, 1975), 220.

SECULAR SONG AND CULTURAL VALUES—BLACK AND WHITE

1. Stanley Edgar Hyman, "The Child Ballad in America," JAF, 70 (1957), 239. See also Tristram P. Coffin, *The British Traditional Ballad in North America* (Philadelphia, 1963), and Roger D. Abrahams, "Patterns of Structure and Role Relationship in the Child Ballad in the United States," *JAF*, 79 (1966), 448-62.
2. Alan Lomax, *The Folk Songs of North America* (Garden City, N.Y., 1960), xvii-xix. For an example of the process Lomax describes, compare the British and American versions of *The Foggy Dew* which he prints in this collection, 89-90.
3. S. I. Hayakawa, "Popular Songs vs. the Facts of Life," *Etc.: General Review of Semantics*, 12 (1955), 83-95.
4. These lists were compiled from the American Society of Composers, Authors and Publishers' publication, *ASCAP Hit Tunes*, which covers the years from 1892 to 1970.
5. *That Old Black Magic*, lyrics by Johnny Mercer, music by Harold Arlen, copyright 1942 by Famous Music Corporation.
6. *Blue Moon*, lyrics by Lorenz Hart, music by Richard Rodgers, copyright 1934 by Metro-Goldwyn-Mayer Inc.
7. *Out of This World*, lyrics by Johnny Mercer, music by Harold Arlen, copyright 1945 by Edwin H. Morris & Company.
8. *Prisoner of Love*, by Leo Robin, Clarence Gaskill and Russ Columbo, copyright 1931 by Edwin H. Morris & Company.
9. *Our Love Is Here To Stay*, by George and Ira Gershwin, copyright 1938 by Gershwin Publishing Corporation.
10. *Out of This World*, lyrics by Johnny Mercer, music by Harold Arlen, copyright 1945 by Edwin H. Morris & Company.
11. These various musical categories and sub-markets, of course, were not mutually exclusive. One could partake of several simultaneously. The neglected subject of Country-Western music is discussed in the "Hillbilly Issue" of *JAF*, 78 (1965);

Bill C. Malone, *Country Music, U.S.A.* (Austin, 1968); D. K. Wilgus, "Country-Western Music and the Urban Hillbilly," in *The Urban Experience and Folk Tradition*, edited by Américo Paredes and Ellen J. Stekert (Austin, 1971).

12. Neil Leonard, *Jazz and the White Americans: The Acceptance of a New Art Form* (Chicago, 1962), 108-19, Appendix B.
13. Godrich and Dixon, *Blues and Gospel Records, 1902-1942,* 10; WPA manuscripts, Archive of Folk Song; Longini, *JAF,* 52 (1939), 99ff.
14. Columbia Records, G31093, *Bessie Smith: Nobody's Blues But Mine.*
15. Bass, *JAF,* 44 (1931), 431; White, *American Negro Folk-Songs,* 396.
16. Sackheim, *Blues Line,* 81.
17. "Death Letter Blues," on Biograph Records, BLP-12013, *Early Leadbelly, 1935-1940.*
18. Sterling Brown, "Blues as Folk Poetry," in Hughes and Bontemps, *Book of Negro Folklore,* 382.
19. Handy, *Blues: An Anthology,* 13.
20. Sackheim, *Blues Line,* 73.
21. "Bird Nest Bound," on Origin Jazz Library Records, OJL-7, *Immortal Charlie Patton,* No. 2.
22. Sackheim, *Blues Line,* 143-44.
23. Sterling Brown, "Blues as Folk Poetry," in Hughes and Bontemps, *Book of Negro Folklore,* 382; Oliver, *Blues Fell This Morning,* 90; Charters, *Poetry of the Blues,* 39.
24. Oliver, "Blues to Drive the Blues Away," in Henthoff and McCarthy, *Jazz,* 90.
25. Odum and Johnson, *Negro Workaday Songs,* 149.
26. Folkways Records, FG 3586, *Big Bill Broonzy Interviewed by Studs Terkel.*
27. "Put It Right Here (or Keep it Out There)," on Columbia Records, G 30450, *Bessie Smith: Empty Bed Blues.* Smith's complaints about men are particularly prominent on Columbia Records, GP 33, *Bessie Smith: The World's Greatest Blues Singer.*
28. "Doggin' Me Around Blues," on Historical Records, HLP-1, *Rare Blues of the Twenties,* Vol. I.
29. "Don't Fish in My Sea," on Biograph Records, BLP-12011, *Oh My Babe Blues: Ma Rainey and Her Georgia Jazz Band,* Vol. 2.
30. Broonzy, *Big Bill Blues,* 32.
31. Sackheim, *Blues Line,* 87; Charters, *Poetry of the Blues,* 64-65; "Deceitful Brown-skin Women," on Biograph Records, BLP-12015, *Blind Lemon Jefferson, 1926-1929,* Vol. 2.
32. "Leavin' Town Blues," on Historical Records, HLP-32, *I'm Wild About My Lovin', 1928-1930.*
33. Charters, *Poetry of the Blues,* 66.
34. Sackheim, *Blues Line,* 143.
35. Handy, *Blues: An Anthology,* 17.
36. Sterling Brown, "Blues as Folk Poetry," in Hughes and Bontemps, *Book of Negro Folklore,* 375.
37. "Going To Move to Alabama," on Origin Jazz Library Records, OJL-1, *Immortal Charlie Patton,* No. 1.
38. Charters, *Poetry of the Blues,* 46.
39. *Ibid.,* 39. Also Oliver, *Conversation,* 100.
40. Newman White papers, Houghton Library, Harvard University.
41. R. Emmet Kennedy, *More Mellows* (New York, 1931), 172-78.

42. Longini, *JAF*, 52 (1939), 103; John and Alan Lomax, *Negro Songs as Sung by Leadbelly*, 134-35; Courlander, *Negro Folk Music, U.S.A.*, 131.

43. Thomas, *PTFS*, 5 (1926), 166. For other versions of this common song, see White, *American Negro Folk-Songs*, 268, and Bass, *JAF*, 44 (1931), 426.

44. Odum, *JAF*, 24 (1911), 277.

45. Webb, *PTFS*, 2 (1923), 47.

46. "A Spoonful Blues," on Origin Jazz Library Records, OJL-7, *Immortal Charlie Patton*, No. 2.

47. Charters, *Poetry of the Blues*, 49.

48. "Southern Blues," on Biograph Records, BLP-12032, *Gertrude 'Ma' Rainey: Queen of the Blues*, Vol. 3.

49. Charters, *Country Blues*, 56.

50. Thomas, *PTFS*, 5 (1926), 162.

51. "Moon Going Down," on Origin Jazz Library Records, OJL-1, *Immortal Charlie Patton*, No. 1.

52. Handy, *Blues: An Anthology*, 13.

53. Biograph Records, BLP 12011, *Oh My Babe Blues: Ma Rainey and Her Georgia Jazz Band*, Vol. 2.

54. Oliver, *Blues Tradition*, 187.

55. Oliver, *Blues Fell This Morning*, 112.

56. Oliver, *Blues Tradition*, 187, 196.

57. Alfred C. Kinsey *et al.*, *Sexual Behavior in the Human Male* (Philadelphia, 1948), and *Sexual Behavior in the Human Female* (Philadelphia, 1953).

58. Lee Rainwater, "Crucible of Identity: The Negro Lower-Class Family," *Daedalus*, 95 (1966), 212n. and *passim*.

59. Clyde Taylor, ed., *Vietnam and Black America* (Garden City, N.Y., 1973), xx.

60. "High Sheriff Blues," on Origin Jazz Library Records, OJL-1, *Immortal Charlie Patton*, No. 1; White, *American Negro Folk-Songs*, 296.

61. Newman White papers, Houghton Library, Harvard University; Odum, *JAF*, 24 (1911), 358-59; John and Alan Lomax, *American Ballads*, 208; Coahoma County, Mississippi, Tape, Archive of Folk Song; "Take a Whiff on Me," on Elektra Records, EKL-301/2, *Leadbelly: The Library of Congress Recordings*.

62. Folkways Records, RBF 14, *Blues Roots / Mississippi*. Also on Historical Records, HLP-31, *Masters of the Blues, 1928-1940*.

63. "Tain't Nobody's Bizness If I Do," on Columbia Records, GP 33, *Bessie Smith: The World's Greatest Blues Singer*. Also Frank Stokes, "Tain't Nobody's Business," on Blues Classics Records, 5, *Country Blues Classics*, Vol. I; Odum, *JAF*, 24 (1911), 275, 357-58.

64. Oster, *Living Country Blues*, 404.

65. Pickens, *American Aesop*, 53.

66. White, *American Negro Folk-Songs*, 355; Niles, *Singing Soldiers*, 26.

67. Coahoma County, Mississippi, Tape, Archive of Folk Song. Newman White dates the popularity of this song from about 1905.

68. Talley, *Negro Folk Rhymes*, 10-11.

69. White, *American Negro Folk-Songs*, 327.

70. Odum, *JAF*, 24 (1911), 285. Also Mary Virginia Bales, "Some Negro Folk-Songs of Texas," *PTFS*, 7 (1928), 104.

71. Oliver, *Blues Tradition*, 114-15; Oster, *Living Country Blues*, 290, 320, 326.

72. White, *American Negro Folk-Songs*, 335.

73. Oliver, *Blues Fell This Morning*, 81.
74. Odum and Johnson, *Negro Workaday Songs*, 146, 123.
75. Timely Records, TI-112, *Collection of Lawrence Gellert*.
76. "Pony Blues," on Origin Jazz Library Records, OJL-7, *Immortal Charlie Patton*, No. 2; Oliver, *Blues Tradition*, 48, 87.
77. John and Alan Lomax, *Negro Songs as Sung by Leadbelly*, 157-59.
78. White, *American Negro Folk-Songs*, 326.
79. Odum, *JAF*, 24 (1911), 375; Odum and Johnson, *Negro Workaday Songs*, 146.
80. White, *American Negro Folk-Songs*, 317-21; Bales, *PTFS*, 7 (1928), 103-4; John and Alan Lomax, *American Ballads*, 246-47.
81. Talley, *Negro Folk Rhymes*, 99; Oliver, *Blues Fell This Morning*, 79.
82. Broonzy, *Big Bill Blues*, 144. Leadbelly used this proverb to argue in favor of brown skin. John and Alan Lomax, *Negro Songs as Sung by Leadbelly*, 216.
83. Odum and Johnson, *Negro Workaday Songs*, 81, 146.
84. Broonzy, *Big Bill Blues*, 144-45.
85. WPA manuscripts, Florida File, Archive of Folk Song.
86. Talley, *Negro Folk Rhymes*, 42-43. Also John and Alan Lomax, *American Ballads*, 50-52.
87. Odum, *JAF*, 24 (1911), 266; Perrow, *JAF*, 28 (1915), 189.
88. Kennedy, *More Mellows*, 161-166.
89. Monroe, *Bayou Ballads*, 14-15. Also Krehbiel, *Afro-American Folk-Songs*, 142; Allen *et al.*, *Slave Songs*, 113.
90. Yetman, ed., *Life Under the "Peculiar Institution,"* 127.
91. Parrish, *Slave Songs*, 38.
92. Waters, *His Eye Is on the Sparrow*, 30.
93. Lena Horne and Richard Schickel, *Lena* (Garden City, N.Y., 1965), 31-32.
94. For some brief but interesting speculations concerning the meaning of this transformation, see Marvin Harris, "The Rites of Summer," *Natural History*, 82 (1973), 20-22.
95. James W. Fernandez, "Persuasions and Performances: Of the Beast in Every Body . . . And the Metaphors of Everyman," *Daedalus*, 101 (1972), 45.
96. *The Autobiography of Malcolm* X, with the assistance of Alex Haley (New York, 1965), 54-56, 59.
97. Tom Davin, "Conversation with James P. Johnson," in Martin Williams, ed., *Jazz Panorama*, 58. Willie the Lion Smith also referred to "Dr. Hart's" preparation being widely used in this period. *Music on My Mind*, 101-2.
98. Philip Roth, *Portnoy's Complaint* (New York, 1968).
99. Adams, *Social Forces*, 26 (1947), 203.
100. Walton, *Music: Black, White and Blue*, 33-34.
101. Ralph Ellison, *Shadow and Act* (New York, 1964), 303-17.
102. Morroe Berger, "Jazz: Resistance to the Diffusion of a Culture Pattern," *JNH*, 32 (1947), 461-94; Aaron H. Esman, "Jazz—A Study in Cultural Conflict," *The American Imago*, 8 (1951), 219-26; Norman M. Margolis, "A Theory on the Psychology of Jazz," *The American Imago*, 11 (1954), 263-91; Leonard, *Jazz and the White Americans*.
103. Louis Armstrong, *Swing That Music* (New York, 1936), 76.
104. Eddie Condon, *We Called It Music* (New York, 1947), 107.
105. Hoagy Carmichael, *The Stardust Road* (New York, 1946), 53.
106. Condon, *We Called It Music*, 107.

107. Carmichael, *Stardust Road*, 16-17.
108. Milton "Mezz" Mezzrow and Bernard Wolfe, *Really the Blues* (New York, 1946), 127.
109. Carmichael, *Stardust Road*, 7-8.
110. Mezzrow and Wolfe, *Really the Blues*, 103-6, 204-5.
111. Benny Goodman and Irving Kolodin, *The Kingdom of Swing* (New York, 1939), 101. Jazz musicians as a separate group are discussed in William Bruce Cameron, "Sociological Notes on the Jam Session," *Social Forces*, 33 (1954), 177-82; Alan P. Merriam and Raymond W. Mack, "The Jazz Community," *Social Forces*, 38 (1960), 211-22; Howard S. Becker, *Outsiders: Studies in the Sociology of Deviance* (New York, 1963), Chaps. 5-6.
112. Norman Mailer, "The White Negro," in *Advertisements for Myself* (New York, 1959), 302-22.
113. Bechet, *Treat It Gentle*, 102.
114. Dixon, "The Music of Harlem," in John Henrik Clarke, ed., *Harlem*, 70.

CHAPTER 5: BLACK LAUGHTER

EPIGRAPH

1. Claude McKay, *Home to Harlem* (New York, 1928), 266-67.

INTRODUCTION

1. James Weldon Johnson, *Along This Way: The Autobiography of James Weldon Johnson* (New York, 1933), 118-20.
2. Claude McKay, "Negro Dancers," in Alain Locke, ed., *The New Negro*, 215.
3. James Weldon Johnson, *Along This Way*, 120.
4. James Weldon Johnson, *The Autobiography of an Ex-Coloured Man* (New York, 1927 ed.), 56.
5. Locke, ed., *The New Negro*, 214.
6. Jessie Fauset, "The Gift of Laughter," in Locke, ed., *The New Negro*, 161-67.
7. Talley, *Negro Folk Rhymes*, 244-45.
8. W. E. B. Du Bois, *Dusk of Dawn: An Essay Toward an Autobiography of a Race Concept* (New York, 1940), 148-49.
9. *Chicago Defender*, June 15, 1935, clipping in WPA manuscripts, New York File, Archive of Folk Song.
10. Theodor Reik, *Jewish Wit* (New York, 1962), 212.

LAUGHING AT THE MAN

1. Henri Bergson, *Laughter: An Essay on the Meaning of the Comic* (London, 1911), 94.
2. In addition to Bergson, discussions of this element of humor include D. H. Monro, *Argument of Laughter* (Notre Dame, Ind., 1963); Ralph Piddington, *The Psychology of Laughter* (London, 1933); Reik, *Jewish Wit*, 208.
3. Bernard, *Retrospections of America, 1797-1811*, 126, 128.

4. SW, 28 (1899), 192-94; Harris, *Uncle Remus: His Songs and His Sayings,* xv; Bacon and Parsons, *JAF,* 35 (1922), 301-10.

5. Lafcadio Hearn, *An American Miscellany,* Albert Mordell, ed. (New York, 1924), I, 160.

6. Parsons, *JAF,* 30 (1917), 186.

7. Fauset, *JAF,* 41 (1928), 550-51; Fauset, *JAF,* 40 (1927), 213, 267-69.

8. Dorson, *Negro Tales from Pine Bluff and Calvin,* 92-95, 250-54; Dorson, *Negro Folktales in Michigan,* 182-85; Dorson, "Negro Tales (Concluded)," *WF,* 13 (1954), 163-67.

9. Bacon and Parsons, *JAF,* 35 (1922), 306.

10. This is one of the most frequently collected Irishman jokes. For two nineteenth-century versions, see *SW,* 28 (1899), 192-93, and Harris, *Uncle Remus: His Songs and His Sayings,* xv. A-T tale type 1319, Pumpkin Sold as an Ass's Egg.

11. SW, 28 (1899), 193-94.

12. *Ibid.,* 193; Bacon and Parsons, *JAF,* 35 (1922), 303.

13. Fauset, *JAF,* 40 (1927), 267.

14. *Ibid.,* 268.

15. Bacon and Parsons, *JAF,* 35 (1922), 309-10.

16. Dorson, *Negro Tales from Pine Bluff and Calvin,* 253.

17. Bacon and Parsons, *JAF,* 35 (1922), 308.

18. *Ibid.*

19. Parsons, *Folk-Lore of the Sea Islands,* 120.

20. Bacon and Parsons, *JAF,* 35 (1922), 302-3.

21. *Ibid.,* 303-4.

22. Parsons, *Folk-Lore of the Sea Islands,* 92.

23. Dorson, *WF,* 13 (1954), 166-67.

24. Seth Scheiner, *Negro Mecca: A History of the Negro in New York City, 1865-1920* (New York, 1965), 130-33.

25. J. Mason Brewer, *Worser Days and Better Times: The Folklore of the North Carolina Negro* (Chicago, 1965), 80.

26. Dorson, *Negro Folktales in Michigan,* 77-78; Pickens, *American Aesop,* 113.

27. Fauset, *JAF,* 41 (1928), 551.

28. Dorson, *Negro Tales from Pine Bluff and Calvin,* 89-90.

29. Pickens, *American Aesop,* 113-15.

30. WPA manuscripts, Archive of Folk Song.

31. Brewer, *Worser Days and Better Times,* 30.

32. *Ibid.,* 86.

33. Coahoma County, Mississippi, Tape, Archive of Folk Song.

34. J. Mason Brewer, *Humorous Folk Tales of the South Carolina Negro* (Orangeburg, S.C., 1945), 7.

35. Arthur J. Prange, Jr., and M. M. Vitols, "Jokes Among Southern Negroes," *Journal of Nervous and Mental Disease,* 136 (1963), 163-64; Kathryn L. Morgan, "Jokes Among Urban Blacks in the North," *Blackfolk: Journal of Afro-American Expressive Culture,* 1 (1973-1974), 26.

36. Russell Middleton and John Moland, "Humor in Negro and White Subcultures," *American Sociological Review,* 24 (1959), 67.

37. Philip Sterling, *Laughing on the Outside* (New York, 1965), 213-14; Abrahams, *Positively Black,* 72; Paulette Cross, "Jokes and Black Consciousness: A Collection with Interviews," *The Folklore Forum,* 2 (1969), 140-41.

38. Morgan, *Blackfolk,* 1 (1973-1974), 28.

39. J. Saunders Redding, *No Day of Triumph* (New York, 1942), 210-11.

40. Ellen Dickson Wilson, "The Aunt Hannah Stories," *SW*, 41 (1912), 43.

41. These stories seem to have been common everywhere and were often told as true. For examples, see Langston Hughes, "Jokes Negroes Tell on Themselves," *Negro Digest*, 9 (1951), 21; Hughes and Bontemps, *Book of Negro Folklore*, 504-5; Brewer, *Worser Days and Better Times*, 104; Spalding, *Encyclopedia of Black Folklore and Humor*, 68; Sterling, *Laughing on the Outside*, 179-80; WPA manuscripts, New York File, interview with Levi C. Hubert, Oct. 18, 1938, Archive of Folk Song; John H. Burma, "Humor as a Technique in Race Conflict," *American Sociological Review*, 2 (1946), 713.

42. Alan Lomax, *Common Ground*, 8 (1948), 51.

43. Dorson, *Negro Tales from Pine Bluff and Calvin*, 123-24.

44. Sterling, *Laughing on the Outside*, 182.

45. Burma, *American Sociological Review*, 2 (1946), 713.

46. Pickens, *American Aesop*, 87-88.

47. Donald C. Simmons, "Protest Humor: Folkloristic Reaction to Prejudice," *American Journal of Psychiatry*, 120 (1963), 569.

48. Hamner Cobbs, "Give Me the Black Belt," *Alabama Review*, 17 (1964), 177; Sterling, *Laughing on the Outside*, 156-57; Dorson, *Negro Tales from Pine Bluff and Calvin*, 118.

49. N. S. Dodge, "Negro Patois and Its Humor," *Appleton's Journal of Popular Literature, Science, and Art*, 3 (1870), 161.

50. Anton C. Zijderveld, "Jokes and Their Relation to Social Reality," *Social Research*, 35 (1968), 286-311.

51. Dodge, *Appleton's Journal*, 3 (1870), 161.

52. Puckett, *Folk Beliefs*, 49; John Dollard, *Caste and Class in a Southern Town* (1937; Anchor paperback ed., 1949), 309-10.

53. *Ibid.*

54. Park, *JNH*, 4 (1919), 118.

55. Hughes, *Negro Digest*, 9 (1951), 22.

56. Alan Lomax, *Common Ground*, 8 (1948), 46.

57. Burma, *American Sociological Review*, 2 (1946), 714.

58. Hughes, *Negro Digest*, 9 (1951), 21; Langston Hughes, *The Book of Negro Humor* (New York, 1966), 13-14; Brewer, *PTFS*, 10 (1932), 53-54; Scarborough, *On the Trail*, 30; WPA manuscripts, New York File, interview with Levi C. Hubert, Archive of Folk Song.

59. Brewer, *Worser Days and Better Times*, 71-73; Brewer, *The Word on the Brazos: Negro Preacher Tales from the Brazos Bottoms of Texas* (Austin, 1953), 92-93; Dorson, *Negro Tales from Pine Bluff and Calvin*, 119-20.

60. Edgar T. Thompson, "The Plantation as a Form of Interracial Society," in Edgar T. Thompson and Everett C. Hughes, eds., *Race: Individual and Collective Behavior* (Glencoe, Ill., 1958), 326; Pickens, *American Aesop*, 71-72.

61. Ray Stannard Baker, *Following the Color Line* (1908; Harper Torchbook ed., 1964), 26.

62. Gunnar Myrdal, *An American Dilemma* (New York, 1962), 961.

63. Morgan, *Blackfolk*, 1 (1973-1974), 25.

64. Sterling, *Laughing on the Outside*, 106.

65. Like many popular jokes, this one was frequently told as a true story. See, for instance, Broonzy, *Big Bill Blues*, 38-39.

66. Cobbs, *Alabama Review*, 17 (1964), 170-71.

67. Dorothy Nelkin, "A Response to Marginality: The Case of Migrant Farm Workers," *British Journal of Sociology*, 20 (1969), 387.
68. Sterling Brown, "Negro Jokes," unpublished ms., 11.
69. Brewer, *Worser Days and Better Times*, 121-22.
70. Sterling, *Laughing on the Outside*, 129; Pickens, *American Aesop*, 19.
71. WPA manuscripts, Florida File, Archive of Folk Song.
72. Sterling, *Laughing on the Outside*, 206; Abrahams, *Positively Black*, 34; Morgan, *Blackfolk*, 1 (1973-1974), 26; Dorson, *Negro Tales from Pine Bluff and Calvin*, 122-23.
73. Abrahams, *Positively Black*, 133.
74. Raven I. McDavid, Jr., "Linguistic Geography and the Study of Folklore," *NYFQ*, 14 (1958), 257-58.
75. Sterling, *Laughing on the Outside*, 81-82. For other jokes on this theme, see Brewer, *Worser Days and Better Times*, 95; Norine Dresser, "The Metamorphosis of the Humor of the Black Man," *NYFQ*, 26 (1970), 224.
76. Sterling, *Laughing on the Outside*, 78; Morgan, *Blackfolk*, 1 (1973-74), 26; Hughes and Bontemps, *Book of Negro Folklore*, 504.
77. Pickens, *American Aesop*, 61-62; Burma, *American Sociological Review*, 2 (1946), 712; Sterling Brown, "Negro Jokes," unpublished ms., 11.
78. *Ibid.*
79. William Henry Hardin, "Old Days at Cold Springs," *PTFS*, 30 (1961), 126-27; Pickens, *American Aesop*, 39-41; Hughes, *Book of Negro Humor*, 262.
80. Louis E. Lomax, "The American Negro's New Comedy Act," *Harper's Magazine*, 222 (1961), 45-46; Sterling, *Laughing on the Outside*, 210.
81. Hughes, *Book of Negro Humor*, 265; Brewer, *Worser Days and Better Times*, 105-6; Jim Haskins, *Jokes from Black Folks* (Garden City, N.Y., 1973), 62-63.
82. For the jokes about Faubus and Wallace, see Hughes, *Book of Negro Humor*, 262, and Alan Dundes, *Mother Wit from the Laughing Barrel* (Englewood Cliffs, N.J., 1973), 620.

THE ECONOMY OF LAUGHTER

1. G. Legman, *Rationale of the Dirty Joke: An Analysis of Sexual Humor* (New York, 1968), 9.
2. "The very essence of Negro humor is the minimal use of words for the maximal effect. The Negro can pack into a few delightful words a long-winded story which might take us five minutes to narrate." (Cobbs, *Alabama Review*, 17 [1964], 174).
3. Sigmund Freud, *Jokes and Their Relation to the Unconscious*, translated by James Strachey (New York, 1963), *passim*.
4. Kenneth Burke, *Attitudes Toward History* (Los Altos, Calif. 1959), 171. Italics in original.
5. Charters, *Country Blues*, 130-31.
6. Dorson, *Negro Tales from Pine Bluff and Calvin*, 121-22, 235-38; Dorson, *MF*, 6 (1956), 19; Spalding, *Encyclopedia of Black Folklore and Humor*, 63, 350-51.
7. William H. Wiggins, Jr., "Jack Johnson as Bad Nigger: The Folklore of His Life," *The Black Scholar*, 2 (1971), 39.
8. Morgan, *Blackfolk*, 1 (1973-1974), 27-28; Spalding, *Encyclopedia of Black Folklore and Humor*, 508-9.

9. Dundes, *Mother Wit*, 612.
10. Girlene Marie Williams, "Negro Stories from the Colorado Valley," *PTFS*, 29 (1959), 164-65.
11. Abrahams, *Positively Black*, 33-34; Sterling, *Laughing on the Outside*, 75.
12. Louis Lomax, *Harper's Magazine*, 222 (1961), 45.
13. Dorson, *Negro Tales from Pine Bluff and Calvin*, 115-16.
14. Wiggins, *Black Scholar*, 2 (1971), 41.
15. Pickens, *American Aesop*, 63-64.
16. Brewer, *Humorous Tales of South Carolina Negroes*, 53.
17. Hughes and Bontemps, *Book of Negro Folklore*, 501.
18. Sterling, *Laughing on the Outside*, 110. Growing up in a Jewish immigrant neighborhood in New York City, I heard this joke told by Jews and about Jews many times. Reik prints a Jewish version in *Jewish Wit*, 43.
19. Hughes, *Book of Negro Humor*, 261; Morgan, *Blackfolk*, 1 (1973-1974), 25.
20. Sterling Brown, "Negro Jokes," unpublished ms., 11; Sterling, *Laughing on the Outside*, 68. Lizzie Lavender, an ex-slave born in 1841, drew the same lesson from Douglass' life: "And yet Frederick Douglass was only half black. I have often thought that if a man who is only half black can become great like that, what may not be achieved by a person who is all black like me?" (James P. Frances, "Mother Lavender and Her Holiday Dinners," *NYFQ*, 8 [1952], 286).
21. Spalding, *Encyclopedia of Black Folklore and Humor*, 520. Again, this is a joke told by other ethnic groups as well. I often heard it told about a Jew who is accidentally converted to Catholicism and rushes to tell his brethren only to be greeted with hostility. "How do you like that," he mutters to himself. "I've been a *goy* only a few hours and already I feel like an anti-Semite."
22. Prange and Vitols, *Journal of Nervous and Mental Disease*, 136 (1963), 164. Hylan Lewis, *Blackways of Kent* (Chapel Hill, 1955), 57, prints a closely related joke concerning hair texture.
23. Louis Lomax, *Harper's Magazine*, 222 (1961), 44-45.
24. Brewer, *Worser Days and Better Times*, 34-36.
25. Dorson, *Negro Folktales in Michigan*, 216n.
26. Odum and Johnson, *Workaday Songs*, 134.
27. WPA, "Negroes of New York City," microfilm in Schomburg Collection; Gellert, *Negro Songs of Protest*, 12-14.
28. Saxon *et al.*, *Gumbo Ya-Ya*, 484.
29. Sackheim, *Blues Line*, 251-52. Paul Oliver has an excellent discussion of the attitudes in blues toward preachers and religion in his *Blues Tradition*, Chap. 2.
30. Coahoma County, Mississippi, Tape, Archive of Folk Song.
31. Brewer, *Dog Ghosts*, 84.
32. Coahoma County, Mississippi, Tape, Archive of Folk Song; Ray B. Browne, "Negro Folktales from Alabama," *SFQ*, 18 (1954), 132; Brewer, *PTFS*, 10 (1932), 36-37.
33. K. Leroy Irvis, "Negro Tales from Eastern New York," *NYFQ*, 11 (1955), 176; Parsons, *Folk-Lore of the Sea Islands*, 57-58; Fauset, *JAF*, 41 (1928), 552. For an example of this joke told as a true story, see Phoebe Beckner Estes, "The Reverend Peter Vinegar," *SFQ*, 23 (1959), 250-51.
34. Sterling, *Laughing on the Outside*, 116-17.
35. *Ibid.*, 118-19.
36. Brewer, *Humorous Folk Tales of the South Carolina Negro*, 36.
37. WPA manuscripts, interview with Rivlana Boynton, Florida File, Archive of

Folk Song; WPA Slave Narratives, interview with Clark Hill (Ark.); Brewer *Dog Ghosts*, 7-9; Bacon and Parsons, *JAF*, 35 (1922), 295.

38. Dorson, *SFQ*, 19 (1955), 111-12.
39. Browne, *SFQ*, 18 (1954), 133.
40. Brewer, *Dog Ghosts*, 45-46.
41. Hughes, *Book of Negro Humor*, 30.
42. Haskins, *Jokes for Black Folks*, 82; Dresser, NYFQ, 26 (1970), 223-24.
43. Smiley, *JAF*, 32 (1919), 373; Guy Johnson, *Folk Culture on St. Helena Island*, 153-54; A. W. Eddins, "Brazos Bottom Philosophy," *PTFS*, 9 (1931), 160-62.
44. Prange and Vitols, *Journal of Nervous and Mental Disease*, 136 (1963), 164.
45. WPA, "Negroes of New York City," microfilm in Schomburg Collection.
46. Brewer, *Dog Ghosts*, 105-9.
47. Lewis, *Blackways of Kent*, 291.
48. Pickens, *American Aesop*, 94-95.
49. K. Leroy Irvis who told this story in 1955 commented, "I can't tell you who told this one to me. It seems as if I have always known it" (*NYFQ*, 11 [1955], 170-71). In Michigan Suggs told a version ending with the line, "My peoples, my peoples won't do" (Dorson, *Negro Tales from Pine Bluff and Calvin*, 183-84).
50. *Ibid.*, 118.
51. Brewer, *Worser Days and Better Times*, 112-13.
52. Irvis, *NYFQ*, 11 (1955), 171-72; Smiley, *JAF*, 32 (1919), 374.
53. Dorson, *American Negro Folktales*, 178-80; WPA manuscripts, Florida File, Archive of Folk Song; Smiley, *JAF*, 32 (1919), 365.
54. Hughes, *Negro Digest*, 9 (1951), 25.
55. Sterling, *Laughing on the Outside*, 169-71; Irvis, *NYFQ*, 11 (1955), 173-74; WPA Slave Narratives, interview with Marion Johnson (Ark.).
56. Prange and Vitols, *Journal of Nervous and Mental Disease*, 136 (1963), 165. Roger Abrahams collected an interesting variant of this joke which he interprets as related to notions of the blacks' superior sexual powers (*Positively Black*, 70).
57. Roger D. Abrahams, *Deep Down in the Jungle . . . : Negro Narrative Folklore from the Streets of Philadelphia* (Hatboro, Pa., 1964), 235.
58. Sterling Brown, "Negro Jokes," unpublished ms., 2.
59. Spalding, *Encyclopedia of Black Folklore and Humor*, 350.
60. Parsons, *JAF*, 30 (1917), 186.
61. Abrahams, *Positively Black*, 98.
62. Carl Carmer, *Stars Fell on Alabama* (New York, 1934), 120-21; Legman, *Rationale of the Dirty Joke*, 312.
63. *Ibid.*, 312-13.
64. Cross, *Folklore Forum*, 2 (1969), 151.
65. Hughes, *Negro Digest*, 9 (1951), 24-25.
66. Cross, *Folklore Forum*, 2 (1969), 141-42; Sterling Brown, "Negro Jokes," unpublished ms., 3.
67. Neil A. Eddington, "Genital Superiority in Oakland Negro Folklore," *The Kroeber Anthropological Society Papers*, No. 33 (1965), 100-101.
68. Abrahams, *Positively Black*, 116.
69. Eddington, *Kroeber Anthropological Society Papers*, No. 33 (1965), 100.
70. *Ibid.*, 99-100; Abrahams, *Positively Black*, 60-61; Legman, *Rationale of the Dirty Joke*, 292, 313; Prange and Vitols, *Journal of Nervous and Mental Disease*, 136 (1963), 165.

71. Martin Grotjahn, *Beyond Laughter: Humor and the Subconscious* (New York, 1966), 23-24.
72. Julius Lester, *To Be a Slave* (New York, 1968), 84.
73. Grotjahn, *Beyond Laughter,* 22-23, 25. Theodor Reik has also argued that this type of humor among Jews does not constitute self-estrangement (*Jewish Wit,* 188-94). For a different perspective, see Bernard Rosenberg and Gilbert Shapiro, "Marginality and Jewish Humor," *Midstream,* 4 (1958), 70-80.
74. Robert Merton, *Social Theory and Social Structure* (New York, 1957), 428-29.
75. Thomas F. Gossett, *Race: The History of an Idea in America* (Dallas, 1963), 364.
76. Abrahams, *Positively Black,* 69-70.
77. Prange and Vitols, *Journal of Nervous and Mental Disease,* 136 (1963), 165; Wiggins, *Black Scholar,* 2 (1971), 42; Hughes and Bontemps, *Book of Negro Folklore,* 509; Dorson, *American Negro Folktales,* 185-86.
78. Russell Middleton, "Negro and White Reactions to Racial Humor," *Sociometry,* 22 (1959), 175-83.
79. Middleton and Moland, *American Sociological Review,* 24 (1959), 61-69.
80. Brewer, *Worser Days and Better Times,* 29-30.
81. Abrahams, *Positively Black,* 70n.
82. Richard Wright, *Black Boy* (Cleveland, 1945), 71.
83. Lewis, *Blackways of Kent,* 200-201.
84. Sterling Brown, "Negro Jokes," unpublished ms., 10.
85. Morgan, *Blackfolk,* 1 (1973-1974), 26-27; Prange and Vitols, *Journal of Nervous and Mental Disease,* 136 (1963), 164.
86. Spalding, *Encyclopedia of Black Folklore and Humor,* 349-50.
87. Hughes, *Book of Negro Humor,* 263.
88. Dorson, *Negro Tales from Pine Bluff and Calvin,* 116-17; Prange and Vitols, *Journal of Nervous and Mental Disease,* 136 (1963), 164.
89. Pickens, *American Aesop,* 82-83.
90. Hughes, *Negro Digest,* 9 (1951), 21.
91. Dollard, *Caste and Class,* 310.
92. Sigmund Freud, "Humour," *International Journal of Psycho-Analysis,* 9 (1928), 1-6. Also Lucille Dooley, "A Note on Humor," *The Psychoanalytic Review,* 21 (1934), 49-57; Kenneth Burke, *Attitudes Toward History,* 43.
93. Prange 'and Vitols, *Journal of Nervous and Mental Disease,* 136 (1963), 164.
94. Sterling, *Laughing on the Outside,* 77-78; Spalding, *Encyclopedia of Black Folklore and Humor,* 65-66.
95. Odum and Johnson, *Negro Workaday Songs,* 85.

THE RITUAL OF INSULT

1. Dick Gregory, *Nigger: An Autobiography* (New York, Pocket Cardinal ed., 1965), 40-42.
2. H. Rap Brown, *Die Nigger Die!* (New York, 1969), 25-26.
3. For descriptions of verbal contests in Oakland, see Mitchell-Kernan, *Language Behavior in a Black Urban Community,* 87-129; in New York, William Labov *et al., A Study of the Non-Standard English of Negro and Puerto Rican Speakers in New York City* (Cooperative Research Project No. 3288, New York, 1968), II, 76-135; and Labov, *Language in the Inner City,* Chap. 8; in Philadelphia, Roger D. Abrahams, "Playing the Dozens," *JAF,* 75 (1962), 209-20, and Ab-

rahams, *Deep Down in the Jungle,* Chap. 2; in Philadelphia and Texas, Abrahams, *Positively Black,* 39-42; in Chicago, Thomas Kochman, "Toward an Ethnography of Black American Speech Behavior," in Norman E. Whitten, Jr., and John F. Szwed, eds., *Afro-American Anthropology* (New York, 1970), 145-62; in Washington, D.C., Lee Rainwater, *Behind Ghetto Walls: Black Families in a Federal Slum* (Chicago, 1970), 277-78, and Ulf Hannerz, *Soulside: Inquiries into Ghetto Culture and Community* (New York, 1969), 129-35.

4. Hannerz, *Soulside,* 133.
5. Abrahams, *JAF,* 75 (1962), 219; Abrahams, *Deep Down in the Jungle,* Chap. 2; Hannerz, *Soulside,* 129-31; Kochman in Whitten and Szwed, eds., *Afro-American Anthropology,* 159.
6. Labov *et al., Non-Standard English of Negro and Puerto Rican Speakers,* II, 100-103.
7. J. Huizinga, *Homo Ludens: A Study of the Play-Element in Culture* (Boston, 1955), 10.
8. Abrahams, *Deep Down in the Jungle,* 62.
9. Mitchell-Kernan, *Language Behavior in a Black Urban Community,* 9.
10. Shapiro and Henthoff, eds., *Hear Me Talkin' to Ya,* 223-24.
11. Jack Olsen, *Black Is Best: The Riddle of Cassius Clay* (New York, Dell ed., 1967), 10.
12. John Dollard, "The Dozens: Dialect of Insult," *The American Imago,* 1 (1939), 3-25.
13. Rattray, *Ashanti,* 156-67; Herskovits, *New World Negro,* 138.
14. Herskovits, *Dahomey,* I, 151-53; Philip Mayer, "The Joking of 'Pals' in Gusii Age-Sets," *African Studies,* 10 (1951), 27-41; Donald Simmons, "Possible West African Sources for the American Negro 'Dozens,'" *JAF,* 76 (1963), 339-40; William Elton, "'Playing the Dozens,'" *American Speech,* 25 (1950), 232-33; Dundes, *Mother Wit,* 295-97.
15. Quoted in Kingsley, *West African Studies,* 319-20.
16. Huizinga, *Homo Ludens,* 65.
17. Herbert Halpert, "A Pattern of Proverbial Exaggeration from West Kentucky," *MF,* 1 (1951), 41-47.
18. Brewer, *Humorous Folk Tales of the South Carolina Negro,* 27-30.
19. Abrahams, *Positively Black,* 40; Labov *et al., Non-Standard English of Negro and Puerto Rican Speakers,* II, 80-81.
20. Thomas, *PTFS,* 5 (1926), 172.
21. Odum, *JAF,* 24 (1911), 276.
22. White, *American Negro Folk-Songs,* 365.
23. Sackheim, *Blues Line,* 119.
24. Oliver, *Blues Tradition,* 240. See also the interview with Perryman in Oliver, *Conversation,* 61-62. An unexpurgated version of the Dozens may be heard on Raglan Records, *The Unexpurgated Folk Songs of Men,* collected by Mack McCormick.
25. Shirley and Driggs, *Book of the Blues,* 228-29.
26. Oliver, *Blues Tradition,* 240.
27. Saxon *et al., Gumbo Ya-Ya,* 448-49.
28. Oster, *Living Country Blues,* 301.
29. Biograph Records, BLP-12013, *Early Leadbelly, 1935-1940.*
30. Danny Barker, "A Memory of King Bolden," *Evergreen Review,* 12 (1965), 68.
31. Coahoma County, Mississippi, Tape, Archive of Folk Song.

32. Abrahams, *Deep Down in the Jungle*, 50n.
33. Oliver, *Blues Tradition*, 230-33.
34. Dollard, *American Imago*, 1 (1939), 14.
35. H. Rap Brown, *Die Nigger Die!*, 27.
36. Joyce A. Ladner, *Tomorrow's Tomorrow: The Black Woman* (Garden City, Anchor book ed., N.Y., 1972), 66.
37. Nikki Giovanni, *Gemini* (New York, 1971), 17.
38. Rainwater, *Behind Ghetto Walls*, 277-78.
39. Abrahams, *Positively Black*, 39.
40. Dollard, *American Imago*, 1 (1939), 20-25. Samuel J. Sperling, "On the Psychodynamics of Teasing," *Journal of the American Psychoanalytic Association*, 1 (1953), 458-83, offers a similar interpretation.
41. Abrahams, *Deep Down in the Jungle*, 56-58; Abrahams, *JAF*, 75 (1962), 209, 213.
42. For a brief discussion of ritual insult among whites, see Labov *et al.*, *Non-Standard English of Negro and Puerto Rican Speakers*, II, 89-90. From my own experience as an adolescent in a German and East European Jewish neighborhood in New York City in the 1940s, I would argue that Labov and his associates put too much emphasis upon the divergent nature of games of ritual insult as played by whites and blacks. In the 1940s we played a game called Slipping which was very close to the Dozens in every respect. I would agree with Labov, however, that for whites the game was much less important and was not a training ground for verbal facility as it was for blacks.
43. *Ibid.*, I, 76-116.
44. Hannerz, *Soulside*, 135.
45. Ralph F. Berdie, whose article "Playing the Dozens," *Journal of Abnormal and Social Psychology*, 42 (1947), 120-21, exaggerates the frequency of violence in the Dozens, comments that the individual who strikes the first physical blow carries the stigma of being unable to "take it."
46. James Weldon Johnson, *Book of American Negro Spirituals*, 174-76.

THE COMMUNITY OF LAUGHTER

1. Bergson, *Laughter*, 3-8.
2. Rose Laub Coser, "Some Social Functions of Laughter: A Study of Humor in a Hospital Setting," *Human Relations*, 12 (1959), 171-82.
3. Bergson, *Laughter*, 6.
4. Stearns, *Jazz Dance*, 246-47.
5. Sterling Brown, "Negro Jokes," unpublished ms., 10-11; Sterling, *Laughing on the Outside*, 96-97.
6. William Schecter, *The History of Negro Humor in America* (New York, 1970), 68.
7. Ann Charters, *Nobody* (New York, 1970), 106.
8. Loma Records, L 5905, *Redd Foxx on the Loose*.
9. Dick Gregory, *From the Back of the Bus*, Bob Orben, ed. (New York, 1962), 21, 62, 68, 76, 111.
10. Schecter, *History of Negro Humor*, 193.
11. My information concerning the number and sales of Moms Mabley's records

comes from the excellent unpublished paper, "Moms Mabley, 'I Got Sumpin' to Tell Ya',' " written by Barbara Walsh in my graduate seminar in 1967. I am indebted to Ms. Walsh also for the Moms Mabley recordings which she collected in the course of her research and generously donated to the Berkeley History Department.

12. Record jacket notes, Mercury SR-61139, *The Best of Moms Mabley.*
13. *Ibid.*
14. Walsh, "Moms Mabley," unpublished seminar paper, 21.
15. Schecter, *History of Negro Humor*, 191.
16. Chess LP 1452, *Moms Mabley at the "Un";* Chess LP 1479, *Moms Mabley: 'I Got Somethin' to Tell You!';* Mercury, SR-61139, *The Best of Moms Mabley.*
17. Mercury, SR-61139, *The Best of Moms Mabley;* Chess LP 1452, *Moms Mabley at the "UN";* Chess LP 1472, *Moms Mabley Breaks It Up;* Chess LP 1463, *Moms Mabley at Geneva Conference;* Chess LP 1447, *Moms Mabley Onstage.*
18. Chess LP 1463, *Moms Mabley at Geneva Conference.*
19. Chess LP 1472, *Moms Mabley Breaks It Up;* Chess LP 1463, *Moms Mabley at Geneva Conference;* Mercury, SR-61139, *The Best of Moms Mabley.*
20. Chess LP 1472, *Moms Mabley Breaks It Up;* Chess LP 1452, *Moms Mabley at the "UN."*
21. Chess LP 1477, *Moms Mabley: Young Men, Si—Old Men, No.*
22. Mercury, SR-61139, *The Best of Moms Mabley.*
23. Chess LP 1477, *Young Men, Si—Old Men, No;* Chess LP 1486, *Moms Wows;* Chess LP 1447, *Moms Mabley Onstage.*
24. Chess LP 1463, *Moms Mabley at Geneva Conference.*
25. Chess LP 1477, *Young Men, Si—Old Men, No.*
26. Mercury, SR-61139, *The Best of Moms Mabley.*
27. Chess LP 1463, *Moms Mabley at Geneva Conference.*
28. Chess LP 1447, *Moms Mabley Onstage.*
29. Walsh, "Moms Mabley," unpublished seminar paper, 39.
30. Mercury Records, SR-60907, *Moms Mabley: Moms the Word.*
31. Walsh, "Moms Mabley," unpublished seminar paper, 13.

CHAPTER 6: A PANTHEON OF HEROES

EPIGRAPH

1. *Southern Road: Poems by Sterling A. Brown* (1932; Beacon ed., 1974), 95-96.

INTRODUCTION

1. Ralph Ellison, *Shadow and Act*, 7-8, 157.
2. Samuel Adams, *Social Forces*, 26 (1947), 202.
3. Coahoma County, Mississippi, Tape, Archive of Folk Song.
4. Bechet, *Treat It Gentle*, 4.
5. Giovanni, *Gemini*, 98.
6. Dorson, *SFQ*, 19 (1955), 105.
7. Abrahams, *Deep Down in the Jungle*, and *Positively Black, passim.*

THE FATE OF THE TRICKSTER

1. WPA manuscripts, South Carolina File, Archive of Folk Song.
2. Hurston, *Mules and Men*, 146-47.
3. Richard Smith, *PTFS*, 25 (1953), 230.
4. Dorson, *Negro Tales from Pine Bluff and Calvin*, 24.
5. *Ibid.*, 13-16.
6. Butler H. Waugh, "Negro Tales of John Kendry from Indianapolis," *MF*, 8 (1958), 132.
7. Parsons, *JAF*, 34 (1921), 11.
8. Harold Courlander, *Terrapin's Pot of Sense* (New York, 1957), 31-32.
9. Abrahams, *Positively Black*, 123.
10. Eddins, *PTFS*, 9 (1931), 153-56. A-T tale type 1030, The Crop Division.
11. Trickster tales featuring Anansi rather than traditional North American black animal tricksters can be found in the New York File of the WPA manuscripts in the Archive of Folk Song and in Fauset, *JAF*, 41 (1928), 531-32.
12. Parsons, *JAF*, 30 (1917), 168-200.
13. Parsons, *Folk-Lore of the Sea Islands*, xiii-xiv, and *passim*, and Parsons, *JAF*, 34 (1921), 1-39.
14. "Folk-Tales from Students in Tuskegee Institute, Alabama," *JAF*, 32 (1919), 397-401; "Folk-Tales from Students in the Georgia State College," *JAF*, 32 (1919), 401-5; "Folklore from St. Helena, South Carolina," *JAF*, 38 (1925), 217-38.
15. Guy Johnson, *Folk Culture on St. Helena Island*, 135-36.
16. Fauset, *JAF*, 41 (1928), 529-57; Fauset, *JAF*, 40 (1927), 213-303.
17. Guy Johnson, *Folk Culture on St. Helena Island*, 135-36.
18. Brewer, *Dog Ghosts*, 50-51.
19. Dorson, *Negro Folktales in Michigan*, 39-40.
20. Michael Quitt, "Some Traditional Negro Tales in the City," *Journal of the Folklore Society of Greater Washington*, 2 (1970-71), 16-18.
21. Richard M. Dorson, "The Astonishing Repertoire of James Douglas Suggs, A Michigan Negro Storyteller," *Michigan History*, 40 (1956), 152-66.
22. Abrahams, *Deep Down in the Jungle*, Chap. 3.
23. Henry C. Davis, "Negro Folk-Lore in South Carolina," *JAF*, 27 (1914), 244-45.
24. WPA manuscripts, Florida File, Archive of Folk Song.
25. Parsons, *Folk-Lore of the Sea Islands*, 8-10, 40-41, 52, 142-43.
26. Parsons, *JAF*, 30 (1917), 174; Newman White, ed., *Frank C. Brown Collection*, I, 703-4; Dorson, *SFQ*, 19 (1955), 106.
27. Dorson, *Negro Tales from Pine Bluff and Calvin*, 169.
28. For texts of *Signifying Monkey*, see Roger Abrahams, *Deep Down in the Jungle*, 136-57; Abrahams, *Positively Black*, 88-91; Bruce Jackson, *"Get Your Ass in the Water and Swim Like Me": Narrative Poetry from Black Oral Tradition* (Cambridge, Mass., 1974), 161-72; Hughes and Bontemps, *Book of Negro Folklore*, 363-66. For a version told in tale rather than toast form, see Dorson, *WF*, 13 (1954), 87-88.
29. For examples, see the two tales of John Blackamore, *ibid.*, 82-84.
30. Mitchell-Kernan, *Language Behavior in a Black Urban Community*, 111-13.
31. Heyward, *Seed from Madagascar*, 57.
32. WPA manuscripts, Mississippi File, Archive of Folk Song.

33. WPA manuscripts, Florida File, Archive of Folk Song.
34. Bruce Jackson, *Wake Up Dead Man*, 10-11, 202-15.
35. Dorson, *Negro Folktales in Michigan*, 194. J. Mason Brewer prints a North Carolina version of this anecdote in *Worser Days and Better Times*, 66.
36. Hannerz, *Soulside*, 108.
37. Bruce Jackson has compiled an excellent collection of such toasts in *"Get Your Ass in the Water and Swim Like Me,"* 95-144.
38. Christina and Richard Milner, *Black Players: The Secret World of Black Pimps* (Bantam ed., New York, 1973), 242.
39. Susan Hall and Bob Adelman, *Gentleman of Leisure: A Year in the Life of a Pimp* (New York, 1972), 4, 15. Also Iceberg Slim, *Pimp: The Story of My Life* (Los Angeles, 1969).
40. Parsons, *JAF*, 34 (1921), 2-3.
41. Backus, *JAF*, 13 (1900), 26-27.
42. John Harrington Cox, "Negro Tales From West Virginia," *JAF*, 47 (1934), 350-51. Motif K311.3, Thief disguises voice and is allowed access to goods (children).
43. Richard M. Dorson, "Negro Tales," *WF*, 13 (1954), 85-86; Dorson, *Negro Folktales in Michigan*, 45-46.
44. Harris, *Nights with Uncle Remus*, 61-68.
45. Abrahams, *Deep Down in the Jungle*, 74-77.
46. John and Alan Lomax, *American Ballads*, 18.

THE SLAVE AS HERO

1. Dorson, *Negro Folktales in Michigan*, 85.
2. Horne and Schickel, *Lena*, 2.
3. Dorson, *MF*, 6 (1956), 14-15.
4. WPA Slave Narratives (Tenn.).
5. WPA, *Negro in Virginia*, 170.
6. WPA manuscripts, Archive of Folk Song.
7. WPA, *Negro in Virginia*, 209.
8. Holiday, *Lady Sings the Blues*, 8-9.
9. Parsons, *Folk-Lore of the Sea Islands*, xxi-xxii.
10. Dorson, *Negro Folktales in Michigan*, 84-85.
11. Yetman, ed., *Life Under the "Peculiar Institution,"* 24.
12. Dorson, *Negro Folktales in Michigan*, 89.
13. Kathryn L. Morgan, "Caddy Buffers: Legends of a Middle Class Negro Family in Philadelphia," *Keystone Folklore Quarterly*, 11 (1966), 86.
14. Compare Bechet, *Treat It Gentle*, Chap. 2, and the legend of Bras Coupé as given in Herbert Asbury, *The French Quarter* (New York, 1936), 244-47.
15. Bechet, *Treat It Gentle*, 13, 49.
16. Dorson, *Negro Tales from Pine Bluff and Calvin*, 174-75.
17. Botkin, ed., *Lay My Burden Down*, xiii.
18. Coahoma County, Mississippi, Tape, Archive of Folk Song.
19. For a wonderfully composite slave trickster tale that includes many of the leading themes of this genre, see Waugh, *MF*, 8 (1958), 126-32. Abundant slave trickster tales can be found in the WPA manuscripts in the Archive of Folk Song as well as in the WPA Slave Narratives.

20. Abrahams, *Positively Black*, 68. Abrahams has other recent Master-John stories on pp. 63-69. See also Dorson, *American Negro Folktales*, 124-71.
21. Dorson, *SFQ*, 19 (1955), 108-9.
22. Dorson, *Negro Folktales in Michigan*, 74.
23. Smiley, *JAF*, 32 (1919), 362.
24. Bechet, *Treat It Gentle*, 6-7.
25. Fisk University, *God Struck Me Dead*, 161.
26. Fisk University, *Unwritten History*, 284-91.
27. WPA, *Negro in Virginia*, 127-28.
28. Morgan, *Keystone Folklore Quarterly*, 11 (1966), 68, 75, and *passim*.
29. Fisk University, *Unwritten History*, 116.
30. *Ibid.*, 139.
31. Yetman, ed., *Life Under the "Peculiar Institution,"* 213.
32. Botkin, ed., *Lay My Burden Down*, 174.
33. WPA Slave Narratives (Tenn.).
34. WPA Slave Narratives (N.C.).
35. Yetman, ed., *Life Under the "Peculiar Institution,"* 253.
36. Dorson, *Negro Folktales in Michigan*, 85-86.
37. Fisk University, *God Struck Me Dead*, 111.
38. Yetman, ed., *Life Under the "Peculiar Institution,"* 130.
39. WPA Slave Narratives (Ala.).
40. Botkin, ed., *Lay My Burden Down*, 175.
41. Yetman, ed., *Life Under the "Peculiar Institution,"* 11-14.
42. *Ibid.*, 293.
43. WPA Slave Narratives (N.C.).
44. Botkin, ed., *Lay My Burden Down*, 55.
45. Bacon and Parsons, *JAF*, 35 (1922), 293.
46. Botkin, ed., *Lay My Burden Down*, 189.
47. Yetman, ed., *Life Under the "Peculiar Institution,"* 302.

THE MODERNIZATION OF THE BLACK HERO

1. Yetman, ed., *Life Under the "Peculiar Institution,"* 110.
2. Botkin, ed., *Lay My Burden Down*, 257.
3. *Ibid.*, 264.
4. Dorson, *Negro Tales from Pine Bluff and Calvin*, 230-35.
5. Morgan, *Keystone Folklore Quarterly*, 11 (1966), 83-84.
6. Alan Lomax, *Common Ground*, 8 (1948), 48-49.
7. Richard M. Dorson, "King Beast of the Forest Meets Man," *SFQ*, 18 (1954), 128.
8. Odum and Johnson, *Negro Workaday Songs*, 65.
9. John Lomax, *Adventures of a Ballad Hunter*, 286-89.
10. Dorson, *Negro Folktales in Michigan*, 180.
11. H. Rap Brown, *Die Nigger Die!*, 27-29.
12. WPA manuscripts, Florida File, Archive of Folk Song.
13. Irvis, *NYFQ*, 11 (1955), 174-75.
14. Brewer, *Dog Ghosts*, 9-14. Similar tales were told about contemporary Negroes. On pp. 20-21 of his collection Brewer prints one about a white sheriff and his black servant. Motif D615, Transformation Combat.

15. Dorson, *Negro Tales from Pine Bluff and Calvin*, 110-11, 182-83.
16. Dorson, *Negro Folktales in Michigan*, 151, 181; Dorson, *SFQ*, 19 (1955), 109.
17. Odum and Johnson, *Negro Workaday Songs*, 59-61; White, *American Negro Folk-Songs*, 349-50.
18. WPA manuscripts, New York File, Archive of Folk Song.
19. Roger D. Abrahams, "The Changing Concept of the Negro Hero," *PTFS*, 31 (1962), 120.
20. Brewer, *American Negro Folklore*, 48.

BAD MEN AND BANDITS

1. Talley, *Negro Folk Rhymes*, 118.
2. Odum and Johnson, *Negro Workaday Songs*, 67.
3. WPA manuscripts, Florida File, Archive of Folk Song.
4. John and Alan Lomax, *Folk Song, U.S.A.*, 313.
5. Oliver, *Blues Fell This Morning*, 194.
6. Charters, *Poetry of the Blues*, 23-24.
7. Oliver, *Blues Fell This Morning*, 193.
8. Thomas, *PTFS*, 5 (1926), 165.
9. White, *American Negro Folk-Songs*, 272.
10. Charters, *Poetry of the Blues*, 32.
11. Oliver, *Blues Fell This Morning*, 201-3.
12. Charters, *Poetry of the Blues*, 47.
13. Oster, *Living Country Blues*, 326-27.
14. John Hardy songs are commonly found in most collections of folksong. An excellent collection of variants was compiled by Louis Chappell and printed in his study, *John Henry*, 129-40. John Harrington Cox, "John Hardy," *JAF*, 32 (1919), 505-20, contains some excellent material on the life of John Hardy in spite of its spurious argument that Hardy and John Henry were the same man.
15. The facts of Slater's life and the legends that grew up around him can be found in Carl Carmer, *Stars Fell on Alabama*, 122-25, and Frederick William Turner, III, *Badmen, Black and White* (unpublished Ph.D. dissertation, University of Pennsylvania, 1965), 377-85.
16. For songs about Railroad Bill, see Perrow, *JAF*, 28 (1915), 155; Carmer, *Stars Fell on Alabama*, 124; Odum, *JAF*, 24 (1911), 290; MacEdward Leach and Horace P. Beck, "Songs From Rappahannock County, Virginia," *JAF*, 63 (1950), 280.
17. For the facts and legends of Harris' life, see Alan Lomax, *Mister Jelly Roll*, 50-52, 122-24; Frederick William Turner, *Badmen, Black and White*, Chap. 9.
18. There is no single collection of black lore concerning figures of this type. One or another of them is present in almost every collection of black songs and toasts but it is necessary to read through many collections to become acquainted with them all. For an introduction to the genre, see the two collections by Odum and Johnson, *Negro and His Songs*, Chap. 7, and *Negro Workaday Songs*, Chap. 4 and Frederick William Turner's 1965 University of Pennsylvania dissertation, *Badmen, Black and White*.
19. John and Alan Lomax, *American Ballads*, 90-91; Hughes and Bontemps, *Book of Negro Folklore*, 354-55.
20. Thomas, *PTFS*, 5 (1926), 171.

21. Abrahams, *Deep Down in the Jungle*, 162-63. For other recent bad man toasts, see Bruce Jackson, "*Get Your Ass in the Water*," 43-93.
22. Interviews with Charles Haffer and Will Starks, Coahoma County, Mississippi, Tape, Archive of Folk Song. There have been numerous speculations that the exploits of Stagolee were based upon incidents occurring either in Memphis or St. Louis. There was in fact a Mississippi steamboat called the *Stacker Lee* owned by the Lee family in Memphis. See John and Alan Lomax, *American Ballads*, 93-94; Wheeler, *Steamboatin' Days*, 99-102; B. A. Botkin in *Standard Dictionary of Folklore, Mythology and Legend*, II, 1080-81. The evidence for Stagolee's historical authenticity is unconvincing. See Richard E. Buehler, "Stacker Lee: A Partial Investigation into the Historicity of a Negro Murder Ballad," *Keystone Folklore Quarterly*, 12 (1967), 187-91.
23. Odum, *JAF*, 24 (1911), 288-89.
24. Dorson, *WF*, 13 (1954), 160-62 (Michigan); Abrahams, *Deep Down in the Jungle*, 123-36 (Philadelphia); Abrahams, *Positively Black*, 45-47 (Texas); Hughes and Bontemps, *Book of Negro Folklore*, 361-63 (New York City); Bruce Jackson, "*Get Your Ass in the Water*," 43-55 (Texas, Chicago, New York State).
25. Odum, *JAF*, 24 (1911), 288.
26. Alan Lomax, *Common Ground*, 8 (1948), 48.
27. Wheeler, *Steamboatin' Days*, 102.
28. Abrahams, *Positively Black*, 45-46.
29. WPA manuscripts, Florida File, Archive of Folk Song.
30. Wheeler, *Steamboatin' Days*, 102.
31. WPA manuscripts, Florida File, Archive of Folk Song.
32. For these atypical variants, see Onah L. Spencer, "Stackalee," *Direction*, 4 (1941), 16; John and Alan Lomax, *American Ballads*, 95; Odum, *JAF*, 24 (1911), 288.
33. Abrams, *Positively Black*, 47.
34. John and Alan Lomax, *American Ballads*, 99; Alan Lomax, *Folk Songs of North America*, 572.
35. John and Alan Lomax, *American Ballads*, 99. Similar versions were collected in Florida, WPA manuscripts, Florida File, Archive of Folk Song, and Harlem, Hughes and Bontemps, *Book of Negro Folklore*, 362-63.
36. Abrahams, *Deep Down in the Jungle*, 130-34; Dorson, *WF*, 13 (1954), 160-62.
37. This collective portrait was derived from Turner, *Badmen, Black and White, passim*; Eric Hobsbawm, *Bandits* (New York, 1969), Chaps. 1-3; Hobsbawm, *Primitive Rebels*, Chaps. 2-3; Kent L. Steckmesser, "Robin Hood and the American Outlaw: A Note on History and Folklore," *JAF*, 79 (1966), 348-55; Mody C. Boatright, "The Western Bad Man as Hero," *PTFS*, 27 (1957), 96-104; Robert H. Byington, "The Frontier Hero: Refinement and Definition," *PTFS*, 30 (1961), 140-55; B. A. Botkin, "Bad Man," *Standard Dictionary of Folklore, Mythology and Legend*, I, 102-3.
38. John and Alan Lomax, *Folk Song U.S.A.*, 283; Alan Lomax, *Folk Songs of North America*, 352.
39. John and Alan Lomax, *American Ballads*, 132-33.
40. Alan Lomax, *Folk Songs of North America*, 437.
41. Hobsbawm, *Bandits*, 41.
42. *Ibid.*, Chap. 4.
43. Alan Lomax, *Common Ground*, 8 (1948), 50; Gellert, *Negro Songs of Protest*, 18-19.
44. Oliver, *Blues Fell This Morning*, 199.

45. The best expression of these attitudes is Abrahams, *Deep Down in the Jungle,* Chap. 3.
46. Hobsbawm, *Bandits,* 21.

THE HERO VS. SOCIETY: JOHN HENRY TO JOE LOUIS

1. See, for instance, H. C. Brearley, "Ba-ad Nigger," *The South Atlantic Quarterly,* 38 (1939), 75-81. Clarence Major in his *Dictionary of Afro-American Slang* (New York, 1970), gives these definitions: *Bad:* "a simple reversal of the white standard, the very best." *Bad nigger:* "a black person who refuses to be meek or who rejects the social terms of poverty and oppression the culture designs for him." *Bad talk:* "revolutionary or radical ideas."
2. Guy Johnson, *John Henry: Tracking Down a Negro Legend* (Chapel Hill, 1929), Chaps. 1-4, 8; Louis W. Chappell, *John Henry: A Folk-Lore Study* (Jena, 1933), Chaps. 1-5. While neither of these exhaustive studies proves the historicity of the John Henry legend, they both make a good case for its probable basis in fact.
3. On this point, see Richard M. Dorson, "The Career of 'John Henry,'" *WF,* 24 (1965), 155-63.
4. Unless otherwise noted, all of the John Henry songs quoted in this section come from the hundreds of variants in Guy Johnson, *John Henry,* and Louis Chappell, *John Henry.* Here, as throughout this study, I have chosen only representative texts.
5. Abrahams, *Deep Down in the Jungle,* 80n.
6. Bruce Jackson, *Wake Up Dead Man,* 235.
7. Both Louis Chappell and Guy Johnson have determined that during the 1870s the steam drill was still primitive enough so that, in certain situations, at least, it was entirely possible for a man of great prowess to beat one in a contest.
8. Guy B. Johnson, "John Henry," *SW,* 56 (1927), 160.
9. Guy Johnson, *John Henry,* 143.
10. Leach and Beck, *JAF,* 63 (1950), 273.
11. White, *American Negro Folk-Songs,* 350; Odum and Johnson, *Negro Workaday Songs,* 59-61; interview with Will Starks, Coahoma County, Mississippi, Tape, Archive of Folk Song.
12. Versions of *Shine* can be found in Saxon *et al., Gumbo Ya-Ya,* 373-74; interviews with David Edwards and O. C. King, Coahoma County, Mississippi, Tape, Archive of Folk Song; Hughes and Bontemps, *Book of Negro Folklore,* 366-67; Hughes, *Book of Negro Humor,* 91-92; Abrahams, *Deep Down in the Jungle,* 111-23; Abrahams, *Positively Black,* 44-45; Eddington, *Kroeber Anthropological Society Papers,* No. 33 (1965), 99-105; Labov *et al., Non-Standard English of Negro and Puerto Rican Speakers,* II, 59-60; Bruce Jackson, "*Get Your Ass in the Water,*" 184-96; Raglan Records, *Unexpurgated Folk Songs of Men,* collected by Mack McCormick. All quotes from *Shine* in this section come from these sources.
13. Major, *Dictionary of Afro-American Slang,* 102.
14. Guy Johnson, *John Henry,* 143-44.
15. Unless otherwise noted, my account of Johnson's career is derived from his autobiography, *Jack Johnson—In the Ring—And Out* (Chicago, 1927, reissued in 1969 as *Jack Johnson is a Dandy*), and Finis Farr's biography, *Black Champion: The Life and Times of Jack Johnson* (London, 1964).

16. James Weldon Johnson, *Black Manhattan* (1930; reprint ed., New York, 1968), 66; Roi Ottley and William J. Weatherby, eds., *The Negro in New York: An Informal Social History* (New York, 1969), 152.
17. Al-Tony Gilmore, *Bad Nigger! The National Impact of Jack Johnson* (Port Washington, N.Y., 1975), 35.
18. *Ibid.*, 37-38.
19. Roi Ottley, *"New World A-Coming": Inside Black America* (Boston, 1943), 192.
20. Armstrong, *Satchmo*, 31.
21. The most complete account of these conflicts is in Gilmore, *Bad Nigger!*, Chap. 3.
22. Farr, *Black Champion*, 116.
23. Brewer, *Worser Days and Better Times*, 107, 178.
24. Spalding, *Encyclopedia of Black Folklore and Humor*, 368-69.
25. Wiggins, *Black Scholar*, 2 (1971), 46.
26. Joe Louis, *My Life Story* (New York, 1947), 92, 54.
27. Horne and Schickel, *Lena*, 75.
28. Ottley, *"New World A-Coming,"* 198-99.
29. *The Autobiography of Malcolm X*, 23.
30. Maya Angelou, *I Know Why the Caged Bird Sings*, 111-15.
31. Claude Brown, *Manchild in the Promised Land* (New York, 1965), 165.
32. WPA manuscripts, File of Children's Rhymes and Verses, Archive of Folk Song.
33. WPA manuscripts, Florida File, Archive of Folk Song.
34. For these and other blues about Joe Louis, see Oliver, *Blues Tradition*, Chap. 5.
35. St. Clair Drake and Horace R. Cayton, *Black Metropolis: A Study of Negro Life in a Northern City* (Harper Torchbook ed., New York, 1962), II, 391.
36. *The Autobiography of Malcolm X*, 23-24.
37. Arthur Waskow, *From Race Riot to Sit-In: 1919 and the 1960s* (Garden City, N.Y., 1966), Chaps. 1-8; William Alan Muraskin, *Middle-Class Blacks in a White Society: Prince Hall Freemasonry in America* (Berkeley, 1975), 220-21.

EPILOGUE

1. William James, *Selected Papers on Philosophy* (New York, 1917), 1-2.
2. Robert Louis Stevenson, *Across the Plains* (London, 1892), 206-28.
3. Abram Kardiner and Lionel Ovesey, *The Mark of Oppression: Explorations in the Personality of the American Negro* (1951; Meridian ed., Cleveland, 1962), 384.
4. L. Singer, "Ethnogenesis and Negro Americans Today," *Social Research*, 29 (1962), 429.
5. Myrdal, *An American Dilemma*, 928-29.
6. E. Franklin Frazier, *The Negro in the United States* (revised ed., New York, 1957), 680-81.
7. Nathan Glazer and Daniel Moynihan, *Beyond the Melting Pot* (Cambridge, Mass., 1963), 53.
8. Abrahams, *Positively Black*, 133-34.
9. Stanford M. Lyman, *The Black American in Sociological Thought* (New York, 1972), 183. Lyman has a number of interesting things to say about the sociological approach to blacks in American society, but for a more cogent and comprehensive approach to the same subject, see Charles A. Valentine, *Culture and Poverty* (Chicago, 1968).

10. Fisk University, *Unwritten History*, 45-46.
11. Recent examples of historical scholarship which pay attention to the folk mind include Blassingame, *The Slave Community;* Genovese, *Roll, Jordan, Roll;* Leon F. Litwack, "Free at Last," in Tamara K. Hareven, ed., *Anonymous Americans* (Englewood Cliffs, N.J., 1971), 131-71, and Professor Litwack's forthcoming study of Negroes during and after the Civil War; Sterling Stuckey, "Through the Prism of Folklore," *Massachusetts Review,* 9 (1968), reprinted in Jules Chametzky and Sidney Kaplan, eds., *Black and White in American Culture: An Anthology from the Massachusetts Review* (New York, 1971), 172-191.
12. Ralph Ellison, "A Very Stern Discipline," *Harpers* (March 1967), 84.
13. Gregory, *Nigger*, 39.
14. Ellison, *Shadow and Act*, 115.

INDEX

Cotton Top Mountain Sanctified Singers, 179
Courlander, Harold, 219, 240
Courtney, John, 371, 404
Covey, Edward, 68-69
Cox, Ida, 232
Cox, John Harrington, 501 *n.* 14
Cragin, Ellen, 393
Creole, 89, 195, 289
Cries, *see* Field Hollers
Crisis, 168
Crockett, Davy, 104, 400
Cromer, Harold, *see* Stump and Stumpy
Crosby, Bing, 356
Cross, James, *see* Stump and Stumpy
Crow, Jim, 192
Cuenta de Nansi, 103
Culpepper, Nicholas, 64
Cultural Self-containment, 138-40
Curaçao, 103, 105
Curry, Ben, 353
Cutting, *see* Dozens

Dahomey, 8-9, 90-91, 103-4, 350
Dance: African influence on, 16; after emancipation, 200-201, 224; and religion, 18, 189; and ring shout, 38; as satire, 17; in slavery, 15-17
Dancer, Earl, 233
Daniel, in slave lore, 23, 37, 50-51, 136
Daniel, Vattel Elbert, 189
Daniels, John, 79
Dauner, Louise, 120
Davenport, Charles, 88
Davenport, Cow Cow, 267
David, in slave lore, 50-51, 385
Davies, Samuel, 21, 61
Davis, Daniel Webster, 150
Dawson, Anthony, 47, 56, 63
Dempsey, Jack, 429
Dennison, Tim, 169
De Paur, Leonard, 202
Dett, R. Nathaniel, 168
Devil, conceptions of: as conjurer, 57; after emancipation, 148, 160, 244, 403, 415; in humor, 302-3, 306, 331; in slave lore, 40, 84, 94, 96
Dialect, *see* Black Language
Dickson, A. F., 44-45
Dillard, J. L., 153-54
Dillinger, John, 413

Dinkie, slave conjurer, 74
Dinwiddie Colored Quartet, 224
Dixon, Luke, 87
Dixon, William, 205, 297
"Doctor Jack," root doctor, 64
Dodds, Baby, 222, 238, 294
Dodds, Johnny, 294
Dodge, N. S., 312
Dollard, John, 313-14, 343, 350, 354, 356
Dolomite, 412
Dorsey, Thomas A., 181-86
Dorson, Richard M., 86, 89-90, 105, 302, 369, 376, 386-87, 401
Douglass, Frederick, 325, 492 *n.* 20; and slave folk beliefs, 67-69, 71; on slave music, 12-13, 51, 192
Dozens, the, 344-58, 496 *n.* 42, *n.* 45
Drake, St. Clair, 438
Dranes, Arizona, 179
Du Bois, W. E. B.: on acculturation, 136, 151; on African influences, 4, 58; on humor, 299-300; on religion, 29; on spirituals, 471 *n.* 53
Dundes, Alan, 462 *n.* 4
Dupree, 242, 412
Dusen, Frankie, 354
Duval, Reggie, 295
Dvořák, Anton, 168
Dwight's Journal of Music, 5

Eberhart, Bradley, 208
Edmonds, Shephard, 17
Edo people, 103
Edwards, Anderson, 48
Edwards, David, 389-90
Edwards, Mrs. I. E., 93
Eisenhower, Dwight, 364
Eisenhower, Mamie, 364
Elder, Callie, 63
Eliade, Mircea, 31
Elkins, Stanley, 54
Ellington, Duke, 200, 349
Ellison, Ralph, 293, 368-69, 405, 445
Emancipation: and acculturation, 139-40; effect on slave language, 138-55; slaves' reaction to, 136-38, 387, 392-93
Emerson, Ralph Waldo, 143
Emmett, Dan, 194
Episcopal Church, 46, 188
Eshu, African trickster, 103
Esman, Aaron, 293